KNIVES
2012

EDITED BY
Joe Kertzman

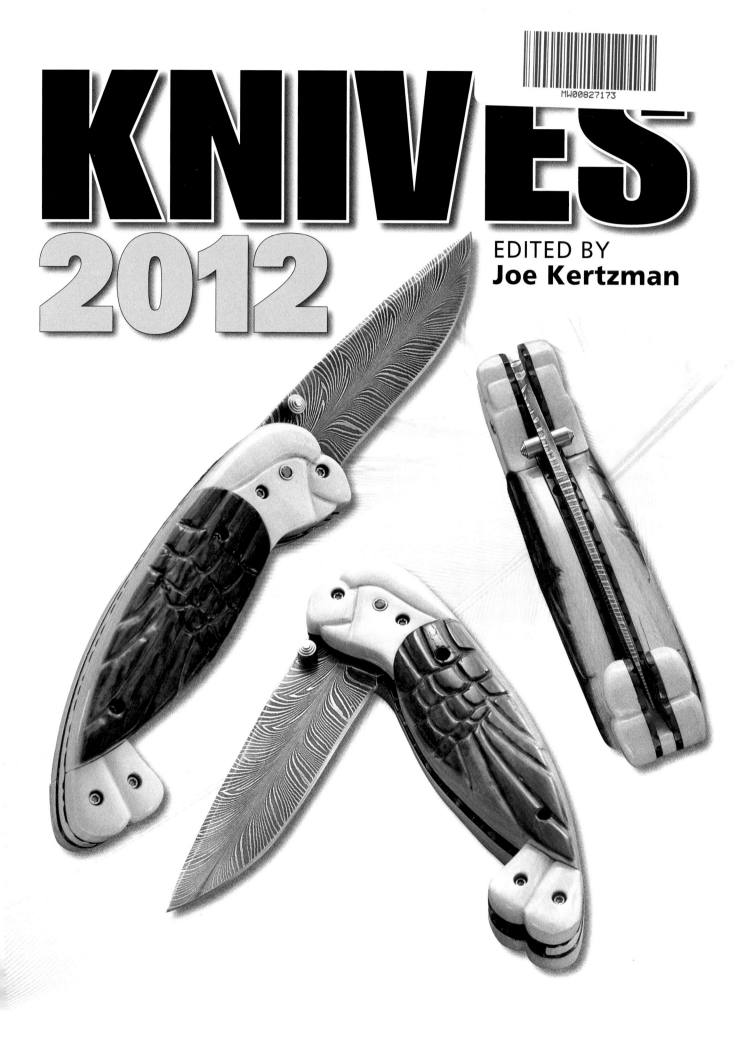

Published by

Krause Publications, a division of F+W Media, Inc.
700 East State Street • Iola, WI 54990-0001
715-445-2214 • 888-457-2873
www.krausebooks.com

To order books or other products call toll-free 1-800-258-0929
or visit us online at www.shopblade.com

Cover photography by Kris Kandler

ISSN: 0277-0725

ISBN-13: 978-1-4402-1687-9
ISBN-10: 1-4402-1687-8

Designed by Kara Grundman
Edited by Corrina Peterson

Printed in the United States of America

Dedication and Acknowledgments

It was right there all along, practically hitting me over the head with its obviousness, looming, leaving hints like handwritten notes passed in an elementary classroom. How could I have missed the signs? They lingered long enough for me to discover them. I struggled as to whom I should dedicate the *KNIVES 2012* book. I had already dedicated the 2010 edition to Ken Warner, and 2011's rendition to Steve Shackleford. My wife and kids had been mentioned in previous editions, as well as my mother and father.

So many people contribute time, effort, innovation and ideas to the world of knives. And there it was, my answer—so many people ... and handmade knives ... and then it finally occurred to me—the Knifemakers' Guild and the American Bladesmith Society (ABS). These are the organizations that further the causes of the handmade knife, that hold classes, benefit their members, organize craftsmen, guide them through newsletters, mission statements and goals, hold and sponsor knife shows, recognize the accomplishments of custom knifemakers, raise them through the ranks, present awards, and rally the troops together when someone's shop burns down, they become ill or pass away. They teach children, alert the media of accomplishments in the knife industry, present a goodwill image, and educate the public on knives as tools and works of art rather than as weapons in the hands of criminals.

Those who sit on the Boards of the Knifemakers' Guild and ABS are mostly knifemakers with a few money and organizational managers, industry professionals, writers, secretaries and accountants thrown in. They pour their hearts and souls into furthering knife causes, and if you think the pay is great, ask ABS Chairman Greg Neely, or Knifemakers' Guild President Gil Hibben, Vice President Wayne Hensley, Secretary-Treasurer W. Lowell Bray Jr., or Directors Gene Baskett, Edmund Davidson, Kevin Hoffman or William C. "Bill" Johnson. Ask Jan DuBois who manages the ABS office, James Batson, director of the Society's many hammer-in's, Cindy Sheely, the store manager, Sally Cassidy who handles membership services, Carolyn Hughes, editor of the *Journal of the American Bladesmith Society*, Scott Taylor, coordinator of community services, or Laura Simmons, Dereck Glaser, Jay Hendrickson, Rick Dunkerley, David Etchieson and Bill Worthen who run the community colleges, museums, expositions and bladesmithing schools. To all of the aforementioned, the members, volunteers, makers, collectors, dealers, purveyors of fine knives, and even to the paid associates, this, the 32nd Edition of the *Knives* annual book, is dedicated to you.

I acknowledge others who, if it wasn't for them, this book would never come to be, folks who not only help this lowly *Knives* editor, but also the knifemakers, engravers, scrimshaw artists, sculptors, carvers, leatherworkers and other artisans who are the featured subjects of the text and photos. It is the photographers to whom I refer and whose efforts I wish to acknowledge. They illustrate knives in a good light, and good lighting, present the forms, shapes and styles in a classy manner, highlighting the features, embellishments, mechanisms and even their inner workings. There are several photographers who have been at this for quite some time, including Eric Eggly of Point Seven Studios, Daniel O'Malley of BladeGallery.com, Terrill Hoffman, Jim and Louise Weyer, Chuck Ward, Jim Cooper of SharpByCoop. com, Buddy Thomason, Bob Glassman of Custom Knife Gallery of Colorado, Mitch Lum, Cory Martin Imaging and Francesco Pachi.

I acknowledge the Publisher of the Firearms/Knives Group, of F+W Media, Jim Schlender, for his support, encouragement, friendship and efforts, Corrina Peterson, who edits these pages, and to the book designer, Kara Grundman. Thank you all. Good work, and keep the faith.

Joe Kertzman

On the Cover

Not many makers have combined basket-weave engraving and Hawaiian pheasant wood on the bolsters and handle, respectively, of a "Mini Bowie" (far left on the front cover), this one with a 4.25-inch W2 blade, but that's just what Michael Vagnino did successfully and beautifully. To the small bowie's immediate right is a William C. "Bill" Johnson dagger featuring a "spiral-fluted," sterling-silver-wire-wrapped mammoth tooth grip of the greenest kind, a 7-inch damascus blade, and a 303 stainless steel guard and pommel. Front and center is a lengthy "Legacy #2" bowie by John White parading a 9.75-inch, four-bar, "modified Turkish twist"-damascus blade, engraved damascus fittings and a pre-ban elephant ivory handle. Brian Hochstrat inlaid and engraved the guard and pommel area in platinum and three colors of gold. By the way, this puppy is of takedown construction. At far right, and at the ready, is Donald Vogt's "Persian Automatic" folder showcasing a carved damascus blade and bolsters, the latter embellished with hand-carved 14k-gold leaf overlays, gold scrolls, and ruby inlays. It also sports a carved black-lip-pearl handle, and a carved-damascus spine that features yet more gold and rubies. Not bad for four knifemakers and a few days' work in their smithies.

Contents

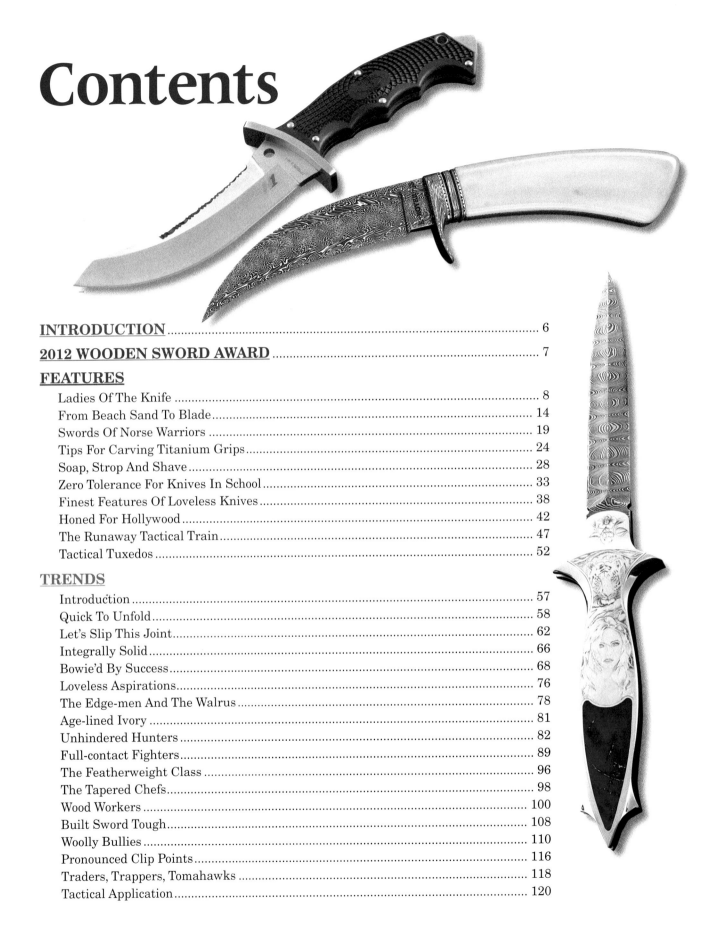

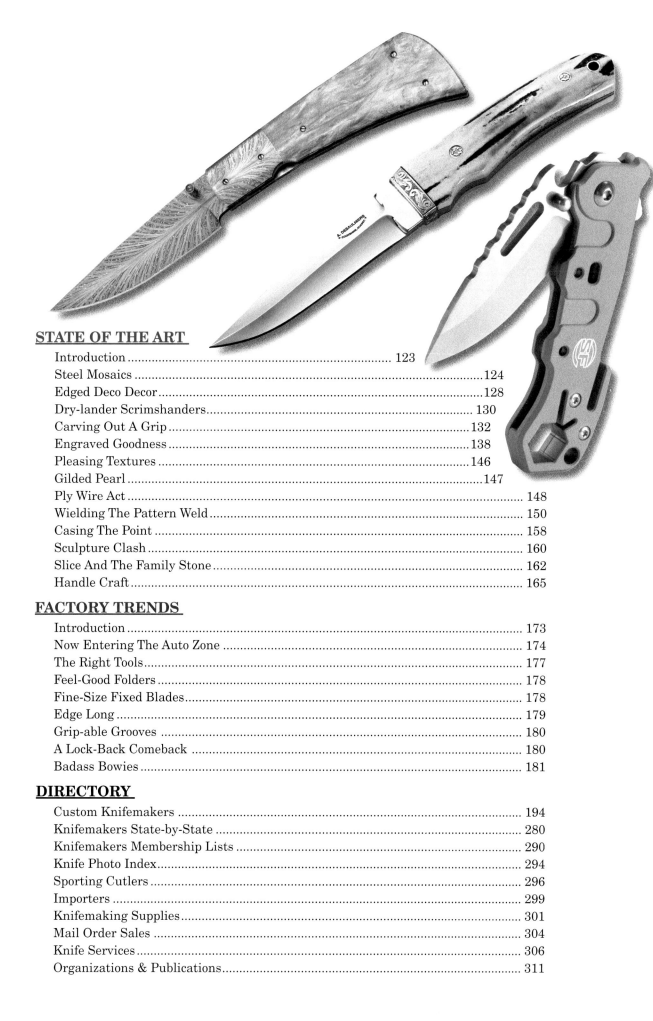

STATE OF THE ART

FACTORY TRENDS

DIRECTORY

Introduction

The young ones are always most excited. They dial up someone on the phone just to talk knives. They can barely contain their enthusiasm, having spent the last 72 hours hammering out their first knife blade, grinding it, belt sanding it, polishing it and pinning stag handle slabs onto the tang. They're running on adrenalin, enthusiasm and caffeine. They have bloodshot eyes, but the perma-grin and dirt smudges won't wipe off their faces. They've discovered an age-old handcraft practiced and perfected for thousands of years, but you couldn't tell them that. They've just discovered something no one else knows about.

It's beautiful, like watching a young girl put a Selena Gomez CD into her pink music player and dance, twirl, sing and silhouette like a prima ballerina. To her, the voice of young Gomez is that of an angel, the first angel, Gabriel, floating notes on billowy clouds. She cares not about virtuosos who've come before, brilliant musicians who've left their hearts and souls on stage, or prodigies of the past.

Witnessing a knifemaker discover his skills is akin to spying a 12-year-old boy who has yet to experience puppy love, and thinks LeBron James is the most fluent, finest basketball player in the world. The pre-teen's eyes sparkle, heart swells, and mind races as he dreams of playing round ball in front of thousands of vocal fans, hustling down the court, blocking every shot, sinking three-pointers and hitting the winning basket at the buzzer. The names Wilt Chamberlain, Kareem Abdul Jabbar, Magic Johnson, Larry Byrd and Michael Jordan are familiar, but they couldn't possibly hold a candle to the new wave of b-ball players, or have been as cool, well dressed, fit, flashy or fluid.

Knifemaking isn't as flashy a pursuit as a pop star or professional basketball player. It's demanding, time consuming and hard work. The hours, days, weeks and years fly by, with more time spent in dirty, noisy, dust-filled shops than outdoors in the wild blue yonder. Yet it's an honorable profession, one where useful tools are built, a few hands are shook, deals are landed and, if lucky, enough dollars make it into the pocket to pay the bills and save for days when the hands won't work as well anymore.

All too soon that young buck has grown into a weathered, experienced knifemaker, perhaps a little slower, but wiser, and with that familiar gleam in his eye. It's the same gleam seen in the eyes of collectors, the much beloved segment of the knife industry, who will share their savings with the artisans they most admire, the LeBron James's of the knife industry, the Selena Gomez's of handmade knives.

Turn the pages slowly. The blades pictured between the covers of *Knives 2012* are some of the finest on the planet, and pouring over them is like seeing the world for the first time, rediscovering one's passion and desires. Such is the power of pristine custom knives.

It's an honor to edit the 32nd Edition of a book that attracts the best knife writers alive, a title known to knifemakers, collectors and enthusiasts across the globe.

In feature articles, respected knife and gun writer Pat Covert covers innovations in tactical folders and fixed blades; knifemaker Matt Cucchiara gives tips on carving titanium handles; accomplished custom maker Tim Zowada explains how he made knife blades from Lake Superior beach sand; Mike Haskew writes about the romance, danger and daring associated with Hollywood movie knives and swords; knifemaker Vincent Evans tells how Anglo-Saxon and Viking swords have inspired him; attorney-at-law Louis P. Nappen takes on the knives-at-school Zero Tolerance policies; collector Don Guild talks up his favorite female knifemakers; and Durwood Hollis delves into the finest features of Bob Loveless knives.

Trends in custom knives this year include the "Quick To Unfold" crowd of fast folders, integrally solid integrals, gilded-pearl-handle art knives, steel mosaics, those aspiring to the greatness of Loveless, walrus knife handles, those with age-lined ivory grips and chef's knives. In the "State of the Art" section, "Edged Deco Décor" sees a resurgence, and "Dry-land Scrimshanders" show their stuff, as do the best knife carvers, engravers, wire and stone inlayers, and sculptors in the business.

To showcase the work of masters is not a job but an honor and pleasure, one this Editor deeply appreciates.

Joe Kertzman

2012 WOODEN SWORD AWARD

Add it to the "things I never thought I'd do" list—give the "Wooden Sword Award" to a knifemaker for fashioning a fantasy piece. As far as can be discerned, this is the first time the award has ever been presented, in 32 editions of the *Knives* annual book, for impeccably crafting a fantasy knife.

Yet when knifemaker Max Berger, who specializes in fantasy and working/using straight knives of his design, contacted this book author via email with images of his latest creation, it was one of those "ah hah!" moments. Max, as it turns out, began with a 1-foot-diameter by 1-foot-high piece of 440C stainless steel that weighed 400 pounds. Using a 4.5-inch band saw, a 12-inch drill press, an 11-amp die grinder and Dremel tool (both with carbide burs) and hand files, he sculpted the "Raven and the Serpent," which includes six honed knife blades in its steely makeup.

Knifemaker Max Berger fashioned the "Raven and the Serpent" fantasy knife sculpture from one piece of 440C stainless steel. It initially measured a foot in diameter by a foot high, and weighed 400 pounds.

Berger sanded the knife sculpture—and it is a sculpture, no two ways about it—using rotary grinding stones, and sandpaper decreasing in grit size from 120-grit paper down to 2,500 grit, leaving a mirror polish. He left the base alone after shaping it with carbide burs, and satin finished the blades with 1,000-grit paper. The entire piece has been heat treated to a rating of 58-60 Rc on the Rockwell Hardness Scale. Amethyst stones at the base provide the finishing touch.

So speaking of final touches, here, with one flourish of an editorial wooden sword, I bestow upon Max Berger the 2012 Wooden Sword Award.

Joe Kertzman

Ladies Of The Knife

Women knifemakers are well established and respected in a field once dominated by men

By Don Guild

On a rainy Friday morning in Georgia, literally hundreds of eyes were searching for that one knife, the *piéce de résistance*, the "it" knife that just knocks you out. That's when I chanced onto a knife that possessed strong, visual intrigue that made me gasp at its velvety smooth opening. As I pressed the release button, I said to myself, "Here's the one that no one else has yet discovered." I nodded at the young lady behind the table, asked about the knife, and my mouth dropped open as she said, "I'm the sole maker, and that knife is dual-action."

The knife turned out to be a jewel of a double-action folding art knife at the BLADE Show in Atlanta, the world's largest show, and it was my introduction to Gail Lunn, the only woman in the world who has made over 100 dual-action autos. How can a gal make such an attractive, masculine piece of mechanical art?

Women and knives, at first glance, seem like honey and nails. So who are these birds, and how many of this species exist? Sure, I know a few, but to really find out, I posed this question to some leading purveyors and longtime collectors: "Off the top of your head, how many women are mak-

Julie Warenski-Erickson has chosen custom knives as her exclusive engraving medium for the past 25 years, and says she likes to make her own pieces, like this California dagger, to give her a nice pallet on which to ply her trade.

Julie Warenski-Erickson engraved and pierced the blade of the curvaceous dagger, further embellishing the piece with gold inlay and engraving along the double guard and pommel. *(Point Seven photo)*

ing knives, and which ones are the best at plying their craft today?"

Their answers surprised me. Since five names kept coming up to dominate a list of 14 women makers, without wishing to snub anyone, I selected the following to interview: Julie Warenski Erickson, Dellana, Harumi Hirayama, Elizabeth Loerchner, and Gail Lunn.

Julie Warenski-Erickson

"My history in the knife business has been engraving. I've been engraving now exclusively on custom knives for 25 years. Over the years, I was slowly given more training in making the knives with Buster," Julie says. (Julie's late first husband, Buster Warenski, is considered one of the most talented art knife makers in history, and is in the *BLADE Magazine* Cutlery Hall Of Fame®.)

"The only thing he didn't teach me was grinding blades. It was after his death that I kicked myself for not learning that part also. My most recent challenge has been grinding blades. The rest

of the knife business I learned from years of experience. My first knife was made in 2005 after the death of Buster. It was a challenge I really needed at the time. That was when Curt Erickson offered

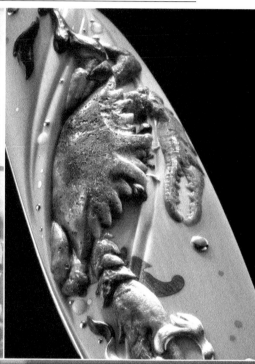

For the "Carps In The Rapid Stream" fixed blade, Harumi Hirayama carved the African Blackwood handle to look like waves through which the pearl-inlaid carp are fighting to swim.

The largest folder Harumi Hirayama has ever made, the Lobster & Crab knife took a decade to fashion and finish, requiring a lot of drawing and planning. It sports a 440C blade, silver bolsters, an ivory handle and various stone, coral, wood, shell, opal, gold and silver inlays.

to teach me to grind blades like Buster had taught him years before.

"I feel so lucky to have been in the knife business for the past 25 years. I cannot think of any other career I could possibly love as much as I love this one. I do work too much. Thank goodness I love what I do. Most of my time is spent engraving. I engrave the few knives I make, as well as all the knives Curt makes, and engraving for other makers and collectors. I probably average a 50-hour workweek.

"The great thing about this profession is that you can either work straight all day, or take time to do other things. Every day is different. As long as I get my work done, I'm on the 'no-plan plan.' I enjoy occasionally making a knife to get the pallet I want for engraving. When I engrave on other makers' knives, I have to work on the pallet I'm given.

"I really admire Harumi for her knifemaking abilities and her dedication to her profession. She is very talented with her designs. I admire Dellana's ability with working her gold designs. I also admire Wolfe Loerchner's daughter. It was really great to hear about a new, young woman knifemaker."

Harumi Hirayama

"When I was a student of Tama Art University, I found a magazine on knives [a precursor to the present *Knife Magazine* of Japan]. That magazine featured a how-to article on making knives," Harumi relates. "I used knives, saws and chisels in class, so I started making knives, naturally. Almost entirely self-taught, I have researched books and studied many antiques and craft pieces.

"[I worked in the] design section of a watch company for two years, and at that time, I came to wish to do custom-made work much more than mass-production goods—hoping each piece would be made as a special order in consultation with each customer. I had my first knife show—the Knifemakers Guild Show—in 1985. As I already have a lifetime of orders, I cannot accept new orders any more. I have a waiting list for cancelled orders or extra pieces for now.

"I don't have many machines. Most of my work is done by hand, so I can only make three to five knives a year nowadays, possibly one main knife or one set with a main piece, and a few other knives. It takes me two to three months or longer to make one folder.

"If I could buy my knives for myself … I know I can not. Instead of buying, I keep drawings, letters and leftover scraps for myself as my treasures. I especially like, sometimes, to see each scrap (cutoff) that I rediscover again in a drawer somewhere. Each material, such as mother-of-pearl, pink pearl, a piece of abalone I used for some butterfly wings, black pearl scraps for cutting out a carp tail and body, mastodon tusk for a cat face, etc., they record the exact shapes of each inlaid piece and each knife handle, as well as record my knifemaking history.

"Each cutoff scrap is the brother or sister to each of my knives because they were once the same piece. These materials are remnants of life, very precious. I feel these small scraps are still alive. My heart goes to my faraway knives owned by someone, somewhere, every time when I see these scraps. This is my small mind trip. This kind of feeling may be a little bit sentimental, but may be natural for a woman, I think."

Gail Lunn

"I used to sit in the shop and watch Larry [Lunn] make his knives," wife, Gail, says. "He eventually encouraged me to try to make one myself, offering me his knowledge and experience. All my life I've worked with my hands on crafts and hobbies, so this was just another new hobby for me. I didn't know at the time that I would become a 'knife-aholic.' I began with a simple folder, although Larry preferred I start on a straight-blade hunter. After grinding many blades, my next step was to use damascus and mosaic damascus on a knife. Then the bountiful amount of new materials added more challenge for me, along with file work, gems, carving, texturing and sculpting.

"Teaching me has been a difficult chore for Larry, and he still has to sit across from me at the dinner table and try to be nice. But he gave me the benefit of his 40-year tool-and-die experience and his many years of knifemaking, without which I would probably not be making knives.

"I visualize the knife in my mind. I dream about knives day and night. I can see a new creation in 3-D and color. I twist and turn the knife, and as the knife develops, I can sometimes see places where I can improve the design or add more detail to give it the 'wow' effect. This is all before starting the actual construction at my bench.

"But one of the hardest aspects of knifemaking to deal with in the beginning was having dirty and/or greasy hands. From

The author calls Gail Lunn "the only woman in the world who has made over 100 dual-action autos," such as her "5th Element" folder featuring a "vines-and-roses"-pattern damascus blade and handle. Other amenities include an opal button, ruby-inlaid thumb stud and back bar, and black-lip-pearl and abalone cabochons. *(Point Seven photo)*

manicured office hands to broken, unpolished nails and gritty hands was sheer misery for a while."

Elizabeth Loerchner

"Knifemaking was something that I had always contemplated, as it has always been a part of my life. However, stepping into the shop next to my father, doing the

caliber of work that he does, was intimidating," Elizabeth admits. "It was after one knife show I attended with my father that I could no longer ignore my desire to step into the shop. I asked my father if he would be willing to teach me and he quickly agreed. The file in my hand felt like an old friend and it did not take me

long to realize that I had found a new passion.

"I consider myself very fortunate to be learning with my father—the knifemaker, I believe, is the best choice [to learn with]. Some of the qualities I would like to learn are an eye for detail and perfection in design and execution. I believe it is also important to learn from the mistakes made by others, especially from someone who has taught himself and can pass on his wealth of experience to the student. I have always enjoyed working with my hands and would not feel the same personal sense of accomplishment if I were to make a knife any other way. Learning from a maker who has always worked with his hands is very important to me.

"My life is my knives! I work seven days a week from about 9 a.m.-2 a.m. in the fall and winter, and I take two part-days off to attend a university school.

"It shocks me every time I see a finished piece I've made. I find it hard to believe that came from an ugly chunk of bar stock. And then I get to pass it on to someone else with the prospect that they

Elizabeth Loerchner filed the 10-inch integral dagger from ½-inch 440C bar stock, adding nickel-damascus and 14k-gold inlays, and giving the piece a nice satin-polished finish.

File-worked damascus inlays follow the swoop of the 416 stainless steel handle scales of Elizabeth Loerchner's 6 ¾-inch lock-back folder.

horse competitions," Dellana details. "I was going to be a vet, but received what appeared to be a great job offer on an Arabian horse farm in Santa Ynez, Calif., so cut my college short and took that job.

"While the horses were wonderful, the owners were not, so I left and returned to my home in Upstate New York. There I took a summer class in metals and jewelry making, and knew that was what I was supposed to do. I continued classes in metals and drawing, and had wonderful teachers in both.

"I think I would have to say the most enjoyable knife project I've ever done was the first knife I made under Jim Schmidt's tutelage. I love to learn, and I had enough metals experience to be patient to see the finished project. My love of learning is a fantastic feeling, particularly in the beginning stages. I had been so excited to see my ideas done, when I started making jewelry, that I didn't always have the patience

to finish them properly and then would be disappointed when I could see flaws in the finished project.

"I also knew on that first knife project that that new 'learning high' doesn't last forever, and to consciously enjoy every moment! So I did, and it was great. And I was skillful enough at finishing metal that I was very satisfied with the first result. It wasn't the most fancy knife I ever made, or the most exciting, but I had such a blissful time during that initial learning phase, I'll never forget that!

"I absolutely love the physical involvement of forging damascus steel.

"I also love making a well-working mechanism. There is a skill level involved that I find very satisfying. And then I get to use the precious gems and gold, and other precious metals, and make a beautiful yet fully functional tool. I just love it!

"There is a lot of satisfaction that comes when the knife goes together for the first time and everything fits perfectly and that strong, solid SNAP happens when you open the blade and it locks in place, and then snaps shut when the lock tip cams over the sweet spot and the blade swings shut of its own accord."

Even Playing Field

These women are exceptional and show what can be done in a once exclusively man's field when one possesses grit, talent and enthusiasm. Now that the door's open, the future appears promising for aspiring women to make beautifully crafted knives.

will experience some of what I experienced in creating the piece."

Dellana

"In my first years at college, I studied animal science, horses being of particular interest to me. I had horses all my life, and showed them in 4H and Arabian

From Beach Sand to Blade

The author explains how he and friends made knife blades from Lake Superior beach sand

By Tim Zowada

Tim Zowada and Kevin Cashen forged three blades from the same iron bloom—Kevin's hunter (center) and the author's hunter and straight razor. In the background is the beach sand and flattened bloom.

The bloom from Kevin Cashen's smelter is shown before cutting.
(Tim Zowada photo)

The smelting of iron is nothing new. Bloomery smelting has been going on for at least the last 3,000 years, and many archaeologists are convinced that iron smelting is much older than that. Bloomery smelting is a time-, materials- and labor-consuming process. A *bloomery* is a type of furnace used for smelting iron from its oxides. It was made obsolete nearly overnight by the introduction of the Bessemer furnace in the mid 1850s. So, how did I get sucked in to the world of turning "dirt" into steel?

I blame the whole thing on knifemaker Kevin Cashen. At the 2006 Ashokan seminar, Michael McCarthy gave an excellent lecture and demonstration on bloomery smelting. He ended up with a large bloom (a mass of wrought iron ready for further working) of low-carbon iron. Although it was interesting to see, it just didn't grab me. I needed steel to make knives, not iron. Smelting iron and all the effort required to get and prepare the ore didn't really interest me. A couple years later, I got *the* phone call from Kevin.

Kevin reminded me that in Michigan we are sitting on top of a lot of iron ore. I knew that, but I didn't have any desire to start digging, roasting and crushing ore. Besides, all the rocky ore was at least four hours away from my home. He then reminded how the Japanese used iron-bearing sand to make sword steel—Tamahagane. I knew he was leading me somewhere. Kevin finally told me that he had found black sand containing the iron ores magnetite and hematite on the south shore of Lake Superior. I had taken the bait. Close to my home, I could get good quality ore ready to put in the smelter. I was hooked! It's all Kevin's fault.

Fluxing the bloom with borax prepares it for the next weld. *(Nathan Zowada photo)*

Shortly thereafter, I found myself on a road trip to Lake Superior, the big lake that singer/songwriter Gordon Lightfoot referred to as "Gitche-Gumee." It was the perfect opportunity to turn work into pleasure. Or, maybe that's pleasure into work? The entire family was piled in the car, complete with buckets and shovels. During the trip I had visions of black beaches with the iron-laden sand just lying there waiting to be scooped

The bloom is prepared for the next fold.
(Nathan Zowada photo)

Kevin Cashen feeds the smelter with charcoal.
(Tim Zowada photo)

up. As with many things in life, the anticipation was better than the reality.

There was black sand on the beach. The trouble was, it was in thin layers. Finding enough to scoop up was difficult and time consuming. Subsequent trips have shown the sand to be, at times, downright elusive. After a while though, you learn where to look. The sand tends to collect mostly near objects on the shore, nearest the water. It's kind of like God's own natural sluice box. After a lot of careful collecting we had three five-gallon buckets of the precious sand. It was time for a smelt.

The folded bloom heats up for the next weld. *(Tim Zowada photo)*

Kevin Cashen's smelter is fiery hot.
(Tim Zowada photo)

Knifemaker Delbert Ealy had also taken a trip to Lake Superior. He got some of the sand and analyzed it. Delbert found his batch of sand was 13 percent hematite and 15 percent magnetite. The balance was mostly silica sand. These numbers vary quite a bit depending on how careful one is while collecting the sand.

I figured the best way to learn how to smelt steel was to visit someone who had already done it. That led me back to Kevin. By this time Kevin had completed six smelts. But, he had never done a smelt using our precious Michigan sand as the source for the iron ore. This was to be a first for both of us.

The Fire Is Lit

The smelting procedure isn't all that difficult, but it is time and labor consuming. First, a fire is lit in the bottom of the smelter, and the air blast is turned on. Charcoal is dumped in the top of the smelter during the preheating cycle, eventually filling it to the top. After the smelter is up to temperature, the ore is added along with more charcoal. You must be careful to not add the ore too quickly, or the smelter temperature will decrease enough that a bloom won't form. The next four hours are spent alternately adding charcoal and sand.

During the smelting process, the silica sand in the mix melts and forms a molten slag. This slag is problematic in that it will clog the air blast if you aren't paying attention. The slag is also a helpful byproduct. It acts as a flux assisting the reduced iron ore to fuse and form the bloom. After an hour or so, excess slag must be drained off or it will block the air completely. After about four hours, draining off the slag becomes a losing battle, and the smelter is shut down.

The next 45 minutes feels like being a kid the day before Christmas. You want to look inside and see what you've got. At the same time, you must wait to allow things to cool and solidify. The bloom forms in the base of the smelter just below the air blast. Digging the non-burnt charcoal from the base and pushing the bloom down from the top allows it to be removed from the bottom of the smelter. Kevin cut the bloom in half. We each had nearly three pounds of high-carbon bloom.

After the smelting stage, the bloom is a rough chunk of metal. In many ways it resembles a clinker from a coal fire. It has pits, voids and remnants of slag and charcoal stuck to it, and inside of it. The carbon content is irregular throughout the bloom. This is where the real work begins.

During the smelting, the goal is to form a bloom that is consistently high in carbon. McCarthy showed us that, by changing the angle of the air blast, we could vary the amount of carbon in the bloom. By keeping the bloom fairly small, and high in carbon, it is possible to avoid the post-smelt sorting process common with the Japanese *tatara* (a traditional smelting furnace) style smelts. The five-to-six-pound blooms can simply be taken out of the smelter, forged down flat, and the folding process begun.

The folding and welding of the bloom make up the refining process. The continued folding closes up voids and works impurities out of the steel. The carbon content is reduced and made consistent throughout the bar of steel.

At first the welding is a bit tricky. The bloom tends to crumble and fall apart. High temperatures and gentle hammer blows must be used to keep things together. After about five folds, the bar starts to "behave," with the crumbling tendency nearly gone and the welding decreasing in difficulty. After weld seven, the steel becomes the easiest welding material I have ever worked with, and meanwhile the folding and welding continues until the resulting bar looks clean of pits and the remnants of the weld seams are gone.

It's Really Steel

The result is a bar of steel! While grinding the surface and taking a couple quick photos, I noticed things still looked a little dirty. There were still some pits and faint weld seams visible. So, it was back to the forge for a couple more folds. The extra folds really cleaned things up. The problem was, the more I forged and welded, the more material was lost via oxidation. After a day and a half of work, the material became quite precious. The tendency was to stop folding early to save material.

My bloom half weighed 2.78 pounds. After the folding and welding I had a bar of steel that weighed 11.7 ounces and was big enough to make a straight razor and utility knife blade.

The forging of the blades is surprisingly easy. It is much easier to forge than the O1-and-L6 damascus I usually make. The lack of alloying elements and low "harden-ability" allow the forging to take place quickly and at relatively low temperatures. The welds don't have any tendency to

Nathan Zowada excavates black, iron-rich sand on the shore of Lake Superior. *(Tim Zowada photo)*

come apart, as is common with modern laminated steels.

The grinding is also easy. The lack of alloying elements leaves the steel very low in abrasion resistance, and a joy to grind. I went through my normal progression of 60-, 220- and 400-grit belts, and the edges were ground to a thickness of .020 inches.

The blades had been forged and ground, and it was time for the heat-treating process. I figured it would heat treat like plain 1084 high-carbon steel. I was wrong. I had become spoiled by modern salt-bath equipment, and quenching in oils and salts. Using a small scrap I had saved, I found that I could harden a 1/8-inch-thick piece to reach a Rockwell hardness of 58 Rc, and a 1/16-inch-thick piece to a rating of 61 Rc by quenching in water. Blinded by the high hardness numbers, I forgot that I had not water-quenched a blade in decades!

The blades were heated to 1,475 degrees in my high-temperature salt bath, and then quenched in water with a rapid agitation. Here is where my problems began. I had forgotten that when quenching in water, the blade edges should be left thicker than when using oil or salts. The thicker edges slow the Martensite (steel crystalline structure) formation and decrease the tendency for the blades to crack. Well, I'm sure you've guessed it by now. My 5-inch utility knife became a 3 5/8 inch hunting knife! The blade had cracked from the edge up two-thirds of the way to the spine. It was a good, although expensive, reminder that smelted steel is entirely different from modern steels.

Later, I heat-treated the shortened hunter one more time. This time I used my salt marquenching set-up. Using an extremely agitated quench, I achieved a Rockwell hardness rating of 50 Rc on the ricasso and about 60 Rc on the edge of the blade. This was much better. In the future, I think I will spend more time experimenting with clay on the blade to produce a *hamon* (temper line), and quenching in fast oil.

Blades At Last

After the heat-treating and final grinding I had a nearly finished hunter and straight razor. All I had to do was polish the blades and fit the handles. Well, if the steel wasn't made like modern steel, wasn't alloyed like modern steel, and wasn't heat-treated like modern steel, why did I think it would polish and etch like modern steel? A lengthy telephone call to knifemaker Rick Barrett helped me get the blades looking good and revealed the layers from the folding.

All that was left was to build the knife handles. In keeping with the "made in Michigan" theme, the handle material came from my home state. The spacer on the hunting knife is float copper from Michigan's Keweenaw Peninsula, the maple handle culled from my firewood pile, and the razor scales are whitetail deer antlers from a buck that was shot by my father-in-law. Even the razor pivot screw was custom made locally for the Hart Steel razor project.

After all this time and work, I was thrilled to find the finished blades performed quite well. The low abrasion resistance makes sharpening the blade and honing the razor simple, but different. In general, using a finer grit stone than normal and using little to no down pressure gave great results on the knife. I got my best edges off of a Spyderco Ultra-Fine grit ceramic stone.

The razor is shaving sharp once a person gets used to the steel. Just a linen and canvas strop will keep the edge shaving smoothly for months. No pastes or abrasives are needed. With this simple steel, the blade should be stropped between passes during a shave. I think that bench hone sharpening will only be required every three to four months.

Of course, once the smelting bug bit me I had to do it again. I built a smelter in my shop, bought up all the charcoal in town, and got more sand. Since the original smelt at Kevin's, I have completed seven smelts at home. I have been tweaking the process to get better, more consistent blooms. I am also re-learning the heat treatment of simple steels. Making steel from sand is truly addictive!

I'm sure this isn't the first time a bloomery-style smelt has been done with Michigan ore. Iron has been mined in Michigan for a long time. Due to the elusive nature of the sand, it is possible this is the first time a smelt has been done with Lake Superior sand.

I don't make any claims that this steel is better, stronger, sharper or longer lasting than other smelted or modern steels. Yet, it is neat stuff, and is quite gratifying to make and use. After fabricating a blade from nothing but sand, the feeling you get while using one is similar to catching a trout on a dry fly you tied, while using a bamboo rod you built—complete satisfaction.

Swords of Norse Warriors Felt Alive!

Anglo-Saxon and Viking swords conjure up images of salty spray and fearsome fighters daring fate and foe

By Vincent Evans

Viking and Anglo-Saxon style swords have inspired modern knife and sword makers for as long as I can remember. You will find a Viking-inspired dagger in Bill Moran's 1974-1975 catalog, and knives made by Kemal (Don Fogg and Murad Sayen) in some early 1980s publications.

The Viking Age spanned the late 8th to 11th centuries. The often-forgotten Anglo-Saxon era in England dates from the early 5th century AD to the Norman Conquest in 1066.

Now, over a millennium later, in the era of high-speed Internet and space-age technology, why does it seem that Viking and Anglo-Saxon style swords are still so popular? Who were the real Vikings, not the Hollywood image of men in horned helmets swinging double-bladed axes? What is it that continues to draw makers and collectors to this style?

Swedish sword smith and designer for Albion Swords, Peter Johnsson says, "The Viking sword is one of the most iconic blades of history. The very name conjures images of salty spray and fearsome fighters daring fate and foe. This image can be so strong that the true nature of their swords is difficult to see in the radiance of the myth. The popular image of the wild and barbaric Norse warrior often

leaves us with preconceived and flawed ideas of what to expect from these weapons. Perhaps in hopes to relate some of the power of this imagery, many replicas today are hopelessly clumsy and crude in comparison to the quality of the ancient blades, and fail to capture anything of their real glory."

Michael "Tinker" Pearce comments, "I was first attracted to Viking swords and knives through an experience with a private collection when I was in my early 20s. The owner of the collection had me put on some cotton gloves and invited me to pick up an actual 10th-century Viking sword. I had never imagined a sword could feel like that. Despite being about 30 inches long and two inches wide at the base, it felt light and lively in the hand; it felt alive! I was hooked. I have never forgotten that feeling, and when I became a sword maker years later, that was my goal—to make swords that would have the feel of that sword."

Kevin Cashen had a similar

experience in handling an original Viking sword. He was further inspired by the high level of metalworking skills by the makers of the original swords, and it challenged and guided him in the direction he chose in his career as a blade smith.

"Like many sword makers I was always fascinated by any swords, but due to the lack of popularity enjoyed by other swords I didn't really appreciate these magnificent blades until I had the opportunity to examine and handle one of them," Cashen says.

"Nobody who has held a

Albion's "Valkyrja" model is inspired by a Finnish find from Suantaka, Tyrvanto, Tavastland.

With a dark-oak handle carved from the rib of a submerged Viking ship, the core of the blade on Jake Powning's "Willowraven" is "interrupted-twist-pattern" damascus, while the edge is 800-layer, pattern-welded steel. The hilt and scabbard fittings are silicon bronze, and the scabbard itself is carved from curly yellow birch that is lined with close-sheered sheep fleece.

real 1,300-year-old, pattern-welded blade can help but be in awe of that level of metalworking skill, and feel challenged to attempt it if they are a smith. Just about every ironworking culture forge welded, piled or folded blade steel, but very few ever did it at this level of sophistication. It was this style of blades that convinced me that I could specialize in European blades for the rest of my career and still only scratch the surface of not only what was possible, but what already had been done by our ancestors only to be forgotten."

Spirit of the Time

Johnsson continues, "We are well served to remember that the

Modeled after Viking swords bearing the names "ULFBERHT" and "INGELRII," Jeff Pringle's sword showcases pattern-welded letters inlaid into carbon steel.

swords of the Vikings were not unique to the Norse warriors. Very much the same blades were used in the East and West, all the way from Kiev to Dublin. These are

swords that express the spirit of a time and a great craft tradition, encompassing a large part of the western Eurasian continent. The tradition has roots in the long-bladed spatha (a straight sword) of the late Roman Empire. Important also are swords from the Far East, brought by the mounted warriors of the Steppe, and the weapons of the Germanic tribes north of the Alps, all these influences being forged together and tempered in the tumultuous times of the Migration Period.

"The sword of the Vikings is therefore the result of a long history of sword making with influences from faraway places and peoples," Johnsson determines. "It is not apart or isolated, but very much belongs to a vast and multifaceted mix of cultures.

"What is most specific is the type of hilts that were favored in different areas and periods," he explains. "We can differentiate between a sword made by Anglo-Saxon, Frankish, Danish, Swedish or Norwegian smiths.

"For me as a sword smith of the 21st century, the greatest inspiration working with these blades is the opportunity to learn from surviving originals—individual expressions of a vast and rich tradition," Johnsson says. "The engineering and design of these weapons are highly accomplished, the subtlety of the shape is easily overlooked by their strong and immediate visual impact. The intricate construction

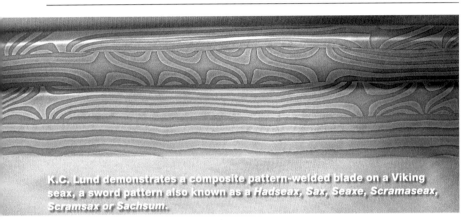

K.C. Lund demonstrates a composite pattern-welded blade on a Viking seax, a sword pattern also known as a *Hadseax, Sax, Seaxe, Scramaseax, Scramsax or Sachsum.*

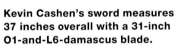

Kevin Cashen's sword measures 37 inches overall with a 31-inch O1-and-L6-damascus blade.
(Steve Dean photo)

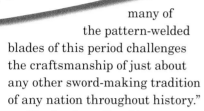

Michael "Tinker" Pearce shows us his version of a Viking sword.

many of the pattern-welded blades of this period challenges the craftsmanship of just about any other sword-making tradition of any nation throughout history."

Stories from the old sagas, and the beauty and craftsmanship of the pattern-welded blades have been a siren's call to modern makers the world over, from the Isle of Skye to the Czech Republic, and from Nova Scotia to the Islands of Hawaii.

Jake Powning remarks, "I am inspired by the ancient European folk culture, and the myths and fables that have been spun from its remains. The closest material culture remaining from this ancient well of inspiration is that of Viking-Age Scandinavia. Pattern welding is a beautiful process that was dear to the Germanic tribes of northern and western Europe from the late Roman period until the end of the Viking Age. For me the opportunity for ornamentation, mythological subject matter, and the alluring beauty of multi-bar pattern welding is too much to resist. The tales of Merlin and Arthur, Beowulf and Grendel, and the great dragon slayers like Sigurd Fafnirsbane come alive in these swords."

In true artist fashion, Powning created his "Vidirhrafn–Willowraven" with a dark oak grip carved from a section of wood from the rib of a submerged Viking ship.

Accomplished Ancients

The creativity afforded the bladesmith is endless. "Pattern welding is what I love to do. I love the complex patterns that can be made with this style of blade, and the variations are endless. It amazes me what the ancients were able to achieve with the patterns in these blades, using very crude tools by our standards today," comments K.C. Lund.

My father, a blacksmith, always had an interest in archaeology and the sea. I was quite

A Rob Miller piece is styled after the Ballinderry sword recovered from an Irish burial.

young when he was inspired to create a Viking sword after reading Eric Oxenstierna's *"The Norsemen."* I don't recall the details, but the memory of listening to an old LP of Wagner's *"Der Ring des Nibelungen"* and seeing the completed sword hanging on the wall left a lasting impression on my young mind. My approach today is a mix of those early impressions and the feeling of an apprentice learning from a skilled craftsman as I try to walk in my master's shoes.

Towards the end of the Viking Age, as better quality ores were mined, pattern-welded swords became less common and homogenous-steel blades more prevalent. Viking swords bearing the names "ULFBERHT" and "INGELRII" appeared—high quality, homogenous-steel blades with pattern-welded letters forged into the blade.

Rob Miller comments, "I love the beauty and elegance of the Viking/Saxon eras, before steel became more homogenized in manufacture; the fact that the sword would often have its own story, passed through generations and imbued with a sense of mystery and awe."

Although most sword makers appreciate swords from many cultures and eras, it is still sad to see the zenith of the pattern-welded blade in Europe pass away. "At the end of the Viking period, pattern welding and ornately decorated hilts are a thing of the past, and there my interest in them fades," laments Jeff Pringle.

Yet, after a millennium, these far-reaching adventurers continue to travel the seas of time and inspire creative minds around the world.

Johnsson concludes, "For a contemporary sword smith, these glorious examples of skillful craftsmanship offer an insight to the mindset and attitude of the ancient smiths. Holding an original sword, experiencing directly its dominating presence and purposeful functionality is awe inspiring. By truly appreciating the real quality of these incredible blades we can also get a glimpse about the reality behind many of the sagas and myths. What we then may see is many times more fantastic than fiction can hope to convey. The intertwined dragons that sleep in the silver of the hilt, the dulled edges that have lost their bite from the gnawing of father time, may yet hope to be brought back to life."

Inspired by swords found in Chertsey, England, and Copenhagen, Denmark, Vince Evans's interpretation of a 10th-century Viking sword includes a composite pattern-welded blade, blued-steel guard and pommel with silver wire inlay, and silver scabbard mounts. *(Point Seven photo)*

Tips for Carving Titanium Grips

Embellishing knife handles takes the redundancy out of knifemaking and adds beauty

By Matt Cucchiara

I thought about carving titanium handle scales from the time I made my first knife. After seeing some of Ken Onion's work at the shows he attended, my search was on for a high-speed, dental-style grinder with carbide dental burrs that would carve into titanium handle scales without taking much time to remove a lot of material.

I searched the Internet and saw some grinders that were fairly expensive, as well as lower-end units that didn't seem like they would stand up to the constant abuse of grinding titanium. I was at a gun show one day and came across a company that sold a mid-range dental lab grinder for carving all types of material. At the show, the representatives allowed me to try their grinder on one of my custom knives I carried at the time. All I can say is that it worked great!

The company can be found online at GraphicTransfer.com. They know their product and stand behind everything they sell with top-notch customer service. I purchased their basic starter kit for right around $750.

I watched the instructional video that came with the kit and sat down with some sticky-back transfer paper to try drawing my own designs that I'd eventually carve into knife handles. That didn't work out very well for me. I found out quickly that I couldn't draw something at the level of detail I wanted. At that time I looked into purchasing clip art in book form and also in digital format from the Internet.

I learned that I needed just the right image or drawing that would give me enough detail for the carving to look cool, but not so much detail that it took too long to carve or just didn't look right on the knife when it was finished.

Brothers Rick and Rudy Lala chose a carved wizard for the "Reptile" model flipper folder. Rick makes the knives and Rudy carves them up!

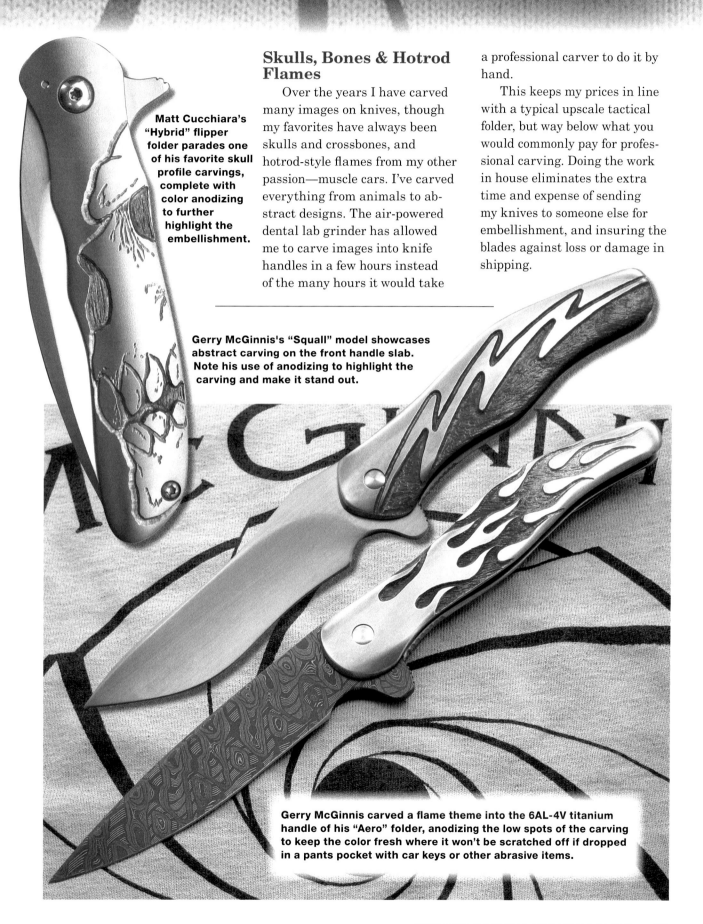

Skulls, Bones & Hotrod Flames

Over the years I have carved many images on knives, though my favorites have always been skulls and crossbones, and hotrod-style flames from my other passion—muscle cars. I've carved everything from animals to abstract designs. The air-powered dental lab grinder has allowed me to carve images into knife handles in a few hours instead of the many hours it would take a professional carver to do it by hand.

This keeps my prices in line with a typical upscale tactical folder, but way below what you would commonly pay for professional carving. Doing the work in house eliminates the extra time and expense of sending my knives to someone else for embellishment, and insuring the blades against loss or damage in shipping.

Matt Cucchiara's "Hybrid" flipper folder parades one of his favorite skull profile carvings, complete with color anodizing to further highlight the embellishment.

Gerry McGinnis's "Squall" model showcases abstract carving on the front handle slab. Note his use of anodizing to highlight the carving and make it stand out.

Gerry McGinnis carved a flame theme into the 6AL-4V titanium handle of his "Aero" folder, anodizing the low spots of the carving to keep the color fresh where it won't be scratched off if dropped in a pants pocket with car keys or other abrasive items.

The author adds some text along the edge of the skull on his small, modified "Severen" flipper folder.

tiresome to grind metal alone in a shop day after day.

The embellishment inspires me to make a particular knife style repeatedly, knowing that by carving a different design on every piece, it brings a truly one-off feel that customers seem to appreciate. Being the sole author of a handmade knife is extremely gratifying to say the least. Many fellow knifemakers helped me in achieving my present skill level, and I try to pass on what I have learned to every novice who

Through the years I have learned what type of carving sells fast and what doesn't when applied to the style of frame-lock flipper folders I now make almost exclusively. It isn't at all uncommon for a knifemaker to experience some level of burnout after fashioning the same style of knife for several years in a row. No matter how much passion is put into the hand-

craft, it makes sense that it would become increasingly

shows an interest in introducing carving to their work. Several makers have also bought identical equipment to mine, and have found it to be perfect for this type of work.

I enjoy flipping through the large collection of clip art I've amassed, finding something I earmarked or thought would look cool someday on one of my flippers. I then get out my small light box, and using the film paper, I transfer the artwork from a page or computer disc onto the paper. Next I use an actual handle slab I will carve, and place it on the drawing to make an outline of the grip over the designed transfer paper. I cut it out to size, peel the paper from the backing and apply it directly onto my semi-finished handle slab. I usually start off with a squared-off

In stunning detail, Rick and Rudy Lala created a dragon-themed "Reptile" flipper folder.

Gerry McGinnis chose an abstract pattern with green anodizing for the "Premonition" model.

carbide dental bit in the grinder to transfer the drawing directly to the handle scale. I remove the transfer paper, or what is left of it, and by looking at the original image I add all the detail work to the handle scale to make the carving really pop. It takes about four different carbide bits to do all the knife carving.

Typically I use a barrel-shaped bit with a round end, one with a square end, and two sizes of round-ball bits. You can do a lot of carving with only these four cutting bits.

Textured Backdrops

It's a good practice to add texture, whether using small lines or full stippling, to the background of a carved image. Applying a variety of finishes on the handle scales can "bring out" the carved image, making it appear to elevate off of the handle slab, which also provides a better, firmer grip on the knife when in use.

I bead-blast the handle slab after carving, then bring the high points of the carving back to a hand-rubbed, satin finish to really make it pop. The use of anodized colors on different carving levels can also make the image stand out and give the knife a brilliant look.

Sometimes a small amount of carving, like a customer's initials, insignia, a badge or emblem, can personalize the knife for the end user. I have further married the carving with the overall design of the knife by extending carved images onto the flat of the blade or up and over the pocket clip. Continuing the embellishment beyond the knife handle seems to complete the package. The carving tool also works well to make thumb-ramp serrations and traction grooves on other areas of the knife.

There is no end in sight for what can be done with knife carving. It is limited only by the imagination. As illustrated herein, a good friend and extraordinary young knifemaker, Gerry McGinnis, and his mother, Kim McGinnis, have come up with some cool designs on his knives. And the custom knives by brothers Rick and Rudy Lala have taken carving to a whole new level.

Only pictures can do justice to Rudy's incredible carved designs, including animals that seemingly come alive on titanium knife handles. Second-to-none is his ability to perform deep 3-D carving, and introduce textures, anodized colors and exotic materials like Timascus. Such boundless creativity benefits not only the knife, but also knife collectors and budding enthusiasts across the globe who've been inspired by the skilled hands of such artists.

Rudy Lala's 3-D carving is a mainstay of knives made by his brother, Rick, including this "Sentry" flipper folder where the embellishment flows seamlessly into the "Lightening Strike" carbon fiber handle.

Soap, Strop and Shave

The quality and diversity of straight razors made a lasting impression on the author

By Richard D. White

It has been over 20 years since I gazed at straight razors with wonderful carved-pearl or tooled-aluminum handles at the Winston Salem Knife Club's annual show, or those showcasing celluloid grips, painted peacocks and Art Deco-style flowing hair. To this day I can picture the scene in my mind. Surrounding the large showroom were amazing knife collections of all kinds, with edged implements carefully mounted on large boards or in original hardware store display cases. Among the magnificent knives were ornate straight razors, neatly lined up in rows or lying in felt-lined trays that comprised each exhibitor's contribution to the show.

One gentleman had his collection housed in "books" of plastic inserts that he lovingly turned, page by page, to reveal straight razors in colors and patterns previously unimaginable to this collector. The prices were perhaps more dramatic than the razors themselves, with the most unique pieces upwards of $100. Although my collecting focus at that time was not directed at straight razors, their quality and diversity made a lasting impression on me.

Unfortunately, the collecting of straight razors has languished over two decades, with the advent of disposable razors and the general public's lack of knowledge and interest in the art of soaping, stropping and shaving.

Like any unusual grip pattern that sets a straight razor apart, diagonal stripes are rare and, thus, desirable. The tang stamps read "Genco"—a W.R. Case trademark—and "Ontario Cutlery."

Collectors recognize the handle material of the razors at top and bottom as "twisted rope" celluloid, while the piece in middle is molded into the form of a woman's flowing hair.

Straight razor collecting has always been an offshoot of knife collecting, with most traditional cutlery companies having also offered a full line of razors. The celluloid on many straight razor handles is the same as that on vintage pocketknife grips. Collectors who focused on particular knife brands, such as Western States Cutlery, Boker or Keen Kutter, also found straight razors among the offerings.

Because the etching on straight razor blades was more ornate than on pocketknives, some collectors favored the former over the latter, and they sought out objects associated with straight razors, including shaving brushes, leather razor strops, cases and hones.

Though there is some modern indifference to antique straight razors, an awakening appears on the horizon, once again placing them in the forefront of collecting.

Shave Ready

Clues to the rising interest in old-time shaving lie in the descriptions of straight razors on Internet auction sites. Words such as "shave ready," lead one to surmise that the razors are being purchased not for their collectible value, but for the use for which they were originally intended. Prices for even the most common straight razors average over $25, with the finest examples climbing back into the $75-$100 range.

Whatever the cause for the sudden revival, collectors who've held on to vintage straight razors for decades are muttering a silent "hallelujah" at the prospect of seeing them gain in value. If a revival is at hand, it begs the question of what type of straight razor to collect. There are thousands available through Internet sites and at most antique and gun shows, with a nearly endless choice of handle materials and company tang stamps.

Collecting Do's and Don'ts

A few considerations and helpful hints ensure an investment in straight razors will pay dividends in the future, and at the same time provide the collector with something he or she can be proud to display.

With few exceptions, stay away from slick-black-handled straight razors. They're akin to *National*

Rare straight-razor handles include mother-of-pearl (bottom), which is difficult to obtain in the length required, and tooled aluminum that was produced during a time when aluminum was rare and quite expensive.

Geographic magazine donations at the local library—millions of them were made, nobody collects them, and consequently they have little or no value. Besides, the handles don't look very good.

Look for razors that have fancy carving or other embellishments on the handles, like celluloid-handle razors, generally in "French Ivory" celluloid, that showcase bamboo, fleur de leis, flowing-hair, entwined-rope, beaded-edge or open-scroll designs. With intricate handles, the straight razors command a high price. The bamboo-designed celluloid straight razors, made by such knife companies as W.R. Case, A.J. Jordan, H. Boker, Clauss, Torrey and Northfield, are especially interesting, complete with lifelike bamboo joints and darkened indentations. A collection of bamboo-style celluloid razors would simultaneously hold value and look breathtaking in a showcase.

Nothing beats fancy handles, whether on pocketknives or straight razors. With alternating stripes of red, orange and yellow, "Candy Stripe" celluloid, used by American and foreign companies, is not only a popular straight razor handle material, but also makes for an outstanding display and a solid basis for a valuable razor collection.

The same goes for other fancy celluloid patterns and colors—variegated onyxes in grays and browns, "checkerboard glitter," multi-colored swirls, and the popular "butter and molasses" celluloid. Look for examples in good condition with brilliantly colored handles.

Sharp Pedigrees

Purchase straight razors made by highly collected pocketknife companies. Like pocketknives, straight razors benefit by having a good pedigree—a name well known and highly collected, like Western States Cutlery. With a significant knife collector following, Western States straight razors command incredible prices when they show up on the Internet. Western States straight razors with fancy celluloid handles, especially in original razor boxes, are a winning formula.

The W.R. Case and Sons Cutlery Co. of Bradford, Pa., has its own collector following. Although

Three W.R. Case and Sons razors are pictured along with an original Case razor strop.

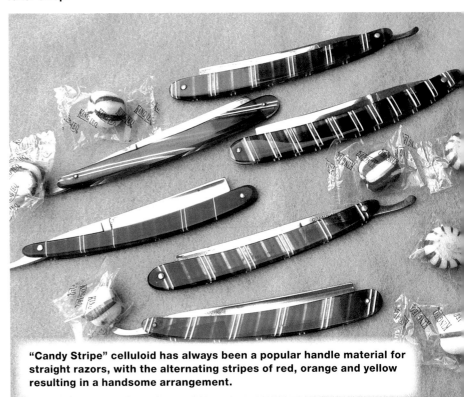

"Candy Stripe" celluloid has always been a popular handle material for straight razors, with the alternating stripes of red, orange and yellow resulting in a handsome arrangement.

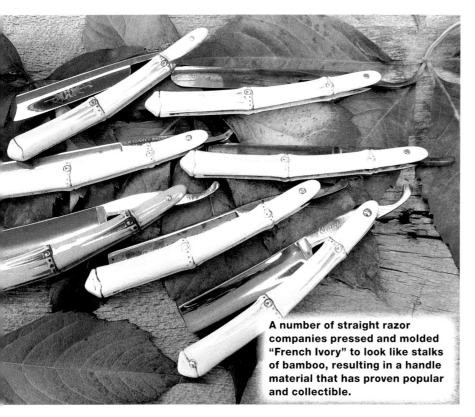

A number of straight razor companies pressed and molded "French Ivory" to look like stalks of bamboo, resulting in a handle material that has proven popular and collectible.

Straight razor collecting can be an exciting and colorful adventure, with handles produced in a variety of schemes, from glittered checkerboards to mottled swirls, "cracked ice," and gorgeous brown and yellow swirls known as "butter and molasses" celluloid.

Be on the lookout for extraordinary features on straight razors, like those with genuine pearl handles. Pearl-handled razors were rarely made and few of those survived, having been dropped and broken over the years. As with pocketknives, pearl is a highly desirable straight razor handle material, particularly because of the length of the pearl required to handle a long, thin straight razor.

Tooled-aluminum-handle straight razors are also rare and quite desirable. There was a time in our history when aluminum was a scarce and precious metal. It wasn't until 1885 that a reasonably cheap method was devised to produce aluminum in quantities large enough to be useful. During this time period, straight razors made with hand-tooled aluminum handles were almost unheard of, and those that survived hold great value.

Straight razors with celluloid handle slabs, and pearl or celluloid tangs are also valuable and collectable. Look for examples that show no signs of cracking around the pivot pin.

As with all collectables, condition is important in regard to knives and straight razors. The highly tempered and thin blades are fragile. I have broken the blade of a straight razor by accidentally dropping it on a cement floor. While a high temper is necessary for a sharp blade and shave, it makes for brittle steel. Steel blades will also rust if they sit in moisture for any length of time, and the resulting metal pits are almost impossible to remove due to the hardness of the steel. Handles are similarly prone to damage. Although celluloid is a durable material, it can crack or

primarily a knife company, Case produced thousands of celluloid razors under a variety of brand names, including the Case name. All of the brands are collectible, and as a crossover for pocket-knife collectors, command high prices. I believe the same value appreciation applies for many

other pocketknife companies, including Clauss, Cattaraugus, Hibbard-Spencer-Bartlett, Schatt and Morgan, Wade and Butcher, Shapleigh Hardware, Wilbert Cutlery, H. Boker and Sons and Union Cutlery, each with a complete line of straight razors in addition to pocketknives.

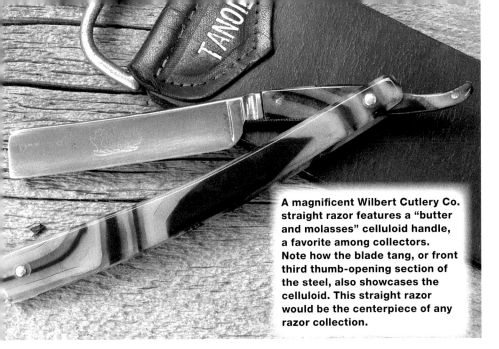

A magnificent Wilbert Cutlery Co. straight razor features a "butter and molasses" celluloid handle, a favorite among collectors. Note how the blade tang, or front third thumb-opening section of the steel, also showcases the celluloid. This straight razor would be the centerpiece of any razor collection.

After applying wax and letting it dry, wipe and polish each blade carefully with a soft towel. This will add a thin, invisible layer of protection to your blades, and will go a long way in protecting the metal from possible contamination from celluloid deterioration. The micro-thin wax layer also protects the blades of the knives and straight razors from fingerprints that can tarnish them. Be careful wiping a knife or straight razor blade with a soft towel to avoid cuts.

The time is right to actively seek out colorful straight razors that are in excellent condition. Looking for razors that have decent pedigrees, and avoiding those with worn or broken blades, will ensure that the money you spend pays dividends in the future. An impressive collection of vintage straight razors is something that you'll be proud to display or take to shows.

warp if exposed to heat, kept in a tight showcase or dropped. Most antiques lose significant value if damaged in some way.

The celluloid handles will deteriorate. The obvious signs are rusting of the blade of the razor itself—as it deteriorates, celluloid gives off a gas that affects the metal it comes in contact with—and crusting and crumbling of the celluloid.

Apply a thin coat of wax on the blades of your knives and straight razors. I learned this technique after noticing that some of my fixed-blade knives were showing signs of rust after being stored in leather sheaths. Even the so-called "vegetable-tanned" leather has enough chemicals in it to affect the knife blades.

Celluloid Stability

Celluloid is still an outstanding straight razor handle material, as evidenced by the millions of knives and razors featuring such colorful synthetic grips. If you ever find that one of your straight razors or pocketknives shows signs of blade rust or that the celluloid seems to be crumbling, separate it from the rest of the collection so that it does not contaminate the remainder of your pieces. In all likelihood, this particular celluloid was poorly made, and is subject to eventual deterioration.

Embellishments on the French-Ivory-celluloid grips include fancy scrollwork, entwined flowers and art deco styling. Note the fine lines, designed to mimic the grains of elephant ivory, of the bottom razor.

Zero Tolerance for Knives in School

How has it evolved into innocent children being expelled from school for having utilitarian knives?

By Louis P. Nappen, J.D., M.A.T.

In Louisiana, an 8-year-old brings her grandfather's pocket watch to show-and-tell. The watch has a chain attached to it with a one-inch pocketknife. The girl is expelled.

In Florida, a 15-year-old has a penknife attached to her belt loop. She uses the knife to cut twine on bales of hay for her horses, but she forgets to remove it before going to school. She is arrested.

In Massachusetts, an 8th-grade honors student confiscates a knife from another student who threatened to hurt his friend. He plans to go to the main office and turn in the knife, but before he can do so, the assistant principal, hearing word of the incident, suspends him for one year because he "possesses" a knife.

In Georgia, a 14-year-old discovers that he inadvertently brought his fishing knife to his middle school. He brings the knife to the office to turn it in. He is arrested, convicted of a felony and expelled.

In New York, a 2-inch pocketknife is found in a high school student's car emergency kit, where he also stores a sleeping bag, bottled water and an MRE. He is an Eagle Scout and believes in being prepared. The previous year, the boy received commendations from the City of

In Georgia, a 14-year-old who discovered that he inadvertently brought his fishing knife to middle school was arrested, convicted of a felony and expelled. The Case Fillet Knife sports a 6-inch blade and leather sheath.

Troy and the Boy Scouts of America for saving a woman's life. He has completed Army basic training and hopes to attend West Point Military Academy. He is suspended for 20 days.

In Washington, a high school sophomore uses his mini Swiss Army pocketknife scissors to trim his hangnails and uses the 1 3/8-inch blade to tighten parts on his skateboard. The knife is attached to his key chain and, after he empties his pockets for a routine security check, he is expelled.

In Texas, a 10-inch bread knife with a rounded point is found in the bed of a 16-year-old's pickup truck parked on school property. This honor student's grandmother had suffered a stroke and was just moved to assisted living. The night before, the student helped deliver his grandmother's household items to Goodwill, and the knife apparently slipped out of one of the boxes. The school board expels him, and orders him to spend a year in a juvenile justice education program.

In New York, a 2-inch pocketknife is found in a high school student's car emergency kit, where he also stores a sleeping bag, bottled water and an MRE. He is an Eagle Scout and believes in being prepared.

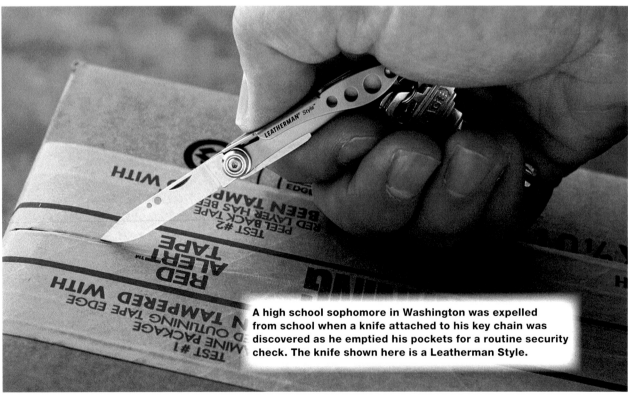

A high school sophomore in Washington was expelled from school when a knife attached to his key chain was discovered as he emptied his pockets for a routine security check. The knife shown here is a Leatherman Style.

In South Carolina, an 11-year-old puts a kitchen knife in her lunchbox to cut her chicken. She is arrested and suspended. Michael Rader's handmade Santoku kitchen knife sports a Bubinga-wood and box-elder handle. (*BladeGallery.com photo*)

A 1st-grader in Delaware brings his Cub Scout fork-spoon-knife pocket utensil to school to use at lunch. The school district committee suspends him for 45 days and recommends that he be placed at a reform school for juvenile delinquents.

In Delaware, a 1st-grader brings his Cub Scout fork-spoon-knife pocket utensil to school to use at lunch. The school district committee suspends him for 45 days and recommends that he be placed at a reform school for juvenile delinquents.

Further in Delaware, a 3rd-grader brings to school a birthday cake, and a knife to cut the cake. The teacher uses the knife to cut the cake, and then reports the student to the principal. He is expelled for a year.

In Colorado, a mother puts a knife in a lunchbox for her 10-year-old daughter to cut an apple. When the girl realizes that the knife might violate school policy, she turns it in to a teacher, who tells her she did the right thing. The girl is expelled.

In South Carolina, an 11-year-old puts a kitchen knife in her lunchbox to cut her chicken at lunch. She is arrested and suspended.

In Rhode Island, a kindergartner brings a plastic knife to school to cut his cookies. He is suspended.

How did it come to this?

In 1990 and 1994, Congress passed "Gun-Free School" Acts. The U.S. Supreme Court found the 1990 Act unconstitutional for exceeding Congressional "Commerce Clause" power. The 1994

Act, however, utilized Congress' grant-in-aid power to force schools to cooperate.

When the federal government offers much-needed funding to states via grant-in-aid, states may, of course, refuse. Yet, this is unlikely. The U.S. Constitution does not mention education, which is, historically, a reserved power of the states. However, after states accept grant-in-aid money to be used for a specific purpose, they have to obey any attached federal requirements.

As part of the 1994 Act, Congress mandated that "each state receiving federal funds shall have in effect a policy requiring the expulsion from school for a period of not less than one year of any student who is determined to have brought a weapon to a school." Upon accepting the money, the states required their school districts to implement policies in line with the federal mandate.

The Act originally defined "weapon" to include only firearms but, thereafter, expanded the definition to include any item that "may be used as a weapon." Accordingly, knives, which were previously tolerated for mere student possession on school grounds, became definitively outlawed.

Statutes and policies often broadly define weapons. Consider, for example, Pennsylvania's Education 24 PS 13-1317.2: "the term 'weapon' shall include, but not be limited to, any knife, cutting instrument, cutting tool, nunchaku, firearm, shotgun, rifle and any other tool, instrument or implement capable of inflicting serious bodily injury." Although the federal Act technically permits case-by-case analyses,

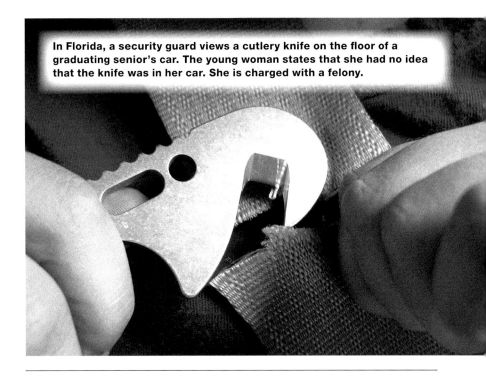

In Florida, a security guard views a cutlery knife on the floor of a graduating senior's car. The young woman states that she had no idea that the knife was in her car. She is charged with a felony.

school administrators fear losing billions of dollars in educational funding if they do not impose a rigid stance. School officials have therefore chosen, by and large, a "zero tolerance" approach whenever a student has been alleged to possess a weapon.

"Zero tolerance" is the common term applied to illegal conduct that imposes mechanical and stiff penalties regardless of individual circumstances. It was first applied during the 1980s "war on drugs." Zero tolerance policies have gotten more expansive, and administrators are not shy to implement strict analysis when students are found to possess anything questionable.

Many educators approve of zero tolerance policies. Such policies deal with issues swiftly, firmly and consistently. They ensure that everyone is treated equally, and allow school officials to avoid politically incorrect decisions. Zero tolerance limits the chances of schools being sued. In response to the 6-year-old with

Cub Scout utensils, the district's president defended the punishment by hypothesizing: What if there was a scuffle and someone pulled out a knife?

Of course, theoretically, anything could be a weapon, from keys, to pencils, to flagpoles. The negative aspects of zero tolerance approaches are vast and varied.

One-size justice does not fit all. Mitigating and aggravating circumstances are not taken into consideration. The policies are enforced regardless of possessors' intentions or age. The policies hurt the very children they supposedly are in place to protect. The long-term effects upon children's reputations, records and continuing education are devastating.

Students do not necessarily learn what they did wrong (assuming they actually did something wrong). Instead of actively engaging in studies, students walk on eggshells not knowing what they might potentially do wrong.

When thorough investigations of circumstances do not occur, the roots of actual problems are not resolved. In 2001, the American Bar Association passed a resolution opposing zero tolerance policies. In 2006, the American Psychological Association reported finding no evidence that zero tolerance policies reduced school violence or improved behaviors. University studies have found that zero tolerance policies are ineffective, particularly since they do not make students feel safer. Other studies suggest that zero tolerance policies are applied disproportionately against minorities, males and students with disabilities.

Overwhelmingly, courts uphold warrantless searches of students' lockers and cars on school grounds. They also uphold the use of metal detector scans. Although students do not shed their rights at the schoolhouse gate, generally, courts have found that the legitimate state interests of student safety and non-disruptive classrooms trumps students' Fourth Amendment rights against unreasonable searches and seizures. Mere "reasonable suspicion" that a particular student has violated a rule is enough to search him or her.

Of course, nobody is arguing that intentionally threatening or actual violent behaviors should not be punished, but the present system is plainly lacking flexibility, equity and discretion.

Some courts are recognizing that zero tolerance policies violate due process or equal protection rights. In many instances, convictions are eventually reduced or overturned. However, this usually takes time and resources, while students remain suspended or otherwise under judicial scrutiny.

Since the 1994 Gun-Free Schools Act technically allows for case-by-case analysis, some state legislatures and governors have begun to amend unjust policies. In 2009, Texas implemented a new state law requiring administrators to consider four factors before determining a weapons infraction: self-defense, intention, disciplinary history and the individual student's mental capacity. In January 2010, Florida revised its policies so that only students who truly pose a threat to school safety are expelled or charged. In March 2010, the Georgia Senate passed a bill requiring a hearing before a student can be taken and charged as a felon, and re-classifying the act as a juvenile delinquency unless the weapon (other than a firearm) was used in an assault.

Many students have been sentenced under zero tolerance policies for possessing penknives. Ironically, penknives are so named because they were used for putting points on quill pens. Students, therefore, were once expected to possess and use penknives in schools. Without penknives at the ready, our forefathers could not have penned our nation's founding documents, which, among other things, ensure due process of law.

Louis P. Nappen, Esq., is a criminal defense attorney in New Jersey. Previously, he was a high school English teacher. He has published several law review articles focusing on the loss of student rights at schools.

In Pennsylvania, a 10-year-old is taken away in handcuffs after scissors are found in her book bag.

Finest Features of Loveless Knives

What makes the knives of Bob Loveless so remarkable, ingenious, significant and beautiful?

The late Robert "Bob" W. Loveless brought beauty and function together in his exquisite knife designs. No doubt his influence on the knife community will continue to be felt for generations to come.

Durwood Hollis was fortunate to spend time in Bob's shop, interview him and write the book *Knifemaking With Bob Loveless*: Build Knives with a Living Legend shortly before the renowned knifemaker left this world.

By Durwood Hollis

By any measure, it would have appeared that the life of Bob Loveless was doomed for failure. Born near the beginning of the Great Depression, his parents divorced only a couple of years after they married. From that point on, Bob was the child of an absentee father. Sent to live with his maternal grandparents on their small 17-acre farm in northeastern Ohio, there was no "Aid for Dependent Children" program, food stamps, or other governmen-

A tapered tang, as illustrated at lower right in the image of a 1960s-era Bob Loveless fighter, is a staple of any Loveless fixed blade. *(SharpByCoop.com photo)*

The author was fortunate to spend time in the shop of Bob Loveless, shown here at his desk, interview him and write the book *Knifemaking With Bob Loveless: Build Knives with a Living Legend.* *(Durwood Hollis image)*

tal social programs designed to provide for the child of a divorced mother.

"We didn't have any money. All we had was a roof over our heads, a garden, a few chickens, a milk cow, and there was game in the surrounding woods," Loveless said.

At an early age, Bob learned to be self-reliant. If he wanted something to play with, it had to be made from whatever he could find. Fortunately, he was

a boy with an imagination and a touch of creative genius. A length of metal tubing and a piece of wood served as a toy gun. And a forked branch was fashioned into a slingshot. However, an impoverished childhood didn't seem to have a negative effect on the young Loveless.

When World War II dawned, Bob was too young for active military service. Not to be deterred, the teenager changed the date on his birth certificate

and joined the Merchant Marine. With a keen mind, a willingness to learn and a solid work ethic, Loveless quickly fit in with the older crew members of whichever ship he was assigned.

"Being part of a crew on a Merchant ship was hard work, but it was better than the alternative I'd left behind in Ohio," Bob said.

When aboard ship, he quickly discovered that his most useful tool was a knife. After reading an article in a popular magazine about Bo Randall, he decided that a Randall knife was what he wanted. Stationed on a ship that was docked near New York City, on his next shore leave Bob went to the famous Abercrombie & Fitch store in Manhattan to see if he could find what he wanted. Unfortunately, the store didn't have any Randall knives

A typical Bob Loveless pouch sheath featured a built-in internal leather cam to prevent a knife from jarring loose and becoming lost in the woods or field. Loveless was not a fan of a "keeper strap" or a "hook and loop" knife-retention sheath.

at the time and there was an extensive waiting list.

Stymied by the failure to obtain the knife he wanted, or even to be put on the waiting list for one, Bob decided to make a knife of his own. On the way back to the ship he asked the cab driver to stop at a wrecking yard. There, he obtained a length of spring steel from a 1930s-vintage Packard automobile. Using the spring steel as the basis for his knife and working over a galley stove during his time off work, Loveless successfully forged his first knife.

"When the knife was finally finished, it seemed to cut well enough. The only problem I had was the edge would chip easily," he said. "Uneducated on how to properly heat-treat and temper a blade, I went to the local library and read up on the subject. Afterward, I took the knife apart and subjected the blade to low heat to draw off some of the hardness, and that solved the edge chipping problem."

First Paycheck

Shortly thereafter, Bob returned to Abercrombie & Fitch and showed the knife to the store manager. The manager was so impressed with Bob's work that he asked if more knives could be made. When Bob answered in the affirmative, he was given a purchase order and a check.

"I guess you could say that was the start of my cutlery career," Bob said. This was the early 1950s, when a knife with a six- or seven-inch blade was thought to be the ultimate game-care tool for hunters. Shaving inches off of what he regarded as both an unbalanced and fragile hunter's tool, Loveless determined that a 3-1/2- or 4-inch blade was stronger and easier to manage.

The question remains: What is it about a Loveless knife that makes it a stand out among other handmade pieces?

Taking one of Loveless' hunting knives in hand, there are some rather obvious elements that come to mind, including a drop-point blade, tapered full-length tang, ambidextrous handle design, mirror-polished blade and a pouch sheath with cam retention.

Prior to Loveless' arrival on the scene, straight or clip-point blade patterns were the most popular. His own hunting experience, however, provided considerable insight into what a hunter needed in a game-care tool. When field-dressing an animal, if the point of the knife is in direct line with the back, or spine, of the blade, it's highly likely that the user will cut into the underlying digestive system and spill the contents into the abdominal cavity.

"Once you accidentally cut

The dropped hunter, shown here with a single brass guard, is the design most associated with Loveless' work.

The knife duo is a prime example of the combined efforts of Bob Loveless and his business partner Jim Merritt, each of whose skills were without peer. *(Durwood Hollis image)*

open the stomach or pierce the guts, then you've got a real mess on your hands," Loveless said.

Thinking outside the box, Bob dropped the point of his hunting knife blade below the direct line of the actual cutting force. This was done using a convex curve to drop the tip well below the blade spine.

The Loveless tapered tang may have come about by accident. Some years ago, a number of blades had come back from heat-treat slightly warped. In order to salvage the work, Loveless simply re-ground the tangs to eliminate the problem. Once that was done, he realized that the balance point of the unfinished blade had shifted. When the guard and handle were attached and the knife finished, the tapered tang provided a mid-point balance favoring superior edge-control management.

Carrying a knife in the field, especially a fixed blade, demands some type of sheath for convenience and to prevent loss. Leather is the traditional sheath material, in that it can be formed to hold almost any fixed-blade knife. When it came to a sheath for one of his knives, Loveless was no exception in his preference for leather.

No Adornment

The Loveless sheath was crafted from 8-9-ounce top-grade leather, without adornment. Instead of a keeper strap, something that he disliked with a passion, Bob utilized a small interior leather cam for knife retention.

"Keeper straps are worthless. Wade through a patch of heavy cover and the strap can [catch on brush or natural obstacles and] come loose. And if it can, it will and there goes your knife. More knives go missing because of keeper strap failure than any other reason. Once one of my knives is secured in its sheath, it won't come out by accident. You have to intentionally remove it by hand," Bob said.

Capitalizing on the popularity of Loveless knives, many modern makers replicate or fashion near copies of various Loveless models. One needs only look through a purveyor's catalog to find Loveless-style knives. Loveless business partner Jim Merritt said, "Bob Loveless was the best knife designer in the world. If that wasn't true, then why does his work continue to be copied so widely?"

Instead of being angered by his imitators, Loveless was gratified. "After all, perfecting your craft and sharing with others is what life is all about," he said.

From a beginning that fore-shadowed failure, Loveless rose to the pinnacle of success. His life story is one that stands as a monument to self-determination, hard work and a willingness to do what was necessary to care for his family.

"For most of my life I worked two jobs. My day job paid most of the bills. And my after hours knife work put groceries on the table," Bob said.

More than anything else, Loveless' intellectual curiosity and "can do" attitude carried him to the top of his profession.

Many so-called knife experts regard the late knifemaker as a Neanderthal because of his strongly held opinions and his railing against many aspects of modern society. "If I am thought to be a Neanderthal, then I am in good company. Those early flint knappers are what gave credit-ability to knifemaking in the first place. I am proud to be a member of man's oldest profession," Bob stated.

On September 1, 2010, Robert Waldorf Loveless stepped quietly away from the campfire of life. What remains is a legacy in steel that will stand as a guidepost for generations of future knifemakers and users alike.

A mirror-polished blade and "Naked Lady" logo are two classic features of a Bob Loveless knife, as evidenced by this authentic Loveless fighter in stag. *(SharpByCoop.com photo)*

Honed For Hollywood

Blades of the silver screen make adventure, romance, danger and daring come alive

By Mike Haskew

John Rambo takes on a powerful enemy against long odds, Hawkeye races to the heroine's rescue, and Captain Hook's namesake glitters in the starlight. Each of these movie icons has something in common when working their magic. They need a sword, knife or tomahawk to do it.

Sometimes the center of attention and sometimes at the hero's side, the blades of the silver screen make adventure, romance, danger and daring come alive. Since the first shout of "Lights! Camera! Action!" they have captured the imagination of the viewer. Some have, in fact, become legends in their own right, such as the Arthur Rhoades' bowie from the classic *Iron Mistress* or the Sylvester Stallone fighters fashioned by the great Jimmy Lile for the first two Rambo films (*First Blood* and *Rambo: First Blood Part II*).

Many knife enthusiasts would agree that it was Lile who brought custom knifemaking mainstream in the early 1980s with his famed Rambo knives.

Through the years, knife collector Joe Musso has become the caretaker of a piece of Hollywood history. A veteran of the film industry himself, working on sto-

Designer Kit Rae has been instrumental in the development and marketing of movie replica swords, including the United Cutlery Dastan Sword from the movie *Prince of Persia*.

ryboards and other projects with studios such as Warner Brothers, Musso frequently visited prop master Rhoades. Over time, he managed to collect several of the *Iron Mistress* blades, including the most famous steel bowie, a collapsible version, several rubber models and a wooden prototype.

For Musso, working in films combines his love of the movies, history and art. Collecting knives seemed to follow suit, and the opportunities to obtain some icons have come along. Among Musso's favorites are knives carried by MacDonald Carey in the 1950 film *Comanche Territory*, and by John Wayne in three movies—the 1942 film *Reap the Wild Wind*, the classic *The Searchers*, and the 1960 film *The Alamo* in which

Duke carried a Ka-Bar with a handle wrapped for a frontier look.

"When they merged the RKO and Paramount studios in the late 1960s, there was a big, empty lot between the two properties owned by the companies," remembered Joe. "Paramount knocked down the fence that separated the studios, and they were throwing stuff away. Inside an old prop chest, I found the Johnny Weismuller *Tarzan* knives I had obsessed over since I was a boy."

Forging a Friendship

Gil Hibben became the heir to Lile, making numerous knives for the Rambo movies and forging a continuing friendship with star Stallone. Hibben, whose other film credits include the Steven Seagal movies *Marked for Death* and *Under Siege*, along with a bowie and Arkansas toothpick for the 2010 Stallone box office hit *The Expendables*, initially made six knives for Rambo III, made some modifications to an existing bowie, and ultimately produced some additional survival knives for the film.

"Here is the thing about movie people," he smiled. "Most of the time they don't know what they are doing, and they are inventing the story as they go along. I make knives for them, and they don't know what they are going to do with them. There are rewards, and there are ups and downs, but I wouldn't trade it for anything."

The popularity of the Rambo knives skyrocketed, and Smoky Mountain Knife Works offered a scaled-down version of the knife from the third movie, expecting to sell about 10,000. Hibben related that 10,000 were sold within days and about 250,000 have been purchased to date.

Designer Kit Rae has been instrumental in the development and marketing of movie replica knives, and United Cutlery has been a leader for more than 20 years. "I have several clients, but United is my largest and the most fun to work with," Rae commented. "The *Rambo III* Hibben bowie was their first true film replica

Knife collector Joe Musso managed to collect several of the *Iron Mistress* blades used in the iconic movie, based on the book by Paul I. Wellman, starring Alan Ladd as Jim Bowie. Ladd used the Iron Mistress to fight Anthony Caruso, who played Bloody Jack Sturdevant. (*photos courtesy of Joe Musso and Warner Bros. Pictures*)

back in 1988. I had been looking for an opportunity to get involved with that, and Gil's original knife was very tool-and-die friendly."

"After *Rambo: First Blood Part II* we immediately moved on to doing licensed replicas of the Jimmy Lile knives from the first two Rambo films," he added.

During the last 20 years, Rae has been a virtual dynamo

Custom knifemaker Darrel Ralph was pleasantly surprised to find out that his big assisted-opening titanium AXD tanto with wild 3-D handle machining appeared in the hit movie *The Expendables*.

in the design and production of sword and knife replicas for the film and gaming industries. He was instrumental in merchandising over 50 swords and other products from the blockbuster *Lord of the Rings* trilogy, and the Khyber Bowie from the 1984 hit *Indiana Jones and the Temple of Doom*. Among his other film replica credits are the Snake Eyes and Storm Shadow katanas from *G.I. Joe: The Rise of Cobra*; the Hibben knives and Mr. Christmas' throwing knives from *The Expendables*; the Connor and Duncan katanas and the Kurgan sword from *Highlander*; the knives from the Arnold Schwarzenegger films *Terminator 2* and *Total Recall*; and the Sands of Time Dagger and Dastan Sword from *Prince of Persia*.

Peter Lyons made Prince Caspian's sword—featured in *The Chronicles of Narnia: Prince Caspian*—at WETA, a conceptual design and physical manufacturing facility servicing the world's entertainment and creative industries.

Taken Aback Blade

Sometimes a custom knifemaker is actually surprised to see his work appear in a feature film. When Darrel Ralph heard that his big assisted-opening titanium AXD tanto with wild 3-D machining on the handle had appeared in *The Expendables*, he was taken aback.

"It blew me away, and I found out Sly's wife had bought the knife for him and that he decided to throw it into the movie," commented Darrel."

Knifemaker Randall King fashioned a knife with a bone handle for the character Chingauchgook from the movie *Last of the Mohicans*. He also made the character Magua's knife with a bear head carved in the walnut handle, as well as special effects pieces.

For the film *Lara Croft: Tomb Raider*, actress Angelina Jolie, reportedly a collector of butterfly knives, sports a beautiful example of Darrel's popular Venturi models.

For Ralph, the film industry has not been limited to features alone. He produced a series of 12 daggers for the *Buffy the Vampire Slayer* television series. "I think it is delicious that the film industry would be an area for involvement," remarked Darrel. "I really do what I do with films because I think it is so cool to have something in a movie or television series."

When the 1992 Daniel Day-Lewis film *Last of the Mohicans* was on location in western North Carolina, knifemakers Daniel Winkler and Randall King seized the opportunity to get involved.

"I did the knife for Chingauchgook, the Mohican father, with a bone handle, and I built it along the interpretations of what Michael Mann, the director, wanted, Randall explained. "It is a dagger of O-1 steel and bluing for an aged patina. I did Magua's knife, with a bear head carved in the walnut handle."

Winkler has long been known for his black-powder period pieces accented by Karen Shook's fine sheath work, and while preparing for an event on the grounds of the famed Biltmore Estate in Asheville, North Carolina, Winkler and Shook heard about the casting call for background characters in *Last of the Mohicans*.

Working with United Cutlery, Kit Rae designed over 50 swords and other products from the blockbuster *Lord of the Rings* trilogy, including the Sting sword carried by the character Frodo.

Historically Correct

"We sat down with Michael Mann and with the prop master and showed them what we did," said Daniel. "They really liked it and saw that we were doing historically correct pieces. Immediately, they gave us orders for four or five."

Among the most prolific of movie-knife makers is Tony Swatton, who founded his company The Sword and the Stone in 1989. Two years later Swatton moved to a new location in Burbank, California, and worked on swords, daggers and the well-known hook for the 1991 Dustin Hoffman film *Hook*.

"I have been making knives since I was 15," said Swatton, "and I started selling my work to studios back in 1987."

Among Swatton's film credits are some of the best-known Hollywood offerings of the past 25 years, including *Zorro, Blade, Master and Commander, Hook*, the four *Pirates of the Caribbean* movies, *Hellboy, The Alamo, Rush Hour 2, The Lion The Witch and the Wardrobe, The Crow 2, Constantine, The Last Samurai*, and *Highlander 4*.

"I think one of my favorite pieces might be Jack Sparrow's sword from *Pirates of the Caribbean*, which has a 24-inch, hollow-ground blade of 5160 steel with a quarter-inch fuller following the curved back edge," Tony related. "I also enjoyed making the bowie knife for *The Alamo* (2004) from 5/16-inch-thick 5160 steel forged to shape with a brass back on the blade."

The blades of the silver screen bring personality, character, action, comedy and excitement to the film industry and provide another venue of expression for the talents of custom makers. The bond between blades and movies is forged for the future as well.

When the RKO and Paramount film studios merged in the late 1960s, collector Joe Musso found the Johnny Weismuller *Tarzan* knives he had obsessed over since he was a boy. The knife at top in the photo is made of foam rubber, and the piece at bottom is wooden. Weissmuller slings Maureen O'Sullivan, as Jane, over his shoulder as he prepares for all comers with his knife from *Tarzan and His Mate*, MGM, 1934. *(photos courtesy of Joe Musso and MGM)*

The Runaway Tactical Train

Hitch a ride or be left behind—the movement toward tactical fixed blades and folders isn't slowing down

By Pat Covert

The penultimate "gent's runt," SOG's aptly named Bluto folder features a short 2.25-inch blade, slick handle and the company's patented Arc-lock.

If you're one who keeps scratching your head wondering when the tactical bubble is going to burst, I've got news for you—it won't be this year. The tactical segment of the knives industry has been strong for successive years, and with it are new design trends and innovations. While there's no question that the wars in the Middle East have had a major impact on the continued popularity of tactical fixed blades, folders and related products, the success of the genre has been fueled even further by the efforts of legislators and other government officials to restrict sales of such knives to consumers.

A U.S. Customs attempt to ban assisted-opening folders, and another recent crackdown in New York State on the sales of just about any folder deemed a "gravity knife" have, if anything, only made the knives more desirable. It's been proven time and again in the firearms market that government intrusion into the ownership of weapons for personal protection increases their sales, and the knife industry is no different. The ironic part of all that, according to American Knife & Tool Institute president Goldie Russell, is that statistics show people are more likely to be killed by lightning in Manhattan

Short and sweet, the Benchmade 755 MPR folder (top) and Boker Pry-mate (bottom) are two hot sellers among the new breed of stubby slicers.

Squatty and easily pocketed, Ka-Bar's drop point and tanto FIN frame-lock folders helped set the tone for the "runt knife" trend.

than by a knife. In reality, self-righteous anti-knife proponents would serve the populace better working toward minimalizing deaths due to hazardous weather if they're truly concerned about saving lives.

The trends in tacticals for 2011 and 2012 include some interesting design piques and a breakout in steel technology, all of which make this an exciting year for the tactical end of the knife industry.

Stubby Is Good

Runts, grunts or blunts—call them what you want—short, stubby knives are hot as a firecracker in both folder and fixed-blade form. Blades have been slowly shrinking since the inception of the modern-day tactical folder in the late 1990s, for a couple of reasons. Many martial arts experts who specialize in edged-weapons combat believe large blades can actually be a hindrance in close-quarters combat. And, more civilians are toting tactical fixed blades and folders and prefer a less obvious daily carry to something large. So there you have it.

The new stubbies are not, however, just downsized designs. The stocky knives tend to have blades shorter and wider in profile as opposed to simply being miniaturized versions of larger fare.

The movement has been building the past few years. Ernie Emerson of Emerson Knives developed a precursor to these knives several years back. His CQC-14 "Snubby" folder sports a full-size handle with a short 2.7-inch blade that is legal in states requiring blades to be under three inches in length, as well as in countries outside the U.S. with similar restrictions. Boker's short cutters from martial artist Chad Los Banos caught on like wildfire since their release roughly two years ago. Likewise, Ka-Bar's stocky, more recent FIN folders, designed by Peter Janda of FIN Designs, have helped set the tone.

The current rash of stubby knives have personalities all their own. Benchmade's wildly popular 755 MPR (Mini Pocket Rocket), a collaborative effort with custom knifemaker Shane Sibert, exemplifies the new breed. With a 2.9-inch blade and a handle just under four inches, the 755 MPR looks like a full-size

Spyderco's ambitious Michael Echanis Warrior represents an expansion of the company's use of H-1 no-rust steel outside the marine/outdoors segments of the knife market.

TOPS Knives' Xc EST Alpha has all the style and grace of an irritated bulldog. The handle scales of this aggressive fixed-blade harbor a hidden compartment for storing survival goodies like matches and fishhooks.

tactical that ran head-long into a freight train. Adding to the knife's puggish posture is a heaping helping of overbuilt construction, with one thick G-10 handle scale on the front side, and a beefy titanium Mono-Lock (frame-lock) on the back.

When was the last time you walked into a store and said, "What have you got in a gent's runt folder?" Probably never, but if you did they'd probably pull out the SOG Bluto. This little bully (5.5 inches opened with a 2.25-inch blade) sports a black-to-blue-faded metallic handle and pugnacious re-curved blade that stays put using SOG's patented Arc-Lock. Sweet!

On the fixed-blade side, Boker USA's hot selling Pry-Mate is a pint-sized fixed blade that

packs a lot of punch. Made of incredibly thick steel, the Jesper Voxnaes design has a short and aggressive wharncliffe blade complemented by a generous black milled-Micarta® handle with loads of grip. Boker USA president Dan Weidner tells *Knives 2012*, "The Pry-Mate is a brute of a knife with a 7mm-thick blade of premium Boehler N690 steel. It's so unique you just have to pick it up."

If you want to get down and dirty, check out TOPS Knives' Xc EST Alpha. This aggressive fixed blade has an ample 4.25-inch orange canvas-Micarta handle with a nifty twist. The scales can be removed to reveal a chamber for storing survival goodies like matches and fishhooks. The Xc EST's blade is 3.25 inches of pig-headed cutting power.

The Kershaw Tilt takes its design cues from a stealth fighter and loads it up with technological advancements like a Bohler Uddeholm Zanax 75/420 composite blade.

CRKT is the first manufacturer to incorporate the IKBS ball bearing system into a factory knife. Shown here are the innovative Ken Onion Eros models

As you can see, there are plenty of stubbies to choose from and it will be interesting to see where this trend goes from here.

Steel Explosion

The days when one premium steel stood out above the rest are a thing of the past. New challengers have entered the blade arena and are giving the top dogs a run for their money, but not without a fight. Crucible Industries, the de facto leader in powder steel technology for knives, is up and running with S35VN, a new alloy developed to replace the popular but aging S30V. Noted knife manufacturer Chris Reeve, perennial winner of *BLADE Magazine's* "Manufacturing Quality Award," had a hand in the development

of the blade steel. According to Reeve, "All my knives will be changing over to S35VN. The reason we researched it was to improve S30V from the standpoints of machining ability and polishing aspects. The corrosion and toughness were improved as well, and the edge retention is excellent." Crucible has also introduced a powdered steel version of the ever-popular D2, dubbed CPM D2.

Giving Crucible a run for its money on the domestic front is Carpenter Steel of Reading, Pa. In recent years the company has developed a whole suite of proprietary (powder technology) knife steels, and the word is getting out. Custom knifemakers Rick Hinderer, who worked with

Carpenter developing several of their steels, and Bob Dozier have used Carpenter steels and rave about their quality. On the factory front, Spyderco—ever the stickler for quality—offered the company's CTS-XHP (an air hardened, high carbon, 440C-type variant) on their Manix 2 model. Poised for a breakout, look for more manufacturers to offer Carpenter steels in the future.

Austrian steel manufacture Bohler Uddeholm is also making a big push in blade steels. Benchmade director of marketing Rob Morrison fills us in on this rising star. "In the past year we've added two steels to our core lineup—M390 and N680—both from Bohler. The M390 is high-performance steel with superior cutting ability and wear resistance. Its unique powder metallurgical process also promotes a uniform carbide distribution and clean steel properties, making M390, popular steel used in surgical cutting instruments and in applications requiring a high finish. The N680 provides excellent corrosion resistance properties, especially in salt water, making it the steel of choice for our water and river knives."

Last but not least, Spyderco continues to broaden its line of knives using non-rusting H-1 stainless steel. Developed by Myodo Corp. in Japan, H-1 steel alloy uses .10 percent nitrogen to replace carbon in achieving its rust-free properties. Spyderco believes in the steel so much, the company purchases all the H-1 that Myodo produces. Initially offered only in its marine/outdoors environment Salt series knives, Spyderco recently took it a step further by offering H-1 on the Michael Echanis Warrior model. Stay tuned, we may be seeing much more of the innovative steel.

Techno Exotica

Ever notice how the automotive manufacturers roll out sports cars and racing vehicles every year to whet the public's appetite? Well, so do knife manufacturers. This keeps the technology and

Slick and beautiful is the best way to describe the Benchmade 8600 Auto-Bedlam. This knife was originally designed for the King of Jordan's private security detail.

design juices flowing inside the company while simultaneously creating brand awareness among customers when it comes time to make their purchases. This year's design wonders are geared to take your breath away, and they will.

Hats off to Columbia River Knife & Tool (CRKT) for being the first manufacturer to incorporate the IKBS (Ikoma Korth Bearing System) ball bearing pivot into a factory folder. Not surprising, CRKT incorporated it into its first two folder collaborations—the Ripple and Eros models—with noted knifemaker Ken Onion. Doug Flagg, CRKT marketing director tells *Knives 2012*, "Ken Onion made his custom versions of the Ripple and Eros with the IKBS, so we wanted to emulate his custom knives as closely as possible. The IKBS makes a knife with a flipper as fast as an assisted-opening knife, plus you can tighten the pivot of a knife much more than a knife with Teflon™ washers. The IKBS virtually eliminates any side-to-side blade movement. Yes, we will use it again! In fact we are doing a knife from Flavio Ikoma, the original inventor of IKBS, for 2012."

The Benchmade 8600 Auto-Bedlam is nothing short of one slick, beautiful folder. It blends the ancient with the modern in spectacular fashion. Originally

designed for the King of Jordan's private security detail, "It combines a number different features: our Auto-AXIS® lock and opener, a unique scimitar-style blade, and contoured G10 handle scales with finger grooves," lends Benchmade's Rob Morrison. We can only guess how many Benchmade fans have written to the company begging for a street-legal manual version!

The Japanese tanto has been a respected member of the tactical knife community for many years now, but SOG's Vulcan brings the blade style up to a new level. Wicked looking with its modernized ultra-sleek handle and gracefully double-ground, re-curved edge, the Vulcan raises the bar for factory tantos to follow.

Kershaw continues to push the right buttons in technology and design as witnessed in its new Tilt folder. The Tilt takes design cues from a stealth fighter and loads it up with technological advancements,

like a Bohler Uddeholm Zanax 75/420 composite blade, titanium frame with carbon fiber overlays, and a specially designed ball bearing pivot. In a nutshell, this knife not only pushes the envelope, but also turns it inside out.

Are these knives harbingers of tactical slice to come? We'll have to wait and see, but it's always nice to know the manufacturers are pushing the tactical edge to its limits. Stay tuned!

Tactical Tuxedos

With the business end of tactical folders taken care of, its time to add a touch of class

By Michael Burch

When you hear the term "tactical knife," you probably envision a fighting knife in the hands of a covert operator in some Third World country. And that is technically what it is since the dictionary describes *tactical* as "weapons employed on the battlefront." Though, as we all know, the knife industry is an ever-evolving beast and so are the terms that define it.

The word tactical is widely used to describe a plethora of custom knives simply because there is no other term for their type. To me, the word pertains to a wide array of knives that are built to be used hard. And while some of the knives are only employed to vigorously invade the daily mail, and possibly sever some twine, it is good to know they could be used for harder work if they were called to task.

I'm not sure who placed the adjective tactical in front of folders, but some say that it was in the mid-'80s when the phrase became popular to describe Bob Terzuola's ATCF (Advanced Technology Combat Folder). Others credit Ernie Emerson's CQC-6 (also called the "Viper 6")—conceived in the late '80s or early '90s—as being the model to help popularize the tactical folder genre. Military personnel heavily employed each of the knives, resulting in tactical market growth that continues strong today.

Bob Terzuola dresses one up in a coated blade with Superconductor bolsters and buffalo-horn handle scales.

Leave it to Michael Burch to fashion a tactical folder in a 3.5-inch 1095 blade with smoky hamon *(temper line)*, integral finger guard/flipper mechanism, mokumé bolsters, titanium liners, the Ikoma Korth Bearing System and spalted-birch handle scales. *(EDC Knives.com photo)*

Once tactical folders became popular, it didn't take long for makers to dress them up. Terzuola put damascus and mokumé bolsters on his knives in the mid-'90s to enhance the plain look of those early blades.

Dressing up battle blades is nothing new. A brief look back in history reveals many ornate versions of purebred fighters that saw battle. No matter the knife, there is always someone who wants a more elaborate one. It can be to show rank, as in officers' swords, or just to signify wealth. One popular example would be, in 1827, when Jim Bowie used the knife (that now bears his name) on a sandbar in Mississippi. It didn't take long before everyone wanted that "knife Bowie used," and versions of the infamous Bowie knife have been made ever since.

During the California gold rush, an economic boom allowed refined men to have their bowies

Material choices for Peter Carey's "Vertigo" model include a Damasteel blade and bolsters (top) with curly-maple handle scales, and Mike Norris ladder-pattern damascus paired with an African blackwood grip at bottom.

Peter Carey's "Rubicon" flipper folder showcases a 3.125-inch twist-pattern Damasteel blade, pocket clip and bolsters, and mammoth-ivory handle scales.

embellished with ivory, sterling silver and much more. Still built to work but made with the gentleman in mind, the resulting knives accented the attire and finery of the time. The era ushered in some of the first fancy fighting knives of modern man.

While dress knives have been around for quite some time, a huge market has evolved as of late simply because customers get the best of both worlds—a hardworking knife that also looks good. There is a feeling of individuality when holding a one-of-a-kind, dressy tactical. And though I like to call them "dress tacticals," other descriptive terms include classy tacticals, "tuxedo tacticals" and, my personal favorite, "Genticals" (Gentlemen's Tacticals), a Ken Onion term.

For the "why" of dressing up tactical folders, that is different for each maker. But like most trends in knifemaking, dress tacticals are market driven.

Business Meets Class

I didn't start building knives with exotic materials until customers asked for them. A lot of my first knives featured titanium handles and frames, and G-10 handle scales. All it took was a bit of customer prodding to get me hooked on fancying them up, and now most all models blend natural and manmade materials. And I must say, when "business" meets "class," the byproduct is a thing of beauty.

An innovative individual, Terzuola was one of the first makers to fashion G-10 handle scales and, along with Michael Walker, began employing titanium folder frames. He also authored *The Tactical Folding*

Jody Muller engraves Japanese warriors into the bolster steel of this fancy piece in a mosaic-damascus blade, titanium liners and a carved mammoth-ivory handle. *(SharpByCoop.com photo)*

Terzuola's current favorite materials are carbon fiber, mammoth ivory, buffalo horn, gemsbok horn, superconductor material and mosaic damascus. At press time, he was taking orders and delivering within 6-9 months.

The best way to contact him is through his email: terzuola@ earthlink.net. You can also find his knives on most of the popular custom knife dealer sites.

Peter Carey was already familiar with metal before getting into knifemaking. He worked with structural steel as a fabricator/erector and also did welding. He built his first knife in 1997, and after reading *The Tactical Folding Knife*, got into building tactical pieces.

Having made his first folder in 2000, it didn't take long for Carey to refine his folder work, and in 2002 he won the "Best Amateur Knife" and "Best Folding Blade" awards at the Knife Expo in Southern California. At the request of his customers, he dressed up his folders and now says the practice has expanded his customer base. "Sixty to seventy percent of my customers want the fancy stuff!" he notes.

Clean Lines & Perfect Mechanics

Carey predicts that dress tacticals will compose one of the longest-lasting knife trends ever. As he reasons, "Why not carry a classy tactical that looks

and exotic materials.

"The market for custom knives has broadened in recent years," he added. "The tactical folder is no longer just a simple, functional implement. Collectors seek more than a defensive tool, they demand style, and inevitably, a variety of new and attractive materials."

Terzuola has devout collectors who own dozens of his knives, and he believes that he attracts new customers and keeps the old ones by offering an ever-growing variety of materials. His case in point: the "U.S.S. Intrepid" edition he made from a sheet of stainless steel taken from the sick bay of the *U.S.S. Intrepid* museum aircraft carrier in New York.

Knife, a book that has started many a knifemaker (myself included) down the path of folder making.

His folders were, and still are, primarily made with combat and self-defense in mind. Yet, in the '90s, when he started using exotic materials to dress up his knives, Terzuola built a solid platinum knife for the Barrett-Smythe Gallery of New York City.

When asked why he began integrating more exotic materials into his knife designs, he replied, "I wanted to appeal to a broader marketplace. My knives had always been highly functional and plain, made for soldiers, law enforcement, etc. I decided to try and be at the forefront of new

cool and is strong enough to handle anything?" A full-time maker who builds mostly folders, Cary fashions knives using the stock-removal method of blade making with the best materials he can buy, and does his own heat-treating to achieve optimal blade performance. His knives are known for their clean lines and perfect mechanics. He is not currently taking orders but can be reached through the email found on his website www. careyblade.com. The best way to get one of his knives is to check with Mark Strauss at www. knifeology.com or Julie Hyman at www.arizona-customknives.com. Carey also attends the BLADE Show in Atlanta, and the Tactical Invitational in Las Vegas.

Jody Muller takes a different approach to dress tacticals. Having made his first knife at 12 years old, Muller worked as a jeweler for a time and his knives show it, parading forged damascus blades and hand engraving. A longtime customer and friend, Lance Abernathy requested a large tactical folder with high-end materials. The product of that design won Muller the "Best Tactical Knife" at that year's Chicago Knife Show.

While he still makes many non-tacticals, Muller says he enjoys building tactical folders because of the complexity of the grinds and the larger, more robust feel of the knives. He also likes that they expand his customer base. As he says, "It allows the tactical and art markets

The "Purgatory Now" double-action auto folder from the hands of Jody Muller measures eight inches open and sports deadly engraving, antique-tortoise-shell grip inlays, stainless overlays and a stainless-damascus blade.
(SharpByCoop.com photo)

to intersect at a common style."

While the style might be different from his pure dress pieces, he still incorporates his jewelry background to create intricate handle inlays and engravings

Bob Terzuola's "Model 7" locking-liner folder sports damascus bolsters, a clean, checkered-mammoth-ivory handle and an 18k-gold thumb stud. *(Duane Weikum, EDC Knives photo)*

on the tactical pieces. Engraving themes include skulls, demons, Japanese woodblock print art and pretty much anything the customer envisions.

Muller's favorite materials include mammoth ivory, meteorite, carbon fiber and mother-of-pearl. His knives are available through online dealers or can be ordered directly from Muller at Mullerforge2@hotmail.com, or by calling 417-752-3260.

In an effort to get a dealer's perspective on dress tacticals, I talked with Duane Weikum of EDC Knives. He indicates that customers are drawn to dress tacticals because they like a little variety in their collection. "A collection of all titanium and Micarta®-handled knives is not so exciting to look at over time. When a maker steps up and puts exotic material on a knife, the collector sits up and takes notice,"

he said. Weikum believes the tedium of building the same knife over and over has gotten many tactical makers to start dressing them up. "The makers can change the pace and challenge themselves by working with different materials, which will also helps to expand their customer base."

Weikum also offered a small list of makers who currently fashion dress tacticals. Though the list is just a small peek into the market, it includes some great makers to check out:

Todd Begg: www.beggknives.com (carbon fiber, copper niobium, damascus, Timascus)
Michael Burch: www.burchtree-blades.com (carbon fiber, copper niobium, damascus, mokumé, superconductor material)
Ernie Emerson: www.emerson-knives.com (damascus and/or mother-of-pearl)

Flavio Ikoma: (carbon fiber, damascus, Timascus) fikoma@itelefonica.com.br
Korth: (hand-carved titanium scales) korthknives@terra.com.br
Charles Marlowe: www.marloweknives.com (carbon fiber, damascus, mammoth ivory, stag)
Tom Mayo: www.mayoknives.com (carbon fiber, damascus, ivory)
Ken Onion: www.kenonionknives.com (damascus, giraffe bone, mother-of-pearl)
Mick Strider: www.striderknives.com (carbon fiber, damascus)

The world of knives is one of constant change, development and evolution. Trends in knifemaking come and go, but the dress tactical genre is here to stay. There will always be a market for knives that work hard and look good doing it. The only changes you'll see are the evolving materials used to dress up the sweet tactical pieces.

Trends

They are faster, stronger, lock up tighter, and have more grooves, dimples and cutouts than their edged ancestors. There is simply no stopping technology and innovation in the knife industry. You can throw recessions, housing market collapses and bank closings at them, but custom knifemakers keep building better blades, plain and simple, end of story.

Well, that's not quite the end. Innovations, or in this case "Trends," include but are not limited to knives with ancient walrus ivory handles that cut better than the tusks from which they were born, other edged beauties with age-lined-ivory handles, as well as full-contact fighters, "Tapered Chefs," traders, trappers and tomahawks, and unhindered hunters.

Some pieces are "Quick to Unfold," while others are "Integrally Solid." Some knifemakers are "Bowie'd By Success," while others aspire to the greatness of Robert W. "Bob" Loveless, who sadly passed away in 2010. Some knives have tactical applications, and other edged tools and weapons are "Woolly Bullies" (with mammoth-ivory handles), "Wood Workers" (with highly figured, grainy grips) or "Built Sword Tough."

Slip-joint folders, fixed blades with pronounced clip points and a "Featherweight Class" of miniature knives round out the Class of 2011-2012, and what a productive, fulfilling and fascinating 365 days it has been.

Quick to Unfold

▶ **DAVID SEATON:** The fast opening, locking-liner folders include ATS-34 and Mike Norris damascus blades, mammoth-ivory and gold-lip mother-of-pearl handles, and fluted-damascus and 14k-gold thumb bobs. *(PointSeven photo)*

◀ **JOE SANGSTER:** The locking-liner folder has it all—an ATS-34 blade, damascus bolsters, black-lip mother-of-pearl handle, gold pins, file-worked back spacer and grooved thumb stud. *(PointSeven photo)*

◀ **NORMAN SANDOW:** The tones are set for the locking-liner folder—a two-tone ATS-34 blade, black-semi-gloss titanium bolsters, jeweled liners, a giraffe-bone handle and a black-lip mother-of-pearl-inlaid thumb stud.

▶ **FRANK DILLUVIO:** The one-hand-opening 440C folder wears stag scales.

▲ **DAVID MOSIER:** The "Frontline" flipper folder employs an Ikoma Korth Bearing System *(IKBS)*, titanium liners and a CPM 154 blade. *(Ward photo)*

▶ **CHUCK GEDRAITIS:** The knifemaker carved the thumb-opening area of the Rob Thomas "Ladder Dot Com"-pattern damascus blade to look like the back of a center-fire gun cartridge, adding heat-colored and textured titanium handle scales for further effect.

▲ **RICHARD S. WRIGHT:** The ambidextrous bolster-release switchblade comes in a Jerry Rados Turkish-twist-damascus blade, a damascus frame, carved integral bolsters, tortoise shell inlays and citrine insets.

◀ **GAIL LUNN:** Just one damascus, 24k-gold and tortoise-shell locking-liner art folder didn't seem **sufficient.** *(PointSeven photo)*

◀ **R.J. MARTIN:** The "Transfusion" gets the blood flowing via a 3 7/8-inch, multi-ground CPM S30V blade, a titanium handle, and carbon-fiber inlays. Roller thrust bearings make for smooth operation. *(PointSeven photo)*

▶ **JODY MULLER, SAM JONES and LANCE ABERNATHY:** Whether plain blade or damascus, G-10 handle scales or carbon fiber, the frame-lock folders are fast and furious. *(SharpByCoop.com photo)*

◀ **MIKKEL WILLUMSEN:** A winning combination for the fast folder includes a 4.5-inch CPM 154 blade with elongated opening hole, milled-titanium bolsters, a carved and textured gray G-10 handle, and an Ikoma Korth Bearing System (IKBS).

▶ **JAMES HARRISON:** An "Uber Crossover" model incorporates integral carved titanium bolsters, a stone-washed S30V blade, carbon fiber handle scales and an Ikoma Korth Bearing System *(IKBS)*.

▶ **GRANT and GAVIN HAWK:** This "S.T.U.D." *(Swift Trigger Under Detent)* folder features a roller thrust bearing system, 3.65-inch, bead-blasted CPM S30V blade, folding side lock and grooved G-10 handle. *(BladeGallery.com photo)*

▶ **SHANE SIBERT:** The "Mini-Pocket Rocket" shoots for the stratosphere donning a 3-inch Chad Nichols damascus blade, a G-10 handle, mono-lock and milled-titanium pocket clip.

► **ALAN BLOOMER:** The giraffe-bone handle is mated with Doug Ponzio damascus bolsters and a 440C blade. *(PointSeven photo)*

► **SCOT MATSUOKA:** Curvaceous cut encompasses a CPM 154 blade, titanium "orange peel" bolsters and a green G-10 handle. *(SharpByCoop.com photo)*

◄ **BRAM FRANK:** Known for his multi-function tactical folders used in pressure-point, hostile and self-defense situations, Frank makes one in a Randall-style grip and feel. *(PointSeven photo)*

► **PETER CAREY:** The "Rubicon" comes to market in a CPM 154 blade, 6AL-4V-titanium frame, carbon-fiber handle scales, and a Timascus thumb stud and underlay.

◄ **DARREL RALPH:** Say "yowza" to the folding, assisted-opening, double-flipper dagger designed in Chad Nichols damascus and a tortoise-shell inlay.

◄ **JOE CASWELL:** The "EDX" model features an in-line clip/lock system that includes an auto-retracting pocket clip and a lockdown pivot, as well as a 6AL-4V titanium frame and stone-washed CPM 154 blade.

Let's Slip This Joint

▶ **KEN COATS:** The wharncliffe folder is a fashion plate in jigged-bone handle scales. *(Cory Martin Imaging)*

▲ **JOHNNY STOUT:** The small folding hunter parades satin-finished CPM 154 blades and green-mammoth-ivory handle scales. *(Johnny Stout photo)*

▲ **RON NEWTON:** Not your ordinary five-blade sowbelly, the dressy piece includes antique-tortoise-shell handle scales, a 14k-gold escutcheon shield, filed Celtic knot patterns on all three back springs, gold-inlaid damascus bolsters, and damascus blades. *(Buddy Thomason photo)*

▶ **TONY BOSE:** A pair of two-blade ATS-34 slip joints sports stag and bone handles with dog's-head shields. *(PointSeven photo)*

▼ **PAUL MYERS:** He liked the full-size, jigged-bone-handle 440C folder so much he built proportionately smaller models to go with the first. *(PointSeven photo)*

▼ **REESE BOSE:** In true slip-joint fashion is a two-blade folder flaunting jigged-bone handle scales, ATS-34 blades and long nail nicks. *(Cory Martin Imaging)*

▼ **RICHARD ROGERS:** The swell-center congress is a black-lip-pearl and ATS-34 beauty. *(SharpByCoop.com photo)*

▲ **BILL RUPLE:** Shield and back-spacer engraving accessorize an ancient-ivory-handle damascus three-blade slip joint. *(PointSeven photo)*

◄ **WESLEY DAVIS:** The Remington reproduction is done in a ladder-pattern-damascus blade and stag handle scales. *(PointSeven photo)*

▲ **JOE KIOUS:** While Wally Hayes forged the damascus blades and bolsters of the slip-joint Barlow, Joe fitted the titanium frame with 1948-vintage pre-ban elephant-ivory handle scales. *(SharpByCoop.com photo)*

◀ **TIM BRITTON:** Black-lip mother-of-pearl and Jim Small's gold inlay and engraving invigorate a BG-42 teardrop jackknife. *(Ward photo)*

▼ **JOEL CHAMBLIN:** Two nail nicks, a bowtie shield and stag handle scales smarten up a clip-point folder. *(PointSeven photo)*

▶ **BRET DOWELL:** The "Back Pocket Folder" might just move to the front considering the jigged-bone handle scales and ATS-34 blade steel. *(Ward photo)*

◀ **TOMMY PLOPPERT:** He calls it a "Zulu spear"-point blade, and it's dressed in stag. *(PointSeven photo)*

◀ **BILL KENNEDY JR.:** Giraffe bone is captured on a 154CM two-blade trapper. *(Ward photo)*

▶ **BILL RUPLE:** The four-blade congress is dressed in antique-tortoise shell and CPM 154 steel. *(Ward photo)*

▶ **ALAN BLOOMER:** The clip-point ATS-34 slip joint is engraved by Tim Adlam and fitted with a green-jigged-bone handle. *(PointSeven photo)*

▼ **TOMONARI HAMADA:** Carved mother-of-pearl, five high-carbon blades and a lot of accessories make up this collector's pack. *(SharpByCoop.com photo)*

▲ **W.J. McDONALD:** A baby bullet-style trapper makes use of Paul Bos heat-treated ATS-34 blade steel, integral stainless steel bolsters and liners, and amber-stag handle scales.

▲ **DANIEL STIDHAM:** Mammoth tooth and damascus define a two-blade folder of the slip-joint variety. *(Main Street Photography)*

◀ **DON HANSON III:** An A.G. Russell pattern, the dress slip joint dons a forged W2 blade, 416 stainless steel bolsters and an antique-elephant-ivory handle. *(SharpByCoop.com photo)*

TRENDS **65**

Integrally Solid

Architects and engineers are known to dissect a problem, take it apart piece by piece, scrutinize it, determine every possible solution, chart the most logical course to take and construct a masterwork based on initial analysis. Integral knife construction solves many problems. To put it simply, with a one-piece knife, there are few parts that can fail, and no joints, pivots, locks or bushings to break.

That doesn't mean an integrally solid knife is easy to make, and in fact it's just the opposite. As with the architect or engineer, detailed planning proves crucial to the overall success of a knifemaking project. There is no room for mistakes when working with a single piece of steel that will ultimately act as the blade,

bolsters, handle and butt end of a knife. Concentration remains necessary to the end. A mistake three-quarters of the way through an integral knife means everything accomplished before the error was fruitless. The entire work is wasted.

The simplest design can be the most terrifying and trying to build, frustratingly difficult to see through to fruition, maddening to manufacture. Yet true knife artisans relish working in an integral world of design where a project is stripped of all extras, down to its bare essentials, true to its form, its beginnings, uncluttered, simplistic and integrally solid.

▼ EDMUND DAVIDSON: Known by knife collectors worldwide for his integral art and utility knives, Edmund makes this one up from a single bar of 154CM steel, adding a sambar stag grip. *(PointSeven photo)*

▶ GEORGE TROUT: The double-guard integral is a slippery slope to climb, but George navigates it perfectly using 440C stainless steel and ironwood. *(PointSeven photo)*

◀ JERRY FISK: An engraved spine and pins dress up an otherwise all-integral 5160 dirk with ironwood handle slabs. *(Ward photo)*

▶ **JOE CASWELL:** Fashioned from ½-inch-thick 154CM steel, the "CK-2" retains thickness throughout the handle for enhanced grip purchase, with weight and balance achieved through deep offset handle grooves.

▲ **JOHN PARKS:** Fossil walrus ivory rounds out the pointedly sharp 5160 integral with a flat-ground blade. *(SharpByCoop.com photo)*

▶ **MIKE QUESENBERRY:** Forged from 1-inch round stock, the integral 52100 hunter sports sambar stag handle slabs, domed nickel-silver pins and a Paul Long leather sheath. *(SharpByCoop.com photo)*

▶ **KARL ANDERSEN:** The Custom Knife Collectors Association chose Karl's integral piece as its 2010 club knife. *(Buddy Thomason photo)*

▶ **SERGE PANCHENKO:** Here's a twist on the integral—a dagger formed from a Nicholson file, stretching 6 7/8 inches overall with a bottle-opener pommel.

Bowie'd By Success

▶ **KENNETH KING:** The bowie is filed with flair and fitted with ancient ivory. *(SharpByCoop.com photo)*

◀ **BRIAN THIE:** The Searles bowie replica, dressed in pre-ban, checkered elephant ivory, nickel silver and 5160 steel, was inspired by a James Batson article in the February 2010 issue of *BLADE® Magazine*. *(Ward photo)*

◀ **BRION TOMBERLIN:** Damascus and ironwood provide plenty of punch to an S-guard bowie. *(Ward photo)*

▶ **JERRY FISK:** The smart-dressed cowboy bowie wears stag, steel and a bowtie guard between the two. *(Ward photo)*

► **JERRY VAN EIZENGA:** Steel and ivory blend seamlessly on an 18-inch 5160 bowie with shapely guard and shield. *(PointSeven photo)*

◄ **MICHAEL O'MACHEARLEY:** A nickel-silver guard and butt cap act as shiny respites for an ancient-walrus-ivory grip and damascus "hugs-and-kisses"-pattern blade. *(PointSeven photo)*

◄ **JAMES BATSON:** A walnut coffin awaits those who challenge the blade. *(PointSeven photo)*

► **MIKE WILLIAMS:** A length of shimmering damascus steel ends in an ancient ivory grip that, in turn, shows through the steel butt cap. *(PointSeven photo)*

◄ **ED BRANDSEY:** The "Bison Bowie" features a 10.5-inch, file-worked 440C blade with a round turquoise insert, a stag handle, ebony spacer, and an S-guard that is inlaid with bison bone on one side and horn on the other. *(Cory Martin image)*

▶ **NICK WHEELER:** A smoky temper line travels nearly the entire length of the W2 blade of a bowie with an equally smoking afzelia-burl grip. *(SharpByCoop.com photo)*

◀ **MICHAEL RUTH SR.:** The damascus weaves a fascinating tale, while the pre-ban-ivory proves a happy ending. *(Ward photo)*

▶ **BILL KIRKES:** The water buffalo horn that hangs onto the tang of a damascus bowie dons a wooden cap. *(Ward photo)*

◀ **JOHN WHITE:** White's winsome D-guard bowie benefits from an "Explosion"-pattern damascus blade, "W's"-pattern guard, twist-damascus frame and a chocolaty mammoth-ivory grip. *(SharpByCoop. com photo)*

◀ **STEVEN RAPP:** The 9-inch CPM 154 blade of the Will & Finck-style bowie flares at one end and tucks neatly into a stag grip at the other. *(PointSeven photo)*

▶ **GARTH HINDMARCH:** The blued mild-steel double guard and file-worked spacers were an inspired choice to transition the 440C blade into the stabilized-giraffe-bone grip.

◀ **TOM FERRY:** A big knife defined by a prominent "S-curve," the Persian-style bowie parades a curvaceous damascus blade, gold-inlaid damascus oval guard and a handsome ancient-ivory handle. *(Buddy Thomason photo)*

▶ **JON CHRISTENSEN:** Don't let the hand-rubbed koa wood finish fool you—the damascus D-guard bowie is all bite with no bark. *(Mitch Lum photo)*

▶ **ALAN HUTCHINSON:** Ebony enriches a 15.25-inch bowie of 5160 steel. *(Ward photo)*

◀ **JOSH SMITH:** The damascus blade of the dog-bone bowie is a long, pointed affair. *(Ward photo)*

◀ **JIM FERGUSON:** The Wostenholm-style bowie is as tapered and true on the desert ironwood end as it is on the niter-blued-damascus side.

◀ MIKE QUESENBERRY: The nearly 10-inch ladder-pattern damascus blade threatens to bury itself clean up to its African-blackwood hilt. *(BladeGallery.com photo)*

▶ STEVEN KOSTER: Ladder-pattern damascus makes up the blade, guard and frame of a rope-file-worked bowie, interrupted only by ebony. *(PointSeven photo)*

▶ TAD LYNCH: The wavy temper line of the W2 blade plays temptress while stag and a pommel cap are equally inviting. *(Ward photo)*

▶ BRUCE BARNETT: The twist-damascus blade of the "Blood, Sweat & Tears" bowie will make you hum a few bars, while the mammoth-ivory grip is sure to get a whistle. *(BladeGallery.com photo)*

▶ ERIC FRITZ: The "Cowboy Bowie" is a damascus and ironwood packhorse if ever there was one. *(BladeGallery.com photo)*

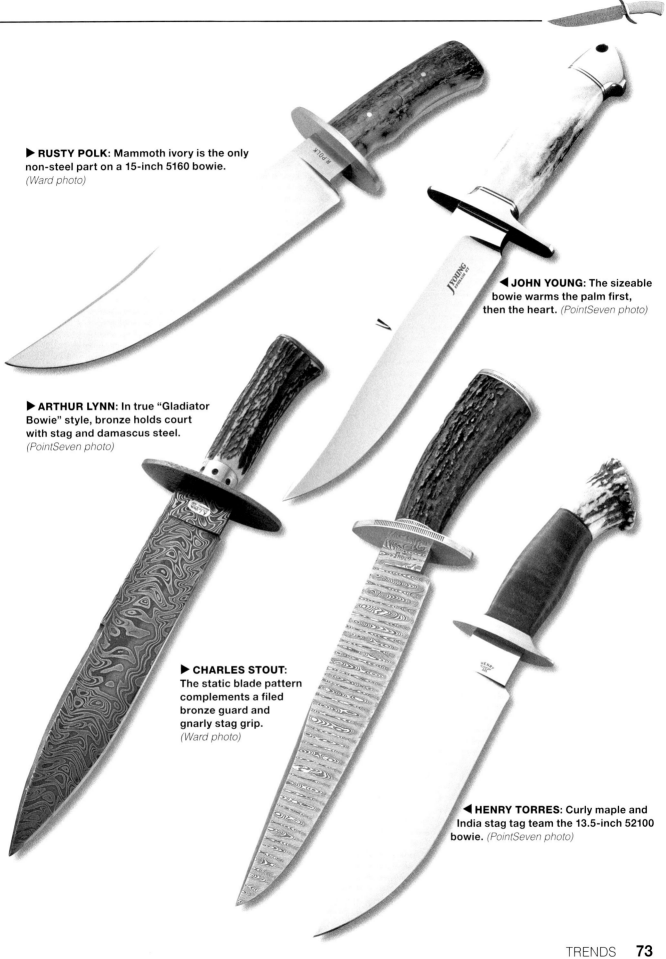

▶ **RUSTY POLK:** Mammoth ivory is the only non-steel part on a 15-inch 5160 bowie. *(Ward photo)*

◀ **JOHN YOUNG:** The sizeable bowie warms the palm first, then the heart. *(PointSeven photo)*

▶ **ARTHUR LYNN:** In true "Gladiator Bowie" style, bronze holds court with stag and damascus steel. *(PointSeven photo)*

▶ **CHARLES STOUT:** The static blade pattern complements a filed bronze guard and gnarly stag grip. *(Ward photo)*

◀ **HENRY TORRES:** Curly maple and India stag tag team the 13.5-inch 52100 bowie. *(PointSeven photo)*

▶ **RONALD WELLING:** The stacked red, black and stainless steel spacers make a nice transition between the stag grip and 10.5-inch damascus blade. *(Ward photo)*

▼ **GARY MULKEY:** It's a steel and stag party. *(Ward photo)*

▶ **DAVID JACKSON:** The stag-handle "Finger Ring Bowie" is worn with pride. *(Ward photo)*

▶ **SHAWN ELLIS:** The classic bowie shape is accomplished through a 10.5-inch W2 blade and a pretty length of ironwood. *(Ward photo)*

◀ **J.R. REEVES:** The 5160 blade sweeps up and the stag handle slopes down. *(Ward photo)*

▶ **J. NEILSON:** One sign of a fine knife is the way makers have been filing the pommels to match the grooves of stag grips, as done on this piece, which also features a 10 5/8-inch random-cut damascus blade and wrought iron fittings. *(Ward photo)*

▶ **DON HANSON III:** The fossil ivory grip has enough character to hold its own against the damascus blade of the "Sloup Creek Bowie." *(Ward photo)*

▼ **PETE CROWL:** Ironwood is a fitting choice for the W2 "Backwoods Bowie." *(Ward photo)*

◀ **J.P. JONES:** Blackwood befits an ATS-34 English bowie. *(Ward photo)*

▲ **T.C. ROBERTS:** A 9-inch blade of Larry Donnelly damascus gets the party started, while a cast bronze guard and butt cap bookend a stag grip.

Loveless Aspirations

It is absolutely amazing the amount of innovations the late Robert W. "Bob" Loveless brought to the table before he passed away on Sept. 2, 2010. Most knife enthusiasts and casual observers could name the "dropped" (drop-point) hunter, ATS-34 blade steel, green canvas-Micarta® handle scales and maybe even the naked lady logo as contributions to the world of handmade knives. At the very least, Loveless popularized the aforementioned.

True knife nuts would include his Lawndale and Delaware Maid knives. But what about chute knives, Big Bear sub-hilt fighters, tapered tangs, New York Specials, and the pieces he made for Abercrombie & Fitch and in collaboration with Schrade Knife Company? Those would have to pass as milestones in the knife industry, as would Loveless sheaths, skinners, semi-skinners and finger-grooved stacked-leather-washer and maroon-Micarta grips. The list goes on.

Many know Loveless as the father of the modern custom knife movement. Along with Richard Barney, Loveless co-wrote *How To Make Knives*, if not *the*, then *one* of the best-selling knife books ever. Loveless had a large following of Japanese knife collectors and enthusiasts, and he is likely one of the five most popular hand-made knifemakers in history.

No wonder so many people aspire to achieve the look, feel and balance of a Loveless knife, using not only similar designs, but materials, innovations, steels and styles. They may be rendi-tions or replicas of originals, but as Loveless once noted about his collaboration with Schrade, if it meant that the average knife user could afford a Loveless pattern, and if the versions of his pieces were well made, then he didn't find anything wrong with that. The knife industry will miss Loveless, and many will aspire to his greatness.

▶ **J.P. JONES**: Loveless first fashioned a chute knife for a Special Operations paratrooper, and this 9-inch ATS-34 and stag version would likely meet with approval. *(Ward photo)*

▶ **ALAIN DESAULNIERS**: Whether the "New York Special" or "Saturday Night Special," either stag-handle ATS-34 fixed blade will work in a pinch. Engravers include Bill Mairns and A. Bruce Bradshaw. *(SharpByCoop.com photo)*

◀ **THAD BUCHANAN**: The Loveless-designed "Junior Bear" incorporates a pre-ban elephant-ivory handle, 416 stainless steel fittings and a 6-inch CPM 154 blade. *(Custom Knife Gallery Of Colorado photo)*

▶ **CHARLES VESTAL:** The Bob Loveless-style fighter is cleanly fit and finished, including a 6.75-inch CPM 154 blade, amboyna-burl grip, red spacers and a tapered tang. *(PointSeven photo)*

▶ **MAMORU SHIGENO:** Two chute knives in stag are a fitting tribute to the late Bob Loveless. *(PointSeven photo)*

◀ **MARCUS LIN:** A rendition of a Loveless "Big Bear" sub-hilt fighter, the ATS-34 fixed blade stretches 14 inches overall and includes green-canvas-Micarta handle scales. *(SharpByCoop.com photo)*

◀ **STEVE LIKARICH:** Carved mother-of-pearl, file-worked bolsters, colored liners and agate balls for the eyes of the "Bird Motif" New York Special define the pretty CPM 154 piece. *(Dave Siegel photo)*

▲ **MARCUS LIN:** In true Loveless fashion, the "New York Special" dons green-canvas-Micarta® handle scales, an ATS-34 blade, red liners and a tapered tang. *(SharpByCoop.com photo)*

The Edge-men and the Walrus

There was a recent article on phenology in the newspaper. Phenology is the study of natural phenomena that recur periodically, such as bird migration, flower blossoming and instinctual animal behavior, and how they relate to the climate and changes in the environment.

As it turns out, there are many phenologists walking among us, people like bird-watchers, hunters, hikers and fishermen who not only spend time in the wilderness, but also enjoy recording what they see. They keep daily logs, and if they continue to do so for a lifetime there's a record of nature's own progression in a certain area for a specific time. This is noteworthy for many reasons, but how it relates to knifemakers and enthusiasts is that it illustrates man's relationship to nature. From the caveman and the wooly mammoth to the upland bird hunter and his dog, man has always communed with nature. There is a mutual respect. To some nature means beauty, to others danger, and still more consider nature the only barometer of truth and tranquility.

The beauty, the respect, the hunter and the hunted perhaps best explain and exemplify a knifemaker's attraction to ancient walrus ivory. It is aesthetically pleasing, stable and a "once-living material," the tusk of a walrus, a beast that has fascinated man for centuries. The excitement, shock and awe that must occur when man encounters such a majestic animal in the wilderness are unimaginable. The tusks that survive are testament to an impressive creature. The makers of man's oldest tool, the knife, have always been in tune with nature, in touch with their innate feelings, their basic instincts, and such is the relationship between the edge-men and the walrus.

▶ **WESLEY DAVIS:** The "D-guard" wraps around the walrus ivory and transitions into an 11-inch ladder-pattern-damascus blade. *(PointSeven photo)*

▶ **BILL MILLER:** Mr. Miller fashions a damascus bowie with a caramel-color, fossil-walrus-ivory handle and a nickel silver guard. *(Ward photo)*

◀ **TERRY VANDEVENTER:** Ancient walrus ivory anchors a 9.5-inch damacus bowie blade. *(SharpByCoop.com photo)*

▶ **SHAWN ELLIS:** A spectacular damascus blade is offset by an impressive length of walrus ivory. *(Ward photo)*

◀ **DAVE COLE:** In picking his palette of colors, the knifemaker chose a bronze guard to bring out the true hues of the fossil walrus ivory. *(Ward photo)*

▼ **KEVIN CASHEN:** The natural beauty of ancient walrus ivory is immortalized on the tang end of an O1-and-L6-damascus blade.

▶ **TAD LYNCH:** The temper line of the forged 1084 blade adds a misty ambiance to nature's own creation, a fossil walrus ivory grip. *(SharpByCoop.com photo)*

◀ **MICHAEL BURCH:** Walrus ivory and W2 steel go together like the wind and a whispering pine. *(SharpByCoop.com photo)*

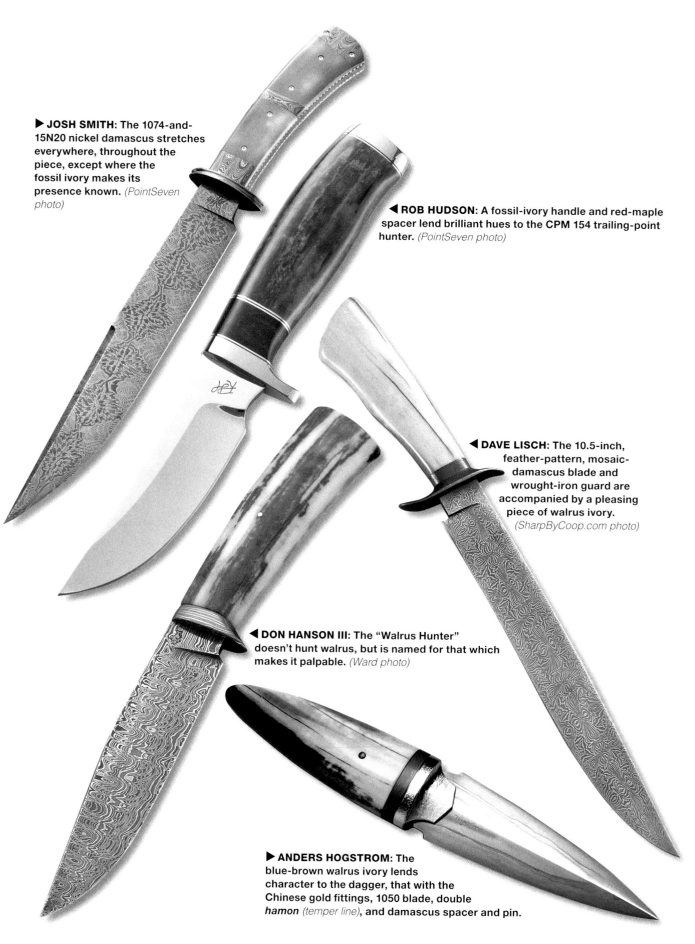

▶ **JOSH SMITH:** The 1074-and-15N20 nickel damascus stretches everywhere, throughout the piece, except where the fossil ivory makes its presence known. *(PointSeven photo)*

◀ **ROB HUDSON:** A fossil-ivory handle and red-maple spacer lend brilliant hues to the CPM 154 trailing-point hunter. *(PointSeven photo)*

◀ **DAVE LISCH:** The 10.5-inch, feather-pattern, mosaic-damascus blade and wrought-iron guard are accompanied by a pleasing piece of walrus ivory. *(SharpByCoop.com photo)*

◀ **DON HANSON III:** The "Walrus Hunter" doesn't hunt walrus, but is named for that which makes it palpable. *(Ward photo)*

▶ **ANDERS HOGSTROM:** The blue-brown walrus ivory lends character to the dagger, that with the Chinese gold fittings, 1050 blade, double *hamon* (temper line), and damascus spacer and pin.

Age-Lined Ivory

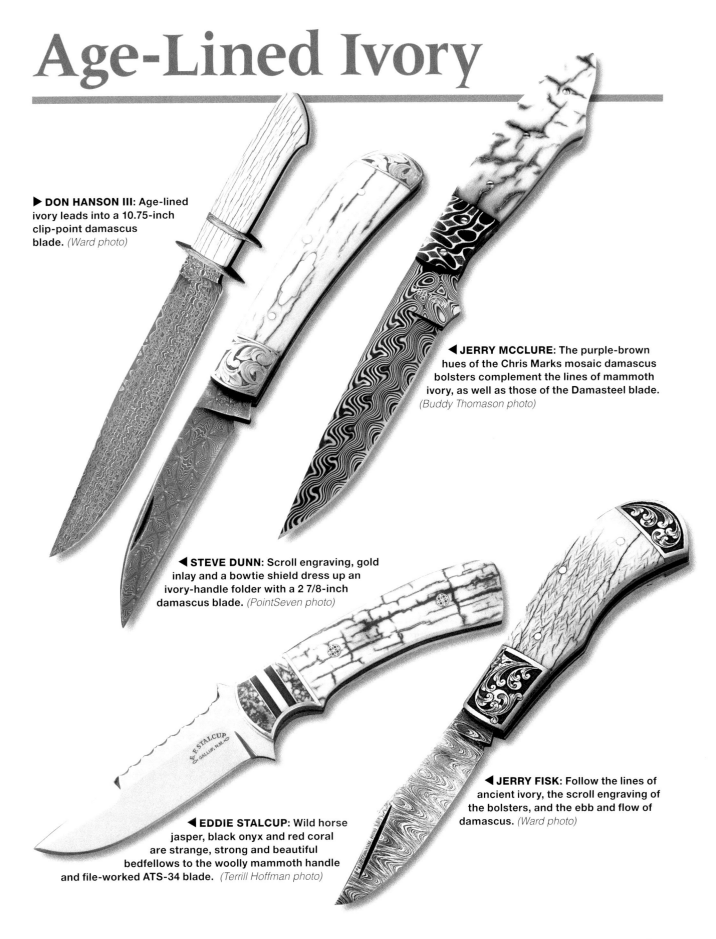

▶ DON HANSON III: Age-lined ivory leads into a 10.75-inch clip-point damascus blade. *(Ward photo)*

◀ JERRY MCCLURE: The purple-brown hues of the Chris Marks mosaic damascus bolsters complement the lines of mammoth ivory, as well as those of the Damasteel blade. *(Buddy Thomason photo)*

◀ STEVE DUNN: Scroll engraving, gold inlay and a bowtie shield dress up an ivory-handle folder with a 2 7/8-inch damascus blade. *(PointSeven photo)*

◀ EDDIE STALCUP: Wild horse jasper, black onyx and red coral are strange, strong and beautiful bedfellows to the woolly mammoth handle and file-worked ATS-34 blade. *(Terrill Hoffman photo)*

◀ JERRY FISK: Follow the lines of ancient ivory, the scroll engraving of the bolsters, and the ebb and flow of damascus. *(Ward photo)*

Unhindered Hunters

They're the bread and butter, or meat and potatoes, of the knife industry. While fancier pieces might make it to a display shelf, case or coffee table, hunting knives generally put food on the kitchen table. They do it in the wet and cold, farm and field, and in the snow and ice. They bump up against blood and fat, meat and hide, bone and brisket, and dirt and grime.

Yet they don't have to be ugly affairs. Many a handmade hunter is finely fit and finished. Grips include highly figured wood with welcoming grains, palpable sambar stag, jigged bone or stacked leather. Brass guards and stainless steel bolsters complement drop-point blades and basket-weave leather pouch sheaths.

The smell of leather, glint of steel and feel of natural, form-fitted knife handles define the custom hunter of the 21st century. The only thing different between modern renditions and their predecessors are years of refinement and technological advances in knifemaking methods. The only thing that stands between them and the job at hand is the skill of the hunter.

There's an innate attraction to an aesthetically pleasing tool designed to fill basic needs, such as providing food or shelter. A hunting knife can accomplish both, and a high-fashion hunter looks good doing it. They are natural, uncomplicated and uninhibited tasks done by unhindered hunters.

▶ **JONATHAN WICK:** The "W's" damascus pattern bounces up and down along the blade edge without sacrificing the quality of the cut. *(PointSeven photo)*

◀**ALBERT TRUJILLO:** Two ATS-34 hunters in camel bone and ironwood would make quick work of even large game. *(PointSeven photo)*

◀ **PETE CROWL:** The slight clip point of the ironwood-handle hunter distinguishes it from its drop-point brethren. *(Ward photo)*

▶ **RALPH RICHARDS:** How can one go wrong with a walnut-handle hunter in a Cru-V Forge blade? *(Ward photo)*

◀ **LIN RHEA:** A small red spacer brings out the amber hue of the stag grip on a 1084 hunter. *(Ward photo)*

◀ **ALAN HUTCHINSON:** The amber of the stag and gold of the bronze highlight the drop-point hunter. *(Ward photo)*

◀ **TOMMY MCNABB:** Carved finger grooves and a file-worked blade spine provide hand and thumb purchase on a swayback skinner with a mirror-polished ATS-34 blade and giraffe-bone handle. *(BladeGallery.com photo)*

▲ **MIKE QUESENBERRY:** The 3.75-inch W2 blade of a hunter is treated to a wispy hamon *(temper line)*, and a fine ebony grip. *(BladeGallery.com photo)*

▶ **JERRY E. JOHNSON:** The antiqued copper guard and pommel are a nice touch on the big-horn-sheep-handle hunter with a fancy Devin Thomas damascus blade.

▶ **RUSSELL TOWNSLEY:** The handle combines giraffe bone with buffalo and caribou horn, not unlike a hunter's dream. *(Ward photo)*

◀ **STUART BARKER:** A Canadian belt knife necessitated a 3.75-inch O1 blade and a stabilized amboyna-burl handle. *(Kam Singh photo)*

◀ **BUTCH DEVERAUX:** The "Buffalo Hunter" is donned in a 52100 blade, sheep-horn handle and a brass guard. *(BladeGallery.com photo)*

◀ **BILL LEVENGOOD:** The knifemaker chose a synthetic G10 handle for the "Nesmuk Hunter" in an ATS-34 blade.

◀ LARRY MCALPINE: Make mine a damascus and deer-antler skinner. *(BladeGallery.com photo)*

▶ EMIL BUCHARSKY: Large details, like the 4.4-inch CPM 154 stainless steel blade and rare high-arctic-musk-ox-horn handle, blend with small details, such as the step-down 416 stainless steel bolsters and mosaic pin, to form a fine hunting knife. *(BladeGallery.com photo)*

▶ DAN DICK: Mosaic-damascus pins attach desert-ironwood scales to the full-tang D-2 blade.

◀ MIKE MANN: The "Buck Skinner" makes use of a flat-ground, satin-finished 15N20 blade, a brass guard and osage-orange-wood handle to part the wild-game gifts. *(BladeGallery.com photo)*

▲▶ TIM HANCOCK: The bone-color stag is a clean look for the damascus upswept hunter with carved and polished nickel silver accouterments. *(PointSeven photo)*

▶ **JERRY FISK:** Even good guys where black, in this case black sheep horn, a silver, grey and black engraved guard and damascus blade. *(PointSeven photo)*

◀ **JOHN BARTLOW:** The "Whitetail Hunter" can hunt what it wants via 3 3/8 inches of ATS-34, a stainless steel guard and sambar-stag handle. *(Buddy Thomason photo)*

◀ **LEON TREIBER:** Amber stag proves popular, this time on a fixed blade hunter of 154CM steel and rope file work. *(Ward photo)*

▼ **AARON WILBURN:** Looking good enough to handle is an Ed Fowler-style "Pronghorn Hunter" fashioned with a sheep-horn grip, black-sheep-horn spacer and a triple-tempered 5160 blade. *(BladeGallery.com photo)*

▶ **MIKE MCCLURE:** Pools of 15N20-and-1080 mosaic damascus form on the blade of a stag-handle hunter. *(BladeGallery.com photo)*

▶ **MICHAEL MILLER:** Maple is a sticky-sweet way to handle a CPM 154 hunter. *(Ward photo)*

◀ **BOB DOZIER:** If Westinghouse only knew how good their yellow linen Micarta® looks on a CTS-40CP-steel, drop-point hunter, they'd market it more to the knife industry. *(SharpByCoop.com photo)*

▶ **RAY KIRK:** The drop-point, through-tang hunter flies its colors—red, white and blue spacers, an amber stag grip and a "firestorm"-pattern-damascus blade. *(Ward photo)*

▶ **ROB HUDSON:** Black ash and sambar stag support a drop-point CPM 154 blade.

◀ **JAMES RODEBAUGH:** Domed handle pins, extensive file work and damascus steel distinguish the exhibition-grade hunter. *(Buddy Thomason photo)*

▶ **ROBERT BEATY:** Swing low and sway back, sweet skinner, coming for to carry you home. *(BladeGallery.com photo)*

▶ **SAMMY FISCHER:** Mastodon ivory gives the "Pro Hunter" model a natural look and feel, complemented by a shapely CPM 154 blade and elongated nickel-silver finger guard. *(Ward photo)*

▶ **DR. JAMES LUCIE:** William Scagel built legendary hunting knives, his spirit kept alive by such flattering replicas as this 1084 upswept hunter with a stacked-leather-washer handle, brass guard and stag pommel.

▶ **ZANE BLACKWELL:** The CPM 154 "Cross Draw" hunter is a full-tang affair, beefy, and with the axis-antler grip pinned to the tang, it's an impressive package. *(Ward photo)*

◀ **MARVIN SOLOMON:** The tight damascus pattern, camel bone grip and nickel silver guard are an amazing combination for a 9-inch skinner with just the right upswept tip. *(Ward photo)*

▶ **ERIK FRITZ:** This one's all about shapes—the pointed 52100 blade, the flared, palm-filling blackwood grip and finger-friendly nickel silver guard. *(BladeGallery.com photo)*

Full-Contact Fighters

The purest form of water is assumed to be vapor. In pure love there would be no outside influence, just unadulterated bliss. The purest form of gold is a panned nugget or mined vein, of pearl is a nacreous inner-shell formation, and of honey is that taken straight from the comb. No one knows what the purest form of knife is, but a chipped or flint-knapped rock is the likely culprit. Yet when you consider modern knives, the fighter is pure in form, intent, integrity and mission.

A fighter is stealth. It wears no finery but that which doubles and triples as necessity and utility. It masks no secondary tasks, and performs no double duty. It fits the hand and stays in the grasp. The blade is guarded, the edge sharp, a secondary edge does the same as the first, only straighter and with more intent. The only reason for a blade belly is cutting once it has pierced, and the only end in sight is that of flared butt or pommel for plying, pounding and palming.

So can straightforward be beautiful? You bet it can. Have you seen an F-19 Stealth Fighter, and did you think it an ugly affair? How about a Raptor, Nighthawk or Mach 2, these of the warp-speed, locked-in and leave-the-horizon-behind kind? There's not room for error when building an elite fighting unit. The tolerance is zero, the fit and finish fine to the point of infinity. This is where the rubber meets the road, the chicken comes home to roost and the rent comes due.

Full contact fighters answer to no one but he who built them, and he who guides their way.

▶ **DAVID BROADWELL:** The temper line of the W2 fighting blade softens its blow, further tamed by the highly patterned ironwood grip and cast-bronze guard. *(Ward photo)*

◀ **GIL HIBBEN:** The first prototype for the movie The Expendables features a Brazilian wood grip, foot-long damascus blade and a brass fitting along its spine. *(SharpByCoop. com photo)*

▲ **BOB DOZIER:** The six-inch fighter is an impressive figure cut from CTS-40CP steel, Westinghouse green linen Micarta®, and a stainless guard. *(SharpByCoop.com photo)*

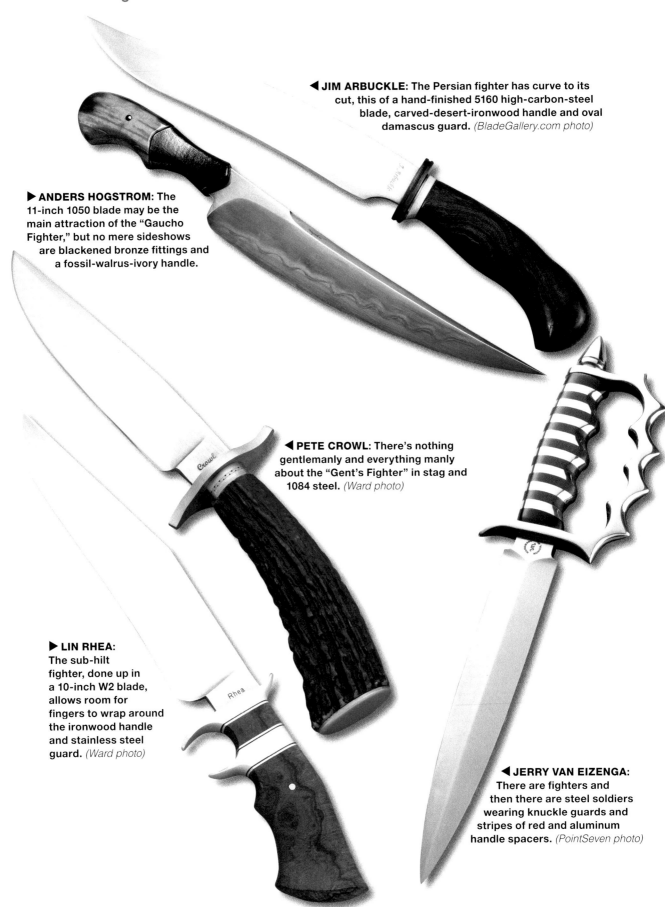

◄ JIM ARBUCKLE: The Persian fighter has curve to its cut, this of a hand-finished 5160 high-carbon-steel blade, carved-desert-ironwood handle and oval damascus guard. *(BladeGallery.com photo)*

► ANDERS HOGSTROM: The 11-inch 1050 blade may be the main attraction of the "Gaucho Fighter," but no mere sideshows are blackened bronze fittings and a fossil-walrus-ivory handle.

◄ PETE CROWL: There's nothing gentlemanly and everything manly about the "Gent's Fighter" in stag and 1084 steel. *(Ward photo)*

► LIN RHEA: The sub-hilt fighter, done up in a 10-inch W2 blade, allows room for fingers to wrap around the ironwood handle and stainless steel guard. *(Ward photo)*

◄ JERRY VAN EIZENGA: There are fighters and then there are steel soldiers wearing knuckle guards and stripes of red and aluminum handle spacers. *(PointSeven photo)*

▶ **RALPH RICHARDS:** Ironwood is a wise and popular choice for modern fighters such as this 16.5-inch piece in 5160 steel. *(Ward photo)*

◀ **SHAWN ELLIS:** The W2 fighter wears a stag grip, 416 stainless steel guard, and a stern demeanor. *(Ward photo)*

◀ **LARRY COX:** Stag actually stabilizes the 1080-and-15N20 pattern of this damascus fighter blade. *(Ward photo)*

▶ **MICHAEL RUTH JR.:** Winner of the American Bladesmith Society 2010 George Peck Award, the 13-inch 5160 fighter in an ivory grip would hunt before it pecked. *(Ward photo)*

◀ **J.R. REEVES:** From its ironwood beginnings to its 5160 point, this one's gonna fight for the right to p-a-r-t-y. *(Ward photo)*

▶ **SCHUYLER LOVESTRAND:** The fixed 154CM fighter is nose-down for effect. *(SharpByCoop.com photo)*

◀ **KUNIHIKO TAMATSU:** Winner of the "Best Fighter" Award at the 2010 BLADE Show, this piece in a blackwood grip and ATS-34 blade had some stiff competition. *(PointSeven photo)*

▼ **BUTCH DEVERAUX:** The "Pronghorn Fighter" was born from the mind of Ed Fowler and fashioned in 52100 steel, a brass guard and sheep-horn handle. *(BladeGallery.com photo)*

◀ **ERIK FRITZ:** The "Little Missouri Fighter" is an amboyna burl and 5160 affair. *(PointSeven photo)*

▶ **J. NEILSON:** The "Combat Version" fighter is forged from 5160 high-carbon steel that is fully quenched and treated with an antiqued finish for corrosion resistance and non-reflectivity. The guard is low-carbon steel and the handle of "burlap Micarta."

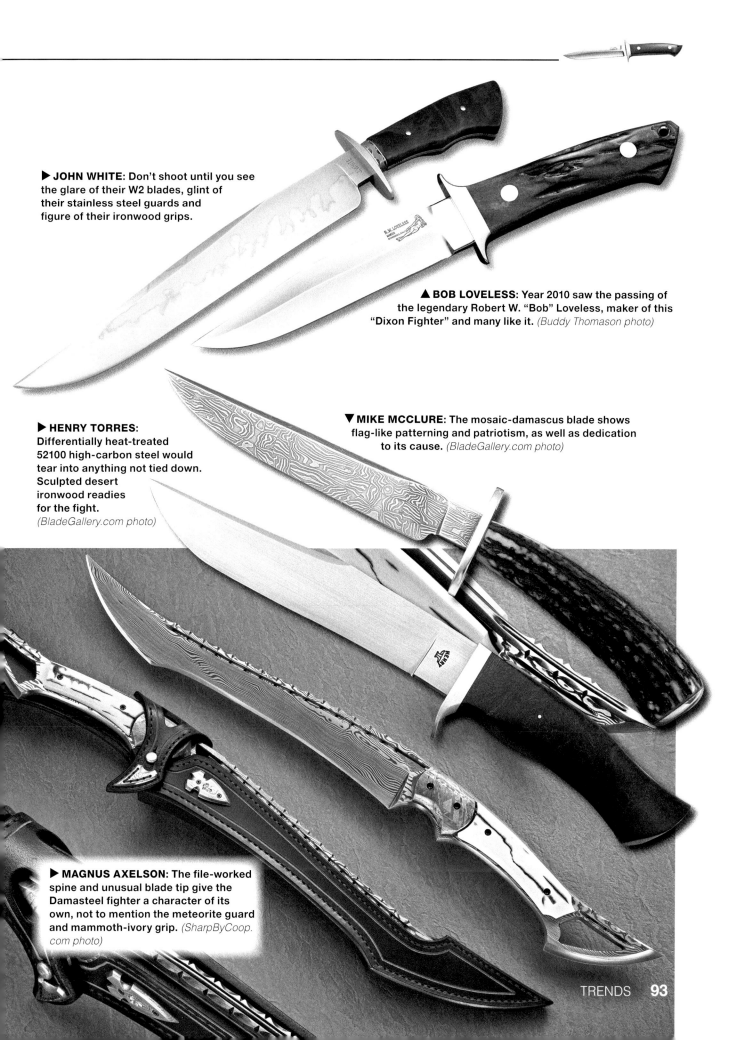

JOHN WHITE: Don't shoot until you see the glare of their W2 blades, glint of their stainless steel guards and figure of their ironwood grips.

BOB LOVELESS: Year 2010 saw the passing of the legendary Robert W. "Bob" Loveless, maker of this "Dixon Fighter" and many like it. *(Buddy Thomason photo)*

HENRY TORRES: Differentially heat-treated 52100 high-carbon steel would tear into anything not tied down. Sculpted desert ironwood readies for the fight. *(BladeGallery.com photo)*

MIKE MCCLURE: The mosaic-damascus blade shows flag-like patterning and patriotism, as well as dedication to its cause. *(BladeGallery.com photo)*

MAGNUS AXELSON: The file-worked spine and unusual blade tip give the Damasteel fighter a character of its own, not to mention the meteorite guard and mammoth-ivory grip. *(SharpByCoop. com photo)*

TRENDS **93**

▶ **BILLYBOB SOWELL:** Walrus ivory counterbalances the W2 blade of the 15.25-inch fighter from the Iron Horse Forge. *(PointSeven photo)*

◀ **MIKE MOONEY:** The 13-inch fighting bowie boasts a 154CM blade, desert ironwood handle, nickel silver guard and vine file work. *(Buddy Thomason photo)*

◀ **KYLE ROYER:** A double-edged W2 fighter with a stag handle, and stainless steel and nickel silver fittings is double, triple and quadruple fun. *(Caleb Royer Studio photo)*

▶ **BILL MILLER:** Blackwood and damascus make for a mean fighter. *(Ward photo)*

▶ **BRION TOMBERLIN:** The personal fighter gets up close and personal with a 5.5-inch 1084 blade, wavy hamon *(temper line)* and blackwood grip. *(Ward photo)*

▲ **JIM HAMMOND:** The maker shows off the tapered tang of his "Endurance" model in a green-linen-Micarta grip. *(SharpByCoop.com photo)*

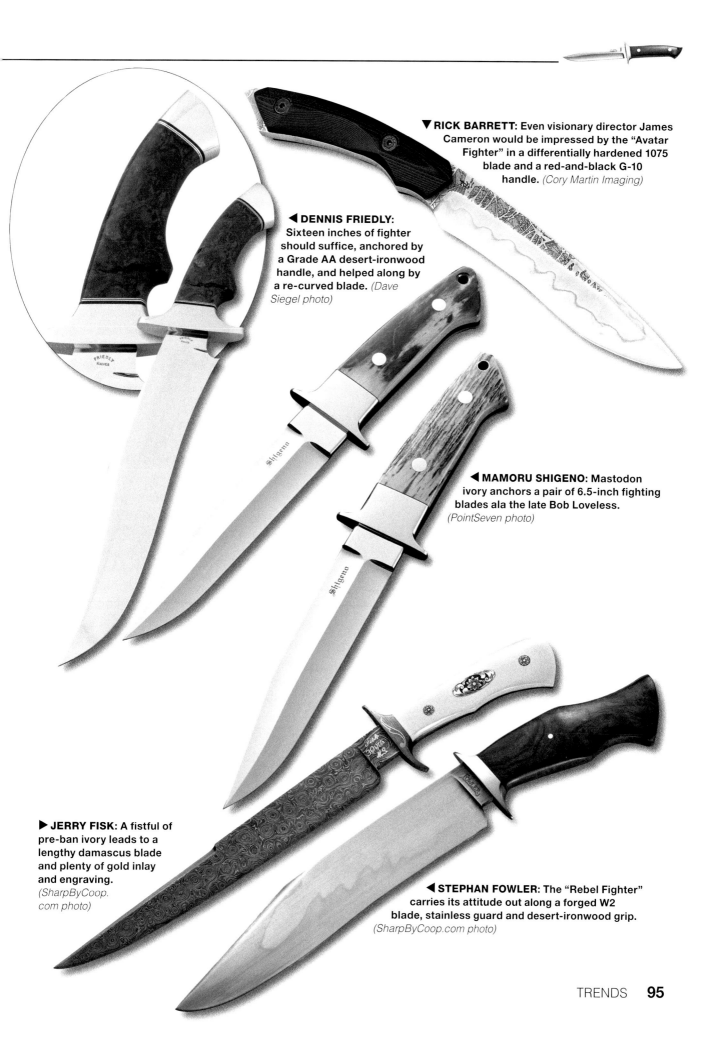

▼ **RICK BARRETT:** Even visionary director James Cameron would be impressed by the "Avatar Fighter" in a differentially hardened 1075 blade and a red-and-black G-10 handle. *(Cory Martin Imaging)*

◄ **DENNIS FRIEDLY:** Sixteen inches of fighter should suffice, anchored by a Grade AA desert-ironwood handle, and helped along by a re-curved blade. *(Dave Siegel photo)*

◄ **MAMORU SHIGENO:** Mastodon ivory anchors a pair of 6.5-inch fighting blades ala the late Bob Loveless. *(PointSeven photo)*

► **JERRY FISK:** A fistful of pre-ban ivory leads to a lengthy damascus blade and plenty of gold inlay and engraving. *(SharpByCoop. com photo)*

◄ **STEPHAN FOWLER:** The "Rebel Fighter" carries its attitude out along a forged W2 blade, stainless guard and desert-ironwood grip. *(SharpByCoop.com photo)*

The Featherweight Class

It's so easy to discount them as shrimps, peewees or diminutive dicers. Sure, there are the old sayings that "size doesn't matter," "good things come in small packages" and "the bigger they are the harder they fall," but those theories can be easily discounted, can't they? I mean, how powerful can a pint-sized fighter be? There is recent proof that those of small stature can throw knockout punches. Or maybe you haven't yet been introduced to Manny Pacquiao. It's not surprising.

Boxing doesn't get the same kind of exposure as it used to in the days of Mohammed Ali, Joe Frazier and George Foreman.

Pacquiao is a professional Filipino boxer who has won world championship belts in more weight classes and divisions—eight total divisions—than any other boxer in history. He is also the first boxer to ever win the lineal championship in four different weight classes. He was named "Fighter of the Decade" for the 2000s by the Boxing Writers Association of America (BWAA). Pacquiao is a three-time BWAA *The Ring* "Fighter of the Year." He is currently the Welterweight World Champion and the number one "pound-for-pound best boxer in the world" as rated by several sporting news and boxing websites, including *The Ring, Sports Illustrated*, ESPN, NBC Sports, Yahoo! Sports, *Sporting Life* and About.com.

Oh, by the way, Pacquiao started his boxing career at age 16 when he stood 4' 11" tall and weighed 98 pounds. His weight for fights has since ranged between 112 and 154 pounds. So size doesn't really matter.

Most of the knives in this "Featherweight Class" aren't meant for fighting anyway, but that's not the point. They can cut it if need be, and cut it they will, no matter the weight class.

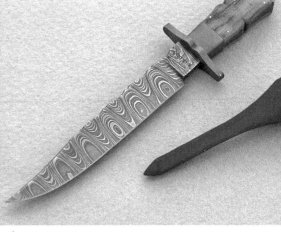

◀ **TY MONTELL:** The miniature trapper features two Devin Thomas "Dot Metrics" stainless-damascus blades, a bark-mastodon-ivory handle and 410 stainless steel bolsters. *(Buddy Thomason photo)*

▶ **LEE FERGUSON:** Pushpins nearly pierce as deep as the 2.25-inch 440C blade of the dagger that also parades titanium fittings and a mother-of-pearl handle. *(Ward photo)*

▲ **BILL DUFF:** The damascus miniature bowie is 2.25 inches overall and sports an antique-ivory grip the size of a golf tee head. *(Ward photo)*

KGA
Presents
Best Miniature
August 28th, 2010

▶ **RUSTY POLK:** A 3-inch damascus blade and even shorter mammoth-ivory handle make up the whole of the miniature bowie. *(Ward photo)*

▼ **YOSHIO SAKAUCHI:** The seven-blade ATS-34 folder with ivory handle scales won the "Yvon Vachon Best Miniature Award" at the 2010 BLADE Show. *(PointSeven photo)*

▲ **MIKE FELLOWS:** The miniature hunter stalks its prey in a "ripple-twist"-pattern damascus blade, stainless steel guard, African blackwood handle and elephant-ivory butt cap.

▲ **JERRY BODNER:** Imagine the look on Billy Bates' face when Jerry asked him to engrave the bolsters of the 3 5/16-inch hunter in an ATS-34 blade and a Rocky Mountain sheep horn handle. Barry Carthers fashioned the undersized sheath. *(PointSeven photo)*

◀ **CRAIG BRASCHLER and MARTIN:** Winner of the "Best Miniature" Award at the 2010 Arkansas Custom Knife Show, the bowie showcases a 2-inch 1095 blade and an ironwood handle with 14 tiny pins. *(Ward photo)*

The Tapered Chefs

They are finally gaining respect, the justice they deserve, their just deserts! Yes, kitchen knives—chef's knives, butcher knives, steak knives, bread knives, serving sets and paring knives—have come of age. They are not only popular, but they've evolved into modern, quality cutlery … trendy and top drawer! No longer are they referred to as slicers, dicers or choppers, and the electric knife—the "Veg-O-Matic"—has long since been relegated to the junk heap. This is not Grandma's cutlery set. And no one sharpens blades on the back of an electric can opener anymore.

Today's kitchen knives include Santokus made popular by Rachael Ray on the Food Network, as well as other Japanese, Chinese, French and American pieces with laminated-steel or damascus blades, fine wood handles, integral bolsters and exotic materials not common in cutlery of days past.

Dimples on the sides of blades prevent food from sticking to the steely surfaces, and though there's a dishwasher in just about every home in America, no self-respecting, stay-at-home mom would ever think about placing the

thousand-dollar medium chef's knife into the same rack with the kids' slimy cereal spoons.

Kitchen knives have gone custom, upper-end and high dollar. At the same pace that kitchens have evolved into high-ceilinged, open-concept entertainment centers with bays, islands and stainless steel appliances, so too has the cutlery used to prepare gourmet food for the guests evolved into techie utensils. These are the knives Paula Dean, Anthony Bourdain and Emeril Lagasse use, the pampered, the trendy, the tried, true, tested and tapered chefs!

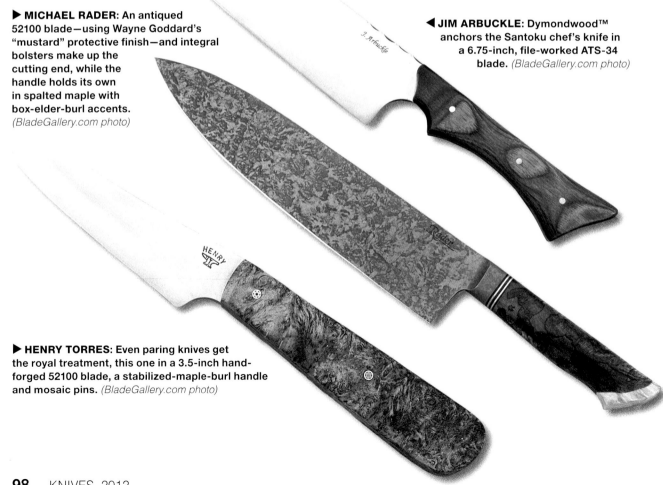

▶ **MICHAEL RADER:** An antiqued 52100 blade—using Wayne Goddard's "mustard" protective finish—and integral bolsters make up the cutting end, while the handle holds its own in spalted maple with box-elder-burl accents. *(BladeGallery.com photo)*

◀ **JIM ARBUCKLE:** Dymondwood™ anchors the Santoku chef's knife in a 6.75-inch, file-worked ATS-34 blade. *(BladeGallery.com photo)*

▶ **HENRY TORRES:** Even paring knives get the royal treatment, this one in a 3.5-inch hand-forged 52100 blade, a stabilized-maple-burl handle and mosaic pins. *(BladeGallery.com photo)*

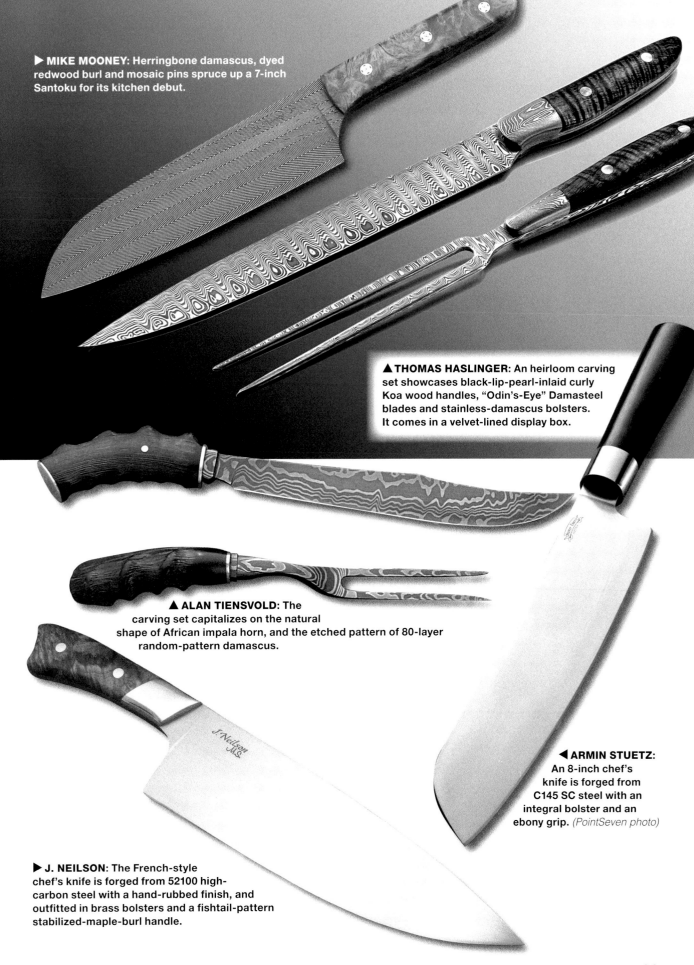

▶ **MIKE MOONEY:** Herringbone damascus, dyed redwood burl and mosaic pins spruce up a 7-inch Santoku for its kitchen debut.

▲**THOMAS HASLINGER:** An heirloom carving set showcases black-lip-pearl-inlaid curly Koa wood handles, "Odin's-Eye" Damasteel blades and stainless-damascus bolsters. It comes in a velvet-lined display box.

▲ **ALAN TIENSVOLD:** The carving set capitalizes on the natural shape of African impala horn, and the etched pattern of 80-layer random-pattern damascus.

◀**ARMIN STUETZ:** An 8-inch chef's knife is forged from C145 SC steel with an integral bolster and an ebony grip. *(PointSeven photo)*

▶ **J. NEILSON:** The French-style chef's knife is forged from 52100 high-carbon steel with a hand-rubbed finish, and outfitted in brass bolsters and a fishtail-pattern stabilized-maple-burl handle.

Wood Workers

▶ **CLARENCE DE YONG:** The Wood Lab handle with mosaic pins is palpable enough to eventually shift attention toward the blade fashioned from a file. *(Cory Martin Imaging)*

▼ **LIN RHEA:** The grains of ironwood are dyed dark enough to deliver "wow factor," and accompanied by a 10-inch W2 blade and 416 stainless steel fittings. *(Ward photo)*

▶ **VINCE EVANS:** The 16th-century Flemish Ballok repro parades a silky smooth stabilized-maple-burl handle, and well finished, gradually tapering 10-inch ladder-pattern-damascus blade. The fittings are engraved steel and silver. *(PointSeven photo)*

▲ **PETER CAREY:** Koa wood lights up the "Firefly," which also features a folding CPM 154 wing and Chad Nichols "bull's-eye"-damascus mid-section.

▲ **BURT FOSTER:** The forge-textured, full-tang, laminated blade is treated to stabilized spalted-maple-burl handle scales and domed nickel-silver pins. *(Buddy Thomason photo)*

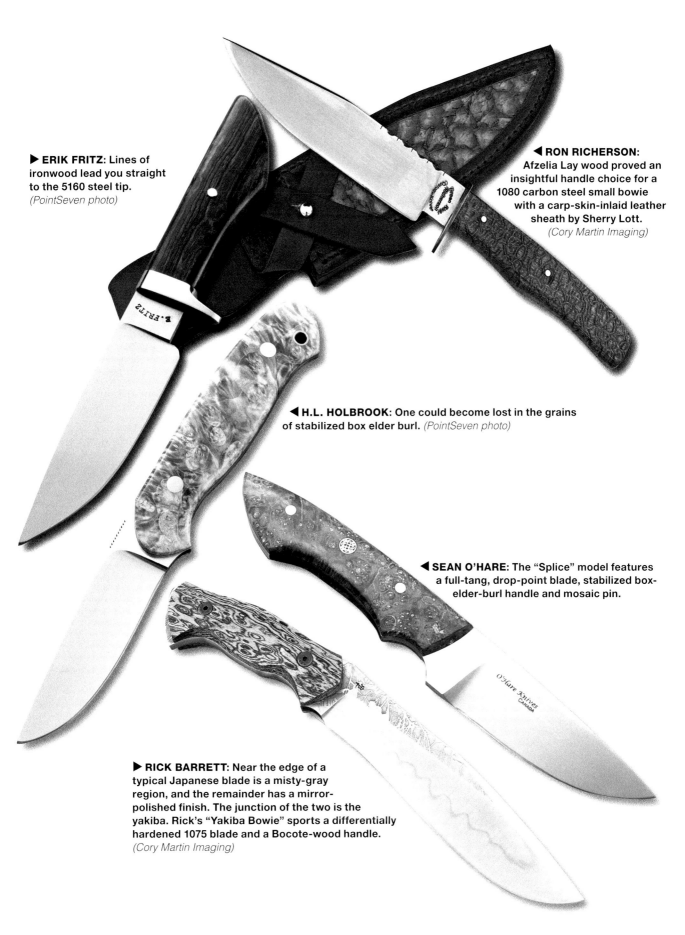

▶ **ERIK FRITZ:** Lines of ironwood lead you straight to the 5160 steel tip. *(PointSeven photo)*

◀ **RON RICHERSON:** Afzelia Lay wood proved an insightful handle choice for a 1080 carbon steel small bowie with a carp-skin-inlaid leather sheath by Sherry Lott. *(Cory Martin Imaging)*

◀ **H.L. HOLBROOK:** One could become lost in the grains of stabilized box elder burl. *(PointSeven photo)*

◀ **SEAN O'HARE:** The "Splice" model features a full-tang, drop-point blade, stabilized box-elder-burl handle and mosaic pin.

▶ **RICK BARRETT:** Near the edge of a typical Japanese blade is a misty-gray region, and the remainder has a mirror-polished finish. The junction of the two is the yakiba. Rick's "Yakiba Bowie" sports a differentially hardened 1075 blade and a Bocote-wood handle. *(Cory Martin Imaging)*

▶ **KEVIN CROSS:** Green, brown and good are the stabilized-cottonwood handle and ancient-ivory bolsters of a CPM 154 drop-point hunter. *(SharpByCoop.com photo)*

▲ **JOHN PARKS:** Amboyna burl enables the 5160 blade with integral bolster. *(SharpByCoop.com photo)*

◀ **KEVIN CASEY:** Tasmanian eucalyptus burl meets feather damascus and a knife shape takes root. *(Buddy Thomason photo)*

◀ **GARY HOUSE:** The curly maple haft makes the damascus pipe tomahawk well worth the heft. The mouthpiece combines blackwood and mammoth ivory. *(PointSeven photo)*

▶ **ANDERS HOGSTROM:** Copper and Amboyna burl blend beautifully on a "Kwaiken" with a 1050 blade and distinct *hamon (temper line).* *(SharpByCoop.com photo)*

▶ **EDMUND DAVIDSON:** The only part not integral to the CPM 154 hunter is the honey of a rosewood handle. *(PointSeven photo)*

▶ **ALLEN NEWBERRY:** The redwood burl of the handle was cut in the 1940s, and accompanies a more modern double-edge 1095 blade and a copper *habaki (ferrule)*. *(Ward photo)*

◀ **DAVID SLOAN:** A prime cut of curly maple anchors a lengthy, 11.25-inch, flat-ground W2 blade with smoky *hamon (temper line)*. *(SharpByCoop.com photo)*

◀ **CRAIG BRASCHLER and MARTIN:** Walnut lends further figure to a 4-inch 1095 drop-point hunter. *(Ward photo)*

▲ **ROB HUDSON:** A maple burl handle is trimmed in buffalo horn and treated to a CPM 154 blade.

▶ **AARON WILBURN:** Considering the effort it took to hand forge, triple quench and double temper the 52100 blade, the least the maker could do was endow it with a Lacewood grip. *(BladeGallery. com photo)*

◀ **BILL AMOUREUX:** There's some swirl to the box elder burl, and some cut to the semi-serrated D2 blade. *(BladeGallery. com photo)*

▶ **GARTH HINDMARCH:** The "River Rapids"-pattern damascus blade washed up some black ash burl.

▼ **DANA HACKNEY:** Bronze and stabilized spalted oak meld like the 1084 and L6 carbon steels the maker forged into a ladder-pattern-damascus blade. *(BladeGallery.com photo)*

▶ **BOB MUNJAS:** The blade is forged from chainsaw blade and 1084 powder steel, the guard is mammoth ivory, copper and reconstituted stone, and the handle is as sturdy as an oak.

▶ **J. NEILSON:** Redwood burl balances out a 15-inch damascus S-guard bowie nicely. *(Ward photo)*

▶ **STUART BARKER:** Stabilized beech wood gets things started on the way to a 7.24-inch O1 blade with integral finger guard. *(Kam Singh photo)*

◀ **NICK WHEELER:** Considering the Afzelia burl handle and 9.5-inch W2 blade with wavy temper line, the bowie that Jim Cooper ordered and commissioned six years ago was well worth the wait. *(SharpByCoop.com photo)*

▼ **MICHAEL RADER:** Dark and light stabilized Koa wood sends the 17-inch David Lisch 1080-and-15N20-damascus blade packin' *(in a good way)*. *(BladeGallery.com photo)*

▶ **MACE VITALE:** The kick-ass 1084-and-15N20-damascus dagger is sent to market in a coffin-style ironwood handle. *(SharpByCoop.com photo)*

▶ **MUDD SHARRIGAN:** Who knew old grape vines made such handsome knife handles as that on the 5160 bowie with all copper fittings?

◀ **MIKE MOONEY:** Snakewood is a striking choice to latch onto a pair of wharncliffe *(top)* and drop-point bird & trout knives.

▶ **JOHN CONWAY:** Imagine how many handles for W2 fighters one can fashion from a redwood tree, though few would look this good. *(BladeGallery.com photo)*

▶ **ROBB GRAY:** The 440C gentleman's field knife is scrolled, engraved, and embellished in another way—with an Amboyna burl and mammoth-ivory grip. *(BladeGallery.com photo)*

▶ **JON P. MOORE:** A select piece of cocobolo wood is partnered with a random-pattern damascus blade.

▶ **BILL HERNDON:** In spalted maple and damascus, the "Bonsai" pruning knife stands tall.

▶ **THOMAS HASLINGER:** Between a satin-finished 154 CM blade with tapered tang and a maple-burl handle, the utility knife shows good balance.

▶ **ALAN HUTCHINSON:** Bird's-eye maple gets "top billing" on the grip of a 5160 utility knife. *(Ward photo)*

◀ **MIKE O'BRIEN:** The look of the curly Koa wood handle of the CPM 154 dagger is like a waistline leading to a buxom top. *(SharpByCoop.com photo)*

◀ **MICHAEL RUTH:** The 1084 blade of the "Sidekick" is paired with a proper ironwood handle. *(Ward photo)*

◀ **ALAN FORNEY:** The 5160 utility knife sports tiger maple digs with copper pins. *(Ward photo)*

Built Sword Tough

◀ **SCOTT SLOBODIAN:** A 22-inch "Honor Wakizashi" pays tribute to Japanese sword smiths via a clay-tempered 1050 high-carbon steel blade with smoky temper line, a basswood hilt stained to resemble bamboo and 14k-gold fittings. Barbara Slobodian engraved the habaki.

soft meets the hard. It's even more astonishing when sword smiths accomplish such feats with much longer blades.

Sword smiths don't stop there, either. Many fashion basket hilts or double hand guards, bronze or copper *habakis* (ferrules), laminated *sayas* (sheaths) or highly finished wood scabbards, cord- or silk-wrapped stingray-skin handles, *menukis* (handle charms), pinned handles, cast bronze pommels, carved grips or wide pattern-welded and plain-steel blades.

There are two-handed swords and those meant for fencing, highly guarded loppers and others with small oval hand guards, shapely pommels and plain handles, and varieties to go around. Yet they all have one thing in common—they're build sword tough and meant to stay that way.

◀ **RICK BARRETT:** The "Krill" contemporary Persian-inspired saber sports a curved 52100-and-A203E damascus blade, a bronze guard and pommel, and a Wenge-wood handle. *(Cory Martin Imaging)*

I f ever there was an area where toughness mattered, it's in a sword blade. Much like a fillet knife, in order to use a sword the way it was originally intended, the steel must flex without breaking. Unlike a fillet knife where the worst that will happen if the blade breaks is that the fish don't make it to the frying pan, if a sword blade breaks in battle, the warrior ends up holding, well, the short end of the stick.

It is amazing to non knife smiths that those who forge steel in home workshops can master their media to the point of heat treating, tempering and quenching blades, thus achieving soft backs, or spines, and hard edges. It is such treatment that ensures cut and flex, and some go as far as clay tempering and etching each blade to show the *hamon*, or temper line, where the

▶ **BILL BURKE:** Start with 185,000-layer folded steel, add a silk-wrapped stingray-skin hilt, top it off with gold and silver insets, and Samurais everywhere start to take notice. *(PointSeven photo)*

▶ **THINUS HERBST:** The "Lion Sword" is done up in an N690 stainless steel blade, a bronze hilt and stainless fittings of the fetching kind.

▶ **ANDERS HOGSTROM:** In the sword cane realm is a two-bar Conny Persson damascus piece with a bronze, copper and damascus hilt inlaid with ivory. The cane is oak. *(SharpByCoop.com*

▶ **STEVE SCHWARZER:** A soft hamon *(temper line)* follows the slight curve of the 1084 blade while a fuller, or blood groove, stretches along the spine. Wally Hostetter is credited for fashioning the fittings and saya (sheath). The leather-wrapped stingray-skin handle is treated to a gold menuki (handle charm). *(PointSeven photo)*

▲ **KEVIN CASHEN:** The "Pappenheimer Rapier" reaches 43 inches overall and is guarded by a basket hilt with a traditional iron-wire-wrapped hilt.

◀ **GARY HOUSE:** The "Sherasaya" is attributed to Bill Burke, while House takes credit for the rest of the work on the W2 sword with poplar hilt. *(PointSeven photo)*

TRENDS **109**

Woolly Bullies

▼ RUSS ANDREWS II: Mammoth ivory makes a sweet damascus integral more palatable. *(SharpByCoop.com photo)*

▶▲ GARY MULKEY: Colors crisscross the mammoth-ivory grip like the lines of the 9-inch damascus bowie blade. *(Ward photo)*

▶ MARVIN WINN: The ATS-34 drop-point hunter distances itself from similar pieces through mammoth ivory, and Roy Finney bolster and pinhead engraving. *(PointSeven photo)*

▶ KIRK REXROAT: A cowboy rides a bronco on the mosaic-damascus bolster of a damascus folder with a bark-mammoth-ivory grip. *(PointSeven photo)*

◀ MICHAEL KINKER: Choosing two slabs of mammoth ivory for the handles of a couple Brooks Bart-engraved 440C fixed blades proved a winning formula. *(PointSeven photo)*

◄ JOEL CHAMBLIN: A foil cutter and corkscrew fold out from the mammoth ivory handle of a clip-point fixed blade. *(Ward photo)*

◄ GENE BASKETT: Somehow the blued damascus steel, mammoth tooth and 18k-gold inlay are color coordinated. *(PointSeven photo)*

◄ WAYNE HENSLEY: The integral D2 fixed blade is literally embellished with a mammoth-tooth grip. *(PointSeven photo)*

► RUSTY POLK: Blue mammoth ivory tames a 10-inch "snake"-pattern damascus bowie blade. *(Ward photo)*

◄ PHIL EVANS: In an 11-inch damascus blade, nickel silver guard and mammoth ivory handle, this one has snap, crackle and pop. *(Ward photo)*

▲ EMIL BUCHARSKY: Mosaic damascus bolsters are dovetailed into the "cracked ice" mammoth ivory scales of a re-curved CPM-D2 folder. *(BladeGallery.com photo)*

▶ JOHN PERRY: The tightly patterned damascus blade and bolsters meet the natural grains of mammoth ivory and come to a mutual understanding. *(Ward photo)*

◀ STEVE CULVER: Mammoth tooth makes an already fascinating 1084- and-15N20-damascus sub-hilt fighter with engraved guard all that much more interesting.

▶ CLIFTON POLK: The colorful ancient ivory grip is bookended by "flame"- damascus bolsters and a fiery clip-pint blade. *(Ward photo)*

▶ DAVID SLOAN: The 10- inch, 280-layer damascus blade with a long clip point is enhanced greatly by a woolly and bully mammoth-ivory grip. *(SharpByCoop.com photo)*

◀ JOHNNY STOUT: The patterns of "raindrop" damascus, engraved bolsters and "crackle" mammoth ivory wander all over "The Nomad." *(Ward photo)*

▼ PETER MARTIN: Green mammoth ivory, blued chevron-pattern-damascus bolsters and a black Turkish damascus blade are a colorful combination. *(Cory Martin Imaging)*

◄ TERRY VANDEVENTER: A "Small Cowboy Bowie" is spurred on by a 6.75-inch mosaic-damascus blade and reined in by a mammoth ivory grip. *(Ward photo)*

◄ CHUCK GEDRAITIS: The hamon *(temper line)* of the snub-nose folder moves from the top swedge of the 1095 blade, through the bolsters and leads into the blue-green mammoth ivory handle scales.

◄ R.J. MARTIN: The flipper folder features a Chad Nichols stainless damascus blade, a 6AL-4V-titanium frame, mammoth-bark-ivory handle inserts and roller thrust bearings. *(SharpByCoop.com photo)*

◄ THOMAS HASLINGER: You just want to palm the premium-mammoth-tooth grip, held in place by small gold pins, of the little boot knife in an integral San Mai damascus blade.

Pronounced Clip Points

◄KEITH BAGLEY: The wide blade leaves more room for admiring the damascus pattern, continued onto the guard, and held in check by a sambar-stag grip. *(PointSeven photo)*

►BRAD SINGLEY: Sheep horn provides hand purchase for a 1080 Southwest bowie with a silicon-bronze guard. *(Ward photo)*

►RICK SMITH: The "Pirate Bowie" is an O1 tool steel swashbuckler with a long clip point, an elk-stag handle and curved mild steel quillion S-guard.

◄ARTHUR LYNN: The 1084-and-15N20-damascus blade cuts and dives like a shark through murky waters, guided by its giraffe-bone tail. *(PointSeven photo)*

◄PETE CROWL: This 5160 clip-point gent's bowie is set up with a stainless-steel and copper guard, and a stag-horn grip. *(Ward photo)*

▶ **LAWRENCE WHITLOCK:** The dark Devin Thomas damascus blade with pronounced clip point lies in stark contrast to the ivory handle, nickel silver fittings and carved guard. *(PointSeven photo)*

▶ **D.R. GOOD:** A clip-point bowie boasts an ivory handle, nickel-silver fittings, a 9.25-inch 6K Stellite blade and a leather sheath inlaid with rattlesnake skin.

▶ **MARVIN SOLOMON:** The clip-nose fighter is done up in a striped damascus blade and wooden grip. *(Ward photo)*

▶ **JOHN HORRIGAN:** The laminated blade with pronounced clip point will woo any onlookers, helped along by gold inlay, engraving, bluing and a walrus-ivory handle. *(Ward photo)*

◀ **JAMES BATSON:** The "Alamo Bowie" enlists an 11.5-inch CruV Forge blade, a forged-iron S-guard and a crown-stag handle. *(Ward photo)*

Traders, Trappers and Tomahawks

◄ RAY RYBAR: "Yesteryear's Armory" includes two tomahawks—one a spike hawk, one a pipe hawk—in curly maple hafts, copper cones, brass tacks and horse hair, and a "herring-bone-damascus" bowie with a stag grip. *(PointSeven photo)*

◄ RICK MARCHAND: The hammer-finished 5160 blade is treated to an aged-like patina to match its hemp-wrapped, distressed-oak handle and exposed copper rivet. *(PointSeven photo)*

◄ SERGE PANCHENKO: A "Relic Wharncliffe" is done in 1080 steel, a mild-steel and copper handle, and brass pins.

▼ EMIL BUCHARSKY: The "Firewater Trader" model is stunningly composed in a 7.25-inch, six-bar composite-damascus blade, hot-blued, engraved and gold-inlaid mild-steel guard and a bark-mammoth-ivory handle. *(BladeGallery.com photo)*

◄ BILL KIRKES: Commemorating the "Trail Of Tears," the bowie boasts a 7-inch 5160 blade, an amber-crown-stag handle, teardrop-shaped grip overlay and an Indianhead-nickel pommel. *(Ward photo)*

▼**JACK A. FULLER:** Engraver Keith Castell created a peace metal to inlay into the head of Jack's two-foot pipe tomahawk that also features an ivory mouthpiece and clean-out plug. *(PointSeven photo)*

▼**LIN RHEA:** A "Trappers Hawk," hafted in curly maple, dons a 1084 bit with a 2.25-inch cutting edge. *(Ward photo)*

▲**JOHN M. COHEA:** A frontier-style rifleman's knife sports a wood handle, a wide drop-point blade in an aged patina and a rawhide sheath with period decoration. *(Buddy Thomason photo)*

▶**BILL BEHNKE:** The flat-ground damascus hatchet head is hafted in ash, and handy to hold. *(SharpByCoop.com photo)*

▲◀**R.W. WILSON:** The pierced heart through the Alabama damascus head of the tomahawk is only one of the decorations with the others including a carved curly maple haft, engraved silver inlays and beaded leather thongs. *(Cory Martin Imaging)*

Tactical Application

▶ **BRAM FRANK:** The maker's style is all his own, this one in a tactical bowie blade, extended flipper/one-hand opener/pressure point mechanism, front lock and indexing dimples. *(PointSeven photo)*

◀ **AARON FREDERICK:** The tactical folder and fixed-blade combination features re-curved blades with large serrations, gut hooks or seat belt cutters, aesthetic holes in the blades, and ivory-Micarta handle scales. *(PointSeven photo)*

▲ **DAVID MOSIER:** The fixed-blade "Karambit" cuts the mustard in a 4-inch CPM 154 blade and G-10 handle scales. *(Ward photo)*

▶ **BRENT BESHARA:** Only the Canadian knifemaker known as "Besh" makes a fixed-blade wharncliffe like this one in O1 tool steel, G-10 handle scales and a signature "Besh Wedge" tip. *(Steve Woods photo)*

▶ **SHANE SIBERT:** The no-frills, all-thrills "Hyperspace Fighter" includes a 9-inch, ¼-inch-thick CPM S30V blade and a "Camo-G-10" handle.

◀ **KEITH OUYE:** The re-curved 1/8-inch-thick CPM 154 blade with swedge along the spine gives the titanium-frame-lock folder the character it deserves to go along with pirate-themed engraving. *(SharpByCoop.com photo)*

▶ **SAL MANARO:** Whether in blued Chad Nichols damascus or plain blade steel, the "Rush" model in anodized-titanium liners and clips, and carbon-fiber handle scales is a smooth operator. *(SharpByCoop.com photo)*

▶ **JASON KNIGHT:** The mid-size military model is outfitted in black canvas Micarta and a hammer-marked blade with finger guard. *(Buddy Thomason photo)*

◀ **JIM HAMMOND:** Between the micro-bead-blasted finish of the 6-inch 440C blade and the black-linen-Micarta® handle, the "Cobra Gold" is a stealth fighter. *(Buddy Thomason photo)*

◀ **JODY MULLER, SAM JONES and LANCE ABERNATHY:** The frame-lock folders come in CPM 154 or "Digi-Camo" 1075 blades, and titanium or orange-G-10 handle scales. *(SharpByCoop.com photo)*

▶ **PAT and WES CRAWFORD:** The "Kasper" model is a classic, tactically attractive design with a skeletonized grip and long top swedge along the blade spine. *(SharpByCoop.com photo)*

▼ **SEAN O'HARE:** Coyote-brown G-10 is a handsome handle choice to go with black G-10 bolsters and a 4.25-inch CPM 154 blade.

▼ **HUMAYD A.R. MAHOMEDY:** An "EDC Shark" is one of the most dangerous predators, this one in a triple-ground, 4.75-inch Bohler N690 blade and carbon fiber handle scales.

▲ **DANIEL WINKLER:** The maker offers the tactical fixed blades with rubber or cord-wrapped grips, and in plain or camouflage blades with saw teeth along their spines. *(SharpByCoop.com photo)*

▲ **JAMES HARRISON:** Follow the holes along the titanium handle frame to the Damasteel blade, Ikoma Korth Bearing System and carved pocket clip.

STATE OF THE ART

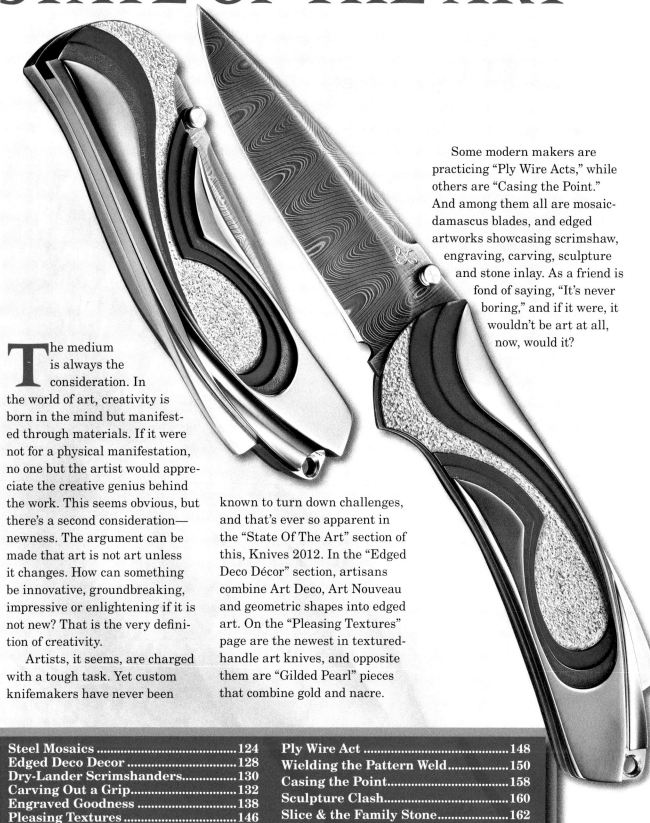

Some modern makers are practicing "Ply Wire Acts," while others are "Casing the Point." And among them all are mosaic-damascus blades, and edged artworks showcasing scrimshaw, engraving, carving, sculpture and stone inlay. As a friend is fond of saying, "It's never boring," and if it were, it wouldn't be art at all, now, would it?

The medium is always the consideration. In the world of art, creativity is born in the mind but manifested through materials. If it were not for a physical manifestation, no one but the artist would appreciate the creative genius behind the work. This seems obvious, but there's a second consideration—newness. The argument can be made that art is not art unless it changes. How can something be innovative, groundbreaking, impressive or enlightening if it is not new? That is the very definition of creativity.

Artists, it seems, are charged with a tough task. Yet custom knifemakers have never been

known to turn down challenges, and that's ever so apparent in the "State Of The Art" section of this, Knives 2012. In the "Edged Deco Décor" section, artisans combine Art Deco, Art Nouveau and geometric shapes into edged art. On the "Pleasing Textures" page are the newest in textured-handle art knives, and opposite them are "Gilded Pearl" pieces that combine gold and nacre.

Steel Mosaics

Ed Fowler penned a feature article for the May 2011 issue of *BLADE Magazine*® in which he outlined "Four Bladesmithing Myths Ed Fowler Style." The myths were untruths as he has come to know them, in his own experience, about forging blades.

The third myth he mentioned is that layered damascus makes a more high-performance blade than a blade forged or made from a single steel. Fowler said he strongly believed this at one time, and started forging damascus blades in pursuit of the high-endurance blade. But, facts as he now knows them, and after years of testing, indicate to him that "blades forged from a single steel can outdistance the performance of layered damascus blades easily, providing, of course, that the quality of the steel is adequate and the methods used are appropriate for developing the steel's maximum potential."

Why bring that up in the "State Of The Art" section of the *KNIVES* annual, a color, coffee-table-style book almost entirely devoted to handmade knives, and in this particular chapter, on the "state of the art" in knives? Because of what Fowler said next: "Damascus in many forms can be beautiful and is totally appropriate for an art knife."

Many using-knife purists don't understand that last part, yet they should for one simple reason—art knives are good for the industry. Collectors are good for the industry. High-dollar, investment-grade knives are good for the industry. The industry thrives on gorgeous damascus, embellished knives. They help keep the industry lucrative so that folks can continue making hunting, camp, fillet, utility and military knives, and actually have a market in which to sell them.

They're gorgeous, particularly mosaic-damascus blades, with patterns as stunning as the glazed titles of the Piazza Vittoria in Palermo, where the most important scenes depict *Orpheus, Alexander the Great's Hunt and the Four Seasons.*

▶ **KYLE ROYER:** A vest fighter, meant for the vest pocket of a well-heeled gentleman, is appropriately outfitted in "basket-weave" mosaic damascus and Alaskan mammoth ivory. *(Caleb Royer Studio photo)*

▶ **STEVEN SKIFF:** The colors of gun-blued Chris Marks damascus please the sense of sight, just as black mammoth ivory plays to a sense of touch, and a 24k-gold thumb stud to a sense of taste and style. *(PointSeven photo)*

◀ **TOM FERRY:** Big details like the San Mai mosaic-damascus blade share billing with such small details as an abalone inlay in a blackwood handle. This one comes with a Paul Long sheath. *(SharpByCoop.com photo)*

▶ **DAVE LISCH:** Place the forefinger through the wrought iron ring, hold onto the fossil-walrus-ivory grip and let the mosaic-damascus fighter blade point you the rest of the way. *(Mitch Lum photo)*

◀ **ED CAFFREY:** Of San Mai mosaic-damascus construction, along with a carved grip and titanium liners, the folder emanates a smoky ambiance reminiscent of the forge from which it came. *(SharpByCoop.com photo)*

▶ **HANK KNICKMEYER:** Cave paintings may have inspired the pattern of the San Mai mosaic-damascus blade, fittingly butted up against a fossil-walrus-artifact handle. *(PointSeven photo)*

▶ **CLIFF PARKER:** It was a mammoth undertaking but the maker forged the blade just the same, adding a musk ox handle. *(PointSeven photo)*

◀ **KIRK REXROAT:** A mosaic bison blade is butted up against a damascus guard, titanium spacers and a walrus-ivory handle. *(PointSeven photo)*

▼**GEORGE GARNER:** Mosaic damascus frames presentation-grade mother-of-pearl, all guarded by a 1095- and-15N20-damascus blade. Other amenities include a sterling silver bail, gold screws and a file-worked back spine and liners. *(Buddy Thomason photo)*

◀**BILL BUXTON:** While the 9 7/8-inch blade is 155-layer "W's"-pattern damascus, the ferrule is a one-of-a-kind mosaic "X" pattern, and the handle is fossilized walrus ivory. *(Buddy Thomason photo)*

▼**JEFF DRISCOLL:** The silver-wire inlay of the sculpted desert ironwood bolster transitions the ebony handle into the Micke Andersson multi-bar mosaic-damascus blade. *(BladeGallery.com photo)*

◀**JERRY MCCLURE:** The blued Joel Davis mosaic-damascus bolsters make a flattering waistcoat accentuating a pearl bottom and twist-pattern Damasteel top. *(SharpByCoop.com photo)*

▶**ANDERS HEDLUND:** The maker's vision of what "Butterfly Heaven" looks like is done using media like "butterfly"- and "flowers"-pattern mosaic damascus, engraving, 18k-gold inlays and mammoth ivory.

◀**TOBBE LUNDSTROM:** The mosaic damascus blade forged by Mattias Styrefors depicts a stegosaurus lumbering away from stacked up fossil-walrus and fossil-mammoth ivory. *(BladeGallery.com photo)*

▶ **JON CHRISTENSEN:** A pro at "quilted feathers" mosaic damascus, Jon also shows us his hand at a carved random-damascus handle on the San Francisco folder. *(Mitch Lum photo)*

◀ **MARCELLO GARAU:** A close look reveals why the maker calls it a "turtles"-pattern mosaic-damascus blade, to go along with the ancient tortoise-shell handle and damascus bolsters. *(Francesco Pachi photo)*

▶ **RON NEWTON:** Newton's physics include a "starburst"-pattern damascus blade, damascus escutcheon plate and finial knob, engraving and a dog-bone mammoth-ivory handle. *(Ward photo)*

◀ **DON HANSON III:** When you have a colorful slab of mammoth ivory, some "Goblin" mosaic damascus and titanium at your disposal, why not use them on a dress tactical folder? *(SharpByCoop.com photo)*

▶ **GRAHAM FREDEEN:** "Flaming Rose" mosaic damascus sprouts from stabilized California buckeye burl. *(SharpByCoop.com photo)*

◀ **MIKE FELLOWS:** Carved hippo tooth ivory allows the mosaic-damascus blade and bolsters of the "Duchess" to breathe.

Edged Deco Decor

One of the reasons why, after 32 annual editions, the *Knives* book remains so popular with knife collectors, makers, professionals and general enthusiasts is that it is formulated to track trends and art movements within the blade community. The full-color book succeeds at this through its "Trends" and "State Of The Art" sections.

Though some knife enthusiasts prefer straightforward, well-made, clean hunters, bowies, skinners and fillet knives, and others gravitate toward art, collector and fantasy pieces, there is common ground. As in the fields of art, music and fashion, the extreme designs, the over-the-edge art and wild or questionable fashion statements help steer the more reserved, middle-ground practitioners in a direction. In other words,

those who tend toward practical knife patterning borrow a few of the more reasonable yet edgy design elements from the art, collector and fantasy pieces, or at the very least they are influenced by them, and incorporate them sensibly into their own patterns.

There has been a movement the last couple years in the collector-knife community toward art deco and art nouveau designs, particularly on higher-end pieces aimed toward those who appreciate the artistic genres. Now there is a new movement, one in which the lines are blurred between art deco, art nouveau, geometric shapes and general embellishments on fine art knives. Call it "Edged Deco Décor," if you will.

◄ **DES HORN:** The maker describes his Damasteel lock-back folder as displaying "Prism-art," highlighted by 18k-gold pins, bale and screws. *(Francesco Pachi photo)*

▶ **ROGER BERGH:** The geometric damascus guards and carved blade shape give the blackwood-handle bowie a hot little hybrid look and feel. *(SharpByCoop.com photo)*

▲ **STEPHEN OLSZEWSKI:** The double-action dagger struts its Art Deco stuff via bronze, copper, sterling silver and 14k-gold bolsters, a walrus-ivory handle carved to reveal a long-armed female bedecked in a fancy armband, and a Jerry Rados ladder-pattern-damascus blade.

▶ **KEN STEIGERWALT:** Here's a "Deco Dagger" in Mike Norris damascus, a carved damascus frame, and black-lip-pearl and 18k-gold inlays. *(SharpByCoop.com photo)*

▼ **TOM OVEREYNDER:** Engraved by Amayak Stepanyan, the damascus folder is heavily influenced by a popular 1920s Parisian art movement. *(Buddy Thomason photo)*

▶ **ROGER BERGH:** No matter how the large, guard-less dagger is viewed, it's all about the angles, whether via the damascus blade, mosaic-damascus bolsters or damascus- and gold-inlaid mammoth-ivory grip. *(SharpByCoop.com photo)*

◀ **STEPHEN OLSZEWSKI:** The Art Deco angel has gold-tipped wings, mokumé hair and a copper halo. The damascus blade is the work of Jerry Rados.

▶ **MATTHEW LERCH:** The "Geo Dagger" makes good use of 24k-gold-wire inlays and Rob Thomas's "shark's-tooth" damascus. *(SharpByCoop.com photo)*

Dry-Lander Scrimshanders

◀ **LINDA KARST STONE, SANDRA BRADY** and **CONNIE BELLETT:** The three artists scrimmed bears on walrus-ivory-handle hunters by D' Alton Holder, and allowed Bruce Christensen, Pat Holder and Bruce Shaw to engrave the pieces. *(SharpByCoop.com photo)*

◀ **LINDA KARST STONE:** The artists—knifemaker Edmund Davidson, engraver Jere Davidson and scrimshander Karst Stone—proved no cowardly lions. *(PointSeven photo)*

▶ **SANDRA BRADY:** Warriors rule the wicked world of the ivory handle, framed out in Ray Cover Jr. engraving and a damascus blade by the fighting-knife's maker, Mike Sakmar. *(Cory Martin Imaging)*

▶ **DR. HANS PETER JENSEN:** A Siegfried Rinkes Damasteel locking-liner folder is "undressed up" in "Modern Eve" color scrimshaw of an alluring nude bather.

▲ **NKOSI JUBANE:** A rare parrot flower is immortalized in color within the pores of whale tooth, mounted on the full, tapered tang of a satin-finished N690 blade from knifemaker A.R. Mahomedy, and accompanied by Armin Winkler engraving.

▶ **RONI DIETRICH:** Embellishments on a Howard Hitchmough bowie include Roni's wildlife scrimshaw in ancient walrus ivory, Robert Eggerling damascus, Vinland Damasteel and an 18k-gold name plate. *(PointSeven photo)*

◀ **GARY WILLIAMS:** With so much to appreciate on the Dennis Friedly bowie—as in the Gil Rudolph engraving and gold inlay of brush, thorns, a bald eagle and acorns—it's the scrimshaw of a Native American and wildcat that focuses the attention. *(PointSeven photo)*

▶ **LINDA KARST STONE:** Edmund Davidson's ivory-handle, integral 154CM fixed blade provides the perfect palette for Jere Davidson engraving and Linda's scrimmed bird-dog scene. *(PointSeven photo)*

▲ **STEPHEN MACKRILL:** The scrimshander applies and flies his colors in the form of a flag—part of "The Patriot" scrimshaw theme done on hippo tooth—with a bald eagle also taking wing, and a mosaic-damascus "flag"-pattern blade to boot. *(PointSeven photo)*

▲ **LINDA KARST STONE:** In 1986, Karst Stone scrimmed a wagon-train motif on the ivory handles of four Smith & Wesson 44/40 Texas Sesquicentennial Wagon Train edition revolvers. Knifemaker Jerry Moen bought the collection, fashioned a matching CPM 154 drop-point hunter, and commissioned Karst Stone to scrimshaw its handle to match those of the guns. Kevin Elkins engraved the bolsters.

STATE OF THE ART **131**

Carving out a Grip

Why take the time? You could find a nice slab of stag, a length of exotic wood, two pieces of pearl with nacre so bright you'd have to wear shades, and apply them to the handle areas of finely crafted knives with nary a care about shaping, carving, sculpting or creating. Why make more work when less will suffice?

It has taken this knife editor a while to figure it out, but the "why" may be answered with a "because they care." This is why knifemakers round knife handles, bevel the edges, tightly fit grips to bolsters and guards, round blade spines, add finger notches,

choils and grooves, include palm swells, taper the tangs and create indexing dimples.

The answer may also be more complicated than "because they care." Knifemaking is a handcraft, and as such it also qualifies as an art form to those who are so creatively inclined. There are people in the world who see beyond the outer layers. Like a mathematician who digs deeply to the root of a problem, artists envision possibilities, and see beauty where none exists, at least to the unenlightened. They envision life forms, landscapes, fictional beings, characters and surreal subtleties where the

common man views things only as they are, or appear to be.

Knife artists not only carve out grips, but niches, livings and places where they feel at home, in wonderful worlds where outside influences barely intrude, and inanimate objects come to life for the enjoyment and benefit of all who care to take a closer look. All that from carved grips? You can bet your knife on it.

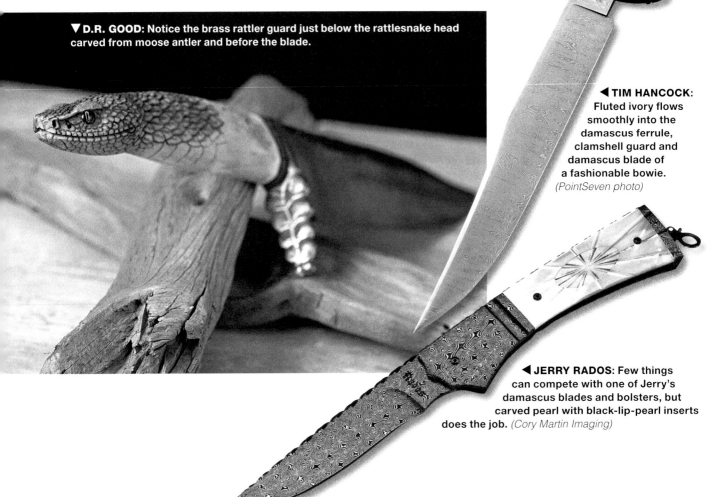

▼ **D.R. GOOD:** Notice the brass rattler guard just below the rattlesnake head carved from moose antler and before the blade.

◄ **TIM HANCOCK:** Fluted ivory flows smoothly into the damascus ferrule, clamshell guard and damascus blade of a fashionable bowie. *(PointSeven photo)*

◄ **JERRY RADOS:** Few things can compete with one of Jerry's damascus blades and bolsters, but carved pearl with black-lip-pearl inserts does the job. *(Cory Martin Imaging)*

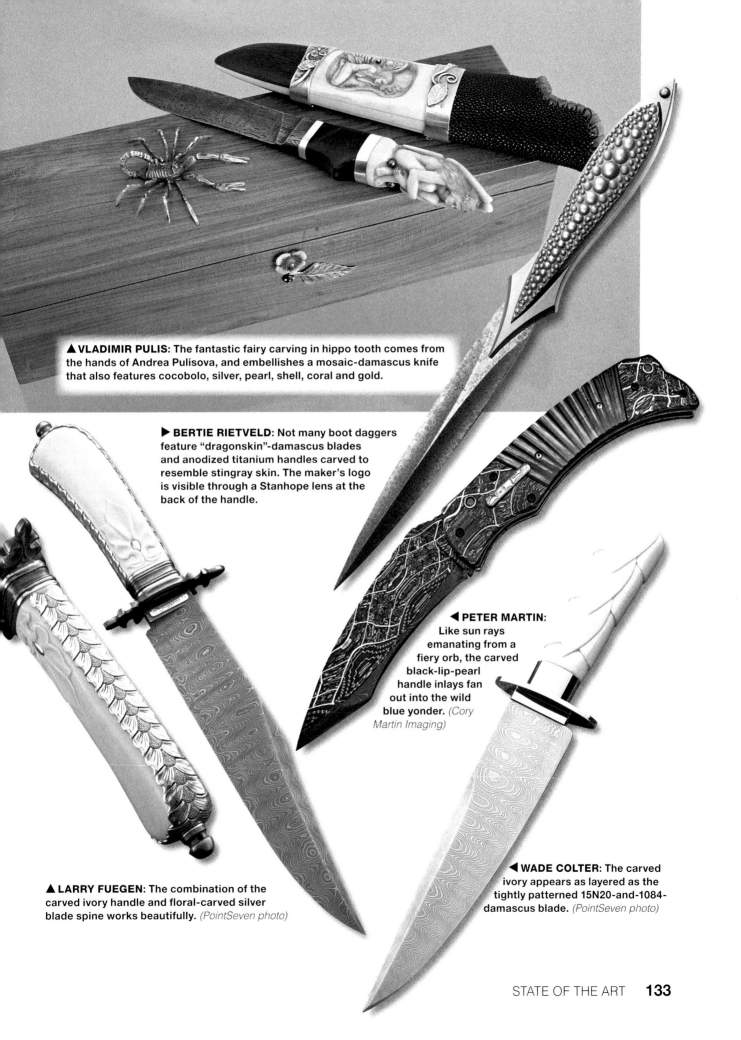

VLADIMIR PULIS: The fantastic fairy carving in hippo tooth comes from the hands of Andrea Pulisova, and embellishes a mosaic-damascus knife that also features cocobolo, silver, pearl, shell, coral and gold.

BERTIE RIETVELD: Not many boot daggers feature "dragonskin"-damascus blades and anodized titanium handles carved to resemble stingray skin. The maker's logo is visible through a Stanhope lens at the back of the handle.

PETER MARTIN: Like sun rays emanating from a fiery orb, the carved black-lip-pearl handle inlays fan out into the wild blue yonder. *(Cory Martin Imaging)*

LARRY FUEGEN: The combination of the carved ivory handle and floral-carved silver blade spine works beautifully. *(PointSeven photo)*

WADE COLTER: The carved ivory appears as layered as the tightly patterned 15N20-and-1084-damascus blade. *(PointSeven photo)*

▶ **JESSE DAVIS:** Carved by D.R. Good, the axis-stag handle snakes its way around to a Chad Nichols damascus blade via way of an amber spacer and nickel-silver guard. *(Ward photo)*

▶ **DANIEL STEPHAN:** The dagger might just be too pretty to push, parading a carved Hank Knickmeyer San Mai damascus blade, a carved mammoth-ivory grip and copper fittings. *(PointSeven photo)*

▲ **DONALD VOGT:** With copper and gold horns molded into the damascus bolsters, and copper claws digging into the carved gold-lip-pearl handle, the knifemaker says the artistic rendering on the automatic dagger represents a bird of prey's talons tearing into flesh.

▼ **TOMMY MCNABB:** Otherworldly would be a good way to describe the one-of-a-kind knife in a hollow-ground Muonionalusta meteorite blade and an antique-bone handle carved in an Asian dragon motif. *(BladeGallery.com photo)*

▲ **MARKKU VILPPOLA:** Carved dyed birch contrasts nicely with the mammoth-ivory, cow-bone and cast-bronze spacers, allowing the damascus blade to stretch out.

▶ **ROBERT SMITH:** A bird's-beak guard perches atop the feathered mammoth-ivory grip of a boot knife in Mike Norris damascus. *(Ward photo)*

▼ **HIDETOSHI NAKAYAMA:** A netsuke *(small sculpture)* artist plies his trade, carving the fossil-mammoth-ivory grip of a two-blade D2 folder into a gecko sunning itself on a bamboo stalk. *(BladeGallery.com photo)*

▶ **CHARLIE and HARRY MATHEWS:** Raised leaf carvings embellish the walrus-ivory grip of a CPM-3V Scandinavian-style fixed blade. *(SharpByCoop.com photo)*

▶ **LEON TREIBER:** The carved lines don't halt, but keep going from the fluted walrus grip through the jeweler's bronze bolsters of the lock-back folder. *(Ward photo)*

▶ **LOWELL BRAY:** In handling the damascus fixed blade, the maker enlisted David Semone to carve an eagle and one of its feathers just below the surface of the highly figured stag. *(PointSeven photo)*

STATE OF THE ART **135**

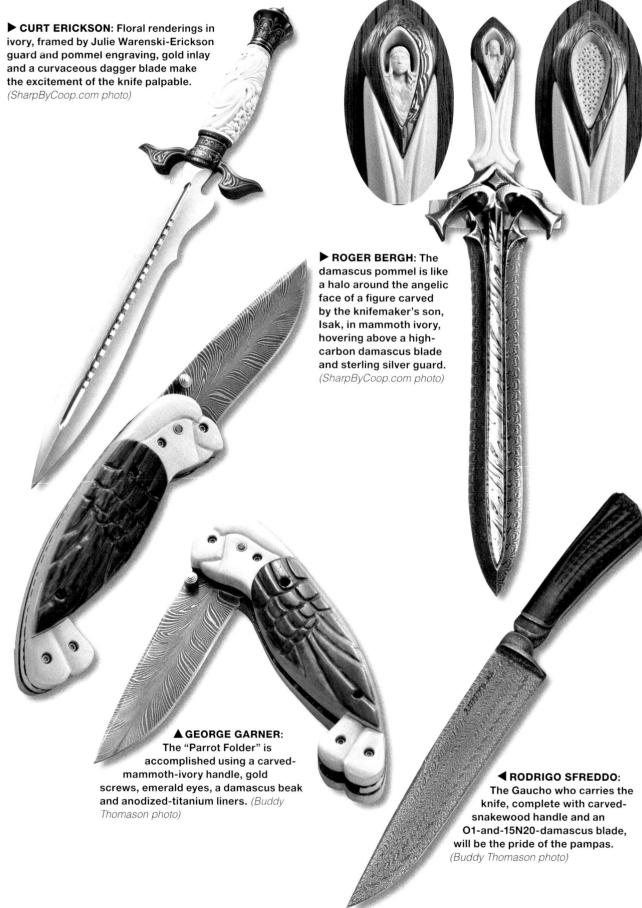

▶ **CURT ERICKSON:** Floral renderings in ivory, framed by Julie Warenski-Erickson guard and pommel engraving, gold inlay and a curvaceous dagger blade make the excitement of the knife palpable. *(SharpByCoop.com photo)*

▶ **ROGER BERGH:** The damascus pommel is like a halo around the angelic face of a figure carved by the knifemaker's son, Isak, in mammoth ivory, hovering above a high-carbon damascus blade and sterling silver guard. *(SharpByCoop.com photo)*

▲ **GEORGE GARNER:** The "Parrot Folder" is accomplished using a carved-mammoth-ivory handle, gold screws, emerald eyes, a damascus beak and anodized-titanium liners. *(Buddy Thomason photo)*

◀ **RODRIGO SFREDDO:** The Gaucho who carries the knife, complete with carved-snakewood handle and an O1-and-15N20-damascus blade, will be the pride of the pampas. *(Buddy Thomason photo)*

▶ **JAY HENDRICKSON:** Maple-leaf carvings, and just the right amount of red dye, enhance the curly-maple handle of a 5160 bowie. *(SharpByCoop.com photo)*

◀ **ROBERT KOVACIK:** The "Mustang Bowie" bucks trends by wearing an unusual Buxus-wood handle and 440C blade engraved in an Arizona-teepee and landscape motif.

◀ **JEREMY MARSH:** The high-relief brickwork carving and color anodizing put the building blocks in place for a spectacular Damasteel flipper folder. *(SharpByCoop.com photo)*

▶ **GAWIE HERBST:** Only bronze fittings would do for the fluted, carved and textured black-ivory handle of the K110 dagger.

◀ **ANDERS HEDLUND:** In cutting out the dark-brown mammoth ivory, engraving a handle shield, inlaying gold, sapphire, pearl and amethysts, and working with Johan Gustavsson and Doug Ponzio damascus, the maker further cemented his place of honor in the world of art knives.

◀ **JERRY FISK:** The swirls never stop on the fluted-handle dirk in ivory, damascus and gold inlay, and in this case that's a good thing. *(Ward photo)*

Engraved Goodness

▶ **BRIAN HOCHSTRAT:** It took four views to show how Brian sexed up each bolster of a Joe Kious damascus auto dagger, as well as underneath each of the sliding antique-tortoise-shell handle slabs. *(Buddy Thomason photo)*

▶ **BARBARA SLOBODIAN:** The knife embellishment is an ancient Korean gilding technique—Keum-boo—incorporating thin sheets of pure gold-to-silver, in this case engraved in a fanciful dragon motif, and accompanying the Poul Strand "explosion"-pattern-damascus blade of a Scott Slobodian folder.

▶ **LEON TREIBER:** The "Ranger" lock-back folder is the beneficiary of gold-inlaid and engraved bolsters, and handle decorations in the form of a jeweler's-bronze pistol and Texas Ranger shield. *(Ward photo)*

▶ **BRIAN HOCHSTRAT:** "Days Gone By" cowboy-and-Indian engraving, gold pins and shield, and an antique Remington-bone handle dress up a T.R. Overeynder slip-joint folder. *(PointSeven photo)*

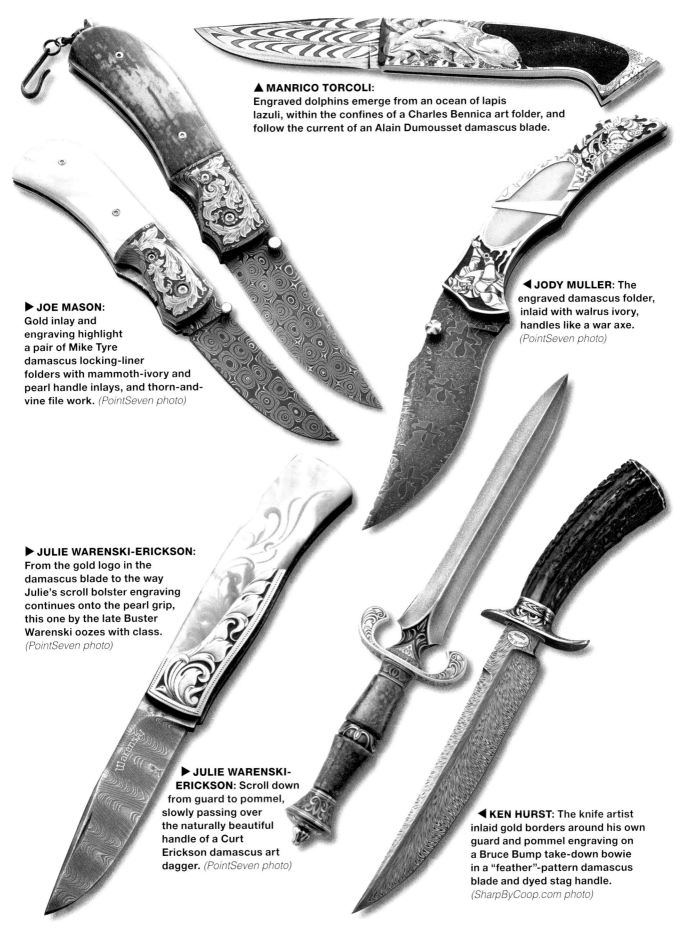

▲ MANRICO TORCOLI:
Engraved dolphins emerge from an ocean of lapis lazuli, within the confines of a Charles Bennica art folder, and follow the current of an Alain Dumousset damascus blade.

► JOE MASON:
Gold inlay and engraving highlight a pair of Mike Tyre damascus locking-liner folders with mammoth-ivory and pearl handle inlays, and thorn-and-vine file work. *(PointSeven photo)*

◄ JODY MULLER: The engraved damascus folder, inlaid with walrus ivory, handles like a war axe. *(PointSeven photo)*

► JULIE WARENSKI-ERICKSON:
From the gold logo in the damascus blade to the way Julie's scroll bolster engraving continues onto the pearl grip, this one by the late Buster Warenski oozes with class. *(PointSeven photo)*

► JULIE WARENSKI-ERICKSON: Scroll down from guard to pommel, slowly passing over the naturally beautiful handle of a Curt Erickson damascus art dagger. *(PointSeven photo)*

◄ KEN HURST: The knife artist inlaid gold borders around his own guard and pommel engraving on a Bruce Bump take-down bowie in a "feather"-pattern damascus blade and dyed stag handle. *(SharpByCoop.com photo)*

GIL RUDOLPH: A ladder-pattern damascus D-guard bowie by Ron Newton sports a fossil-walrus-ivory handle, 24-carat raised-gold inlays, and floral engraving. *(Ward photo)*

▲ MARIAN SAWBY: The gold-and-copper bolster engraving is a perfect complement to the copper-infused quartz handle inlays of a Scott Sawby folder. *(BladeGallery.com photo)*

▲ WALLY HAYES: Battling ancient Asian beasts takes its toll, but the damascus folder stood up well. *(PointSeven photo)*

▶ LISA TOMLIN: A golden bird in the bush is worth two in the handle, complete with black-lip-pearl inlays, of a Howard Hitchmough Damasteel art folder. *(PointSeven photo)*

◀ GIL RUDOLPH: A Dennis Friedly pearl-handle chute knife is decked out in gold inlay, engraving and six small diamonds. *(Dave Siegel photo)*

▶ SHANE TAYLOR: Like sands through an hourglass, so are the days numbered. Damascus and ancient ivory complete the piece. *(PointSeven photo)*

▶ **JERE DAVIDSON:** When Edmund Davidson is done cutting, pounding, wrestling, finishing and polishing the integral drop-point hunters, friend and collaborator Jere engraves them before the ivory handle slabs are added. *(PointSeven photo)*

▶ **RICK DUNKERLEY:** He forged the mosaic-damascus blade, carved the fossil-walrus-ivory handle, engraved the bolsters and back bar, planted a sapphire in the thumb stud and took a nap. *(PointSeven photo)*

▶ **JULIE WARENSKI-ERICKSON:** Don Lozier's takedown dagger is a delight in Jerry Rados "Turkish" damascus, a hot-blued handle, and engraved guard and rear bolster. *(PointSeven photo)*

▲ **RAY COVER JR.:** Horns aplenty enrich a threesome of John Young upswept fixed-blade hunters. *(SharpByCoop.com photo)*

► **BRUCE SHAW:** Classic wildlife and scroll engraving dress up a W.E. Ankrom folding hunter in an ATS-34 blade and rosewood handle scales. *(Gallagher photo)*

► **TOM FERRY:** Full handle engraving enhances the "Chaos Folder" that includes a 3.5-inch mosaic-damascus blade and a 416 stainless steel frame. *(Mitch Lum photo)*

◄ **TIM BRITTON:** The "Baby Bullet" lock-back folder showcases sapphire-inlaid, hand-engraved bolsters, diamond-inlaid pins and an exhibition-grade Fiji fire-pearl handle. *(Ward photo)*

▼ **SIMON LYTTON:** Beryllium copper proved a good engraving medium on Jerry McClure's pearl-handle Damasteel folder with a Cognac-diamond thumb stud. *(Buddy Thomason photo)*

► **LEE GRIFFITH:** The Mike Norris damascus blade of Warren Osborne's lock-back folder is as unsettled as the West that's depicted in the bolster engraving, and as busy as the Rocky Butte jasper stone inlay. *(Ward photo)*

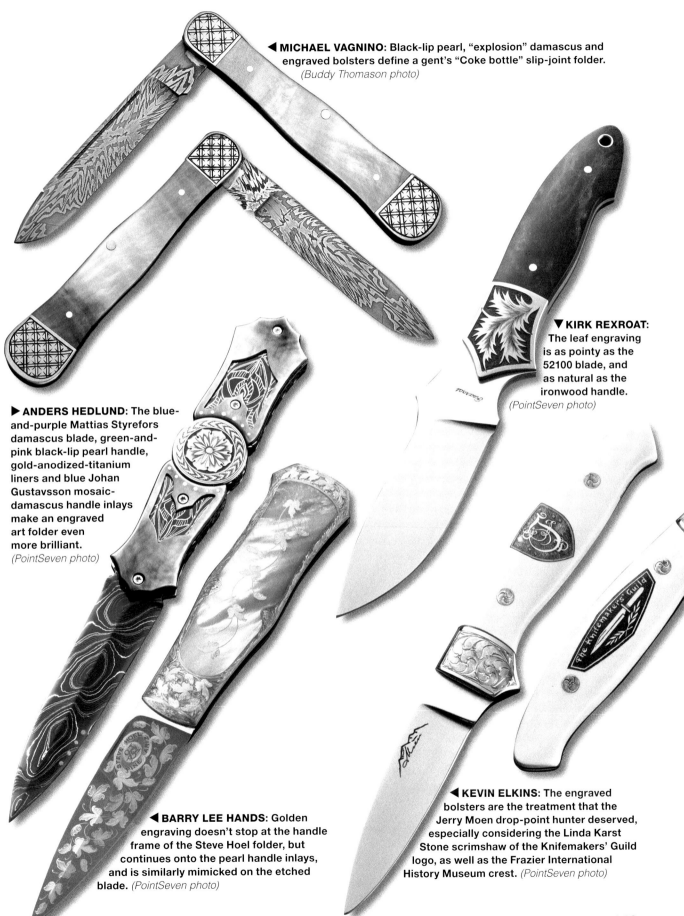

◄ **MICHAEL VAGNINO:** Black-lip pearl, "explosion" damascus and engraved bolsters define a gent's "Coke bottle" slip-joint folder. *(Buddy Thomason photo)*

▼ **KIRK REXROAT:** The leaf engraving is as pointy as the 52100 blade, and as natural as the ironwood handle. *(PointSeven photo)*

► **ANDERS HEDLUND:** The blue-and-purple Mattias Styrefors damascus blade, green-and-pink black-lip pearl handle, gold-anodized-titanium liners and blue Johan Gustavsson mosaic-damascus handle inlays make an engraved art folder even more brilliant. *(PointSeven photo)*

◄ **BARRY LEE HANDS:** Golden engraving doesn't stop at the handle frame of the Steve Hoel folder, but continues onto the pearl handle inlays, and is similarly mimicked on the etched blade. *(PointSeven photo)*

◄ **KEVIN ELKINS:** The engraved bolsters are the treatment that the Jerry Moen drop-point hunter deserved, especially considering the Linda Karst Stone scrimshaw of the Knifemakers' Guild logo, as well as the Frazier International History Museum crest. *(PointSeven photo)*

◄ **BRUCE SHAW:** The dovetailed, engraved bolsters transition the "rose"-pattern-Damasteel blade into the Arizona desert ironwood handle and mosaic pins of Sean O'Hare's "Kestrel-B" fixed blade.

► **GLENN WATERS:** Golden butterflies and blossoms grace the Timascus handle and Barry Gallagher damascus blade.

◄ **LISA TOMLIN:** "Delilah" is the name of the sweetheart on the titanium handle of the Keith Ouye flipper folder fashioned to ride low in the pocket. *(SharpByCoop.com photo)*

► **LESTER BRYANT:** Even bubbles and shells are depicted on the fish-themed bolsters of a Tim Britton two-blade gent's folder with black-lip-pearl handle inlays and 15 faceted diamond inlays. *(Ward photo)*

► **STEVE DUNN:** Josh Smith called on his buddy Steve to engrave the 18k-gold frame of the fossil-walrus-ivory-handle damascus bowie. *(SharpByCoop.com photo)*

▶ **AAD VAN RYSWYK:** Bolster engraving of saber tooth tigers and a caveman family, outlined in gold, is a fitting subject matter for a mammoth-ivory-handle damascus folder.

▼ **MARK WALDROP:** A stag handle is made more staggering by the gold inlay and scroll engraving on a William Pease CPM-154 inter-frame folder. *(PointSeven photo)*

▼ **JACK LEVIN:** One of Jack's signature pop-up shield folders, this one is fully engraved with a portrait of King Rudolf II executed in a grotesque manner as a composition of different fruits and vegetables. *(Francesco Pachi photo)*

▶ **SHAUN and SHARLA HANSEN:** A couple wild ones grace the frame of a damascus folding dagger with blue lapis-lazuli stone inlays. *(PointSeven photo)*

◀ **JULIE WARENSKI-ERICKSON:** It has to be intimidating to be called upon to engrave a Steven Rapp California bowie with gold-quartz inlays and a golden frame. *(PointSeven photo)*

◀ **JIM SMALL:** The crackled mammoth-ivory grip of the Johnny Stout locking-liner folder is as appealing as the engraved and gold inlaid bolsters and the Devin Thomas damascus blade. *(Johnny Stout image)*

Pleasing Textures

▶ **PETER CAREY:** Electrons would flow easily through the "Superconductor" bolsters and into the carbon-fiber handle scales and CPM 154 blade.

◀ **LAURENT DOUSSOT:** The handle frame is carved, textured and anodized titanium sweeping its way into a hollow-ground ladder-pattern stainless-damascus blade.
(SharpByCoop.com photo)

◀ **BILL COYE:** The "Oscar Mike" model dons a 4.5-inch 154CM blade, a grooved G-10 handle, Corby bolts and a Kydex® sheath.
(Ward photo)

◀ **ANDRE VAN HEERDEN:** Through 3-D texturing, the G10 handle scales are made to look like reptile skin, and check out the fang on the fine specimen.
(BladeGallery.com photo)

▶ **ANDRE THORBURN:** Textured like cells under a microscope, the 304 stainless steel bolsters give birth to a stabilized-giraffe-bone handle and a hand-rubbed 19C27 blade.
(BladeGallery.com photo)

Gilded Pearl

◄ **DON HANSON III:** It's all carved gold until the shock and awe wears off, and one discovers the inlaid black lip pearl and dazzling damascus blades. *(SharpByCoop.com photo)*

◄ **RON NEWTON:** The "gilded" part is the 24k-gold overlay on the engraved 410 stainless steel handle, while the "pearl" part comes in the form of a black-lip mother-of-pearl underlay, all complementing a "feather"-pattern-damascus blade and a carved blue steel guard. *(Ward photo)*

◄ **KOJI HARA:** Thanks to engraved gold overlays by Nobu Mukaizura, a dragon breathes multi-karat fire all over the black-lip-pearl and abalone grip of a damascus folder. *(SharpByCoop.com photo)*

◄ **RICK DUNKERLEY:** Gold lip pearl and gold-wire inlay go together like a damascus blade and handle frame. *(PointSeven photo)*

▶ **REINHARD TSCHAGER:** A golden crown frames out diamonds, blue sapphire, abalone and mother-of-pearl. A few gold pins, a little steel, and an art knife takes form.

Ply Wire Act

▶ **KYLE ROYER:** If Argentium-silver-wire inlay happens to be your thing, you'll love the wrapped and fluted premium mammoth ivory handle of the ladder-pattern-damascus dagger. *(Caleb Royer image)*

▼ **MICHAEL RUTH:** The outer ridges of a fluted-African-blackwood handle worked perfectly for twisted-wire overlays that lead to a ladder-pattern-damascus blade. *(Ward photo)*

▲ **JOE KEESLAR:** The "Southwest Bowie," forged from a file with much of the rasp still showing, parades engraved integral bolsters and a wire-inlaid maple handle. *(Ward photo)*

◀ **A.G. BARNES:** Poker anyone? The "Gambler's Bowie" has some poke of its own in the form of a 9-inch 5160 blade and a silver- and ivory-inlaid curly maple handle. *(PointSeven photo*

◀ **RON NEWTON:** Twisted wire resembles tire tread on the grip of the damascus and black-pearl bowie. *(Ward photo)*

▶ **ANDRE THORBURN:** Though the cutting edge and blade spine of the folder are Sandvik 19C27 steel, the inner core is Ettoré Gianferrari "pinstripe"-high-carbon damascus, as is the pearl-inlaid handle with gold-wire decoration. *(SharpByCoop.com photo)*

▶ **LARRY NEWTON:** Diamond and gold inlays dress up a damascus folder with mastodon-ivory grip. *(PointSeven photo)*

◀ **E. JAY HENDRICKSON:** Fine silver wire inlay leads to a silver Pope & Young arrowhead on the curly maple handle of a 5160 fixed blade. *(SharpByCoop.com photo)*

◀ **MICHAEL RADER:** For his master smith's quillion dagger, the maker combined a 10.25-inch damascus blade with a nickel-silver-wire-wrapped Koa and blackwood handle. And for his next act ... *(PointSeven photo)*

▲ **W.E. ANKROM:** The Gil Rudolph 24k-gold-wire scrollwork on the bolsters of the folding hunter is nothing short of inspired, as is the Mike Norris damascus blade and fossil-walrus-ivory handle. *(Neal Lafave photo)*

Wielding the Pattern Weld

▶ **SHANE TAYLOR:** Seven-and-three-quarter inches of damascus terminate in a file-worked, tapered tang tucked neatly under mammoth-ivory handle slabs. *(PointSeven photo)*

◀ **KYLE ROYER:** The "bill" of the "Hawkbill Hunter" is 1080-and-15N20 "W's"-pattern damascus extending from a fossil ivory torso. *(Caleb Royer Studio photo)*

◀ **CLIFF PARKER:** Damascus and mammoth ivory enhance the slim profile of the finely fit and finished gentleman's folder. *(PointSeven photo)*

◀ **STAN WILSON:** The skin of the dragon proved as fiery as its breath, and as hot as its black-lip-pearl body. Bertie Rietveld gets credit for forge-welding the steel. *(SharpByCoop.com photo)*

▶ **RON RICHERSON:** Ladder-pattern damascus climbs up and down a 10-inch bowie blade anchored by Sambar stag. *(Cory Martin Imaging)*

◀ **MIKE WILLIAMS:** No mere blips on a radar screen, the lines of damascus bounce along the edge, enhanced by a swedge on the spine, a mammoth-ivory grip and blued O1 fittings. *(Ward photo)*

▼ **MARVIN SOLOMON:** The skinner wears a devilish grin on its face, hinting toward dark beginnings. *(Ward photo)*

▶ **GARY ROOT:** While Dave Marlatt transformed the stag grip into an eagle head, Ray Rybar used his own eagle eye to forge the San Mai damascus blade, and Gary added a mokumé guard, brass and damascus fittings, and a Brazilian gold ferrule. *(Kris Kandler photo)*

▶ **CHARLES BENNICA:** Parading its chevrons is a soldier in red coral and stainless steel. Owen Wood forged the folding dagger blade.

▼ **DON HANSON III:** Between the black-as-night steel and the white-as-a-ghost pearl, it's red hot. *(Cory Martin Imaging)*

◀ **BERTIE RIETVELD:** Named after a small African bird that sings sweet songs, the "Tinktinkie" preens a colorful, distal-tapered "Dragonskin"-damascus blade, a mammoth-ivory handle, 24k-gold inlays and a Stanhope lens through which the maker's logo is visible.

STATE OF THE ART   **151**

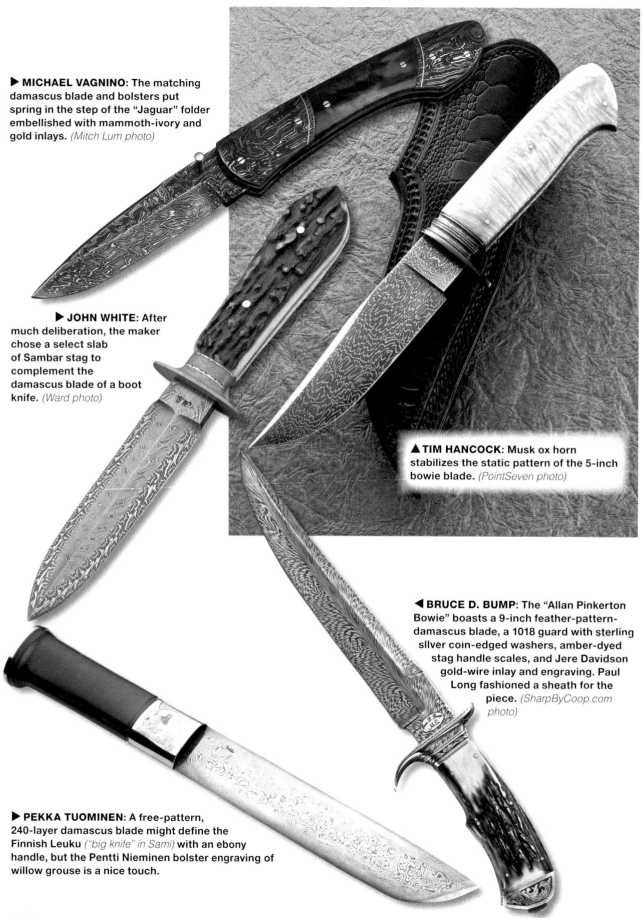

▶ **MICHAEL VAGNINO:** The matching damascus blade and bolsters put spring in the step of the "Jaguar" folder embellished with mammoth-ivory and gold inlays. *(Mitch Lum photo)*

▶ **JOHN WHITE:** After much deliberation, the maker chose a select slab of Sambar stag to complement the damascus blade of a boot knife. *(Ward photo)*

▲ **TIM HANCOCK:** Musk ox horn stabilizes the static pattern of the 5-inch bowie blade. *(PointSeven photo)*

◀ **BRUCE D. BUMP:** The "Allan Pinkerton Bowie" boasts a 9-inch feather-pattern-damascus blade, a 1018 guard with sterling sIlver coin-edged washers, amber-dyed stag handle scales, and Jere Davidson gold-wire inlay and engraving. Paul Long fashioned a sheath for the piece. *(SharpByCoop.com photo)*

▶ **PEKKA TUOMINEN:** A free-pattern, 240-layer damascus blade might define the Finnish **Leuku** *("big knife" in Sami)* with an ebony handle, but the Pentti Nieminen bolster engraving of willow grouse is a nice touch.

▼JERRY JOHNSON: A hand-carved copper guard protects the hand from sliding off the elk antler handle, past the mammoth-tooth and turquoise spacers, and onto the Devin Thomas damascus blade.

▶ RUSTY POLK: The dagger wears the "snake"-pattern damascus blade like its own skin, while mammoth ivory acts as a natural appendage. *(Ward photo)*

◀MIKKEL WILLUMSEN: Blending Chad Nichols and Joel Davis damascus with carbon fiber proved a winning combination for a file-worked tactical folder including an Ikoma Korth Bearing System.

◀PETER CAREY: The "Nitro Flipper" is a knockout in "Infinity" Damasteel, titanium and mother-of-pearl.

▲ MARK NEVLING: An electrical discharge sent a shockwave across the damascus bowie blade, grounded only by a mokumé guard, ebony spacer and fossil-walrus-ivory handle.

▶ **MIKE FELLOWS:** The mosaic-damascus blade, and elephant ivory handle and butt cap turn the "mini" into a "mighty."

▼ **JERRY MCCLURE:** The lines of Damasteel direct the Gibeon meteorite handle scales to their place in the knife galaxy. Domed gold pins map the Big Dipper and Little Dipper on each side of the grip.

▶ **TERRY VANDEVENTER:** It would be tough to ruffle the feather-damascus blade of the Sambar-stag-handle hunter.

▶ **CLIFF POLK:** A clip-point auto folder is a web of amazing damascus interrupted only by mammoth ivory and file work. *(Ward photo)*

▶ **ANDERS HOGSTROM:** Japanese chisels are exotically alluring in Damasteel and ebony.

▼ HENRY TORRES: The maker set the bar high with the four-bar 15N20-and-1084 damascus blade, getting over the top with a damascus oval guard and butt cap, an India stag handle and a hand-stitched Kenny Rowe sheath. *(BladeGallery.com photo)*

▶ JODY MULLER: From the "basket-weave"-pattern damascus blade to engraved bolsters and tiger coral handle slabs, this one remains on the **move.** *(BladeGallery.com photo)*

▼ J. NEILSON: Accessorized by mammoth-ivory handle scales, the "wave"-pattern damascus blade and mosaic-damascus bolsters are nice cuts of **cloth.** *(Ward photo)*

▲ MIKE QUESENBERRY: The integral damascus blade and bolsters are the sales clincher of a Sambar-stag-handle knife. *(BladeGallery.com photo)*

▶ REINHARD TSCHAGER: If you look closely at the bail of the integral "Snake" dagger, in Johann Ebner damascus, it is a white gold snake head with diamond inlays.

▼**JERRY PARTRIDGE:** The "Rock Star" folding razor adds Alabama Damascus and ebony wood to its repertoire. *(Bob Mills photo)*

▶**STEVE KOSTER:** If anything can keep pace with the pattern of the 10.5-inch, 352-layer damascus blade and integral bolsters, it's a fiddle-back-walnut handle. *(PointSeven photo)*

▶**JERRY FISK:** To commemorate 30 years of knifemaking, Jerry sends the "Personal Bowie" to market in a damascus blade and ancient ivory grip that rise to the occasion. *(SharpByCoop.com photo)*

▶**WADE COLTER:** While blackwood caresses the hand, damascus stings whatever with which it comes into contact. *(PointSeven photo)*

◀**ERIK FRITZ:** Follow the damascus to the sweet spot of the bowie blade, and back to the cocobolo handle scales. *(PointSeven photo)*

▶ **CRAIG STEKETEE**: Danger: Damascus bowie with coffin-shaped ancient ivory handle ahead. *(Buddy Thomason photo)*

◀ **LARRY INMAN:** Ribbons of damascus help define the award-winning hunter handled in ironwood. *(Ward photo)*

BRANSON
HAMMER-IN
&
KNIFE SHOW

BEST
HUNTER

2010

▶ **FRANK DILLUVIO:** Mother-of-pearl neither competes with nor shies away from the Bob Eggerling damascus blade and bolsters.

◀ **RYAN MINCHEW:** The "5-Turn Damasteel" blade definitely gets things rolling, as do heat-colored damascus bolsters and a mammoth-ivory handle. *(Kayla Minchew photo)*

STATE OF THE ART **157**

Casing the Point

To consider them afterthoughts is shortsighted at least, and naïve at the extreme end. So much time and effort is spent fashioning a fine handmade knife, and such an enormous amount of research and money is dedicated to patterns, designs, materials, steels, bolsters, guards, liners, locks and mechanisms, that sheaths often take a backseat, or are saved for last when the chips are down (literally) and the knives are ready for sale.

Yet sheaths and pouches are arguably as important as the knives they hold and secure. Imagine a fixed blade without a sheath. How would you carry it? Where would you put it? Could you leave it dangle from your hip, point swaying in the breeze, edge swinging like a pendulum? Of course not, so knifemakers have either learned to make sheaths, or formed relationships with leatherworkers and sheath makers.

Speaking of forming, most modern sheaths, even those with snap closures, loops and flaps, are formed to the knife blades to hold them taut, so they won't fall out when carried over rough terrain, during hard-fought battles or when taken on a hunt, safari or a rapid ride. Sheath making is an art form all to itself, often learned through trial and error, and where patience is a virtue. The fine folks that case the point, after all, are always ahead of the crowd scouting out better ways of doing things, and keeping the rest of us safe in the meantime.

▶ **LARRY PARSONS:** The leather sheath is embossed, stamped, sewn, layered, inlaid and even engraved, and such is the handcraft. The wood handle looks sweet sticking out of the snapped loop. *(Ward photo)*

◀ **JONATHAN WICK:** If the crinkly copper and silver sheath doesn't leave you smitten, the mesquite-burl-handle damascus fixed blade will do the trick. *(PointSeven photo)*

◀ **ROBERT SCHRAP:** The pouch sheath is cowhide under an alligator back strap.

▶ **ROBERT SCHRAP:** The pouch sheath features a full stingray-skin overlay, and a nice loop laced with leather string.

KENNY ROWE: Knifemaker Jerry Fisk is so prolific, he keeps Kenny busier than a cobbler fashioning leather sheaths for his fixed blades. *(Ward photo)*

JOHN COHEA: The rawhide sheath shows Native American influences, including horsehair tassels, beads and copper decorations. It protects a stag-handle damascus bowie like a brave warrior. *(Ward photo)*

CRAIG BRASCHLER: Equipped with an engraved nickel-silver throat and tip, the pigskin sheath isn't for tossing, but for keeping all the players safe. *(Ward photo)*

LARRY PARSONS: The Concho-style sheath features skillfully embossed and engraved shell-like decorations, as well as stylish reptile skin inlay. *(Ward photo)*

STATE OF THE ART **159**

Sculpture Clash

None of the knives on this and the facing page will be displayed on cement pedestals in New York's Central Park or London's Hyde Park. Nor will they find a permanent home in the Art Institute of Chicago, the Louvre of Paris, Metropolitan Museum of Art in New York or the Boston Museum of Fine Art. Few will grace the rotundas or commons at Yale, Harvard, Stanford or Notre Dame.

Yet, in their own edged way, these are world-class sculptures. They deserve media attention, accolades and private showings. Consuming them with a little glass of wine and some finger snacks would be a wonderful way to absorb their beauty. Sure, some are a little rough around the edges, too pointed, or possibly guarded. They aren't conducive to frames, satin pillows or lighted turntables, but wall hangers they are, and appreciated they shall be.

The "State Of The Art" section of the Knives annual book seems a fitting place to let the little sculptures clash, so let's display the artistic wares in our own museum of fine art, and open it up to public viewing only when we're good and ready.

◄► JOHN BARDSLEY: The knifemaker calls the creation, accomplished in 440C and giraffe bone, "Nothing Better To Do," and we're all glad he was bored that day. *(SharpByCoop. com photo)*

◄ GAIL LUNN: The diamond-eyed scorpion renders its prey incapacitated using a five-bar composite-damascus stinger. *(PointSeven photo)*

▼JAY FISHER: The maker says he hopes his knife sculpture in hot-blued O1 tool steel, gold, olivine, silicon bronze, rosewood, coral and nebula stone is as inspiring as his fascination with the ancient seas and the myths and legends that surround them.

AEGIR

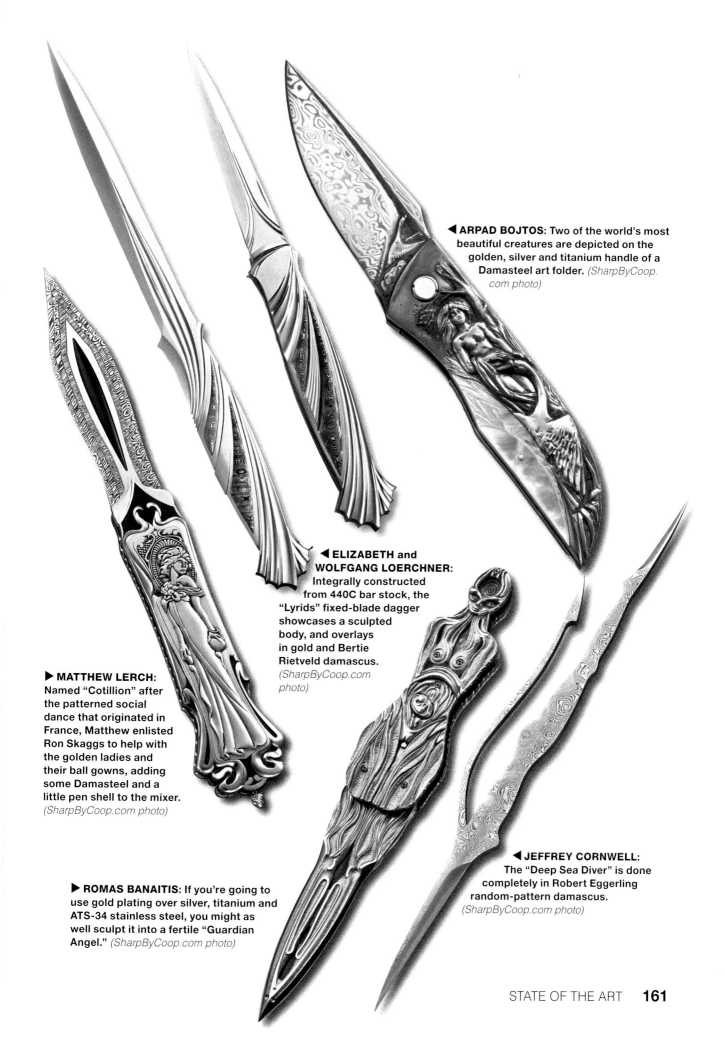

◀ **ARPAD BOJTOS:** Two of the world's most beautiful creatures are depicted on the golden, silver and titanium handle of a Damasteel art folder. *(SharpByCoop. com photo)*

◀ **ELIZABETH and WOLFGANG LOERCHNER:** Integrally constructed from 440C bar stock, the "Lyrids" fixed-blade dagger showcases a sculpted body, and overlays in gold and Bertie Rietveld damascus. *(SharpByCoop.com photo)*

▶ **MATTHEW LERCH:** Named "Cotillion" after the patterned social dance that originated in France, Matthew enlisted Ron Skaggs to help with the golden ladies and their ball gowns, adding some Damasteel and a little pen shell to the mixer. *(SharpByCoop.com photo)*

▶ **ROMAS BANAITIS:** If you're going to use gold plating over silver, titanium and ATS-34 stainless steel, you might as well sculpt it into a fertile "Guardian Angel." *(SharpByCoop.com photo)*

◀ **JEFFREY CORNWELL:** The "Deep Sea Diver" is done completely in Robert Eggerling random-pattern damascus. *(SharpByCoop.com photo)*

STATE OF THE ART **161**

Slice & the Family Stone

Isn't it interesting that "Sly and the Family Stone" was the first major American rock band to have a racially integrated and multi-gender lineup? They also recorded five Billboard Hot 100 hits. But it's the diversity issue that's intriguing, as it directly relates to the knives and knife-handle and spacer materials herein. As there are no two snowflakes or fingerprints alike, neither are there two stones that are exact in being or likeness. Each has its own character, color and clarity. Each is exclusive as a mineral. Each is different.

Knifemakers are no dummies. These facts have not gone unnoticed.

They embrace diversity and individualism. And if you've ever sat down and shot the breeze with a knifemaker, talked, had a discussion, asked questions, you realize that finding a niche, a specialty, a voice, look and feel, achieving individuality and style is an underlying goal of all blade artisans. One way knifemakers achieve the goal is through diversity of materials, or by using a single material that, by its very nature, is diverse. Such would include ivory, pearl, wood or stone.

Stones within the "Slice & the Family Stone" lineup include lapis lazuli, turquoise, ammonite, ruby, opal, garnet, emerald, sapphire, diamond, Verdite, jasper and jade. The colors would make rainbows green with envy, the character like that of an elder statesman, or better yet, a statesman's wife, the clarity as if seeing things for the first time, from the eyes of a newborn baby, or an enlightened empathetic person, a reborn sinner. Yes, knifemakers are individuals. They are also a family. And the family stone is a diverse group of individuals who've come together for a common cause.

▼ **THOMAS HASLINGER:** Named "Thus Spoke Zarathustra," after the Friedrich Nietzsche book, the Persian folder glows with a lustrous hot-blued finish, gold wire inlays, ammonite insets within flame-shaped handle cutouts, and a faceted princess garnet for elegance. The blade is Mike Norris damascus.

◄ **EMIL BUCHARSKY:** For his "Willow" model, Emil combined a five-bar, composite twist-pattern-damascus blade with ammonite stone "leaves" and 18k-gold "branches."
(BladeGallery.com photo)

▶ **DALE SANDRONE:** Reconstituted turquoise may not be the stone of choice for gemologists, but it works beautifully here for highlighting a S90V, stag-handle drop-point hunter.
(Cory Martin Imaging)

▼ **REINHARD TSCHAGER:** Just when you thought there was nothing new in knives, Reinhard fashions a blade from a manta ray stinger. The jewel pendant folder also showcases damascus, yellow and white gold, diamonds, a sapphire and emeralds.

▶ **AAD VAN RYSWYK:** They slid open the ancient Egyptian tombstone made of blue lapis lazuli to discover white and yellow gold, and hand-forged damascus.

▼ **RICHARD S. WRIGHT:** The bolsters of the switchblade are bronze, in a diamond pattern, with a 5 millimeter lab-grown ruby on each side, all accompanied by pre-ban elephant-ivory handle slabs and a Doug Ponzio damascus blade.

▲ **GAYLE BRADLEY:** Lapis lazuli is the stone that brings green and rust coloring to the Sandvik steel slip-joint folder.
(SharpByCoop.com photo)

◀ **DON LOZIER:** A take-down dagger engraved by Julie Warenski-Erickson, the art knife combines a Jerry Rados damascus blade with a hot-blued handle and ruby inlays planted in just the right places.
(PointSeven photo)

▶ **KENNETH KING:** You don't need a lot of turquoise to accessorize a damascus and mammoth-ivory bowie. *(SharpByCoop.com photo)*

▶ **JESSE DAVIS:** Turquoise, desert ironwood and file-worked nickel silver triple-team a 440C dagger. *(Weyer photo)*

▼ **YASUTAKA WADA:** It's jade in spades, and a hot little ATS-34 fixed blade at that.

◀ **GAWIE HERBST:** Wrapping fingers around the green Verdite handle is a cool, empowering feeling, akin to toting a dazzling damascus blade with carved bronze fittings.

▲ **JAY FISHER:** The polished Sampson Peak jasper called for hand-engraved bookends between which to sit, and a mirror-polished 440C blade.

Handle Craft

With all of the technological advances in blade steel, powder metallurgy, assisted-opening folder mechanisms and handle materials, it might be easy to forget that knifemaking is a handcraft. Perhaps it doesn't seem like a handcraft when blades can be cut out on CNC machines, power hammers pound steel, and cams, bushings and roller bearings populate the pivot areas of modern folding knives.

Yet there are those who continue to practice traditional methods of bladesmithing and knifemaking, whether that is through coal-fired forges, hand-finished blades, carved grips or precision fitting of folder springs, liners and blades. Many know that forging damascus or single steels, with an eye toward

hardness, wear resistance and proper heat treatment, takes knowledge, time, patience and persistence.

There is "sweat equity" involved in handcrafts, and very few art outlets, including knifemaking, make the practitioners wealthy. Rich in spirit and experience, maybe, but monetary rewards are seldom showered on handcrafters. Corporate bonuses are not doled out quarterly.

The knife grips showcased herein took some handwork,

diligence and talent to create. They were built for the love of fashioning fine cutting instruments, because tradition still matters, handwork still pays off and talent should be used and shared. There is pride in practicing a handcraft, and in this case, handle craft, and the results are breathtaking and humbling.

◄ **MARK KNAPP: A** hand fit and finished kudu-horn, walrus-ivory and sunken-oak handle anchors the hunter, which also sports a damascus blade, and mokumé guard and butt cap. *(SharpByCoop.com photo)*

▶ **ZAZA REVISHVILI: Hand filigree work** and gemstone inlays are Revishvili staples, and with damascus daggers this gorgeous, why not carry on as usual? *(PointSeven photo)*

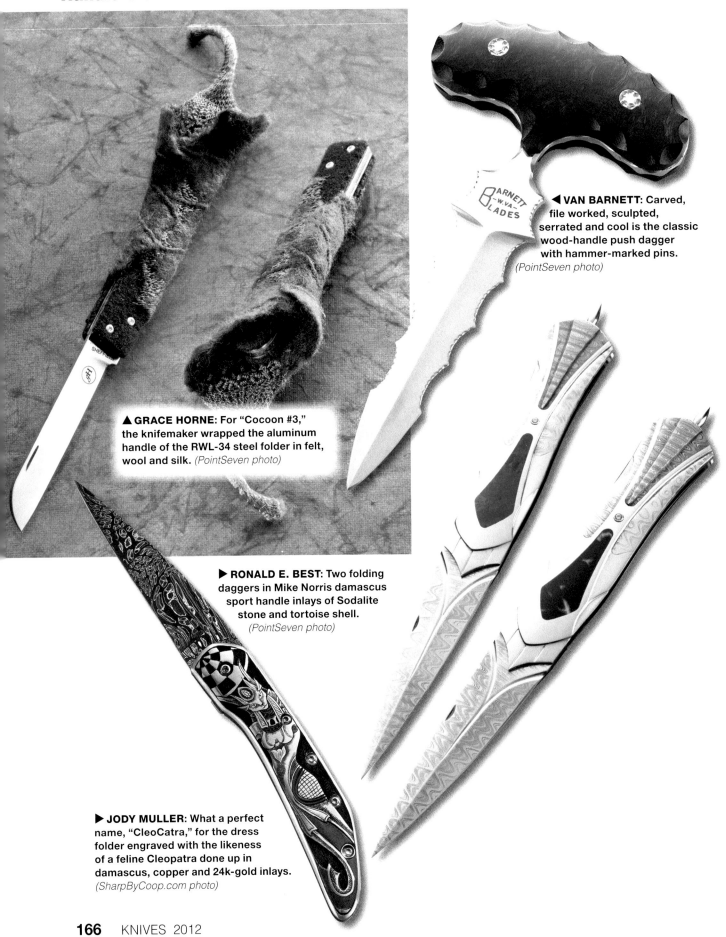

▲ GRACE HORNE: For "Cocoon #3," the knifemaker wrapped the aluminum handle of the RWL-34 steel folder in felt, wool and silk. *(PointSeven photo)*

◄ VAN BARNETT: Carved, file worked, sculpted, serrated and cool is the classic wood-handle push dagger with hammer-marked pins. *(PointSeven photo)*

▶ RONALD E. BEST: Two folding daggers in Mike Norris damascus sport handle inlays of Sodalite stone and tortoise shell. *(PointSeven photo)*

▶ JODY MULLER: What a perfect name, "CleoCatra," for the dress folder engraved with the likeness of a feline Cleopatra done up in damascus, copper and 24k-gold inlays. *(SharpByCoop.com photo)*

▲▶ JOT SINGH KHALSA: Amongst the lapis and damascus of the art dagger is Julie Warenski Erickson carving and engraving, diamonds, and white and yellow gold.

◀PHILIP BOOTH: Flames and skulls, including those forged into a Doug Ponzio damascus blade, are appropriate attire for the "Hotrod" auto folder with an exhaust header that acts as the blade release. *(SharpByCoop.com photo)*

◀BUSTER WARENSKI: The late great knifemaker presented the French main gauche parrying dagger at the 1993 Art Knife Invitational, including a carved, engraved and file-worked silver basket, fluted-black-marble handle, silver rope trim, 700 diamonds and 40 rubies. *(SharpByCoop.com photo)*

▼ **VLADIMIR PULIS:** We begin with a battle scene carved in ostrich bone, and travel through damascus to a place where gold and silver abound.

▼ **EMIL BUCHARSKY:** Ammonite inlays practically leap off the carved damascus handle of the illustrious locking-liner folder. *(BladeGallery.com photo)*

▲ **ALAN WARREN:** What better way to hold a fighting dagger than with mammoth molar, blackwood and pre-ban elephant ivory? *(BladeGallery.com photo)*

▲ **LONNIE HANSEN:** Flowered vines climb the hickory haft to the sculpted 52100 head that includes forward and reverse chevrons, a chalice-shaped hammer and a heart pierced through the blade. *(BladeGallery.com photo)*

▶ **STEVE CULVER:** The engraved handle frame and caustic blued fittings were inspired choices to frame out the abalone handle inlay and complement the 1084-and-15N20-damascus dagger blade.

▼ **KEN ONION:** Whether sculpted to cut, or a sculpture itself, the damascus and titanium folder is a vision. The inset shows a sweet titanium pocket clip and wavy frame-lock cutout. *(PointSeven photo)*

▶ **A.G. BARNES:** Silver wire inlays and a silver star enhance the carved and smoothed fiddleback-maple grip of a 5160 bowie. *(PointSeven photo)*

◀ **DONALD VOGT:** Spring flowers have nothing over the carved mother-of-pearl, 14k-gold and damascus automatic art folder with a sapphire mounted in the flora and a diamond in the rough.

▶ **TOBBE LUNDSTROM:** The puukko is a stunner, from the five-bar Mattias Styrefors damascus blade to the stacked fossil-walrus-ivory and woolly-mammoth-bone handle with a dinosaur-pattern-damascus inlay. *(BladeGallery.com photo)*

◀ **MARCELLO GARAU:** Damascus makes a beeline from the bolsters, through mother-of-pearl handle scales and to the blade of the folding dagger. *(Francesco Pachi photo)*

▶ **STEVE JERNIGAN:** The steely spine wends its way through black-lip pearl to connect a golden lizard head, engraved by Tim George, to its curly tail. Pearl inlays line up along the spine of this damascus gecko. *(PointSeven photo)*

◀ **WARREN OSBORNE:** Few inter-frame folders feature three inlays, but that's the case with the antique-tortoise-shell-inlaid, lock-back dagger that includes a step-down bolster and stainless damascus blade. *(PointSeven photo)*

◀ **STEVEN RAPP:** An ATS-34 San Francisco dirk is outfitted in abalone and zigzags of stainless steel. *(Ward photo)*

◀ **R.B. JOHNSON:** Mosaics of mammoth ivory make up the handles of two folders with Devin Thomas stainless damascus blades, mosaic-damascus bolsters, titanium liners, gold-plated screws and black-diamond-inlaid thumb studs. *(Cory Martin Imaging)*

▼ **HARUMI HIRAYAMA:** A feminine touch has never been so apparent as on the mother-of-pearl knife handle inlaid with white- and pink-shell orchid flowers.

▶ **REINHARD TSCHAGER:** The full-integral ATS-34 jewel knife sports coral, jet and gold inlays, as well as a gold chain with pendant.

▶ **THINUS HERBST:** A boot knife of black ivory, bronze and pierced damascus is hot to trot.

◀ **ANDRE THORBURN:** The smooth-operating, satin-finished Sandvik 19C27 blade unfolds from an engraved stainless steel handle with inlays of Ettoré Gianferrari mosaic damascus and black-lip pearl. *(Dorian Spence photo)*

▶ **GLENN WATERS:** Items peeking out from around the silk-bound stingray-skin handle of the "RaiJin Tactical Fighter" include engraved and inlaid gold, colorful Timascus, a titanium menuki *(handle charm)*, and engraving of FuJin (the god of wind) and RaiJin (god of thunder.)

▶ **JOE OLSON:** The king of enamel knife handle inlays shows us one depicting "Diana the Huntress" accompanied by a "wildlife"-mosaic-damascus blade. *(SharpByCoop.com photo)*

◀ **STEPHEN OLSZEWSKI:**
The "Art Deco Ram's Head"
folder is aptly named for the 14k-gold
ram's head bolster, a carved Jerry Rados
damascus blade, and an engraved,
sterling-silver-overlaid Robert
Eggerling damascus grip.

▶ **PETER MARTIN:** The file-worked integral
handle frame gives the illusion of rope
lassoed around a heat-colored damascus
inlay. Notice the anvil-shaped cutout.
(Cory Martin Imaging)

◀ **MARDI MESHEJIAN:** The appealing
grip of the dagger showcases fossilized
bone accented by anodized titanium and
cast *shibuichi*—a copper alloy that can
be patinated into subtle shades of blue or
green. *(SharpByCoop.com photo)*

▶ **BILLY MACE IMEL:** The "Split-
Branch Poignard" wraps itself around
the hand, endears itself via a fluted-ivory
grip and stings just the same with a pierced
440C blade. *(SharpByCoop.com photo)*

FACTORY TRENDS

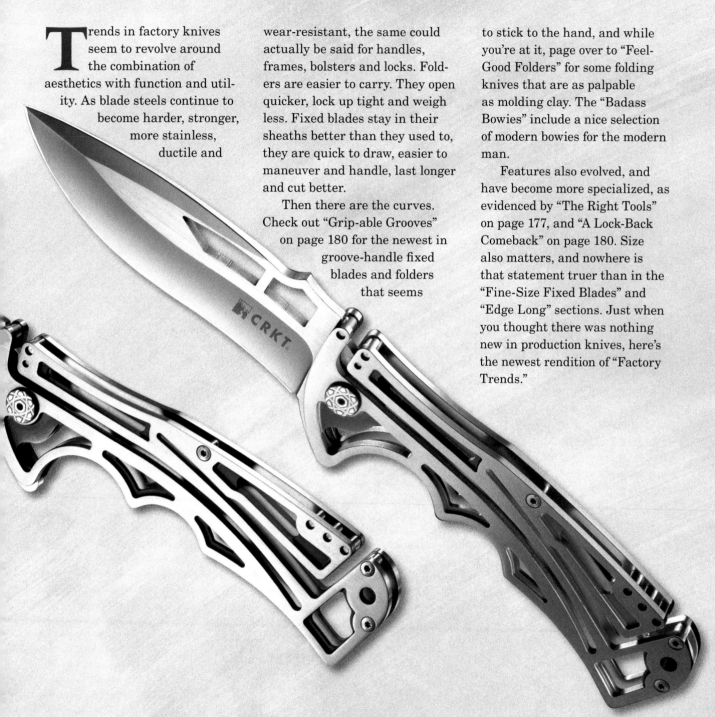

Trends in factory knives seem to revolve around the combination of aesthetics with function and utility. As blade steels continue to become harder, stronger, more stainless, ductile and wear-resistant, the same could actually be said for handles, frames, bolsters and locks. Folders are easier to carry. They open quicker, lock up tight and weigh less. Fixed blades stay in their sheaths better than they used to, they are quick to draw, easier to maneuver and handle, last longer and cut better.

Then there are the curves. Check out "Grip-able Grooves" on page 180 for the newest in groove-handle fixed blades and folders that seems to stick to the hand, and while you're at it, page over to "Feel-Good Folders" for some folding knives that are as palpable as molding clay. The "Badass Bowies" include a nice selection of modern bowies for the modern man.

Features also evolved, and have become more specialized, as evidenced by "The Right Tools" on page 177, and "A Lock-Back Comeback" on page 180. Size also matters, and nowhere is that statement truer than in the "Fine-Size Fixed Blades" and "Edge Long" sections. Just when you thought there was nothing new in production knives, here's the newest rendition of "Factory Trends."

Now Entering the Auto Zone

Tactical operators, police and rescue personnel appreciate today's fast-firing, fully automatic knives

Text and photos by Dexter Ewing

Much of what law enforcement and military personnel do in the line of duty to serve our country and local communities requires training and quality equipment. From apparel to firearms, they rely on quality gear to help defend what is good and right in this country. Knives play an important role in keeping the peace and protecting the communities, serving dual roles as back-up weapons and cutting tools. Auto-opening knives are sold only to qualified fire, rescue, law enforcement and military personnel, a practice strictly enforced by the federal government.

Not every fireman, policeman, soldier or search-and-rescue officer qualifies for the right to carry autos, and each is advised to check local and state laws prior to purchase. There are plenty of automatic knives geared towards the tactical market, and many are built tough and rugged to withstand hard use in harsh environments. In short, they are built to last a lifetime with minimal maintenance.

Nearly all the major manufacturers and distributors of manual, one-hand-opening tactical folders offer at least one or more

The Benchmade AFO II exhibits all the hallmarks of a great working auto folder, including an ergonomic handle, integral double guard and drop-point blade.

Pro-Tech and custom knifemaker Allen Elishewitz teamed up on the "Doru," a stylish yet hardworking auto folder.

The SOG TAC ST-06 folder features a re-curved AUS-8 blade, secondary safety and an aluminum handle with finger grooves.

An all-business folder geared toward military and law enforcement, the Zero Tolerance 0650 is based on a Grant and Gavin Hawk design. It showcases ZT's exclusive CrossFire™—an auto opener and safety in one mechanism.

autos. In examining some of the current models on the market, it becomes apparent that they are engineered with the endgame in mind of protecting and serving.

Benchmade Knife Co. has long been recognized as a leader in automatic tactical folders. Having seen plenty of action in U.S. military zones all over the globe, Benchmade autos exude manufacturing quality and boast the finest materials. One such time-tested knife fashioned for rugged use is the Model 9050 AFO (Armed Forces Only.) It has an ergonomic grip with an expanded front hand guard, a drop-point blade and a plunge-lock button release.

A couple years ago, Benchmade redesigned the AFO slightly, making it beefier and incorporating a few new enhancements meant to make a great design even better. The result is the Model 9051 AFO II. "The AFO II is designed for all active military and law enforcement," says Josh Harrell, international military sales rep for Benchmade. "This safety rescue knife focuses on one-handed opening and can be used across all branches of the military."

For the AFO II, Benchmade concentrated on improving the original AFO design, which first entered the market in 1997. Some of the major enhancements include a larger push button for better access with gloved hands, an open handle spine for ease of cleaning via compressed air or running water, an enlarged finger guard at the pivot area, and a pommel striker at the butt end of the handle for breaking glass.

"Two blade shapes are offered on the AFO II to give more options to the end user," Harrell explains. "The classic drop-point blade style (model 9051) mimics the 9050 original design and is used as more of a slicing tool, while the tanto blade style (model 9052) is a better piercing tool and provides more tip strength."

In either style, the AFO II proves a formidable cutting tool via its 3.5-inch, premium 154CM stainless steel blade. The ergonomic, machined T6-6061 aluminum handle boasts a Type III hard-coat anodized finish to guard against wear and achieve a subdued non-reflective exterior. A reversible pocket clip can be used in the tip-up or tip-down carry configuration, and either model is available in black-coated or satin-finished blades.

Off to the Races!

"It was at the Santa Barbara Custom Knife Show that Allen Elishewitz and I struck up a conversation about a collaborative knife," begins Dave Wattenberg, president of Pro-Tech Knives. Wattenberg picked a particularly handsome knife off Elishewitz's table. "A couple months later he sent me a custom auto version of it," Wattenberg enthuses, "and we were off to the races!" Thus, was the birth of the Pro-Tech Doru automatic, a production version of Elishewitz's original folder.

"It's got super-fast action, a recessed and secure push button, an innovative blade shape that is good looking, and a great multi-task design," says Wattenberg of his production version. The 154CM stainless steel blade measures 3.5 inches in length and is complemented by a T6-6061 aluminum handle with a hard-coat anodized finish. The firing button sits in a machined recess in the handle, requiring deliberate movement to fire the blade, and thus preventing accidental blade deployment. The Doru includes a pocket clip for tip-down carry, and a ballistic nylon belt sheath, giving the end user two carry options.

Speaking of carrying the Doru, Wattenberg says the knife is already in the hands of capable and trained individuals. "We sent some of the Doru's to soldiers in Iraq, Afghanistan and other overseas bases. We've shipped Doru models to the U.S.M.C. Recon units, Navy SEALs, and officers of the CEXC in Iraq," he notes.

In addition to the knife's growing acceptance in the military arena, Wattenberg says it's gaining attention in the law enforcement community. Pro-Tech currently offers the auto in three distinct grades geared toward all segments of the tactical market. The base model features an aluminum handle and a plain or partially serrated, satin-finished blade. "It's an awesome knife at an excellent price point," Wattenberg offers.

The tactical models are considered an upgrade, as they "offer some extra machining across the handle spine area for a good grip, and tungsten-DLC-coated black blades," according to Wattenberg. These truly are the core tactical-grade models of the Doru lineup.

Pro-Tech also markets some mid-range Doru pieces featuring aluminum handles with various inlays ranging from ivory to Micarta®, cocobolo wood and several colors of G-10. And the *crème de la crème* is the limited-edition versions. "Each year we plan to offer a limited-edition Doru made of either a titanium or 416 stainless steel frame, damascus blade steel, and high-end handle material," cites Wattenberg. These pieces are individually serial numbered and limited editions.

No stranger to the tactical market, SOG Specialty Knives & Tools boasts a diverse line of fixed blades and folders for law enforcement, military and search-and-rescue teams. While the company already offers a few automatic folders, the SOG TAC ST-06 is the latest and perhaps the most visually exciting auto on the market.

"The philosophy on the ST-06 was to add a unique and functional blade shape to our popular line of automatic knives," says SOG marketing director Chris Cashbaugh. "We have had good success with the other, more tactical blade shapes and we thought that adding a blade that was a little more practical would be a good boost to the line."

Glowing Crosshairs

The ST-06 showcases a 3.5-inch, re-curved, drop-point AUS-8 stainless steel blade, and a full, unsharpened swedge along the spine that gives it a dramatic and somewhat aggressive appearance. SOG offers the blade in a satin or black titanium-nitride-coated finish. The handle is machined out of T6-6061 aluminum and features prominent finger grooves for a good grip. The SOG name is machined into the grip with the "O" being a glow-in-the-dark reticle, or crosshairs, as seen in rifle sites.

"We have one of the thinnest handles available and it is pretty cool that we can pack a powerful auto-opening blade in such a thin product," Cashbaugh points out.

The ST-06 is indeed one of the thinnest autos on the market today. SOG's trademark reversible bayonet-style pocket clip allows deep pocket, low-profile carry. A sliding safety switch prevents unwanted firing of the blade, and acts as a secondary lock when the blade is open.

"We have shipped the autos to a few law enforcement departments here in Washington State, California and Arizona," Cashbaugh begins, "and to the Border Patrol, DEA and other government agencies." The SOG TAC ST-06 carries a manufacturer's suggested retail price of $180-$200, depending on blade version and finish, a great value in tactical automatic openers.

The KAI USA Zero Tolerance knife line has proven to be a serious player in tactical folders and fixed blades, with the company now offering two auto-opening folders. The ZT 0650 is based on a design by Grant and Gavin Hawk, a father and son knifemaking team from Idaho. A straightforward working folder built to survive harsh environment, the ZT 0650 features a combination release and safety mechanism. It also parades a 3.75-inch, modified-clip-point 154CM stainless steel blade with black tungsten-DLC coating for further corrosion resistance and anti-reflective qualities.

The clip point excels in piercing, while the slight curve to the belly gives the 0650 excellent slicing capabilities. A T6-6061 aircraft-grade aluminum handle and textured G-10 overlays promote a secure grip with or without gloved hands, and a CrossFire™ release with safety further separates the 0650 from the competition.

"The CrossFire lock ensures there is no chance the blade will accidentally deploy," states KAI's director of sales and marketing, Thomas Welk, adding that one button operates the lock release and safety. "With the CrossFire lock, you have both functions in one mechanism and in one location."

To deploy the 0650 there are two distinct actions. First, you slide the CrossFire button toward the handle spine to disengage the safety. Then, by pulling back on the button in the direction of the butt end of the handle, the blade is released. "You use two actions," Welk says, "but because both are located in one place on the knife handle, the whole operation is much faster from start to finish."

While the ZT 0650 is not issued to any particular military or law enforcement unit, Welk says there are many individual military and law enforcement members who have purchased the 0650 for their own use, and the company has received positive feedback concerning its design and materials, including comments regarding the lock and safety. "The CrossFire lock is effortless to use and we haven't heard about any problems, misfires or accidental openings," Welk summarizes.

Automatics represent the latest in what the knife industry has to offer in terms of design and materials. Manufactured by some of the best in the business, auto-opening folders are becoming user friendly, increasingly rugged and more popular than ever.

The Right Tools

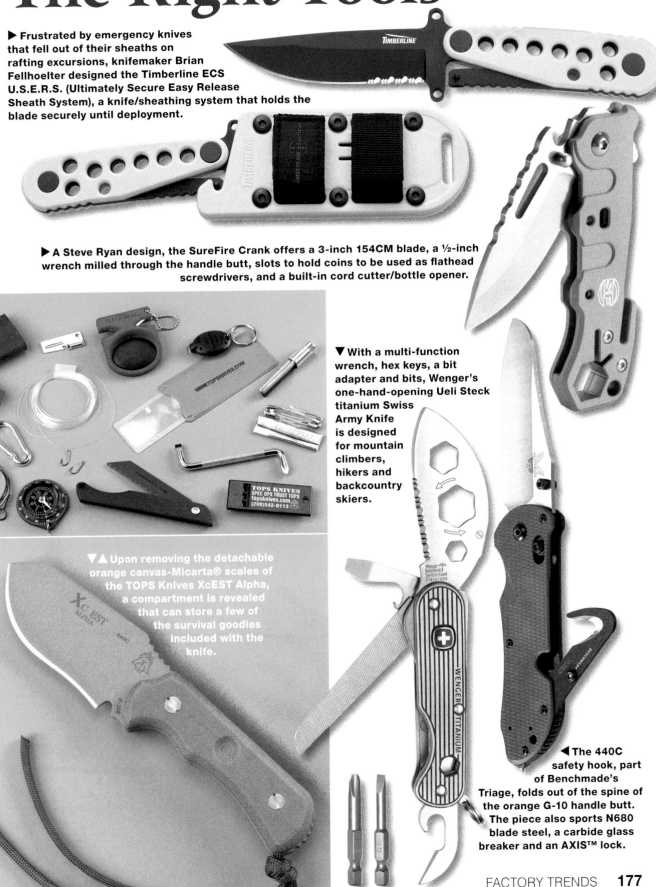

▶ Frustrated by emergency knives that fell out of their sheaths on rafting excursions, knifemaker Brian Fellhoelter designed the Timberline ECS U.S.E.R.S. (Ultimately Secure Easy Release Sheath System), a knife/sheathing system that holds the blade securely until deployment.

▶ A Steve Ryan design, the SureFire Crank offers a 3-inch 154CM blade, a ½-inch wrench milled through the handle butt, slots to hold coins to be used as flathead screwdrivers, and a built-in cord cutter/bottle opener.

▼ With a multi-function wrench, hex keys, a bit adapter and bits, Wenger's one-hand-opening Ueli Steck titanium Swiss Army Knife is designed for mountain climbers, hikers and backcountry skiers.

▼▲ Upon removing the detachable orange canvas-Micarta® scales of the TOPS Knives XcEST Alpha, a compartment is revealed that can store a few of the survival goodies included with the knife.

◀ The 440C safety hook, part of Benchmade's Triage, folds out of the spine of the orange G-10 handle butt. The piece also sports N680 blade steel, a carbide glass breaker and an AXIS™ lock.

Feel-Good Folders

◀ Designed by Kirk Rexroat, the Al Mar Knives Shrike folder showcases textured G-10 handle scales and a VG-10 stainless steel blade.

◀ The W.R. Case & Sons 611 1/2L SS Cheetah offers a palm-leaf design on its bolsters and smooth bone handle.

▲ Blade Magazine's 2010 American-Made Knife Of The Year®, the Kershaw Tilt comes with a 4-inch blade that is a composite of a Vanax 75 cutting edge and a 400 series stainless steel spine.

◀ The assisted-opening thumb stud of the Kershaw Echelon hovers in the middle of an oversized blade cutout. The 3.25-inch blade is Sandvik 14C28N stainless steel, and the handle is translucent G-10.

Fine-Size Fixed Blades

◀ Primarily a neck or boot knife, the Benchmade Heckler & Koch 14536 "Instigator" exhibits a number of modern-day, tactical-fixed-blade attributes—lightweight, compact, easy to carry, and with a good blade-to-handle ratio.

▶ The Gerber Basic (top) and Ka-Bar Becker K-13 Remora (bottom) are similar in size. While the Remora parades a skeletonized grip, the Basic sports "TacHide"™ (textured rubber) handle overlays.

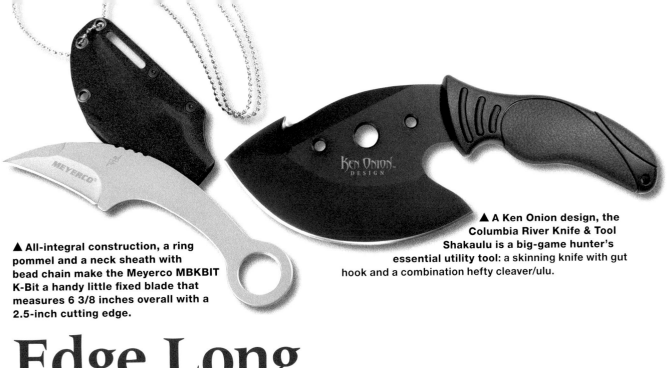

▲ All-integral construction, a ring pommel and a neck sheath with bead chain make the Meyerco MBKBIT K-Bit a handy little fixed blade that measures 6 3/8 inches overall with a 2.5-inch cutting edge.

▲ A Ken Onion design, the Columbia River Knife & Tool Shakaulu is a big-game hunter's essential utility tool: a skinning knife with gut hook and a combination hefty cleaver/ulu.

Edge Long

▶ Shaolin monks reportedly use the traditional Jie Dao as a multipurpose tool. The 11 5/8-inch carbon steel blade of CAS Hanwei's repro emerges from a bamboo handle and traditional steel fittings.

▼ The forward weighting of the carbon steel blade enhances the hack-and-chop uses of Gerber's Bear Grylls Parang. It includes a nylon sheath and Grylls' "Priorities of Survival" pocket guide.

▼ All black, including a titanium-nitride-coated AUS-8 stainless blade and GRN handle, the Force has the look with which SOG Specialty Knives & Tools has become synonymous.

Grip-able Grooves

▶ Buck Knives and TOPS Knives collaborate on the CSAR-T that features a 4.5-inch, modified-tanto blade, grooved "Rocky Mountain Tread" G-10 scales, and an extended pommel that acts as an impact tool and multi-function hex driver.

◀ Mantis Knife Co. utilized a specific type of soft rubber with a composition identical to that used on racecar tires for the handle of the TP-2CM The Principal.

◀ Danish maker Jesper Voxnaes' 11.5-inch design for the Boker Plus Collection is based on his Ripley model, which was inspired by Sigourney Weaver's lead character in the Alien series of movies. The blade is 440C stainless with a dramatic choil, and the handle is 3-D contoured Micarta®.

A Lock-Back Comeback

▶ The SOGzilla RSP-21 from SOG Specialty Knives & Tools features a 4.75-inch blade of 8Cr13MoV stainless steel and a red injection-molded, two-way textured handle.

◀ Boker offers the Fellow Damascus lock-back folder in a 3.25-inch blade of Devin Thomas "basket-weave" stainless damascus.

◀ The Outdoor Edge Flip n' Blaze Saw/Combo are mid-lock/front-lock folders. The skinning, gutting and saw blades are all 8Cr13MoV stainless, and the handles are Kraton® rubber.

▼ H1 steel, which is reportedly 100 percent rustproof, comprises the 3-inch blade of the Spyderco Salt I lock-back folder.

▲ What Spyderco's Sal Glesser said is the "best lock-back folder in the world," the Native 5 is also the company's first production folder made with CPM-S35VN stainless steel.

Badass Bowies

▼ Kit Rae of United Cutlery says the large, 10.5-inch taper-ground blade of the Serpentine Survival Bowie makes it most suitable for chopping wood or brush, and it fills the role of a machete easily.

◀ According to Chris Cashbaugh of SOG Specialty Knives & Tools, the SEAL Pup Elite is the company's best-selling fixed blade among military customers.

◀ The TOPS Prather War Bowie incorporates a 7.25-inch blade of quarter-inch-thick 1095 carbon steel in a Tac-Black™ finish, and a "Rocky Mountain Tread" Micarta® grip.

▼ A supercharged version of KA-BAR's classic 1217 combat/utility knife, the Big Brother features a 9 3/8-inch blade with serrations on the spine and a leather handle.

KNIVES MARKETPLACE

INTERESTING PRODUCT NEWS FOR BOTH THE CUTLER AND THE KNIFE ENTHUSIAST

The companies and individuals represented on the following pages will be happy to provide additional information — feel free to contact them.

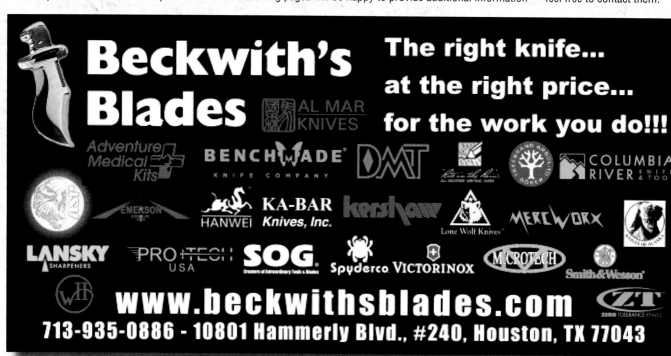
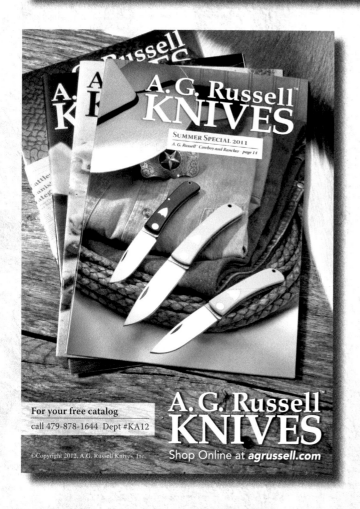

KNIVES MARKETPLACE

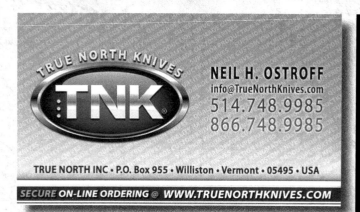
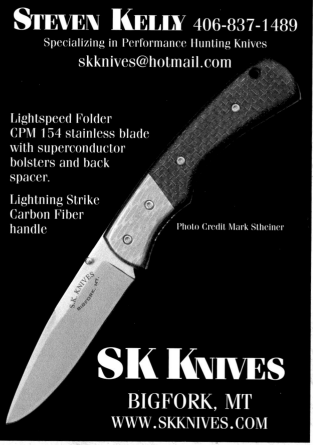

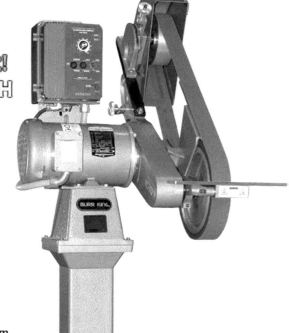

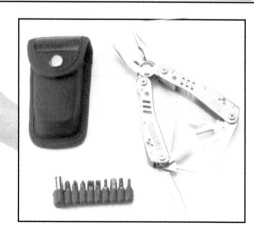

BusseKnives.com

Use it like you hate it

UDDEHOLM VANAX®

Knives made from Uddeholm Vanax steel barely need maintenance. It's a bold statement, we know – but the outstanding corrosion resistance and excellent edge retention of the steel makes for a blade that can handle the roughest conditions.

By exchanging carbon for nitrogen in our third generation powder process, we have given Uddeholm Vanax a different steel structure with superior properties. You can basically use your knife like you hate it. It won't mind.

WHERE KNIFE COLLECTORS CONNECT WITH KNIFEMAKERS

The Knife Showcase at **BladeMag.com** is the premier site for knife-collecting. Chat with knifemakers, visit their blogs, find other collectors, or buy knives. Whatever it is that you love about knife-collecting, you'll find it in the Knife Showcase.

JOIN US TODAY.
click on Knife Showcase at www.BladeMag.com

DIRECTORY

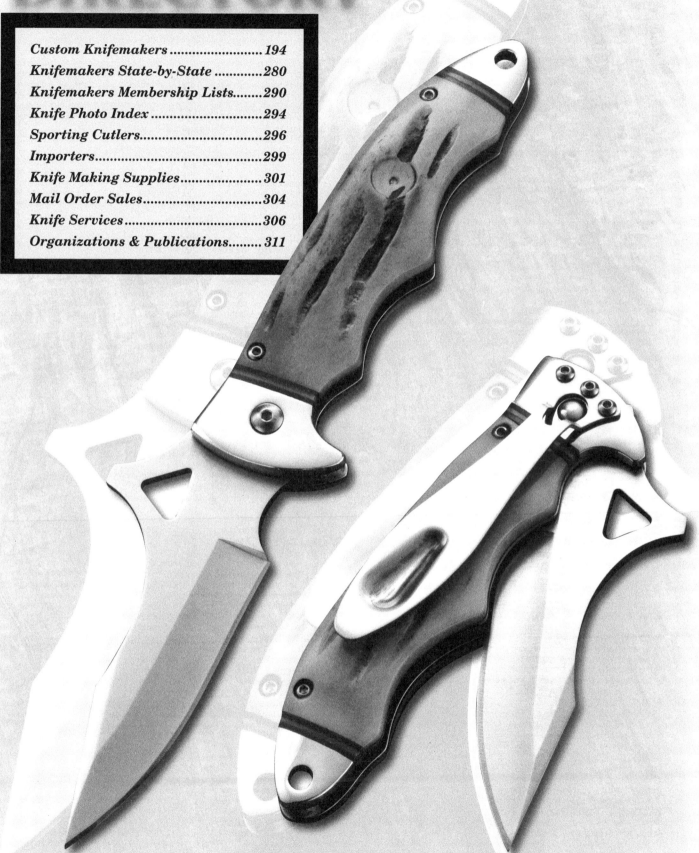

A

ABEGG, ARNIE,
5992 Kenwick Cr, Huntington Beach, CA 92648, Phone: 714-848-5697

ABERNATHY, PAUL J,
3033 Park St., Eureka, CA 95501, Phone: 707-442-3593
Specialties: Period pieces and traditional straight knives of his design and in standard patterns. **Patterns:** Miniature daggers, fighters and swords. **Technical:** Forges and files SS, brass and sterling silver. **Prices:** $100 to $250; some to $500. **Remarks:** Part-time maker. Doing business as Abernathy's Miniatures. **Mark:** Stylized initials.

ACCAWI, FUAD,
131 Bethel Rd, Clinton, TN 37716, Phone: 865-414-4836, gaccawi@comcast.net; Web: www.acremetalworks.com
Specialties: I create one of a kind pieces from small working knives to performance blades and swords. **Patterns:** Styles include, and not limited to hunters, Bowies, daggers, swords, folders and camp knives. **Technical:** I forge primarily 5160, produces own Damascus and does own heat treating. **Prices:** $150 to $3000. **Remarks:** I am a full-time bladesmith. I enjoy producing Persian and historically influenced work. **Mark:** My mark is an eight sided Middle Eastern star with initials in the center.

ACKERSON, ROBIN E,
119 W Smith St, Buchanan, MI 49107, Phone: 616-695-2911

ADAMS, JIM,
1648 Camille Way, Cordova, TN 38016, Phone: 901-326-0441, jim@JimAdamsKnives.com Web: www.jimadamsknives.com
Specialties: Fixed blades in classic design. **Patterns:** Hunters, fighters, and Bowies. **Technical:** Grinds Damascus, O1, others as requested. **Prices:** Starting at $150. **Remarks:** Full-time maker. **Mark:** J. Adams, Cordova, TN.

ADAMS, LES,
6413 NW 200 St, Hialeah, FL 33015, Phone: 305-625-1699
Specialties: Working straight knives of his design. **Patterns:** Fighters, tactical folders, law enforcing autos. **Technical:** Grinds ATS-34, 440C and D2. **Prices:** $100 to $500. **Remarks:** Part-time maker; first knife sold in 1989. **Mark:** First initial, last name, Custom Knives.

ADAMS, WILLIAM D,
PO Box 439, Burton, TX 77835, Phone: 713-855-5643, Fax: 713-855-5638
Specialties: Hunter scalpels and utility knives of his design. **Patterns:** Hunters and utility/camp knives. **Technical:** Grinds 1095, 440C and 440V. Uses stabilized wood and other stabilized materials. **Prices:** $100 to $200. **Remarks:** Part-time maker; first knife sold in 1994. **Mark:** Last name in script.

ADDISON, KYLE A,
588 Atkins Trail, Hazel, KY 42049-8629, Phone: 270-492-8120, kylest2@yahoo.com
Specialties: Hand forged blades including Bowies, fighters and hunters. **Patterns:** Custom leather sheaths. **Technical:** Forges 5160, 1084, and his own Damascus. **Prices:** $175 to $1500. **Remarks:** Part-time maker, first knife sold in 1996. ABS member. **Mark:** First and middle initial, last name under "Trident" with knife and hammer.

ADKINS, LARRY,
10714 East County Rd. 100S, Indianapolis, IN 46231, Phone: 317-838-7292
Specialties: Single blade slip joint folders. Bear Jaw Damascus hunters, Bowies, and fighters. Handles from stag, ossic, pearl, bone, mastodon-mammoth elephant. **Technical:** Forges own Damascus and all high carbon steels. Grinds 5160, 52100, 1095, O1 and L6. **Prices:** $150 and up. **Remarks:** Part-time maker, first knife sold in 2001. **Mark:** L. Adkins.

ADKINS, RICHARD L,
138 California Ct, Mission Viejo, CA 92692-4079

AIDA, YOSHIHITO,
26-7 Narimasu 2-chome, Itabashi-ku, Tokyo 175-0094, JAPAN, Phone: 81-3-3939-0052, Fax: 01-3-3939 0058
Specialties: High-tech working straight knives and folders of his design. **Patterns:** Bowies, lockbacks, hunters, fighters, fishing knives, boots. **Technical:** Grinds CV-134, ATS-34; buys Damascus; works in traditional Japanese fashion for some handles and sheaths. **Prices:** $700 to $1200; some higher. **Remarks:** Full-time maker; first knife sold in 1978. **Mark:** Initial logo and Riverside West.

ALBERICCI, EMILIO,
19 Via Masone, 24100, Bergamo, ITALY, Phone: 01139-35-215120
Specialties: Folders and Bowies. **Patterns:** Collector knives. **Technical:** Uses stock removal with extreme accuracy; offers exotic and high-tech materials. **Prices:** Not currently selling. **Remarks:** Part-time maker. **Mark:** None.

ALBERT, STEFAN,
U Lucenecka 434/4, Filakovo 98604, SLOVAK REPUBLIC, albert@albertknives.com Web: www.albertknives.com
Specialties: Art Knives, Miniatures, Scrimshaw, Bulino. **Prices:** From USD $500 to USD $25000. **Mark:** Albert

ALCORN, DOUGLAS A.,
14687 Fordney Rd., Chesaning, MI 48616, Phone: 989-845-6712, fortalcornknives@centurytel.net
Specialties: Gentleman style and presentation knives. **Patterns:** Hunters, miniatures, and military type fixed blade knives and axes. **Technical:** Blades are stock removal and forged using best quality stainless, carbon, and damascus steels. Handle materials are burls, ivory, pearl, leather and other exotics. **Prices:** $300 and up. **Motto:** Simple, Rugged, Elegant, Handcrafted **Remarks:** Knife maker since 1989 and full time since 1999, Knife Makers Guild (voting member), member of the Bladesmith Society. **Mark:** D.A. Alcorn (Loveless style mark), Maker, Chesaning, MI.

ALDERMAN, ROBERT,
2655 Jewel Lake Rd., Sagle, ID 83860, Phone: 208-263-5996
Specialties: Classic and traditional working straight knives in standard patterns or to customer specs and his design; period pieces. **Patterns:** Bowies, fighters, hunters and utility/camp knives. **Technical:** Casts, forges and grinds 1084; forges and grinds L6 and O1. Prefers an old appearance. **Prices:** $100 to $350; some to $700. **Remarks:** Full-time maker; first knife sold in 1975. Doing business as Trackers Forge. Knife-making school. Two-week course for beginners; covers forging, stock removal, hardening, tempering, case making. All materials supplied; $1250. **Mark:** Deer track.

ALDRETE, BOB,
PO Box 1471, Lomita, CA 90717, Phone: 310-326-3041

ALEXANDER, DARREL,
Box 381, Ten Sleep, WY 82442, Phone: 307-366-2699, dalexwyo@tctwest.net
Specialties: Traditional working straight knives. **Patterns:** Hunters, boots and fishing knives. **Technical:** Grinds D2, 440C, ATS-34 and 154CM. **Prices:** $75 to $120; some to $250. **Remarks:** Full-time maker; first knife sold in 1983. **Mark:** Name, city, state.

ALEXANDER, EUGENE,
Box 540, Ganado, TX 77962-0540, Phone: 512-771-3727

ALEXANDER, OLEG, Cossack Blades,
15460 Stapleton Way, Wellington, FL 33414, Phone: 443-676-6111, Web: www.cossackblades.com
Technical: All knives are made from hand-forged Damascus (3-4 types of steel are used to create the Damascus) and have a HRC of 60-62. Handle materials are all natural, including various types of wood, horn, bone and leather. Embellishments include the use of precious metals and stones, including gold, silver, diamonds, rubies, sapphires and other unique materials. All knives include hand-made leather sheaths, and some models include wooden presentation boxes and display stands. **Prices:** $395 to over $10,000, depending on design and materials used. **Remarks:** Full-time maker, first knife sold in 1993. **Mark:** Rectangle enclosing a stylized Cyrillic letter "O" overlapping a stylized Cyrillic "K."

ALLEN, MIKE "WHISKERS",
12745 Fontenot Acres Rd, Malakoff, TX 75148, Phone: 903-489-1026, whiskersknives@aol.com; Web: www.whiskersknives.com
Specialties: Working and collector-quality lockbacks, liner locks, automatic folders and assisted openers of his own proprietary mechanisms. **Patterns:** Folders and fixed blades. **Technical:** Makes Damascus, 440C and ATS-34, engraves. **Prices:** $200 and up. **Remarks:** Full-time maker since 1984. **Mark:** Whiskers and month and year.

ALLRED, BRUCE F,
1764 N. Alder, Layton, UT 84041, Phone: 801-825-4612, allredbf@msn.com
Specialties: Custom hunting and utility knives. **Patterns:** Custom designs that include a unique grind line, thumb and mosaic pins. **Technical:** ATS-34, 154CM and 440C. **Remarks:** The handle material includes but not limited to Micarta (in various colors), natural woods and reconstituted stone.

ALLRED, ELVAN,
31 Spring Terrace Court, St. Charles, MO 63303, Phone: 636-936-8871, allredknives@yahoo.com; Web: www.allredcustomknives.com
Specialties: Innovative sculpted folding knives designed by Elvan's son Scott that are mostly one of a kind. **Patterns:** Mostly folders but some high-end straight knives. **Technical:** ATS-34 SS, 440C SS, stainless Damascus, S30V, 154cm; inlays are mostly natural materials such as pearl, coral, ivory, jade, lapis, and other precious stone. **Prices:** $500 to $4000, some higher. **Remarks:** Started making knives in the shop of Dr. Fred Carter in the early 1990s. Full-time maker since 2006, first knife sold in 1993. Take some orders but work mainly on one-of-a-kind art knives. **Mark:** Small oval with signature Eallred in the center and handmade above.

ALVERSON, TIM (R.V.),
622 Homestead St., Moscow, ID 83843, Phone: 208-874-2277, alvie35@yahoo.com Web: cwknives.blogspot.com
Specialties: Fancy working knives to customer specs; other types on request. **Patterns:** Bowies, daggers, folders and miniatures. **Technical:** Grinds 440C, ATS-34; buys some Damascus. **Prices:** Start at $100. **Remarks:** Full-time maker; first knife sold in 1981. **Mark:** R.V.A. around rosebud.

AMERI, MAURO,
Via Riaello No. 20, Trensasco St Olcese, 16010 Genova, ITALY, Phone: 010-8357077
Specialties: Working and using knives of his design. **Patterns:** Hunters, Bowies and utility/camp knives. **Technical:** Grinds 440C, ATS-34 and 154CM. Handles in wood or Micarta; offers sheaths. **Prices:** $200 to $1200. **Remarks:** Spare-time maker; first knife sold in 1982. **Mark:** Last name, city.

AMMONS, DAVID C,
6225 N. Tucson Mtn. Dr, Tucson, AZ 85743, Phone: 520-307-3585
Specialties: Will build to suit. **Patterns:** Yours or his. **Prices:** $250 to $2000. **Mark:** AMMONS.

AMOUREUX, A W,
PO Box 776, Northport, WA 99157, Phone: 509-732-6292
Specialties: Heavy-duty working straight knives. **Patterns:** Bowies, fighters, camp knives and hunters for world-wide use. **Technical:** Grinds 440C, ATS-34 and 154CM. **Prices:** $80 to $2000. **Remarks:** Full-time maker; first knife sold in 1974. **Mark:** ALSTAR.

ANDERS, DAVID,
157 Barnes Dr, Center Ridge, AR 72027, Phone: 501-893-2294
Specialties: Working straight knives of his design. **Patterns:** Bowies, fighters and hunters. **Technical:** Forges 5160, 1080 and Damascus. **Prices:** $225 to $3200. **Remarks:** Part-time maker; first knife sold in 1988. Doing business as Anders Knives. **Mark:** Last name/MS.

ANDERS, JEROME,
14560 SW 37th St, Miramar, FL 33027, Phone: 305-613-2990, web:www.andersknives.com
Specialties: Case handles and pin work. **Patterns:** Layered and mosiac steel. **Prices:** $275 and up. **Remarks:** All his knives are truly one-of-a-kind. **Mark:** J. Anders in half moon.

ANDERSEN, HENRIK LEFOLII,
Jagtvej 8, Groenholt, 3480, Fredensborg, DENMARK, Phone: 0011-45-48483026
Specialties: Hunters and matched pairs for the serious hunter. **Technical:** Grinds A2; uses materials native to Scandinavia. **Prices:** Start at $250. **Remarks:** Part-time maker; first knife sold in 1985. **Mark:** Initials with arrow.

ANDERSEN, KARL B.,
1699 N. Bluebell Bend Rd., Watseka, IL 60970, Phone: 815-644-0127, Karl@andersenforge.com Web: www.andersenforge.com
Specialties: Hunters, Bowies, Fighters, Camp knives forged from high carbon tool steels and Andersen Forge Damascus. **Technical:** All types of materials used. Exotic inlay materials and silver wire embellishments utilized. **Prices:** Starting at $450 and up. **Remarks:** Full-time maker. ABS Journeyman Smith. All knives sole authorship. Andersen Forge was instrumental in paving the way for take-down knife construction to be more recognized and broadly accepted in knife making today. **Mark:** Andersen in script on obverse. J.S. on either side, depending on knife.

ANDERSON, GARY D,
2816 Reservoir Rd, Spring Grove, PA 17362-9802, Phone: 717-229-2665
Specialties: From working knives to collectors quality blades, some folders. **Patterns:** Traditional and classic designs; customer patterns welcome. **Technical:** Forges Damascus carbon and stainless steels. Offers silver inlay, mokume, filework, checkering. **Prices:** $250 and up. **Remarks:** Part-time maker; first knife sold in 1985. Some engraving, scrimshaw and stone work. **Mark:** GAND, MS.

ANDERSON, MARK ALAN,
1176 Poplar St, Denver, CO 80220, mcantdrive95@comcast.net; Web: www.malancustomknives.com
Specialties: Stilettos. Automatics of several varieties and release mechanisms. **Patterns:** Drop point hunters, sub hilt fighters & drop point camp knives. **Technical:** Almost all my blades are hollow ground. **Prices:** $200 to $1800. **Remarks:** Focusing on fixed blade hunting, skinning & fighting knives now. **Mark:** Dragon head.

ANDERSON, MEL,
29505 P 50 Rd, Hotchkiss, CO 81419-8203, Phone: 970-872-4882, Fax: 970-872-4882, artnedge1@wmconnect.com
Specialties: Full-size, miniature and one-of-a-kind straight knives and folders of his design. **Patterns:** Tantos, Bowies, daggers, fighters, hunters and pressure folders. **Technical:** Grinds 440C, 5160, D2, 1095. **Prices:** Start at $145. **Remarks:** Knifemaker and sculptor, full-time maker; first knife sold in 1987. **Mark:** Scratchy Hand.

ANDERSON, TOM,
955 Canal Rd. Extd., Manchester, PA 17345, Phone: 717-266-6475, andersontech1@comcast.net Web: artistryintitanium.com
Specialties: Battle maces and war hammers.

ANDREWS, ERIC,
132 Halbert Street, Grand Ledge, MI 48837, Phone: 517-627-7304
Specialties: Traditional working and using straight knives of his design. **Patterns:** Full-tang hunters, skinners and utility knives. **Technical:** Forges carbon steel; heat-treats. All knives come with sheath; most handles are of wood. **Prices:** $80 to $160. **Remarks:** Part-time maker; first knife sold in 1990. Doing business as The Tinkers Bench.

ANDREWS, RUSS,
PO Box 7732, Sugar Creek, MO 64054, Phone: 816-252-3344, russandrews@sbcglobal.net; Web:wwwrussandrewsknives.com
Specialties: Hand forged bowies & hunters. **Mark:** E. R. Andrews II. ERAII.

ANGELL, JON,
22516 East C R1474, Hawthorne, FL 32640, Phone: 352-475-5380, syrjon@aol.com

ANKROM, W.E.,
14 Marquette Dr, Cody, WY 82414, Phone: 307-587-3017, weankrom@hotmail.com
Specialties: Best quality folding knives of his design. Bowies, fighters, chute knives, boots and hunters. **Patterns:** Lock backs, liner locks, single high art. **Technical:** ATS-34 commercial Damascus, CPM 154 steel. **Prices:** $500 and up. **Remarks:** Full-time maker; first knife sold in 1975. **Mark:** Name or name, city, state.

ANSO, JENS,
GL. Skanderborgvej, 116, 8472 Sporup, DENMARK, Phone: 45 86968826, info@ansoknives.com; Web: www.ansoknives.com
Specialties: Working knives of his own design. **Patterns:** Balisongs, swords, folders, drop-points, sheepsfoots, hawkbill, tanto, recurve. **Technical:** Grinds RWL-34 Damasteel S30V, CPM 154CM. Handrubbed or beadblasted finish. **Price:** $400 to $1200, some up to $3500. **Remarks:** Full-time maker since January 2002. First knife sold 1997. Doing business as ANSOKNIVES. **Mark:** ANSO and/or ANSO with logo.

ANTONIO JR., WILLIAM J,
6 Michigan State Dr, Newark, DE 19713-1161, Phone: 302-368-8211, antonioknives@aol.com
Specialties: Fancy working straight knives of his design. **Patterns:** Hunting, survival and fishing knives. **Technical:** Grinds D2, 440C and 154CM; offers stainless Damascus. **Prices:** $125 to $395; some to $900. **Remarks:** Part-time maker; first knife sold in 1978. **Mark:** Last name.

APELT, STACY E,
8076 Moose Ave, Norfolk, VA 23518, Phone: 757-583-5872, sapelt@cox.net
Specialties: Exotic wood and burls, ivories, Bowies, custom made knives to order. **Patterns:** Bowies, hunters, fillet, professional cutlery and Japanese style blades and swords. **Technical:** Hand forging, stock removal, scrimshaw, carbon, stainless and Damascus steels. **Prices:** $65 to $5000. **Remarks:** Professional Goldsmith. **Mark:** Stacy E. Apelt - Norfolk VA.

APPLEBY, ROBERT,
746 Municipal Rd, Shickshinny, PA 18655, Phone:570-864-0879, applebyknives@yahoo.com; Web: www.applebyknives.com
Specialties: Working using straight knives and folders of his own and popular and historical designs. **Patterns:** Variety of straight knives and folders. **Technical:** Hand forged or grinds O1, 1084, 5160, 440C, ATS-34, commercial Damascus, makes own sheaths. **Prices:** Starting at $75. **Remarks:** Part-time maker, first knife sold in 1995. **Mark:** APPLEBY over SHICKSHINNY, PA.

APPLETON, RON,
315 Glenn St, Bluff Dale, TX 76433, Phone: 254-728-3039, ron@helovesher.com; Web: http://community.webshots.com/user/angelic574
Specialties: One-of-a-kind folding knives. **Patterns:** Unique folding multi-locks and high-tech patterns. **Technical:** All parts machined, D2, S7, 416, 440C, 6A14V et.al. **Prices:** Start at $9500. **Remarks:** Spare-time maker; first knife sold in 1996. **Mark:** Initials with anvil or initials within arrowhead, signed and dated.

ARBUCKLE, JAMES M,
114 Jonathan Jct, Yorktown, VA 23693, Phone: 757-867-9578, a_r_buckle@hotmail.com
Specialties: One-of-a-kind of his design; working knives. **Patterns:** Mostly chef's knives and hunters. **Technical:** Forged and stock removal blades using exotic hardwoods, natural materials, Micarta and stabilized woods. Forge 5160, 1084 and O1; stock removal D2, ATS-34, 440C. Makes own pattern welded steel. **Prices:** $195 to $700. **Remarks:** Forge, grind, heat-treat, finish and embellish all knives himself. Does own leatherwork. Part-time maker. ABS Journeyman smith 2007; ASM member. **Mark:** J. Arbuckle or J. ARBUCKLE MAKER.

ARCHER, RAY AND TERRI,
4207 South 28 St., Omaha, NE 68107, Phone: 402-505-3084, archerrt@cox.net
Specialties: Back to basics high finish working knives and upscale. **Patterns:** Hunters/skinners, camping. **Technical:** Flat grinds ATS-34, 440C, S30V. Buys Damascus. **Price:** $100 to $500, some higher. **Remarks:** Full time makers. Make own sheaths; first knife sold 1994. Member of PKA & OK CA (Oregon Knife Collector Assoc.). **Mark:** Last name over city and state.

ARDWIN, COREY,
4700 North Cedar, North Little Rock, AR 72116, Phone: 501-791-0301, Fax: 501-791-2974, Boog@hotmail.com

ARM-KO KNIVES,
PO Box 76280, Marble Ray 4035 KZN, SOUTH AFRICA, Phone: 27 31 5771451, arm-koknives.co.za; Web: www.arm-koknives.co.za
Specialties: They will make what your fastidious taste desires. Be it cool collector or tenacious tactical with handles of mother-of-pearl, fossil & local ivories. Exotic dye/stabilized burls, giraffe bone, horns, carbon fiber, g10, and titanium etc. **Technical:** Via stock removal, grinding Damasteel, carbon & mosaic. Damascus, ATS-34, N690, 440A, 440B, 12C27, RWL34 and high carbon EN 8, 5160 all heat treated in house. **Prices:** From $200 and up. **Remarks:** Father a part-time maker for well over 10 years and member of Knifemakers Guild in SA. Son full-time maker over 3 years. **Mark:** Logo of initials A R M and H A R M "Edged Tools."

ARMS, ERIC,
11153 7 Mile Road, Tustin, MI 49688, Phone: 231-829-3726, ericarms@netonecom.net
Specialties: Working hunters, high performance straight knives. **Patterns:** Variety of hunters, scagel style, Ed Fowler design and drop point. **Technical:** Forge 52100, 5160, 1084 hand grind, heat treat, natural handle, stag horn, elk, big horn, flat grind, convex, all leather sheath work. **Prices:** Starting at $150 **Remarks:** Part-time maker **Mark:** Eric Arms

ARNOLD, JOE,
47 Patience Cres, London, Ont., CANADA N6E 2K7, Phone: 519-686-2623
Specialties: Traditional working and using straight knives of his design and to customer specs. **Patterns:** Fighters, hunters and Bowies. **Technical:** Grinds 440C, ATS-34 and 5160. **Prices:** $75 to $500; some to $2500. **Remarks:** Part-time maker; first knife sold in 1988. **Mark:** Last name, country.

ARROWOOD—BANKS

ARROWOOD, DALE,
556 Lassetter Rd, Sharpsburg, GA 30277, Phone: 404-253-9672
Specialties: Fancy and traditional straight knives of his design and to customer specs. Patterns: Bowies, fighters and hunters. Technical: Grinds ATS-34 and 440C; forges high-carbon steel. Engraves and scrimshaws. Prices: $125 to $200; some to $245. Remarks: Part-time maker; first knife sold in 1989. Mark: Anvil with an arrow through it; Old English "Arrowood Knives."

ASHBY, DOUGLAS,
10123 Deermont Trail, Dallas, TX 75243, Phone: 214-929-7531
Specialties: Traditional and fancy straight knives and folders of his design or to customer specs. Patterns: Skinners, hunters, utility/camp knives, locking liner folders. Technical: Grinds ATS-34, commercial Damascus, and other steels on request. Prices: $125 to $1000. Remarks: Part-time maker; first knife sold in 1990. Mark: Name, city.

ASHWORTH, BOYD,
1510 Bullard Place, Powder Springs, GA 30127, Phone: 770-422-9826, boydashworth@comcast.net; Web: www.boydashworthknives.com
Specialties: Turtle folders. Fancy Damascus locking folders. Patterns: Fighters, hunters and gents. Technical: Forges own Damascus; offers filework; uses exotic handle materials. Prices: $500 to $2500. Remarks: Part-time maker; first knife sold in 1993. Mark: Last name.

ATHEY, STEVE,
3153 Danube Way, Riverside, CA 92503, Phone: 951-850-8612, stevelonnie@yahoo.com
Specialties: Stock removal. Patterns: Hunters & Bowies. Prices: $100 to $500. Remarks: Part-time maker. Mark: Last name with number on blade.

ATKINS, JIM,
760 270th Ave, Frederic, WI 54837, Phone: 715-472-8510, jubjub223@gmail.com
Specialties: Hardworking combat and hunting knives. Technical: Forging recycled 5160. Stock removal with O1. Handles of Micarta and natural materials. Remarks: Part-time maker since 2000. Mark: Stylized initials.

ATKINSON, DICK,
General Delivery, Wausau, FL 32463, Phone: 850-638-8524
Specialties: Working straight knives and folders of his design; some fancy. Patterns: Hunters, fighters, boots; locking folders in interframes. Technical: Grinds A2, 440C and 154CM. Likes filework. Prices: $85 to $300; some exceptional knives. Remarks: Full-time maker; first knife sold in 1977. Mark: Name, city, state.

AYARRAGARAY, CRISTIAN L.,
Buenos Aires 250, (3100) Parana-Entre Rios, ARGENTINA, Phone: 043-231753
Specialties: Traditional working straight knives of his design. Patterns: Fishing and hunting knives. Technical: Grinds and forges carbon steel. Uses native Argentine woods and deer antler. Prices: $150 to $250; some to $400. Remarks: Full-time maker; first knife sold in 1980. Mark: Last name, signature.

B

BAARTMAN, GEORGE,
PO Box 1116, Bela-Bela 0480, Limpopo, SOUTH AFRICA, Phone: 27 14 736 4036, Fax: 086 636 3408, thabathipa@gmail.com
Specialties: Fancy and working LinerLock® folders of own design and to customers specs. Specialize in pattern filework on liners. Patterns: LinerLock® folders. Technical: Grinds 12C27, ATS-34, and Damascus, prefer working with stainless damasteel. Hollow grinds to hand-rubbed and polished satin finish. Enjoys working with mammoth, warthog tusk and pearls. Prices: Folders from $380 to $1000. Remarks: Part-time maker. Member of the Knifemakers Guild of South Africa since 1993. Mark: BAARTMAN.

BACHE-WIIG, TOM,
N-5966, Eivindvik, NORWAY, Phone: 475-778-4290, Fax: 475-778-1099, tom.bache-wiig@enivest.net; Web: tombachewiig.com
Specialties: High-art and working knives of his design. Patterns: Hunters, utility knives, hatchets, axes and art knives. Technical: Grinds Uddeholm Elmax, powder metallurgy tool stainless steel. Handles made of rear burls of Nordic woods stabilized with vacuum/high-pressure technique. Prices: $430 to $900; some to $2300. Remarks: Part-time maker; first knife sold 1988. Mark: Etched name and eagle head.

BACON, DAVID R.,
906 136th St E, Bradenton, FL 34202-9694, Phone: 813-996-4289

BAGLEY, R. KEITH,
OLD PINE FORGE, 4415 Hope Acres Dr, White Plains, MD 20695, Phone: 301-932-0990, oldpineforge@hotmail.com
Specialties: Hand-made Damascus hunters, skinners, Bowies. Technical: Use ATS-34, 5160, O1, 1085, 1095. Patterns: Ladder-wave lightning bolt. Price: $275 to 750. Remarks: Farrier for 25 years, blacksmith for 25 years, knifemaker for 10 years. Mark: KB inside horseshoe and anvil.

BAILEY, I.R.,
Lamorna Cottage, Common End, Colkirk, ENGLAND NR 21 7JD, Phone: 01-328-856-183, irbailey1975@tiscali.co.uk Web: irbailey.co.uk
Specialties: Hunters, utilities, Bowies, camp knives, fighters. Mainly influenced by Moran, Loveless and Lile. Technical: Primarily stock removal using flat ground 1095, 1075, and 80CrV2. Occasionally forges including own basic Damascus. Uses both native and exotic hardwoods, stag, Leather, Micarta and other synthetic handle materials, with brass or 301 stainless fittings. Does some filework and leather tooling. Does own heat treating. Remarks: Part-time maker since 2005. All knives and sheaths are sole authorship. Mark: Last name stamped.

BAILEY, JOSEPH D.,
3213 Jonesboro Dr, Nashville, TN 37214, Phone: 615-889-3172, jbknfemkr@aol.com
Specialties: Working and using straight knives; collector pieces. Patterns: Bowies, hunters, tactical, folders. Technical: 440C, ATS-34, Damascus and wire Damascus. Offers scrimshaw. Prices: $85 to $1200. Remarks: Part-time maker; first knife sold in 1988. Mark: Joseph D Bailey Nashville Tennessee.

BAILEY, RYAN,
4185 S. St. Rt. 605, Galena, OH 43021, Phone: 740-965-9970, dr@darrelralph.com; Web: www.darrelralph.com
Specialties: Fancy, high-art, high-tech, collectible straight knives and folders of his design and to customer specs; unique mechanisms, some disassemble. Patterns: Daggers, fighters and swords. Technical: Does own Damascus and forging from high-carbon. Embellishes with file work and gold work. Prices: $200 to $2500. Remarks: Full-time maker; first knife sold in 1999. Doing business as Briar Knives. Mark: RLB.

BAKER, HERB,
14104 NC 87 N, Eden, NC 27288, Phone: 336-627-0338

BAKER, RAY,
PO Box 303, Sapulpa, OK 74067, Phone: 918-224-8013
Specialties: High-tech working straight knives. Patterns: Hunters, fighters, Bowies, skinners and boots of his design and to customer specs. Technical: Grinds 440C, 1095 spring steel or customer request; heat-treats. Custom-made scabbards for any knife. Prices: $125 to $500; some to $1000. Remarks: Full-time maker; first knife sold in 1981. Mark: First initial, last name.

BAKER, WILD BILL,
Box 361, Boiceville, NY 12412, Phone: 914-657-8646
Specialties: Primitive knives, buckskinners. Patterns: Skinners, camp knives and Bowies. Technical: Works with L6, files and rasps. Prices: $100 to $350. Remarks: Part-time maker; first knife sold in 1989. Mark: Wild Bill Baker, Oak Leaf Forge, or both.

BALBACH, MARKUS,
Heinrich - Worner - Str 3, 35789 Weilmunster-Laubuseschbach/Ts., GERMANY 06475-8911, Fax: 912986, Web: www.schmiede-balbach.de
Specialties: High-art knives and working/using straight knives and folders of his design and to customer specs. Patterns: Hunters and daggers. Technical: Stainless steel, one of Germany's greatest Smithies. Supplier for the forges of Solingen. Remarks: Full-time maker; first knife sold in 1984. Doing business as Schmiedewerkstatte M. Balbach. Mark: Initials stamped inside the handle.

BALL, BUTCH,
2161 Reedsville Rd., Floyd, VA 24091, Phone: 540-392-3485, ballknives@yahoo.com
Specialties: Fancy and Tactical Folders and Automatics. Patterns: Fixed and folders. Technical: Use various Damascus and ATS34, 154cm. Prices: $300 - $1500. Remarks: Part-time maker. Sold first knife in 1990. Mark: Ball or BCK with crossed knives.

BALL, KEN,
127 Sundown Manor, Mooresville, IN 46158, Phone: 317-834-4803
Specialties: Classic working/using straight knives of his design and to customer specs. Patterns: Hunters and utility/camp knives. Technical: Flat-grinds ATS-34. Offers filework. Prices: $150 to $400. Remarks: Part-time maker; first knife sold in 1994. Doing business as Ball Custom Knives. Mark: Last name.

BALLESTRA, SANTINO,
via D. Tempesta 11/17, 18039 Ventimiglia (IM), ITALY 0184-215228, ladasin@libero.it
Specialties: Using and collecting straight knives. Patterns: Hunting, fighting, skinners, Bowies, medieval daggers and knives. Technical: Forges ATS-34, D2, O2, 1060 and his own Damascus. Uses ivory and silver. Prices: $500 to $2000; some higher. Remarks: Full-time maker; first knife sold in 1979. Mark: First initial, last name.

BALLEW, DALE,
PO Box 1277, Bowling Green, VA 22427, Phone: 804-633-5701
Specialties: Miniatures only to customer specs. Patterns: Bowies, daggers and fighters. Technical: Files 440C stainless; uses ivory, abalone, exotic woods and some precious stones. Prices: $100 to $800. Remarks: Part-time maker; first knife sold in 1988. Mark: Initials and last name.

BANAITIS, ROMAS,
84 Winthrop St., Medway, MA 02053, Phone: 774-248-5851, rbanaitis@verizon.net
Specialties: Designing art and fantasy knives. Patterns: Folders, daggers and fixed blades. Technical: Hand-carved blades, handles and fittings in stainless steel, sterling silver and titanium. Prices: Moderate to upscale. Remarks: First knife sold in 1996. Mark: Romas Banaitis.

BANKS, DAVID L.,
99 Blackfoot Ave, Riverton, WY 82501, Phone: 307-856-3154/Cell: 307-851-5599

Specialties: Heavy-duty working straight knives. **Patterns:** Hunters, Bowies and camp knives. **Technical:** Forges Damascus 1084-15N20, L6-W1 pure nickel, 5160, 52100 and his own Damascus; differential heat treat and tempers. Handles made of horn, antlers and exotic wood. Hand-stitched harness leather sheaths. **Prices:** $300 to $2000. **Remarks:** Part-time maker. **Mark:** Banks Blackfoot forged Dave Banks and initials connected.

BARDSLEY, NORMAN P.,
197 Cottage St, Pawtucket, RI 02860, Phone: 401-725-9132, norman.bardsley@verizon.net
Specialties: Working and fantasy knives. **Patterns:** Fighters, boots, fantasy, renaissance and native American in upscale and presentation fashion. **Technical:** Grinds all steels and Damascus. Uses exotic hides for sheaths. **Prices:** $100 to $15,000. **Remarks:** Full-time maker. **Mark:** Last name in script with logo.

BAREFOOT, JOE W.,
1654 Honey Hill, Wilmington, NC 28442, Phone: 910-641-1143
Specialties: Working straight knives of his design. **Patterns:** Hunters, fighters and boots; tantos and survival knives. **Technical:** Grinds D2, 440C and ATS-34. Mirror finishes. Uses ivory and stag on customer request only. **Prices:** $50 to $160; some to $500. **Remarks:** Part-time maker; first knife sold in 1980. **Mark:** Bare footprint.

BARKER, JOHN,
5725 Boulder Bluff Dr., Cumming, GA 30040, Phone: 678-357-8586, barkerknives@bellsouth.net Web: www.barkerknives.com
Specialties: Tactical fixed blades and folders. **Technical:** Stock removal method and CPM and Carpenter powdered technology steels. **Prices:** $150 and up. **Remarks:** First knife made 2006. **Mark:** Snarling dog with "Barker" over the top of its head and "Knives" below.

BARKER, REGGIE,
603 S Park Dr, Springhill, LA 71075, Phone: 318-539-2958, wrbarker@cmaaccess.com; Web: www.reggiebarkerknives.com
Specialties: Camp knives and hatchets. **Patterns:** Bowie, skinning, hunting, camping, fighters, kitchen or customer design. **Technical:** Forges carbon steel and own pattern welded steels. **Prices:** $225 to $2000. **Remarks:** Full-time maker. Winner of 1999 and 2000 Spring Hammering Cutting contest. Winner of Best Value of Show 2001; Arkansas Knife Show and Journeyman Smith. Border Guard Forge. **Mark:** Barker JS.

BARKER, ROBERT G.,
2311 Branch Rd, Bishop, GA 30621, Phone: 706-769-7827
Specialties: Traditional working/using straight knives of his design. **Patterns:** Bowies, hunters and utility knives, ABS Journeyman Smith. **Technical:** Hand forged carbon and Damascus. Forges to shape high-carbon 5160, cable and chain. Differentially heat-treats. **Prices:** $200 to $500; some to $1000. **Remarks:** Spare-time maker; first knife sold in 1987. **Mark:** BARKER/J.S.

BARKER, STUART,
14 Belvoir Close, Oadby, Leicester, England LE2 4SG, Phone: +447887585411, sc_barker@hotmail.com Web: www.barkerknives.co.uk
Specialties: Fixed blade working knives of his design. **Patterns:** Kitchen, hunter, utility/camp knives. **Technical:** Grinds O1, Rw134 & Damasteel, hand rubbed or shot blast finishes. **Prices:** $150 - $500 **Remarks:** Part-time maker, first knife sold 2006. **Mark:** Last initial

BARKES, TERRY,
14844 N. Bluff Rd., Edinburgh, IN 46124, Phone: 812-526-6390, knifenpocket@sbcglobal.net; Web:http:// my.hsonline.net/wizard/TerryBarkesKnives.htm
Specialties: Traditional working straight knives of his designs. **Patterns:** Drop point hunters, boot knives, skinning, fighter, utility, all purpose, camp, and grill knives. **Technical:** Grinds 1095 - 1084 - 52100 - 01, Hollow grinds and flat grinds. Hand rubbed finish from 400 to 2000 grit or High polish buff. Hard edge and soft back, heat treat by maker. Likes File work, natural handle material, bone, stag, water buffalo horn, wildbeast bone, ironwood. **Prices:** $200 and up **Remarks:** Full-time maker, first knifge sold in 2005. Doing business as Barkes Knife Shop. **Marks:** Barkes - USA, Barkes Double Arrow - USA

BARLOW, JANA POIRIER,
3820 Borland Cir, Anchorage, AK 99517, Phone: 907-243-4581

BARNES, AUBREY G.,
11341 Rock Hill Rd, Hagerstown, MD 21740, Phone: 301-223-4587, a.barnes@myactv.net
Specialties: Classic Moran style reproductions and using knives of his own design. **Patterns:** Bowies, hunters, fighters, daggers and utility/camping knives. **Technical:** Forges 5160, 1085, L6 and Damascus, Silver wire inlays. **Prices:** $500 to $5000. **Remarks:** Full-time maker; first knife sold in 1992. Doing business as Falling Waters Forge. **Mark:** First and middle initials, last name, M.S.

BARNES, GARY L.,
Box 138, New Windsor, MD 21776-0138, Phone: 410-635-6243, Fax: 410-635-6243, mail@glbarnes.com; Web: www.glbarnes.com or www.barnespneumatic.com
Specialties: Ornate button lock Damascus folders. **Patterns:** Barnes original. **Technical:** Forges own Damascus. **Prices:** Average $2500. **Remarks:** ABS Master Smith since 1983. **Mark:** Hand engraved logo of letter B pierced by dagger.

BARNES, GREGORY,
266 W Calaveras St, Altadena, CA 91001, Phone: 626-398-0053, snake@annex.com

BARNES, JACK,
PO Box 1315, Whitefish, MT 59937-1315, Phone: 406-862-6078

BARNES, JIM,
PO BOX 50, Christoval, TX 76935, Phone: 325-896-7819
Specialties: Traditional and working straight and folder knives of all designs. Standard or customer request specialties.
Technical: Grinds ATS-34, 440C, and D2 heat treats. All folders have filework.
Prices: Start at $175 for straight and start at $275 for folders.
Remarks: Full-time maker first knife sold in 1984. DBA Jim Barnes Custom Knives
Mark: Logo with Name City and State

BARNES, MARLEN R.,
904 Crestview Dr S, Atlanta, TX 75551-1854, Phone: 903-796-3668, MRBlives@worldnet.att.net
Specialties: Hammer forges random and mosaic Damascus. **Patterns:** Hatchets, straight and folding knives. **Technical:** Hammer forges carbon steel using 5160, 1084 and 52100 with 15N20 and 203E nickel. **Prices:** $150 and up. **Remarks:** Part-time maker; first knife sold 1999. **Mark:** Script M.R.B., other side J.S.

BARNES, WENDELL,
PO Box 272, Clinton, MT 59825, Phone: 406-825-0908
Specialties: Working straight knives. **Patterns:** Hunters, folders, neck knives. **Technical:** Grinds 440C, ATS-34, D2 and Damascus. **Prices:** Start at $75. **Remarks:** Spare-time maker; first knife sold in 1996. **Mark:** First initial, split heart, last name.

BARNES JR., CECIL C.,
141 Barnes Dr, Center Ridge, AR 72027, Phone: 501-893-2267

BARNETT, BRUCE,
PO Box 447, Mundaring 6073, Western Australia, Phone: 61-8-92955502, bruce@barnettcustomknives.com; web: www.barnettcustomknives.com
Specialties: Most types of fixed blades, folders, carving sets. **Patterns:** Hunters, Bowies, Camp Knives, Fighters, Lockback and Slipjoint Folders. **Prices:** $175 up
Remarks: Part time maker. Member Australian Knifemakers Guild and American Bladesmith Society. **Mark:** Barnett

BARNETT, VAN,
BARNETT INT'L INC, 1135 Terminal Way Ste #209, Reno, NV 89502, Phone: 304-727-5512, artknife@suddenlink.net; Web: www.VanBarnett.com
Specialties: Collector grade one-of-a-kind / embellished high art daggers and art folders. **Patterns:** Art daggers and folders. **Technical:** Forges and grinds own Damascus. **Prices:** Upscale. **Remarks:** Designs and makes one-of-a-kind highly embellished art knives using high karat gold, diamonds and other gemstones, pearls, stone and fossil ivories, carved steel guards and blades, all knives are carved and or engraved, does own engraving, carving and other embellishments, sole authorship; full-time maker since 1981. Does one high art collaboration a year with Dellana. Member of ABS. Member Art Knife Invitational Group (AKI) **Mark:** V. H. Barnett or Van Barnett in script.

BARR, JUDSON C.,
1905 Pickwick Circle, Irving, TX 75060, Phone: 972-790-7195, judsonbarrknives@yahoo.com
Specialties: Bowies. **Patterns:** Sheffield and Early American. **Technical:** Forged carbon steel and Damascus. Also stock removal. **Remarks:** Journeyman member of ABS. **Mark:** Barr.

BARRETT, RICK L. (TOSHI HISA),
18943 CR 18, Goshen, IN 46528, Phone: 574-533-4297, barrettrick@hotmail.com
Specialties: Japanese-style blades from sushi knives to katana and fantasy pieces. **Patterns:** Swords, axes, spears/lances, hunter and utility knives. **Technical:** Forges and grinds Damascus and carbon steels, occasionally uses stainless. **Prices:** $250 to $4000+. **Remarks:** Full-time bladesmith, jeweler. **Mark:** Japanese mei on Japanese pieces and stylized initials.

BARRON, BRIAN,
123 12th Ave, San Mateo, CA 94402, Phone: 650-341-2683
Specialties: Traditional straight knives. **Patterns:** Daggers, hunters and swords. **Technical:** Grinds 440C, ATS-34 and 1095. Sculpts bolsters using an S-curve. **Prices:** $130 to $270; some to $1500. **Remarks:** Part-time maker; first knife sold in 1993. **Mark:** Diamond Drag "Barron."

BARRY, SCOTT,
Box 354, Laramie, WY 82073, Phone: 307-721-8038, scottyb@uwyo.edu
Specialties: Currently producing mostly folders, also make fixed blade hunters & fillet knives. **Technical:** Steels used are 440/C, ATS/34, 154/CM, S30V, Damasteel & Mike Norris stainless Damascus. **Prices:** Range from $300 $1000. **Remarks:** Part-time maker. First knife sold in 1972. **Mark:** DSBarry, etched on blade.

BARRY III, JAMES J.,
115 Flagler Promenade No., West Palm Beach, FL 33405, Phone: 561-832-4197
Specialties: High-art working straight knives of his design also high art tomahawks. **Patterns:** Hunters, daggers and fishing knives. **Technical:** Grinds 440C only. Prefers exotic materials for handles. Most knives embellished with filework, carving and scrimshaw. Many pieces designed to stand unassisted. **Prices:** $500 to $10,000. **Remarks:** Part-time maker; first knife sold in 1975. Guild member (Knifemakers) since 1991. **Mark:** Branded initials as a J and B together.

BARTH, J.D.,
101 4th St, PO Box 186, Alberton, MT 59820, Phone: 406-722-4557, mtdeerhunter@blackfoot.net; Web: www.jdbarthcustomknives.com
Specialties: Working and fancy straight knives of his design. LinerLock® folders, stainless and Damascus, fully file worked, nitre bluing. Technical: Grinds ATS-34, 440-C, stainless and carbon Damascus. Uses variety of natural handle materials and Micarta. Likes dovetailed bolsters. Filework on most knives, full and tapered tangs. Makes custom fit sheaths for each knife. Mark: Name over maker, city and state.

BARTLOW, JOHN,
5078 Coffeen Ave, Sheridan, WY 82801, Phone: 307 673-4941, bartlow@bresnan.net
Specialties: Working hunters, greenriver skinners, classic capers and bird & trouts. Technical: ATS-34, CPM154, Damascus available on all linerlocks. Prices: Full-time maker, guild member from 1988. Mark: Bartlow, Sheridan WYO.

BASKETT, BARBARA,
427 Sutzer Ck Rd, Eastview, KY 42732, Phone: 270-862-5019, baskettknives@windstream.net
Specialties: Hunters and LinerLocks. Technical: 440-C, CPM 154, S30V. Prices: $250 and up. Mark: B. Baskett.

BASKETT, LEE GENE,
427 Sutzer Ck. Rd., Eastview, KY 42732, Phone: 270-862-5019, Fax: Cell: 270-766-8724, baskettknives@hotmail.com Web: www.baskettknives.com
Specialties: Fancy working knives and fancy art pieces, often set up in fancy desk stands.
Patterns: Fighters, Bowies, and Surival Knives; lockback folders and liner locks along with traditional styles. Cutting competition knives.
Technical: Grinds O1, 440-c, S30V, power CPM154, CPM 4, D2, buys Damascus. Filework provided on most knives.
Prices: $250 and up.
Remarks: Part-time maker, first knife sold in 1980.
Mark: Baskett

BASSETT, DAVID J.,
P.O. Box 69-102, Glendene, Auckland 0645, NEW ZEALAND, Phone: 64 9 818 9083, Fax: 64 9 818 9013, david@customknifemaking.co.nz; Web:www.customknifemaking.co.nz
Specialties: Working/using knives. Patterns: Hunters, fighters, boot, skinners, tanto. Technical: Grinds 440C, 12C27, D2 and some Damascus via stock removal method. Prices: $150 to $500. Remarks: Part-time maker, first knife sold in 2006. Also carries range of natural and synthetic handle material, pin stock etc. for sale. Mark: Name over country in semi-circular design.

BATLEY, MARK S.,
PO Box 217, Wake, VA 23176, Phone: 804 776-7794

BATSON, JAMES,
176 Brentwood Lane, Madison, AL 35758
Specialties: Forged Damascus blades and fittings in collectible period pieces. Patterns: Integral art knives, Bowies, folders, American-styled blades and miniatures. Technical: Forges carbon steel and his Damascus. Prices: $150 to $1800; some to $4500. Remarks: Semi retired full-time maker; first knife sold in 1978. Mark: Name, bladesmith with horse's head.

BATSON, RICHARD G.,
6591 Waterford Rd, Rixeyville, VA 22737, Phone: 540-937-2318
Specialties: Military, utility and fighting knives in working and presentation grade. Patterns: Daggers, combat and utility knives. Technical: Grinds O1, 1095 and 440C. Etches and scrimshaws; offers polished, Parkerized finishes. Prices: $350 to $1500. Remarks: Semi-retired, limit production. First knife sold in 1958. Mark: Bat in circle, hand-signed and serial numbered.

BATTS, KEITH,
450 Manning Rd, Hooks, TX 75561, Phone: 903-277-8466, kbatts@valornet.com
Specialties: Working straight knives of his design or to customer specs. Patterns: Bowies, hunters, skinners, camp knives and others. Technical: Forges 5160 and his Damascus; offers filework Prices: $245 to $895. Remarks: Part-time maker; first knife sold in 1988. Mark: Last name.

BAUCHOP, ROBERT,
PO Box 330, Munster, Kwazulu-Natal 4278, SOUTH AFRICA, Phone: +27 39 3192449
Specialties: Fantasy knives; working and using knives of his design and to customer specs. Patterns: Hunters, swords, utility/camp knives, diver's knives and large swords. Technical: Grinds Sandvick 12C27, D2, 440C. Uses South African hardwoods red ivory, wild olive, African blackwood, etc. on handles. Prices: $200 to $800; some to $2000. Remarks: Full-time maker; first knife sold in 1986. Doing business as Bauchop Custom Knives and Swords. Mark: Viking helmet with Bauchop (bow and chopper) crest.

BAXTER, DALE,
291 County Rd 547, Trinity, AL 35673, Phone: 256-355-3626, dale@baxterknives.com
Specialties: Bowies, fighters, and hunters. Patterns: No patterns: all unique true customs. Technical: Hand forge and hand finish. Steels: 1095 and L6 for carbon blades, 1095/L6 for Damascus. Remarks: Full-time bladesmith and sold first knife in 1998. Mark: Dale Baxter (script) and J.S. on reverse.

BEAM, JOHN R.,
1310 Foothills Rd, Kalispell, MT 59901, Phone: 406-755-2593
Specialties: Classic, high-art and working straight knives of his design. Patterns: Bowies and hunters. Technical: Grinds 440C, Damascus and scrap. Prices: $175 to $600; some to $3000. Remarks: Part-time maker; first knife sold in 1950. Doing business as Beam's Knives. Mark: Beam's Knives.

BEASLEY, GENEO,
PO Box 339, Wadsworth, NV 89442, Phone: 775-575-2584

BEATTY, GORDON H.,
121 Petty Rd, Seneca, SC 29672, Phone: 864-882-6278
Specialties: Working straight knives, some fancy. Patterns: Traditional patterns, mini-skinners and letter openers. Technical: Grinds 440C, D2 and ATS-34; makes knives one-at-a-time. Prices: $75 to $450. Remarks: Part-time maker; first knife sold in 1982. Mark: Name.

BEATY, ROBERT B.,
CUTLER, 1995 Big Flat Rd, Missoula, MT 59804, Phone: 406-549-1818
Specialties: Plain and fancy working knives and collector pieces; will accept custom orders. Patterns: Hunters, Bowies, utility, kitchen and camp knives; locking folders. Technical: Grinds D-2, ATS-34, Dendritic D-2, makes all tool steel Damascus, forges 1095, 5160, 52100. Prices: $150 to $600, some to $1100. Remarks: Full-time maker; first knife sold 1995. Mark: Stainless: First name, middle initial, last name, city and state. Carbon: Last name stamped on Ricasso.

BEAUCHAMP, GAETAN,
125 de la Rivire, Stoneham, PQ, CANADA G3C 0P6, Phone: 418-848-1914, Fax: 418-848-6859, knives@gbeauchamp.ca; Web: www.gbeauchamp.ca
Specialties: Working knives and folders of his design and to customer specs. Patterns: Hunters, fighters, fantasy knives. Technical: Grinds ATS-34, 440C, Damascus. Scrimshaws on ivory; specializes in buffalo horn and black backgrounds. Offers a variety of handle materials. Prices: Start at $250. Remarks: Full-time maker; first knife sold in 1992. Mark: Signature etched on blade.

BECKER, FRANZ,
AM Kreuzberg 2, 84533, Marktl/Inn, GERMANY 08678-8020
Specialties: Stainless steel knives in working sizes. Patterns: Semi- and full-integral knives; interframe folders. Technical: Grinds stainless steels; likes natural handle materials. Prices: $200 to $2000. Mark: Name, country.

BEERS, RAY,
8 Manorbrook Rd, Monkton, MD 21111, Phone: Summer 410-472-2229

BEERS, RAY,
2501 Lakefront Dr, Lake Wales, FL 33898, Phone: Winter 863-696-3036, rbknives@copper.net

BEETS, MARTY,
390 N 5th Ave, Williams Lake, BC, CANADA V2G 2G4, Phone: 250-392-7199
Specialties: Working and collectable straight knives of his own design. Patterns: Hunter, skinners, Bowies and utility knives. Technical: Grinds 440C-does all his own work including heat treating. Uses a variety of handle material specializing in exotic hardwoods, antler and horn. Price: $125 to $400. Remarks: Wife, Sandy does handmade/hand stitched sheaths. First knife sold in 1988. Business name Beets Handmade Knives.

BEGG, TODD M.,
420 169 St S, Spanaway, WA 98387, Phone: 253-531-2113, tntbegg@comcast.net Web: www.beggknives.com
Specialties: High-grade tacticle folders and fixed blades. Patterns: Folders, integrals, fighters. Technical: Specializes in flipper folders using "IK135" bearing system. Price: $400 - $15,000. Remarks: Uses modern designs and materials.

BEHNKE, WILLIAM,
8478 Dell Rd, Kingsley, MI 49649, Phone: 231-263-7447, bill@billbehnkeknives.com Web: www.billbehnkeknives.com
Specialties: Hunters, belt knives, folders, hatchets and tomahawks. Patterns: Traditional styling in moderate-sized straight and folding knives. Technical: Forges own Damascus, W-2 and CRU Forge V. Prices: $150 to $2000. Remarks: Part-time maker. Mark: Bill Behnke Knives.

BELL, DON,
Box 98, Lincoln, MT 59639, Phone: 406-362-3208, dlb@linctel.net
Patterns: Folders, hunters and custom orders. Technical: Carbon steel 52100, 5160, 1095, 1084. Making own Damascus. Flat grinds. Natural handle material including fossil, ivory, pearl, & ironwork. Remarks: Full-time maker. First knife sold in 1999. Mark: Last name.

BELL, DONALD,
2 Division St, Bedford, Nova Scotia, CANADA B4A 1Y8, Phone: 902-835-2623, donbell@accesswave.ca; Web: www.bellknives.com
Specialties: Fancy knives: carved and pierced folders of his own design. Patterns: Locking folders, pendant knives, jewelry knives. Technical: Grinds Damascus, pierces and carves blades. Prices: $500 to $2000, some to $3000. Remarks: Spare-time maker; first knife sold in 1993. Mark: Bell symbol with first initial inside.

BELL, MICHAEL,
88321 N Bank Lane, Coquille, OR 97423, Phone: 541-396-3605, michael@dragonflyforge.com; Web: www. Dragonflyforge.com
Specialties: Full line of combat quality Japanese swords. Patterns: Traditional tanto to katana. Technical: Handmade steel and welded cable. Prices: Swords from bare blades to complete high art $1500 to $28,000. Remarks: Studied with Japanese master Nakajima Muneyoshi. Instruction in sword crafts. Working in partnership with son, Gabriel. Mark: Dragonfly in shield or tombo kunimitsu.

BELL, TONY,
PO Box 24, Woodland, AL 36280, Phone: 256-449-2655, tbell905@aol.com
Specialties: Hand forged period knives and tomahawks. Art knives and knives made for everyday use. Technical: Makes own Damascus. Forges 1095, 5160,1080,L6 steels. Does own heat treating. Prices: $75-$1200. Remarks: Full time maker. Mark: Bell symbol with initial T in the middle.

BENDIK, JOHN,
7076 Fitch Rd, Olmsted Falls, OH 44138

BENJAMIN JR., GEORGE,
3001 Foxy Ln, Kissimmee, FL 34746, Phone: 407-846-7259
 Specialties: Fighters in various styles to include Persian, Moro and military. **Patterns:** Daggers, skinners and one-of-a-kind grinds. **Technical:** Forges O1, D2, A2, 5160 and Damascus. Favors Pakkawood, Micarta, and mirror or Parkerized finishes. Makes unique para-military leather sheaths. **Prices:** $150 to $600; some to $1200. **Remarks:** Doing business as The Leather Box. **Mark:** Southern Pride Knives.

BENNETT, BRETT C,
4717 Sullivan St, Cheyenne, WY 82009, Phone: 307-220-3919, brett@bennettknives.com; Web: www.bennettknives.com
 Specialties: Hand-rubbed finish on all blades. **Patterns:** Most fixed blade patterns. **Technical:** ATS-34, D-2, 1084/15N20 Damascus, 1084 forged. **Prices:** $100 and up. **Mark:** "B.C. Bennett" in script or "Bennett" stamped in script.

BENNETT, GLEN C,
5821 S Stewart Blvd, Tucson, AZ 85706

BENNETT, PETER,
PO BOX 143, Engadine N.S.W. 2233, AUSTRALIA, Phone: 02-520-4975 (home), Fax: 02-528-8219 (work)
 Specialties: Fancy and embellished working and using straight knives to customer specs and in standard patterns. **Patterns:** Fighters, hunters, bird/trout and fillet knives. **Technical:** Grinds 440C, ATS-34 and Damascus. Uses rare Australian desert timbers for handles. **Prices:** $90 to $500; some to $1500. **Remarks:** Full-time maker; first knife sold in 1985. **Mark:** First and middle initials, last name; country.

BENNICA, CHARLES,
11 Chemin du Salet, 34190 Moules et Baucels, FRANCE, Phone: +33 4 67 73 42 40, cbennica@bennica-knives.com; Web: www.bennica-knives.com
 Specialties: Fixed blades and folding knives; the latter with slick closing mechanisms with push buttons to unlock blades. Unique handle shapes, signature to the maker. **Technical:** 416 stainless steel frames for folders and ATS-34 blades. Also specializes in Damascus.

BENSINGER, J. W.,
583 Jug Brook Rd., Marshfield, VT 05658, Phone: 802-917-1789, jwbensinger@gmail.com Web: www.vermontbladesmith.com
 Specialties: Working hunters, bowies for work and defense, and Finnish patterns. Occasional folders. **Technical:** High performance handforged knives in 5160, 52100, 1080, and in-house damascus. **Prices:** Range from $130 for simple bushcraft knives to $500 for larger knives. Damascus prices on request. **Remarks:** First knife made in 1980 or so. Full-time maker. Customer designs welcome. **Mark:** "JWB" and year in cursive.

BENSON, DON,
2505 Jackson St #112, Escalon, CA 95320, Phone: 209-838-7921
 Specialties: Working straight knives of his design. **Patterns:** Axes, Bowies, tantos and hunters. **Technical:** Grinds 440C. **Prices:** $100 to $150; some to $400. **Remarks:** Spare-time maker; first knife sold in 1980. **Mark:** Name.

BENTLEY, C L,
2405 Hilltop Dr, Albany, GA 31707, Phone: 912-432-6656

BER, DAVE,
656 Miller Rd, San Juan Island, WA 98250, Phone: 206-378-7230
 Specialties: Working straight and folding knives for the sportsman; welcomes customer designs. **Patterns:** Hunters, skinners, Bowies, kitchen and fishing knives. **Technical:** Forges and grinds saw blade steel, wire Damascus, O1, L6, 5160 and 440C. **Prices:** $100 to $300; some to $500. **Remarks:** Full-time maker; first knife sold in 1985. **Mark:** Last name.

BERG, LOTHAR,
37 Hillcrest Ln, Kitchener ON, CANADA NZK 1S9, Phone: 519-745-3260; 519-745-3260

BERGER, MAX A.,
5716 John Richard Ct, Carmichael, CA 95608, Phone: 916-972-9229, bergerknives@aol.com
 Specialties: Fantasy and working/using straight knives of his design. **Patterns:** Fighters, hunters and utility/camp knives. **Technical:** Grinds ATS-34 and 440C. Offers fileworks and combinations of mirror polish and satin finish blades. **Prices:** $200 to $600; some to $2500. **Remarks:** Part-time maker; first knife sold in 1992. **Mark:** Last name.

BERGH, ROGER,
Dalkarlsa 291, 91598 Bygdea, SWEDEN, Phone: 469-343-0061, knivroger@hotmail.com; Web: www.rogerbergh.com
 Specialties: Collectible all-purpose straight-blade knives. Damascus steel blades, carving and artistic design knives are heavily influenced by nature and have an organic hand crafted feel.

BERGLIN, BRUCE D,
17441 Lake Terrace Place, Mount Vernon, WA 98274, Phone: 360-422-8603, bruce@berglins.com
 Specialties: Working and using fixed blades and folders of his own design. **Patterns:** Hunters, boots, bowies, utility, liner locks and slip joints some with vintage finish. **Technical:** Forges carbon steel, grinds carbon steel. Prefers natural handle material. **Prices:** Start at $300. **Remarks:** Part-time maker since 1998. **Mark:** First initial, middle initial and last name, surrounded with an oval.

BERTOLAMI, JUAN CARLOS,
Av San Juan 575, Neuquen, ARGENTINA 8300, fliabertolami@infovia.com.ar
 Specialties: Hunting and country labor knives. All of them unique high qual-

ity pieces and supplies collectors too. **Technical:** Austrian stainless steel and elephant, hippopotamus and orca ivory, as well as ebony and other fine woods for the handles.

BERTUZZI, ETTORE,
Via Partigiani 3, 24068 Seriate (Bergamo), ITALY, Phone: 035-294262, Fax: 035-294262
 Specialties: Classic straight knives and folders of his design, to customer specs and in standard patterns. **Patterns:** Bowies, hunters and locking folders. **Technical:** Grinds ATS-34, D3, D2 and various Damascus. **Prices:** $300 to $500. **Remarks:** Part-time maker; first knife sold in 1993. **Mark:** Name etched on ricasso.

BESEDICK, FRANK E,
1257 Country Club Road, Monongahela, PA 15063-1057, Phone: 724-292-8016, bxtr.bez3@verizon.net
 Specialties: Traditional working and using straight knives of his design. **Patterns:** Hunters, utility/camp knives and miniatures; buckskinner blades and tomahawks. **Technical:** Forges and grinds 5160, O1 and Damascus. Offers filework and scrimshaw. **Prices:** $75 to $300; some to $750. **Remarks:** Part-time maker; first knife sold in 1990. **Mark:** Name or initials.

BESHARA, BRENT (BESH),
PO BOX 557, Holyrood, NL, CANADA A0A 2R0, Phone: 705-428-3152, BESH@beshknives.com Web: www.beshknives.com
 Specialties: Tactical/utility fighting fixed blades and folders. **Patterns:** BESH Wedge, daggers, fighters boot, neck and custom designs. **Technical:** Custom design work, grinds 0-1, D-2, 440C. Offers kydex sheaths and does own Paragon heat treating. **Prices:** Start at $165. **Remarks:** Inventor of BESH Wedge, custom maker and designer since 2000. Retired Special Forces, Navy bomb disposal diver. Lifelong martial artist. **Mark:** "BESH" stamped.

BEST, RON,
1489 Adams Lane, Stokes, NC 27884, Phone: 252-714-1264, ronbestknives@msn.com; Web: www.ronbestknives.com
 Specialties: All integral fixed knives, interframe.**Patterns:** Bowies, hunters, fighters, fantasy, daggers & swords. **Technical:** Grinds 440C, D-2 and ATS-34. **Prices:** $600 to $8000.

BETANCOURT, ANTONIO L.,
5718 Beefwood Ct., St. Louis, MO 63129, Phone: 314-306-1869, bet2001@charter.net
 Specialties: One-of-a-kind fixed blades and art knives. **Patterns:** Hunters and Bowies with embellished handles. **Technical:** Uses cast sterling silver and lapidary with fine gemstones, fossil ivory, and scrimshaw. Grinds Damascus and 440C. **Prices:** $100 to $800. **Remarks:** Part-time maker, first knife sold in 1974. **Mark:** Initials in cursive.

BEUKES, TINUS,
83 Henry St, Risiville, Vereeniging 1939, SOUTH AFRICA, Phone: 27 16 423 2053
 Specialties: Working straight knives. **Patterns:** Hunters, skinners and kitchen knives. **Technical:** Grinds D2, 440C and chain, cable and stainless Damascus. **Prices:** $80 to $180. **Remarks:** Part-time maker; first knife sold in 1993. **Mark:** Full name, city, logo.

BEVERLY II, LARRY H,
PO Box 741, Spotsylvania, VA 22553, Phone: 540-898-3951
 Specialties: Working straight knives, slip-joints and liner locks. Welcomes customer designs. **Patterns:** Bowies, hunters, guard less fighters and miniatures. **Technical:** Grinds 440C, A2 and O1. **Prices:** $125 to $1000. **Remarks:** Part-time maker; first knife sold in 1986. **Mark:** Initials or last name in script.

BEZUIDENHOUT, BUZZ,
PO BOX 28284, Malvern, KZN, SOUTH AFRICA 4055, Phone: 031-4632827, Fax: 031-4632827, buzzbee@mweb.co.za
 Specialties: Working and Fancy Folders, my or customer design.**Patterns:** Boots, hunters, kitchen knives and utility/camp knives. **Technical:** Use 12-C-27 + stainless damascus, some carbon damascus. Uses local hardwoods, horn: kudu, impala, buffalo, giraffe bone and ivory for handles. **Prices:** $250 to upscale. **Remarks:** Part-time maker; first knife sold in 1985. Member S.A. Knife Makers Guild**Mark:** First name with a bee emblem.

BIGGERS, GARY,
VENTURA KNIVES, 1278 Colina Vista, Ventura, CA 93003, Phone: 805-658-6610, Fax: 805-658-6610
 Specialties: Fixed blade knives of his design. **Patterns:** Hunters, boots/fighters, Bowies and utility knives. **Technical:** Grinds ATS-34, O1 and commercial Damascus. **Prices:** $150 to $550. **Remarks:** Part-time maker: first knife sold in 1996. Doing business as Ventura Knives. **Mark:** First and last name, city and state.

BILLGREN, PER,
Stallgatan 9, S815 76 Soderfors, SWEDEN, Phone: +46 293 30600, Fax: +46 293 30124, mail@damasteel.se Web:www.damasteel.se
 Specialties: Damasteel, stainless Damascus steels. **Patterns:** Bluetongue, Heimskringla, Muhammad's ladder, Rose, Twist, Odin's eye, Vinland, Hakkapelliitta. **Technical:** Modern Damascus steel made by patented powder metallurgy method. **Prices:** $80 to $180. **Remarks:** Damasteel is available through distributors around the globe.

BINGENHEIMER, BRUCE,
553 Tiffany Dr., Spring Creek, NV 89815, Phone: 775-934-6295, mbing@citlink.net
 Specialties: Forging fixed blade hunters, bowies, fighters. **Technical:** Forges own Damascus. Steel choices 5160, 1084. Damascus steels 15N20, 1080. **Prices:** $300 and up. **Remarks:** ABS Journeyman Smith 2010. Member of Montana Knife Makers Association and Oregon Knife Collector's Association. **Mark:** Bingenheimer (arched over) M B.

custom knifemakers

BIRDWELL, IRA LEE,
PO Box 1448, Congress, AZ 85332, Phone: 928-925-3258, heli.ira@gmail.com
Specialties: Special orders. **Mark:** Engraved signature.

BIRNBAUM, EDWIN,
9715 Hamocks Blvd I 206, Miami, FL 33196

BISH, HAL,
9347 Sweetbriar Trace, Jonesboro, GA 30236, Phone: 770-477-2422, halbish@hp.com

BISHER, WILLIAM (BILL),
1015 Beck Road, Denton, NC 27239, Phone: 336-859-4686, blackturtleforge@wildblue.net;Web: www.blackturtleforge.com
Specialties: Period pieces, also contemporary belt knives, friction folders. **Patterns:** Own design, hunters, camp/utility, Bowies, belt axes, neck knives, carving sets. **Technical:** Forges straight high carbon steels, and own Damascus, grinds ATS34 and 154CM. Uses natural handle materials (wood, bone, stag horn), micarta and stabilized wood.**Prices:** Starting at $75 - $2500. **Remarks:** President North Carolina Custom Knifemakers Guild, member ABS, Full-time maker as of 2007, first knife made 1989, all work in house, blades and sheaths **Mark:** Last name under crown and turtle

BIZZELL, ROBERT,
145 Missoula Ave, Butte, MT 59701, Phone: 406-782-4403, patternweld@yahoo.com
Specialties: Damascus Bowies. **Patterns:** Composite, mosaic and traditional. **Technical:** Fixed blades & LinerLock® folders. **Prices:** Fixed blades start at $275. Folders start at $500. **Remarks:** Currently not taking orders. **Mark:** Hand signed.

BLACK, EARL,
3466 South, 700 East, Salt Lake City, UT 84106, Phone: 801-466-8395
Specialties: High-art straight knives and folders; period pieces. **Patterns:** Boots, Bowies and daggers; lockers and gents. **Technical:** Grinds 440C and 154CM. Buys some Damascus. Scrimshaws and engraves. **Prices:** $200 to $1800; some to $2500 and higher. **Remarks:** Full-time maker; first knife sold in 1980. **Mark:** Name, city, state.

BLACK, SCOTT,
27100 Leetown Rd, Picayune, MS 39466, Phone: 601-799-5939, copperheadforge@telepak.net
Specialties: Friction folders; fighters. **Patterns:** Bowies, fighters, hunters, smoke hawks, friction folders, daggers. **Technical:** All forged, all work done by him, own hand-stitched leather work; own heat-treating. **Prices:** $100 to $2200. **Remarks:** ABS Journeyman Smith. Cabel / Damascus/ High Carbone. **Mark:** Hot Mark - Copperhead Snake.

BLACK, TOM,
921 Grecian NW, Albuquerque, NM 87107, Phone: 505-344-2549, blackknives@comcast.net
Specialties: Working knives to fancy straight knives of his design. **Patterns:** Drop-point skinners, folders, using knives, Bowies and daggers. **Technical:** Grinds 440C, 154CM, ATS-34, A2, D2 and Damascus. Offers engraving and scrimshaw. **Prices:** $250 and up; some over $8500. **Remarks:** Full-time maker; first knife sold in 1970. **Mark:** Name, city.

BLACKWELL, ZANE,
PO BOX 234, Eden, TX 76837, Phone: 325-869-8821, blackwellknives@hotmail.com
Specialties: Hunters and slipjoint folders. **Patterns:** Drop point fixed-blade hunter and classic slipjoint patterns. **Prices:** Hunters start at $200, folders at $250. **Mark:** Name and Eden, Texas.

BLACKWOOD, NEIL,
7032 Willow Run, Lakeland, FL 33813, Phone: 863-701-0126, neil@blackwoodknives.com; Web: www.blackwoodknives.com
Specialties: Fixed blades and folders. **Technical:** Blade steels D2 Talonite, Stellite, CPM S30V and RWL 34. Handle materials: G-10 carbon fiber and Micarta in the synthetics: giraffe bone and exotic woods on the natural side. **Remarks:** Makes everything from the frames to the stop pins, pivot pins: everything but the stainless screws; one factory/custom collaboration (the Hybrid Hunter) with Outdoor Edge is in place and negotiations are under way for one with Benchmade.

BLANCHARD, G R (GARY),
PO BOX 292, Dandridge, TN 37725, Phone: 865-397-9515, blanchardcustomknives@yahoo.com; Web: www.blanchardscutlery.com
Specialties: Fancy folders with patented button blade release and high-art straight knives of his design. **Patterns:** Boots, daggers and locking folders. **Technical:** Grinds 440C and ATS-34 and Damascus. Engraves his knives. **Prices:** $1500 to $18,000 or more. **Remarks:** Full-time maker; first knife sold in 1989. **Mark:** First and middle initials, last name or last name only.

BLAUM, ROY,
319 N Columbia St, Covington, LA 70433, Phone: 985-893-1060
Specialties: Working straight knives and folders of his design; lightweight easy-open folders. **Patterns:** Hunters, boots, fishing and woodcarving/whittling knives. **Technical:** Grinds A2, D2, O1, 154CM and ATS-34. Offers leatherwork. **Prices:** $40 to $800; some higher. **Remarks:** Full-time maker; first knife sold in 1976. **Mark:** Engraved signature or etched logo.

BLOODWORTH CUSTOM KNIVES,
3502 W. Angelica Dr., Meridian, ID 83646, Phone: 208-888-7778
Patterns: Working straight knives, hunters, skinners, bowies, utility knives of his designs or customer specs. Scagel knives. Period knives and traditional frontier knives and sheaths. **Technical:** Grinds D2, ATS34, 154CM, 5160, 01, Damascus, Heat treats, natural and composite handle materials. **Prices:** $185.00 to $1,500. **Remarks:** Roger Smith knife maker. Full-time maker; first knife sold in 1978 **Mark:** Sword over BLOODWORTH.

BLOOMER, ALAN T,
PO Box 154, 116 E 6th St, Maquon, IL 61458, Phone: 309-875-3583, alant.bloomer@winco.net
Specialties: Folders & straight knives & custom pen maker. **Patterns:** All kinds. **Technical:** Does own heat treating. **Prices:** $400 to $1000. **Remarks:** Part-time maker. No orders. **Mark:** Stamp Bloomer.

BLUM, KENNETH,
1729 Burleson, Brenham, TX 77833, Phone: 979-836-9577
Specialties: Traditional working straight knives of his design. **Patterns:** Camp knives, hunters and Bowies. **Technical:** Forges 5160; grinds 440C and D2. Uses exotic woods and Micarta for handles. **Prices:** $150 to $300. **Remarks:** Part-time maker; first knife sold in 1978. **Mark:** Last name on ricasso.

BOARDMAN, GUY,
39 Mountain Ridge R, New Germany 3619, SOUTH AFRICA, Phone: 031-726-921
Specialties: American and South African-styles. **Patterns:** Bowies, American and South African hunters, plus more. **Technical:** Grinds Bohler steels, some ATS-34. **Prices:** $100 to $600. **Remarks:** Part-time maker; first knife sold in 1986. **Mark:** Name, city, country.

BOCHMAN, BRUCE,
183 Howard Place, Grants Pass, OR 97526, Phone: 541-471-1985, 183bab@echoweb.net
Specialties: Hunting, fishing, bird and tactical knives. **Patterns:** Hunters, fishing and bird knives. **Technical:** ATS34, 154CM, mirror or satin finish. **Prices:** $250 to $350; some to $750. **Remarks:** Part-time maker; first knife sold in 1977. **Mark:** Hand made by B. Bochman.

BODEN, HARRY,
Via Gellia Mill, Bonsall Matlock, Derbyshire DE4 2AJ, ENGLAND, Phone: 0629-825176
Specialties: Traditional working straight knives and folders of his design. **Patterns:** Hunters, locking folders and utility/camp knives. **Technical:** Grinds Sandvik 12C27, D2 and O1. **Prices:** £70 to £150; some to £300. **Remarks:** Full-time maker; first knife sold in 1986. **Mark:** Full name.

BODNER, GERALD "JERRY",
4102 Spyglass Ct, Louisville, KY 40229, Phone: 502-968-5946
Specialties: Fantasy straight knives in standard patterns. **Patterns:** Bowies, fighters, hunters and micro-miniature knives. **Technical:** Grinds Damascus, 440C and D2. Offers filework. **Prices:** $35 to $180. **Remarks:** Part-time maker; first knife sold in 1993. **Mark:** Last name in script and JAB in oval above knives.

BODOLAY, ANTAL,
Rua Wilson Soares Fernandes #31, Planalto, Belo Horizonte MG-31730-700, BRAZIL, Phone: 031-494-1885
Specialties: Working folders and fixed blades of his design or to customer specs; some art daggers and period pieces. **Patterns:** Daggers, hunters, locking folders, utility knives and Khukris. **Technical:** Grinds D6, high-carbon steels and 420 stainless. Forges files on request. **Prices:** $30 to $350. **Remarks:** Full-time maker; first knife sold in 1965. **Mark:** Last name in script.

BOEHLKE, GUENTER,
Parkstrasse 2, 56412 Grossholbach, GERMANY 2602-5440, Boehlke-Messer@t-online.de; Web: www.boehlke-messer.de
Specialties: Classic working/using straight knives of his design. **Patterns:** Hunters, utility/camp knives and ancient remakes. **Technical:** Grinds Damascus, CPM-T-440V and 440C. Inlays gemstones and ivory. **Prices:** $220 to $700; some to $2000. **Remarks:** Spare-time maker; first knife sold in 1985. **Mark:** Name, address and bow and arrow.

BOGUSZEWSKI, PHIL,
PO Box 99329, Lakewood, WA 98499, Phone: 253-581-7096, knives01@aol.com
Specialties: Working folders—some fancy—mostly of his design. **Patterns:** Folders, slip-joints and lockers; also makes anodized titanium frame folders. **Technical:** Grinds BG42 and Damascus; offers filework. **Prices:** $550 to $3000. **Remarks:** Full-time maker; first knife sold in 1979. **Mark:** Name, city and state.

BOJTOS, ARPAD,
Dobsinskeho 10, 98403 Lucenec, SLOVAKIA, Phone: 00421-47 4333512, botjos@stonline.sk; Web: www.arpadbojtos.sk
Specialties: Art knives. **Patterns:** Daggers, fighters and hunters. **Technical:** Grinds ATS-34. Carves on steel, handle materials and sheaths. **Prices:** $5000 to $10,000; some over. **Remarks:** Full-time maker; first knife sold in 1990. **Mark:** AB.

BOLEWARE, DAVID,
PO Box 96, Carson, MS 39427, Phone: 601-943-5372
Specialties: Traditional and working/using straight knives of his design, to

customer specs and in standard patterns. **Patterns:** Bowies, hunters and utility/camp knives. **Technical:** Grinds ATS-34, 440C and Damascus. **Prices:** $85 to $350; some to $600. **Remarks:** Part-time maker; first knife sold in 1989. **Mark:** First and last name, city, state.

BOLEY, JAMIE,
PO Box 477, Parker, SD 57053, Phone: 605-297-0014, jamie@polarbearforge.com
Specialties: Working knives and historical influenced reproductions. **Patterns:** Hunters, skinners, scramasaxes, and others.**Technical:** Forges 5160, O1, L6, 52100, W1, W2 makes own Damascus. **Prices:** Starts at $125. **Remarks:** Part-time maker. **Mark:** Polar bear paw print with name on the left side and Polar Bear Forge on the right.

BONASSI, FRANCO,
Via Nicoletta 4, Pordenone 33170, ITALY, Phone: 0434-550821, frank.bonassi@alice.it
Specialties: Fancy and working one-of-a-kind folder knives of his design. **Patterns:** Folders, linerlocks and back locks. **Technical:** Grinds CPM, ATS-34, 154CM and commercial Damascus. Uses only titanium foreguards and pommels. **Prices:** Start at $350. **Remarks:** Spare-time maker; first knife sold in 1988. Has made cutlery for several celebrities; Gen. Schwarzkopf, Fuzzy Zoeller, etc. **Mark:** FRANK.

BOOCO, GORDON,
175 Ash St, PO Box 174, Hayden, CO 81639, Phone: 970-276-3195
Specialties: Fancy working straight knives of his design and to customer specs. **Patterns:** Hunters and Bowies. **Technical:** Grinds 440C, D2 and A2. Heat-treats. **Prices:** $150 to $350; some $600 and higher. **Remarks:** Part-time maker; first knife sold in 1984. **Mark:** Last name with push dagger artwork.

BOOS, RALPH,
6018-37A Avenue NW, Edmonton, Alberta, CANADA T6L 1H4, Phone: 780-463-7094
Specialties: Classic, fancy and fantasy miniature knives and swords of his design or to customer specs. **Patterns:** Bowies, daggers and swords. **Technical:** Hand files O1, stainless and Damascus. Engraves and carves. Does heat bluing and acid etching. **Prices:** $125 to $350; some to $1000. **Remarks:** Part-time maker; first knife sold in 1982. **Mark:** First initials back to back.

BOOTH, PHILIP W,
301 S Jeffery Ave, Ithaca, MI 48847, Phone: 989-875-2844, Web: wwwphilipbooth.com
Specialties: Folding knives of his design using various mechanisms. **Patterns:** "Minnow" folding knives, a series of small folding knives started in 1996 and changing yearly. One of a kind hot-rod car themed folding knives. **Technical:** Grinds ATS-34, 1095 and commercial Damascus. Offers gun blue finishes and file work. **Prices:** $200 and up. **Remarks:** Part-time maker, first knife sold in 1991. **Mark:** Last name or name with city and map logo.

BORGER, WOLF,
Benzstrasse 8, 76676 Graben-Neudorf, GERMANY, Phone: 07255-72303, Fax: 07255-72304, wolf@messerschmied.de; Web: www.messerschmied.de
Specialties: High-tech working and using straight knives and folders, many with corkscrews or other tools, of his design. **Patterns:** Hunters, Bowies and folders with various locking systems. **Technical:** Grinds 440C, ATS-34 and CPM. Uses stainless Damascus. **Prices:** $250 to $900; some to $1500. **Remarks:** Full-time maker; first knife sold in 1975. **Mark:** Howling wolf and name; first name on Damascus blades.

BOSE, REESE,
PO Box 61, Shelburn, IN 47879, Phone: 812-397-5114
Specialties: Traditional working and using knives in standard patterns and multi-blade folders. **Patterns:** Multi-blade slip-joints. **Technical:** ATS-34, D2 and CPM 440V. **Prices:** $275 to $1500. **Remarks:** Full-time maker; first knife sold in 1992. Photos by Jack Busfield. **Mark:** R. Bose.

BOSE, TONY,
7252 N. County Rd, 300 E., Shelburn, IN 47879-9778, Phone: 812-397-5114
Specialties: Traditional working and using knives in standard patterns; multi-blade folders. **Patterns:** Multi-blade slip-joints. **Technical:** Grinds commercial Damascus, ATS-34 and D2. **Prices:** $400 to $1200. **Remarks:** Full-time maker; first knife sold in 1972. **Mark:** First initial, last name, city, state.

BOSSAERTS, CARL,
Rua Albert Einstein 906, 14051-110, Ribeirao Preto, S.P., BRAZIL, Phone: 016 633 7063
Specialties: Working and using straight knives of his design, to customer specs and in standard patterns. **Patterns:** Hunters, fighters and utility/camp knives. **Technical:** Grinds ATS-34, 440V and 440C; does filework. **Prices:** 60 to $400. **Remarks:** Part-time maker; first knife sold in 1992. **Mark:** Initials joined together.

BOST, ROGER E,
30511 Cartier Dr, Palos Verdes, CA 90275-5629, Phone: 310- 541-6833, rogerbost@cox.net
Specialties: Hunters, fighters, boot, utility. **Patterns:** Loveless-style. **Technical:** ATS-34, 60-61RC, stock removal and forge. **Prices:** $300 and up. **Remarks:** First knife sold in 1990. Cal. Knifemakers Assn., ABS. **Mark:** Diamond with initials inside and Palos Verdes California around outside.

BOSWORTH, DEAN,
329 Mahogany Dr, Key Largo, FL 33037, Phone: 305-451-1564, DLBOZ@bellsouth.net
Specialties: Free hand hollow ground working knives with hand rubbed satin finish, filework and inlays. **Patterns:** Bird and Trout, hunters, skinners, fillet, Bowies, miniatures. **Technical:** Using 440C, ATS-34, D2, Meier Damascus, custom wet formed sheaths. **Prices:** $250 and up. **Remarks:** Part-time maker; first knife made in 1985. Member Florida Knifemakers Assoc. **Mark:** BOZ stamped in block letters.

BOURBEAU, JEAN YVES,
15 Rue Remillard, Notre Dame, Ile Perrot, Quebec, CANADA J7V 8M9, Phone: 514-453-1069
Specialties: Fancy/embellished and fantasy folders of his design. **Patterns:** Bowies, fighters and locking folders. **Technical:** Grinds 440C, ATS-34 and Damascus. Carves precious wood for handles. **Prices:** $150 to $1000. **Remarks:** Part-time maker; first knife sold in 1994. **Mark:** Interlaced initials.

BOWLES, CHRIS,
PO Box 985, Reform, AL 35481, Phone: 205-375-6162
Specialties: Working/using straight knives, and period pieces. **Patterns:** Utility, tactical, hunting, neck knives, machetes, and swords. **Grinds:** 0-1, 154 cm, BG-42, 440V. **Prices:** $50 to $400 some higher. **Remarks:** Full-time maker. **Mark:** Bowles stamped or Bowles etched in script.

BOXER, BO,
LEGEND FORGE, 6477 Hwy 93 S #134, Whitefish, MT 59937, Phone: 505-799-0173, legendforge@aol.com; Web: www.legendforgesknives.com
Specialties: Handmade hunting knives, Damascus hunters. Most are antler handled. Also, hand forged Damascus steel. **Patterns:** Hunters and Bowies. **Prices:** $125 to $2500 on some very exceptional Damascus knives. Remarks: Makes his own custom leather sheath stamped with maker stamp. His knives are used by the outdoorsman of the Smoky Mountains, North Carolina, and the Rockies of Montana and New Mexico. Spends one-half of the year in Montana and the other part of the year in Taos, New Mexico. **Mark:** The name "Legend Forge" hand engraved on every blade.

BOYD, FRANCIS,
1811 Prince St, Berkeley, CA 94703, Phone: 510-841-7210
Specialties: Folders and kitchen knives, Japanese swords. **Patterns:** Push-button sturdy locking folders; San Francisco-style chef's knives. **Technical:** Forges and grinds; mostly uses high-carbon steels. **Prices:** Moderate to heavy. **Remarks:** Designer. **Mark:** Name.

BOYE, DAVID,
PO Box 1238, Dolan Springs, AZ 86441, Phone: 800-853-1617, Fax: 928-767-4273, boye@cltlink.net; Web: www.boyeknives.com
Specialties: Folders and Boye Basics. Forerunner in the use of dendritic steel and dendritic cobalt for blades. **Patterns:** Lockback folders and fixed blade sheath knives in cobalt. **Technical:** Casts blades in cobalt. **Prices:** From $129 to $360. **Remarks:** Part-time maker; author of *Step-by-Step Knifemaking*. **Mark:** Name.

BOYES, TOM,
731 Jean Ct, Addison, WI 53002, Phone: 262-391-2172
Specialties: Hunters, working knives. **Technical:** Grinds ATS-34, 440C, O1 tool steel and Damascus. **Prices:** $60 to $1000. **Remarks:** First knife sold in 1998. Doing business as R. Boyes Knives.

BOYSEN, RAYMOND A,
125 E St Patrick, Rapid Ciy, SD 57701, Phone: 605-341-7752
Specialties: Hunters and Bowies. **Technical:** High performance blades forged from 52100 and 5160. **Prices:** $200 and up. **Remarks:** American Bladesmith Society Journeyman Smith. Part-time bladesmith. **Mark:** BOYSEN.

BRACK, DOUGLAS D,
1591 Los Angeles Ave #8, Ventura, CA 93004, Phone: 805-659-1505
Specialties: Fighters, daggers, boots, Bowies. **Patterns:** One of a kind. **Technical:** Grinds 440-ATS, own Damascus. **Prices:** $300 to $3000. **Remarks:** Full-time maker; first knife sold in 1984. **Mark:** tat.

BRADBURN, GARY,
BRADBURN CUSTOM CUTLERY, 1714 Park Place, Wichita, KS 67203, Phone: 316-640-5684, gary@bradburnknives.com; Web:www.bradburnknives.com
Specialties: Specialize in clay-tempered Japanese-style knives and swords. **Patterns:** Also Bowies and fighters. **Technical:** Forge and/or grind carbon steel only. **Prices:** $150 to $1200. **Mark:** Initials GB stylized to look like Japanese character.

BRADFORD, GARRICK,
582 Guelph St, Kitchener ON, CANADA N2H-5Y4, Phone: 519-576-9863

BRADLEY, DENNIS,
178 Bradley Acres Rd, Blairsville, GA 30512, Phone: 706-745-4364, bzbtaz@brmemc.net Web: www.dennisbradleyknives.com
Specialties: Working straight knives and folders, some high-art. **Patterns:** Hunters, boots and daggers; slip-joints and two-blades. **Technical:** Grinds ATS-34, D2, 440C and commercial Damascus. **Prices:** $100 to $500; some to $2000. **Remarks:** Part-time maker; first knife sold in 1973. **Mark:** BRADLEY KNIVES in double heart logo.

BRADLEY, JOHN,
PO Box 33, Pomona Park, FL 32181, Phone: 386-649-4739, johnbradleyknives@yahoo.com
Specialties: Fixed-blade using and art knives; primitive folders. **Patterns:** Skinners, Bowies, camp knives and primitive knives. **Technical:** Forged and ground 52100, 1095, O1 and Damascus. **Prices:** $250 to $2000. **Remarks:** Full-time maker; first knife sold in 1988. **Mark:** Last name.

BRANDSEY, EDWARD P,
4441 Hawkridge Ct, Janesville, WI 53546, Phone: 608-868-9010, ebrandsey@centurytel.net
   Patterns: Large bowies, hunters, neck knives and buckskinner-styles. Native American influence on some. An occasional tanto, art piece. Does own scrimshaw. See Egnath's second book. Now making locking liner folders. **Technical:** ATS-34, CPM154, 440-C, 0-1, and some Damascus. Paul Bos treating past 20 years. **Prices:** $250 to $600; some to $3000. **Remarks:** Full-time maker. First knife sold in 1973. **Mark:** Initials connected - registered Wisc. Trademark since March 1983.

BRANDT, MARTIN W,
833 Kelly Blvd, Springfield, OR 97477, Phone: 541-747-5422, oubob747@aol.com

BRANTON, ROBERT,
PO BOX 807, Awendaw, SC 29429, Phone: 843-928-3624, www.brantonknives.com
   Specialties: Working straight knives of his design or to customer specs; throwing knives. **Patterns:** Hunters, fighters and some miniatures. **Technical:** Grinds ATS-34, A2 and 1050; forges 5160, O1. Offers hollow- or convex-grinds. **Prices:** $25 to $400. **Remarks:** Part-time maker; first knife sold in 1985. Doing business as Pro-Flyte, Inc. **Mark:** Last name; or first and last name, city, state.

BRASCHLER, CRAIG W.,
HC4 Box 667, Doniphan, MO 63935, Phone: 573-996-5058
   Specialties: Art knives, Bowies, utility hunters, slip joints, miniatures, engraving. **Technical:** Flat grinds. Does own selective heat treating. Does own engraving. **Prices:** Starting at $200. **Remarks:** Full-time maker since 2003. **Mark:** Braschler over Martin Oval stamped.

BRATCHER, BRETT,
11816 County Rd 302, Plantersville, TX 77363, Phone: 936-894-3788, Fax: (936) 894-3790, brett_bratcher@msn.com
   Specialties: Hunting and skinning knives. **Patterns:** Clip and drop point. Hand forged. **Technical:** Material 5160, D2, 1095 and Damascus. **Price:** $200 to $500. **Mark:** Bratcher.

BRAY JR., W LOWELL,
6931 Manor Beach Rd, New Port Richey, FL 34652, Phone: 727-846-0830, brayknives@aol.com Web: www.brayknives.com
   Specialties: Traditional working and using straight knives and collector pieces. **Patterns:** One of a kind pieces, hunters, fighters and utility knives. **Technical:** Grinds 440C and ATS-34; forges 52100 and Damascus. **Prices:** $125 to $800. **Remarks:** Spare-time maker; first knife sold in 1992. **Mark:** Lowell Bray Knives in shield or Bray Primative in shield.

BREED, KIM,
733 Jace Dr, Clarksville, TN 37040, Phone: 931-980-4956, sfbreed@yahoo.com
   Specialties: High end through working folders and straight knives. **Patterns:** Hunters, fighters, daggers, Bowies. His design or customers. Likes one-of-a-kind designs. **Technical:** Makes own Mosiac and regular Damascus, but will use stainless steels. Offers filework and sculpted material. **Prices:** $150 to $2000. **Remarks:** Full-time maker. First knife sold in 1990. **Mark:** Last name.

BREND, WALTER,
4094 Columbia Hwy., Ridge Springs, SC 29129, Phone: 256-736-3520, walterbrend@hotmail.com Web: www.brendknives.com
   Specialties: Tactical-style knives, fighters, automatics. **Technical:** Grinds D-Z and 440C blade steels, 154CM steel. **Prices:** Micarta handles, titanium handles.

BRENNAN, JUDSON,
PO Box 1165, Delta Junction, AK 99737, Phone: 907-895-5153, Fax: 907-895-5404
   Specialties: Period pieces. **Patterns:** All kinds of Bowies, rifle knives, daggers. **Technical:** Forges miscellaneous steels. **Prices:** Upscale, good value. **Remarks:** Muzzle-loading gunsmith; first knife sold in 1978. **Mark:** Name.

BRESHEARS, CLINT,
1261 Keats, Manhattan Beach, CA 90266, Phone: 310-372-0739, Fax: 310-372-0739, breshears1@verizon.net; Web: www.clintknives.com
   Specialties: Working straight knives and folders. **Patterns:** Hunters, Bowies and survival knives. Folders are mostly hunters. **Technical:** Grinds 440C, 154CM and ATS-34; prefers mirror finishes. **Prices:** $125 to $750; some to $1800. **Remarks:** Part-time maker; first knife sold in 1978. **Mark:** First name.

BREUER, LONNIE,
PO Box 877384, Wasilla, AK 99687-7384
   Specialties: Fancy working straight knives. **Patterns:** Hunters, camp knives and axes, folders and Bowies. **Technical:** Grinds 440C, AEB-L and D2; likes wire inlay, scrimshaw, decorative filing. **Prices:** $60 to $150; some to $300. **Remarks:** Part-time maker; first knife sold in 1977. **Mark:** Signature.

BRITTON, TIM,
PO Box 71, Bethania, NC 27010, Phone: 366-923-2062, timbritton@yahoo.com; Web: www.timbritton.com
   Specialties: Small and simple working knives, sgian dubhs, slip joint folders and special tactical designs. **Technical:** Forges and grinds stainless steel. **Prices:** $165 to ???. **Remarks:** Veteran knifemaker. **Mark:** Etched signature.

BROADWELL, DAVID,
PO Box 4314, Wichita Falls, TX 76308, Phone: 940-692-1727, david@broadwellstudios.com; Web: www.broadwellstudios.com
   Specialties: Sculpted high-art straight and folding knives. **Patterns:** Daggers, sub-hilted fighters, folders, sculpted art knives and some Bowies. **Technical:** Grinds mostly Damascus; carves; prefers natural handle materials, including stone. Some embellishment. **Prices:** $500 to $4000; some higher. **Remarks:** Full-time maker since 1989; first knife sold in 1981. **Mark:** Stylized emblem bisecting "B"/with last name below.

BROCK, KENNETH L,
PO Box 375, 207 N Skinner Rd, Allenspark, CO 80510, Phone: 303-747-2547, brockknives@nedernet.net
   Specialties: Custom designs, full-tang working knives and button lock folders of his design. **Patterns:** Hunters, miniatures and minis. **Technical:** Flat-grinds D2 and 440C; makes own sheaths; heat-treats. **Prices:** $75 to $800. **Remarks:** Full-time maker; first knife sold in 1978. **Mark:** Last name, city, state and serial number.

BRODZIAK, DAVID,
27 Stewart St, Albany, Western Australia, AUSTRALIA 6330, Phone: 61 8 9841 3314, Fax: 61898115065, brodziakm@net.net.au; Web: www.brodziakcustomknives.com

BROMLEY, PETER,
BROMLEY KNIVES, 1408 S Bettman, Spokane, WA 99212, Phone: 509-534-4235, Fax: 509-536-2666
   Specialties: Period Bowies, folder, hunting knives; all sizes and shapes. **Patterns:** Bowies, boot knives, hunters, utility, folder, working knives. **Technical:** High-carbon steel (1084, 1095 and 5160). Stock removal and forge. **Prices:** $85 to $750. **Remarks:** Almost full-time, first knife sold in 1987. A.B.S. Journeyman Smith. **Mark:** Bromley, Spokane, WA.

BROOKER, DENNIS,
55858 260th Ave., Chariton, IA 50049, Phone: 641-862-3263, dbrooker@dbrooker.com Web: www.dbrooker.com
   Specialties: Fancy straight knives and folders of his design. Obsidian and glass knives. **Patterns:** Hunters, folders and boots. **Technical:** Forges and grinds. Full-time engraver and designer; instruction available. **Prices:** Moderate to upscale. **Remarks:** Part-time maker. Takes no orders; sells only completed work. **Mark:** Name.

BROOKS, BUZZ,
2345 Yosemite Dr, Los Angles, CA 90041, Phone: 323-256-2892

BROOKS, MICHAEL,
2811 64th St, Lubbock, TX 79413, Phone: 806-438-3862, chiang@clearwire.net
   Specialties: Working straight knives of his design or to customer specs. **Patterns:** Martial art, Bowies, hunters, and fighters. **Technical:** Grinds 440C, D2 and ATS-34; offers wide variety of handle materials. **Prices:** $75 & up. **Remarks:** Part-time maker; first knife sold in 1985. **Mark:** Initials.

BROOKS, STEVE R,
1610 Dunn Ave, Walkerville, MT 59701, Phone: 406-782-5114, Fax: 406-782-5114, steve@brooksmoulds.com; Web: brooksmoulds.com
   Specialties: Working straight knives and folders; period pieces. **Patterns:** Hunters, Bowies and camp knives; folding lockers, axes, tomahawks and buckskinner knives; swords and stilettos. **Technical:** Damascus and mosaic Damascus. Some knives come embellished. **Prices:** $400 to $2000. **Remarks:** Full-time maker; first knife sold in 1982. **Mark:** Lazy initials.

BROOME, THOMAS A,
1212 E. Aliak Ave, Kenai, AK 99611-8205, Phone: 907-283-9128, tomlei@ptialaska.ent; Web: www.alaskanknives.com
   Specialties: Working hunters and folders **Patterns:** Traditional and custom orders. **Technical:** Grinds ATS-34, BG-42, CPM-S30V. **Prices:** $175 to $350. **Remarks:** Full-time maker; first knife sold in 1979. Doing business as Thom's Custom Knives, Alaskan Man O; Steel Knives. **Mark:** Full name, city, state.

BROTHERS, DENNIS L,
2007 Kent Rd., Oneonta, AL 35121, Phone: 205-466-3276, blademan@brothersblades.com Web: www.brothersblades.com
   Specialties: Fixed blade hunting/working knives of maker's deigns. Works with customer designed specifications. **Patterns:** Hunters, camp knives, kitchen/utility, bird, and trout. Standard patterns and customer designed. **Technical:** Stock removal. Works with stainless and tool steels. SS cryo-treatment. Hollow and flat grinds. **Prices:** $100 - $300. **Remarks:** Sole authorship knives and customer leather sheaths. Part-time maker. **Mark:** "D.L. Brothers, 4B, Oneonta, AL" on obverse side of blade.

BROTHERS, ROBERT L,
989 Philpott Rd, Colville, WA 99114, Phone: 509-684-8922
   Specialties: Traditional working and using straight knives and folders of his design and to customer specs. **Patterns:** Bowies, fighters and hunters. **Technical:** Grinds D2; forges Damascus. Makes own Damascus from saw steel wire rope and chain; part-time goldsmith and stone-setter. **Prices:** $100 to $400; some higher. **Remarks:** Part-time maker; first knife sold in 1986. **Mark:** Initials and year made.

BROUS, JASON,
5940 Matthews St., Goleta, CA 93110, Phone: 805-717-7192, contact@brousblades.com Web: www.brousblades.com
   Patterns: Mostly fixed blades. **Technical:** Stock removal method using D2, CPM 154, 440c, ATS-34 or 1095 steels. **Prices:** $100 - $400. **Remarks:** Started May 2010.

BROWER, MAX,
2016 Story St, Boone, IA 50036, Phone: 515-432-2938, mbrower@mchsi.com
Specialties: Working/using straight knives. **Patterns:** Bowies, hunters and boots. **Technical:** Grinds 440C and ATS-34. **Prices:** Start at $150. **Remarks:** Spare-time maker; first knife sold in 1981. **Mark:** Last name.

BROWN, DENNIS G,
1633 N 197th Pl, Shoreline, WA 98133, Phone: 206-542-3997, denjilbro@msn.com

BROWN, HAROLD E,
3654 NW Hwy 72, Arcadia, FL 34266, Phone: 863-494-7514, brknives@strato.net
Specialties: Fancy and exotic working knives. **Patterns:** Folders, slip-lock, locking several kinds. **Technical:** Grinds D2 and ATS-34. Embellishment available. **Prices:** $175 to $1000. **Remarks:** Part-time maker; first knife sold in 1976. **Mark:** Name and city with logo.

BROWN, JIM,
1097 Fernleigh Cove, Little Rock, AR 72210

BROWN, ROB E,
PO Box 15107, Emerald Hill 6011, Port Elizabeth, SOUTH AFRICA, Phone: 27-41-3661086, Fax: 27-41-4511731, rbknives@global.co.za
Specialties: Contemporary-designed straight knives and period pieces. **Patterns:** Utility knives, hunters, boots, fighters and daggers. **Technical:** Grinds 440C, D2, ATS-34 and commercial Damascus. Knives mostly mirror finished; African handle materials. **Prices:** $100 to $1500. **Remarks:** Full-time maker; first knife sold in 1985. **Mark:** Name and country.

BROWNE, RICK,
980 West 13th St, Upland, CA 91786, Phone: 909-985-1728
Specialties: Sheffield pattern pocket knives. **Patterns:** Hunters, fighters and daggers. No heavy-duty knives. **Technical:** Grinds ATS-34. **Prices:** Start at $450. **Remarks:** Part-time maker; first knife sold in 1975. **Mark:** R.E. Browne, Upland, CA.

BROWNING, STEVEN W,
3400 Harrison Rd, Benton, AR 72015, Phone: 501-316-2450

BRUCE, RICHARD L.,
13174 Surcease Mine Road, Yankee Hill, CA 95965, Phone: 530-532-0880, Richardkarenbruce@yahoo.com
RL Bruce Custom Knives

BRUCE, RICHARD L.,
13174 Surcease Mine Road, Yankee Hill, CA 95965, Phone: 530-532-0880, richardkarenbruce@yahoo.com
Specialties: Working straight knives. Prefers natural handle material; stag bone and woods. Admires the classic straight knife look. **Patterns:** Hunters, Fighters, Fishing Knives. **Technical:** Uses 01, 1095, L6, W2 steel. Stock removal method, flat grind, heat treats and tempers own knives. Builds own sheaths; simple but sturdy. **Prices:** $150-$400. **Remarks:** Sold first knife in 2006; part-time maker. **Mark:** RL Bruce.

BRUNCKHORST, LYLE,
COUNTRY VILLAGE, 23706 7th Ave SE Ste B, Bothell, WA 98021, Phone: 425-402-3484, bronks@bronksknifeworks.com; Web: www.bronksknifeworks.com
Specialties: Forges own Damascus with 1084 and 15N20, forges 5160, 52100. Grinds CPM 154 CM, ATS-34, S30V. Hosts Biannual Northwest School of Knifemaking and Northwest Hammer In. Offers online and in-house sharpening services and knife sharpeners. Maker of the Double L Hoofknife. Traditional working and using knives, the new patent pending Xross-Bar Lock folders, tomahawks and irridescent RR spike knives. **Patterns:** Damascus Bowies, hunters, locking folders and featuring the ultra strong locking tactical folding knives. **Prices:** $185 to $1500; some to $3750. **Remarks:** Full-time maker; first knife made in 1976. **Mark:** Bucking horse or bronk.

BRUNER JR., FRED BRUNER BLADES,
E10910 W Hilldale Dr, Fall Creek, WI 54742, Phone: 715-877-2496, brunerblades@msn.com
Specialties: Pipe tomahawks, swords, makes his own. **Patterns:** Drop point hunters. **Prices:** $65 to $1500. **Remarks:** Voting member of the Knifemakers Guild. **Mark:** Fred Bruner.

BRYAN, TOM,
14822 S Gilbert Rd, Gilbert, AZ 85296, Phone: 480-812-8529
Specialties: Straight and folding knives. **Patterns:** Drop-point hunter fighters. **Technical:** ATS-34, 154CM, 440C and A2. **Prices:** $150 to $800. **Remarks:** Part-time maker; sold first knife in 1994. DBA as T. Bryan Knives. **Mark:** T. Bryan.

BUCHANAN, THAD,
THAD BUCHANAN CUSTOM KNIVES, 915 NW Perennial Way, Prineville, OR 97754, Phone: 541-416-2556, knives@crestviewcable.com; Web: www.buchananblades.com
Specialties: Fixed blades. **Patterns:** Various hunters, trout, bird, utility, boots & fighters, including most Loveless patterns. **Technical:** Stock removal, high polish, variety handle materials. **Prices:** $450 to $2000. **Remarks:** 2005 and 2008 Blade Magazine handmade award for hunter/utility. 2006 Blade West best fixed blade award; 2008 Blade West best hunter/utility. **Mark:** Thad Buchanan Oregon USA.

BUCHMAN, BILL,
63312 South Rd, Bend, OR 97701-9027, Phone: 541-382-8851
Specialties: Leather cutting knives for saddle makers and leather crafters. **Patterns:** Many. **Technical:** Sandkik-Swedish carbon steel. **Prices:** Varies: $35 to $130. **Remarks:** Full-time maker; first knife sold in 1982. **Mark:** BB & # of knife on large knives - no mark on small knives.

BUCHNER, BILL,
PO Box 73, Idleyld Park, OR 97447, Phone: 541-498-2247, blazinhammer@earthlink.net; Web: www.home.earthlin.net/~blazinghammer
Specialties: Working straight knives, kitchen knives and high-art knives of his design. **Technical:** Uses W1, L6 and his own Damascus. Invented "spectrum metal" for letter openers, folder handles and jewelry. Likes sculpturing and carving in Damascus. **Prices:** $40 to $3000; some higher. **Remarks:** Full-time maker; first knife sold in 1978. **Mark:** Signature.

BUCKBEE, DONALD M,
243 South Jackson Trail, Grayling, MI 49738, Phone: 517-348-1386
Specialties: Working straight knives, some fancy, in standard patterns; concentrating on kitchen knives. **Patterns:** Kitchen knives, hunters, Bowies. **Technical:** Grinds D2, 440C, ATS-34. Makes ultra-lights in hunter patterns. **Prices:** $100 to $250; some to $350. **Remarks:** Part-time maker; first knife sold in 1984. **Mark:** Antlered bee—a buck bee.

BUCKNER, JIMMIE H,
PO Box 162, Putney, GA 31782, Phone: 229-436-4182
Specialties: Camp knives, Bowies (one-of-a-kind), liner-lock folders, tomahawks, camp axes, neck knives for law enforcement and hide-out knives for body guards and professional people. **Patterns:** Hunters, camp knives, Bowies. **Technical:** Forges 1084, 5160 and Damascus (own), own heat treats. **Prices:** $195 to $795 and up. **Remarks:** Full-time maker; first knife sold in 1980, ABS Master Smith. **Mark:** Name over spade.

BUDELL, MICHAEL,
1100-A South Market St, Brenham, TX 77833, Phone: 979-836-0098, mbbudell@att.net
Specialties: Slip Joint Folders. **Technical:** Grinds 01, 440C. File work springs, blades and liners. Natural material scales giraffe, mastadon ivory, elephant ivory, and jigged bone. **Prices:** $175 - $350. **Remarks:** Part-time maker; first knife sold 2006. **Mark:** XA

BUEBENDORF, ROBERT E,
108 Lazybrooke Rd, Monroe, CT 06468, Phone: 203-452-1769
Specialties: Traditional and fancy straight knives of his design. **Patterns:** Hand-makes and embellishes belt buckle knives. **Technical:** Forges and grinds 440C, O1, W2, 1095, his own Damascus and 154CM. **Prices:** $200 to $500. **Remarks:** Full-time maker; first knife sold in 1978. **Mark:** First and middle initials, last name and MAKER.

BULLARD, BENONI,
4416 Jackson 4, Bradford, AR 72020, Phone: 501-344-2672, benandbren@earthlink.net
Specialties: Bowies and hunters. **Patterns:** Camp knives, bowies, hunters, slip joints, folders, lock blades, miniatures, Hawks Tech. **Technical:** Makes own Damascus. Forges 5160, 1085, 15 N 20. Favorite is 5160. **Prices:** $150 - $1500. **Remarks:** Part-time maker. Sold first knife in 2006. **Mark:** Benoni with a star over the letter i.

BULLARD, RANDALL,
7 Mesa Dr., Canyon, TX 79015, Phone: 806-655-0590
Specialties: Working/using straight knives and folders of his design or to customer specs. **Patterns:** Hunters, locking folders and slip-joint folders. **Technical:** Grinds O1, ATS-34 and 440C. Does file work. **Prices:** $125 to $300; some to $500. **Remarks:** Part-time maker; first knife sold in 1993. Doing business as Bullard Custom Knives. **Mark:** First and middle initials, last name, maker, city and state.

BULLARD, TOM,
117 MC 8068, Flippin, AR 72634, Phone: 870-453-3421, tbullard@southshore.com; Web: www.southshore.com/~tombullard
Specialties: Traditional folders and hunters. **Patterns:** Bowies, hunters, single and 2-blade trappers, lockback folders. **Technical:** Grinds 440-C, ATS-34, 0-1, commercial Damascus. **Prices:** $150 and up. **Remarks:** Offers filework and engraving by Norvell Foster and Terry Thies. Does not make screw-together knives. **Mark:** T Bullard.

BUMP, BRUCE D.,
1103 Rex Ln, Walla Walla, WA 99362, Phone: 509 522-2219, brucebump1@gmail.com; Web: www.brucebumpknives.com
Specialties: "One-of-a-kind" folders to cut and shoots. **Patterns:** Damascus patterns including feather patterns. **Technical:** Dual threat weapons of his own design. **Prices:** Call for prices. **Remarks:** Full-time maker ABS mastersmith 2003. **Mark:** Bruce D. Bump "Custom", Bruce D. Bump "MS".

BURDEN, JAMES,
405 Kelly St, Burkburnett, TX 76354

BURGER, FRED,
Box 436, Munster 4278, Kwa-Zulu Natal, SOUTH AFRICA, Phone: 27 39 3192316, info@swordcane.com; Web: www.swordcane.com
Specialties: Sword canes, folders, and fixed blades. **Patterns:** 440C and carbon steel blades. **Technical:** Double hollow ground and Poniard-style blades. **Prices:** $300 to $3000. **Remarks:** Full-time maker with son, Barry, since 1987. Member South African Guild. **Mark:** Last name in oval pierced by a dagger.

BURGER, PON,
12 Glenwood Ave, Woodlands, Bulawayo, ZIMBABWE 75514
Specialties: Collector's items. **Patterns:** Fighters, locking folders of traditional styles, buckles. **Technical:** Scrimshaws 440C blade. Uses polished buffalo horn with brass fittings. Cased in buffalo hide book. **Prices:** $450 to $1100. **Remarks:** Full-time maker; first knife sold in 1973. Doing business as Burger Products. **Mark:** Spirit of Africa.

BURGER, TIAAN,
69 Annie Botha Ave, Riviera, Pretoria, South Africa, tiaan_burger@hotmail.com
Specialties: Sliplock and multi-blade folder. **Technical:** High carbon or stainless with African handle materials **Remarks:** Occasional fixed blade knives.

BURKE, BILL,
12 Chapman Lane, Boise, ID 83716, Phone: 208-336-3792, billburke@bladegallery.com
Specialties: Hand-forged working knives. **Patterns:** Fowler pronghorn, clip point and drop point hunters. **Technical:** Forges 52100 and 5160. Makes own Damascus from 15N20 and 1084. **Prices:** $450 and up. **Remarks:** Dedicated to fixed-blade high-performance knives. ABS Journeyman. Also makes "Ed Fowler" miniatures. **Mark:** Initials connected.

BURKE, DAN,
22001 Ole Barn Rd, Edmond, OK 73003, Phone: 405-341-3406, Fax: 405-340-3333, burkeknives@aol.com
Specialties: Slip joint folders. **Patterns:** Traditional folders. **Technical:** Grinds D2 and BG-42. Prefers natural handle materials; heat-treats. **Prices:** $440 to $1900. **Remarks:** Full-time maker; first knife sold in 1976. **Mark:** First initial and last name.

BURNLEY, LUCAS,
1005 La Font Rd. SW, Albuquerque, NM 87105, Phone: 505-265-4297, burnleyknives@comcast.net
Specialties: Contemporary tactical fixed blade, and folder designs, some art knives. **Patterns:** Hybrids, neo Japanese, defensive, utility and field knives. **Technical:** Grinds CPM154, A2, D2, BG42, Stainless Damascus as well as titanium and aerospace composites. **Prices:** Most models $150 - $1000. Some specialty pieces higher. **Remarks:** Full-time maker, first knife sold in 2003. **Mark:** Last name, Burnley Knives, or Burnley Design.

BURRIS, PATRICK R,
11078 Crystal Lynn Ct, Jacksonville, FL 32226, Phone: 904-757-3938, keenedge@comcast.net
Specialties: Traditional straight knives. **Patterns:** Hunters, Bowies, locking liner folders. **Technical:** Flat grinds CPM stainless and Damascus. **Remarks:** Offers filework, embellishment, exotic materials and Damascus **Mark:** Last name in script.

BURROWS, CHUCK,
WILD ROSE TRADING CO, 289 La Posta Canyon Rd, Durango, CO 81303, Phone: 970-259-8396, chuck@wrtcleather.com; Web: www.wrtcleather.com
Specialties: Presentation knives, hawks, and sheaths based on the styles of the American frontier incorporating carving, beadwork, rawhide, braintan, and other period correct materials. Also makes other period style knives such as Scottish Dirks and Moorish jambiyahs. **Patterns:** Bowies, Dags, tomahawks, war clubs, and all other 18th and 19th century frontier style edged weapons and tools. **Technical:** Carbon steel only: 5160, 1080/1084, 1095, O1, Damascus-Our Frontier Shear Steel, plus other styles available on request. Forged knives, hawks, etc. are made in collaborations with bladesmiths. Gib Guignard (under the name of Cactus Rose) and Mark Williams (under the name UB Forged). Blades are usually forge finished and all items are given an aged period look. **Prices:** $500 plus. **Remarks:** Full-time maker, first knife sold in 1973. 40+ years experience working leather. **Mark:** A lazy eight or lazy eight with a capital T at the center. On leather either the lazy eight with T or a WRTC makers stamp.

BURROWS, STEPHEN R,
1020 Osage St, Humboldt, KS 66748, Phone: 816-921-1573
Specialties: Fantasy straight knives of his design, to customer specs and in standard patterns; period pieces. **Patterns:** Fantasy, bird and trout knives, daggers, fighters and hunters. **Technical:** Forges 5160 and 1095 high-carbon steel, O1 and his Damascus. Offers lost wax casting in bronze or silver of cross guards and pommels. **Prices:** $65 to $600; some to $2000. **Remarks:** Full-time maker; first knife sold in 1983. Doing business as Gypsy Silk. **Mark:** Etched name.

BUSCH, STEVE,
1989 Old Town Loop, Oakland, OR 97462, Phone: 541-459-2833, steve@buschcustomknives.com; Web: www.buschcustomknives.blademakers.com
Specialties: D/A automatic right and left handed, folders, fixed blade working mainly in Damascus file work, functional art knives, nitrate bluing, heat bluing most all scale materials. **Prices:** $150 to $2000. **Remarks:** Trained under Vallotton family 3 1/2 years on own since 2002. **Mark:** Signature and date of completion on all knives.

BUSFIELD, JOHN,
153 Devonshire Circle, Roanoke Rapids, NC 27870, Phone: 252-537-3949, Fax: 252-537-8704, busfield@charter.net; Web: www.busfieldknives.com
Specialties: Investor-grade folders; high-grade working straight knives. **Patterns:** Original price-style and trailing-point interframe and sculpted-frame folders, drop-point hunters and semi-skinners. **Technical:** Grinds 154CM and ATS-34. Offers interframes, gold frames and inlays; uses jade, agate and lapis. **Prices:** $275 to $2000. **Remarks:** Full-time maker; first knife sold in 1979. **Mark:** Last name and address.

BUSSE, JERRY,
11651 Co Rd 12, Wauseon, OH 43567, Phone: 419-923-6471
Specialties: Working straight knives. **Patterns:** Heavy combat knives and camp knives. **Technical:** Grinds D2, A2, INFI. **Prices:** $1100 to $3500. **Remarks:** Full-time maker; first knife sold in 1983. **Mark:** Last name in logo.

BUTLER, BART,
822 Seventh St, Ramona, CA 92065, Phone: 760-789-6431

BUTLER, JOHN,
777 Tyre Rd, Havana, FL 32333, Phone: 850-539-5742
Specialties: Hunters, Bowies, period. **Technical:** Damascus, 52100, 5160, L6 steels. **Prices:** $80 and up. **Remarks:** Making knives since 1986. Journeyman (ABS). **Mark:** JB.

BUTLER, JOHN R,
20162 6th Ave N E, Shoreline, WA 98155, Phone: 206-362 3847, rjjjrb@sprynet.com

BUXTON, BILL,
155 Oak Bend Rd, Kaiser, MO 65047, Phone: 573-348-3577, camper@yhti.net; Web: www.billbuxtonknives.com
Specialties: Forged fancy and working straight knives and folders. Mostly one-of-a-kind pieces. **Patterns:** Fighters, daggers, Bowies, hunters, linerlock folders, axes and tomahawks. **Technical:** Forges 52100, 0-1, 1080. Makes own Damascus (mosaic and random patterns) from 1080, 1095, 15n20, and powdered metals 1084 and 4800a. Offers sterling silver inlay, n/s pin patterning and pewter pouring on axe and hawk handles. **Prices:** $300 to $1500. **Remarks:** Full-time maker, sold first knife in 1998. **Mark:** First and last name.

BYBEE, BARRY J,
795 Lock Rd. E, Cadiz, KY 42211-8615
Specialties: Working straight knives of his design. **Patterns:** Hunters, fighters, boot knives, tantos and Bowies. **Technical:** Grinds ATS-34, 440C. Likes stag and Micarta for handle materials. **Prices:** $125 to $200; some to $1000. **Remarks:** Part-time maker; first knife sold in 1968. **Mark:** Arrowhead logo with name, city and state.

BYRD, WESLEY L,
189 Countryside Dr, Evensville, TN 37332, Phone: 423-775-3826, w.l.byrd@worldnet.att.net
Specialties: Hunters, fighters, Bowies, dirks, sgian dubh, utility, and camp knives. **Patterns:** Wire rope, random patterns. Twists, W's, Ladder, Kite Tail. **Technical:** Uses 52100, 1084, 5160, L6, and 15n20. **Prices:** Starting at $180. **Remarks:** Prefer to work with customer for their design preferences. ABS Journeyman Smith. **Mark:** BYRD, WB <X.

C

CABE, JERRY (BUDDY),
62 McClaren Ln, Hattieville, AR 72063, Phone: 501-354-3581

CABRERA, SERGIO B,
24500 Broad Ave, Wilmington, CA 90744

CAFFREY, EDWARD J,
2608 Central Ave West, Great Falls, MT 59404, Phone: 406-727-9102, caffreyknives@gmail.com; Web: www.caffreyknives.net
Specialties: One-of-a-kind using and collector quality pieces. Will accept some customer designs. **Patterns:** Bowies, folders, hunters, fighters, camp/utility, tomahawks and hatchets. **Technical:** Forges all types of Damascus, specializing in Mosaic Damascus, 52100, 5160, 1080/1084 and most other commonly forged steels. **Prices:** Starting at $185; typical hunters start at $400; collector pieces can range into the thousands. **Remarks:** Offers one-on-one basic and advanced bladesmithing classes. ABS Mastersmith. Full-time maker. **Mark:** Stamped last name and MS on straight knives. Etched last name with MS on folders.

CALDWELL, BILL,
255 Rebecca, West Monroe, LA 71292, Phone: 318-323-3025
Specialties: Straight knives and folders with machined bolsters and liners. **Patterns:** Fighters, Bowies, survival knives, tomahawks, razors and push knives. **Technical:** Owns and operates a very large, well-equipped blacksmith and bladesmith shop with six large forges and eight power hammers. **Prices:** $400 to $3500; some to $10,000. **Remarks:** Full-time maker and self-styled blacksmith; first knife sold in 1962. **Mark:** Wild Bill and Sons.

CALLAHAN, F TERRY,
PO Box 880, Boerne, TX 78006, Phone: 830-981-8274, Fax: 830-981-8279, ftclaw@gvtc.com
Specialties: Custom hand-forged edged knives, collectible and functional. **Patterns:** Bowies, folders, daggers, hunters & camp knives . **Technical:** Forges 5160, 1095 and his own Damascus. Offers filework and handmade sheaths. **Prices:** $125 to $2000. **Remarks:** First knife sold in 1990. ABS/Journeyman Bladesmith. **Mark:** Initials inside a keystone symbol.

CALVERT JR., ROBERT W (BOB),
911 Julia, Rayville, LA 71269, Phone: 318-728-4113 ext. 2, Fax: (318) 728-0000, rcalvert1@gmail.com
Specialties: Using and hunting knives; your design or his. Since 1990. **Pat-**

terns: Forges own Damascus; all patterns. **Technical:** 5160, D2, 52100, 1084. Prefers natural handle material. **Prices:** $250 and up. **Remarks:** TOMB Member, ABS. Journeyman Smith. ABS Board of directors **Mark:** Calvert (Block) J S.

CAMERER, CRAIG,
3766 Rockbridge Rd, Chesterfield, IL 62630, Phone: 618-753-2147, craig@ camererknives.com; Web: www.camererknives.com
Specialties: Everyday carry knives, hunters and Bowies. **Patterns:** D-guard, historical recreations and fighters. **Technical:** Most of his knives are forged to shape. **Prices:** $100 and up. **Remarks:** Member of the ABS and PKA. Journeymen Smith ABS.

CAMERON, RON G,
PO Box 183, Logandale, NV 89021, Phone: 702-398-3356, rntcameron@mvdsl.com
Specialties: Fancy and embellished working/using straight knives and folders of his design. **Patterns:** Bowies, hunters and utility/camp knives. **Technical:** Grinds ATS-34, AEB-L and Devin Thomas Damascus or own Damascus from 1084 and 15N20. Does filework, fancy pins, mokume fittings. Uses exotic hardwoods, stag and Micarta for handles. Pearl & mammoth ivory. **Prices:** $175 to $850 some to $1000. **Remarks:** Part-time maker; first knife sold in 1994. Doing business as Cameron Handmade Knives. **Mark:** Last name, town, state or last name.

CAMPBELL, DICK,
196 Graham Rd, Colville, WA 99114, Phone: 509-684-6080, dicksknives@aol.com
Specialties: Working straight knives, folders & period pieces. **Patterns:** Hunters, fighters, boots: 19th century Bowies, Japanese swords and daggers. **Technical:** Grinds 440C, 154CM. **Prices:** $200 to $2500. **Remarks:** Full-time maker. First knife sold in 1975. **Mark:** Name.

CAMPBELL, DOUG,
46 W Boulder Rd., McLeod, MT 59052, Phone: 406-222-8153, dkcampbl@ yahoo.com
Specialties: Sole authorship of most any fixed blade knife. **Patterns:** Capers, hunters, camp knives, bowies, fighters. **Technical:** Forged from 1084, 5160, 52100, and self forged pattern-welded Damascus. **Prices:** $150-$750. **Remarks:** Part-time knifesmith. Built first knife in 1987, tried to make every knife since better than the one before. Pursuing ABS JS stamp. **Mark:** Grizzly track surrounded by a C.

CAMPOS, IVAN,
R.XI de Agosto 107, Tatui, SP, BRAZIL 18270-000, Phone: 00-55-15-2518092, Fax: 00-55-15-2594368, ivan@ivancampos.com; Web: www.ivancampos.com
Specialties: Brazilian handmade and antique knives.

CANDRELLA, JOE,
1219 Barness Dr, Warminster, PA 18974, Phone: 215-675-0143
Specialties: Working straight knives, some fancy. **Patterns:** Daggers, boots, Bowies. **Technical:** Grinds 440C and 154CM. **Prices:** $100 to $200; some to $1000. **Remarks:** Part-time maker; first knife sold in 1985. Does business as Franjo. **Mark:** FRANJO with knife as J.

CANNADY, DANIEL L,
Box 301, 358 Parkwood Terrace, Allendale, SC 29810, Phone: 803-584-2813, Fax: 803-584-2813
Specialties: Working straight knives and folders in standard patterns. **Patterns:** Drop-point hunters, Bowies, skinners, fishing knives with concave grind, steak knives and kitchen cutlery. **Technical:** Grinds D2, 440C and ATS-34. **Prices:** $65 to $325; some to $1000. **Remarks:** Full-time maker; first knife sold in 1980. **Mark:** Last name above Allendale, S.C.

CANOY, ANDREW B,
3420 Fruchey Ranch Rd, Hubbard Lake, MI 49747, Phone: 810-266-6039, canoy1@shianet.org

CANTER, RONALD E,
96 Bon Air Circle, Jackson, TN 38305, Phone: 731-668-1780, canterr@charter.net
Specialties: Traditional working knives to customer specs. **Patterns:** Beavertail skinners, Bowies, hand axes and folding lockers. **Technical:** Grinds 440C, Micarta & deer antler. **Prices:** $75 and up. **Remarks:** Spare-time maker; first knife sold in 1973. **Mark:** Three last initials intertwined.

CANTRELL, KITTY D,
19720 Hwy 78, Ramona, CA 92076, Phone: 760-788-8304

CAPDEPON, RANDY,
553 Joli Rd, Carencro, LA 70520, Phone: 318-896-4113, Fax: 318-896-8753
Specialties: Straight knives and folders of his design. **Patterns:** Hunters and locking folders. **Technical:** Grinds ATS-34, 440C and D2. **Prices:** $200 to $600. **Remarks:** Part-time maker; first knife made in 1992. Doing business as Capdepon Knives. **Mark:** Last name.

CAPDEPON, ROBERT,
829 Vatican Rd, Carencro, LA 70520, Phone: 337-896-8753, Fax: 318-896-8753
Specialties: Traditional straight knives and folders of his design. **Patterns:** Boots, hunters and locking folders. **Technical:** Grinds ATS-34, 440C and D2. Hand-rubbed finish on blades. Likes natural horn materials for handles, including ivory. Offers engraving. **Prices:** $250 to $750. **Remarks:** Full-time maker; first knife made in 1992. **Mark:** Last name.

CAREY, PETER,
P.O. Box 4712, Lago Vista, TX 78645, Phone: 512-358-4839, Web: www.careyblade.com
Specialties: Tactical folders, Every Day Carry to presentation grade. Working straight knives, hunters, and tactical. **Patterns:** High-tech patterns of his own design, Linerlocks, Framelocks, Flippers. **Technical:** Hollow grinds CPM154, S30V, 154cm, stainless Damascus, Talonite, Stellite. Uses titanium, carbon fiber, G10, and select natural handle materials. **Prices:** Starting at $450. **Remarks:** Full-time maker, first knife sold in 2002. **Mark:** Last name in diamond.

CARLISLE, JEFF,
PO Box 282 12753 Hwy 200, Simms, MT 59477, Phone: 406-264-5693

CAROLINA CUSTOM KNIVES, SEE TOMMY MCNABB,

CARPENTER, RONALD W,
Rt. 4 Box 323, Jasper, TX 75951, Phone: 409-384-4087

CARR, JOSEPH E.,
W183 N8974 Maryhill Drive, Menomonee Falls, WI 53051, Phone: 920-625-3607, carsmith1@SBCGlobal.net; Web: Hembrook3607@charter.net
Specialties: JC knives. **Patterns:** Hunters, Bowies, fighting knives, every day carries. **Technical:** Grinds ATS-34 and Damascus. **Prices:** $200 to $750. **Remarks:** Full-time maker for 2 years, being taught by Ron Hembrook.

CARR, TIM,
3660 Pillon Rd, Muskegon, MI 49445, Phone: 231-766-3582, tim@ blackbearforgemi.com Web:www.blackbearforgemi.com
Specialties: Hunters, camp knives. **Patterns:** His or yours. **Technical:** Hand forges 5160, 52100 and Damascus. **Prices:** $125 to $700. **Remarks:** Part-time maker. **Mark:** The letter combined from maker's initials TRC.

CARRILLO, DWAINE,
C/O AIRKAT KNIVES, 1021 SW 15th St, Moore, OK 73160, Phone: 405-503-5879, Web: www.airkatknives.com

CARROLL, CHAD,
12182 McClelland, Grant, MI 49327, Phone: 231-834-9183, CHAD724@msn.com
Specialties: Hunters, Bowies, folders, swords, tomahawks. **Patterns:** Fixed blades, folders. **Prices:** $100 to $2000. **Remarks:** ABS Journeyman May 2002. **Mark:** A backwards C next to a forward C, maker's initials.

CARSON, HAROLD J "KIT",
1076 Brizendine Lane, Vine Grove, KY 40175, Phone: 270 877-6300, Fax: 270 877 6338, KCKnives@bbtel.com; Web: www.kitcarsonknives.com/album
Specialties: Military fixed blades and folders; art pieces. **Patterns:** Fighters, D handles, daggers, combat folders and Crosslock-styles, tactical folders, tactical fixed blades. **Technical:** Grinds Stellite 6K, Talonite, CPM steels, Damascus. **Prices:** $400 to $750; some to $5000. **Remarks:** Full-time maker; first knife sold in 1973. **Mark:** Name stamped or engraved.

CARTER, FRED,
5219 Deer Creek Rd, Wichita Falls, TX 76302, Phone: 904-723-4020
Specialties: High-art investor-class straight knives; some working hunters and fighters. **Patterns:** Classic daggers, Bowies; interframe, stainless and blued steel folders with gold inlay. **Technical:** Grinds a variety of steels. Uses no glue or solder. Engraves and inlays. **Prices:** Generally upscale. **Remarks:** Full-time maker. **Mark:** Signature in oval logo.

CARTER, MIKE,
2522 Frankfort Ave, Louisville, KY 40206, Phone: 502-387-4844, mike@ cartercrafts.com Web: www.cartercrafts.com
Remarks: Voting Member Knifemakers Guild

CARTER, MURRAY M,
22097 NW West Union Rd, Hillsboro, OR 97124, Phone: 503-447-1029, murray@ cartercutlery.com; Web: www.cartercutlery.com
Specialties: Traditional Japanese cutlery, utilizing San soh ko (three layer) or Kata-ha (two layer) blade construction. Laminated neck knives, traditional Japanese etc. **Patterns:** Works from over 200 standard Japanese and North American designs. **Technical:** Hot forges and cold forges Hitachi white steel #1, Hitachi blue super steel exclusively. **Prices:** $800 to $10,000. **Remarks:** Owns and operates North America's most exclusive traditional Japanese bladesmithing school; web site available at which viewers can subscribe to 10 free knife sharpening and maintenance reports. **Mark:** Name in cursive, often appearing with Japanese characters. **Other:** Very interestng and informative monthly newsletter.

CASEY, KEVIN,
10583 N. 42nd St., Hickory Corners, MI 49060, Phone: 269-719-7412, kevincasey@tds.net; Web: www.kevincaseycustomknives.com
Specialties: Fixed blades and folders. **Patterns:** Liner lock folders and feather Damascus pattern, mammoth ivory. **Technical:** Forges Damascus and carbon steels. **Prices:** Starting at $500 - $2500. **Remarks:** Member ABS, Knifemakers Guild, Custom Knifemakers Collectors Association.

CASHEN, KEVIN R,
5615 Tyler St, Hubbardston, MI 48845, Phone: 989-981-6780, kevin@ cashenblades.com; Web: www.cashenblades.com
Specialties: Working straight knives, high art pattern welded swords, traditional renaissance and ethnic pieces. **Patterns:** Hunters, Bowies, utility knives, swords, daggers. **Technical:** Forges 1095, 1084 and his own O1/L6 Damascus. **Prices:** $100 to $4000+. **Remarks:** Full-time maker; first knife sold in 1985. Doing business as Matherton Forge. **Mark:** Black letter Old English initials and Master Smith stamp.

CASTEEL, DIANNA,
PO Box 63, Monteagle, TN 37356, Phone: 931-212-4341, ddcasteel@charter. net; Web: www.casteelcustomknives.com
Specialties: Small, delicate daggers and miniatures; most knives one-of-a-kind. **Patterns:** Daggers, boot knives, fighters and miniatures. **Technical:** Grinds 440C. Offers stainless Damascus. **Prices:** Start at $350; miniatures start at $250. **Remarks:** Full-time maker. **Mark:** Di in script.

CASTEEL, DOUGLAS,
PO Box 63, Monteagle, TN 37356, Phone: 931-212-4341, Fax: 931-723-1856, ddcasteel@charter.net; Web: www.casteelcustomknives.com
Specialties: One-of-a-kind collector-class period pieces. **Patterns:** Daggers, Bowies, swords and folders. **Technical:** Grinds 440C. Offers gold and silver castings.Offers stainless Damascus **Prices:** Upscale. **Remarks:** Full-time maker; first knife sold in 1982. **Mark:** Last name.

CASTELLUCIO, RICH,
220 Stairs Rd, Amsterdam, NY 12010, Phone: 518-843-5540, rcastellucio@ nycap.rr.com
Patterns: Bowies, push daggers, and fantasy knives. **Technical:** Uses ATS-34, 440C, 154CM. I use stabilized wood, bone for the handles. Guards are made of copper, brass, stainless, nickle, and mokume.

CASWELL, JOE,
173 S Ventu Park Rd, Newbury, CA 91320, Phone: 805-499-0707, Web:www. caswellknives.com
Specialties: Historic pattern welded knives and swords, hand forged. Also high precision folding and fixed blade "gentleman" and "tactical" knives of his design, period firearms. Inventor of the "In-Line" retractable pocket clip for folding knives. **Patterns:**Hunters, tactical/utility, fighters, bowies, daggers, pattern welded medieval swords, precision folders. **Technical:**Forges own Damascus especially historic forms. Sometimes uses modern stainless steels and Damascus of other makers. Makes some pieces entirely by hand, others using the latest CNC techniques and by hand. Makes sheaths too. **Prices:**$100-$5,500. **Remarks:**Full time makers since 1995. Making mostly historic recreations for exclusive clientele. Recently moving into folding knives and 'modern' designs. **Mark:**CASWELL or CASWELL USA Accompanied by a mounted knight logo.

CATOE, DAVID R,
4024 Heutte Dr, Norfolk, VA 23518, Phone: 757-480-3191
Technical: Does own forging, Damascus and heat treatments. **Price:** $200 to $500; some higher. **Remarks:** Part-time maker; trained by Dan Maragni 1985-1988; first knife sold 1989. **Mark:** Leaf of a camellia.

CAWTHORNE, CHRISTOPHER A,
PO Box 604, Wrangell, AK 99929, Phone: 661-902-3724, chriscawthorne@ hotmail.com
Specialties: High-carbon steel, cable wire rope, silver wire inlay. **Patterns:** Forge welded Damascus and wire rope, random pattern. **Technical:** Hand forged, 50 lb. little giant power hammer, W-2, 0-1, L6, 1095. **Prices:** $650 to $2500. **Remarks:** School ABS 1985 w/Bill Moran, hand forged, heat treat. **Mark:** Cawthorne, forged in stamp.

CECCHINI, GUSTAVO T.,
R. XV Novembro 2841, Sao Jose Rio Preto SP, 15015110, Phone: 55 1732224267, tomaki@terra.com.be Web: www.gtcknives.com
Specialties: Tactical and HiTech folders. **Technical:** Stock removal. Stainless steel fixed blades. S30V, S35Vn, S90V, CowryX, Damasteel, Chad Nichols SS damascus, RWL 34, CPM 154 CM, BG 42. **Prices:** $500 - $1500. **Remarks:** Full-time since 2004. **Mark:** Tang Stamp "GTC"

CEPRANO, PETER J.,
213 Townsend Brooke Rd., Auburn, ME 04210, Phone: 207-786-5322, bpknives@gmail.com
Specialties: Traditional working/using straight knives; tactical/defense straight knives. Own designs or to a customer's specs. **Patterns:** Hunters, skinners, utility, Bowies, fighters, camp and survival, neck knives. **Technical:** Forges 1095, 5160, W2, 52100 and old files; grinds CPM154cm, ATS-34, 440C, D2, CPMs30v, Damascus from other makes and other tool steels. Hand-sewn and tooled leather and Kydex sheaths. **Prices:** Starting at $125. **Remarks:** Full-time maker, first knife sold in 2001. Doing business as Big Pete Knives. **Mark:** Bold BPK over small BigPeteKnivesUSA.

CHAFFEE, JEFF L,
14314 N. Washington St, PO Box 1, Morris, IN 47033, Phone: 812-212-6188
Specialties: Fancy working and utility folders and straight knives. **Patterns:** Fighters, dagger, hunter and locking folders. **Technical:** Grinds commercial Damascus, 440C, ATS-34, D2 and O1. Prefers natural handle materials. **Prices:** $350 to $2000. **Remarks:** Part-time maker; first knife sold in 1988. **Mark:** Last name.

CHAMBERLAIN, CHARLES R,
PO Box 156, Barren Springs, VA 24313-0156, Phone: 703-381-5137

CHAMBERLAIN, JON A,
15 S. Lombard, E. Wenatchee, WA 98802, Phone: 509-884-6591
Specialties: Working and kitchen knives to customer specs; exotics on special order. **Patterns:** Over 100 patterns in stock. **Technical:** Prefers ATS-34, D2, L6 and Damascus. **Prices:** Start at $50. **Remarks:** First knife sold in 1986. Doing business as Johnny Custom Knifemakers. **Mark:** Name in oval with city and state enclosing.

CHAMBERLIN, JOHN A,
11535 Our Rd., Anchorage, AK 99516, Phone: 907-346-1524, Fax: 907-562-4583
Specialties: Art and working knives. **Patterns:** Daggers and hunters; some folders. **Technical:** Grinds ATS-34, 440C, A2, D2 and Damascus. Uses Alaskan handle materials such as oosic, jade, whale jawbone, fossil ivory. **Prices:** Start at $200. **Remarks:** Favorite knives to make are double-edged. Does own heat treating and cryogenic deep freeze. Full-time maker; first knife sold in 1984. **Mark:** Name over English shield and dagger.

CHAMBLIN, JOEL,
960 New Hebron Church Rd, Concord, GA 30206, Phone: 678-588-6769, chamblinknives@yahoo.com Web: chamblinknives.com
Specialties: Fancy and working folders. **Patterns:** Fancy locking folders, traditional, multi-blades and utility. **Technical:** Uses ATS-34, CPM 154, and commercial Damascus. Offers filework. **Prices:** Start at $400. **Remarks:** Full-time maker; first knife sold in 1989. **Mark:** Last name.

CHAMPION, ROBERT,
7001 Red Rock Rd., Amarillo, TX 79118, Phone: 806-622-3970
Specialties: Traditional working straight knives. **Patterns:** Hunters, skinners, camp knives, Bowies, daggers. **Technical:** Grinds 440C and D2. **Prices:** $100 to $600. **Remarks:** Part-time maker; first knife sold in 1979. Stream-line hunters. **Mark:** Last name with dagger logo, city and state.

CHAPO, WILLIAM G,
45 Wildridge Rd, Wilton, CT 06897, Phone: 203-544-9424
Specialties: Classic straight knives and folders of his design and to customer specs; period pieces. **Patterns:** Boots, Bowies and locking folders. **Technical:** Forges stainless Damascus. Offers filework. **Prices:** $750 and up. **Remarks:** Full-time maker; first knife sold in 1989. **Mark:** First and middle initials, last name, city, state.

CHARD, GORDON R,
104 S. Holiday Lane, Iola, KS 66749, Phone: 620-365-2311, Fax: 620-365-2311, gchard@cox.net
Specialties: High tech folding knives in one-of-a-kind styles. **Patterns:** Liner locking folders of own design. Also fixed blade Art Knives. **Technical:** Clean work with attention to fit and finish. Blade steel mostly ATS-34 and 154CM, some CPM440V Vaso Wear and Damascus. **Prices:** $150 to $2500. **Remarks:** First knife sold in 1983. **Mark:** Name, city and state surrounded by wheat on each side.

CHASE, ALEX,
208 E. Pennsylvania Ave., DeLand, FL 32724, Phone: 386-734-9918, chase8578@ bellsouth.net
Specialties: Historical steels, classic and traditional straight knives of his design and to customer specs. **Patterns:** Art, fighters, hunters and Japanese style. **Technical:** Forges O1-L6 Damascus, meteoric Damascus, 52100, 5160; uses fossil walrus and mastodon ivory etc. **Prices:** $150 to $1000; some to $3500. **Remarks:** Full-time maker. Guild member since 1996. Doing business as Confederate Forge. **Mark:** Stylized initials-A.C.

CHASE, JOHN E,
217 Walnut, Aledo, TX 76008, Phone: 817-441-8331, jchaseknives@sbcglobal. net
Specialties: Straight high-tech working knives in standard patterns or to customer specs. **Patterns:** Hunters, fighters, daggers and Bowies. **Technical:** Grinds D2, O1, 440C; offers mostly satin finishes. **Prices:** Start at $265. **Remarks:** Part-time maker; first knife sold in 1974. **Mark:** Last name in logo.

CHAUVIN, JOHN,
200 Anna St, Scott, LA 70583, Phone: 337-237-6138, Fax: 337-230-7980
Specialties: Traditional working and using straight knives of his design, to customer specs and in standard patterns. **Patterns:** Bowies, fighters, and hunters. **Technical:** Grinds ATS-34, 440C and O1 high-carbon. Paul Bos heat treating. Uses ivory, stag, oosic and stabilized Louisiana swamp maple for handle materials. Makes sheaths using alligator and ostrich. **Prices:** $200 and up. Bowies start at $500. **Remarks:** Part-time maker; first knife sold in 1995. **Mark:** Full name, city, state.

CHAUZY, ALAIN,
1 Rue de Paris, 21140 Seur-en-Auxios, FRANCE, Phone: 03-80-97-03-30, Fax: 03-80-97-34-14
Specialties: Fixed blades, folders, hunters, Bowies-scagel-style. **Technical:** Forged blades only. Steels used XC65, 07C, and own Damascus. **Prices:** Contact maker for quote. **Remarks:** Part-time maker. **Mark:** Number 2 crossed by an arrow and name.

CHEATHAM, BILL,
PO Box 636, Laveen, AZ 85339, Phone: 602-237-2786, blademan76@aol.com
Specialties: Working straight knives and folders. **Patterns:** Hunters, fighters, boots and axes; locking folders. **Technical:** Grinds 440C. **Prices:** $150 to $350; exceptional knives to $600. **Remarks:** Full-time maker; first knife sold in 1976. **Mark:** Name, city, state.

CHERRY, FRANK J,
3412 Tiley N.E., Albuquerque, NM 87110, Phone: 505-883-8643

CHEW, LARRY,
515 Cleveland Rd Unit A-9, Granbury, TX 76049, Phone: 817-573-8035, chewman@swbell.net; Web: www.voodooinside.com
Specialties: High-tech folding knives. **Patterns:** Double action automatic and manual folding patterns of his design. **Technical:** CAD designed folders utilizing roller bearing pivot design known as "VooDoo." Double action automatic folders with a variety of obvious and disguised release mechanisms, some

with lock-outs. **Prices:** Manual folders start at $475, double action autos start at $750. **Remarks:** Made and sold first knife in 1988, first folder in 1989. Full-time maker since 1997. **Mark:** Name and location etched in blade, Damascus autos marked on spring inside frame. Earliest knives stamped LC.

CHINNOCK, DANIEL T.,
380 River Ridge Dr., Union, MO 63084, Phone: 314-276-6936, Web: www.DanChinnock.com; email: Sueanddanc@cs.com
Specialties: One of a kind folders in Damascus and Mammoth Ivory. Performs intricate pearl inlays into snake wood and giraffe bone. Makes matching ivory pistol grips for colt 1911's and Colt SAA. **Patterns:** New folder designs each year, thin ground and delicate gentleman's folders, large "hunting" folders in stainless Damascus and CPM154. Several standard models carried by Internet dealers. **Prices:** $500-$1500 **Remarks:** Full-time maker in 2005 and a voting member of the Knifemakers Guild. Performs intricate file work on all areas of knife. **Mark:** Signature on inside of backbar, starting in 2009 blades are stamped with a large "C" and "Dan" buried inside the "C".

CHOATE, MILTON,
1665 W. County 17-1/2, Somerton, AZ 85350, Phone: 928-627-7251, mccustom@juno.com
Specialties: Classic working and using straight knives of his design, to customer specs and in standard patterns. **Patterns:** Bowies, hunters and utility/camp knives. **Technical:** Grinds 440C; grinds and forges 1095 and 5160. Does filework on top and guards on request. **Prices:** $200 to $800. **Remarks:** Full-time maker, first knife made in 1990. All knives come with handmade sheaths by Judy Choate. **Mark:** Knives marked "Choate."

CHOMILIER, ALAIN AND JORIS,
20 rue des Hauts de Chanturgue, 63100 Clermont-Ferrand, France, Phone: + 33 4 73 25 64 47, jo_chomilier@yahoo.fr
Specialties: One-of-a-kind knives; exclusive designs; art knives in carved patinated bronze, mainly folders, some straight knives and art daggers. **Patterns:** Liner-lock, side-lock, button-lock, lockback folders. **Technical:** Grind carbon and stainless damascus; also carve and patinate bronze. **Prices:** $400 to $3000, some to $4000. **Remarks:** Spare-time makers; first knife sold in 1995; Use fossil stone and ivory, mother-of-pearl, (fossil) coral, meteorite, bronze, gemstones, high karat gold. **Mark:** A. J. Chomilier in italics.

CHRISTENSEN, JON P,
516 Blue Grouse, Stevensville, MT 59870, Phone: 406-697-8377, jpcknives@gmail.com; Web: www.jonchristensenknives.com
Specialties: Hunting/utility knives, folders, art knives. **Patterns:** Mosaic damascus **Technical:** Sole authorship, forges 01, 1084, 52100, 5160, Damascus from 1084/15N20. **Prices:** $220 and up. **Remarks:** ABS Mastersmith, first knife sold in 1999. **Mark:** First and middle initial surrounded by last initial.

CHURCHMAN, T W (TIM),
475 Saddle Horn Drive, Bandera, TX 78003, Phone: 830-796-8350
Specialties: Fancy and traditional straight knives. Bird/trout knives of his design and to customer specs. **Patterns:** Bird/trout knives, Bowies, daggers, fighters, boot knives, some miniatures. **Technical:** Grinds 440C, D2 and 154CM. Offers stainless fittings, fancy filework, exotic and stabilized woods, elk and other antler, and hand sewed lined sheaths. Also flower pins as a style. **Prices:** $350 to $450; some to $2,250. **Remarks:** Part-time maker; first knife made in 1981 after reading "*KNIVES '81.*" Doing business as "Custom Knives Churchman Made." **Mark:** "Churchman" over Texas outline, "Bandera" under.

CLAIBORNE, JEFF,
1470 Roberts Rd, Franklin, IN 46131, Phone: 317-736-7443, jeff@claiborneknives.com; Web: www.claiborneknives.com
Specialties: Multi blade slip joint folders. All one-of-a-kind by hand, no jigs or fixtures, swords, straight knives, period pieces, camp knives, hunters, fighters, ethnic swords all periods. Handle: uses stag, pearl, oosic, bone ivory, mastadon-mammoth, elephant or exotic woods. **Technical:** Forges high-carbon steel, makes Damascus, forges cable grinds, O1, 1095, 5160, 52100, L6. **Prices:** $250 and up. **Remarks:** Part-time maker; first knife sold in 1989. **Mark:** Stylized initials in an oval.

CLAIBORNE, RON,
2918 Ellistown Rd, Knox, TN 37924, Phone: 615-524-2054, Bowie@icy.net
Specialties: Multi-blade slip joints, swords, straight knives. **Patterns:** Hunters, daggers, folders. **Technical:** Forges Damascus: mosaic, powder mosaic. Prefers bone and natural handle materials; some exotic woods. **Prices:** $125 to $2500. **Remarks:** Part-time maker; first knife sold in 1979. Doing business as Thunder Mountain Forge Claiborne Knives. **Mark:** Claiborne.

CLARK, D E (LUCKY),
413 Lyman Lane, Johnstown, PA 15909-1409
Specialties: Working straight knives and folders to customer specs. **Patterns:** Customer designs. **Technical:** Grinds D2, 440C, 154CM. **Prices:** $100 to $200; some higher. **Remarks:** Part-time maker; first knife sold in 1975. **Mark:** Name on one side; "Lucky" on other.

CLARK, HOWARD F,
115 35th Pl, Runnells, IA 50237, Phone: 515-966-2126, howard@mvforge.com; Web: mvforge.com
Specialties: Currently Japanese-style swords. **Patterns:** Katana. **Technical:** Forges L6 and 1086. **Prices:** $1200 to 5000. **Remarks:** Full-time maker; first knife sold in 1979. Doing business as Morgan Valley Forge. **Prior Mark:** Block letters and serial number on folders; anvil/initials logo on straight knives. **Current Mark:** Two character kanji "Big Ear."

CLARK, NATE,
604 Baird Dr, Yoncalla, OR 97499, nateclarkknives@hotmail.com; Web: www.nateclarkknives.com
Specialties: Automatics (push button and hidden release) ATS-34 mirror polish or satin finish, Damascus, pearl, ivory, abalone, woods, bone, Micarta, G-10, filework and carving and sheath knives. **Prices:** $100 to $2500. **Remarks:** Full-time knifemaker since 1996. **Mark:** Nate Clark on spring, spacer or blade.

CLARK, R W,
R.W. CLARK CUSTOM KNIVES, 17602 W. Eugene Terrace, Surprise, AZ 85388-5047, Phone: 909-279-3494, info@rwclarkknives.com
Specialties: Military field knives and Asian hybrids. Hand carved leather sheaths. **Patterns:** Fixed blade hunters, field utility and military. Also presentation and collector grade knives. **Technical:** First maker to use liquid metals LM1 material in knives. Other materials include S30V, O1, stainless and carbon Damascus. **Prices:** $75 to $2000. Average price $300. **Remarks:** Started knifemaking in 1990, full-time in 2000. **Mark:** R.W. Clark, Custom, Corona, CA in standard football shape. Also uses three Japanese characters, spelling Clark, on Asian Hybrids.

CLAY, WAYNE,
Box 125B, Pelham, TN 37366, Phone: 931-467-3472, Fax: 931-467-3076
Specialties: Working straight knives and folders in standard patterns. **Patterns:** Hunters and kitchen knives; gents and hunter patterns. **Technical:** Grinds ATS-34. **Prices:** $125 to $500; some to $1000. **Remarks:** Full-time maker; first knife sold in 1978. **Mark:** Name.

CLINCO, MARCUS,
821 Appelby Street, Venice, CA 90291, Phone: 818-610-9640, marcus@clincoknives.com
Specialties: I make mostly fixed blade knives with an emphasis on everyday working and tactical models. Most of my knives are stock removal with the exception of my sole authored damascus blades. I have several integral models including a one piece tactical model named the viper. **Technical:** Most working knife models in ATS 34. Integrals in O-1, D-2 and 440 C. Damascus in 1080 and 15 N 20. Large camp and Bowie models in 5160 and D-2. Handle materials used include micarta, stabilized wood, G-10 and occasionally stag and ivory. **Prices:** $200 - $600.

COATS, KEN,
317 5th Ave, Stevens Point, WI 54481, Phone: 715-544-0115, kandk_c@charter.net
Specialties: Does own jigged bone scales **Patterns:** Traditional slip joints - shadow patterns **Technical:** ATS-34 Blades and springs. Milled frames. Grinds ATS-34, 440C. Stainless blades and backsprings. Does all own heat treating and freeze cycle. Blades are drawn to 60RC. Nickel silver or brass bolsters on folders are soldered, neutralized and pinned. Handles are jigged bone, hardwoods antler, and Micarta. Cuts and jigs own bone, usually shades of brown or green. **Prices:** $300 and up

COCKERHAM, LLOYD,
1717 Carolyn Ave, Denham Springs, IA 70726, Phone: 225-665-1565

COFFEY, BILL,
68 Joshua Ave, Clovis, CA 93611, Phone: 559-299-4259
Specialties: Working and fancy straight knives and folders of his design. **Patterns:** Hunters, fighters, utility, LinerLock® folders and fantasy knives. **Technical:** Grinds 440C, ATS-34, A-Z and commercial Damascus. **Prices:** $250 to $1000; some to $2500. **Remarks:** Full-time maker. First knife sold in 1993. **Mark:** First and last name, city, state.

COFFMAN, DANNY,
541 Angel Dr S, Jacksonville, AL 36265-5787, Phone: 256-435-1619
Specialties: Straight knives and folders of his design. Now making liner locks for $650 to $1200 with natural handles and contrasting Damascus blades and bolsters. **Patterns:** Hunters, locking and slip-joint folders. **Technical:** Grinds Damascus, 440C and D2. Offers filework and engraving. **Prices:** $100 to $400; some to $800. **Remarks:** Spare-time maker; first knife sold in 1992. Doing business as Customs by Coffman. **Mark:** Last name stamped or engraved.

COHEA, JOHN M,
114 Rogers Dr., Nettleton, MS 38855, Phone: 662-322-5916, jhncohea@hotmail.com Web: http://jmcknives.blademakers.com
Specialties: Frontier style knives, hawks, and leather. **Patterns:** Bowies, hunters, patch/neck knives, tomahawks, and friction folders. **Technical:** Makes both forged and stock removal knives using high carbon steels and damascus. Uses natural handle materials that include antler, bone, ivory, horn, and figured hardwoods. Also makes rawhide covered sheaths that include fringe, tacks, antique trade beads, and other period correct materials. **Prices:** $100 - $1500, some higher. **Remarks:** Part-time maker, first knife sold in 1999. **Mark:** COHEA stamped on riccasso.

COHEN, N J (NORM),
2408 Sugarcone Rd, Baltimore, MD 21209, Phone: 410-484-3841, inquiry@njcknives.com; Web:www.njcknives.com
Specialties: Working class knives. **Patterns:** Hunters, skinners, bird knives, push daggers, boots, kitchen and practical customer designs. **Technical:** Stock removal 440C, ATS-34. Uses Micarta, Corian. Some woods and stabilized woods in handles. **Prices:** $50 to $250. **Remarks:** Part-time maker; first knife sold in 1982. **Mark:** NJC engraved.

COHEN, TERRY A,
PO Box 406, Laytonville, CA 95454
   Specialties: Working straight knives and folders. **Patterns:** Bowies to boot knives and locking folders; mini-boot knives. **Technical:** Grinds stainless; hand rubs; tries for good balance. **Prices:** $85 to $150; some to $325. **Remarks:** Part-time maker; first knife sold in 1983. **Mark:** TERRY KNIVES, city and state.

COIL, JIMMIE J,
2936 Asbury Pl, Owensboro, KY 42303, Phone: 270-684-7827
   Specialties: Traditional working and straight knives of his design. **Patterns:** Hunters, Bowies and fighters. **Technical:** Grinds 440C, ATS-34 and D2. Blades are flat-ground with brush finish; most have tapered tang. Offers filework. **Prices:** $65 to $250; some to $750. **Remarks:** Spare-time maker; first knife sold in 1974. **Mark:** Name.

COLE, DAVE,
620 Poinsetta Dr, Satellite Beach, FL 32937, Phone: 321-773-1687, Web: http://dcknivesandleather.blademakers.com
   Specialties: Fixed blades and friction folders of his design or customers. **Patterns:** Utility, hunters, and Bowies. **Technical:** Grinds O1, 1095, 1080, Damascus; prefers natural handle materials. Full custom sheathmaker specializing in inlays, exotics, lacing. **Prices:** $100 and up. **Remarks:** Part-time maker, custom sheath services for others; first knife sold in 1991. **Mark:** D Cole.

COLE, JAMES M,
505 Stonewood Blvd, Bartonville, TX 76226, Phone: 817-430-0302, dogcole@swbell.net

COLE, WELBORN I,
365 Crystal Ct, Athens, GA 30606, Phone: 404-261-3977
   Specialties: Traditional straight knives of his design. **Patterns:** Hunters. **Technical:** Grinds 440C, ATS-34 and D2. Good wood scales. **Prices:** NA. **Remarks:** Full-time maker; first knife sold in 1983. **Mark:** Script initials.

COLEMAN, JOHN A,
7325 Bonita Way, Citrus Heights, CA 95610-3003, Phone: 916-335-1568, slimsknifes@yahoo.com
   Specialties: Minis, hunters, bowies of his design or yours. **Patterns:** Plain to fancy file back working knives. **Technical:** Grinds 440C, ATS-34, 145CM, D2, 1095, 5160, 01. Some hand-forged blades. Exotic woods bone, antler and some ivory. **Prices:** $100 to $500. **Remarks:** Does some carving in handles. Part-time maker. First knife sold in 1989. OKCA 2010 Award winner for best mini of show. **Mark:** Cowboy setting on log whittling Slim's Custom Knives above cowboy and name and state under cowboy.

COLLINS, LYNN M,
138 Berkley Dr, Elyria, OH 44035, Phone: 440-366-7101
   Specialties: Working straight knives. **Patterns:** Field knives, boots and fighters. **Technical:** Grinds D2, 154CM and 440C. **Prices:** Start at $150. **Remarks:** Spare-time maker; first knife sold in 1980. **Mark:** Initials, asterisks.

COLTER, WADE,
PO Box 2340, Colstrip, MT 59323, Phone: 406-748-4573
   Specialties: Fancy and embellished straight knives, folders and swords of his design; historical and period pieces. **Patterns:** Bowies, swords and folders. **Technical:** Hand forges 52100 ball bearing steel and L6, 1090, cable and chain Damascus from 5N20 and 1084. Carves and makes sheaths. **Prices:** $250 to $3500. **Remarks:** Part-time maker; first knife sold in 1990. Doing business as "Colter's Hell" Forge. **Mark:** Initials on left side ricasso.

CONKLIN, GEORGE L,
Box 902, Ft. Benton, MT 59442, Phone: 406-622-3268, Fax: 406-622-3410, 7bbgrus@3rivers.net
   Specialties: Designer and manufacturer of the "Brisket Breaker." **Patterns:** Hunters, utility/camp knives and hatchets. **Technical:** Grinds 440C, ATS-34, D2, 1095, 154CM and 5160. Offers some forging and heat-treats for others. Offers some jewelling. **Prices:** $65 to $200; some to $1000. **Remarks:** Full-time maker. Doing business as Rocky Mountain Knives. **Mark:** Last name in script.

CONLEY, BOB,
1013 Creasy Rd, Jonesboro, TN 37659, Phone: 423-753-3302
   Specialties: Working straight knives and folders. **Patterns:** Lockers, two-blades, gents, hunters, traditional-styles, straight hunters. **Technical:** Grinds 440C, 154CM and ATS-34. Engraves. **Prices:** $250 to $450; some to $600. **Remarks:** Full-time maker; first knife sold in 1979. **Mark:** Full name, city, state.

CONN JR., C T,
206 Highland Ave, Attalla, AL 35954, Phone: 205-538-7688
   Specialties: Working folders, some fancy. **Patterns:** Full range of folding knives. **Technical:** Grinds O2, 440C and 154CM. **Prices:** $125 to $300; some to $600. **Remarks:** Part-time maker; first knife sold in 1982. **Mark:** Name.

CONNOLLY, JAMES,
2486 Oro-Quincy Hwy, Oroville, CA 95966, Phone: 530-534-5363, rjconnolly@sbcglobal.net
   Specialties: Classic working and using knives of his design. **Patterns:** Boots, Bowies, daggers and swords. **Technical:** Grinds ATS-34, BG42, A2, O1. **Prices:** $100 to $500; some to $1500. **Remarks:** Part-time maker; first knife sold in 1980. Doing business as Gold Rush Designs. **Mark:** First initial, last name, Handmade.

CONNOR, JOHN W,
PO Box 12981, Odessa, TX 79768-2981, Phone: 915-362-6901

CONNOR, MICHAEL,
Box 502, Winters, TX 79567, Phone: 915-754-5602
   Specialties: Straight knives, period pieces, some folders. **Patterns:** Hunters to camp knives to traditional locking folders to Bowies. **Technical:** Forges 5160, O1, 1084 steels and his own Damascus. **Prices:** Moderate to upscale. **Remarks:** Spare-time maker; first knife sold in 1974. ABS Master Smith 1983. **Mark:** Last name, M.S.

CONTI, JEFFREY D,
21104 75th St E, Bonney Lake, WA 98390, Phone: 253-447-4660, Fax: 253-512-8629
   Specialties: Working straight knives. **Patterns:** Fighters and survival knives; hunters, camp knives and fishing knives. **Technical:** Grinds D2, 154CM and O1. Engraves. **Prices:** Start at $80. **Remarks:** Part-time maker; first knife sold in 1980. Does own heat treating. **Mark:** Initials, year, steel type, name and number of knife.

CONWAY, JOHN,
13301 100th Place NE, Kirkland, WA 98034, Phone: 425-823-2821, jcknives@verizon.net
   Specialties: Folders; working and Damascus. Straight knives, camp, utility and fighting knives. **Patterns:** LinerLock® folders of own design. Hidden tang straight knives of own design. **Technical:** Flat grinds forged carbon steels and own Damascus steel, including mosaic. **Prices:** $300 to $850. **Remarks:** Part-time maker since 1999. **Mark:** Oval with stylized initials J C inset.

COOGAN, ROBERT,
1560 Craft Center Dr, Smithville, TN 37166, Phone: 615-597-6801, http://iweb.tntech.edu/rcoogan/
   Specialties: One-of-a-kind knives. **Patterns:** Unique items like ulu-style Appalachian herb knives. **Technical:** Forges; his Damascus is made from nickel steel and W1. **Prices:** Start at $100. **Remarks:** Part-time maker; first knife sold in 1979. **Mark:** Initials or last name in script.

COOK, JAMES R,
455 Anderson Rd, Nashville, AR 71852, Phone: 870 845 5173, jr@jrcookknives.com; Web: www.jrcookknives.com
   Specialties: Working straight knives and folders of his design or to customer specs. **Patterns:** Bowies, hunters and camp knives. **Technical:** Forges 1084 and high-carbon Damascus. **Prices:** $500 to $5500. **Remarks:** Full-time maker; first knife sold in 1986. **Mark:** First and middle initials, last name.

COOK, LOUISE,
475 Robinson Ln, Ozark, IL 62972, Phone: 618-777-2932
   Specialties: Working and using straight knives of her design and to customer specs; period pieces. **Patterns:** Bowies, hunters and utility/camp knives. **Technical:** Forges 5160. Filework; pin work; silver wire inlay. **Prices:** Start at $50/inch. **Remarks:** Part-time maker; first knife sold in 1990. Doing business as Panther Creek Forge. **Mark:** First name and Journeyman stamp on one side; panther head on the other.

COOK, MIKE,
475 Robinson Ln, Ozark, IL 62972, Phone: 618-777-2932
   Specialties: Traditional working and using straight knives of his design and to customer specs. **Patterns:** Bowies, hunters and utility/camp knives. **Technical:** Forges 5160. Filework; pin work. **Prices:** Start at $50/inch. **Remarks:** Spare-time maker; first knife sold in 1991. **Mark:** First initial, last name and Journeyman stamp on one side; panther head on the other.

COOK, MIKE A,
10927 Shilton Rd, Portland, MI 48875, Phone: 517-242-1352, macook@hughes.net Web: www.artofishi.com
   Specialties: Fancy/embellished and period pieces of his design. **Patterns:** Daggers, fighters and hunters. **Technical:** Stone bladed knives in agate, obsidian and jasper. Scrimshaws; opal inlays. **Prices:** $60 to $300; some to $800. **Remarks:** Part-time maker; first knife sold in 1988. Doing business as Art of Ishi. **Mark:** Initials and year.

COOMBS JR., LAMONT,
546 State Rt 46, Bucksport, ME 04416, Phone: 207-469-3057, Fax: 207-469-3057, theknifemaker@hotmail.com; Web: www.knivesby.com/coomb-knives.html
   Specialties: Classic fancy and embellished straight knives; traditional working and using straight knives. Knives of his design and to customer specs. **Patterns:** Hunters, folders and utility/camp knives. **Technical:** Hollow- and flat-grinds ATS-34, 440C, A2, D2 and O1; grinds Damascus from other makers. **Prices:** $100 to $500; some to $3500. **Remarks:** Full-time maker; first knife sold in 1988. **Mark:** Last name on banner, handmade underneath.

COON, RAYMOND C,
21135 S.E. Tillstrom Rd, Gresham, OR 97080, Phone: 503-658-2252, Raymond@damascusknife.com; Web: Damascusknife.com
   Specialties: Working straight knives in standard patterns. **Patterns:** Hunters, Bowies, daggers, boots and axes. **Technical:** Forges high-carbon steel and Damascus or 97089. **Prices:** Start at $235. **Remarks:** Full-time maker; does own leatherwork, makes own Damascus, daggers; first knife sold in 1995. **Mark:** First initial, last name.

COOPER, PAUL,
9 Woods St., Woburn, MA 01801, Phone: 781-938-0519, byksm@yahoo.com
Specialties: Forged, embellished, hand finished fixed-blade knives. **Patterns:** One of a kind designs, often inspired by traditional and historic pieces. **Technical:** Works in tool steel, damascus and natural materials. **Prices:** $500 - $2000. **Remarks:** Part-time maker, formally apprenticed under J.D. Smith. Sold first piece in 2006. **Mark:** Letter C inside bleeding heart.

COPELAND, THOM,
171 Country Line Rd S, Nashville, AR 71852, tcope@cswnet.com
Specialties: Hand forged fixed blades; hunters, Bowies and camp knives. **Remarks:** Member of ABS and AKA (Arkansas Knifemakers Association). **Mark:** Copeland.

COPPINS, DANIEL,
7303 Sherrard Rd, Cambridge, OH 43725, Phone: 740-439-4199
Specialties: Grinds 440 C, D-2. Antler handles. **Patterns:** Drop point hunters, fighters, Bowies, bird and trout daggers. **Prices:** $40 to $800. **Remarks:** Sold first knife in 2002. **Mark:** DC.

CORBY, HAROLD,
218 Brandonwood Dr, Johnson City, TN 37604, Phone: 423-926-9781
Specialties: Large fighters and Bowies; self-protection knives; art knives. Along with art knives and combat knives, Corby now has a all new automatic MO.PB1, also side lock MO LL-1 with titanium liners G-10 handles. **Patterns:** Sub-hilt fighters and hunters. **Technical:** Grinds 154CM, ATS-34 and 440C. **Prices:** $200 to $6000. **Remarks:** Full-time maker; first knife sold in 1969. Doing business as Knives by Corby. **Mark:** Last name.

CORDOVA, JOSEPH G,
PO Box 977, Peralta, NM 87042, Phone: 505-869-3912, kcordova@rt66.com
Specialties: One-of-a-kind designs, some to customer specs. **Patterns:** Fighter called the 'Gladiator', hunters, boots and cutlery. **Technical:** Forges 1095, 5160; grinds ATS-34, 440C and 154CM. **Prices:** Moderate to upscale. **Remarks:** Full-time maker; first knife sold in 1953. Past chairman of American Bladesmith Society. **Mark:** Cordova made.

CORKUM, STEVE,
34 Basehoar School Rd, Littlestown, PA 17340, Phone: 717-359-9563, sco7129849@aol.com; Web: www.hawknives.com

COSTA, SCOTT,
409 Coventry Rd, Spicewood, TX 78669, Phone: 830-693-3431
Specialties: Working straight knives. **Patterns:** Hunters, skinners, axes, trophy sets, custom boxed steak sets, carving sets and bar sets. **Technical:** Grinds D2, ATS-34, 440 and Damascus. Heat-treats. **Prices:** $225 to $2000. **Remarks:** Full-time maker; first knife sold in 1985. **Mark:** Initials connected.

COTTRILL, JAMES I,
1776 Ransburg Ave, Columbus, OH 43223, Phone: 614-274-0020
Specialties: Working straight knives of his design. **Patterns:** Caters to the boating and hunting crowd; cutlery. **Technical:** Grinds O1, D2 and 440C. Likes filework. **Prices:** $95 to $250; some to $500. **Remarks:** Full-time maker; first knife sold in 1977. **Mark:** Name, city, state, in oval logo.

COURTNEY, ELDON,
2718 Bullinger, Wichita, KS 67204, Phone: 316-838-4053
Specialties: Working straight knives of his design. **Patterns:** Hunters, fighters and one-of-a-kinds. **Technical:** Grinds and tempers L6, 440C and spring steel. **Prices:** $100 to $500; some to $1500. **Remarks:** Full-time maker; first knife sold in 1977. **Mark:** Full name, city and state.

COURTOIS, BRYAN,
3 Lawn Ave, Saco, ME 04072, Phone: 207-282-3977, bryancourtois@verizon.net; Web: http://mysite.verizon.net/vzeui2z01
Specialties: Working straight knives; prefers customer designs, no standard patterns. **Patterns:** Functional hunters; everyday knives. **Technical:** Grinds 440C or customer request. Hollow-grinds with a variety of finishes. Specializes in granite handles and custom skeleton knives. **Prices:** Start at $75. **Remarks:** Part-time maker; first knife sold in 1988. Doing business as Castle Knives. **Mark:** A rook chess piece machined into blade using electrical discharge process.

COUSINO, GEORGE,
7818 Norfolk, Onsted, MI 49265, Phone: 517-467-4911, cousinoknives@yahoo.com; Web: www.cousinoknives.com
Specialties: Hunters, Bowies using knives. **Patterns:** Hunters, Bowies, buckskinners, folders and daggers. **Technical:** Grinds 440C. **Prices:** $95 to $300. **Remarks:** Part-time maker; first knife sold in 1981. **Mark:** Last name.

COVER, RAYMOND A,
1206 N Third St, Festus, MO 63028-1628, Phone: 636-937-5955
Specialties: High-tech working straight knives and folders in standard patterns. **Patterns:** Slip joint folders, two-bladed folders. **Technical:** Grinds D2, and ATS-34. **Prices:** $165 to $250; some to $400. **Remarks:** Part-time maker; first knife sold in 1974. **Mark:** Name.

COWLES, DON,
1026 Lawndale Dr, Royal Oak, MI 48067, Phone: 248-541-4619, don@cowlesknives.com; Web: www.cowlesknives.com
Specialties: Straight, non-folding pocket knives of his design. **Patterns:** Gentlemen's pocket knives. **Technical:** Grinds CPM154, S30V, Damascus, Talonite. Engraves; pearl inlays in some handles. **Prices:** Start at $300. **Remarks:** Full-time maker; first knife sold in 1994. **Mark:** Full name with oak leaf.

COX, COLIN J,
107 N. Oxford Dr, Raymore, MO 64083, Phone: 816-322-1977, Colin4knives@aol.com; Web: www.colincoxknives.com
Specialties: Working straight knives and folders of his design; period pieces. **Patterns:** Hunters, fighters and survival knives. Folders, two-blades, gents and hunters. **Technical:** Grinds D2, 440C, 154CM and ATS-34. **Prices:** $125 to $750; some to $4000. **Remarks:** Full-time maker; first knife sold in 1981. **Mark:** Full name, city and state.

COX, LARRY,
701 W. 13th St, Murfreesboro, AR 71958, Phone: 870-258-2429, Fax: Cell: 870-557-8062
Patterns: Hunters, camp knives, Bowies, and skinners. **Technical:** Forges carbon steel 1084, 1080, 15N29, 5160 and Damascus. Forges own pattern welded Damascus as well as doing own heat treat. **Prices:** $150 and up. **Remarks:** Sole ownership; knives and sheaths. Part-time maker; first knife sold in 2007. Member ABS and Arkansas Knifemakers Association. **Mark:** COX.

COX, SAM,
1756 Love Springs Rd, Gaffney, SC 29341, Phone: 864-489-1892
Remarks: Started making knives in 1981 for another maker. 1st knife sold under own name in 1983. Full-time maker 1985-2009. Retired in 2010. Now part time. **Mark:** Different logo each year.

CRAIG, ROGER L,
2617 SW Seabrook Ave, Topeka, KS 66614, Phone: 785-249-4109
Specialties: Working and camp knives, some fantasy; all his design. **Patterns:** Fighters, hunter. **Technical:** Grinds 1095 and 5160. Most knives have file work. **Prices:** $50 to $250. **Remarks:** Part-time maker; first knife sold in 1991. Doing business as Craig Knives. **Mark:** Last name-Craig.

CRAIN, JACK W,
PO Box 212, Granbury, TX 76048, jack@jackcrainknives.com Web: www.jackcrainknives.com
Specialties: Fantasy and period knives; combat and survival knives. **Patterns:** One-of-a-kind art or fantasy daggers, swords and Bowies; survival knives. **Technical:** Forges Damascus; grinds stainless steel. Carves. **Prices:** $350 to $2500; some to $20,000. **Remarks:** Full-time maker; first knife sold in 1969. Designer of the knives seen in the films *Dracula 2000*, *Executive Decision*, *Demolition Man*, *Predator I* and *II*, *Commando*, *Die Hard I* and *II*, *Road House*, *Ford Fairlane* and *Action Jackson*, and television shows *War of the Worlds*, *Air Wolf*, *Kung Fu: The Legend Cont.* and *Tales of the Crypt*. **Mark:** Stylized crane.

CRAMER, BRENT,
PO BOX 99, Wheatland, IN 47597, Phone: 812-881-9961, Bdcramer@juno.com Web: BDCramerKnives.com
Specialties: Traditional and custom working and using knives. **Patterns:** Traditional single blade slip-joint folders and standard fixed blades. **Technical:** Stock removal only. Pivot bushing construction on folders. Steel: D-2, 154 CM, ATS-34, CPM-D2, CPM-154CM, 0-1, 52100, A-2. All steels heat treated in shop with LN Cryo. Handle Material: Stag, Bone, Wood, Ivory, and Micarta. **Prices:** $150 - $550. **Remarks:** Part-time maker. First fixed blade sold in 2003. First folder sold in 2007. **Mark:** BDC and B.D.Cramer.

CRAWFORD, PAT AND WES,
205 N. Center, West Memphis, AR 72301, Phone: 870-732-2452, patcrawford1@earthlink.com; Web: www.crawfordknives.com
Specialties: Stainless steel Damascus. High-tech working self-defense and combat types and folders. **Patterns:** Tactical-more fancy knives now. **Technical:** Grinds S30V. **Prices:** $400 to $2000. **Remarks:** Full-time maker; first knife sold in 1973. **Mark:** Last name.

CRAWLEY, BRUCE R,
16 Binbrook Dr, Croydon 3136 Victoria, AUSTRALIA
Specialties: Folders. **Patterns:** Hunters, lockback folders and Bowies. **Technical:** Grinds 440C, ATS-34 and commercial Damascus. Offers filework and mirror polish. **Prices:** $160 to $3500. **Remarks:** Part-time maker; first knife sold in 1990. **Mark:** Initials.

CRENSHAW, AL,
Rt 1 Box 717, Eufaula, OK 74432, Phone: 918-452-2128
Specialties: Folders of his design and in standard patterns. **Patterns:** Hunters, locking folders, slip-joint folders, multi blade folders. **Technical:** Grinds 440C, D2 and ATS-34. Does filework on back springs and blades; offers scrimshaw on some handles. **Prices:** $150 to $300; some higher. **Remarks:** Full-time maker; first knife sold in 1981. Doing business as A. Crenshaw Knives. **Mark:** First initial, last name, Lake Eufaula, state stamped; first initial last name in rainbow; Lake Eufaula across bottom with Okla. in middle.

CRIST, ZOE,
2274 Deep Gap Rd., Flat Rock, NC 28731, Phone: 828-685-0147, zoe@zoecristknives.com Web: www.zoecristknives.com
Specialties: Mosaic and classic pattern Damascus. Custom Damascus and traditional Damascus working and art knives. Also makes Mokume. Works to customer specs. **Patterns:** All Damascus hunters, bowies, fighters, neck, boot, and high-end art knives. **Technical:** Makes all his own Damascus Steel from 1095, L6, 15n20. Forges all knives, heat treats, filework, differential heat treating. **Prices:** $150 - $2500. **Remarks:** Full-time maker, has been making knives since 1988, went full-time 2009. Also makes own leather sheaths. **Mark:** Small "z" with long tail on left side of blade at ricasso.

CROCKFORD, JACK,
1859 Harts Mill Rd, Chamblee, GA 30341, Phone: 770-457-4680
   Specialties: Lockback folders. **Patterns:** Hunters, fishing and camp knives, traditional folders. **Technical:** Grinds A2, D2, ATS-34 and 440C. Engraves and scrimshaws. **Prices:** Start at $175. **Remarks:** Part-time maker; first knife sold in 1975. **Mark:** Name.

CROSS, KEVIN,
PO Box 38, Higganum, CT 06441, Phone: 860-345-3949, kevincross@comcast.net
   Specialties: Working/using and presentation grade fixed-blade knives. Also, kitchen knives with custom handles. **Patterns:** Hunters, skinners, fighters. Bowies, camp knives. **Technical:** Stock removal maker. Uses O1, 1095, 154 CPM as well as Damascus from Eggerling, Ealy, Donnelly, Nichols, Barr and others. Most handles are natural materials such as burled and spalted woods, stag and ancient ivory. **Prices:** $200 - $1,200. **Remarks:** Part-time maker. First knife sold around 1997. **Mark:** Name, city and state.

CROSS, ROBERT,
RMB 200B, Manilla Rd, Tamworth 2340, NSW, AUSTRALIA, Phone: 067-618385

CROTTS, DAN,
PO Box 68, Elm Springs, AR 72728, Phone: 479-248-7116, dancrottsknives@yahoo.com Web: www.facebook.com/dancrottsknives
   Specialties: User grade, hunting, tactical and folders. **Technical:** High-end tool steel. **Prices:** $2200. **Remarks:** Specializes in making performance blades. **Mark:** Crotts.

CROWDER, ROBERT,
Box 1374, Thompson Falls, MT 59873, Phone: 406-827-4754
   Specialties: Traditional working knives to customer specs. **Patterns:** Hunters, Bowies, fighters and fillets. **Technical:** Grinds ATS-34, 154CM, 440C, Vascowear and commercial Damascus. **Prices:** $225 to $500; some to $2500. **Remarks:** Full-time maker; first knife sold in 1985. **Mark:** R Crowder signature & Montana.

CROWELL, JAMES L,
PO Box 822, 676 Newnata Cutoff, Mtn. View, AR 72560, Phone: 870-746-4215, crowellknives@yahoo.com
   Specialties: Bowie knives; fighters and working knives. **Patterns:** Hunters, fighters, Bowies, daggers and folders. Period pieces: War hammers, Japanese and European. **Technical:** Forges 10 series carbon steels as well as O1, L6 and his own Damascus. **Prices:** $425 to $4500; some to $7500. **Remarks:** Full-time maker; first knife sold in 1980. Earned ABS Master Bladesmith in 1986. **Mark:** A shooting star.

CROWL, PETER,
5786 County Road 10, Waterloo, IN 46793, Phone: 260-488-2532, pete@petecrowlknives.com; Web: www.petecrowlknives.com
   Specialties: Bowie, hunters. **Technical:** Forges 5160, 1080, W2, 52100. **Prices:** $200 and up. **Remarks:** ABS Journeyman smith. **Mark:** Last name in script.

CROWNER, JEFF,
1565 Samuel Drive, Cottage Grove, OR 97424, Phone: 541-201-3182, Fax: 541-579-3762
   Specialties: Custom knife maker. I make some of the following: wilderness survival blades, martial art weapons, hunting blades. **Technical:** I differentially heat treat every knife. I use various steels like 5160, L-6, Cable Damascus, 52100, 6150, and some stainless types. I use the following for handle materials: TeroTuf by Columbia Industrial products and exotic hardwoods and horn. I make my own custom sheaths as well with either kydex or leather.

CROWTHERS, MARK F,
PO Box 4641, Rolling Bay, WA 98061-0641, Phone: 206-842-7501

CUCCHIARA, MATT,
387 W. Hagler, Fresno, CA 93711, Phone: 559-917-2328, matt@cucchiaraknives.com Web: www.cucchiaraknives.com
   Specialties: I make large and small, plain or hand carved Ti handled Tactical framelock folders. All decoration and carving work done by maker. Also known for my hand carved Ti pocket clips. **Prices:** Start at around $400 and go as high as $1500 or so.

CULVER, STEVE,
5682 94th St, Meriden, KS 66512, Phone: 785-484-0146, Web: www.culverart.com
   Specialties: Edged tools and weapons, collectible and functional. **Patterns:** Bowies, daggers, swords, hunters, folders and edged tools. **Technical:** Forges carbon steels and his own pattern welded steels. **Prices:** $500 to $5,000. **Remarks:** Full-time maker; first knife sold in 1989. **Mark:** Last name, M. S.

CUMMING, BOB,
CUMMING KNIVES, 35 Manana Dr, Cedar Crest, NM 87008, Phone: 505-286-0509, cumming@comcast.net; Web: www.cummingknives.com
   Specialties: One-of-a-kind exhibition grade custom Bowie knives, exhibition grade and working hunters, bird & trout knives, salt and fresh water fillet knives. Low country oyster knives, custom tanto's plains Indian style sheaths & custom leather, all types of exotic handle materials, scrimshaw and engraving. Added folders in 2006. Custom oyster knives. **Prices:** $95 to $3500 and up. **Remarks:** Mentored by the late Jim Nolen, sold first knife

in 1978 in Denmark. Retired U.S. Foreign Service Officer. Member NCCKG. **Mark:** Stylized CUMMING.

CURTISS, STEVE L,
PO Box 448, Eureka, MT 59914, Phone: 406-889-5510, Fax: 406-889-5510, slc@bladerigger.com; Web: http://www.bladerigger.com
   Specialties: True custom and semi-custom production (SCP), specialized concealment blades; advanced sheaths and tailored body harnessing systems. **Patterns:** Tactical/personal defense fighters, swords, utility and custom patterns. **Technical:** Grinds A2 and Talonite®; heat-treats. Sheaths: Kydex or Kydex-lined leather laminated or Kydex-lined with Rigger Coat™. Exotic materials available. **Prices:** $50 to $10,000. **Remarks:** Full-time maker. Doing business as Blade Rigger L.L.C. Martial artist and unique defense industry tools and equipment. **Mark:** For true custom: Initials and for SCP: Blade Rigger.

CUTE, THOMAS,
State Rt 90-7071, Cortland, NY 13045, Phone: 607-749-4055
   Specialties: Working straight knives. **Patterns:** Hunters, Bowies and fighters. **Technical:** Grinds O1, 440C and ATS-34. **Prices:** $100 to $1000. **Remarks:** Full-time maker; first knife sold in 1974. **Mark:** Full name.

D

DAILEY, G E,
577 Lincoln St, Seekonk, MA 02771, Phone: 508-336-5088, gedailey@msn.com; Web: www.gedailey.com
   Specialties: One-of-a-kind exotic designed edged weapons. **Patterns:** Folders, daggers and swords. **Technical:** Reforges and grinds Damascus; prefers hollow-grinding. Engraves, carves, offers filework and sets stones and uses exotic gems and gold. **Prices:** Start at $1100. **Remarks:** Full-time maker. First knife sold in 1982. **Mark:** Last name or stylized initialed logo.

DAKE, C M,
19759 Chef Menteur Hwy, New Orleans, LA 70129-9602, Phone: 504-254-0357, Fax: 504-254-9501
   Specialties: Fancy working folders. **Patterns:** Front-lock lockbacks, button-lock folders. **Technical:** Grinds ATS-34 and Damascus. **Prices:** $500 to $2500; some higher. **Remarks:** Full-time maker; first knife sold in 1988. Doing business as Bayou Custom Cutlery. **Mark:** Last name.

DAKE, MARY H,
Rt 5 Box 287A, New Orleans, LA 70129, Phone: 504-254-0357

DALLYN, KELLY,
124 Deerbrook Place S.E., Calgary, AB, CANADA T2J 6J5, Phone: 403-475-3056, info@dallyn-knives.com Web: dallyn-knives.com
   Specialties: Kitchen, utility, and hunting knives

DAMASTEEL STAINLESS DAMASCUS,
3052 Isim Rd., Norman, OK 73026, Phone: 888-804-0683; 405-321-3614, damascus@newmex.com; Web: www.ssdamacus.com
   Patterns: Rose, Odin's eye, 5, 20, 30 twists Hakkapelitta, TNT, and infinity, Big Rose, Mumin

DAMLOVAC, SAVA,
10292 Bradbury Dr, Indianapolis, IN 46231, Phone: 317-839-4952
   Specialties: Period pieces, fantasy, Viking, Moran type all Damascus daggers. **Patterns:** Bowies, fighters, daggers, Persian-style knives. **Technical:** Uses own Damascus, some stainless, mostly hand forges. **Prices:** $150 to $2500; some higher. **Remarks:** Full-time maker; first knife sold in 1993. Specialty, Bill Moran all Damascus dagger sets, in Moran-style wood case. **Mark:** "Sava" stamped in Damascus or etched in stainless.

D'ANDREA, JOHN,
8517 N Linwood Loop, Citrus Springs, FL 34433-5045, Phone: 352-489-2803, jpda@optonline.net
   Specialties: Fancy working straight knives and folders with filework and distinctive leatherwork. **Patterns:** Hunters, fighters, daggers, folders and an occasional sword. **Technical:** Grinds ATS-34, 154CM, 440C and D2. **Prices:** $220 to $1000. **Remarks:** Part-time maker; first knife sold in 1986. **Mark:** First name, last initial imposed on samurai sword.

D'ANGELO, LAURENCE,
14703 NE 17th Ave, Vancouver, WA 98686, Phone: 360-573-0546
   Specialties: Straight knives of his design. **Patterns:** Bowies, hunters and locking folders. **Technical:** Grinds D2, ATS-34 and 440C. Hand makes all sheaths. **Prices:** $100 to $200. **Remarks:** Full-time maker; first knife sold in 1987. **Mark:** Football logo—first and middle initials, last name, city, state, Maker.

DANIEL, TRAVIS E,
PO Box 1223, Thomaston, GA 30286, Phone: 252-362-1229, tedsknives@mail.com
   Specialties: Traditional working straight knives of his design or to customer specs. **Patterns:** Hunters, fighters and utility/camp knives. **Technical:** Grinds ATS-34, 440-C, 154CM, forges his own Damascus. Stock removal. **Prices:** $90 to $1200. **Remarks:** Full-time maker; first knife sold in 1976. **Mark:** TED.

DANIELS, ALEX,
1416 County Rd 415, Town Creek, AL 35672, Phone: 256-685-0943, akdknives@hughes.net
   Specialties: Working and using straight knives and folders; period pieces, reproduction Bowies. **Patterns:** Mostly reproduction Bowies but offers full

line of knives. **Technical:** BG-42, 440C, 1095, 52100 forged blades. **Prices:** $350 to $2500. **Remarks:** Full-time maker; first knife sold in 1963. **Mark:** First and middle initials, last name, city and state.

DANNEMANN, RANDY,
RIM RANCH, 27752 P25 Rd, Hotchkiss, CO 81419
    Specialties: Classic pattern working hunters, skinners, bird, trout, kitchen & utility knives. **Technical:** Grinds 440C, 154CM, & D2 steel, in house heat treating and cryogenic enhancement. Custom fitted leather sheath for every hunting style knife, both serialized. Uses imported hardwoods, stag, or Micarta for handles. **Price:** $140 to $240 some higher. **Remarks:** First knife sold 1974. **Mark:** R. Dannemann Colorado or stamped Dannemann.

DARBY, DAVID T,
30652 S 533 Rd, Cookson, OK 74427, Phone: 918-457-4868, knfmkr@fullnet.net
    Specialties: Forged blades only, all styles. **Prices:** $350 and up. **Remarks:** ABS Journeyman Smith. **Mark:** Stylized quillion dagger incorporates last name (Darby).

DARBY, JED,
7878 E Co Rd 50 N, Greensburg, IN 47240, Phone: 812-663-2696
    Specialties: Traditional working/using straight knives of his design and to customer specs. **Patterns:** Bowies, hunters and utility/camp knives. **Technical:** Grinds 440C, ATS-34 and Damascus. **Prices:** $70 to $550; some to $1000. **Remarks:** Full-time maker; first knife sold in 1992. Doing business as Darby Knives. **Mark:** Last name and year.

DARBY, RICK,
71 Nestingrock Ln, Levittown, PA 19054
    Specialties: Working straight knives. **Patterns:** Boots, fighters and hunters with mirror finish. **Technical:** Grinds 440C and CPM440V. **Prices:** $125 to $300. **Remarks:** Part-time maker; first knife sold in 1974. **Mark:** First and middle initials, last name.

DARCEY, CHESTER L,
1608 Dominik Dr, College Station, TX 77840, Phone: 979-696-1656, DarceyKnives@yahoo.com
    Specialties: Lockback, LinerLock® and scale release folders. **Patterns:** Bowies, hunters and utilities. **Technical:** Stock removal on carbon and stainless steels, forge own Damascus. **Prices:** $200 to $1000. **Remarks:** Part-time maker, first knife sold in 1999. **Mark:** Last name in script.

DARK, ROBERT,
2218 Huntington Court, Oxford, AL 36203, Phone: 256-831-4645, dark@darkknives.com; Web: www.darkknives.com
    Specialties: Fixed blade working knives of maker's designs. Works with customer designed specifications. **Patterns:** Hunters, Bowies, camp knives, kitchen/utility, bird and trout. Standard patterns and customer designed. **Technical:** Forged and stock removal. Works with high carbon, stainless and Damascus steels. Hollow and flat grinds. **Prices:** $175 to $750. **Remarks:** Sole authorship knives and custom leather sheaths. Full-time maker. **Mark:** "R Dark" on left side of blade.

DARPINIAN, DAVE,
PO Box 2643, Olathe, KS 66063, Phone: 913-244-7114, darpo1956@yahoo.com Web: www.kansasknives.org
    Specialties: Hunters, fighters, utilities, lock back folders. **Patterns:** Full range of straight knives including art daggers and short swords. **Technical:** Art grinds, Damascus, 1095, 1084, 5160, Clay temper hammon, Stock removal and forging. **Prices:** $300 to $1000. **Remarks:** First knife sold in 1986, part-time maker. **Mark:** Last name.

DAVIDSON, EDMUND,
3345 Virginia Ave, Goshen, VA 24439, Phone: 540-997-5651, Web: www.edmunddavidson.com
    Specialties: High class art integrals. **Patterns:** Many hunters and art models. **Technical:** CPM 154-CM. **Prices:** $100 to infinity. **Remarks:** Full-time maker; first knife sold in 1986. **Mark:** Name in deer head or custom logos.

DAVIDSON, LARRY,
14249 River Rd., New Braunfels, TX 78132, Phone: 830-214-5144, lazza@davidsonknives.com; Web: www.davidsonknives.com

DAVIS, BARRY L,
4262 US 20, Castleton, NY 12033, Phone: 518-477-5036, daviscustomknives@yahoo.com
    Specialties: Collector grade Damascus folders. Traditional designs with focus on turn-of-the-century techniques employed. Sole authorship. Forges own Damascus, does all carving, filework, gold work and piquet. Uses only natural handle material. Enjoys doing multi-blade as well as single blade folders and daggers. **Prices:** Prices range from $2000 to $7000. **Remarks:** First knife sold in 1980.

DAVIS, CHARLIE,
ANZA KNIVES, PO Box 710806, Santee, CA 92072, Phone: 619-561-9445, Fax: 619-390-6283, sales@anzaknives.com; Web: www.anzaknives.com
    Specialties: Fancy and embellished working straight knives of his design. **Patterns:** Hunters, camp and utility knives. **Technical:** Grinds high-carbon files. **Prices:** $20 to $185, custom depends. **Remarks:** Full-time maker; first knife sold in 1980. Now offers custom. **Mark:** ANZA U.S.A.

DAVIS, DON,
8415 Coyote Run, Loveland, CO 80537-9665, Phone: 970-669-9016, Fax: 970-669-8072
    Specialties: Working straight knives in standard patterns or to customer

specs. **Patterns:** Hunters, utility knives, skinners and survival knives. **Technical:** Grinds 440C, ATS-34. **Prices:** $75 to $250. **Remarks:** Full-time maker; first knife sold in 1985. **Mark:** Signature, city and state.

DAVIS, JESSE W,
7398A Hwy 3, Sarah, MS 38665, Phone: 662-382-7332, jandddvais1@earthlink.net
    Specialties: Working straight knives and boots in standard patterns and to customer specs. **Patterns:** Boot knives, daggers, fighters, subhilts & Bowies. **Technical:** Grinds A2, D2, 440C and commercial Damascus. **Prices:** $125 to $1000. **Remarks:** Full-time maker; first knife sold in 1977. Former member Knifemakers Guild (in good standing). **Mark:** Name or initials.

DAVIS, JOEL,
74538 165th, Albert Lea, MN 56007, Phone: 507-377-0808, joelknives@yahoo.com
    Specialties: Complete sole authorship presentation grade highly complex pattern-welded mosaic Damascus blade and bolster stock. **Patterns:** To date Joel has executed over 900 different mosaic Damascus patterns in the past four years. Anything conceived by maker's imagination. **Technical:** Uses various heat colorable "high vibrancy" steels, nickel 200 and some powdered metal for bolster stock only. Uses 1095, 1075 and 15N20. High carbon steels for cutting edge blade stock only. **Prices:** 15 to $50 per square inch and up depending on complexity of pattern. **Remarks:** Full-time mosaic Damascus metal smith focusing strictly on never-before-seen mosaic patterns. Most of maker's work is used for art knives ranging between $1500 to $4500.

DAVIS, JOHN,
235 Lampe Rd, Selah, WA 98942, Phone: 509-697-3845, 509-945-4570, jdwelds@charter.net
    Specialties: Damascus and mosaic Damascus, working knives, working folders, art knives and art folders. **Technical:** Some ATS-34 and stainless Damascus. Embellishes with fancy stabilized wood, mammoth and walrus ivory. **Prices:** Start at $150. **Remarks:** Part-time maker; first knife sold in 1996. **Mark:** Name city and state on Damascus stamp initials; name inside back RFR.

DAVIS, STEVE,
3370 Chatsworth Way, Powder Springs, GA 30127, Phone: 770-427-5740, bsdavis@bellsouth.net
    Specialties: Gents and ladies folders. **Patterns:** Straight knives, slip-joint folders, locking-liner folders. **Technical:** Grinds ATS-34 forges own Damascus. Offers filework; prefers hand-rubbed finishes and natural handle materials. Uses pearl, ivory, stag and exotic woods. **Prices:** $250 to $800; some to $1500. **Remarks:** Full-time maker; first knife sold in 1988. Doing business as Custom Knives by Steve Davis. **Mark:** Name engraved on blade.

DAVIS, TERRY,
Box 111, Sumpter, OR 97877, Phone: 541-894-2307
    Specialties: Traditional and contemporary folders. **Patterns:** Multi-blade folders, whittlers and interframe multiblades; sunfish patterns. **Technical:** Flat-grinds ATS-34. **Prices:** $400 to $1000; some higher. **Remarks:** Full-time maker; first knife sold in 1985. **Mark:** Name in logo.

DAVIS, VERNON M,
2020 Behrens Circle, Waco, TX 76705, Phone: 254-799-7671
    Specialties: Presentation-grade straight knives. **Patterns:** Bowies, daggers, boots, fighters, hunters and utility knives. **Technical:** Hollow-grinds 440C, ATS-34 and D2. Grinds an aesthetic grind line near choil. **Prices:** $125 to $550; some to $5000. **Remarks:** Part-time maker; first knife sold in 1980. **Mark:** Last name and city inside outline of state.

DAVIS, W C,
1955 S 1251 Rd, El Dorado Springs, MO 64744, Phone: 417-876-1259
    Specialties: Fancy working straight knives and folders. **Patterns:** Folding lockers and slip-joints; straight hunters, fighters and Bowies. **Technical:** Grinds A2, ATS-34, 154, CPM T490V and CPM 530V. **Prices:** $100 to $300; some to $1000. **Remarks:** Full-time maker; first knife sold in 1972. **Mark:** Name.

DAVIS JR., JIM,
5129 Ridge St, Zephyrhills, FL 33541, Phone: 813-779-9213 813-469-4241 Cell, jimdavisknives@aol.com
    Specialties: Presentation-grade fixed blade knives w/composite hidden tang handles. Employs a variety of ancient and contemporary ivories. **Patterns:** One-of-a-kind gents, personal, and executive knives and hunters w/unique cam-lock pouch sheaths and display stands. **Technical:** Flat grinds ATS-34 and stainless Damascus w/most work by hand w/assorted files. **Prices:** $300 and up. **Remarks:** Full-time maker, first knives sold in 2000. **Mark:** Signature w/printed name over "HANDCRAFTED."

DAVISON, TODD A.,
415 So. Reed, Lyons, KS 67554, Phone: 620-894-0402, todd@tadscustomknives.com; Web: www.tadscustomknives.com
    Specialties: Making working/using and collector folders of his design. All knives are truly made one of a kind. Each knife has a serial number inside the liner. **Patterns:** Single and double blade traditional slip-joint pocket knives. **Technical:** Free hand hollow ground blades, hand finished. Using only the very best materials possible. Holding the highest standards to fit & finish and detail. Does his own heat treating. ATS34 and D2 steel. **Prices:** $450 to $900, some higher. **Remarks:** Full time maker, first knife sold in 1981. **Mark:** T.A. DAVISON stamped.

DAWKINS, DUDLEY L,
221 NW Broadmoor Ave., Topeka, KS 66606-1254, Phone: 785-235-0468, dawkind@sbcglobal.net
Specialties: Stylized old or "Dawkins Forged" with anvil in center. New tang stamps. **Patterns:** Straight knives. **Technical:** Mostly carbon steel; some Damascus-all knives forged. **Prices:** $175 and up. **Remarks:** All knives supplied with wood-lined sheaths. Also make custom wood-lined sheaths $55 and up. ABS Member, sole authorship. **Mark:** Stylized "DLD or Dawkins Forged with anvil in center.

DAWSON, BARRY,
7760 E Hwy 69, Prescott Valley, AZ 86314, Phone: 928-255-9830, dawsonknives@yahoo.com; Web: www.dawsonknives.com
Specialties: Samurai swords, combat knives, collector daggers, tactical, folding and hunting knives. **Patterns:** Offers over 60 different models. **Technical:** Grinds 440C, ATS-34, own heat-treatment. **Prices:** $75 to $1500; some to $5000. **Remarks:** Full-time maker; first knife sold in 1975. **Mark:** Last name, USA in print or last name in script.

DAWSON, LYNN,
7760 E Hwy 69 #C-5 157, Prescott Valley, AZ 86314, Phone: 928-713-2812, lynnknives@yahoo.com; Web: www.lynnknives.com
Specialties: Swords, hunters, utility, and art pieces. **Patterns:** Over 25 patterns to choose from. **Technical:** Grinds 440C, ATS-34, own heat treating. **Prices:** $80 to $1000. **Remarks:** Custom work and her own designs. **Mark:** The name "Lynn" in print or script.

DE MARIA JR., ANGELO,
12 Boronda Rd, Carmel Valley, CA 93924, Phone: 831-659-3381, Fax: 831-659-1315, angelodemaria1@mac.com
Specialties: Damascus, fixed and folders, sheaths. **Patterns:** Mosiac and random. **Technical:** Forging 5160, 1084 and 15N20. **Prices:** $200+. **Remarks:** Part-time maker. **Mark:** Angelo de Maria Carmel Valley, CA etch or AdM stamp.

DEAN, HARVEY J,
3266 CR 232, Rockdale, TX 76567, Phone: 512-446-3111, Fax: 512-446-5060, dean@tex1.net; Web: www.harveydean.com
Specialties: Collectible, functional knives. **Patterns:** Bowies, hunters, folders, daggers, swords, battle axes, camp and combat knives. **Technical:** Forges 1095, O1 and his Damascus. **Prices:** $350 to $10,000. **Remarks:** Full-time maker; first knife sold in 1981. **Mark:** Last name and MS.

DEBAUD, JAKE,
2403 Springvale Lane, Dallas, TX 75234, Phone: 214-916-1891, jake.debaud@gmail.com Web: www.debaudknives.com
Specialties: Custom damascus art knives, hunting knives and tactical knives. **Technical:** A2, D2, 01, 1095 and some stainless if requested ATS-34 or 154CM and S30V. **Remarks:** Full-time maker. Have been making knives for three years.

DEBRAGA, JOSE C,
1341 9e Rue, Trois Rivieres, Quebec, CANADA G8Y 2Z2, Phone: 418-948-0105, Fax: 819-840-5864, josecdebragaglovetrotter.net; Web: www.geocities.com/josedebraga
Specialties: Art knives, fantasy pieces and working knives of his design or to customer specs. **Patterns:** Knives with sculptured or carved handles, from miniatures to full-size working knives. **Technical:** Grinds and hand-files 440C and ATS-34. A variety of steels and handle materials available. Offers lost wax casting. **Prices:** Start at $300. **Remarks:** Full-time maker; wax modeler, sculptor and knifemaker; first knife sold in 1984. **Mark:** Initials in stylized script and serial number.

DEBRAGA, JOVAN,
141 Notre Dame des Victoir, Quebec, CANADA G2G 1J3, Phone: 418-997-0819/418-877-1915, jovancdebraga@msn.com
Specialties: Art knives, fantasy pieces and working knives of his design or to customer specs. **Patterns:** Knives with sculptured or carved handles, from miniatures to full-sized working knives. **Technical:** Grinds and hand-files 440C, and ATS-34. A variety of steels and handle materials available. **Prices:** Start at $300. **Remarks:** Full time maker. Sculptor and knifemaker. First knife sold in 2003. **Mark:** Initials in stylized script and serial number.

DEL RASO, PETER,
28 Mayfield Dr, Mt. Waverly, Victoria, 3149, AUSTRALIA, Phone: 613 98060644, delraso@optusnet.com.au
Specialties: Fixed blades, some folders, art knives. **Patterns:** Daggers, Bowies, tactical, boot, personal and working knives. **Technical:** Grinds ATS-34, commercial Damascus and any other type of steel on request. **Prices:** $100 to $1500. **Remarks:** Part-time maker, first show in 1993. **Mark:** Maker's surname stamped.

DELAROSA, JIM,
2116 N Pontiac Dr, Janesville, WI 53545, Phone: 262-617-1685, d-knife@hotmail.com
Specialties: Working straight knives and folders of his design or customer specs. **Patterns:** Hunters, skinners, fillets, utility and locking folders. **Technical:** Grinds ATS-34, 440-C, D2, O1 and commercial Damascus. **Prices:** $100 to $500; some higher. **Remarks:** Part-time maker. **Mark:** First and last name.

DELL, WOLFGANG,
Am Alten Berg 9, D-73277 Owen-Teck, GERMANY, Phone: 49-7021-81802, wolfgang@dell-knives.de; Web: www.dell-knives.de
Specialties: Fancy high-art straight of his design and to customer specs. **Patterns:** Fighters, hunters, Bowies and utility/camp knives. **Technical:** Grinds ATS-34, RWL-34, Elmax, Damascus (Fritz Schneider). Offers high gloss finish and engraving. **Prices:** $500 to $1000; some to $1600. **Remarks:** Full-time maker; first knife sold in 1992. **Mark:** Hopi hand of peace.

DELLANA,
STARLANI INT'L INC, 1135 Terminal Way Ste #209, Reno, NV 89502, Phone: 304-727-5512, dellana@dellana.cc; Web: www.dellana.cc
Specialties: Collector grade fancy/embellished high art folders and art daggers. **Patterns:** Locking folders and art daggers. **Technical:** Forges her own Damascus and W-2. Engraves, does stone setting, filework, carving and gold/platinum fabrication. Prefers exotic, high karat gold, platinum, silver, gemstone and mother-of-pearl handle materials. **Price:** Upscale. **Remarks:** Sole authorship, full-time maker, first knife sold in 1994. Also does one high art collaboration a year with Van Barnett. Member: Art Knife Invitational and ABS. **Mark:** First name.

DELONG, DICK,
PO Box 1024, Centerville, TX 75833-1024, Phone: 903-536-1454
Specialties: Fancy working knives and fantasy pieces. **Patterns:** Hunters and small skinners. **Technical:** Grinds and files O1, D2, 440C and Damascus. Offers cocobolo and Osage orange for handles. **Prices:** Start at $50. **Remarks:** Part-time maker. Member of Art Knife Invitational. Voting member of Knifemakers Guild. Member of ABS. **Mark:** Last name; some unmarked.

DEMENT, LARRY,
PO Box 1807, Prince Fredrick, MD 20678, Phone: 410-586-9011
Specialties: Fixed blades. **Technical:** Forged and stock removal. **Prices:** $75 to $200. **Remarks:** Affordable, good feelin', quality knives. Part-time maker.

DEMPSEY, DAVID,
1644 Bass Rd, Apt 2202, Macon, GA 31210, Phone: 229-244-9101, dempsey@dempseyknives.com; Web: www.dempseyknives.com
Specialties: Tactical, utility, working, classic straight knives. **Patterns:** Fighters, tantos, hunters, neck, utility or customer design. **Technical:** Grinds carbon steel and stainless including S30V (differential heat treatment), stainless steel. **Prices:** Start at $150 for neck knives. **Remarks:** Full-time maker. First knife sold 1998. **Mark:** First and last name over knives.

DEMPSEY, GORDON S,
PO Box 7497, N. Kenai, AK 99635, Phone: 907-776-8425
Specialties: Working straight knives. **Patterns:** Pattern welded Damascus and carbon steel blades. **Technical:** Pattern welded Damascus and carbon steel. **Prices:** $80 to $250. **Remarks:** Part-time maker; first knife sold in 1974. **Mark:** Name.

DENNEHY, JOHN D,
2959 Zachary Drive, Loveland, CO 80537, Phone: 970-218-7128, www.thewildirishrose.com
Specialties: Working straight knives, throwers, and leatherworker's knives. **Technical:** 440C, & O1, heat treats own blades, part-time maker, first knife sold in 1989. **Patterns:** Small hunting to presentation Bowies, leatherworks round and head knives. **Prices:** $200 and up. **Remarks:** Custom sheath maker, sheath making seminars at the Blade Show.

DENNING, GENO,
CAVEMAN ENGINEERING, 135 Allenvalley Rd, Gaston, SC 29053, Phone: 803-794-6067, cden101656@aol.com; Web: www.cavemanengineering.com
Specialties: Mirror finish. **Patterns:** Hunters, fighters, folders. **Technical:** ATS-34, 440V, S-30-V D2. **Prices:** $100 and up. **Remarks:** Full-time maker since 1996. Sole income since 1999. Instructor at Montgomery Community College (Grinding Blades). A director of SCAK: South Carolina Association of Knifemakers. **Mark:** Troy NC.

DERESPINA, RICHARD,
, Willow Grove, PA, Phone: 917-843-7627, derespinaknives@yahoo.com Web: www.derespinaknives.com
Specialties: Custom fixed blades and folders, Kris and Karambit. **Technical:** I use the stock removal method. Steels I use are S30V, 154CM, D2, 440C, BG42. Handles made of G10 particularly Micarta, etc. **Prices:** $150 to $550 depending on model. **Remarks:** Full-time maker. **Mark:** My etched logos are two, my last name and Brooklyn NY mark as well as the Star/Yin Yang logo. The star being both representative of various angles of attack common in combat as well as being three triangles, each points to levels of metaphysical understanding. The Yin and Yang have my company initials on each side D & K. Yin and Yang shows the ever present physics of life.

DERINGER, CHRISTOPH,
625 Chemin Lower, Cookshire, Quebec, CANADA J0B 1M0, Phone: 819-345-4260, cdsab@sympatico.ca
Specialties: Traditional working/using straight knives and folders of his design and to customer specs. **Patterns:** Boots, hunters, folders, art knives, kitchen knives and utility/camp knives. **Technical:** Forges 5160, O1 and Damascus. Offers a variety of filework. **Prices:** Start at $250. **Remarks:** Full-time maker; first knife sold in 1989. **Mark:** Last name stamped/engraved.

DERR, HERBERT,
413 Woodland Dr, St. Albans, WV 25177, Phone: 304-727-3866
Specialties: Damascus one-of-a-kind knives, carbon steels also. **Patterns:** Birdseye, ladder back, mosaics. **Technical:** All styles functional as well as artistically pleasing. **Prices:** $90 to $175 carbon, Damascus $250 to $800. **Remarks:** All Damascus made by maker. **Mark:** H.K. Derr.

DESAULNIERS, ALAIN,
100 Pope Street, Cookshire, Quebec, Canada J0B 1M0, pinklaperez@sympatico.ca Web: www.desoknives.com
Specialties: Mostly Loveless style knives. **Patterns:** Double grind fighters, hunters, daggers, etc. **Technical:** Stock removal, ATS-34, CPM. High-polished blades, tapered tangs, high-quality handles. **Remarks:** Full-time. Collaboration with John Young. **Prices:** $425 and up. **Mark:** Name and city in logo.

DESROSIERS, ADAM,
PO Box 1954, Petersburg, AK 99833, Phone: 907-518-4570, adam@alaskablades.com Web: www.alaskablades.com
Specialties: High performance, forged, carbon steel and damascus camp choppers, and hunting knives. Hidden tang, full tang, and full integral construction. High performance heat treating. Knife designs inspired by life in Alaskan bush. **Technical:** Hand forges tool steels and damascus. Sole authorship. Full range of handle materials, micarta to Ivory. Preferred steels: W-2, O-1, L-6, 15n20, 1095. **Prices:** $200 - $3000. **Remarks:** ABS member. Has trained with Masters around the world. **Mark:** DrsRosiers over Alaska, underlined with a rose.

DESROSIERS, HALEY,
PO Box 1954, Petersburg, AK 99833, Phone: 907-518-1416, haley@alaskablades.com Web: www.alaskablades.com
Specialties: Hunting knives and a few choppers **Technical:** Forged using 1084, W2 and Damascus (usually made of 1080, 1084, 15n20). **Prices:** $175 - $400. **Remarks:** Forged first knife in 2001. Part-time bladesmith all year except for commercial fishing season. **Mark:** Capital HD.

DETMER, PHILLIP,
14140 Bluff Rd, Breese, IL 62230, Phone: 618-526-4834, jpdetmer@att.net
Specialties: Working knives. **Patterns:** Bowies, daggers and hunters. **Technical:** Grinds ATS-34 and D2. **Prices:** $60 to $400. **Remarks:** Part-time maker; first knife sold in 1977. **Mark:** Last name with dagger.

DEUBEL, CHESTER J.,
6211 N. Van Ark Rd., Tucson, AZ 85743, Phone: 520-444-5246, cjdeubel@yahoo.com; Web: www.cjdeubel.com
Specialties: Fancy working straight knives and folders of his or customer design, with intricate file work. **Patterns:** Fighters, Bowies, daggers, hunters, camp knives, and cowboy. **Technical:** Flat guard, hollow grind, antiqued, all types Damascus, 154cpm Stainsteel, high carbon steel, 440c Stainsteel. **Prices:** From $250 to $3500. **Remarks:** Started making part-time in 1980; went to full-time in 2000. Don Patch is my engraver. **Mark:** C.J. Deubel.

DI MARZO, RICHARD,
1417 10th St S, Birmingham, AL 35205, Phone: 205-252-3331
Specialties: Handle artist. Scrimshaw carvings.

DIAZ, JOSE,
409 W. 12th Ave, Ellensburg, WA 98926, jose@diaztools.com Web: www.diaztools.com
Specialties: Affordable custom user-grade utility and camp knives. Also makes competition cutting knives. **Patterns:** Mas. **Technical:** Blade materials range from high carbon steels and Damascus to high performance tool and stainless steels. Uses both forge and stock removal methods in shaping the steel. Handle materials include Tero Tuf, Black Butyl Burl, Micarta, natural woods and G10. **Prices:** $65-$700. **Remarks:** Part-time knife maker; made first knife in 2008. **Mark:** Reclining tree frog with a smile, and "Diaz Tools."

DICK, DAN,
P.O. Box 2303, Hutchinson, KS 67504-2303, Phone: 620-669-6805, Dan@DanDickKnives.com; Web: www.dandickknives.com
Specialties: Traditional working/using fixed bladed knives of maker's design. **Patterns:** Hunters, Skinners, Utility, Kitchen, Tactical, Bowies. **Technical:** Stock removal maker using D2. Prefers such materials as exotic and fancy burl woods. Makes his own sheaths, all leather with tooling. **Prices:** $80 and up. **Remarks:** Part-time maker since 2006. **Marks:** Name in outline border of Kansas.

DICKERSON, GAVIN,
PO Box 7672, Petit 1512, SOUTH AFRICA, Phone: +27 011-965-0988, Fax: +27 011-965-0988
Specialties: Straight knives of his design or to customer specs. **Patterns:** Hunters, skinners, fighters and Bowies. **Technical:** Hollow-grinds D2, 440C, ATS-34, 12C27 and Damascus upon request. Prefers natural handle materials; offers synthetic handle materials. **Prices:** $190 to $2500. **Remarks:** Part-time maker; first knife sold in 1982. **Mark:** Name in full.

DICKISON, SCOTT S,
179 Taylor Rd, Fisher Circle, Portsmouth, RI 02871, Phone: 401-847-7398, squared22@cox .net; Web: http://members.cox.net/squared22
Specialties: Working and using straight knives and locking folders of his design and automatics. **Patterns:** Trout knives, fishing and hunting knives. **Technical:** Forges and grinds commercial Damascus and D2, O1. Uses natural handle materials. **Prices:** $400 to $750; some higher. **Remarks:** Part-time maker; first knife sold in 1989. **Mark:** Stylized initials.

DICRISTOFANO, ANTHONY P,
PO Box 2369, Northlake, IL 60164, Phone: 847-845-9598, sukemitsu@sbcglobal.net Web: www.namahagesword.com
Specialties: Japanese-style swords. **Patterns:** Katana, Wakizashi, Otanto, Kozuka. **Technical:** Tradition and some modern steels. All clay tempered and traditionally hand polished using Japanese wet stones. **Remarks:** Part-time maker. **Prices:** Varied, available on request. **Mark:** Blade tang signed in "SUKEMITSU."

DIETZ, HOWARD,
421 Range Rd, New Braunfels, TX 78132, Phone: 830-885-4662
Specialties: Lock-back folders, working straight knives. **Patterns:** Folding hunters, high-grade pocket knives. ATS-34, 440C, CPM 440V, D2 and stainless Damascus. **Prices:** $300 to $1000. **Remarks:** Full-time gun and knifemaker; first knife sold in 1995. **Mark:** Name, city, and state.

DIETZEL, BILL,
PO Box 1613, Middleburg, FL 32068, Phone: 904-282-1091
Specialties: Forged straight knives and folders. **Patterns:** His interpretations. **Technical:** Forges his Damascus and other steels. **Prices:** Middle ranges. **Remarks:** Likes natural materials; uses titanium in folder liners. Master Smith (1997). **Mark:** Name.

DIGANGI, JOSEPH M,
Box 950, Santa Cruz, NM 87567, Phone: 505-753-6414, Fax: 505-753-8144, Web: www.digangidesigns.com
Specialties: Kitchen and table cutlery. **Patterns:** French chef's knives, carving sets, steak knife sets, some camp knives and hunters. Holds patents and trademarks for "System II" kitchen cutlery set. **Technical:** Grinds ATS-34. **Prices:** $150 to $595; some to $1200. **Remarks:** Full-time maker; first knife sold in 1983. **Mark:** DiGangi Designs.

DILL, DAVE,
7404 NW 30th St, Bethany, OK 73008, Phone: 405-789-0750
Specialties: Folders of his design. **Patterns:** Various patterns. **Technical:** Hand-grinds 440C, ATS-34. Offers engraving and filework on all folders. **Prices:** Starting at $450. **Remarks:** Full-time maker; first knife sold in 1987. **Mark:** First initial, last name.

DILL, ROBERT,
1812 Van Buren, Loveland, CO 80538, Phone: 970-667-5144, Fax: 970-667-5144, dillcustomknives@msn.com
Specialties: Fancy and working knives of his design. **Patterns:** Hunters, Bowies and fighters. **Technical:** Grinds 440C and D2. **Prices:** $100 to $800. **Remarks:** Full-time maker; first knife sold in 1984. **Mark:** Logo stamped into blade.

DILLUVIO, FRANK J,
311 Whitetail Dr., Prudenville, MI 48651, Phone: 989-202-4051, fjdknives@hotmail.com; Web: www.fdilluviocustomknives.com
Specialties: Folders, fixed blades. **Patterns:** Many. **Technical:** Grinds 440-c, D-2. Precision fits. **Prices:** $225 and up. **Remarks:** Full-time maker; first knife sold in 1984. **Mark:** Name and state.

DION, GREG,
3032 S Jackson St, Oxnard, CA 93033, Phone: 519-981-1033
Specialties: Working straight knives, some fancy. Welcomes special orders. **Patterns:** Hunters, fighters, camp knives, Bowies and tantos. **Technical:** Grinds ATS-34, 154CM and 440C. **Prices:** $85 to $300; some to $600. **Remarks:** Part-time maker; first knife sold in 1985. **Mark:** Name.

DIOTTE, JEFF,
DIOTTE KNIVES, 159 Laurier Dr, LaSalle Ontario, CANADA N9J 1L4, Phone: 519-978-2764

DIPPOLD, AL,
90 Damascus Ln, Perryville, MO 63775, Phone: 573-547-1119, adippold@midwest.net
Specialties: Fancy one-of-a-kind locking folders. **Patterns:** Locking folders. **Technical:** Forges and grinds mosaic and pattern welded Damascus. Offers filework on all folders. **Prices:** $500 to $3500; some higher. **Remarks:** Full-time maker; first knife sold in 1980. **Mark:** Last name in logo inside of liner.

DISKIN, MATT,
PO Box 653, Freeland, WA 98249, Phone: 360-730-0451
Specialties: Damascus autos. **Patterns:** Dirks and daggers. **Technical:** Forges mosaic Damascus using 15N20, 1084, 02, 06, L6; pure nickel. **Prices:** Start at $500. Remarks; Full-time maker. **Mark:** Last name.

DIXON JR., IRA E,
PO Box 2581, Ventura, CA 93002-2581, irasknives@yahoo.com
Specialties: Utilitarian straight knives of his design. **Patterns:** Camp, hunters, fighters, utility knives and art knives. **Technical:** Grinds CPM, S30V, 1095, Damascus and D2. **Prices:** $200 to $1500. **Remarks:** Part-time maker; first knife sold in 1993. **Mark:** First name, Handmade.

DOBRATZ, ERIC,
25371 Hillary Lane, Laguna Hills, CA 92653, Phone: 949-233-5170, knifesmith@gmail.com
Specialties: Differentially quenched blades with Hamon of his design or with customer input. **Patterns:** Hunting, camp, kitchen, fighters, bowies, traditional tanto, and unique fixed blade designs. **Technical:** Hand-forged high carbon and damascus. Prefers natural material for handles; rare/exotic woods and stag, but also uses micarta and homemade synthetic materials. **Prices:** $150 - $1500. **Remarks:** Part-time maker; first knife made in 1995. **Mark:** Stylized Scarab beetle.

DODD—DROST

DODD, ROBERT F,
4340 E Canyon Dr, Camp Verde, AZ 86322, Phone: 928-567-3333, rfdknives@commspeed.net; Web: www.rfdoddknives.com
Specialties: Folders, fixed blade hunter/skinners, Bowies, daggers. Patterns: Drop point. Technical: ATS-34 and Damascus. Prices: $250 and up. Remarks: Hand tooled leather sheaths. Mark: R. F. Dodd, Camp Verde AZ.

DOGGETT, BOB,
1310 Vinetree Rd, Brandon, FL 33510, Phone: 813-205-5503, dogman@tampabay.rr.com; Web: www.doggettcustomknives.com
Specialties: Clean, functional working knives. Patterns: Classic-styled hunter, fighter and utility fixed blades; liner locking folders. Technical: Uses stainless steel and commercial Damascus, 416 stainless for bolsters and hardware, hand-rubbed satin finish, top quality handle materials and titanium liners on folders. Prices: Start at $175. Remarks: Part-time maker. Mark: Last name.

DOIRON, DONALD,
6 Chemin Petit Lac des Ced, Messines, PQ, CANADA J0X-2J0, Phone: 819-465-2489

DOMINY, CHUCK,
PO Box 593, Colleyville, TX 76034, Phone: 817-498-4527
Specialties: Titanium LinerLock® folders. Patterns: Hunters, utility/camp knives and LinerLock® folders. Technical: Grinds 440C and ATS-34. Prices: $250 to $3000. Remarks: Full-time maker; first knife sold in 1976. Mark: Last name.

DOOLITTLE, MIKE,
13 Denise Ct, Novato, CA 94947, Phone: 415-897-3246
Specialties: Working straight knives in standard patterns. Patterns: Hunters and fishing knives. Technical: Grinds 440C, 154CM and ATS-34. Prices: $125 to $200; some to $750. Remarks: Part-time maker; first knife sold in 1981. Mark: Name, city and state.

DORNELES, LUCIANO OLIVERIRA,
Rua 15 De Novembro 2222, Nova Petropolis, RS, BRAZIL 95150-000, Phone: 011-55-54-303-303-90, tchebufalo@hotmail.com
Specialties: Traditional "true" Brazilian-style working knives and to customer specs. Patterns: Brazilian hunters, utility and camp knives, Bowies, Dirk. A master at the making of the true "Faca Campeira Gaucha," the true camp knife of the famous Brazilian Gauchos. A Dorneles knife is 100 percent hand-forged with sledge hammers only. Can make spectacular Damascus hunters/daggers. Technical: Forges only 52100 and his own Damascus, can put silver wire inlay on customer design handles on special orders; uses only natural handle materials. Prices: $250 to $1000. Mark: Symbol with L. Dorneles.

DOTSON, TRACY,
1280 Hwy C-4A, Baker, FL 32531, Phone: 850-537-2407
Specialties: Folding fighters and small folders. Patterns: LinerLock® and lockback folders. Technical: Hollow-grinds ATS-34 and commercial Damascus. Prices: Start at $250. Remarks: Part-time maker; first knife sold in 1995. Mark: Last name.

DOUCETTE, R,
CUSTOM KNIVES, 112 Memorial Dr, Brantford, Ont., CANADA N3R 5S3, Phone: 519-756-9040, randy@randydoucetteknives.com; Web: www.randydoucetteknives.com
Specialties: Filework, tactical designs, multiple grinds. Patterns: Tactical folders, fancy folders, daggers, tantos, karambits. Technical: All knives are handmade. The only outsourcing is heat treatment. Prices: $500 to $2,500. Remarks: Full-time knifemaker; 2-year waiting list. Mark: R. Doucette

DOUGLAS, JOHN J,
506 Powell Rd, Lynch Station, VA 24571, Phone: 804-369-7196
Specialties: Fancy and traditional straight knives and folders of his design and to customer specs. Patterns: Locking folders, swords and sgian dubhs. Technical: Grinds 440C stainless, ATS-34 stainless and customer's choice. Offers newly designed non-pivot uni-lock folders. Prefers highly polished finish. Prices: $160 to $1400. Remarks: Full-time maker; first knife sold in 1975. Doing business as Douglas Keltic. Mark: Stylized initial. Folders are numbered; customs are dated.

DOURSIN, GERARD,
Chemin des Croutoules, F 84210, Pernes les Fontaines, FRANCE
Specialties: Period pieces. Patterns: Liner locks and daggers. Technical: Forges mosaic Damascus. Prices: $600 to $4000. Remarks: First knife sold in 1983. Mark: First initial, last name and I stop the lion.

DOUSSOT, LAURENT,
1008 Montarville, St. Bruno, Quebec, CANADA J3V 3T1, Phone: 450-441-3298, doussot@skalja.com; Web: www.skalja.com, www.doussot-knives.com
Specialties: Fancy and embellished folders and fantasy knives. Patterns: Fighters and locking folders. Technical: Grinds ATS-34 and commercial Damascus. Scale carvings on all knives; most bolsters are carved titanium. Prices: $350 to $3000. Remarks: Part-time maker; first knife was sold in 1992. Mark: Stylized initials inside circle.

DOWELL, T M,
139 NW St Helen's Pl, Bend, OR 97701, Phone: 541-382-8924, Fax: 541-382-8924, tmdknives@webtv.net
Specialties: Integral construction in hunting knives. Patterns: Limited to featherweights, lightweights, integral hilt and caps. Technical: Grinds D-2,

BG-42 and Vasco wear. Prices: $275 and up. Remarks: Full-time maker; first knife sold in 1967. Mark: Initials logo.

DOWNIE, JAMES T,
1295 - 906 Sandy Lane, Sarnia, Ontario, CANADA N7V 4K5, Phone: 519-491-8234, Web: www.ckg.org (click on members page)
Specialties: Serviceable straight knives and folders; period pieces. Patterns: Hunters, Bowies, camp knives, fillet and miniatures. Technical: Grinds D2, 440C and ATS-34, Damasteel, stainless steel Damascus. Prices: $150 and up. Remarks: Full-time maker, first knife sold in 1978. Mark: Signature of first and middle initials, last name.

DOWNING, LARRY,
12268 State Route 181 N, Bremen, KY 42325, Phone: 270-525-3523, larrydowning@bellsouth.net; Web: www.downingknives.com
Specialties: Working straight knives and folders. Patterns: From mini-knives to daggers, folding lockers to interframes. Technical: Forges and grinds 154CM, ATS-34 and his own Damascus. Prices: $195 to $950; some higher. Remarks: Part-time maker; first knife sold in 1979. Mark: Name in arrowhead.

DOWNING, TOM,
2675 12th St, Cuyahoga Falls, OH 44223, Phone: 330-923-7464
Specialties: Working straight knives; period pieces. Patterns: Hunters, fighters and tantos. Technical: Grinds 440C, ATs-34 and CPM-T-440V. Prefers natural handle materials. Prices: $150 to $900, some to $1500. Remarks: Part-time maker; first knife sold in 1979. Mark: First and middle initials, last name.

DOWNS, JAMES F,
2247 Summit View Rd, Powell, OH 43065, Phone: 614-766-5350, jfdowns1@yahoo.com
Specialties: Working straight knives of his design or to customer specs. Patterns: Folders, Bowies, boot, hunters, utility. Technical: Grinds 440C and other steels. Prefers mastodon ivory, all pearls, stabilized wood and elephant ivory. Prices: $75 to $1200. Remarks: Full-time maker; first knife sold in 1980. Mark: Last name.

DOX, JAN,
Zwanebloemlaan 27, B 2900 Schoten, BELGIUM, Phone: 32 3 658 77 43, jan.dox@scarlet.be
Specialties: Working/using knives, from kitchen to battlefield. Patterns: Own designs, some based on traditional ethnic patterns (Scots, Celtic, Scandinavian and Japanese) or to customer specs. Technical: Grinds D2/A2 and stainless, forges carbon steels, convex edges. Handles: Wrapped in modern or traditional patterns, resin impregnated if desired. Natural or synthetic materials, some carved. Prices: $50 and up. Remarks: Spare-time maker, first knife sold 2001. Mark: Name or stylized initials.

DOZIER, BOB,
PO Box 1941, Springdale, AR 72765, Phone: 888-823-0023/479-756-0023, Fax: 479-756-9139, info@dozierknives.com; Web www.dozierknives.com
Specialties: Using knives (fixed blades and folders). Patterns: Some fine collector-grade knives. Technical: Uses D2. Prefers Micarta handle material. Prices: Using knives: $195 to $700. Remarks: Full-time maker; first knife sold in 1965. No longer doing semi-handmade line. Mark: State, made, last name in a circle (for fixed blades); Last name with arrow through 'D' and year over name (for folders).

DRAPER, AUDRA,
#10 Creek Dr, Riverton, WY 82501, Phone: 307-856-6807 or 307-851-0426 cell, adraper@wyoming.com; Web: www.draperknives.com
Specialties: One-of-a-kind straight and folding knives. Also pendants, earring and bracelets of Damascus. Patterns: Design custom knives, using, Bowies and minis. Technical: Forge Damascus; heat-treats all knives. Prices: Vary depending on item. Remarks: Full-time maker; master bladesmith in the ABS. Member of the PKA; first knife sold in 1995, Mark: Audra.

DRAPER, MIKE,
#10 Creek Dr, Riverton, WY 82501, Phone: 307-856-6807, adraper@wyoming.com
Specialties: Mainly folding knives in tactical fashion, occasonal fixed blade. Patterns: Hunters, Bowies and camp knives, tactical survival. Technical: Grinds S30V stainless steel. Prices: Starting at $250+. Remarks: Full-time maker; first knife sold in 1996. Mark: Initials M.J.D. or name, city and state.

DREW, GERALD,
213 Hawk Ridge Dr, Mill Spring, NC 28756, Phone: 828-713-4762
Specialties: Blade ATS-34 blades. Straight knives. Patterns: Hunters, camp knives, some Bowies and tactical. Technical: ATS-34 preferred. Price: $65 to $400. Mark: GL DREW.

DRISCOLL, MARK,
4115 Avoyer Pl, La Mesa, CA 91941, Phone: 619-670-0695, markdriscoll91941@yahoo.com
Specialties: High-art, period pieces and working/using knives of his design or to customer specs; some fancy. Patterns: Swords, Bowies, fighters, daggers, hunters and primitive (mountain man-styles). Technical: Forges 52100, 5160, O1, L6, 1095, 15n20, W-2 steel and makes his own Damascus and mokume; also does multiple quench heat treating. Uses exotic hardwoods, ivory and horn, offers fancy file work, carving, scrimshaws. Prices: $150 to $550; some to $1500. Remarks: Part-time maker; first knife sold in 1986. Doing business as Mountain Man Knives. Mark: Double "M."

DROST, JASON D,
Rt 2 Box 49, French Creek, WV 26218, Phone: 304-472-7901

Specialties: Working/using straight knives of his design. **Patterns:** Hunters and utility/camp knives. **Technical:** Grinds 154CM and D2. **Prices:** $125 to $5000. **Remarks:** Spare-time maker; first knife sold in 1995. **Mark:** First and middle initials, last name, maker, city and state.

DROST, MICHAEL B,
Rt 2 Box 49, French Creek, WV 26218, Phone: 304-472-7901
  Specialties: Working/using straight knives and folders of all designs. **Patterns:** Hunters, locking folders and utility/camp knives. **Technical:** Grinds ATS-34, D2 and CPM-T-440V. Offers dove-tailed bolsters and spacers, filework and scrimshaw. **Prices:** $125 to $400; some to $740. **Remarks:** Full-time maker; first knife sold in 1990. Doing business as Drost Custom Knives. **Mark:** Name, city and state.

DRUMM, ARMIN,
Lichtensteinstrasse 33, D-89160 Dornstadt, GERMANY, Phone: 49-163-632-2842, armin@drumm-knives.de; Web: www.drumm-knives.de
  Specialties: One-of-a-kind forged and Damascus fixed blade knives and folders. **Patterns:** Classic Bowie knives, daggers, fighters, hunters, folders, swords. **Technical:** Forges own Damascus and carbon steels, filework, carved handles. **Prices:** $250 to $800, some higher. **Remarks:** First knife sold in 2001, member of the German Knifemakers Guild. **Mark:** First initial, last name.

DUFF, BILL,
2801 Ash St, Poteau, OK 74953, Phone: 918-647-4458
  Specialties: Straight knives and folders, some fancy. **Patterns:** Hunters, folders and miniatures. **Technical:** Grinds 440-C and commercial Damascus. **Prices:** $200 to $1000 some higher. **Remarks:** First knife some in 1976. **Mark:** Bill Duff.

DUFOUR, ARTHUR J,
8120 De Armoun Rd, Anchorage, AK 99516, Phone: 907-345-1701
  Specialties: Working straight knives from standard patterns. **Patterns:** Hunters, Bowies, camp and fishing knives—grinded thin and pointed. **Technical:** Grinds 440C, ATS-34, AEB-L. Tempers 57-58R; hollow-grinds. **Prices:** $135; some to $250. **Remarks:** Part-time maker; first knife sold in 1970. **Mark:** Prospector logo.

DUGDALE, DANIEL J,
11 Eleanor Road, Walpole, MA 02081, Phone: 508-668-3528, dlpdugdale@comcast.net
  Specialties: Button-lock and straight knives of his design. **Patterns:** Utilities, hunters, skinners, and tactical. **Technical:** Falt grinds D-2 and 440C, aluminum handles with anodized finishes. **Prices:** $150 to $500. **Remarks:** Part-time maker since 1977. **Mark:** Deer track with last name, town and state.

DUNCAN, RON,
1432 County Road 1635, Cairo, MO 65239, www.duncanmadeknives.com
  Remarks: Duncan Made Knives

DUNKERLEY, RICK,
PO Box 601, Lincoln, MT 59639, Phone: 406-210-4101, rick@dunkerleyhandmadeknives.com Web: www.dunkerleyknives.com
  Specialties: Mosaic Damascus folders and carbon steel utility knives. **Patterns:** One-of-a-kind folders, standard hunters and utility designs. **Technical:** Forges 52100, Damascus and mosaic Damascus. Prefers natural handle materials. **Prices:** $200 and up. **Remarks:** Full-time maker; first knife sold in 1984, ABS Master Smith. Doing business as Dunkerley Custom Knives. Dunkerley handmade knives, sole authorship. **Mark:** Dunkerley, MS.

DUNN, CHARLES K,
17740 GA Hwy 116, Shiloh, GA 31826, Phone: 706-846-2666
  Specialties: Fancy and working straight knives and folders of his design and to customer specs. **Patterns:** Bowies, hunters and locking folders. **Technical:** Grinds 440C and ATS-34. Engraves; filework offered. **Prices:** $75 to $300. **Remarks:** Part-time maker; first knife sold in 1988. **Mark:** First initial, last name, city, state.

DUNN, STEVE,
376 Biggerstaff Rd, Smiths Grove, KY 42171, Phone: 270-563-9830, dunndeal@verizon.net; Web: www.stevedunnknives.com
  Specialties: Working and using straight knives of his design; period pieces. Also offer engraving & gold inlays. **Patterns:** Hunters, skinners, Bowies, fighters, camp knives, folders, swords and battle axes. **Technical:** Forges own Damascus, 1075, 15N20, 52100, 1084, L6. **Prices:** Moderate to upscale. **Remarks:** Full-time maker; first knife sold in 1990. **Mark:** Last name and MS.

DURAN, JERRY T,
PO Box 80692, Albuquerque, NM 87198-0692, Phone: 505-873-4676, jtdknives@hotmail.com; Web: www.kmg.org/jtdknives
  Specialties: Tactical folders, Bowies, fighters, liner locks, autopsy and hunters. **Patterns:** Folders, Bowies, hunters and tactical knives. **Technical:** Forges own Damascus and forges carbon steel. **Prices:** Moderate to upscale. **Remarks:** Full-time maker; first knife sold in 1978. **Mark:** Initials in elk rack logo.

DURHAM, KENNETH,
BUZZARD ROOST FORGE, 10495 White Pike, Cherokee, AL 35616, Phone: 256-359-4287, www.home.hiwaay.net/~jamesd/
  Specialties: Bowies, dirks, hunters. **Patterns:** Traditional patterns. **Technical:** Forges 1095, 5160, 52100 and makes own Damascus. **Prices:** $85 to $1600. **Remarks:** Began making knives about 1995. Received Journeyman stamp 1999. Got Master Smith stamp in 2004. **Mark:** Bull's head with Ken Durham above and Cherokee AL below.

DURIO, FRED,
144 Gulino St, Opelousas, LA 70570, Phone: 337-948-4831/cell 337-351-2652, fdurio@yahoo.com
  Specialties: Folders. **Patterns:** Liner locks; plain and fancy. **Technical:** Makes own Damascus. **Prices:** Moderate to upscale. **Remarks:** Full-time maker. **Mark:** Last name-Durio.

DUVALL, FRED,
10715 Hwy 190, Benton, AR 72015, Phone: 501-778-9360
  Specialties: Working straight knives and folders. **Patterns:** Locking folders, slip joints, hunters, fighters and Bowies. **Technical:** Grinds D2 and CPM440V; forges 5160. **Prices:** $100 to $400; some to $800. **Remarks:** Part-time maker; first knife sold in 1973. **Mark:** Last name.

DWYER, DUANE,
120 N. Pacific St., L7, San Marcos, CA 92069, Phone: 760-471-8275, striderknives@aol.com Web: www.striderknives.com
  Specialties: Primarily tactical. **Patterns:** Fixed and folders. **Technical:** Primarily stock removal specializing in highly technical materials. **Prices:** $100 and up, based on the obvious variables. **Remarks:** Full-time maker since 1996.

DYER, DAVID,
4531 Hunters Glen, Granbury, TX 76048, Phone: 817-573-1198
  Specialties: Working skinners and early period knives. **Patterns:** Customer designs, his own patterns. **Technical:** Coal forged blades; 5160 and 52100 steels. Grinds D2, 1095, L6. **Prices:** $150 for neck knives and small (3" to 3-1/2"). To $600 for large blades and specialty blades. **Mark:** Last name DYER electro etched.

DYESS, EDDIE,
1005 Hamilton, Roswell, NM 88201, Phone: 505-623-5599, eddyess@msn.com
  Specialties: Working and using straight knives in standard patterns. **Patterns:** Hunters and fighters. **Technical:** Grinds 440C, 154CM and D2 on request. **Prices:** $150 to $300, some higher. **Remarks:** Spare-time maker; first knife sold in 1980. **Mark:** Last name.

DYRNOE, PER,
Sydskraenten 10, Tulstrup, DK 3400 Hilleroed, DENMARK, Phone: +45 42287041
  Specialties: Hand-crafted knives with zirconia ceramic blades. **Patterns:** Hunters, skinners, Norwegian-style tolle knives, most in animal-like ergonomic shapes. **Technical:** Handles of exotic hardwood, horn, fossil ivory, etc. Norwegian-style sheaths. **Prices:** Start at $500. **Remarks:** Part-time maker in cooperation with Hans J. Henriksen; first knife sold in 1993. **Mark:** Initial logo.

E

EAKER, ALLEN L,
416 Clinton Ave Dept KI, Paris, IL 61944, Phone: 217-466-5160
  Specialties: Traditional straight knives and folders of his design. **Patterns:** Hunters, locking folders and slip-joint folders. **Technical:** Grinds 440C; inlays. **Prices:** $125 to $325; some to $500. **Remarks:** Spare-time maker; first knife sold in 1994. **Mark:** Initials in tankard logo stamped on tang, serial number on back side.

EALY, DELBERT,
PO Box 121, Indian River, MI 49749, Phone: 231-238-4705

EATON, FRANK L JR,
41 Vista Woods Rd, Stafford, VA 22556, Phone: 540-657-6160, FEton2@aol.com
  Specialties: Full tang/hidden tang fixed working and art knives of his own design. **Patterns:** Hunters, skinners, fighters, Bowies, tacticals and daggers. **Technical:** Stock removal maker, prefer using natural materials. **Prices:** $175 to $400. **Remarks:** Part-time maker - Active Duty Airborn Ranger-Making 4 years. **Mark:** Name over 75th Ranger Regimental Crest.

EATON, RICK,
313 Dailey Rd, Broadview, MT 59015, Phone: 406-667-2405, rick@eatonknives.com; Web: www.eatonknives.com
  Specialties: Interframe folders and one-hand-opening side locks. **Patterns:** Bowies, daggers, fighters and folders. **Technical:** Grinds 154CM, ATS-34, 440C and other maker's Damascus. Offers high-quality hand engraving, Bulino and gold inlay. **Prices:** Upscale. **Remarks:** Full-time maker; first knife sold in 1982. **Mark:** Full name or full name and address.

EBISU, HIDESAKU,
3-39-7 Koi Osako Nishi Ku, Hiroshima City, JAPAN 733 0816

ECHOLS, ROGER,
46 Channing Rd, Nashville, AR 71852-8588, Phone: 870-451-9089, blademanechols@aol.com
  Specialties: Liner locks, auto-scale release, lock backs. **Patterns:** His or yours. **Technical:** Autos. **Prices:** $500 to $1700. **Remarks:** Likes to use pearl, ivory and Damascus the most. Made first knife in 1984. Part-time maker; tool and die maker by trade. **Mark:** Name.

EDDY, HUGH E,
211 E Oak St, Caldwell, ID 83605, Phone: 208-459-0536

EDEN, THOMAS,
PO Box 57, Cranbury, NJ 08512, Phone: 609-371-0774, njirrigation@msn.com
Specialties: Chef's knives. Patterns: Fixed blade, working patterns, hand forged. Technical: Damascus. Remarks: ABS Smith. Mark: Eden (script).

EDGE, TOMMY,
1244 County Road 157, Cash, AR 72421, Phone: 501-477-5210, tedge@tex.net
Specialties: Fancy/embellished working knives of his design. Patterns: Bowies, hunters and utility/camping knives. Technical: Grinds 440C, ATS-34 and D2. Makes own cable Damascus; offers filework. Prices: $70 to $250; some to $1500. Remarks: Part-time maker; first knife sold in 1973. Mark: Stamped first initial, last name and stenciled name, city and state in oval shape.

EDMONDS, WARRICK,
Adelaide Hills, South Australia, Phone: 61-8-83900339, warrick@riflebirdknives.com Web: www.riflebirdknives.com
Specialties: Fixed blade knives with select and highly figured exotic or unique Australian wood handles. Themed collectors knives to individually designed working knives from Damascus, RWL34, 440C or high carbon steels. Patterns: Hunters, utilities and workshop knives, cooks knives with a Deco to Modern flavour. Hand sewn individual leather sheaths. Technical: Stock removal using only steel from well known and reliable sources. Prices: $250Aust to $1000Aust. Remarks: Part-time maker since 2004. Mark: Name stamped into sheath.

EDWARDS, FAIN E,
PO Box 280, Topton, NC 28781, Phone: 828-321-3127

EDWARDS, MITCH,
303 New Salem Rd, Glasgow, KY 42141, Phone: 270-404-0758 / 270-404-0758, medwards@glasgow-ky.com; Web: www.traditionalknives.com
Specialties: Period pieces. Patterns: Neck knives, camp, rifleman and Bowie knives. Technical: All hand forged, forges own Damascus O1, 1084, 1095, L6, 15N20. Prices: $200 to $1000. Remarks: Journeyman Smith. Mark: Broken heart.

EHRENBERGER, DANIEL ROBERT,
1213 S Washington St, Mexico, MO 65265, Phone: 573-633-2010
Specialties: Affordable working/using straight knives of his design and to custom specs. Patterns: 10" western Bowie, fighters, hunting and skinning knives. Technical: Forges 1085, 1095, his own Damascus and cable Damascus. Prices: $80 to $500. Remarks: Full-time maker, first knife sold 1994. Mark: Ehrenberger JS.

EIRICH, WILLIAM,
61535 S. Hwy 97, Ste. 9-163, Bend, OR 97702, Phone: 541-408-2364, tapejet@live.com
Specialties: Hunting, folders, other. Technical: Stock removal. 154CM, 1050, M390, 5160, 01, 52100, ATS-34. Prices: $200 and up. Remarks: First knife made 2004. Mark: Circle with an "E" in the center and a wing to the right of the circle with the name "Eirich" below framed by dots.

EKLUND, MAIHKEL,
Fone Stam V9, S-820 41 Farila, SWEDEN, info@art-knives.com; Web: www.art-knives.com
Specialties: Collector-grade working straight knives. Patterns: Hunters, Bowies and fighters. Technical: Grinds ATS-34, Uddeholm and Dama steel. Engraves and scrimshaws. Prices: $200 to $2000. Remarks: Full-time maker; first knife sold in 1983. Mark: Initials or name.

ELDRIDGE, ALLAN,
7731 Four Winds Dr, Ft. Worth, TX 76133, Phone: 817-370-7778
Specialties: Fancy classic straight knives in standard patterns. Patterns: Hunters, Bowies, fighters, folders and miniatures. Technical: Grinds O1 and Damascus. Engraves silver-wire inlays, pearl inlays, scrimshaws and offers filework. Prices: $50 to $500; some to $1200. Remarks: Spare-time maker; first knife sold in 1965. Mark: Initials.

ELISHEWITZ, ALLEN,
3960 Lariat Ridge, New Braunfels, TX 78132, Phone: 830-899-5356, allen@elishewitzknives.com; Web: elishewitzknives.com
Specialties: Collectible high-tech working straight knives and folders of his design. Patterns: Working, utility and tactical knives. Technical: Designs and uses innovative locking mechanisms. All designs drafted and field-tested. Prices: $600 to $1000. Remarks: Full-time maker; first knife sold in 1989. Mark: Gold medallion inlaid in blade.

ELLEFSON, JOEL,
PO Box 1016, 310 S 1st St, Manhattan, MT 59741, Phone: 406-284-3111
Specialties: Working straight knives, fancy daggers and one-of-a-kinds. Patterns: Hunters, daggers and some folders. Technical: Grinds A2, 440C and ATS-34. Makes own mokume in bronze, brass, silver and shibuishi; makes brass/steel blades. Prices: $100 to $500; some to $2000. Remarks: Part-time maker; first knife sold in 1978. Mark: Stylized last initial.

ELLERBE, W B,
3871 Osceola Rd, Geneva, FL 32732, Phone: 407-349-5818
Specialties: Period and primitive knives and sheaths. Patterns: Bowies to patch knives, some tomahawks. Technical: Grinds Sheffield O1 and files. Prices: Start at $35. Remarks: Full-time maker; first knife sold in 1971. Doing business as Cypress Bend Custom Knives. Mark: Last name or initials.

ELLIOTT, JERRY,
4507 Kanawha Ave, Charleston, WV 25304, Phone: 304-925-5045, elliottknives@verizon.net
Specialties: Classic and traditional straight knives and folders of his design and to customer specs. Patterns: Hunters, locking folders and Bowies. Technical: Grinds ATS-34, 154CM, O1, D2 and T-440-V. All guards silver-soldered; bolsters are pinned on straight knives, spot-welded on folders. Prices: $80 to $265; some to $1000. Remarks: Full-time maker; first knife sold in 1972. Mark: First and middle initials, last name, knife maker, city, state.

ELLIS, DAVE/ABS MASTERSMITH,
770 Sycamore Ave., Suite 122 Box 451, Vista, CA 92083, Phone: 760-945-7177, www.exquisiteknives.com
Specialties: Bowies, utility and combat knives. Patterns: Using knives to art quality pieces. Technical: Forges 5160, L6, 52100, cable and his own Damascus steels. Prices: $300 to $4000. Remarks: Part-time maker. California's first ABS Master Smith. Mark: Dagger-Rose with name and M.S. mark.

ELLIS, WILLIAM DEAN,
2767 Edgar Ave, Sanger, CA 93657, Phone: 559-314-4459, urleebird@comcast.net; Web: www.billysblades.com
Specialties: Classic and fancy knives of his design. Patterns: Boots, fighters and utility knives. Technical: Grinds ATS-34, D2 and Damascus. Offers tapered tangs and six patterns of filework; tooled multi-colored sheaths. Prices: $250 to $1500 Remarks: Part-time maker; first knife sold in 1991. Doing business as Billy's Blades. Also make shave-ready straight razors for actual use. Mark: "B" in a five-point star next to "Billy," city and state within a rounded-corner rectangle.

ELLIS, WILLY B,
4941 Cardinal Trail, Palm Harbor, FL 34683, Phone: 727-942-6420, Web: www.willyb.com
Specialties: One-of-a-kind high art and fantasy knives of his design. Occasional customs full size and miniatures. Patterns: Bowies, fighters, hunters and others. Technical: Grinds 440C, ATS-34, 1095, carbon Damascus, ivory bone, stone and metal carving. Prices: $175 to $15,000. Remarks: Full-time maker, first knife made in 1973. Member Knifemakers Guild. Jewel setting inlays. Mark: Willy B. or WB'S C etched or carved.

ELROD, ROGER R,
58 Dale Ave, Enterprise, AL 36330, Phone: 334-347-1863

EMBRETSEN, KAJ,
FALUVAGEN 67, S-82830 Edsbyn, SWEDEN, Phone: 46-271-21057, Fax: 46-271-22961, kay.embretsen@telia.com Web: www.embretsenknives.com
Specialties: Damascus folding knives. Patterns: Uses mammoth ivory and some pearl. Technical: Uses own Damascus steel. Remarks: Full time since 1983. Prices: $2500 to $8000. Mark: Name inside the folder.

EMERSON, ERNEST R,
PO Box 4180, Torrance, CA 90510-4180, Phone: 310-212-7455, info@emersonknives.com; Web: www.emersonknives.com
Specialties: High-tech folders and combat fighters. Patterns: Fighters, LinerLock® combat folders and SPECWAR combat knives. Technical: Grinds 154CM and Damascus. Makes folders with titanium fittings, liners and locks. Chisel grind specialist. Prices: $550 to $850; some to $10,000. Remarks: Full-time maker; first knife sold in 1983. Mark: Last name and Specwar knives.

ENCE, JIM,
145 S 200 East, Richfield, UT 84701, Phone: 435-896-6206
Specialties: High-art period pieces (spec in California knives) art knives. Patterns: Art, boot knives, fighters, Bowies and occasional folders. Technical: Grinds 440C for polish and beauty boys; makes own Damascus. Prices: Upscale. Remarks: Full-time maker; first knife sold in 1977. Does own engraving, gold work and stone work. Guild member since 1977. Founding member of the AKI. Mark: Ence, usually engraved.

ENGLAND, VIRGIL,
1340 Birchwood St, Anchorage, AK 99508, Phone: 907-274-9494, WEB:www.virgilengland.com
Specialties: Edged weapons and equipage, one-of-a-kind only. Patterns: Axes, swords, lances and body armor. Technical: Forges and grinds as pieces dictate. Offers stainless and Damascus. Prices: Upscale. Remarks: A veteran knifemaker. No commissions. Mark: Stylized initials.

ENGLE, WILLIAM,
16608 Oak Ridge Rd, Boonville, MO 65233, Phone: 816-882-6277
Specialties: Traditional working and using straight knives of his design. Patterns: Hunters, Bowies and fighters. Technical: Grinds 440C, ATS-34 and 154 CM. Prices: $250 to $500; some higher. Remarks: Part-time maker; first knife sold in 1982. All knives come with certificate of authenticity. Mark: Last name in block lettering.

ENGLISH, JIM,
14586 Olive Vista Dr., Jamul, CA 91935, Phone: 619-669-0833
Specialties: High-quality working straight knives. **Patterns:** Hunters, fighters, skinners, tantos, utility and fillet knives, Bowies and *san-mai* Damascus Bowies. **Technical:** Hollow-grind 440C by hand. Feature linen Micarta handles, desert ironwood, many different woods, stabilized woods, nickel-silver handle bolts and handmade sheaths. **Prices:** $125 to $600. **Remarks:** Company name is Mountain Home Knives. **Mark:** Mountain Home Knives.

ENGLISH, JIM,
14586 Olive Vista Dr, Jamul, CA 91935, Phone: 619-669-0833
Specialties: Traditional working straight knives to customer specs. **Patterns:** Hunters, Bowies, fighters, tantos, daggers, boot and utility/camp knives. **Technical:** Grinds 440C, ATS-34, commercial Damascus and customer choice. **Prices:** $130 to $350. **Remarks:** Part-time maker; first knife sold in 1985. In addition to custom line, also does business as Mountain Home Knives. **Mark:** Double "A," Double "J" logo.

ENNIS, RAY,
1220S 775E, Ogden, UT 84404, Phone: 800-410-7603, Fax: 501-621-2683, nifmakr@hotmail.com; Web:www.ennis-entrekusa.com

ENOS III, THOMAS M,
12302 State Rd 535, Orlando, FL 32836, Phone: 407-239-6205, tmenos3@att.net
Specialties: Heavy-duty working straight knives; unusual designs. **Patterns:** Swords, machetes, daggers, skinners, filleting, period pieces. **Technical:** Grinds 440C, D2, 154CM. **Prices:** $75 to $1500. **Remarks:** Full-time maker; first knife sold in 1972. Will be making his own designs. Send SASE for listing of items for sale. **Mark:** Name in knife logo and year, type of steel and serial number.

ENTIN, ROBERT,
127 Pembroke St 1, Boston, MA 02118

EPTING, RICHARD,
4021 Cody Dr, College Station, TX 77845, Phone: 979-690-6496, rgeknives@hotmail.com; Web: www.eptingknives.com
Specialties: Folders and working straight knives. **Patterns:** Hunters, Bowies, and locking folders. **Technical:** Forges high-carbon steel and his own Damascus. **Prices:** $200 to $800; some to $1800. **Remarks:** Part-time maker, first knife sold 1996. **Mark:** Name in arch logo.

ERICKSON, L.M.,
1379 Black Mountain Cir, Ogden, UT 84404, Phone: 801-737-1930
Specialties: Straight knives; period pieces. **Patterns:** Bowies, fighters, boots and hunters. **Technical:** Grinds 440C, 154CM and commercial Damascus. **Prices:** $200 to $900; some to $5000. **Remarks:** Part-time maker; first knife sold in 1981. **Mark:** Name, city, state.

ERICKSON, WALTER E.,
22280 Shelton Tr, Atlanta, MI 49709, Phone: 989-785-5262, wberic@racc2000.com
Specialties: Unusual survival knives and high-tech working knives. **Patterns:** Butterflies, hunters, tantos. **Technical:** Grinds ATS-34 or customer choice. **Prices:** $150 to $500; some to $1500. **Remarks:** Full-time maker; first knife sold in 1981. **Mark:** Using pantograph with assorted fonts (no longer stamping).

ERIKSEN, JAMES THORLIEF,
dba VIKING KNIVES, 3830 Dividend Dr, Garland, TX 75042, Phone: 972-494-3667, Fax: 972-235-4932, VikingKnives@aol.com
Specialties: Heavy-duty working and using straight knives and folders utilizing traditional, Viking original and customer specification patterns. Some high-tech and fancy/embellished knives available. **Patterns:** Bowies, hunters, skinners, boot and belt knives, utility/camp knives, fighters, daggers, locking folders, slip-joint folders and kitchen knives. **Technical:** Hollow-grinds 440C, D2, ASP-23, ATS-34, 154CM, Vascowear. **Prices:** $150 to $300; some to $600. **Remarks:** Full-time maker; first knife sold in 1985. Doing business as Viking Knives. For a color catalog showing 50 different models, mail $5 to above address. **Mark:** VIKING or VIKING USA for export.

ERNEST, PHIL (PJ),
PO Box 5240, Whittier, CA 90607-5240, Phone: 562-556-2324, hugger883562@yahoo.com; Web:www.ernestcustomknives.com
Specialties: Fixed blades. **Patterns:** Wide range. Many original as well as hunters, camp, fighters, daggers, bowies and tactical. Specialzin in Wharncliff's of all sizes. **Technical:** Grinds commercial Damascus, Mosaid Damascus. ATS-34, and 440C. Full Tangs with bolsters. Handle material includes all types of exotic hardwood, abalone, peal mammoth tooth, mammoth ivory, Damascus steel and Mosaic Damascus. **Remarks:** Full time maker. First knife sold in 1999. **Prices:** $200 to $1800. Some to $2500. **Mark:** Owl logo with PJ Ernest Whittier CA or PJ Ernest.

ESSEGIAN, RICHARD,
7387 E Tulare St, Fresno, CA 93727, Phone: 309-255-5950
Specialties: Fancy working knives of his design; art knives. **Patterns:** Bowies and some small hunters. **Technical:** Grinds A2, D2, 440C and 154CM. Engraves and inlays. **Prices:** Start at $600. **Remarks:** Part-time maker; first knife sold in 1986. **Mark:** Last name, city and state.

ETZLER, JOHN,
11200 N Island, Grafton, OH 44044, Phone: 440-748-2460, jetzler@bright.net; Web: members.tripod.com/~etzlerknives/
Specialties: High-art and fantasy straight knives and folders of his design and to customer specs. **Patterns:** Folders, daggers, fighters, utility knives. **Technical:** Forges and grinds nickel Damascus and tool steel; grinds stainless steels. Prefers exotic, natural materials. **Prices:** $250 to $1200; some to $6500. **Remarks:** Full-time maker; first knife sold in 1992. **Mark:** Name or initials.

EVANS, BRUCE A,
409 CR 1371, Booneville, MS 38829, Phone: 662-720-0193, beknives@avsia.com; Web: www.bruceevans.homestead.com/open.html
Specialties: Forges blades. **Patterns:** Hunters, Bowies, or will work with customer. **Technical:** 5160, cable Damascus, pattern welded Damascus. **Prices:** $200 and up. **Mark:** Bruce A. Evans Same with JS on reverse of blade.

EVANS, CARLTON,
PO Box 46, Gainesville, TX 76241, Phone: 817-886-9231, carlton@carltonevans.com; Web: www.carltonevans.com
Specialties: High end folders and fixed blades. **Technical:** Uses the stock removal methods. The materials used are of the highest quality. **Remarks:** Full-time knifemaker, voting member of Knifemakers Guild, member of the Texas Knifemakers and Collectors Association.

EVANS, PHIL,
594 SE 40th, Columbus, KS 66725, Phone: 620-249-0639, phil@glenviewforge.com Web: www.glenviewforge.com
Specialties: Working knives, hunters, skinners, also enjoys making Bowies and fighters, high carbon or Damascus. **Technical:** Forges own blades and makes own Damascus. Uses all kinds of ancient Ivory and bone. Stabilizes own native hardwoods. **Prices:** $150 - $1,500. **Remarks:** Part-time maker. Made first knife in 1995. **Mark:** EVANS.

EVANS, RONALD B,
209 Hoffer St, Middleton, PA 17057-2723, Phone: 717-944-5464

EVANS, VINCENT K AND GRACE,
HC 1 Box 5275, Keaau, HI 96749-9517, Phone: 808-966-8978, evansvk@gmail.com Web: www.picturetrail.com/vevans
Specialties: Period pieces; swords. **Patterns:** Scottish, Viking, central Asian. **Technical:** Forges 5160 and his own Damascus. **Prices:** $700 to $4000; some to $8000. **Remarks:** Full-time maker; first knife sold in 1983. **Mark:** Last initial with fish logo.

EWING, JOHN H,
3276 Dutch Valley Rd, Clinton, TN 37716, Phone: 865-457-5757, johnja@comcast.net
Specialties: Working straight knives, hunters, camp knives. **Patterns:** Hunters. **Technical:** Grinds 440-D2. Forges 5160, 1095 prefers forging. **Prices:** $150 to $2000. **Remarks:** Part-time maker; first knife sold in 1985. **Mark:** First initial, last name, some embellishing done on knives.

F

FANT JR., GEORGE,
1983 CR 3214, Atlanta, TX 75551-6515, Phone: (903) 846-2938

FARID R, MEHR,
8 Sidney Close, Tunbridge Wells, Kent, ENGLAND TN2 5QQ, Phone: 011-44-1892 520345, farid@faridknives.com; Web: www.faridknives.com
Specialties: Hollow handle survival knives. High tech folders. **Patterns:** Flat grind blades & chisel ground LinerLock® folders. **Technical:** Grinds 440C, CPMT-440V, CPM-420V, CPM-15V, CPM5125V, and T-1 high speed steel. **Prices:** $550 to $5000. **Remarks:** Full-time maker; first knife sold in 1991. **Mark:** First name stamped.

FARR, DAN,
285 Glen Ellyn Way, Rochester, NY 14618, Phone: 585-721-1388
Specialties: Hunting, camping, fighting and utility. **Patterns:** Fixed blades. **Technical:** Forged or stock removal. **Prices:** $150 to $750.

FASSIO, MELVIN G,
420 Tyler Way, Lolo, MT 59847, Phone: 406-273-9143
Specialties: Working folders to customer specs. **Patterns:** Locking folders, hunters and traditional-style knives. **Technical:** Grinds 440C. **Prices:** $125 to $350. **Remarks:** Part-time maker; first knife sold in 1975. **Mark:** Name and city, dove logo.

FAUCHEAUX, HOWARD J,
PO Box 206, Loreauville, LA 70552, Phone: 318-229-6467
Specialties: Working straight knives and folders; period pieces. Also a hatchet with capping knife in the handle. **Patterns:** Traditional locking folders, hunters, fighters and Bowies. **Technical:** Forges W2, 1095 and his own Damascus; stock removal D2. **Prices:** Start at $200. **Remarks:** Full-time maker; first knife sold in 1969. **Mark:** Last name.

FAUST, DICK,
624 Kings Hwy N, Rochester, NY 14617, Phone: 585-544-1948, dickfaustknives@mac.com
Specialties: High-performance working straight knives. **Patterns:** Hunters and utility/camp knives. **Technical:** Hollow grinds 154CM full tang. Exotic woods, stag and Micarta handles. Provides a custom leather sheath with each knife. **Prices:** From $200 to $600, some higher. **Remarks:** Full-time maker. **Mark:** Signature.

FAUST, JOACHIM,
Kirchgasse 10, 95497 Goldkronach, GERMANY

FECAS, STEPHEN J,
1312 Shadow Lane, Anderson, SC 29625, Phone: 864-287-4834, Fax: 864-287-4834

Specialties: Front release lock backs, liner locks. Folders only. **Patterns:** Gents folders. **Technical:** Grinds ATS-34, Damascus-Ivories and pearl handles. **Prices:** $650 to $1200. **Remarks:** Full-time maker since 1980. First knife sold in 1977. All knives hand finished to 1500 grit. **Mark:** Last name signature.

FELIX, ALEXANDER,
PO Box 4036, Torrance, CA 90510, Phone: 310-320-1836, sgiandubh@dslextreme.com

Specialties: Straight working knives, fancy ethnic designs. **Patterns:** Hunters, Bowies, daggers, period pieces. **Technical:** Forges carbon steel and Damascus; forged stainless and titanium jewelry, gold and silver casting. **Prices:** $110 and up. **Remarks:** Jeweler, ABS Journeyman Smith. **Mark:** Last name.

FELLOWS, MIKE,
PO Box 162, Mosselbay 6500, SOUTH AFRICA, Phone: 27 82 960 3868, karatshin@gmail.com

Specialties: Miniatures, art knives and folders with occasionally hunters and skinners. **Patterns:** Own designs. **Technical:** Uses own Damascus. **Prices:** Upon request. **Remarks:** Use only indigenous materials. Exotic hard woods, horn & ivory. Does all own embellishments. **Mark:** "SHIN" letter from Hebrew alphabet over Hebrew word "Karat." **Other:** Member of knifemakers guild of Southern Africa.

FERGUSON, JIM,
32131 Via Bande, Temecula, CA 92592, Phone: 951-302-0267, Web: www.twistednickel.com www.howtomakeaknife.net

Specialties: Nickel Damascus, Bowies, daggers, push blades. Also makes swords, battle axes and utilities. **Patterns:** All styles. **Technical:** Sells in U.S. and Canada. **Prices:** $350 to $600, some to $1000. **Mark:** Jim Ferguson/USA. Also makes swords, battle axes and utilities.

FERGUSON, JIM,
PO Box 301, San Angelo, TX 76902, Phone: 915-651-6656

Specialties: Straight working knives and folders. **Patterns:** Working belt knives, hunters, Bowies and some folders. **Technical:** Grinds ATS-34, D2 and Vascowear. Flat-grinds hunting knives. **Prices:** $200 to $600; some to $1000. **Remarks:** Full-time maker; first knife sold in 1987. **Mark:** First and middle initials, last name.

FERGUSON, LEE,
1993 Madison 7580, Hindsville, AR 72738, Phone: 479-443-0084, info@fergusonknives.com; Web: www.fergusonknives.com

Specialties: Straight working knives and folders, some fancy. **Patterns:** Hunters, daggers, swords, locking folders and slip-joints. **Technical:** Grinds D2, 440C and ATS-34; heat-treats. **Prices:** $50 to $600; some to $4000. **Remarks:** Full-time maker; first knife sold in 1977. **Mark:** Full name.

FERGUSON, LINDA,
1993 Madison 7580, Hindsville, AR 72738, Phone: 479-443-0084, info@fergusonknives.com: Web: www.fergusonknives.com

Specialties: Mini knives. **Patterns:** Daggers & hunters. **Technical:** Hollow ground, stainless steel or Damascus. **Prices:** $65 to $250. **Remarks:** 2004 member Knifemakers Guild, Miniature Knifemakers Society. **Mark:** LF inside a Roman numeral 2.

FERRARA, THOMAS,
122 Madison Dr, Naples, FL 33942, Phone: 813-597-3363, Fax: 813-597-3363

Specialties: High-art, traditional and working straight knives and folders of all designs. **Patterns:** Boots, Bowies, daggers, fighters and hunters. **Technical:** Grinds 440C, D2 and ATS-34; heat-treats. **Prices:** $100 to $700; some to $1300. **Remarks:** Part-time maker; first knife sold in 1983. **Mark:** Last name.

FERRIER, GREGORY K,
3119 Simpson Dr, Rapid City, SD 57702, Phone: 605-342-9280

FERRY, TOM,
16005 SE 322nd St, Auburn, WA 98092, Phone: 253-939-4468, tomferryknives@Q.com; Web: tomferryknives.com

Specialties: Presentation grade knives. **Patterns:** Folders and fixed blades. **Technical:** Specialize in Damascus and engraving. **Prices:** $500 and up. **Remarks:** DBA: Soos Creek Ironworks. ABS Master Smith. **Mark:** Combined T and F in a circle and/or last name.

FILIPPOU, IOANNIS-MINAS,
7 Krinis Str Nea Smyrni, Athens 17122, GREECE, Phone: (1) 935-2093

FINCH, RICKY D,
2446 Hwy. 191, West Liberty, KY 41472, Phone: 606-743-7151, finchknives@mrtc.com; Web: www.finchknives.com

Specialties: Traditional working/using straight knives of his design or to customer spec. **Patterns:** Hunters, skinners and utility/camp knives. LinerLock® of his design. **Technical:** Grinds 440C, ATS-34 and CPM154, hand rubbed stain finish, use Micarta, stabilized wood, natural and exotic. **Prices:** $85 to $225. **Remarks:** Part-time maker, first knife made 1994. Doing business as Finch Knives. **Mark:** Last name inside outline of state of Kentucky.

FIORINI, BILL,
703 W. North St., Grayville, IL 62844, Phone: 618-375-7191, smallflowerlonchura@yahoo.com

Specialties: Fancy working knives. **Patterns:** Hunters, boots, Japanese-style knives and kitchen/utility knives and folders. **Technical:** Forges own Damascus, mosaic and mokune-gane. **Prices:** Full range. **Remarks:** Full-time metal smith researching pattern materials. **Mark:** Orchid crest with name KOKA in Japanese.

FISHER, JAY,
1405 Edwards, Clovis, NM 88101, jayfisher@jayfisher.com Web: www.JayFisher.com

Specialties: High-art, working and collector's knives of his design and client's designs. Military working and commemoratives. Gemstone handles, Locking combat sheaths. **Patterns:** Hunters, daggers, folding knives, museum pieces and high-art sculptures. **Technical:** 440C, ATS-34, CPMS30V, D2, O1, CPM154CM, CPMS35VN. Prolific maker of stone-handled knives and swords. **Prices:** $850 to $150,000. **Remarks:** Full-time maker; first knife sold in 1980. High resolution etching, computer and manual engraving. **Mark:** Signature "JaFisher"

FISHER, LANCE,
9 Woodlawn Ave., Pompton Lakes, NJ 07442, Phone: 973-248-8447, lance.fisher@sandvik.com

Specialties: Wedding cake knives and servers, forks, etc. Including velvet lined wood display cases. **Patterns:** Drop points, upswept skinners, Bowies, daggers, fantasy, medieval, San Francisco style, chef or kitchen cutlery. **Technical:** Stock removal method only. Steels include but are not limited to CPM 154, D2, CPM S35VN, CPM S90V and Sandvik 13C26. Handle materials include stag, sheep horn, exotic woods, micarta, and G10 as well as reconstituted stone. **Prices:** $350 - $2000. **Remarks:** Part-time maker, will become full-time on retirement. Made and sold first knife in 1981 and has never looked back. **Mark:** Tang stamp.

FISHER, THEO (TED),
8115 Modoc Lane, Montague, CA 96064, Phone: 916-459-3804

Specialties: Moderately priced working knives in carbon steel. **Patterns:** Hunters, fighters, kitchen and buckskinner knives, Damascus miniatures. **Technical:** Grinds ATS-34, L6 and 440C. **Prices:** $65 to $165; exceptional knives to $300. **Remarks:** First knife sold in 1981. **Mark:** Name in banner logo.

FISK, JERRY,
10095 Hwy 278 W, Nashville, AR 71852, Phone: 870-845-4456, jerry@fisk-knives.com; Web: wwwfisk-knives.com

Specialties: Edged weapons, collectible and functional. **Patterns:** Bowies, daggers, swords, hunters, camp knives and others. **Technical:** Forges carbon steels and his own pattern welded steels. **Prices:** $250 to $15,000. **Remarks:** National living treasure. **Mark:** Name, MS.

FISTER, JIM,
PO Box 307, Simpsonville, KY 40067

Specialties: One-of-a-kind collectibles and period pieces. **Patterns:** Bowies, camp knives, hunters, buckskinners, and daggers. **Technical:** Forges, 1085, 5160, 52100, his own Damascus, pattern and turkish. **Prices:** $150 to $2500. **Remarks:** Part-time maker; first knife sold in 1982. **Mark:** Name and MS.

FITCH, JOHN S,
45 Halbrook Rd, Clinton, AR 72031-8910, Phone: 501-893-2020

FITZGERALD, DENNIS M,
4219 Alverado Dr, Fort Wayne, IN 46816-2847, Phone: 219-447-1081

Specialties: One-of-a-kind collectibles and period pieces. **Patterns:** Skinners, fighters, camp and utility; period pieces. **Technical:** Forges 1085, 1095, L6, 5160, 52100, his own pattern and Turkish Damascus. **Prices:** $100 to $500. **Remarks:** Part-time maker; first knife sold in 1985. Doing business as The Ringing Circle. **Mark:** Name and circle logo.

FLINT, ROBERT,
2902 Aspen, Anchorage, AK 99517, Phone: 907-243-6706

Specialties: Working straight knives and folders. **Patterns:** Utility, hunters, fighters and gents. **Technical:** Grinds ATS-34, BG-42, D2 and Damascus. **Prices:** $150 and up. **Remarks:** Part-time maker, first knife sold in 1998. **Mark:** Last name; stylized initials.

FLOURNOY, JOE,
5750 Lisbon Rd, El Dorado, AR 71730, Phone: 870-863-7208, flournoy@ipa.net

Specialties: Working straight knives and folders. **Patterns:** Hunters, Bowies, camp knives, folders and daggers. **Technical:** Forges only high-carbon steel, steel cable and his own Damascus. **Prices:** $350 Plus. **Remarks:** First knife sold in 1977. **Mark:** Last name and MS in script.

FLYNT, ROBERT G,
15173 Christy Lane, Gulfport, MS 39503, Phone: 228-265-0410, flyntstoneknives@bellsouth.net Web: www.flyntstoneknifeworks.com

Specialties:
All types of fixed blades: Drop point, clip point, trailing point, bull nose hunters, tactical, fighters and Bowies. Folders I've made include liner lock, slip joint and lock back styles.
Technical: Using 154 cm, cpm154, ats34, 440c, cpm3v and 52100 steel, most of my blades are made by stock removal, hollow and flat grind methods. I do forge some cable Damascus and use numerous types of Damascus that is purchased in billets from various makers. All file work and bluing is done by me.

I have made handles from a variety of wood, bone and horn materials, including some with wire inlay and other embellishments. Most knives are sold with custom fit leather sheaves most include exotic skin inlay when appropriate. **Prices:** $150 and up depending on embellishments on blade and sheath. **Remarks:** Full time maker. First knife made in 1966. **Mark:** Last name in cursive letters or a knife striking a flint stone.

FOGARIZZU, BOITEDDU,
via Crispi 6, 07016 Pattada, ITALY
Specialties: Traditional Italian straight knives and folders. **Patterns:** Collectible folders. **Technical:** forges and grinds 12C27, ATS-34 and his Damascus. **Prices:** $200 to $3000. **Remarks:** Full-time maker; first knife sold in 1958. **Mark:** Full name and registered logo.

FOGG, DON,
98 Lake St., Auburn, ME 04210, Phone: 205-483-0822, dfogg@dfoggknives.com; Web: www.dfoggknives.com
Specialties: Swords, daggers, Bowies and hunting knives. **Patterns:** Collectible folders. **Technical:** Hand-forged high-carbon and Damascus steel. **Prices:** $200 to $5000. **Remarks:** Full-time maker; first knife sold in 1976. **Mark:** 24K gold cherry blossom.

FONTENOT, GERALD J,
901 Maple Ave, Mamou, LA 70554, Phone: 318-468-3180

FORREST, BRIAN,
FORREST KNIVES, PO Box 203, Descanso, CA 91916, Phone: 619-445-6343, forrestknives@hotmail.com; Web: www.forrestknives.com
Specialties: Forged tomahawks, working knives, big Bowies. **Patterns:** Traditional and extra large Bowies. **Technical:** Hollow grinds: 440C, 1095, S160 Damascus. **Prices:**"$125 and up. **Remarks:** Member of California Knifemakers Association. Full-time maker. First knife sold in 1971. **Mark:** Forrest USA/Tomahawks marked FF (Forrest Forge).

FORTHOFER, PETE,
5535 Hwy 93S, Whitefish, MT 59937, Phone: 406-862-2674
Specialties: Interframes with checkered wood inlays; working straight knives. **Patterns:** Interframe folders and traditional-style knives; hunters, fighters and Bowies. **Technical:** Grinds D2, 440C, 154CM and ATS-34. **Prices:** $350 to $2500; some to $1500. **Remarks:** Part-time maker; full-time gunsmith. First knife sold in 1979. **Mark:** Name and logo.

FORTUNE PRODUCTS, INC.,
205 Hickory Creek Rd, Marble Falls, TX 78654, Phone: 830-693-6111, Fax: 830-693-6394, Web: www.accusharp.com
Specialties: Knife sharpeners.

FOSTER, AL,
118 Woodway Dr, Magnolia, TX 77355, Phone: 936-372-9297
Specialties: Straight knives and folders. **Patterns:** Hunting, fishing, folders and Bowies. **Technical:** Grinds 440-C, ATS-34 and D2. **Prices:** $100 to $1000. **Remarks:** Full-time maker; first knife sold in 1981. **Mark:** Scorpion logo and name.

FOSTER, BURT,
23697 Archery Range Rd, Bristol, VA 24202, Phone: 276-669-0121, burt@burtfoster.com; Web:www.burtfoster.com
Specialties: Working straight knives, laminated blades, and some art knives of his design. **Patterns:** Bowies, hunters, daggers. **Technical:** Forges 52100, W-2 and makes own Damascus. Does own heat treating. **Remarks:** ABS MasterSmith. Full-time maker, believes in sole authorship. **Mark:** Signed "BF" initials.

FOSTER, NORVELL C,
7945 Youngsford Rd, Marion, TX 78124-1713, Phone: 830-914-2078
Specialties: Engraving; ivory handle carving. **Patterns:** American-large and small scroll-oak leaf and acorns. **Prices:** $25 to $400. **Remarks:** Have been engraving since 1957. **Mark:** N.C. Foster - Marion - Tex and current year.

FOSTER, R L (BOB),
745 Glendale Blvd, Mansfield, OH 44907, Phone: 419-756-6294

FOSTER, RONNIE E,
95 Riverview Rd., Morrilton, AR 72110, Phone: 501-354-5389
Specialties: Working, using knives, some period pieces, work with customer specs. **Patterns:** Hunters, fighters, Bowies, liner-lock folders, camp knives. **Technical:** Forge-5160, 1084, O1, 15N20-makes own Damascus. **Prices:** $200 (start). **Remarks:** Part-time maker. First knife sold 1994. **Mark:** Ronnie Foster MS.

FOSTER, TIMOTHY L,
723 Sweet Gum Acres Rd, El Dorado, AR 71730, Phone: 870-863-6188

FOWLER, CHARLES R,
226 National Forest Rd 48, Ft McCoy, FL 32134-9624, Phone: 904-467-3215

FOWLER, ED A.,
Willow Bow Ranch, PO Box 1519, Riverton, WY 82501, Phone: 307-856-9815
Specialties: High-performance working and using straight knives. **Patterns:** Hunter, camp, bird, and trout knives and Bowies. New model, the gentleman's Pronghorn. **Technical:** Low temperature forged 52100 from virgin 5-1/2 round bars, multiple quench heat treating, engraves all knives, all handles domestic sheep horn processed and aged at least 5 years. Makes heavy duty hand-stitched waxed harness leather pouch type sheathes. **Prices:** $800 to $7000. **Remarks:** Full-time maker. First knife sold in 1962. **Mark:** Initials connected.

FOWLER, JERRY,
610 FM 1660 N, Hutto, TX 78634, Phone: 512-846-2860, fowler@inetport.com
Specialties: Using straight knives of his design. **Patterns:** A variety of hunting and camp knives, combat knives. Custom designs considered. **Technical:** Forges 5160, his own Damascus and cable Damascus. Makes sheaths. Prefers natural handle materials. **Prices:** Start at $150. **Remarks:** Part-time maker; first knife sold in 1986. Doing business as Fowler Forge Knife Works. **Mark:** First initial, last name, date and J.S.

FOX, PAUL,
4721 Rock Barn Rd, Claremont, NC 28610, Phone: 828-459-2000, jessepfox@gmail.com
Specialties: Unique locking mechanisms. **Patterns:** Pen knives, one-of-a-kind tactical knives. **Technical:** All locking mechanisms are his. **Prices:** $350 and up. **Remarks:** First knife sold in 1976. Guild member since 1977. **Mark:** Fox, P Fox, Paul Fox. Cuts out all parts of knives in shop.

FRALEY, D B,
1355 Fairbanks Ct, Dixon, CA 95620, Phone: 707-678-0393, dbtfnives@sbcglobal.net; Web:www.dbfraleyknives.com
Specialties Usable gentleman's fixed blades and folders. **Patterns:** Foure folders in four different sizes in liner lock and frame lock. **Technical:** Grinds CPMS30V, 154, 6K stellite. **Prices:** $250 and up. **Remarks:** Part time maker. First knife sold in 1990. **Mark:** First and middle initials, last name over a buffalo.

FRAMSKI, WALTER P,
24 Rek Ln, Prospect, CT 06712, Phone: 203-758-5634

FRANCE, DAN,
Box 218, Cawood, KY 40815, Phone: 606-573-6104
Specialties: Traditional working and using straight knives of his design. **Patterns:** Hunters, Bowies and utility/camp knives. **Technical:** Forges and grinds O1, 5160 and L6. **Prices:** $35 to $125; some to $350. **Remarks:** Spare-time maker; first knife sold in 1985. **Mark:** First name.

FRANCIS, JOHN D,
FRANCIS KNIVES, 18 Miami St., Ft. Loramie, OH 45845, Phone: 937-295-3941, jdfrancis@roadrunner.com
Specialties: Utility and hunting-style fixed bladed knives of 440 C and ATS-34 steel; Micarta, exotic woods, and other types of handle materials. **Prices:** $90 to $150 range. **Remarks:** Exceptional quality and value at factory prices. **Mark:** Francis-Ft. Loramie, OH stamped on tang.

FRANK, HEINRICH H,
1147 SW Bryson St, Dallas, OR 97338, Phone: 503-831-1489, Fax: 503-831-1489
Specialties: High-art investor-class folders, handmade and engraved. **Patterns:** Folding daggers, hunter-size folders and gents. **Technical:** Grinds 07 and O1. **Prices:** $4800 to $16,000. **Remarks:** Full-time maker; first knife sold in 1965. Doing business as H.H. Frank Knives. **Mark:** Name, address and date.

FRANKLIN, MIKE,
9878 Big Run Rd, Aberdeen, OH 45101, Phone: 937-549-2598, Web: www.mikefranklinknives.com, hawgcustomknives.com
Specialties: High-tech tactical folders. **Patterns:** Tactical folders. **Technical:** Grinds CPM-T-440V, 440-C, ATS-34; titanium liners and bolsters; carbon fiber scales. Uses radical grinds and severe serrations. **Prices:** $100 to $1000. **Remarks:** Full-time maker; first knife sold in 1969. All knives made one at a time, 100% by the maker. **Mark:** Stylized boar with HAWG.

FRAPS, JOHN R,
3810 Wyandotte Tr, Indianapolis, IN 46240-3422, Phone: 317-849-9419, jfraps@att.net; Web: www.frapsknives.com
Specialties: Working and collector grade LinerLock® and slip joint folders. **Patterns:** One-of-a kind linerlocks and traditional slip joints. **Technical:** Flat and hollow grinds ATS-34, Damascus, Talonite, CPM S30V, 154Cm, Stellite 6K; hand rubbed or mirror finish. **Prices:** $200 to $1500, some higher. **Remarks:** Voting member of the Knifemaker's Guild; Full-time maker; first knife sold in 1997. **Mark:** Cougar Creek Knives and/or name.

FRAZIER, JIM,
6315 Wagener Rd., Wagener, SC 29164, Phone: 803-564-6467, jbfrazierknives@hotmail.com Web: www.jbfrazierknives.com
Specialties: Hunters, semi skinners, bird and trout, folders, many patterns of own design with George Herron/Geno Denning influence. **Technical:** Stock removal maker using CPM-154, ATS-34, S30-V, D2. Hollow grind, mainly mirror finish, some satin finish. Prefer to use natural handle material such as stag, horn, mammoth ivory, highly figured woods, some micarta, others on request. Makes own leather sheaths on 1958 straight needle stitcher. **Prices:** $300. **Remarks:** Part-time maker since 1989. **Mark:** JB Frazier in arch with Knives under it.Stamp on sheath is outline of state of SC, JB Frazier Knives Wagener SC inside outline.

FRAZIER, RON,
2107 Urbine Rd, Powhatan, VA 23139, Phone: 804-794-8561
Specialties: Classy working knives of his design; some high-art straight knives. **Patterns:** Wide assortment of straight knives, including miniatures and push knives. **Technical:** Grinds 440C; offers satin, mirror or sand finishes. **Prices:** $85 to $700; some to $3000. **Remarks:** Full-time maker; first knife sold in 1976. **Mark:** Name in arch logo.

FRED, REED WYLE,
3149 X S, Sacramento, CA 95817, Phone: 916-739-0237
Specialties: Working using straight knives of his design. **Patterns:** Hunting and camp knives. **Technical:** Forges any 10 series, old files and carbon steels. Offers initialing upon request; prefers natural handle materials. **Prices:** $30 to $300. **Remarks:** Part-time maker; first knife sold in 1994. Doing business as R.W. Fred Knifemaker. **Mark:** Engraved first and last initials.

FREDEEN, GRAHAM,
5121 Finadene Ct., Colorado Springs, CO 80916, Phone: 719-331-5665, fredeenblades@hotmail.com Web: www.fredeenblades.com
Specialties: Working class knives to high-end custom knives. Traditional pattern welding and mosaic Damascus blades.**Patterns:** All types: Bowies, fighters, hunters, skinners, bird and trout, camp knives, utility knives, daggers, etc. Occasionally swords, both European and Asian.**Technical:** Differential heat treatment and Hamon. Damascus steel rings and jewelry. Hand forged blades and Damascus steel. High carbon blade steels: 1050, 1075/1080, 1084, 1095, 5160, 52100, W1, W2, O1, 15n20**Prices:** $100 - $2,000. **Remarks:** Sole authorship. Part-time maker. First blade produced in 2005. Member of American Bladesmith Society and Professional Knifemaker's Association **Mark:** "Fredeen" etched on the ricasso or on/along the spine of the blade.

FREDERICK, AARON,
459 Brooks Ln, West Liberty, KY 41472-8961, Phone: 606-7432015, aaronf@mrtc.com; Web: www.frederickknives.com
Specialties: Makes most types of knives, but as for now specializes in the Damascus folder. Does all own Damascus and forging of the steel. Also prefers natural handle material such as ivory and pearl. Prefers 14k gold screws in most of the knives he do. Also offer several types of file work on blades, spacers, and liners. Has just recently started doing carving and can do a limited amount of engraving.

FREER, RALPH,
114 12th St, Seal Beach, CA 90740, Phone: 562-493-4925, Fax: same, ralphfreer@adelphia.net
Specialties: Exotic folders, liner locks, folding daggers, fixed blades. **Patters:** All original. **Technical:** Lots of Damascus, ivory, pearl, jeweled, thumb studs, carving ATS-34, 420V, 530V. **Prices:** $400 to $2500 and up. **Mark:** Freer in German-style text, also Freer shield.

FREY JR., W FREDERICK,
305 Walnut St, Milton, PA 17847, Phone: 570-742-9576, wffrey@ptd.net
Specialties: Working straight knives and folders, some fancy. **Patterns:** Wide range miniatures, boot knives and lock back folders. **Technical:** Grinds A2, O1 and D2; vaseo wear, cru-wear and CPM S60V and CPM S90V. **Prices:** $100 to $250; some to $1200. **Remarks:** Spare-time maker; first knife sold in 1983. All knives include quality hand stitched sheaths. **Mark:** Last name in script.

FRIEDLY, DENNIS E,
12 Cottontail Lane E, Cody, WY 82414, Phone: 307-527-6811, friedlyknives@hotmail.com Web: www.friedlyknives.com
Specialties: Fancy working straight knives and daggers, lock back folders and liner locks. Also embellished bowies. **Patterns:** Hunters, fighters, short swords, minis and miniatures; new line of full-tang hunters/boots. **Technical:** Grinds 440C, commercial Damascus, mosaic Damascus and ATS-34 blades; prefers hidden tangs and full tangs. Both flat and hollow grinds. **Prices:** $350 to $2500. Some to $10,000. **Remarks:** Full-time maker; first knife sold in 1972. **Mark:** D.E. Friedly-Cody, WY. Friedly Knives

FRIGAULT, RICK,
3584 Rapidsview Dr, Niagara Falls, Ont., CANADA L2G 6C4, Phone: 905-295-6695, rfrigualt@cogeco.ca; Web: www.rfrigaultknives.ca
Specialties: Fixed blades. **Patterns:** Hunting, tactical and large Bowies. **Technical:** Grinds ATS-34, 440-C, D-2, CPMS30V, CPMS60V, CPMS90V, BG42 and Damascus. Use G-10, Micarta, ivory, antler, ironwood and other stabilized woods for carbon fiber handle material. Makes leather sheaths by hand. Tactical blades include a Concealex sheath made by "On Scene Tactical." **Remarks:** Sold first knife in 1997. Member of Canadian Knifemakers Guild. **Mark:** RFRIGAULT.

FRITZ, ERIK L,
837 River St Box 1203, Forsyth, MT 59327, Phone: 406-351-1101, tacmedic45@yahoo.com
Specialties: Forges carbon steel 1084, 5160, 52100 and Damascus. **Patterns:** Hunters, camp knives, bowies and folders as well as forged tactical. **Technical:** Forges own Mosaic and pattern welded Damascus as well as doing own heat treat. **Prices:** A$200 and up. **Remarks:** Sole authorship knives and sheaths. Part time maker first knife sold in 2004. ABS member. **Mark:** E. Fritz in arc on left side ricasso.

FRITZ, JESSE,
900 S. 13th St, Slaton, TX 79364, Phone: 806-828-5083
Specialties: Working and using straight knives in standard patterns. **Patterns:** Hunters, utility/camp knives and skinners with gut hook, Bowie knives, kitchen carving sets by request. **Technical:** Grinds 440C, O1 and 1095. Uses 1095 steel. Fline-napped steel design, blued blades, filework and machine jewelling. Inlays handles with turquoise, coral and mother-of-pearl. Makes sheaths. **Prices:** $85 to $275; some to $500. **Mark:** Last name only (FRITZ).

FRIZZELL, TED,
14056 Low Gap Rd, West Fork, AR 72774, Phone: 501-839-2516, mmhwaxes@aol.com Web: www.mineralmountain.com
Specialties: Swords, axes and self-defense weapons. **Patterns:** Small skeleton knives to large swords. **Technical:** Grinds 5160 almost exclusively—1/4" to 1/2"— bars some O1 and A2 on request. All knives come with Kydex sheaths. **Prices:** $45 to $1200. **Remarks:** Full-time maker; first knife sold in 1984. Doing business as Mineral Mountain Hatchet Works. Wholesale orders welcome. **Mark:** A circle with line in the middle; MM and HW within the circle.

FRONEFIELD, DANIEL,
20270 Warriors Path, Peyton, CO 80831, Phone: 719-749-0226, dfronfld@hiwaay.com
Specialties: Fixed and folding knives featuring meteorites and other exotic materials. **Patterns:** San-mai Damascus, custom Damascus. **Prices:** $500 to $3000.

FROST, DEWAYNE,
1016 Van Buren Rd, Barnesville, GA 30204, Phone: 770-358-1426, lbrtyhill@aol.com
Specialties: Working straight knives and period knives. **Patterns:** Hunters, Bowies and utility knives. **Technical:** Forges own Damascus, cable, etc. as well as stock removal. **Prices:** $150 to $500. **Remarks:** Part-time maker ABS Journeyman Smith. **Mark:** Liberty Hill Forge Dewayne Frost w/liberty bell.

FRUHMANN, LUDWIG,
Stegerwaldstr 8, 84489 Burghausen, GERMANY
Specialties: High-tech and working straight knives of his design. **Patterns:** Hunters, fighters and boots. **Technical:** Grinds ATS-34, CPM-T-440V and Schneider Damascus. Prefers natural handle materials. **Prices:** $200 to $1500. **Remarks:** Spare-time maker; first knife sold in 1990. **Mark:** First initial and last name.

FUEGEN, LARRY,
617 N Coulter Circle, Prescott, AZ 86303, Phone: 928-776-8777, fuegen@cableone.net; Web: www.larryfuegen.com
Specialties: High-art folders and classic and working straight knives. **Patterns:** Forged scroll folders, lockback folders and classic straight knives. **Technical:** Forges 5160, 1095 and his own Damascus. Works in exotic leather; offers elaborate filework and carving; likes natural handle materials, now offers own engraving. **Prices:** $600 to $12,000. **Remarks:** Full-time maker; first knife sold in 1975. Sole authorship on all knives. ABS Mastersmith. **Mark:** Initials connected.

FUJIKAWA, SHUN,
Sawa 1157 Kaizuka, Osaka 597 0062, JAPAN, Phone: 81-724-23-4032, Fax: 81-726-23-9229
Specialties: Folders of his design and to customer specs. **Patterns:** Locking folders. **Technical:** Grinds his own steel. **Prices:** $450 to $2500; some to $3000. **Remarks:** Part-time maker.

FUJISAKA, STANLEY,
45-004 Holowai St, Kaneohe, HI 96744, Phone: 808-247-0017, s.fuj@earthlink.net
Specialties: Fancy working straight knives and folders. **Patterns:** Hunters, boots, personal knives, daggers, collectible art knives. **Technical:** Grinds 440C, 154CM and ATS-34; clean lines, inlays. **Prices:** $400 to $2000; some to $6000. **Remarks:** Full-time maker; first knife sold in 1984. **Mark:** Name, city, state.

FUKUTA, TAK,
38-Umeagae-cho, Seki-City, Gifu-Pref, JAPAN, Phone: 0575-22-0264
Specialties: Bench-made fancy straight knives and folders. **Patterns:** Sheffield-type folders, Bowies and fighters. **Technical:** Grinds commercial Damascus. **Prices:** Start at $300. **Remarks:** Full-time maker. **Mark:** Name in knife logo.

FULLER, BRUCE A,
1305 Airhart Dr, Baytown, TX 77520, Phone: 281-427-1848, fullcoforg@aol.com
Specialties: One-of-a-kind working/using straight knives and folders of his designs. **Patterns:** Bowies, hunters, folders, and utility/camp knives. **Technical:** Forges high-carbon steel and his own Damascus. Prefers El Solo Mesquite and natural materials. Offers filework. **Prices:** $200 to $500; some to $1800. **Remarks:** Spare-time maker; first knife sold in 1991. Doing business as Fullco Forge. **Mark:** Fullco, M.S.

FULLER, JACK A,
7103 Stretch Ct, New Market, MD 21774, Phone: 301-798-0119
Specialties: Straight working knives of his design and to customer specs. **Patterns:** Fighters, camp knives, hunters, tomahawks and art knives. **Technical:** Forges 5160, O1, W2 and his own Damascus. Does silver wire inlay and own leather work, wood lined sheaths for big camp knives. **Prices:** $400 and up. **Remarks:** Part-time maker. Master Smith in ABS; first knife sold in 1979. **Mark:** Fuller's Forge, MS.

FULTON, MICKEY,
406 S Shasta St, Willows, CA 95988, Phone: 530-934-5780
Specialties: Working straight knives and folders of his design. **Patterns:** Hunters, Bowies, lockback folders and steak knife sets. **Technical:** Hand-filed, sanded, buffed ATS-34, 440C and A2. **Prices:** $65 to $600; some to $1200. **Remarks:** Full-time maker; first knife sold in 1979. **Mark:** Signature.

G

GADBERRY, EMMET,
82 Purple Plum Dr, Hattieville, AR 72063, Phone: 501-354-4842

GADDY, GARY LEE,
205 Ridgewood Lane, Washington, NC 27889, Phone: 252-946-4359
Specialties: Working/using straight knives of his design; period pieces. **Patterns:** Bowies, hunters, utility/camp knives, oyster knives. **Technical:** Grinds ATS-34, O1; forges 1095. **Prices:** $175+ **Remarks:** Spare-time maker; first knife sold in 1991. No longer accepts orders. **Mark:** Quarter moon stamp.

GAETA, ANGELO,
R. Saldanha Marinho, 1295 Centro Jau, SP-17201-310, BRAZIL, Phone: 0146-224543, Fax: 0146-224543
Specialties: Straight using knives to customer specs. **Patterns:** Hunters, fighting, daggers, belt push dagger. **Technical:** Grinds D6, ATS-34 and 440C stainless. Titanium nitride golden finish upon request. **Prices:** $60 to $300. **Remarks:** Full-time maker; first knife sold in 1992. **Mark:** First initial, last name.

GAETA, ROBERTO,
Rua Mandissununga 41, Sao Paulo, BRAZIL 05619-010, Phone: 11-37684626, karlaseno@uol.com.br
Specialties: Wide range of using knives. **Patterns:** Brazilian and North American hunting and fighting knives. **Technical:** Grinds stainless steel; likes natural handle materials. **Prices:** $500 to $800. **Remarks:** Full-time maker; first knife sold in 1979. **Mark:** BOB'G.

GAINES, BUDDY,
GAINES KNIVES, 155 Red Hill Rd., Commerce, GA 30530, Web: www.gainesknives.com
Specialties: Collectible and working folders and straight knives. **Patterns:** Folders, hunters, Bowies, tactical knives. **Technical:** Forges own Damascus, grinds ATS-34, D2, commercial Damascus. Prefers mother-of-pearl and stag. **Prices:** Start at $200. **Remarks:** Part-time maker, sold first knife in 1985. **Mark:** Last name.

GAINEY, HAL,
904 Bucklevel Rd, Greenwood, SC 29649, Phone: 864-223-0225, Web: www.scak.org
Specialties: Traditional working and using straight knives and folders. **Patterns:** Hunters, slip-joint folders and utility/camp knives. **Technical:** Hollow-grinds ATS-34 and D2; makes sheaths. **Prices:** $95 to $145; some to $500. **Remarks:** Full-time maker; first knife sold in 1975. **Mark:** Eagle head and last name.

GALLAGHER, BARRY,
135 Park St, Lewistown, MT 59457, Phone: 406-538-7056, Web: www.gallagherknives.com
Specialties: One-of-a-kind Damascus folders. **Patterns:** Folders, utility to high art, some straight knives, hunter, Bowies, and art pieces. **Technical:** Forges own mosaic Damascus and carbon steel, some stainless. **Prices:** $400 to $5000+. **Remarks:** Full-time maker; first knife sold in 1993. Doing business as Gallagher Custom Knives. **Mark:** Last name.

GAMBLE, FRANK,
4676 Commercial St SE #26, Salem, OR 97302, Phone: 503-581-7993, gamble6831@comcast.net
Specialties: Fantasy and high-art straight knives and folders of his design. **Patterns:** Daggers, fighters, hunters and special locking folders. **Technical:** Grinds 440C and ATS-34; forges Damascus. Inlays; offers jewelling. Prices $150 to $10,000. **Remarks:** Full-time maker; first knife sold in 1976. **Mark:** First initial, last name.

GAMBLE, ROGER,
18515 N.W. 28th Pl., Newberry, FL 32669, ROGERLGAMBLE@COX.NET
Specialties: Traditional working/using straight knives and folders of his design. **Patterns:** Liner locks and hunters. **Technical:** Grinds ATS-34 and Damascus. **Prices:** $150 to $2000. **Remarks:** Part-time maker; first knife sold in 2012. Doing business as Gamble Knives. **Mark:** First name in a fan of cards over last name.

GANN, TOMMY,
2876 State Hwy. 198, Canton, TX 75103, Phone: 903-848-9375
Specialties: Art and working straight knives of my design or customer preferences/design. **Patterns:** Bowie, fighters, hunters, daggers. **Technical:** Forges Damascus 52100 and grinds ATS-34 and D2. **Prices:** $200 to $2500. **Remarks:** Full-time knifemaker, first knife sold in 2002. ABS journey bladesmith. **Mark:** TGANN.

GANSHORN, CAL,
123 Rogers Rd., Regina, Saskatchewan, CANADA S4S 6T7, Phone: 306-584-0524
Specialties: Working and fancy fixed blade knives. **Patterns:** Bowies, hunters, daggers, and filleting. **Technical:** Makes own forged Damascus billets, ATS, salt heat treating, and custom forges and burners. **Prices:** $250 to $1500. **Remarks:** Part-time maker. **Mark:** Last name etched in ricasso area.

GARAU, MARCELLO,
Via Alagon 42, 09170, Oristano, Italy, Phone: 00393479073454, marcellogarau@libero.it Web: www.knifecreator.com
Specialties: Mostly lock back folders with interframe. **Technical:** Forges own damascus for both blades and frames. **Prices:** 200 - 1800 Euro. **Remarks:** Full-time maker; first knife made in 1995. Attends Milano Knife Show and ECCKSHOW yearly. **Mark:** M.Garau inside handle.

GARCIA, MARIO EIRAS,
R. Edmundo Scanapieco, 300 Caxingui, Sao Paulo SP-05516-070, BRAZIL, Fax: 011-37214528
Specialties: Fantasy knives of his design; one-of-a-kind only. **Patterns:** Fighters, daggers, boots and two-bladed knives. **Technical:** Forges car leaf springs. Uses only natural handle material. **Prices:** $100 to $200. **Remarks:** Part-time maker; first knife sold in 1976. **Mark:** Two "B"s, one opposite the other.

GARNER, GEORGE,
7527 Calhoun Dr. NE, Albuquerque, NM 87109, Phone: 505-797-9317, razorbackblades@msn.com Web: www.razorbackblades.com
Specialties: High art locking liner folders and Daggers of his own design. Working and high art straight knives. **Patterns:** Bowies, daggers, fighters and locking liner folders. **Technical:** Grinds 440C, CPM-154, ATS34 and others. Damascus, Mosaic Damascus and Mokume. Makes own custom leather sheaths. **Prices:** $150 - $2,500. **Remarks:** Part-time maker since 1993. Full-time maker as of 2012. Company name is Razorback Blades. **Mark:** GEORGE GARNER.

GARNER, LARRY W,
13069 FM 14, Tyler, TX 75706, Phone: 903-597-6045, lwgarner@classicnet.net
Specialties: Fixed blade hunters and Bowies. **Patterns:** His designs or yours. **Technical:** Hand forges 5160. **Prices:** $200 to $500. **Remarks:** Apprentice bladesmith. **Mark:** Last name.

GARVOCK, MARK W,
RR 1, Balderson, Ont., CANADA K1G 1A0, Phone: 613-833-2545, Fax: 613-833-2208, garvock@travel-net.com
Specialties: Hunters, Bowies, Japanese, daggers and swords. **Patterns:** Cable Damascus, random pattern welded or to suit. **Technical:** Forged blades; hi-carbon. **Prices:** $250 to $900. **Remarks:** CKG member and ABS member. Shipping and taxes extra. **Mark:** Big G with M in middle.

GAUDETTE, LINDEN L,
5 Hitchcock Rd, Wilbraham, MA 01095, Phone: 413-596-4896
Specialties: Traditional working knives in standard patterns. **Patterns:** Broad-bladed hunters, Bowies and camp knives; wood carver knives; locking folders. **Technical:** Grinds ATS-34, 440C and 154CM. **Prices:** $150 to $400; some higher. **Remarks:** Full-time maker; first knife sold in 1975. **Mark:** Last name in Gothic logo; used to be initials in circle.

GEDRAITIS, CHARLES J,
GEDRAITIS HAND CRAFTED KNIVES, 444 Shrewsbury St, Holden, MA 01520, Phone: 508-963-1861, gedraitisknives@yahoo.com; Web: www.gedraitisknives.com
Specialties: One-of-a-kind folders & automatics of his own design. **Patterns:** One-of-a-kind. **Technical:** Forges to shape mostly stock removal. **Prices:** $300 to $2500. **Remarks:** Full-time maker. **Mark:** 3 scallop shells with an initial inside each one: CJG.

GEISLER, GARY R,
PO Box 294, Clarksville, OH 45113, Phone: 937-383-4055, ggeisler@in-touch.net
Specialties: Period Bowies and such; flat ground. **Patterns:** Working knives usually modeled close after an existing antique. **Technical:** Flat grinds 440C, A2 and ATS-34. **Prices:** $300 and up. **Remarks:** Part-time maker; first knife sold in 1982. **Mark:** G.R. Geisler Maker; usually in script on reverse side because maker is left-handed.

GEORGE, HARRY,
3137 Old Camp Long Rd, Aiken, SC 29805, Phone: 803-649-1963, hdkk-george@scescape.net
Specialties: Working straight knives of his design or to customer specs. **Patterns:** Hunters, skinners and utility knives. **Technical:** Grinds ATS-34. Prefers natural handle materials, hollow-grinds and mirror finishes. **Prices:** Start at $70. **Remarks:** Part-time maker; first knife sold in 1985. Trained under George Herron. Member SCAK. Member Knifemakers Guild. **Mark:** Name, city, state.

GEORGE, LES,
6521 Fenwick Dr., Corpus Christi, TX 78414, Phone: 361-288-9777, les@georgeknives.com; Web: www.georgeknives.com
Specialties: Tactical frame locks and fixed blades. **Patterns:** Folders, balisongs, and fixed blades. **Technical:** CPM154, S30V, Chad Nichols Damascus. **Prices:** $200 to $800. **Remarks:** Full-time maker, first knife sold in 1992. Doing business as www.georgeknives.com. **Mark:** Last name over logo.

GEORGE, TOM,
550 Aldbury Dr, Henderson, NV 89014, tagmaker@aol.com
Specialties: Working straight knives, display knives, custom meat cleavers, and folders of his design. **Patterns:** Hunters, Bowies, daggers, buckskinners, swords and folders. **Technical:** Uses D2, 440C, ATS-34 and 154CM. **Prices:** $500 to $13,500. **Remarks:** Custom orders not accepted "at this time". Full-time maker. First knife1982; first 350 knives were numbered; after that no numbers. Almost all his knives today are Bowies and swords. Creator and maker of the "Past Glories" series of knives. **Mark:** Tom George maker.

GEPNER, DON,
2615 E Tecumseh, Norman, OK 73071, Phone: 405-364-2750
Specialties: Traditional working and using straight knives of his design. **Patterns:** Bowies and daggers. **Technical:** Forges his Damascus, 1095 and 5160. **Prices:** $100 to $400; some to $1000. **Remarks:** Spare-time maker; first knife sold in 1991. Has been forging since 1954; first edged weapon made at 9 years old. **Mark:** Last initial.

GERNER, THOMAS,
PO Box 301 Walpole, Western Australia, AUSTRALIA 6398, gerner@bordernet.com.au; Web: www.deepriverforge.com
Specialties: Forged working knives; plain steel and pattern welded. **Patterns:** Tries most patterns heard or read about. **Technical:** 5160, L6, O1, 52100 steels; Australian hardwood handles. **Prices:** $220 and up. **Remarks:** Achieved ABS Master Smith rating in 2001. **Mark:** Like a standing arrow and a leaning cross, T.G. in the Runic (Viking) alphabet.

GIAGU, SALVATORE AND DEROMA MARIA ROSARIA,
Via V Emanuele 64, 07016 Pattada (SS), ITALY, Phone: 079-755918, Fax: 079-755918, coltelligiagupattada@tiscali.it Web: www.culterpattada.it
Specialties: Using and collecting traditional and new folders from Sardegna. **Patterns:** Folding, hunting, utility, skinners and kitchen knives. **Technical:** Forges ATS-34, 440, D2 and Damascus. **Prices:** $200 to $2000; some higher. **Mark:** First initial, last name and name of town and muflon's head.

GIBERT, PEDRO,
Los Alamos 410, 8370 San Martin de los Andes Neuquen, ARGENTINA, Phone: 054-2972-410868, rosademayo@infovia.com.ar
Specialties: Hand forges: Stock removal and integral. High quality artistic knives of his design and to customer specifications. **Patterns:** Country (Argentine gaucho-style), knives, folders, Bowies, daggers, hunters. Others upon request. **Technical:** Blade: Bohler k110 Austrian steel (high resistance to waste). Handles: (Natural materials) ivory elephant, killer whale, hippo, walrus tooth, deer antler, goat, ram, buffalo horn, bone, rhea, sheep, cow, exotic woods (South America native woods) hand carved and engraved guards and blades. Stainless steel guards, finely polished: semi-matte or shiny finish. Sheaths: Raw or tanned leather, hand-stitched; rawhide or cotton yarn embroidered. Box: One wood piece, hand carved. Wooden hinges and locks. **Prices:** $600 and up. **Remarks:** Full-time maker. Made first knife in 1987. **Mark:** Only a rose logo. Buyers initials upon request.

GIBO, GEORGE,
PO Box 4304, Hilo, HI 96720, Phone: 808-987-7002, geogibo@hilo808.net
Specialties: Straight knives and folders. **Patterns:** Hunters, bird and trout, utility, gentlemen and tactical folders. **Technical:** Grinds ATS-34, BG-42, Talonite, Stainless Steel Damascus. **Prices:** $250 to $1000. **Remarks:** Spare-time maker; first knife sold in 1995. **Mark:** Name, city and state around Hawaiian "Shaka" sign.

GIBSON SR., JAMES HOOT,
90 Park Place Ave., Bunnell, FL 32110, Phone: 386-437-4383, hootsknives.aol.com
Specialties: Bowies, folders, daggers, and hunters. **Patterns:** Most all. **Technical:** ATS-440C hand cut and grind. Also traditional old fashioned folders. **Prices:** $250 to $3000. **Remarks:** 100 percent handmade. **Mark:** HOOT

GILBERT, CHANTAL,
291 Rue Christophe-Colomb est #105, Quebec City Quebec, CANADA G1K 3T1, Phone: 418-525-6961, Fax: 418-525-4666, gilbertc@medion.qc.ca; Web: www.chantalgilbert.com
Specialties: Straight art knives that may resemble creatures, often with wings, shells and antennae, always with a beak of some sort, fixed blades in a feminine style. **Technical:** ATS-34 and Damascus. Handle materials usually silver that she forms to shape via special molds and a press; ebony and fossil ivory. **Prices:** Range from $500 to $4000. **Remarks:** Often embellishes her art knives with rubies, meteorite, 18k gold and similar elements.

GILBREATH, RANDALL,
55 Crauswell Rd, Dora, AL 35062, Phone: 205-648-3902
Specialties: Damascus folders and fighters. **Patterns:** Folders and fixed blades. **Technical:** Forges Damascus and high-carbon; stock removal stainless steel. **Prices:** $300 to $1500. **Remarks:** Full-time maker; first knife sold in 1979. **Mark:** Name in ribbon.

GILJEVIC, BRANKO,
35 Hayley Crescent, Queanbeyan 2620, N.S.W., AUSTRALIA 0262977613
Specialties: Classic working straight knives and folders of his design. **Patterns:** Hunters, Bowies, skinners and locking folders. **Technical:** Grinds 440C. Offers acid etching, scrimshaw and leather carving. **Prices:** $150 to $1500. **Remarks:** Part-time maker; first knife sold in 1987. Doing business as Sambar Custom Knives. **Mark:** Company name in logo.

GINGRICH, JUSTIN,
325 North Linton Street, Blue Earth, MN 56013, Phone: 507-230-0398, justin@rangerknives.com Web: www.rangerknives.com
Specialties: Anything from bushcraft to tactical, heavy on the tactical. **Patterns:** Fixed blades and folders. **Technical:** Uses all types of steel and handle material, method is stock-removal. **Prices:** $30 - $1000. **Remarks:** Full-time maker. **Mark:** Tang stamp is the old Ranger Knives logo.

GIRAFFEBONE INC.,
3052 Isim Road, Norman, OK 73026, Phone: 888-804-0683; 405-321-3614, sandy@giraffebone.com; Web: www.giraffebone.com
Specialties: Giraffebone, horns, African hardwoods, and mosaic Damascus

GIRTNER, JOE,
409 Catalpa Ave, Brea, CA 92821, Phone: 714-529-2388, conceptsinknives@aol.com
Specialties: Art knives and miniatures. **Patterns:** Mainly Damascus (some carved). **Technical:** Many techniques and materials combined. Wood carving knives and tools, hunters, custom orders. **Prices:** $55 to $3000. **Mark:** Name.

GITTINGER, RAYMOND,
6940 S Rt 100, Tiffin, OH 44883, Phone: 419-397-2517

GLOVER, RON,
100 West Church St., Mason, OH 45040, Phone: 513-404-7107, r.glover@zoomtown.com
Specialties: High-tech working straight knives and folders. **Patterns:** Hunters to Bowies; some interchangeable blade models; unique locking mechanisms. **Technical:** Grinds 440C, 154CM; buys Damascus. **Prices:** $70 to $500; some to $800. **Remarks:** Part-time maker; first knife sold in 1981. **Mark:** Name in script.

GLOVER, WARREN D,
dba BUBBA KNIVES, PO Box 475, Cleveland, GA 30528, Phone: 706-865-3998, Fax: 706-348-7176, warren@bubbaknives.net; Web: www.bubbaknives.net
Specialties: Traditional and custom working and using straight knives of his design and to customer request. **Patterns:** Hunters, skinners, bird and fish, utility and kitchen knives. **Technical:** Grinds 440, ATS-34 and stainless steel Damascus. **Prices:** $75 to $400 and up. **Remarks:** Full-time maker; sold first knife in 1995. **Mark:** Bubba, year, name, state.

GODDARD, WAYNE,
473 Durham Ave, Eugene, OR 97404, Phone: 541-689-8098, wgoddard44@comcast.net
Specialties: Working/using straight knives and folders. **Patterns:** Hunters and folders. **Technical:** Works exclusively with wire Damascus and his own-pattern welded material. **Prices:** $250 to $4000. **Remarks:** Full-time maker; first knife sold in 1963. **Mark:** Blocked initials on forged blades; regular capital initials on stock removal.

GODLESKY, BRUCE F.,
1002 School Rd., Apollo, PA 15613, Phone: 724-840-5786, brucegodlesky@yahoo.com; Web: www.birdforge.com
Specialties: Working/using straight knives and tomahawks, mostly forged. **Patterns:** Hunters, birds and trout, fighters and tomahawks. **Technical:** Most forged, some stock removal. Carbon steel only. 5160, O-1, W2, 10xx series. Makes own Damascus and welded cable. **Prices:** Starting at $75. **Mark:** BIRDOG FORGE.

GOERS, BRUCE,
3423 Royal Ct S, Lakeland, FL 33813, Phone: 941-646-0984
Specialties: Fancy working and using straight knives of his design and to customer specs. **Patterns:** Hunters, fighters, Bowies and fantasy knives. **Technical:** Grinds ATS-34, some Damascus. **Prices:** $195 to $600; some to $1300. **Remarks:** Part-time maker; first knife sold in 1990. Doing business as Vulture Cutlery. **Mark:** Buzzard with initials.

GOFOURTH, JIM,
3776 Aliso Cyn Rd, Santa Paula, CA 93060, Phone: 805-659-3814
Specialties: Period pieces and working knives. **Patterns:** Bowies, locking folders, patent lockers and others. **Technical:** Grinds A2 and 154CM. **Prices:** Moderate. **Remarks:** Spare-time maker. **Mark:** Initials interconnected.

GOLDBERG, DAVID,
321 Morris Rd, Ft Washington, PA 19034, Phone: 215-654-7117, david@goldmountainforge.com; Web: www.goldmountainforge.com
Specialties: Japanese-style designs, will work with special themes in Japanese genre. **Patterns:** Kozuka, Tanto, Wakazashi, Katana, Tachi, Sword canes, Yari and Naginata. **Technical:** Forges his own Damascus and makes his own handmade tamehagane steel from straw ash, iron, carbon and clay. Uses traditional materials, carves fittings handles and cases. Hardens all blades in traditional Japanese clay differential technique. **Remarks:** Full-time maker; first knife sold in 1987. Japanese swordsmanship teacher (jaido) and Japanese self-defense teach (aikido). **Mark:** Name (kinzan) in Japanese Kanji on Tang under handle.

GOLDEN, RANDY,
6492 Eastwood Glen Dr, Montgomery, AL 36117, Phone: 334-271-6429, rgolden1@mindspring.com
Specialties: Collectable quality hand rubbed finish, hunter, camp, Bowie straight knives, custom leather sheaths with exotic skin inlays and tooling. **Technical:** Stock removal ATS-34, CPM154, S30V and BG-42. Natural handle materials primarily stag and ivory. **Prices:** $500 to $1500. **Remarks:** Full-time maker, member Knifemakers Guild, first knife sold in 2000. **Mark:** R. R. Golden Montgomery, AL.

GONZALEZ, LEONARDO WILLIAMS,
Ituzaingo 473, Maldonado, CP 20000, URUGUAY, Phone: 598 4222 1617, Fax: 598 4222 1617, willyknives@hotmail.com
Specialties: Classic high-art and fantasy straight knives; traditional working

and using knives of his design, in standard patterns or to customer specs. **Patterns:** Hunters, Bowies, daggers, fighters, boots, swords and utility/camp knives. **Technical:** Forges and grinds high-carbon and stainless Bohler steels. **Prices:** $100 to $2500. **Remarks:** Full-time maker; first knife sold in 1985. **Mark:** Willy, whale, R.O.U.

GOO, TAI,
5920 W Windy Lou Ln, Tucson, AZ 85742, Phone: 520-744-9777, taigoo@msn.com; Web: www.taigoo.com
Specialties: High art, neo-tribal, bush and fantasy. **Technical:** Hand forges, does own heat treating, makes own Damascus. **Prices:** $150 to $500 some to $10,000. **Remarks:** Full-time maker; first knife sold in 1978. **Mark:** Chiseled signature.

GOOD, D.R.,
D.R. Good Custom Knives and Weaponry, 6125 W. 100 S., Tipton, IN 46072, Phone: 765-963-6971, drntammigood@bluemarble.net
Specialties: Working knives, own design, Scagel style, "critter" knives, carved handles. **Patterns:** Bowies, large and small, neck knives and miniatures. Offers carved handles, snake heads, eagles, wolves, bear, skulls. **Technical:** Damascus, some stelite, 6K, pearl, ivory, moose. **Prices:** $150 - $1500. **Remarks:** Full-time maker. First knife was Bowie made from a 2-1/2 truck bumper in military. **Mark:** D.R. Good in oval and for minis, DR with a buffalo skull.

GOODE, BEAR,
PO Box 6474, Navajo Dam, NM 87419, Phone: 505-632-8184
Specialties: Working/using knives of his design and in standard patterns. **Patterns:** Bowies, hunters and utility/camp knives. **Technical:** Grinds 440C, ATS-34, 154-CM; forges and grinds 1095, 5160 and other steels on request; uses Damascus. **Prices:** $60 to $225; some to $500 and up. **Remarks:** Part-time maker; first knife sold in 1993. Doing business as Bear Knives. **Mark:** First and last name with a three-toed paw print.

GOODE, BRIAN,
203 Gordon Ave, Shelby, NC 28152, Phone: 704-434-6496, web:www.bgoodeknives.com
Specialties: Flat ground working knives with etched/antique or brushed finish. **Patterns:** Field, camp, hunters, skinners, survival, kitchen, maker's design or yours. Currently full tang only with supplied leather sheath. **Technical:** 0-1, D2 and other ground flat stock. Stock removal and differential heat treat preferred. Etched antique/etched satin working finish preferred. Micarta and hardwoods for strength. **Prices:** $150 to $700. **Remarks:** Part-time maker and full-time knife lover. First knife sold in 2004. **Mark:** B. Goode with NC separated by a feather.

GOODPASTURE, TOM,
13432 Farrington Road, Ashland, VA 23005, Phone: 804-752-8363, rtg007@aol.com; web: goodpastureknives.com
Specialties: Working/using straight knives of his own design, or customer specs. File knives and primative reproductions. **Patterns:** Hunters, bowies, small double-edge daggers, kitchen, custom miniatures and camp/utility. **Technical:** Stock removal, D-2, 0-1, 12C27, 420 HC, 52100. Forged blades of W-2, 1084, and 1095. Flat grinds only. **Prices:** $60 - $300. **Remarks:** Part-time maker, first knife sold at Blade Show 2005. Lifetime guarantee and sharpening. **Mark:** Early mark were initials RTG, current mark: Goodpasture.

GORDON, LARRY B,
23555 Newell Cir W, Farmington Hills, MI 48336, Phone: 248-477-5483, lbgordon1@aol.com
Specialties: Folders, small fixed blades. New design rotating scale release automatic. **Patterns:** Rotating handle locker. Ambidextrous fire (R&L) **Prices:** $450 minimum. **Remarks:** High line materials preferred. **Mark:** Gordon.

GORENFLO, JAMES T (JT),
9145 Sullivan Rd, Baton Rouge, LA 70818, Phone: 225-261-5868
Specialties: Traditional working and using straight knives of his design. **Patterns:** Bowies, hunters and utility/camp knives. **Technical:** Forges 5160, 1095, 52100 and his own Damascus. **Prices:** Start at $200. **Remarks:** Part-time maker; first knife sold in 1992. **Mark:** Last name or initials, J.S. on reverse.

GOSSMAN, SCOTT,
PO Box 41, Whiteford, MD 21160, Phone: 410-452-8456, scott@gossmanknives.com Web:www.gossmanknives.com
Specialties: Heavy duty knives for big game hunting and survival. **Patterns:** Drop point spear point hunters. Large camp/survival knives. **Technical:** Grinds D-2, A2, O1 and 57 convex grinds and edges. **Price:** $100 to $350 some higher. **Remarks:** Full time maker does business as Gossman Knives. **Mark:** Gossman and steel type.

GOTTAGE, DANTE,
43227 Brooks Dr, Clinton Twp., MI 48038-5323, Phone: 810-286-7275
Specialties: Working knives of his design or to customer specs. **Patterns:** Large and small skinners, fighters, Bowies and fillet knives. **Technical:** Grinds O1, 440C and 154CM and ATS-34. **Prices:** $150 to $600. **Remarks:** Part-time maker; first knife sold in 1975. **Mark:** Full name in script letters.

GOTTAGE, JUDY,
43227 Brooks Dr, Clinton Twp., MI 48038-5323, Phone: 586-286-7275, jgottage@remaxmetropolitan.com
Specialties: Custom folders of her design or to customer specs. **Patterns:** Interframes or integral. **Technical:** Stock removal. **Prices:** $300 to $3000.

Remarks: Full-time maker; first knife sold in 1980. **Mark:** Full name, maker in script.

GOTTSCHALK, GREGORY J,
12 First St. (Ft. Pitt), Carnegie, PA 15106, Phone: 412-279-6692
Specialties: Fancy working straight knives and folders to customer specs. **Patterns:** Hunters to tantos, locking folders to minis. **Technical:** Grinds 440C, 154CM, ATS-34. Now making own Damascus. Most knives have mirror finishes. **Prices:** Start at $150. **Remarks:** Part-time maker; first knife sold in 1977. **Mark:** Full name in crescent.

GOUKER, GARY B,
PO Box 955, Sitka, AK 99835, Phone: 907-747-3476
Specialties: Hunting knives for hard use. **Patterns:** Skinners, semi-skinners, and such. **Technical:** Likes natural materials, inlays, stainless steel. **Prices:** Moderate. **Remarks:** New Alaskan maker. **Mark:** Name.

GRAHAM, GORDON,
3145 CR 4008, New Boston, TX 75570, Phone: 903-293-2610, Web: www.grahamknives.com
Prices: $325 to $850. **Mark:** Graham.

GRANGER, PAUL J,
704 13th Ct. SW, Largo, FL 33770-4471, Phone: 727-953-3249, grangerknives@live.com Web: http://palehorsefighters.blogspot.com
Specialties: Working straight knives of his own design and a few folders. **Patterns:** 2.75" to 4" work knives, tactical knives and Bowies from 5"-9." **Technical:** Grinds CPM154-CM, ATS-34 and forges 52100 and 1084. Offers filework. **Prices:** $95 to $500. **Remarks:** Part-time maker since 1997. Sold first knife in 1997. Doing business as Granger Knives and Pale Horse Fighters. Member of ABS and Florida Knifemakers Association. **Mark:** "Granger" or "Palehorse Fighters."

GRAVELINE, PASCAL AND ISABELLE,
38, Rue de Kerbrezillic, 29350 Moelan-sur-Mer, FRANCE, Phone: 33 2 98 39 73 33, atelier.graveline@wanadoo.fr; Web: www.graveline-couteliers.com
Specialties: French replicas from the 17th, 18th and 19th centuries. **Patterns:** Traditional multi-blade pocket knives; traveling knives, fruit knives and fork sets; puzzle knives and friend's knives; rivet less knives. **Technical:** Grind 12C27, ATS-34, Damascus and carbon steel. **Prices:** $500 to $5000. **Remarks:** Full-time makers; first knife sold in 1992. **Mark:** Last name over head of ram.

GRAVES, DAN,
4887 Dixie Garden Loop, Shreveport, LA 71105, Phone: 318-865-8166, Web: wwwtheknifemaker.com
Specialties: Traditional forged blades and Damascus. **Patterns:** Bowies (D guard also), fighters, hunters, large and small daggers. **Remarks:** Full-time maker. **Mark:** Initials with circle around them.

GRAY, BOB,
8206 N Lucia Court, Spokane, WA 99208, Phone: 509-468-3924
Specialties: Straight working knives of his own design or to customer specs. **Patterns:** Hunter, fillet and carving knives. **Technical:** Forges 5160, L6 and some 52100; grinds 440C. **Prices:** $100 to $600. **Remarks:** Part-time knifemaker; first knife sold in 1991. Doing business as Hi-Land Knives. **Mark:** HI-L.

GRAY, DANIEL,
GRAY KNIVES, 686 Main Rd., Brownville, ME 04414, Phone: 207-965-2191, mail@grayknives.com; Web: www.grayknives.com
Specialties: Straight knives, fantasy, folders, automatics and traditional of his own design. **Patterns:** Automatics, fighters, hunters. **Technical:** Grinds O1, 154CM and D2. **Prices:** From $155 to $750. **Remarks:** Full-time maker; first knife sold in 1974. **Mark:** Gray Knives.

GREBE, GORDON S,
PO Box 296, Anchor Point, AK 99556-0296, Phone: 907-235-8242
Specialties: Working straight knives and folders, some fancy. **Patterns:** Tantos, Bowies, boot fighter sets, locking folders. **Technical:** Grinds stainless steels; likes 1/4" inch stock and glass-bead finishes. **Prices:** $75 to $250; some to $2000. **Remarks:** Full-time maker; first knife sold in 1968. **Mark:** Initials in lightning logo.

GRECO, JOHN,
100 Mattie Jones Rd, Greensburg, KY 42743, Phone: 270-932-3335, johngreco@grecoknives.com; Web: www.grecoknives.com
Specialties: Folders. **Patterns:** Tactical, fighters, camp knives, short swords. **Technical:** Stock removal carbon steel. **Prices:** Affordable. **Remarks:** Full-time maker since 1979. First knife sold in 1979. **Mark:** GRECO

GREEN, BILL,
6621 Eastview Dr, Sachse, TX 75048, Phone: 972-463-3147
Specialties: High-art and working straight knives and folders of his design and to customer specs. **Patterns:** Bowies, hunters, kitchen knives and locking folders. **Technical:** Grinds ATS-34, D2 and 440V. Hand-tooled custom sheaths. **Prices:** $70 to $350; some to $750. **Remarks:** Part-time maker; first knife sold in 1990. **Mark:** Last name.

GREEN, WILLIAM (BILL),
46 Warren Rd, View Bank Vic., AUSTRALIA 3084, Fax: 03-9459-1529
Specialties: Traditional high-tech straight knives and folders. **Patterns:** Japanese-influenced designs, hunters, Bowies, folders and miniatures. **Technical:** Forges O1, D2 and his own Damascus. Offers lost wax castings for bolsters and pommels. Likes natural handle materials, gems, silver and gold. **Prices:** $400 to $750; some to $1200. **Remarks:** Full-time maker. **Mark:** Initials.

GREENAWAY, DON,
3325 Dinsmore Tr, Fayetteville, AR 72704, Phone: 501-521-0323

GREENE, CHRIS,
707 Cherry Lane, Shelby, NC 28150, Phone: 704-434-5620

GREENE, DAVID,
570 Malcom Rd, Covington, GA 30209, Phone: 770-784-0657
Specialties: Straight working using knives. **Patterns:** Hunters. **Technical:** Forges mosaic and twist Damascus. Prefers stag and desert ironwood for handle material.

GREENE, STEVE,
DUNN KNIVES INC, PO Box 307 1449 Nocatee St., Intercession City, FL 33848, Phone: 800-245-6483, steve.greene@dunnknives.com; Web: www.dunnknives.com
Specialties: Skinning & fillet knives. **Patterns:** Skinners, drop points, clip points and fillets. **Technical:** S60V, S90V and 20 CV powdered metal steel. **Prices:** $90 to $250. **Mark:** Dunn by Greene and year. **Remarks:** Full-time knifemaker. First knife sold in 1972.

GREENFIELD, G O,
2605 15th St #310, Everett, WA 98201, garyg1946@yahoo.com
Specialties: High-tech and working straight knives and folders of his design. **Patterns:** Boots, daggers, hunters and one-of-a-kinds. **Technical:** Grinds ATS-34, D2, 440C and T-440V. Makes sheaths for each knife. **Prices:** $100 to $800; some to $10,000. **Remarks:** Part-time maker; first knife sold in 1978. **Mark:** Springfield®, serial number.

GREGORY, MICHAEL,
211 Calhoun Rd, Belton, SC 29627, Phone: 864-338-8898
Specialties: Working straight knives and folders. **Patterns:** Hunters, tantos, locking folders and slip-joints, boots and fighters. **Technical:** Grinds 440C, 154CM and ATS-34; mirror finishes. **Prices:** $95 to $200; some to $1000. **Remarks:** Part-time maker; first knife sold in 1980. **Mark:** Name, city in logo.

GREINER, RICHARD,
1073 E County Rd 32, Green Springs, OH 44836

GREISS, JOCKL,
Herrenwald 15, D 77773 Schenkenzell, GERMANY, Phone: +49 7836 95 71 69 or +49 7836 95 55 76, www.jocklgreiss@yahoo.com
Specialties: Classic and working using straight knives of his design. **Patterns:** Bowies, daggers and hunters. **Technical:** Uses only Jerry Rados Damascus. All knives are one-of-a-kind made by hand; no machines are used. **Prices:** $700 to $2000; some to $3000. **Remarks:** Full-time maker; first knife sold in 1984. **Mark:** An "X" with a long vertical line through it.

GREY, PIET,
PO Box 363, Naboomspruit 0560, SOUTH AFRICA, Phone: 014-743-3613
Specialties: Fancy working and using straight knives of his design. **Patterns:** Fighters, hunters and utility/camp knives. **Technical:** Grinds ATS-34 and AEB-L; forges and grinds Damascus. Solder less fitting of guards. Engraves and scrimshaws. **Prices:** $125 to $750; some to $1500. **Remarks:** Part-time maker; first knife sold in 1970. **Mark:** Last name.

GRIFFIN, RENDON AND MARK,
9706 Cedardale, Houston, TX 77055, Phone: 713-468-0436
Specialties: Working folders and automatics of their designs. **Patterns:** Standard lockers and slip-joints. **Technical:** Most blade steels; stock removal. **Prices:** Start at $350. **Remarks:** Rendon's first knife sold in 1966; Mark's in 1974. **Mark:** Last name logo.

GRIFFIN JR., HOWARD A,
14299 SW 31st Ct, Davie, FL 33330, Phone: 954-474-5406, mgriffin18@aol.com
Specialties: Working straight knives and folders. **Patterns:** Hunters, Bowies, locking folders with his own push-button lock design. **Technical:** Grinds 440C. **Prices:** $100 to $200; some to $500. **Remarks:** Part-time maker; first knife sold in 1983. **Mark:** Initials.

GRIMES, MARK,
PO BOX 1293, Bedford, TX 76095, Phone: 817-416-7507
Specialties: Qs. **Patterns:** Hunters, fighters, bowies. **Technical:** Custom hand forged 1084 steel blades full and hidden tang, heat treating, sheathes. **Prices:** $150-$400. **Remarks:** Part-time maker, first knife sold in 2009. **Mark:** Last name.

GROSPITCH, ERNIE,
18440 Amityville Dr, Orlando, FL 32820, Phone: 407-568-5438, shrpknife@aol.com; Web: www.erniesknives.com
Specialties: Bowies, hunting, fishing, kitchen, lockback folders, leather craft. **Patterns:** His design or customer. **Technical:** Stock removal using most available steels. **Prices:** $140 and up. **Remarks:** Full-time maker, sold first knife in 1990. Mark: Etched name/maker city and state.

GROSS, W W,
109 Dylan Scott Dr, Archdale, NC 27263-3858
Specialties: Working knives. **Patterns:** Hunters, boots, fighters. **Technical:** Grinds. **Prices:** Moderate. **Remarks:** Full-time maker. **Mark:** Name.

GROSSMAN, STEWART,
24 Water St #419, Clinton, MA 01510, Phone: 508-365-2291; 800-mysword
Specialties: Miniatures and full-size knives and swords. **Patterns:** One-of-a-kind miniatures—jewelry, replicas—and wire-wrapped figures. Full-size art, fantasy and combat knives, daggers and modular systems. **Technical:** Forges and grinds most metals and Damascus. Uses gems, crystals, electronics and motorized mechanisms. **Prices:** $20 to $300; some to $4500 and higher. **Remarks:** Full-time maker; first knife sold in 1985. **Mark:** G1.

GRUSSENMEYER, PAUL G,
310 Kresson Rd, Cherry Hill, NJ 08034, Phone: 856-428-1088, pgrussentne@comcast.net; Web: www.pgcarvings.com
Specialties: Assembling fancy and fantasy straight knives with his own carved handles. **Patterns:** Bowies, daggers, folders, swords, hunters and miniatures. **Technical:** Uses forged steel and Damascus, stock removal and knapped obsidian blades. **Prices:** $250 to $4000. **Remarks:** Spare-time maker; first knife sold in 1991. **Mark:** First and last initial hooked together on handle.

GUARNERA, ANTHONY R,
42034 Quail Creek Dr, Quartzhill, CA 93536, Phone: 661-722-4032
Patterns: Hunters, camp, Bowies, kitchen, fighter knives. **Technical:** Forged and stock removal. **Prices:** $100 and up.

GUINN, TERRY,
13026 Hwy 6 South, Eastland, TX 76448, Phone: 254-629-8603, Web: www.terryguinn.com
Specialties: Working fixed blades and balisongs. **Patterns:** Almost all types of folding and fixed blades, from patterns and "one of a kind". **Technical:** Stock removal all types of blade steel with preference for air hardening steel. Does own heat treating, all knives Rockwell tested in shop. **Prices:** $200 to $2,000. **Remarks:** Part time maker since 1982, sold first knife 1990. **Mark:** Full name with cross in the middle.

GUNTER, BRAD,
13 Imnaha Rd., Tijeras, NM 87059, Phone: 505-281-8080

GUNTHER, EDDIE,
11 Nedlands Pl Burswood, 2013 Auckland, NEW ZEALAND, Phone: 006492722373, eddit.gunther49@gmail.com
Specialties: Drop point hunters, boot, Bowies. All mirror finished. **Technical:** Grinds D2, 440C, 12c27. **Prices:** $250 to $800. **Remarks:** Part-time maker, first knife sold in 1986. **Mark:** Name, city, country.

GURGANUS, CAROL,
2553 NC 45 South, Colerain, NC 27924, Phone: 252-356-4831, Fax: 252-356-4650
Specialties: Working and using straight knives. **Patterns:** Fighters, hunters and kitchen knives. **Technical:** Grinds D2, ATS-34 and Damascus steel. Uses stag, and exotic wood handles. **Prices:** $100 to $300. **Remarks:** Part-time maker; first knife sold in 1992. **Mark:** Female symbol, last name, city, state.

GURGANUS, MELVIN H,
2553 NC 45 South, Colerain, NC 27924, Phone: 252-356-4831, Fax: 252-356-4650
Specialties: High-tech working folders. **Patterns:** Leaf-lock and back-lock designs, bolstered and interframe. **Technical:** D2 and 440C; Heat-treats, carves and offers lost wax casting. **Prices:** $300 to $3000. **Remarks:** Part-time maker; first knife sold in 1983. **Mark:** First initial, last name and maker.

GUTHRIE, GEORGE B,
1912 Puett Chapel Rd, Bassemer City, NC 28016, Phone: 704-629-3031
Specialties: Working knives of his design or to customer specs. **Patterns:** Hunters, boots, fighters, locking folders and slip-joints in traditional styles. **Technical:** Grinds D2, 440C and 154CM. **Prices:** $105 to $300; some to $450. **Remarks:** Part-time maker; first knife sold in 1978. **Mark:** Name in state.

H

HACKNEY, DANA A.,
33 Washington St., Monument, CO 80132, Phone: 719-481-3940, shacknee@peoplepc.com
Specialties: Hunters, bowies, and everyday carry knives, and some kitchen cutlery. **Technical:** Forges 1080 series, 5160, 0-1, W-2, and his own damascus. Uses 13C26 mostly for stainless knives. **Prices:** $100 and up. **Remarks:** Sole ownership knives and sheaths. Part-time maker. Sold first knife in 2005. ABS, MKA, and PKA member. **Mark:** Last name, HACKNEY on left-side ricasso.

HAGEN, DOC,
PO Box 58, 41780 Kansas Point Ln, Pelican Rapids, MN 56572, Phone: 218-863-8503, dochagen@gmail.com; Web: www.dochagencustomknives.com
Specialties: Folders. Autos:bolster release-dual action. Slipjoint folders**Patterns:** Defense-related straight knives; wide variety of folders. **Technical:** Dual action release, bolster release autos. **Prices:** $300 to $800; some to $3000. **Remarks:** Full-time maker; first knife sold in 1975. Makes his own Damascus. **Mark:** DOC HAGEN in shield, knife, banner logo; or DOC.

HAGGERTY, GEORGE S,
PO Box 88, Jacksonville, VT 05342, Phone: 802-368-7437, swewater@sover.net
Specialties: Working straight knives and folders. **Patterns:** Hunters, claws, camp and fishing knives, locking folders and backpackers. **Technical:** Forges and grinds W2, 440C and 154CM. **Prices:** $85 to $300. **Remarks:** Part-time maker; first knife sold in 1981. **Mark:** Initials or last name.

HAGUE, GEOFF,
Unit 5, Project Workshops, Laines Farm, Quarley, SP11 8PX, UK, Phone: (+44) 01672-870212, Fax: (+44) 01672 870212, geoff@hagueknives.com; Web: www.hagueknives.com
Specialties: Quality folding knives. **Patterns:** Back lock, locking liner, slip joint, and friction folders. **Technical:** RWL34, D2, titanium, and some gold decoraqtion. Mainly natural handle materials. **Prices:** $900 to $2,000. **Remarks:** Full-time maker. **Mark:** Last name.

HAINES, JEFF HAINES CUSTOM KNIVES,
901 A E. Third St., Wauzeka, WI 53826, Phone: 608-875-5325, jeffhaines@centurytel.net
Patterns: Hunters, skinners, camp knives, customer designs welcome. **Technical:** Forges 1095, 5160, and Damascus, grinds A2. **Prices:** $50 and up. **Remarks:** Part-time maker since 1995. **Mark:** Last name.

HALFRICH, JERRY,
340 Briarwood, San Marcos, TX 78666, Phone: 512-353-2582, Fax: 512-392-3659, jerryhalfrich@grandecom.net; Web: www.halfrichknives.com
Specialties: Working knives and specialty utility knives for the professional and serious hunter. Uses proven designs in both straight and folding knives. Plays close attention to fit and finish. Art knives on special request. **Patterns:** Hunters, skinners, lock back liner lock. **Technical:** Grinds both flat and hollow D2, damasteel, BG42 makes high precision folders. **Prices:** $300 to $600, sometimes $1000. **Remarks:** Full-time maker since 2000. DBA Halfrich Custom Knives. **Mark:** Halfrich, San Marcos, TX in a football shape.

HALL, JEFF,
PO Box 435, Los Alamitos, CA 90720, Phone: 562-594-4740, jhall10176@aol.com
Specialties: Collectible and working folders of his design. **Technical:** Grinds S30V, 154CM, and various makers' Damascus. **Patterns:** Fighters, gentleman's, hunters and utility knives. **Prices:** $400 to $600; some to $1000. **Remarks:** Full-time maker. First knife sold 1998. **Mark:** Last name.

HALLIGAN, ED,
14 Meadow Way, Sharpsburg, GA 30277, Phone: 770-251-7720, Fax: 770-251-7720
Specialties: Working straight knives and folders, some fancy. **Patterns:** Liner locks, hunters, skinners, boots, fighters and swords. **Technical:** Grinds ATS-34; forges 5160; makes cable and pattern Damascus. **Prices:** $160 to $2500. **Remarks:** Full-time maker; first knife sold in 1985. Doing business as Halligan Knives. **Mark:** Last name, city, state and USA.

HAMLET JR., JOHNNY,
300 Billington, Clute, TX 77531, Phone: 979-265-6929, nifeman@swbell.net; Web: www.hamlets-handmade-knives.com
Specialties: Working straight knives and folders. **Patterns:** Hunters, fighters, fillet and kitchen knives, locking folders. Likes upswept knives and trailing-points. **Technical:** Grinds 440C, D2, ATS-34. Makes sheaths. **Prices:** $125 and up. **Remarks:** Full-time maker; sold first knife in 1988. **Mark:** Hamlet's Handmade in script.

HAMMOND, HANK,
189 Springlake Dr, Leesburg, GA 31763, Phone: 229-434-1295, godogs57@bellsouth.net
Specialties: Traditional hunting and utility knives of his design. Will also design and produce knives to customer's specifications. **Patterns:** Straight or sheath knives, hunters skinners as well as Bowies and fighters. **Technical:** Grinds (hollow and flat grinds) CPM 154CM, ATS-34. Also uses Damascus and forges 52100. Offers filework on blades. Handle materials include all exotic woods, red stag, sambar stag, deer, elk, oosic, bone, fossil ivory, Micarta, etc. All knives come with sheath handmade for that individual knife. **Prices:** $100 up to $500. **Remarks:** Part-time maker. Sold first knife in 1981. Doing business as Double H Knives. **Mark:** "HH" inside 8 point deer rack.

HAMMOND, JIM,
PO Box 486, Arab, AL 35016, Phone: 256-586-4151, Fax: 256-586-0170, jim@jimhammondknives.com; Web: www.jimhammondknives.com
Specialties: High-tech fighters and folders. **Patterns:** Proven-design fighters. **Technical:** Grinds 440C, 440V, S30V and other specialty steels. **Prices:** $385 to $1200; some to $9200. **Remarks:** Full-time maker; first knife sold in 1977. Designer for Columbia River Knife and Tool. **Mark:** Full name, city, state in shield logo.

HANCOCK, TIM,
10805 N. 83rd St, Scottsdale, AZ 85260, Phone: 480-998-8849
Specialties: High-art and working straight knives and folders of his design and to customer preferences. **Patterns:** Bowies, fighters, daggers, tantos, swords, folders. **Technical:** Forges Damascus and 52100; grinds ATS-34. Makes Damascus. Silver-wire inlays; offers carved fittings and file work. **Prices:** $500 to $10,000. **Remarks:** Full-time maker; first knife sold in 1988. Master Smith ABS. **Mark:** Last name or heart.

HAND, BILL,
PO Box 717, 1103 W. 7th St., Spearman, TX 79081, Phone: 806-659-2967, Fax: 806-659-5139, klinker@arn.net
Specialties: Traditional working and using straight knives and folders of his design or to customer specs. **Patterns:** Hunters, Bowies, folders and fighters. **Technical:** Forges 5160, 52100 and Damascus. **Prices:** Start at $150. **Remarks:** Part-time maker; Journeyman Smith. Current delivery time 12 to 16 months. **Mark:** Stylized initials.

HANSEN, LONNIE,
PO Box 4956, Spanaway, WA 98387, Phone: 253-847-4632, lonniehansen@msn.com; Web: lchansen.com
Specialties: Working straight knives of his design. **Patterns:** Tomahawks, tantos, hunters, fillet. **Technical:** Forges 1086, 52100, grinds 440V, BG-42. **Prices:** Starting at $300. **Remarks:** Part-time maker since 1989. **Mark:** First initial and last name. Also first and last initial.

HANSEN, ROBERT W,
35701 University Ave NE, Cambridge, MN 55008, Phone: 763-689-3242
Specialties: Working straight knives, folders and integrals. **Patterns:** From hunters to minis, camp knives to miniatures; folding lockers and slip-joints in original styles. **Technical:** Grinds O1, 440C and 154CM; likes filework. **Prices:** $100 to $450; some to $600. **Remarks:** Part-time maker; first knife sold in 1983. **Mark:** Fish with last initial inside.

HANSON III, DON L.,
PO Box 13, Success, MO 65570-0013, Phone: 573-674-3045, Web: www.sunfishforge.com; Web: www.donhansonknives.com
Specialties: One-of-a-kind Damascus folders and forged fixed blades. **Patterns:** Small, fancy pocket knives, large folding fighters and Bowies. **Technical:** Forges own pattern welded Damascus, file work and carving also carbon steel blades with hamons. **Prices:** $800 and up. **Remarks:** Full-time maker, first knife sold in 1984. ABS mastersmith. **Mark:** Sunfish.

HARA, KOUJI,
292-2 Osugi, Seki-City, Gifu-Pref. 501-3922, JAPAN, Phone: 0575-24-7569, Fax: 0575-24-7569, info@knifehousehara.com; Web: www.knifehousehara.com
Specialties: High-tech and working straight knives of his design; some folders. **Patterns:** Hunters, locking folders and utility/camp knives. **Technical:** Grinds Cowry X, Cowry Y and ATS-34. Prefers high mirror polish; pearl handle inlay. **Prices:** $400 to $2500. **Remarks:** Full-time maker; first knife sold in 1980. Doing business as Knife House "Hara." **Mark:** First initial, last name in fish.

HARDY, DOUGLAS E,
114 Cypress Rd, Franklin, GA 30217, Phone: 706-675-6305

HARDY, SCOTT,
639 Myrtle Ave, Placerville, CA 95667, Phone: 530-622-5780, Web: www.innercite.com/~shardy
Specialties: Traditional working and using straight knives of his design. **Patterns:** Most anything with an edge. **Technical:** Forges carbon steels. Japanese stone polish. Offers mirror finish; differentially tempers. **Prices:** $100 to $1000. **Remarks:** Part-time maker; first knife sold in 1982. **Mark:** First initial, last name and Handmade with bird logo.

HARKINS, J A,
PO Box 218, Conner, MT 59827, Phone: 406-821-1060, kutter@customknives.net; Web: customknives.net
Specialties: OTFs. **Patterns:** OTFs, Automatics, Folders. **Technical:** Grinds ATS-34. Engraves; offers gem work. **Prices:** $1500 and up. **Remarks:** Celebrating 20th year as full-time maker . **Mark:** First and middle initials, last name.

HARLEY, LARRY W,
348 Deerfield Dr, Bristol, TN 37620, Phone: 423-878-5368 (shop)/Cell 423-571-0638, Fax: 276-466-6771, Web: www.lonesomepineknives.com
Specialties: One-of-a-kind Persian in one-of-a-kind Damascus. Working knives, period pieces. **Technical:** Forges and grinds ATS-34, 440c, L6, 15, 20, 1084, and 52100. **Patterns:** Full range of straight knives, tomahawks, razors, buck skinners and hog spears. **Prices:** $200 and up. **Mark:** Pine tree.

HARLEY, RICHARD,
348 Deerfield Dr, Bristol, TN 37620, Phone: 423-878-5368/423-571-0638
Specialties: Hunting knives, Bowies, friction folders, one-of-a-kind. **Technical:** Forges 1084, S160, 52100, Lg. **Prices:** $150 to $1000. **Mark:** Pine tree with name.

HARM, PAUL W,
818 Young Rd, Attica, MI 48412, Phone: 810-724-5582, harm@blclinks.net
Specialties: Early American working knives. **Patterns:** Hunters, skinners, patch knives, fighters, folders. **Technical:** Forges and grinds 1084, O1, 52100 and own Damascus. **Prices:** $75 to $1000. **Remarks:** First knife sold in 1990. **Mark:** Connected initials.

HARNER, LLOYD R. "BUTCH",
4865 Hanover Rd., Hanover, PA 17331, harnerknives@gmail.com; Web: www.harnerknives.com
Specialties: Kitchen knives and razors. **Technical:** CPM3V, CPM154, and crucible super-alloy blade steels. **Remarks:** Full-time maker since 2007. **Mark:** Maker's name, "L R Harner."

HARRINGTON, ROGER,
P.O. Box 157, Battle, East Sussex, ENGLAND TN 33 3 DD, Phone: 0854-838-7062, info@bisonbushcraft.co.uk; Web: www.bisonbushcraft.co.uk
Specialties: Working straight knives to his or customer's designs, flat saber Scandinavia-style grinds on full tang knives, also hollow and convex grinds. **Technical:** Grinds O1, D2, Damascus. **Prices:** $200 to $800. **Remarks:** First knife made by hand in 1997 whilst traveling around the world. **Mark:** Bison with bison written under.

HARRIS, CASS,
19855 Fraiser Hill Ln, Bluemont, VA 20135, Phone: 540-554-8774, Web: www.tdogforge.com
Prices: $160 to $500.

HARRIS, JAY,
991 Johnson St, Redwood City, CA 94061, Phone: 415-366-6077
Specialties: Traditional high-tech straight knives and folders of his design. **Patterns:** Daggers, fighters and locking folders. **Technical:** Uses 440C, ATS-34 and CPM. **Prices:** $250 to $850. **Remarks:** Spare-time maker; first knife sold in 1980.

HARRIS, JEFFERY A,
214 Glen Cove Dr, Chesterfield, MO 63017, Phone: 314-469-6317, Fax: 314-469-6374, jeffro135@aol.com
Remarks: Purveyor and collector of handmade knives.

HARRIS, JOHN,
14131 Calle Vista, Riverside, CA 92508, Phone: 951-653-2755, johnharrisknives@yahoo.com
Specialties: Hunters, daggers, Bowies, bird and trout, period pieces, Damascus and carbon steel knives, forged and stock removal. **Prices:** $200 to $1000.

HARRIS, RALPH DEWEY,
2607 Bell Shoals Rd, Brandon, FL 33511, Phone: 813-681-5293, Fax: 813-654-8175
Specialties: Collector quality interframe folders. **Patterns:** High tech locking folders of his own design with various mechanisms. **Technical:** Grinds 440C, ATS-34 and commercial Damascus. Offers various frame materials including 416ss, and titanium; file worked frames and his own engraving. **Prices:** $400 to $3000. **Remarks:** Full-time maker; first knife sold in 1978. **Mark:** Last name, or name and city.

HARRISON, BRIAN,
BFH KNIVES, 2359 E Swede Rd, Cedarville, MI 49719, Phone: 906-484-2012, bfhknives@easternup.net; Web: www.bfhknives.com
Specialties: High grade fixed blade knives. **Patterns:** Many sizes & variety of patterns from small pocket carries to large combat and camp knives. Mirror and bead blast finishes. All handles of high grade materials from ivory to highly figured stabilized woods to stag, deer & moose horn and Micarta. Hand sewn fancy sheaths for pocket or belt. **Technical:** Flat & hollow grinds usually ATS-34 but some O1, L6 and stellite 6K. **Prices:** $150 to $1200. **Remarks:** Full-time maker, sole authorship. Made first knife in 1980, sold first knife in 1999. Received much knowledge from the following makers: George Young, Eric Erickson, Webster Wood, Ed Kalfayan who are all generous men. **Mark:** Engraved blade outline w/BFH Knives over the top edge, signature across middle & Cedarville, MI underneath.

HARRISON, JIM (SEAMUS),
721 Fairington View Dr, St. Louis, MO 63129, Phone: 314-894-2525, jrh@seamusknives.com; Web: www.seamusknives.com
Specialties: "Crossover" folders, liner-locks and frame-locks. **Patterns:** Uber, Author, Skyyy Folders, Grant Survivor, Fixed blade. **Technical:** Use CPM S30V and 154, Stellite 6k and S.S. Damascus by Norris, Thomas and Damasteel. **Prices:** Folders $375 to $1,000. **Remarks:** Full-time maker since 2008, Maker since 1999. **Mark:** Seamus

HARSEY, WILLIAM H,
82710 N. Howe Ln, Creswell, OR 97426, Phone: 519-895-4941, harseyjr@cs.com
Specialties: High-tech kitchen and outdoor knives. **Patterns:** Folding hunters, trout and bird folders; straight hunters, camp knives and axes. **Technical:** Grinds; etches. **Prices:** $125 to $300; some to $1500. Folders start at $350. **Remarks:** Full-time maker; first knife sold in 1979. **Mark:** Full name, state, U.S.A.

HART, BILL,
647 Cedar Dr, Pasadena, MD 21122, Phone: 410-255-4981
Specialties: Fur-trade era working straight knives and folders. **Patterns:** Springback folders, skinners, Bowies and patch knives. **Technical:** Forges and stock removes 1095 and 5160 wire Damascus. **Prices:** $100 to $600. **Remarks:** Part-time maker; first knife sold in 1986. **Mark:** Name.

HARTMAN, ARLAN (LANNY),
6102 S Hamlin Cir, Baldwin, MI 49304, Phone: 231-745-4029
Specialties: Working straight knives and folders. **Patterns:** Drop-point hunters, coil spring lockers, slip-joints. **Technical:** Flat-grinds D2, 440C and ATS-34. **Prices:** $300 to $2000. **Remarks:** Part-time maker; first knife sold in 1982. **Mark:** Last name.

HARTMAN, TIM,
3812 Pedroncelli Rd NW, Albuquerque, NM 87107, Phone: 505-385-6924, tbonz1@comcast.net
Specialties: Exotic wood scales, sambar stag, filework, hunters. **Patterns:** Fixed blade hunters, skinners, utility and hiking. **Technical:** 154CM, Ats-34 and D2. Mirror finish and contoured scales. **Prices:** Start at $200-$450. **Remarks:** Started making knives in 2004. **Mark:** 3 lines Ti Hartman, Maker, Albuquerque NM

HARVEY, HEATHER,
HEAVIN FORGE, PO Box 768, Belfast 1100, SOUTH AFRICA, Phone: 27-13-253-0914, heather@heavinforge.co.za; Web: www.heavinforge.co.za
Specialties: Integral hand forged knives, traditional African weapons, primitive folders and by-gone forged-styles. **Patterns:** All forged knives, war axes, spears, arrows, forks, spoons, and swords. **Technical:** Own carbon Damascus and mokume. Also forges stainless, brass, copper and titanium. Traditional forging and heat-treatment methods used. **Prices:** $300 to $5000, average $1000. **Remarks:** Full-time maker and knifemaking instructor. Master bladesmith with ABS. First Damascus sold in 1995, first knife sold in 1998. Often collaborate with husband, Kevin (ABS MS) using the logo "Heavin." **Mark:** First name and sur name, oval shape with "M S" in middle.

HARVEY, KEVIN,
HEAVIN FORGE, PO Box 768, Belfast 1100, SOUTH AFRICA, Phone: 27-13-253-0914, info@heavinforge.co.za Web: www.heavinforge.co.za
Specialties: Large knives of presentation quality and creative art knives. **Patterns:** Fixed blades of Bowie, dagger and fighter-styles, occasionally folders and swords. **Technical:** Stock removal of stainless and forging of carbon steel and own Damascus. Indigenous African handle materials preferred. Own engraving Often collaborate with wife, Heather (ABS MS) under the logo "Heavin." **Prices:** $500 to $5000 average $1500. **Remarks:** Full-time maker and knifemaking instructor. Master bladesmith with ABS. First knife sold in 1984. **Mark:** First name and surname, oval with "M S" in the middle.

HARVEY, MAX,
14 Bass Rd, Bull Creek, Perth 6155, Western Australia, AUSTRALIA, Phone: 09-332-7585
Specialties: Daggers, Bowies, fighters and fantasy knives. **Patterns:** Hunters, Bowies, tantos and skinners. **Technical:** Hollow-and flat-grinds 440C, ATS-34, 154CM and Damascus. Offers gem work. **Prices:** $250 to $4000. **Remarks:** Part-time maker; first knife sold in 1981. **Mark:** First and middle initials, last name.

HARVEY, MEL,
P.O. Box 176, Nenana, AK 99760, Phone: 907-832-5560, tinker1@nenana.net
Specialties: Fixed blade knives for hunting and fishing. **Patterns:** Hunters, skinners. **Technical:** Stock removal on ATS-34, 440C, 01, 1095; Damascus blades using 1095 and 15N20. **Prices:** Starting at $350. **Remarks:** New maker. **Mark:** HARVEY-HOUSE.

HASLINGER, THOMAS,
164 Fairview Dr SE, Calgary, AB, CANADA T2H 1B3, Phone: 403-253-9628, Web: www.haslinger-knives.com
Specialties: One-of-a-kind using, working and art knives HCK signature sweeping grind lines. Maker of New Generation Chef series. Differential heat treated stainless steel. **Patterns:** No fixed patterns, likes to work with customers on design. **Technical:** Grinds various specialty alloys, including Damascus, High end satin finish. Prefers natural handle materials e.g. ancient ivory stag, pearl, abalone, stone and exotic woods. Does inlay work with stone, some sterling silver, niobium and gold wire work. Custom sheaths using matching woods or hand stitched with unique leather like sturgeon, Nile perch or carp. Offers engraving. **Prices:** $300 and up. **Remarks:** Full-time maker; first knife sold in 1994. Doing business as Haslinger Custom Knives. **Mark:** Two marks used, high end work uses stylized initials, other uses elk antler with Thomas Haslinger, Canada, handcrafted above.

HAWES, CHUCK,
HAWES FORGE, PO Box 176, Weldon, IL 61882, Phone: 217-736-2479
Specialties: 95 percent of all work in own Damascus. **Patterns:** Slip-joints liner locks, hunters, Bowie's, swords, anything in between. **Technical:** Forges everything, uses all high-carbon steels, no stainless. **Prices:** $150 to $4000. **Remarks:** Like to do custom orders, his style or yours. Sells Damascus. Full-time maker since 1995. **Mark:** Small football shape. Chuck Hawes maker Weldon, IL.

HAWK, GRANT AND GAVIN,
Box 401, Idaho City, ID 83631, Phone: 208-392-4911, Web: www.9-hawkknives.com
Specialties: Large folders with unique locking systems D.O.G. lock, toad lock. **Technical:** Grinds ATS-34, titanium folder parts. **Prices:** $450 and up. **Remarks:** Full-time maker. **Mark:** First initials and last names.

HAWKINS, BUDDY,
PO Box 5969, Texarkana, TX 75505-5969, Phone: 903-838-7917, buddyhawkins@cableone.net

HAWKINS, RADE,
110 Buckeye Rd, Fayetteville, GA 30214, Phone: 770-964-1177, Fax: 770-306-2877, radeh@bellsouth.net; Web: wwwhawkinscustomknives.com
Specialties: All styles. **Patterns:** All styles. **Technical:** Grinds and forges. Makes own Damascus **Prices:** Start at $190. **Remarks:** Full-time maker; first knife sold in 1972. Member knifemakers guild, ABS Journeyman Smith. **Mark:** Rade Hawkins Custom Knives.

HAYES, SCOTTY,
Texarkana College, 2500 N Robinson Rd., Tesarkana, TX 75501, Phone: 903-838-4541, ext. 3236, Fax: 903-832-5030, shayes@texakanacollege.edu; Web: www.americanbladesmith.com/2005ABSo/o20schedule.htm
Specialties: ABS School of Bladesmithing.

HAYES, WALLY,
9960, 9th Concession, RR#1, Essex, Ont., CANADA N8M-2X5, Phone: 519-776-1284, Web: www.hayesknives.com
Specialties: Classic and fancy straight knives and folders. **Patterns:** Daggers,

Bowies, fighters, tantos. **Technical:** Forges own Damascus and O1; engraves. **Prices:** $150 to $14,000. **Mark:** Last name, M.S. and serial number.

HAYNES, JERRY,
260 Forest Meadow Dr, Gunter, TX 75058, Phone: 903-433-1424, jhaynes@arrow-head.com; Web: http://www.arrow-head.com
Specialties: Working straight knives and folders of his design, also historical blades. **Patterns:** Hunters, skinners, carving knives, fighters, renaissance daggers, locking folders and kitchen knives. **Technical:** Grinds ATS-34, CPM, Stellite 6K, D2 and acquired Damascus. Prefers exotic handle materials. Has B.A. in design. Studied with R. Buckminster Fuller. **Prices:** $200 to $1200. **Remarks:** Part-time maker. First knife sold in 1953. **Mark:** Arrowhead and last name.

HAYS, MARK,
HAYS HANDMADE KNIVES, 1008 Kavanagh Dr., Austin, TX 78748, Phone: 512-292-4410, markhays@austin.rr.com
Specialties: Working straight knives and folders. Patterns inspired by Randall and Stone. **Patterns:** Bowies, hunters and slip-joint folders. **Technical:** 440C stock removal. Repairs and restores Stone knives. **Prices:** Start at $200. **Remarks:** Part-time maker, brochure available, with Stone knives 1974-1983, 1990-1991. **Mark:** First initial, last name, state and serial number.

HEADRICK, GARY,
122 Wilson Blvd, Juane Les Pins, FRANCE 06160, Phone: 033 0610282885, headrick-gary@wanadoo.fr
Specialties: Hi-tech folders with natural furnishings. Back lock & back spring. **Patterns:** Damascus and mokumes. **Technical:** Self made Damascus all steel (no nickel). **Prices:** $500 to $2000. **Remarks:** Full-time maker for last 7 years. German Guild-French Federation. 10 years active. **Mark:** HEADRICK on ricosso is new marking.

HEANEY, JOHN D,
9 Lefe Court, Haines City, FL 33844, Phone: 863-422-5823, jdh199@msn.com; Web: www.heaneyknives.com
Specialties: Forged 5160, O1 and Damascus. Prefers using natural handle material such as bone, stag and ivory. Plans on using some of the various ivories on future knives. **Prices:** $250 and up.**Remarks:** ABS member. Received journeyman smith stamp in June. **Mark:** Heaney JS.

HEASMAN, H G,
28 St Mary's Rd, Llandudno, N. Wales, UNITED KINGDOM LL302UB, Phone: (UK)0492-876351
Specialties: Miniatures only. **Patterns:** Bowies, daggers and swords. **Technical:** Files from stock high-carbon and stainless steel. **Prices:** $400 to $600. **Remarks:** Part-time maker; first knife sold in 1975. Doing business as Reduced Reality. **Mark:** NA.

HEATH, WILLIAM,
PO Box 131, Bondville, IL 61815, Phone: 217-863-2576
Specialties: Classic and working straight knives, folders. **Patterns:** Hunters and Bowies LinerLock® folders. **Technical:** Grinds ATS-34, 440C, 154CM, Damascus, handle materials Micarta, woods to exotic materials snake skins cobra, rattle snake, African flower snake. Does own heat treating. **Prices:** $75 to $300 some $1000. **Remarks:** Full-time maker. First knife sold in 1979. **Mark:** W. D. HEATH.

HEBEISEN, JEFF,
310 19th Ave N, Hopkins, MN 55343, Phone: 952-935-4506, jhebeisen@peoplepc.com
Specialties: One of a kind fixed blade of any size up to 16". **Patterns:** Miniature, Hunters, Skinners, Daggers, Bowies, Fighters and Neck knives. **Technical:** Stock removal using CPM-154, D2, 440C. Handle mterial varies depending on intended use, mostly natural materials such as bone, horn, antler, and wood. Filework on many. Heavy duty sheaths made to fit. **Prices:** From $100 to $750. **Remarks:** Full-time maker. First knife sold in 2007. **Mark:** Arched name over buffalo skull.

HEDGES, DEE,
192 Carradine Rd., Bedfordale, WA Australia 6112, dark_woods_forge@yahoo.com.au
Patterns: Makes any and all patterns and style of blades from working blades to swords to Japanese inspired. Favors exotic and artistic variations and unique one-off pieces. **Technical:** Forges all blades from a range of steels, favoring 1084, W2, 52100, 5160 and Damascus steels he makes from a 1084/15n20 mix. **Prices:** Start at $200. **Remarks:** Full-time bladesmith and jeweller. Started making knives professionally in 1999, earning my Journeyman Smith rating in 2010. **Mark:** "Dark Woods" atop an ivy leaf, with "Forge" underneath.

HEDLUND, ANDERS,
Samstad 400, 454 91, Brastad, SWEDEN, Phone: 46-523-139 48, anderskniv@passagen.se; Web: http://hem.passagen.se/anderskniv
Specialties: Fancy high-end collectible folders, high-end collectible Nordic hunters with leather carvings on the sheath. Carvings combine traditional designs with own designs. **Patterns:** Own designs. **Technical:** Grinds most steels, but prefers mosaic Damascus and RWL-34. Prefers mother-of-pearl, mammoth, and mosaic steel for folders. Prefers desert ironwood, mammoth, stabilized arctic birch, willow burl, and Damascus steel or RWL-34 for stick tang knives. **Prices:** Starting at $750 for stick tang knives and staring at $1500 for folders. **Remarks:** Part-time maker, first knife sold in 1988. Nordic champion (five countries) several times and Swedish champion 20 times in different classes. **Mark:** Stylized initials or last name.

HEDRICK, DON,
131 Beechwood Hills, Newport News, VA 23608, Phone: 757-877-8100, donaldhedrick@cox.net
Specialties: Working straight knives; period pieces and fantasy knives. **Patterns:** Hunters, boots, Bowies and miniatures. **Technical:** Grinds 440C and commercial Damascus. Also makes micro-mini Randall replicas. **Prices:** $150 to $550; some to $1200. **Remarks:** Part-time maker; first knife sold in 1982. **Mark:** First initial, last name in oval logo.

HEFLIN, CHRISTOPHER M,
6013 Jocely Hollow Rd, Nashville, TN 37205, Phone: 615-352-3909, blix@bellsouth.net

HEGWALD, J L,
1106 Charles, Humboldt, KS 66748, Phone: 316-473-3523
Specialties: Working straight knives, some fancy. **Patterns:** Makes Bowies, miniatures. **Technical:** Forges or grinds O1, L6, 440C; mixes materials in handles. **Prices:** $35 to $200; some higher. **Remarks:** Part-time maker; first knife sold in 1983. **Mark:** First and middle initials.

HEHN, RICHARD KARL,
Lehnmuehler Str 1, 55444 Dorrebach, GERMANY, Phone: 06724 3152
Specialties: High-tech, full integral working knives. **Patterns:** Hunters, fighters and daggers. **Technical:** Grinds CPM T-440V, CPM T-420V, forges his own stainless Damascus. **Prices:** $1000 to $10,000. **Remarks:** Full-time maker; first knife sold in 1963. **Mark:** Runic last initial in logo.

HEIMDALE, J E,
7749 E 28 CT, Tulsa, OK 74129, Phone: 918-640-0784, heimdale@sbcglobal.net
Specialties: Art knives **Patterns:** Bowies, daggers **Technical:** Makes all-components and handles - exotic woods and sheaths. Uses Damascus blades by other Blademakers, notably R.W. Wilson. **Prices:** $300 and up. **Remarks:** Part-time maker. First knife sold in 1999. **Marks:** JEHCO

HEINZ, JOHN,
611 Cafferty Rd, Upper Black Eddy, PA 18972, Phone: 610-847-8535, Web: www.herugrim.com
Specialties: Historical pieces / copies. **Technical:** Makes his own steel. **Prices:** $150 to $800. **Mark:** "H."

HEITLER, HENRY,
8106 N Albany, Tampa, FL 33604, Phone: 813-933-1645
Specialties: Traditional working and using straight knives of his design and to customer specs. **Patterns:** Fighters, hunters, utility/camp knives and fillet knives. **Technical:** Flat-grinds ATS-34; offers tapered tangs. **Prices:** $135 to $450; some to $600. **Remarks:** Part-time maker; first knife sold in 1990. **Mark:** First initial, last name, city, state circling double H's.

HELSCHER, JOHN W,
2645 Highway 1, Washington, IA 52353, Phone: 319-653-7310

HELTON, ROY,
HELTON KNIVES, 2941 Comstock St., San Diego, CA 92111, Phone: 858-277-5024

HEMBROOK, RON,
HEMBROOK KNIVES, PO Box 201, Neosho, WI 53059, Phone: 920-625-3607, rhembrook3607@charter.net; Web: www.hembrookcustomknives.com
Specialties: Hunters, working knives. **Technical:** Grinds ATS-34, 440C, O1 and Damascus. **Prices:** $125 to $750, some to $1000. **Remarks:** First knife sold in 1980. **Mark:** Hembrook plus a serial number. Part-time maker, makes hunters, daggers, Bowies, folders and miniatures.

HEMPERLEY, GLEN,
13322 Country Run Rd, Willis, TX 77318, Phone: 936-228-5048, hemperley.com
Specialties: Specializes in hunting knives, does fixed and folding knives.

HENDRICKS, SAMUEL J,
2162 Van Buren Rd, Maurertown, VA 22644, Phone: 703-436-3305
Specialties: Integral hunters and skinners of his design. **Patterns:** Boots, hunters and locking folders. **Technical:** Grinds ATS-34, 440C and D2. Integral liners and bolsters of N-S and 7075 T6 aircraft aluminum. Does leatherwork. **Prices:** $50 to $250; some to $500. **Remarks:** Full-time maker; first knife sold in 1992. **Mark:** First and middle initials, last name, city and state in football-style logo.

HENDRICKSON, E JAY,
4204 Ballenger Creek Pike, Frederick, MD 21703, Phone: 301-663-6923, Fax: 301-663-6923, ejayhendrickson@comcast.net
Specialties: Specializes in silver wire inlay. **Patterns:** Bowies, Kukri's, camp, hunters, and fighters. **Technical:** Forges 06, 1084, 5160, 52100, D2, L6 and W2; makes Damascus. Moran-styles on order. **Prices:** $400 to $5000. **Remarks:** Full-time maker; first knife sold in 1975. **Mark:** Last name, M.S.

HENDRICKSON, SHAWN,
2327 Kaetzel Rd, Knoxville, MD 21758, Phone: 301-432-4306
Specialties: Hunting knives. **Patterns:** Clip points, drop points and trailing point hunters. **Technical:** Forges 5160, 1084 and L6. **Prices:** $175 to $400.

HENDRIX, JERRY,
HENDRIX CUSTOM KNIVES, 175 Skyland Dr. Ext., Clinton, SC 29325, Phone: 864-833-2659, jhendrix@backroads.net
Specialties: Traditional working straight knives of all designs. **Patterns:** Hunters, utility, boot, bird and fishing. **Technical:** Grinds ATS-34 and 440C. **Prices:** $85 to $275. **Remarks:** Full-time maker. Hand stitched, waxed leather sheaths. **Mark:** Full name in shape of knife.

HENDRIX, WAYNE,
9636 Burton's Ferry Hwy, Allendale, SC 29810, Phone: 803-584-3825, Fax: 803-584-3825, w.hendrixknives@gmail.com Web: www.hendrixknives.com
Specialties: Working/using knives of his design. **Patterns:** Hunters and fillet knives. **Technical:** Grinds ATS-34, D2 and 440C. **Prices:** $100 and up. **Remarks:** Full-time maker; first knife sold in 1985. **Mark:** Last name.

HENRIKSEN, HANS J,
Birkegaardsvej 24, DK 3200 Helsinge, DENMARK, Fax: 45 4879 4899
Specialties: Zirconia ceramic blades. **Patterns:** Customer designs. **Technical:** Slip-cast zirconia-water mix in plaster mould; offers hidden or full tang. **Prices:** White blades start at $10cm; colored +50 percent. **Remarks:** Part-time maker; first ceramic blade sold in 1989. **Mark:** Initial logo.

HENSLEY, WAYNE,
PO Box 904, Conyers, GA 30012, Phone: 770-483-8938
Specialties: Period pieces and fancy working knives. **Patterns:** Boots to Bowies, locking folders to miniatures. Large variety of straight knives. **Technical:** Grinds ATS-34, 440C, D2 and commercial Damascus. **Prices:** $85 and up. **Remarks:** Full-time maker; first knife sold in 1974. **Mark:** Last name.

HERB, MARTIN,
2500 Starwood Dr, Richmond, VA 23229

HERBST, GAWIE,
PO Box 59158, Karenpark 0118, Akasia, South Africa, Phone: +27 72 060 3687, Fax: +27 12 549 1876, gawie@herbst.co.za Web: www.herbst.co.za
Specialties: Hunters, Utility knives, Art knives and Liner lock folders.

HERBST, PETER,
Komotauer Strasse 26, 91207 Lauf a.d. Pegn., GERMANY, Phone: 09123-13315, Fax: 09123-13379
Specialties: Working/using knives and folders of his design. **Patterns:** Hunters, fighters and daggers; interframe and integral. **Technical:** Grinds CPM-T-440V, UHB-Elmax, ATS-34 and stainless Damascus. **Prices:** $300 to $3000; some to $8000. **Remarks:** Full-time maker; first knife sold in 1981. **Mark:** First initial, last name.

HERBST, THINUS,
PO Box 59158, Karenpark 0118, Akasia, South Africa, Phone: +27 82 254 8016, thinus@herbst.co.za; Web: www.herbst.co.za
Specialties: Plain and fancy working straight knives of own design and liner lock folders. **Patterns:** Hunters, utility knives, art knives, and liner lock folders. **Technical:** Prefer exotic materials for handles. Most knives embellished with file work, carving and scrimshaw. **Prices:** $200 to $2000. **Remarks:** Full-time maker, member of the Knifemakers Guild of South Africa.

HERMAN, TIM,
517 E. 126 Terrace, Olathe, KS 66061-2731, Phone: 913-839-1924, HermanKnives@comcast.net
Specialties: Investment-grade folders of his design; interframes and bolster frames. **Patterns:** Interframes and new designs in carved stainless. **Technical:** Grinds ATS-34 and damasteel Damascus. Engraves and gold inlays with pearl, jade, lapis and Australian opal. **Prices:** $1500 to $20,000 and up. **Remarks:** Full-time maker; first knife sold in 1978. Inventor of full-color bulino engraving since 1993. **Mark:** Etched signature.

HERNDON, WM R "BILL",
32520 Michigan St, Acton, CA 93510, Phone: 661-269-5860, Fax: 661-269-4568, bherndons1@roadrunner.com
Specialties: Straight knives, plain and fancy. **Technical:** Carbon steel (white and blued), Damascus, stainless steels. **Prices:** Start at $175. **Remarks:** Full-time maker; first knife sold in 1976. American Bladesmith Society journeyman smith. **Mark:** Signature and/or helm logo.

HERRING, MORRIS,
Box 85 721 W Line St, Dyer, AR 72935, Phone: 501-997-8861, morrish@ipa.com

HETHCOAT, DON,
Box 1764, Clovis, NM 88101, Phone: 575-762-5721, dhethcoat@plateautel.net; Web: www.donhethcoat.com
Specialties: Liner lock-locking and multi-blade folders **Patterns:** Hunters, Bowies. **Technical:** Grinds stainless; forges Damascus. **Prices:** Moderate to upscale. **Remarks:** Full-time maker; first knife sold in 1969. **Mark:** Last name on all.

HIBBEN, DARYL,
PO Box 172, LaGrange, KY 40031-0172, Phone: 502-222-0983, dhibben1@bellsouth.net
Specialties: Working straight knives, some fancy to customer specs. **Patterns:** Hunters, fighters, Bowies, short sword, art and fantasy. **Technical:** Grinds 440C, ATS-34, 154CM, Damascus; prefers hollow-grinds. **Prices:** $275 and up. **Remarks:** Full-time maker; first knife sold in 1979. **Mark:** Etched full name in script.

HIBBEN, GIL,
PO Box 13, LaGrange, KY 40031, Phone: 502-222-1397, Fax: 502-222-2676, gil@hibbenknives.com Web: www.hibbenknives.com
Specialties: Working knives and fantasy pieces to customer specs. **Patterns:** Full range of straight knives, including swords, axes and miniatures; some locking folders. **Technical:** Grinds ATS-34, 440C and D2. **Prices:** $300 to $2000; some to $10,000. **Remarks:** Full-time maker; first knife sold in 1957.

Maker and designer of *Rambo III* knife; made swords for movie *Marked for Death* and throwing knife for movie *Under Seige*; made belt buckle knife and knives for movie *Perfect Weapon*; made knives featured in movie *Star Trek the Next Generation* , *Star Trek Nemesis*. 1990 inductee Cutlery Hall of Fame; designer for United Cutlery. Official klingon armourer for Star Trek, over 37 movies and TV productions. Celebrating 50 years since first knife sold. **Mark:** Hibben Knives. City and state, or signature.

HIBBEN, JOLEEN,
PO Box 172, LaGrange, KY 40031, Phone: 502-222-0983, dhibben1@bellsouth.net
Specialties: Miniature straight knives of her design; period pieces. **Patterns:** Hunters, axes and fantasy knives. **Technical:** Grinds Damascus, 1095 tool steel and stainless 440C or ATS-34. Uses wood, ivory, bone, feathers and claws on/for handles. **Prices:** $60 to $600. **Remarks:** Spare-time maker; first knife sold in 1991. Design knives, make & tool leather sheaths. Produced first inlaid handle in 2005, used by Daryl on a dagger. **Mark:** Initials or first name.

HIBBEN, WESTLEY G,
14101 Sunview Dr, Anchorage, AK 99515
Specialties: Working straight knives of his design or to customer specs. **Patterns:** Hunters, fighters, daggers, combat knives and some fantasy pieces. **Technical:** Grinds 440C mostly. Filework available. **Prices:** $200 to $400; some to $3000. **Remarks:** Part-time maker; first knife sold in 1988. **Mark:** Signature.

HICKS, GARY,
341 CR 275, Tuscola, TX 79562, Phone: 325-554-9762

HIELSCHER, GUY,
PO Box 992, 6550 Otoe Rd., Alliance, NE 69301, Phone: 308-762-4318, g-hielsc@bbcwb.net Web: www.ghknives.com
Specialties: Working Damascus fixed blade knives. **Patterns:** Hunters, fighters, capers, skinners, bowie, drop point. **Technical:** Forges own Damascus using 1018 and 0-1 tool steels. **Prices:** $285 and up. **Remarks:** Member of PKA. Part-time maker; sold first knife in 1988. **Mark:** Arrowhead with GH inside.

HIGH, TOM,
5474 S 1128 Rd, Alamosa, CO 81101, Phone: 719-589-2108, www.rockymountainscrimshaw.com
Specialties: Hunters, some fancy. **Patterns:** Drop-points in several shapes; some semi-skinners. Knives designed by and for top outfitters and guides. **Technical:** Grinds ATS-34; likes hollow-grinds, mirror finishes; prefers scrimable handles. **Prices:** $300 to $8000.. **Remarks:** Full-time maker; first knife sold in 1965. Limited edition wildlife series knives. **Mark:** Initials connected; arrow through last name.

HILKER, THOMAS N,
PO Box 409, Williams, OR 97544, Phone: 541-846-6461
Specialties: Traditional working straight knives and folders. **Patterns:** Folding skinner in two sizes, Bowies, fork and knife sets, camp knives and interchangeable. **Technical:** Grinds D2, 440C and ATS-34. Heat-treats. **Prices:** $50 to $350; some to $400. Doing business as Thunderbolt Artisans. Only limited production models available; not currently taking orders. **Remarks:** Full-time maker; first knife sold in 1983. **Mark:** Last name.

HILL, HOWARD E,
41785 Mission Lane, Polson, MT 59860, Phone: 406-883-3405, Fax: 406-883-3486, knifeman@bigsky.net
Specialties: Autos, complete new design, legal in Montana (with permit). **Patterns:** Bowies, daggers, skinners and lockback folders. **Technical:** Grinds 440C; uses micro and satin finish. **Prices:** $150 to $1000. **Remarks:** Full-time maker; first knife sold in 1981. **Mark:** Persuader.

HILL, RICK,
20 Nassau, Maryville, IL 62062-5618, Phone: 618-288-4370
Specialties: Working knives and period pieces to customer specs. **Patterns:** Hunters, locking folders, fighters and daggers. **Technical:** Grinds D2, 440C and 154CM; forges his own Damascus. **Prices:** $75 to $500; some to $3000. **Remarks:** Part-time maker; first knife sold in 1983. **Mark:** Full name in hill shape logo.

HILL, STEVE E,
40 Rand Pond Rd, Goshen, NH 03752, Phone: 603-863-4762, Fax: 603-863-4762, kingpirateboy2@juno.com; Web: www.stevehillknives.com
Specialties: Fancy manual and automatic LinerLock® folders, small fixed blades and classic Bowie knives. **Patterns:** Classic to cool folding and fixed blade designs. **Technical:** Grinds Damascus and occasional 440C, D2. Prefers natural handle materials; offers elaborate filework, carving, and inlays. **Prices:** $400 to $6000, some higher. **Remarks:** Full-time maker; first knife sold in 1978. Google search: Steve Hill custom knives. **Mark:** First initial, last name and handmade. (4400, D2). Damascus folders: mark inside handle.

HILLMAN, CHARLES,
225 Waldoboro Rd, Friendship, ME 04547, Phone: 207-832-4634
Specialties: Working knives of his own or custom design. Heavy Scagel influence. **Patterns:** Hunters, fishing, camp and general utility. Occasional folders. **Technical:** Grinds D2 and 440C. File work, blade and handle carving, engraving. Natural handle materials-antler, bone, leather, wood, horn. Sheaths made to order. **Prices:** $60 to $500. **Remarks:** Part-time maker; first knife sold 1986. **Mark:** Last name in oak leaf.

HINDERER, RICK,
5373 Columbus Rd., Shreve, OH 44676, Phone: 330-263-0962, Fax: 330-263-0962, rhind64@earthlink.net; Web: www.rickhindererknives.com
Specialties: Working tactical knives, and some one-of-a kind. **Patterns:** Makes his own. **Technical:** Grinds Duratech 20 CV and CPM S30V. **Prices:** $150 to $4000. **Remarks:** Full-time maker doing business as Rick Hinderer Knives, first knife sold in 1988. **Mark:** R. Hinderer.

HINDMARCH, GARTH,
PO Box 135, Carlyle SK S0C 0R0, CANADA, Phone: 306-453-2568
Specialties: Working and fancy straight knives, Bowies. **Patterns:** Hunters, skinners, Bowies. **Technical:** Grind 440C, ATS-34, some Damascus. **Prices:** $175 - $700. **Remarks:** Part-time maker; first knife sold 1994. All knives satin finish. Does file work, offers engraving, stabilized wood, Giraffe bone, some Micarta. **Mark:** First initial last name, city, province.

HINK III, LES,
1599 Aptos Lane, Stockton, CA 95206, Phone: 209-547-1292
Specialties: Working straight knives and traditional folders in standard patterns or to customer specs. **Patterns:** Hunting and utility/camp knives; others on request. **Technical:** Grinds carbon and stainless steels. **Prices:** $80 to $200; some higher. **Remarks:** Part-time maker; first knife sold in 1980. **Mark:** Last name, or last name 3.

HINMAN, THEODORE,
186 Petty Plain Road, Greenfield, MA 01301, Phone: 413-773-0448, armenemargosian@verizon.net
Specialties: Tomahawks and axes. Offers classes in bladesmithing and toolmaking.

HINSON AND SON, R,
2419 Edgewood Rd, Columbus, GA 31906, Phone: 706-327-6801
Specialties: Working straight knives and folders. **Patterns:** Locking folders, liner locks, combat knives and swords. **Technical:** Grinds 440C and commercial Damascus. **Prices:** $200 to $450; some to $1500. **Remarks:** Part-time maker; first knife sold in 1983. Son Bob is co-worker. **Mark:** HINSON, city and state.

HINTZ, GERALD M,
5402 Sahara Ct, Helena, MT 59602, Phone: 406-458-5412
Specialties: Fancy, high-art, working/using knives of his design. **Patterns:** Bowies, hunters, daggers, fish fillet and utility/camp knives. **Technical:** Forges ATS-34, 440C and D2. Animal art in horn handles or in the blade. **Prices:** $75 to $400; some to $1000. **Remarks:** Part-time maker; first knife sold in 1980. Doing business as Big Joe's Custom Knives. Will take custom orders. **Mark:** F.S. or W.S. with first and middle initials and last name.

HIRAYAMA, HARUMI,
4-5-13 Kitamachi, Warabi City, Saitama Pref. 335-0001, JAPAN, Phone: 048-443-2248, Fax: 048-443-2248, Web: www.ne.jp/asahi/harumi/knives
Specialties: High-tech working knives of her design. **Patterns:** Locking folders, interframes, straight gents and slip-joints. **Technical:** Grinds 440C or equivalent; uses natural handle materials and gold. **Prices:** Start at $1500. **Remarks:** Part-time maker; first knife sold in 1985. **Mark:** First initial, last name.

HIROTO, FUJIHARA,
2-34-7 Koioosako Nishi-ku Hiroshima-city, Hiroshima, JAPAN, Phone: 082-271-8389, fjhr8363@crest.ocn.ne.jp

HITCHMOUGH, HOWARD,
95 Old Street Rd, Peterborough, NH 03458-1637, Phone: 603-924-9646, Fax: 603-924-9595, howard@hitchmoughknives.com; Web: www.hitchmoughknives.com
Specialties: High class folding knives. **Patterns:** Lockback folders, liner locks, pocket knives. **Technical:** Uses ATS-34, stainless Damascus, titanium, gold and gemstones. Prefers hand-rubbed finishes and natural handle materials. **Prices:** $2500 - $7500. **Remarks:** Full-time maker; first knife sold in 1967. **Mark:** Last name.

HOBART, GENE,
100 Shedd Rd, Windsor, NY 13865, Phone: 607-655-1345

HOCKENSMITH, DAN,
12620 WCR 108, Carr, CO 80612, Phone: 970-231-6506, blademan@skybeam.com
Specialties: Traditional working and using straight knives of his design. **Patterns:** Hunters, Bowies, folders and utility/camp knives. **Technical:** Uses his Damascus, 5160, carbon steel, 52100 steel and 1084 steel. Hand forged. **Prices:** $250 to $1500. **Remarks:** Part-time maker; first knife sold in 1987. **Mark:** Last name or stylized "D" with H inside.

HODGE III, JOHN,
422 S 15th St, Palatka, FL 32177, Phone: 904-328-3897
Specialties: Fancy straight knives and folders. **Patterns:** Various. **Technical:** Pattern-welded Damascus—"Southern-style." **Prices:** To $1000. **Remarks:** Part-time maker; first knife sold in 1981. **Mark:** JH3 logo.

HOEL, STEVE,
PO Box 283, Pine, AZ 85544, Phone: 602-476-4278
Specialties: Investor-class folders, straight knives and period pieces of his design. **Patterns:** Folding interframes lockers and slip-joints; straight Bowies, boots and daggers. **Technical:** Grinds 154CM, ATS-34 and commercial Damascus. **Prices:** $600 to $1200; some to $7500. **Remarks:** Full-time maker. **Mark:** Initial logo with name and address.

HOFER, LOUIS,
BOX 125, Rose Prairie, B.C., CANADA V0C 2H0, Phone: 250-827-3999, ldhofer@xplornet.com
Specialties: Damascus knives, working knives, fixed blade bowies, daggers. **Patterns:** Hunting, skinning, custom. **Technical:** Wild damascus, random damascus. **Prices:** $450 and up. **Remarks:** Part-time maker since 1995. **Mark:** Logo of initials.

HOFFMAN, JAY,
Hoffman Haus Knives, 911 W Superior St., Munising, MI 49862, Phone: 906-387-3440, hoffmanhaus1@yahoo.com Web: www.hoffmanhausknives.com
Technical: Scrimshaw, metal carving, own casting of hilts and pommels, etc. Most if not all leather work for sheaths. **Remarks:** Has been making knives for 50 + years. Professionally since 1991. **Mark:** Early knives marked "Hoffman Haus" and year. Now marks "Hoffman Haus Knives" on the blades. Starting in 2010 uses heraldic device.

HOFFMAN, KEVIN L,
28 Hopeland Dr, Savannah, GA 31419, Phone: 912-920-3579, Fax: 912-920-3579, kevh052475@aol.com; Web: www.KLHoffman.com
Specialties: Distinctive folders and fixed blades. **Patterns:** Titanium frame lock folders. **Technical:** Sculpted guards and fittings cast in sterling silver and 14k gold. Grinds ATS-34, CPM S30V Damascus. Makes kydex sheaths for his fixed blade working knives. **Prices:** $400 and up. **Remarks:** Full-time maker since 1981. **Mark:** KLH.

HOGAN, THOMAS R,
2802 S. Heritage Ave, Boise, ID 83709, Phone: 208-362-7848

HOGSTROM, ANDERS T,
Halmstadsvagen 36, 121 53, Johanneshov, SWEDEN, Phone: 46 702 674 574, andershogstrom@hotmail.com or info@andershogstrom.com; Web: www.andershogstrom.com
Specialties: Short and long daggers, fighters and swords For select pieces makes wooden display stands. **Patterns:** Daggers, fighters, short knives and swords and an occasional sword. **Technical:** Grinds 1050 High Carbon, Damascus and stainless, forges own Damasus on occasion, fossil ivories. Does clay tempering and uses exotic hardwoods. **Prices:** Start at $850. **Marks:** Last name in maker's own signature.

HOKE, THOMAS M,
3103 Smith Ln, LaGrange, KY 40031, Phone: 502-222-0350
Specialties: Working/using knives, straight knives. Own designs and customer specs. **Patterns:** Daggers, Bowies, hunters, fighters, short swords. **Technical:** Grind 440C, Damascus and ATS-34. Filework on all knives. Tooling on sheaths (custom fit on all knives). Any handle material, mostly exotic. **Prices:** $100 to $700; some to $1500. **Remarks:** Full-time maker, first knife sold in 1986. **Mark:** Dragon on banner which says T.M. Hoke.

HOLBROOK, H L,
PO Box 483, Sandy Hook, KY 41171, Phone: Home: 606-738-9922 Cell: 606-794-1497, hhknives@mrtc.com
Specialties: Traditional working using straight knives of his design, to customer specs and in standard patterns. Stabilized wood. **Patterns:** Hunters, mild tacticals and neck knives with kydex sheaths. **Technical:** Grinds CPM154CM, 154CM. Blades have hand-rubbed satin finish. Uses exotic woods, stag and Micarta. Hand-sewn sheath with each straight knife. **Prices:** $100 - $300. **Remarks:** Part-time maker; first knife sold in 1983. Doing business as Holbrook Knives. **Mark:** Name, city, state.

HOLDER, D'ALTON,
18910 McNeil Rd., Wickenburg, AZ 85390, Phone: 928-684-2025, Fax: 623-878-3964, dholderknives@cox.net; Web: d'holder.com
Specialties: Deluxe working knives and high-art hunters. **Patterns:** Drop-point hunters, fighters, Bowies. **Technical:** Grinds ATS-34; uses amber and other materials in combination on stick tangs. **Prices:** $400 to $1000; some to $2000. **Remarks:** Full-time maker; first knife sold in 1966. **Mark:** D'HOLDER, city and state.

HOLLOWAY, PAUL,
714 Burksdale Rd, Norfolk, VA 23518, Phone: 757-547-6025
Specialties: Working straight knives and folders to customer specs. **Patterns:** Lockers and slip-joints; fighters and boots; fishing and push knives, from swords to miniatures. **Technical:** Grinds A2, D2, 154CM, 440C and ATS-34. **Prices:** $210 to $1500; some to $1200. **Remarks:** Part-time maker; first knife sold in 1981. **Mark:** Name and city in logo.

HOOK, BOB,
3247 Wyatt Rd, North Pole, AK 99705, Phone: 907-488-8886, grayling@alaska.net; Web: www.alaskaknifeandforge.com
Specialties: Forged carbon steel. Damascus blades. **Patterns:** Pronghorns, bowies, drop point hunters and knives for the kitchen. **Technical:** 5160, 52100, carbon steel and 1084 and 15N20 pattern welded steel blades are hand forged. Heat treated and ground by maker. Handles are natural materials from Alaska. I favor sole authorship of each piece. **Prices:** $300-$1000. **Remarks:** Journeyman smith with ABS. I have attended the Bill Moran School of Bladesmithing. Knife maker since 2000. **Mark:** Hook.

HORN, DES,
PO Box 322, Onrusrivier 7201, SOUTH AFRICA, Phone: 27283161795, Fax: +27866280824, deshorn@usa.net
Specialties: Folding knives. **Patterns:** Ball release side lock mechanism and interframe automatics. **Technical:** Prefers working in totally stainless materials. **Prices:** $800 to $7500. **Remarks:** Full-time maker. Enjoys working in gold, titanium, meteorite, pearl and mammoth. **Mark:** Des Horn.

HORN, JESS,
2526 Lansdown Rd, Eugene, OR 97404, Phone: 541-463-1510, jandahorn@earthlink.net
Specialties: Investor-class working folders; period pieces; collectibles. **Patterns:** High-tech design and finish in folders; liner locks, traditional slip-joints and featherweight models. **Technical:** Grinds ATS-34, 154CM. **Prices:** Start at $1000. **Remarks:** Full-time maker; first knife sold in 1968. **Mark:** Full name or last name.

HORNE, GRACE,
The Old Public Convenience, 469 Fulwood Road, Sheffield, UNITED KINGDOM S10 3QA, gracehorne@hotmail.co.uk Web: www.gracehorn.co.uk
Specialties: Knives of own design, mainly slip-joint folders. **Technical:** Grinds RWL34, Damasteel and own Damascus for blades. Scale materials vary from traditional (coral, wood, precious metals, etc) to unusual (wool, fabric, felt, etc), **Prices:** $500 - $1500 **Remarks:** Part-time maker. **Mark:** 'gH' and 'Sheffield'.

HORRIGAN, JOHN,
433 C.R. 200 D, Burnet, TX 78611, jhorrigan@yahoo.com Web: www.eliteknives.com
Specialties: High-end custom knives. **Prices:** $200 - $5500. **Remarks:** Part-time maker. Obtained Mastersmith stamp 2005. First knife made in 1982. **Mark:** Horrigan M.S.

HORTON, SCOT,
PO Box 451, Buhl, ID 83316, Phone: 208-543-4222
Specialties: Traditional working stiff knives and folders. **Patterns:** Hunters, skinners, utility, hatchets and show knives. **Technical:** Grinds ATS-34 and D-2 tool steel. **Prices:** $400 to $2500. **Remarks:** First knife sold in 1990. **Mark:** Full name in arch underlined with arrow, city, state.

HOSSOM, JERRY,
3585 Schilling Ridge, Duluth, GA 30096, Phone: 770-449-7809, jerry@hossom.com; Web: www.hossom.com
Specialties: Working straight knives of his own design. **Patterns:** Fighters, combat knives, modern Bowies and daggers, modern swords, concealment knives for military and LE uses. **Technical:** Grinds 154CM, S30V, CPM-3V, CPM-154 and stainless Damascus. Uses natural and synthetic handle materials. **Prices:** $350-1500, some higher. **Remarks:** Full-time maker since 1997. First knife sold in 1983. **Mark:** First initial and last name, includes city and state since 2002.

HOSTETLER, LARRY,
10626 Pine Needle Dr., Fort Pierce, FL 34945, Phone: 772-465-8352, hossknives@bellsouth.net Web: www.hoss-knives.com
Specialties: EDC working knives and custom collector knives. Utilizing own designs and customer designed creations. Maker uses a wide variety of exotic materials. **Patterns:** Bowies, hunters and folders. **Technical:** Stock removal, grinds ATS-34, carbon and stainless Damascus, embellishes most pieces with file work. **Prices:** $200 - $1500. Some custom orders higher. **Remarks:** Motto: "EDC doesn't have to be ugly." First knife made in 2001, part-time maker, voting member in the Knife Maker's Guild. Doing business as "Hoss Knives." **Mark:** "Hoss" etched into blade with a turn of the century fused bomb in place of the "O" in Hoss.

HOUSE, CAMERON,
2001 Delaney Rd Se, Salem, OR 97306, Phone: 503-585-3286, chouse357@aol.com
Specialties: Working straight knives. **Patterns:** Hunters, Bowies, fighters. **Technical:** Grinds ATS-34, 530V, 154CM. **Remarks:** Part-time maker, first knife sold in 1993. **Prices:** $150 and up. **Mark:** HOUSE.

HOUSE, GARY,
2851 Pierce Rd, Ephrata, WA 98823, Phone: 509-754-3272, spindry101@aol.com
Specialties: Mosaic Damascus bar stock. Forged blades. **Patterns:** Unlimited, SW Indian designs, geometric patterns, using 1084, 15N20 and some nickel. Bowies, hunters and daggers. **Technical:** Forged company logos and customer designs in mosaic damascus. **Prices:** $500 & up. **Remarks:** Some of the finest and most unique patterns available. ABS Journeyman Smith. **Marks:** Initials GTH, G hanging T, H.

HOUSE, NATHAN,
4 East HaneKamp St., Lonaconing, MD 21539, Phone: 301-463-3613, poppyhouse@verizon.net Web: www.houseknives.com
Specialties: User style knives that are wicked sharp and are meant to cut. **Technical:** Stock removal and favorite steel D2. **Prices:** $185 - $250. **Remarks:** Full-time maker. **Mark:** "House Knives" in a circle.

HOWARD, DURVYN M,
4220 McLain St S, Hokes Bluff, AL 35903, Phone: 256-492-5720, Fax: Cell: 256-504-1853
Specialties: Collectible upscale folders; one-of-a-kind, gentlemen's folders. Multiple patents. **Patterns:** Conceptual designs; each unique and different. **Technical:** Uses natural and exotic materials and precious metals. **Prices:** $5000 to $25,000. **Remarks:** Full-time maker; by commission or available work. Work displayed at select shows, K.G. Show etc. **Mark:** Howard: new for 2000; Howard in Garamond Narrow "etched."

HOWE, TORI,
30020 N Stampede Rd, Athol, ID 83801, Phone: 208-449-1509, wapiti@knifescales.com; Web: www.knifescales.com
Specialties Custom knives, knife scales & Damascus blades. **Remarks:** Carry James Luman polymer clay knife scales.

HOWELL, JASON G,
1112 Sycamore, Lake Jackson, TX 77566, Phone: 979-297-9454, tinyknives@yahoo.com; Web:www.howellbladesmith.com
Specialties: Fixed blades and LinerLock® folders. Makes own Damascus. **Patterns:** Clip and drop point. **Prices:** $150 to $750. **Remarks:** Likes making Mosaic Damascus out of the ordinary stuff. Member of TX Knifemakers and Collectors Association; apprentice in ABS; working towards Journeyman Stamp. **Mark:** Name, city, state.

HOWELL, LEN,
550 Lee Rd 169, Opelika, AL 36804, Phone: 334-749-1942
Specialties: Traditional and working knives of his design and to customer specs. **Patterns:** Buckskinner, hunters and utility/camp knives. **Technical:** Forges cable Damascus, 1085 and 5160; makes own Damascus. **Mark:** Engraved last name.

HOWELL, TED,
1294 Wilson Rd, Wetumpka, AL 36092, Phone: 205-569-2281, Fax: 205-569-1764
Specialties: Working/using straight knives and folders of his design; period pieces. **Patterns:** Bowies, fighters, hunters. **Technical:** Forges 5160, 1085 and cable. Offers light engraving and scrimshaw; filework. **Prices:** $75 to $250; some to $450. **Remarks:** Part-time maker; first knife sold in 1991. Doing business as Howell Co. **Mark:** Last name, Slapout AL.

HOWSER, JOHN C,
54 Bell Ln, Frankfort, KY 40601, Phone: 502-875-3678
Specialties: Slip joint folders (old patterns-multi blades). **Patterns:** Traditional slip joint folders, lockbacks, hunters and fillet knives. **Technical:** Steel S30V, CPM154, ATS-34 and D2. **Prices:** $200 to $600 some to $800. **Remarks:** Full-time maker; first knife sold in 1974. **Mark:** Signature or stamp.

HOY, KEN,
54744 Pinchot Dr, North Fork, CA 93643, Phone: 209-877-7805

HRISOULAS, JIM,
SALAMANDER ARMOURY, 284-C Lake Mead Pkwy #157, Henderson, NV 89105, Phone: 702-566-8551, www.atar.com
Specialties: Working straight knives; period pieces. **Patterns:** Swords, daggers and sgian dubhs. **Technical:** Double-edged differential heat treating. **Prices:** $85 to $175; some to $600 and higher. **Remarks:** Full-time maker; first knife sold in 1973. Author of *The Complete Bladesmith, The Pattern Welded Blade* and *The Master Bladesmith*. Doing business as Salamander Armory. **Mark:** 8R logo and sword and salamander.

HUCKABEE, DALE,
254 Hwy 260, Maylene, AL 35114, Phone: 205-664-2544, dalehuckabee@hotmail.com
Specialties: Fixed blade hunter and Bowies of his design. **Technical:** Steel used: 5160, 1084, and Damascus. **Prices:** $225 and up, depending on materials used. **Remarks:** Hand forged. Journeyman Smith. Part-time maker. **Mark:** Stamped Huckabee J.S.

HUCKS, JERRY,
KNIVES BY HUCKS, 1807 Perch Road, Moncks Corner, SC 29461, Phone: 843-761-6481, knivesbyhucks@netrockets.com
Specialties: Oyster knives, hunters, Bowies, fillets. Bowies are the maker's favorite with stag & ivory. **Patterns:** Yours and his. **Technical:** ATS-34, BG-42, CPM-154, maker's cable Damascus, also 1084 & 15N20. **Prices:** $125 and up. **Remarks:** Full-time maker, retired as a machinist in 1990. Makes sheaths sewn by hand with some carving. **Mark:** Robin Hood hat with moncke corner, S.C. in oval.

HUDSON, ANTHONY B,
PO Box 368, Amanda, OH 43102, Phone: 740-969-4200, jjahudson@wmconnect.com
Specialties: Hunting knives, fighters, survival. **Remarks:** ABS Journeyman Smith. **Mark:** A.B. HUDSON.

HUDSON, C ROBBIN,
497 Groton Hollow Rd, Rummney, NH 03266, Phone: 603-786-9944
Specialties: High-art working knives. **Patterns:** Hunters, Bowies, fighters and kitchen knives. **Technical:** Forges W2, nickel steel, pure nickel steel, composite and mosaic Damascus; makes knives one-at-a-time. **Prices:** 500 to $1200; some to $5000. **Remarks:** Full-time maker; first knife sold in 1970. **Mark:** Last name and MS.

HUDSON, ROB,
340 Roush Rd, Northumberland, PA 17857, Phone: 570-473-9588, robscustknives@aol.com Web:www.robscustomknives.com
Specialties: Presentation hunters and Bowies. **Technical:** Hollow grinds CPM-154 stainless and stainless Damascus. **Prices:** $400 to $2000. **Remarks:** Full-time maker. Does business as Rob's Custom Knives. **Mark:** Capital R, Capital H in script.

HUDSON, ROBERT,
3802 Black Cricket Ct, Humble, TX 77396, Phone: 713-454-7207
Specialties: Working straight knives of his design. **Patterns:** Bowies, hunters, skinners, fighters and utility knives. **Technical:** Grinds D2, 440C, 154CM and commercial Damascus. **Prices:** $85 to $350; some to $1500. **Remarks:** Part-time maker; first knife sold in 1980. **Mark:** Full name, handmade, city and state.

HUGHES, DAN,
301 Grandview Bluff Rd, Spencer, TN 38585, Phone: 931-946-3044
Specialties: Working straight knives to customer specs. **Patterns:** Hunters, fighters, fillet knives. **Technical:** Grinds 440C and ATS-34. **Prices:** $55 to $175; some to $300. **Remarks:** Part-time maker; first knife sold in 1984. **Mark:** Initials.

HUGHES, DARYLE,
10979 Leonard, Nunica, MI 49448, Phone: 616-837-6623, hughes.builders@verizon.net
Specialties: Working knives. **Patterns:** Buckskinners, hunters, camp knives, kitchen and fishing knives. **Technical:** Forges and grinds 52100 and Damascus. **Prices:** $125 to $1000. **Remarks:** Part-time maker; first knife sold in 1979. **Mark:** Name and city in logo.

HUGHES, ED,
280 1/2 Holly Lane, Grand Junction, CO 81503, Phone: 970-243-8547, edhughes26@msn.com
Specialties: Working and art folders. **Patterns:** Buys Damascus. **Technical:** Grinds stainless steels. Engraves. **Prices:** $300 and up. **Remarks:** Full-time maker; first knife sold in 1978. **Mark:** Name or initials.

HUGHES, LAWRENCE,
207 W Crestway, Plainview, TX 79072, Phone: 806-293-5406
Specialties: Working and display knives. **Patterns:** Bowies, daggers, hunters, buckskinners. **Technical:** Grinds D2, 440C and 154CM. **Prices:** $125 to $300; some to $2000. **Remarks:** Full-time maker; first knife sold in 1979. **Mark:** Name with buffalo skull in center.

HULETT, STEVE,
115 Yellowstone Ave, West Yellowstone, MT 59758-0131, Phone: 406-646-4116, Web: www.seldomseenknives.com
Specialties: Classic, working/using knives, straight knives, folders. Your design, custom specs. **Patterns:** Utility/camp knives, hunters, and LinerLock folders, lock back pocket knives. **Technical:** Grinds 440C stainless steel, O1 Carbon, 1095. Shop is retail and knife shop; people watch their knives being made. We do everything in house: "all but smelt the ore, or tan the hide." **Prices:** Strarting $250 to $7000. **Remarks:** Full-time maker; first knife sold in 1994. **Mark:** Seldom seen knives/West Yellowstone Montana.

HULL, MICHAEL J,
1330 S Hermits Circle, Cottonwood, AZ 86326, Phone: 928-634-2871, mjwhull@earthlink.net
Specialties: Period pieces and working knives. **Patterns:** Hunters, fighters, Bowies, camp and Mediterranean knives, etc. **Technical:** Grinds 440C, ATS-34 and BG42 and S30V. **Prices:** $125 to $750; some to $1000. **Remarks:** Due to health reasons, I have had to go part time; make knives of my design only and when able. First knife sold in 1983. **Mark:** Name, city, state.

HULSEY, HOYT,
379 Shiloh, Attalla, AL 35954, Phone: 256-538-6765
Specialties: Traditional working straight knives and folders of his design. **Patterns:** Hunters and utility/camp knives. **Technical:** Grinds 440C, ATS-34, O1 and A2. **Prices:** $75 to $250. **Remarks:** Part-time maker; first knife sold in 1989. **Mark:** Hoyt Hulsey Attalla AL.

HUME, DON,
2731 Tramway Circle NE, Albuquerque, NM 87122, Phone: 505-796-9451

HUMENICK, ROY,
PO Box 55, Rescue, CA 95672
Specialties: Multiblade folders. **Patterns:** Original folder and fixed blade designs, also traditional patterns. **Technical:** Grinds premium steels and Damascus. **Prices:** $350 and up; some to $1500. **Remarks:** First knife sold in 1984. **Mark:** Last name in ARC.

HUMPHREY, LON,
83 Wilwood Ave., Newark, OH 43055, Phone: 740-644-1137, ironcrossforge@hotmail.com
Specialties: Hunters, tacticals, and bowie knives. **Prices:** I make knives that start in the $150 range and go up to $1000 for a large bowie. **Remarks:** Has been blacksmithing since age 13 and progressed to the forged blade.

HUMPHREYS, JOEL,
90 Boots Rd, Lake Placid, FL 33852, Phone: 863-773-0439
Specialties: Traditional working/using straight knives and folders of his design and in standard patterns. **Patterns:** Hunters, folders and utility/camp knives. **Technical:** Grinds ATS-34, D2, 440C. All knives have tapered tangs, mitered bolster/handle joints, handles of horn or bone fitted sheaths. **Prices:** $135 to $225; some to $350. **Remarks:** Part-time maker; first knife sold in 1990. Doing business as Sovereign Knives. **Mark:** First name or "H" pierced by arrow.

HUNT, MAURICE,
10510 NCR 650 E, Brownsburg, IN 46112, Phone: 317-892-2982, mdhuntknives@juno.com
Patterns: Bowies, hunters, fighters. **Prices:** $200 to $800. **Remarks:** Part-time maker. Journeyman Smith.

HUNTER, HYRUM,
285 N 300 W, PO Box 179, Aurora, UT 84620, Phone: 435-529-7244
Specialties: Working straight knives of his design or to customer specs. **Patterns:** Drop and clip, fighters dagger, some folders. **Technical:** Forged from two-piece Damascus. **Prices:** Prices are adjusted according to size, complexity and material used. **Remarks:** Will consider any design you have. Part-time maker; first knife sold in 1990. **Mark:** Initials encircled with first initial and last name and city, then state. Some patterns are numbered.

HUNTER, RICHARD D,
7230 NW 200th Ter, Alachua, FL 32615, Phone: 386-462-3150
Specialties: Traditional working/using knives of his design or customer suggestions; filework. **Patterns:** Folders of various types, Bowies, hunters, daggers. **Technical:** Traditional blacksmith; hand forges high-carbon steel (5160, 1084, 52100) and makes own Damascus; grinds 440C and ATS-34. **Prices:** $200 and up. **Remarks:** Part-time maker; first knife sold in 1992. **Mark:** Last name in capital letters.

HURST, COLE,
1583 Tedford, E. Wenatchee, WA 98802, Phone: 509-884-9206
Specialties: Fantasy, high-art and traditional straight knives. **Patterns:** Bowies, daggers and hunters. **Technical:** Blades are made of stone; handles are made of stone, wood or ivory and embellished with fancy woods, ivory or antlers. **Prices:** $100 to $300; some to $2000. **Remarks:** Spare-time maker; first knife sold in 1985. **Mark:** Name and year.

HURST, JEFF,
PO Box 247, Rutledge, TN 37861, Phone: 865-828-5729, jhurst@esper.com
Specialties: Working straight knives and folders of his design. **Patterns:** Tomahawks, hunters, boots, folders and fighters. **Technical:** Forges W2, O1 and his own Damascus. Makes mokume. **Prices:** $250 to $600. **Remarks:** Full-time maker; first knife sold in 1984. Doing business as Buzzard's Knob Forge. **Mark:** Last name; partnered knives are marked with Newman L. Smith, handle artisan, and SH in script.

HUSIAK, MYRON,
PO Box 238, Altona 3018, Victoria, AUSTRALIA, Phone: 03-315-6752
Specialties: Straight knives and folders of his design or to customer specs. **Patterns:** Hunters, fighters, lock-back folders, skinners and boots. **Technical:** Forges and grinds his own Damascus, 440C and ATS-34. **Prices:** $200 to $900. **Remarks:** Part-time maker; first knife sold in 1974. **Mark:** First initial, last name in logo and serial number.

HUTCHESON, JOHN,
SURSUM KNIFE WORKS, 1237 Brown's Ferry Rd., Chattanooga, TN 37419, Phone: 423-667-6193, sursum5071@aol.com; Web: www.sursumknife.com
Specialties: Straight working knives, hunters. **Patterns:** Customer designs, hunting, speciality working knives. **Technical:** Grinds D2, S7, O1 and 5160, ATS-34 on request. **Prices:** $100 to $300, some to $600. **Remarks:** First knife sold 1985, also produces a mid-tech line. Doing business as Sursum Knife Works. **Mark:** Family crest boar's head over 3 arrows.

HUTCHINSON, ALAN,
315 Scenic Hill Road, Conway, AR 72034, Phone: 501-470-9653, mama_wolfie@yahoo.com
Specialties: Bowie knives, fighters and working/hunter knives. **Technical:** Forges 10 series carbon steels as well as 5160 and 01. **Prices:** Range from $150 and up. **Remarks:** Prefers natural handle materials, full-time maker, first forged blade in 1970. **Mark:** Last name.

HYTOVICK, JOE "HY",
14872 SW 111th St, Dunnellon, FL 34432, Phone: 800-749-5339, Fax: 352-489-3732, hyclassknives@aol.com
Specialties: Straight, folder and miniature. **Technical:** Blades from Wootz, Damascus and Alloy steel. **Prices:** To $5000. **Mark:** HY.

I

IAMES, GARY,
PO Box 8493, South Lake, Tahoe, CA 96158, Phone: 530-541-2250, iames@charter.net
Specialties: Working and fancy straight knives and folders. **Patterns:** Bowies, hunters, wedding sets and liner locking folders. **Technical:** Grinds 440C, ATS-34, forges 5160 and 1080, makes Damascus. **Prices:** $300 and up. **Mark:** Initials and last name, city or last name.

IKOMA, FLAVIO,
R Manoel Rainho Teixeira 108-Pres, Prudonte SP19031-220, BRAZIL, Phone: 0182-22-0115, fikoma@itelesonica.com.br
Specialties: Tactical fixed blade knives, LinerLock® folders and balisongs. **Patterns:** Utility and defense tactical knives built with hi-tech materials. **Technical:** Grinds S30V and Damasteel. **Prices:** $500 to $1000. **Mark:** Ikoma hand made beside Samurai

IMBODEN II, HOWARD L.,
620 Deauville Dr, Dayton, OH 45429, Phone: 513-439-1536
Specialties: One-of-a-kind hunting, flint, steel and art knives. **Technical:** Forges and grinds stainless, high-carbon and Damascus. Uses obsidian, cast sterling silver, 14K and 18K gold guards. Carves ivory animals and more. **Prices:** $65 to $25,000. **Remarks:** Full-time maker; first knife sold in 1986. Doing business as Hill Originals. **Mark:** First and last initials, II.

IMEL, BILLY MACE,
1616 Bundy Ave, New Castle, IN 47362, Phone: 765-529-1651
Specialties: High-art working knives, period pieces and personal cutlery. **Patterns:** Daggers, fighters, locking folders and slip-joints with interframes. **Technical:** Grinds D2, 440C and 154CM. **Prices:** $300 to $2000; some to $6000. **Remarks:** Part-time maker; first knife sold in 1973. **Mark:** Name in monogram.

custom knifemakers

IRIE, MICHAEL L,
MIKE IRIE HANDCRAFT, 1606 Auburn Dr., Colorado Springs, CO 80909, Phone: 719-572-5330, mikeirie@aol.com
Specialties: Working fixed blade knives and handcrafted blades for the do-it-yourselfer. **Patterns:** Twenty standard designs along with custom. **Technical:** Blades are ATS-34, BG-43, 440C with some outside Damascus. **Prices:** Fixed blades $95 and up, blade work $45 and up. **Remarks:** Formerly dba Wood, Irie and Co. with Barry Wood. Full-time maker since 1991. **Mark:** Name.

IRON WOLF FORGE, SEE NELSON KEN,

ISAO, OHBUCHI,
702-1 Nouso Yame-City, Fukuoka, JAPAN, Phone: 0943-23-4439, www.5d. biglobe.ne.jp/~ohisao/

ISHIHARA, HANK,
86-18 Motomachi, Sakura City, Chiba Pref., JAPAN, Phone: 043-485-3208, Fax: 043-485-3208
Specialties: Fantasy working straight knives and folders of his design. **Patterns:** Boots, Bowies, daggers, fighters, hunters, fishing, locking folders and utility camp knives. **Technical:** Grinds ATS-34, 440C, D2, 440V, CV-134, COS25 and Damascus. Engraves. **Prices:** $250 to $1000; some to $10,000. **Remarks:** Full-time maker; first knife sold in 1987. **Mark:** HANK.

J

JACKS, JIM,
344 S. Hollenbeck Ave, Covina, CA 91723-2513, Phone: 626-331-5665
Specialties: Working straight knives in standard patterns. **Patterns:** Bowies, hunters, fighters, fishing and camp knives, miniatures. **Technical:** Grinds Stellite 6K, 440C and ATS-34. **Prices:** Start at $100. **Remarks:** Spare-time maker; first knife sold in 1980. **Mark:** Initials in diamond logo.

JACKSON, CHARLTON R,
6811 Leyland Dr, San Antonio, TX 78239, Phone: 210-601-5112

JACKSON, DAVID,
214 Oleander Ave, Lemoore, CA 93245, Phone: 559-925-8547, jnbcrea@lemoorenet.com
Specialties: Forged steel. **Patterns:** Hunters, camp knives, Bowies. **Prices:** $150 and up. **Mark:** G.D. Jackson - Maker - Lemoore CA.

JACKSON, JIM,
1 Jesus Hospital, High St. Bray, ENGLAND SL6 2AN, Phone: 01628-620026, jlandsejackson@btconnect.com
Specialties: Large Bowies, concentrating on form and balance; collector quality Damascus daggers. **Patterns:** With fancy filework and engraving available. **Technical:** Forges O1, 5160 and 1084 and 15N20 Damascus. **Remarks:** Part-time maker. All knives come with a custom tooled leather swivel sheath of exotic material. No orders currently undertaken. **Mark:** Jackson England with in a circle M.S.

JACQUES, ALEX,
16 Tupelo Rd., Wakefield, RI 02879, Phone: 617-771-4441, customrazors@gmail.com Web: www.customrazors.com
Specialties: Functional, fully custom STRAIGHT RAZORS. **Technical:** Damascus, 01, CPM154, and various other high carbon and stainless steels using the stock removal method. **Prices:** $350 - $1000. **Remarks:** Slowly transitioning to full-time maker; first knife made in 2008. **Mark:** Jack-O-Lantern logo with "A. Jacques" underneath.

JAKSIK JR., MICHAEL,
427 Marschall Creek Rd, Fredericksburg, TX 78624, Phone: 830-997-1119
Mark: MJ or M. Jaksik.

JARVIS, PAUL M,
30 Chalk St, Cambridge, MA 02139, Phone: 617-547-4355 or 617-666-9090
Specialties: High-art knives and period pieces of his design. **Patterns:** Japanese and Mid-Eastern knives. **Technical:** Grinds Myer Damascus, ATS-34, D2 and O1. Specializes in height-relief Japanese-style carving. Works with silver, gold and gems. **Prices:** $200 to $17,000. **Remarks:** Part-time maker; first knife sold in 1978.

JEAN, GERRY,
25B Cliffside Dr, Manchester, CT 06040, Phone: 860-649-6449
Specialties: Historic replicas. **Patterns:** Survival and camp knives. **Technical:** Grinds A2, 440C and 154CM. Handle slabs applied in unique tongue-and-groove method. **Prices:** $125 to $250; some to $1000. **Remarks:** Spare-time maker; first knife sold in 1973. **Mark:** Initials and serial number.

JEFFRIES, ROBERT W,
Route 2 Box 227, Red House, WV 25168, Phone: 304-586-9780, wvknifeman@hotmail.com; Web: www.jeffrieskniveswv.tripod.com
Specialties: Hunters, Bowies, daggers, lockback folders and LinerLock push buttons. **Patterns:** Skinning types, drop points, typical working hunters, folders one-of-a-kind. **Technical:** Grinds all types of steel. Makes his own Damascus. **Prices:** $125 to $600. Private collector pieces to $3000. **Remarks:** Starting engraving. Custom folders of his design. Part-time maker since 1988. **Mark:** Name etched or on plate pinned to blade.

JENKINS, MITCH,
194 East 500 South, Manti, Utah 84642, Phone: 435-813-2532, mitch.jenkins@gmail.com Web: MitchJenkinsKnives.com
Specialties: Hunters, working knives. **Patterns:** Johnson and Loveless

Style. Drop points, skinners and semi-skinners, Capers and utilities. **Technical:** 154CM and ATS-34. Experimenting with S30V and love working with Damascus on occasion. **Prices:** $150 and up. **Remarks:** Slowly transitioning to full-time maker; first knife made in 2008. **Mark:** Jenkins Manti, Utah and M. Jenkins, Utah.

JENSEN, JOHN LEWIS,
JENSEN KNIVES, PO Box 50041, Pasadena, CA 91116, Phone: 323-559-7454, Fax: 626-449-1148, john@jensenknives.com; Web: www.jensenknives.com
Specialties: Designer and fabricator of modern, original one-of-a-kind, hand crafted, custom ornamental edged weaponry. Combines skill, precision, distinction and the finest materials, geared toward the discriminating art collector. **Patterns:** Folding knives and fixed blades, daggers, fighters and swords. **Technical:** High embellishment, BFA 96 Rhode Island School of Design: jewelry and metalsmithing. Grinds 440C, ATS-34, Damascus. Works with custom made Damascus to his specs. Uses gold, silver, gemstones, pearl, titanium, fossil mastodon and walrus ivories. Carving, file work, soldering, deep etches Damascus, engraving, layers, bevels, blood grooves. Also forges his own Damascus. **Prices:** Start at $10,000. **Remarks:** Available on a first come basis and via commission based on his designs. Knifemakers Guild voting member and ABS apprenticesmith and member of the Society of North American Goldsmiths. **Mark:** Maltese cross/butterfly shield.

JERNIGAN, STEVE,
3082 Tunnel Rd., Milton, FL 32571, Phone: 850-994-0802, Fax: 850-994-0802, jerniganknives@mchsi.com
Specialties: Investor-class folders and various theme pieces. **Patterns:** Array of models and sizes in side plate locking interframes and conventional liner construction. **Technical:** Grinds ATS-34, CPM-T-440V and Damascus. Inlays mokume (and minerals) in blades and sculpts marble cases. **Prices:** $650 to $1800; some to $6000. **Remarks:** Full-time maker, first knife sold in 1982. **Mark:** Last name.

JOBIN, JACQUES,
46 St Dominique, Levis Quebec, CANADA G6V 2M7, Phone: 418-833-0283, Fax: 418-833-8378
Specialties: Fancy and working straight knives and folders; miniatures. **Patterns:** Minis, fantasy knives, fighters and some hunters. **Technical:** ATS-34, some Damascus and titanium. Likes native snake wood. Heat-treats. **Prices:** Start at $250. **Remarks:** Full-time maker; first knife sold in 1986. **Mark:** Signature on blade.

JOEHNK, BERND,
Posadowskystrasse 22, 24148 Kiel, GERMANY, Phone: 0431-7297705, Fax: 0431-7297705
Specialties: One-of-a-kind fancy/embellished and traditional straight knives of his design and from customer drawing. **Patterns:** Daggers, fighters, hunters and letter openers. **Technical:** Grinds and file 440C, ATS-34, powder metal orgical, commercial Damascus and various stainless and corrosion-resistant steels. **Prices:** Upscale. **Remarks:** Likes filework. Leather sheaths. Offers engraving. Part-time maker; first knife sold in1990. Doing business as metal design kiel. All knives made by hand. **Mark:** From 2005 full name and city, with certificate.

JOHANNING CUSTOM KNIVES, TOM,
1735 Apex Rd, Sarasota, FL 34240 9386, Phone: 941-371-2104, Fax: 941-378-9427, Web: www.survivalknives.com
Specialties: Survival knives. **Prices:** $375 to $775.

JOHANSSON, ANDERS,
Konstvartarevagen 9, S-772 40 Grangesberg, SWEDEN, Phone: 46 240 23204, Fax: +46 21 358778, www.scrimart.u.se
Specialties: Scandinavian traditional and modern straight knives. **Patterns:** Hunters, fighters and fantasy knives. **Technical:** Grinds stainless steel and makes own Damascus. Prefers water buffalo and mammoth for handle material. **Prices:** Start at $100. **Remarks:** Spare-time maker; first knife sold in 1994. Works together with scrimshander Vlveca Sahlin. **Mark:** Stylized initials.

JOHNS, ROB,
1423 S. Second, Enid, OK 73701, Phone: 405-242-2707
Specialties: Classic and fantasy straight knives of his design or to customer specs; fighters for use at Medieval fairs. **Patterns:** Bowies, daggers and swords. **Technical:** Forges and grinds 440C, D2 and 5160. Handles of nylon, walnut or wire-wrap. **Prices:** $150 to $350; some to $2500. **Remarks:** Full-time maker; first knife sold in 1980. **Mark:** Medieval Customs, initials.

JOHNSON, C E GENE,
1240 Coan Street, Chesterton, IN 46304, Phone: 219-787-8324, ddjlady55@aol.com
Specialties: Lock-back folders and springers of his design or to customer specs. **Patterns:** Hunters, Bowies, survival lock-back folders. **Technical:** Grinds D2, 440C, A18, O1, Damascus; likes filework. **Prices:** $100 to $2000. **Remarks:** Full-time maker; first knife sold in 1975. **Mark:** Gene.

JOHNSON, DAVID A,
1791 Defeated Creek Rd, Pleasant Shade, TN 37145, Phone: 615-774-3596, artsmith@mwsi.net

JOHNSON, GORDEN W,
5426 Sweetbriar, Houston, TX 77017, Phone: 713-645-8990
Specialties: Working knives and period pieces. **Patterns:** Hunters, boots and Bowies. **Technical:** Flat-grinds 440C; most knives have narrow tang. **Prices:** $90 to $450. **Remarks:** Full-time maker; first knife sold in 1974. **Mark:** Name, city, state.

JOHNSON, GORDON A.,
981 New Hope Rd, Choudrant, LA 71227, Phone: 318-768-2613
Specialties: Using straight knives and folders of my design, or customers. Offering filework and hand stitched sheaths. **Patterns:** Hunters, bowies, folders and miniatures. **Technical:** Forges 5160, 1084, 52100 and my own Damascus. Some stock removal on working knives and miniatures. **Prices:** Mid range. **Remarks:** First knife sold in 1990. ABS apprentice smith. **Mark:** Interlocking initials G.J. or G. A. J.

JOHNSON, JERRY,
PO Box 491, Spring City, Utah 84662, Phone: 435-851-3604, Web: sanpetesilver.com
Specialties: Hunter, fighters, camp. **Patterns:** Multiple. **Prices:** $225 - $3000. **Mark:** Jerry E. Johnson Spring City, UT in several fonts.

JOHNSON, JOHN R,
PO Box 246, New Buffalo, PA 17069, Phone: 717-834-6265, jrj@jrjknives.com; Web: www.jrjknives.com
Specialties: Working hunting and tactical fixed blade sheath knives. **Patterns:** Hunters, tacticals, Bowies, daggers, neck knives and primitives. **Technical:** Flat, convex and hollow grinds. ATS-34, CPM154CM, L6, O1, D2, 5160, 1095 and Damascus. **Prices:** $60 to $700. **Remarks:** Full-time maker, first knife sold in 1996. Doing business as JRJ Knives. Custom sheath made by maker for every knife, **Mark:** Initials connected.

JOHNSON, JOHN R,
5535 Bob Smith Ave, Plant City, FL 33565, Phone: 813-986-4478, rottyjohn@msn.com
Specialties: Hand forged and stock removal. **Technical:** High tech. Folders. **Mark:** J.R. Johnson Plant City, FL.

JOHNSON, MIKE,
38200 Main Rd, Orient, NY 11957, Phone: 631-323-3509, mjohnsoncustomknives@hotmail.com
Specialties: Large Bowie knives and cutters, fighters and working knives to customer specs. **Technical:** Forges 5160, O1. **Prices:** $325 to $1200. **Remarks:** Full-time bladesmith. **Mark:** Johnson.

JOHNSON, R B,
Box 11, Clearwater, MN 55320, Phone: 320-558-6128, Fax: 320-558-6128, rbjohnson@mywdo.com or rb@rbjohnsonknives.com; Web: rbjohnsonknives.com
Specialties: Liner locks with titanium, mosaic Damascus. **Patterns:** LinerLock® folders, skeleton hunters, frontier Bowies. **Technical:** Damascus, mosaic Damascus, A-2, O1, 1095. **Prices:** $200 and up. **Remarks:** Full-time maker since 1973. Not accepting orders. **Mark:** R B Johnson (signature).

JOHNSON, RANDY,
2575 E Canal Dr, Turlock, CA 95380, Phone: 209-632-5401
Specialties: Folders. **Patterns:** Locking folders. **Technical:** Grinds Damascus. **Prices:** $200 to $400. **Remarks:** Spare-time maker; first knife sold in 1989. Doing business as Puedo Knifeworks. **Mark:** PUEDO.

JOHNSON, RICHARD,
W165 N10196 Wagon Trail, Germantown, WI 53022, Phone: 262-251-5772, rlj@execpc.com; Web: http://www.execpc.com/~rlj/index.html
Specialties: Custom knives and knife repair.

JOHNSON, RUFFIN,
215 LaFonda Dr, Houston, TX 77060, Phone: 281-448-4407
Specialties: Working straight knives and folders. **Patterns:** Hunters, fighters and locking folders. **Technical:** Grinds 440C and 154CM; hidden tangs and fancy handles. **Prices:** $450 to $650; some to $1350. **Remarks:** Full-time maker; first knife sold in 1972. **Mark:** Wolf head logo and signature.

JOHNSON, RYAN M,
3103 Excelsior Ave., Signal Mountain, TN 37377, Phone: 866-779-6922, rmjtactical@gmail.com Web: www.rmjforge.com www.rmjtactical.com
Specialties: Historical and Tactical Tomahawks. Some period knives and folders. **Technical:** Forges a variety of steels including own Damascus. **Prices:** $500 - $1200 **Remarks:** Full-time maker began forging in 1986. **Mark:** Sledge-hammer with halo.

JOHNSON, STEVEN R,
202 E 200 N, PO Box 5, Manti, UT 84642, Phone: 435-835-7941, Fax: 435-835-7941, srj@mail.manti.com; Web: www.srjknives.com
Specialties: Investor-class working knives. **Patterns:** Hunters, fighters, boots. **Technical:** Grinds 154-CM, ATS-34, CPM 154-CM. **Prices:** $1,500 to $20,000. **Remarks:** Full-time maker; first knife sold in 1972. Also see SR Johnson forum on www.knifenetwork.com. **Mark:** Registered trademark, including name, city, state, and optional signature mark.

JOHNSON, TOMMY,
144 Poole Rd., Troy, NC 27371, Phone: 910-975-1817, tommy@tjohnsonknives.com Web: www.tjohnsonknives.com
Specialties: Straight knives for hunting, fishing, utility, and linerlock and slip joint folders since 1982.

JOHNSON, WM. C. "BILL",
225 Fairfield Pike, Enon, OH 45323, Phone: 937-864-7802, wjohnson64@woh.RR.com
Patterns: From hunters to art knives as well as custom canes, some with blades. **Technical:** Stock removal method utilizing 440C, ATS34, 154CPM, and custom Damascus. **Prices:** $175 to over $2500, depending on design, materials, and embellishments. **Remarks:** Full-time maker. First knife made

in 1978. Member of the Knifemakers Guild since 1982. **Mark:** Crescent shaped WM. C. "BILL" JOHNSON, ENON OHIO. Also uses an engraved or electro signature on some art knives and on Damascus blades.

JOHNSTON, DR. ROBT,
PO Box 9887 1 Lomb Mem Dr, Rochester, NY 14623

JOKERST, CHARLES,
9312 Spaulding, Omaha, NE 68134, Phone: 402-571-2536
Specialties: Working knives in standard patterns. **Patterns:** Hunters, fighters and pocketknives. **Technical:** Grinds 440C, ATS-34. **Prices:** $90 to $170. **Remarks:** Spare-time maker; first knife sold in 1984. **Mark:** Early work marked RCJ; current work marked with last name and city.

JONES, BARRY M AND PHILLIP G,
221 North Ave, Danville, VA 24540, Phone: 804-793-5282
Specialties: Working and using straight knives and folders of their design and to customer specs; combat and self-defense knives. **Patterns:** Bowies, fighters, daggers, swords, hunters and LinerLock® folders. **Technical:** Grinds 440C, ATS-34 and D2; flat-grinds only. All blades hand polished. **Prices:** $100 to $1000, some higher. **Remarks:** Part-time makers; first knife sold in 1989. **Mark:** Jones Knives, city, state.

JONES, CURTIS J,
210 Springfield Ave, Washington, PA 15301-5244, Phone: 724-225-8829
Specialties: Big Bowies, daggers, his own style of hunters. **Patterns:** Bowies, daggers, hunters, swords, boots and miniatures. **Technical:** Grinds 440C, ATS-34 and D2. Fitted guards only; does not solder. Heat-treats. Custom sheaths: hand-tooled and stitched. **Prices:** $125 to $1500; some to $3000. **Remarks:** Full-time maker; first knife sold in 1975. Mail orders accepted. **Mark:** Stylized initials on either side of three triangles interconnected.

JONES, ENOCH,
7278 Moss Ln, Warrenton, VA 20187, Phone: 540-341-0292
Specialties: Fancy working straight knives. **Patterns:** Hunters, fighters, boots and Bowies. **Technical:** Forges and grinds O1, W2, 440C and Damascus. **Prices:** $100 to $350; some to $1000. **Remarks:** Part-time maker; first knife sold in 1982. **Mark:** First name.

JONES, FRANKLIN (FRANK) W,
6030 Old Dominion Rd, Columbus, GA 31909, Phone: 706-563-6051, frankscuba@bellsouth.net
Specialties: Traditional/working/tactical/period straight knives of his or your design. **Patterns:** Hunters, skinners, utility/camp, Bowies, fighters, kitchen, neck knives, Harley chains. **Technical:** Forges using 5160, O1, 52100, 1084 1095 and Damascus. Also stock removal of stainless steel. **Prices:** $150 to $1000. **Remarks:** Full-time, American Bladesmith Society Journeyman Smith. **Mark:** F.W. Jones, Columbus, GA.

JONES, JACK P.,
17670 Hwy. 2 East, Ripley, MS 38663, Phone: 662-837-3882, jacjones@ripleycable.net
Specialties: Working knives in classic design. **Patterns:** Hunters, fighters, and Bowies. **Technical:** Grinds ATS-34, D2, A2, CPM-154 CM. **Prices:** $200 and up. **Remarks:** Full-time maker since retirement in 2005, first knife sold in 1976. **Mark:** J.P. Jones, Ripley, MS.

JONES, JOHN,
62 Sandy Creek Rd, Gympie, Queensland 4570, AUSTRALIA, Phone: 07-54838731, jaj36@bigpond.com
Specialties: Straight knives, gents folders and folders. **Patterns:** Hunters, Bowies, and art knives. **Technical:** Grinds 440C, AT34, Damasteel. **Prices:** $250 to $2000. **Remarks:** Using knives and collectibles. Prefer natural materials. Full-time maker. **Mark:** Jones in script and year of manufacture.

JONES, JOHN A,
779 SW 131 Hwy, Holden, MO 64040, Phone: 816-850-4318
Specialties: Working, using knives. Hunters, skinners and fighters. **Technical:** Grinds D2, O1, 440C, 1095. Prefers forging; creates own Damascus. File working on most blades. **Prices:** $50 to $500. **Remarks:** Part-time maker; first knife sold in 1996. Doing business as Old John Knives. **Mark:** OLD JOHN and serial number.

JONES, ROGER MUDBONE,
GREENMAN WORKSHOP, 320 Prussia Rd, Waverly, OH 45690, Phone: 740-739-4562, greenmanworkshop@yahoo.com
Specialties: Working in cutlery to suit working woodsman and fine collector. **Patterns:** Bowies, hunters, folders, hatchets in both period and modern style, scale miniatures a specialty. **Technical:** All cutlery hand forged to shape with traditional methods; multiple quench and draws, limited Damascus production hand carves wildlife and historic themes in stag/antler/ivory, full line of functional and high art leather. All work sole authorship. **Prices:** $50 to $5000 **Remarks:** Full-time maker/first knife sold in 1979. **Mark:** Stamped R. Jones hand made or hand engraved sig. W/Bowie knife mark.

K

K B S, KNIVES,
RSD 181, North Castlemaine, Vic 3450, AUSTRALIA, Phone: 0011 61 3 54 705864, Fax: 0011 61 3 54 706233
Specialties: Bowies, daggers and miniatures. **Patterns:** Art daggers, traditional Bowies, fancy folders and miniatures. **Technical:** Hollow or flat grind, most steels. **Prices:** $200 to $600+. **Remarks:** Full-time maker; first knife sold in 1983. **Mark:** Initials and address in Southern Cross motif.

KACZOR, TOM,
375 Wharncliffe Rd N, Upper London, Ont., CANADA N6G 1E4, Phone: 519-645-7640

KAGAWA, KOICHI,
1556 Horiyamashita, Hatano-Shi, Kanagawa, JAPAN
　　Specialties: Fancy high-tech straight knives and folders to customer specs. Patterns: Hunters, locking folders and slip-joints. Technical: Uses 440C and ATS-34. Prices: $500 to $2000; some to $20,000. Remarks: Part-time maker; first knife sold in 1986. Mark: First initial, last name-YOKOHAMA.

KAIN, CHARLES,
KAIN DESIGNS, 1736 E. Maynard Dr., Indianapolis, IN 46227, Phone: 317-781-9549, Fax: 317-781-8521, charles@kaincustomknives.com; Web: www.kaincustomknives.com
　　Specialties: Unique Damascus art folders. Patterns: Any. Technical: Specialized & patented mechanisms. Remarks: Unique knife & knife mechanism design. Mark: Kain and Signet stamp for unique pieces.

KAJIN, AL,
PO Box 1047, 342 South 6th Ave, Forsyth, MT 59327, Phone: 406-346-2442, kajinknives@cablemt.net
　　Specialties: Utility/working knives, hunters, kitchen cutlery. Produces own Damascus steel from 15N20 and 1084 and cable. Forges 52100, 5160, 1084, 15N20 and O1. Stock removal ATS-34, D2, O1, and L6. Patterns: All types, especially like to work with customer on their designs. Technical: Maker since 1989. ABS member since 1995. Does own differential heat treating, cryogenic soaking when appropriate. Does all leather work. Prices: Stock removal starts at $250. Forged blades and Damascus starts at $300. Kitchen cutlery starts at $100. Remarks: Likes to use exotic woods. Mark: Interlocked AK on forged blades, etched stylized Kajin in outline of Montana on stock removal knives.

KANDA, MICHIO,
7-32-5 Shinzutumi-cho, Shunan-shi, Yamaguchi 7460033, JAPAN, Phone: 0834-62-1910, Fax: 011-81-83462-1910
　　Specialties: Fantasy knives of his design. Patterns: Animal knives. Technical: Grinds ATS-34. Prices: $300 to $3000. Remarks: Full-time maker; first knife sold in 1985. Doing business as Shusui Kanda. Mark: Last name inside "M."

KANKI, IWAO,
691-2 Tenjincho, Ono-City, Hyogo, JAPAN 675-1316, Phone: 07948-3-2555, Web: www.chiyozurusadahide.jp
　　Specialties: Plane, knife. Prices: Not determined yet. Remarks:Masters of traditional crafts designated by the Minister of International Trade and Industry (Japan). Mark: Chiyozuru Sadahide.

KANSEI, MATSUNO,
109-8 Uenomachi Nishikaiden, Gitu-city, JAPAN 501-1168, Phone: 81-58-234-8643
　　Specialties: Folders of original design. Patterns: LinerLock® folder. Technical: Grinds VG-10, Damascus. Prices: $350 to $2000. Remarks: Full-time maker. First knife sold in 1993. Mark: Name.

KANTER, MICHAEL,
ADAM MICHAEL KNIVES, 14550 West Honey Ln., New Berlin, WI 53151, Phone: 262-860-1136, mike@adammichaelknives.com; Web: www.adammichaelknives.com
　　Specialties: Fixed blades and folders. Patterns: Drop point hunters, Bowies and fighters. Technical: Jerry Rados Damascus, BG42, CPM, S60V and S30V. Prices: $375 and up. Remarks: Ivory, mammoth ivory, stabilized woods, and pearl handles. Mark: Engraved Adam Michael.

KARP, BOB,
PO Box 47304, Phoenix, AZ 85068, Phone: 602 870-1234
602 870-1234, Fax: 602-331-0283
　　Remarks: Bob Karp "Master of the Blade."

KATO, SHINICHI,
Rainbow Amalke 402, Ohoragnchi, Nakashidami, Moriyama-ku Nagoya, JAPAN 463-0002, Phone: 81-52-736-6032, skato-402@u0l.gate01.com
　　Specialties: Flat grind and hand finish. Patterns: Bowie, fighter. Hunting and folding knives. Technical: Hand forged,flat grind. Prices: $100 to $2000. Remarks: Part-time maker. Mark: Name.

KATSUMARO, SHISHIDO,
2-6-11 Kamiseno Aki-ku, Hiroshima, JAPAN, Phone: 090-3634-9054, Fax: 082-227-4438, shishido@d8.dion.ne.jp

KAUFFMAN, DAVE,
4 Clark Creek Loop, Montana City, MT 59634, Phone: 406-442-9328
　　Specialties: Field grade and exhibition grade hunting knives and ultra light folders. Patterns: Fighters, Bowies and drop-point hunters. Technical: S30V and SS Damascus. Prices: $155 to $1200. Remarks: Full-time maker; first knife sold in 1989. On the cover of Knives '94. Mark: First and last name, city and state.

KAWASAKI, AKIHISA,
11-8-9 Chome Minamiamachi, Suzurandai Kita-Ku, Kobe, JAPAN, Phone: 078-593-0418, Fax: 078-593-0418
　　Specialties: Working/using knives of his design. Patterns: Hunters, kit camp knives. Technical: Forges and grinds Molybdenum Panadium. Grinds ATS-34 and stainless steel. Uses Chinese Quince wood, desert ironwood and cow leather. Prices: $300 to $800; some to $1000. Remarks: Full-time maker. Mark: A.K.

KAY, J WALLACE,
332 Slab Bridge Rd, Liberty, SC 29657

KAZSUK, DAVID,
PO Box 39, Perris, CA 92572-0039, Phone: 909-780-2288, ddkaz@hotmail.com
　　Specialties: Hand forged. Prices: $150+. Mark: Last name.

KEARNEY, JAROD,
1505 Parkersburg Turnpike, Swoope, VA 24479, jarodkearney@gmail.com Web: www.jarodkearney.com
　　Patterns: Bowies, skinners, hunters, Japanese blades, Sgian Dubhs

KEESLAR, JOSEPH F,
391 Radio Rd, Almo, KY 42020, Phone: 270-753-7919, Fax: 270-753-7919, sjkees@apex.net
　　Specialties: Classic and contemporary Bowies, combat, hunters, daggers and folders. Patterns: Decorative filework, engraving and custom leather sheaths available. Technical: Forges 5160, 52100 and his own Damascus steel. Prices: $300 to $3000. Remarks: Full-time maker; first knife sold in 1976. ABS Master Smith. Mark: First and middle initials, last name in hammer, knife and anvil logo, M.S.

KEESLAR, STEVEN C,
115 Lane 216 Hamilton Lake, Hamilton, IN 46742, Phone: 260-488-3161, sskeeslar@hotmail.com
　　Specialties: Traditional working/using straight knives of his design and to customer specs. Patterns: Bowies, hunters, utility/camp knives. Technical: Forges 5160, files 52100 Damascus. Prices: $100 to $600; some to $1500. Remarks: Part-time maker; first knife sold in 1976. ABS member. Mark: Fox head in flames over Steven C. Keeslar.

KEETON, WILLIAM L,
6095 Rehobeth Rd SE, Laconia, IN 47135-9550, Phone: 812-969-2836, wlkeeton@hughes.net; Web: www.keetoncustomknives.com
　　Specialties: Plain and fancy working knives. Patterns: Hunters and fighters; locking folders and slip-joints. Names patterns after Kentucky Derby winners. Technical: Grinds any of the popular alloy steels. Prices: $185 to $8000. Remarks: Full-time maker; first knife sold in 1971. Mark: Logo of key.

KEHIAYAN, ALFREDO,
Cuzco 1455 Ing. Maschwitz, CP B1623GXU Buenos Aires, ARGENTINA, Phone: 54-03488-442212, Fax: 54-077-75-4493-5359, alfredo@kehiayan.com.ar; Web: www.kehiayan.com.ar
　　Specialties: Functional straight knives. Patterns: Utility knives, skinners, hunters and boots. Technical: Forges and grinds SAE 52.100, SAE 6180, SAE 9260, SAE 5160, 440C and ATS-34, titanium with nitride. All blades mirror-polished; makes leather sheath and wood cases. Prices: $70 to $800; some to $6000. Remarks: Full-time maker; first knife sold in 1983. Some knives are satin finish (utility knives). Mark: Name.

KEISUKE, GOTOH,
105 Cosumo-City, Otozu 202 Ohita-city, Ohita, JAPAN, Phone: 097-523-0750, k-u-an@ki.rim.or.jp

KELLER, BILL,
12211 Las Nubes, San Antonio, TX 78233, Phone: 210-653-6609
　　Specialties: Primarily folders, some fixed blades. Patterns: Autos, liner locks and hunters. Technical: Grinds stainless and Damascus. Prices: $400 to $1000, some to $4000. Remarks: Part-time maker, first knife sold 1995. Mark: Last name inside outline of Alamo.

KELLEY, GARY,
17485 SW Pheasant Lane, Aloha, OR 97006, Phone: 503-649-7867, garykelley@theblademaker.com; Web: wwwtheblademaker.com
　　Specialties: Primitive knives and blades. Patterns: Fur trade era rifleman's knives, tomahawks, and hunting knives. Technical: Hand-forges and precision investment casts. Prices: $35 to $125. Remarks: Family business. Doing business as The Blademaker. Mark: Fir tree logo.

KELLY, DAVE,
865 S. Shenandoah St., Los Angeles, CA 90035, Phone: 310-657-7121, dakcon@sbcglobal.net
　　Specialties: Collector and user one-of-a-kind (his design) fixed blades, liner lock folders, and leather sheaths. Patterns: Utility and hunting fixed blade knives with hand-sewn leather sheaths, Gentleman liner lock folders. Technical: Grinds carbon steels, hollow, convex, and flat. Offers clay differentially hardened blades, etched and polished. Uses Sambar stag, mammoth ivory, and high-grade burl woods. Hand-sewn leather sheaths for fixed blades and leather pouch sheaths for folders. Prices: $250 to $750, some higher. Remarks: Full-time maker, first knife made in 2003. Mark: First initial, last name with large K.

KELLY, STEVEN,
11407 Spotted Fawn Ln., Bigfork, MT 59911, Phone: 406-837-1489, www.skknives.com
　　Technical: Damascus from 1084 or 1080 and 15n20. 52100.

KELSEY, NATE,
3401 Cherry St, Anchorage, AK 99504, Phone: 907-360-4469, edgealaska@mac.com; Web: www.edgealaska.com
　　Specialties: Hand forges or stock removal traditional working knives of own or customer design. Forges own Damascus, makes custom leather sheaths, does fine engraving and scrimshaw. Technical: Forges 52100, 1084/15N20, 5160. Grinds ATS-34, 154CM. Prefers natural handle materials. Prices: $300

to \$1500. **Remarks:** Part-time maker since 1990. Member ABS, Arkansas Knifemakers Assoc. **Mark:** Name and city.

KELSO, JIM,
577 Collar Hill Rd, Worcester, VT 05682, Phone: 802-229-4254, Fax: 802-229-0595, kelsonmaker@gmail.com; Web:www.jimkelso.com
Specialties: Fancy high-art straight knives and folders that mix Eastern and Western influences. Only uses own designs. **Patterns:** Daggers, swords and locking folders. **Technical:** Grinds only custom Damascus. Works with top Damascus bladesmiths. **Prices:** \$6000 to \$20,000. **Remarks:** Full-time maker; first knife sold in 1980. **Mark:** Stylized initials.

KEMP, LAWRENCE,
8503 Water Tower Rd, Ooltewah, TN 37363, Phone: 423-344-2357, larry@kempknives.com Web: www.kempknives.com
Specialties: Bowies, hunters and working knives. **Patterns:** Bowies, camp knives, hunters and skinners. **Technical:** Forges carbon steel, and his own Damascus. **Prices:** \$250 to \$1500. **Remarks:** Part-time maker, first knife sold in 1991. ABS Journeyman Smith since 2006. **Mark:** L.A. Kemp.

KENNEDY JR., BILL,
PO Box 850431, Yukon, OK 73085, Phone: 405-354-9150
Specialties: Working straight knives and folders. **Patterns:** Hunters, minis, fishing, and pocket knives. **Technical:** Grinds D2, 440C, ATS-34, BG42. **Prices:** \$110 and up. **Remarks:** Part-time maker; first knife sold in 1980. **Mark:** Last name and year made.

KERANEN, PAUL,
4122 S. E. Shiloh Ct., Tacumseh, KS 66542, Phone: 785-220-2141, paul@pkknives.com Web: www.pkknives.com
Specialties: Specializes in Japanese style knives and swords. Most clay tempered with hamon. **Patterns:** Does bowies, fighters and hunters. **Technical:** Forges and grinds carbons steel only. Make my own Damascus. **Prices:** \$75 to \$800. **Mark:** PK etched.

KERN, R W,
20824 Texas Trail W, San Antonio, TX 78257-1602, Phone: 210-698-2549, rkern@ev1.net
Specialties: Damascus, straight and folders. **Patterns:** Hunters, Bowies and folders. **Technical:** Grinds ATS-34, 440C and BG42. Forges own Damascus. **Prices:** \$200 and up. **Remarks:** First knives 1980; retired; work as time permits. Member ABS, Texas Knifemaker and Collectors Association. **Mark:** Outline of Alamo with kern over outline.

KEYES, DAN,
6688 King St, Chino, CA 91710, Phone: 909-628-8329

KEYES, GEOFF P.,
13027 Odell Rd NE, Duvall, WA 98019, Phone: 425-844-0758, 5ef@polarisfarm.com; Web: www5elementsforge.com
Specialties: Working grade fixed blades, 19th century style gents knives. **Patterns:** Fixed blades, your design or mine. **Technical:** Hnad-forged 5160, 1084, and own Damascus. **Prices:** \$200 and up. **Remarks:** Geoff Keyes DBA 5 Elements Forge, ABS Journeyman Smith. **Mark:** Early mark KEYES etched in script. New mark as of 2009: pressed GPKeyes.

KHALSA, JOT SINGH,
368 Village St, Millis, MA 02054, Phone: 508-376-8162, Fax: 508-532-0517, jotkhalsa@comcast.net; Web: www.khalsakirpans.com, www.lifeknives.com, and www.thekhalsaraj.com
Specialties: Liner locks, one-of-a-kind daggers, swords, and kirpans (Sikh daggers) all original designs. **Technical:** Forges own Damascus, uses others high quality Damascus including stainless, and grinds stainless steels. Uses natural handle materials frequently unusual minerals. Pieces are frequently engraved and more recently carved. **Prices:** Start at \$700.

KHARLAMOV, YURI,
Oboronnay 46, 2, Tula, 300007, RUSSIA
Specialties: Classic, fancy and traditional knives of his design. **Patterns:** Daggers and hunters. **Technical:** Forges only Damascus with nickel. Uses natural handle materials; engraves on metal, carves on nut-tree; silver and pearl inlays. **Prices:** \$600 to \$2380; some to \$4000. **Remarks:** Full-time maker; first knife sold in 1988. **Mark:** Initials.

KI, SHIVA,
5222 Ritterman Ave, Baton Rouge, LA 70805, Phone: 225-356-7274, shivakicustomknives@netzero.net; Web: www.shivakicustomknives.com
Specialties: Working straight knives and folders. **Patterns:** Emphasis on personal defense knives, martial arts weapons. **Technical:** Forges and grinds; makes own Damascus; prefers natural handle materials. **Prices:** \$550 to \$10,000. **Remarks:** Full-time maker; first knife sold in 1981. **Mark:** Name with logo.

KIEFER, TONY,
112 Chateaugay Dr, Pataskala, OH 43062, Phone: 740-927-6910
Specialties: Traditional working and using straight knives in standard patterns. **Patterns:** Bowies, fighters and hunters. **Technical:** Grinds 440C and D2; forges D2. Flat-grinds Bowies; hollow-grinds drop-point and trailing-point hunters. **Prices:** \$110 to \$300; some to \$200. **Remarks:** Spare-time maker; first knife sold in 1988. **Mark:** Last name.

KILBY, KEITH,
1902 29th St, Cody, WY 82414, Phone: 307-587-2732
Specialties: Works with all designs. **Patterns:** Mostly Bowies, camp knives and hunters of his design. **Technical:** Forges 52100, 5160, 1095, Damascus

and mosaic Damascus. **Prices:** \$250 to \$3500. **Remarks:** Part-time maker; first knife sold in 1974. Doing business as Foxwood Forge. **Mark:** Name.

KILEY, MIKE AND JANDY,
ROCKING K KNIVES, 1325 Florida, Chino Valley, AZ 86323, Phone: 928-910-2647
Specialties: Period knives for cowboy action shooters and mountain men. **Patterns:** Bowies, drop-point hunters, skinners, sheepsfoot blades and spear points. **Technical:** Steels are 1095, 0-1, Damascus and others upon request. Handles include all types of wood, with cocobolo, ironwood, rosewood, maple and bacote being favorites as well as buffalo horn, stag, elk antler, mammoth ivory, giraffe boon, sheep horn and camel bone. **Prices:** \$100 to \$500 depending on style and materials. Hand-tooled leather sheaths by Jan and Mike. **Mark:** Stylized K on one side; Kiley on the other.

KILPATRICK, CHRISTIAN A,
6925 Mitchell Ct, Citrus Hieghts, CA 95610, Phone: 916-729-0733, crimsonkil@gmail.com; Web:www.crimsonknives.com
Specialties: All forged weapons (no firearms) from ancient to modern. All blades produced are first and foremost useable tools, and secondly but no less importantly, artistic expressions. **Patterns:** Hunters, bowies, daggers, swords, axes, spears, boot knives, bird knives, ethnic blades and historical reproductions. Customer designs welcome. **Technical:** Forges and grinds, makes own Damascus. Does file work. **Prices:** \$125 to \$3200. **Remarks:** 26 year part time maker. First knife sold in 2002.

KIMBERLEY, RICHARD L.,
86-B Arroyo Hondo Rd, Santa Fe, NM 87508, Phone: 505-820-2727
Specialties: Fixed-blade and period knives. **Technical:** O1, 52100, 9260 steels. **Remarks:** Member ABS. Marketed under "Kimberleys of Santa Fe." **Mark:** "By D. KIMBERLEY SANTA FE NM."

KIMSEY, KEVIN,
198 Cass White Rd. NW, Cartersville, GA 30121, Phone: 770-387-0779 and 770-655-8879
Specialties: Tactical fixed blades and folders. **Patterns:** Fighters, folders, hunters and utility knives. **Technical:** Grinds 440C, ATS-34 and D2 carbon. **Prices:** \$100 to \$400; some to \$600. **Remarks:** Three-time *Blade* magazine award winner, knifemaker since 1983. **Mark:** Rafter and stylized KK.

KING, BILL,
14830 Shaw Rd, Tampa, FL 33625, Phone: 813-961-3455, billkingknives@yahoo.com
Specialties: Folders, lockbacks, liner locks, automatics and stud openers. **Patterns:** Wide varieties; folders. **Technical:** ATS-34 and some Damascus; single and double grinds. Offers filework and jewel embellishment; nickel-silver Damascus and mokume bolsters. **Prices:** \$150 to \$475; some to \$850. **Remarks:** Full-time maker; first knife sold in 1976. All titanium fitting on liner-locks; screw or rivet construction on lock-backs. **Mark:** Last name in crown.

KING, FRED,
430 Grassdale Rd, Cartersville, GA 30120, Phone: 770-382-8478, Web: http://www.fking83264@aol.com
Specialties: Fancy and embellished working straight knives and folders. **Patterns:** Hunters, Bowies and fighters. **Technical:** Grinds ATS-34 and D2; forges 5160 and Damascus. Offers filework. **Prices:** \$100 to \$3500. **Remarks:** Spare-time maker; first knife sold in 1984. **Mark:** Kings Edge.

KING, JASON M,
5170 Rockenham Rd, St. George, KS 66423, Phone: 785-494-8377, Web: www.jasonmkingknives.com
Specialties: Working and using straight knives of his design and sometimes to customer specs. Some slip joint and lockback folders. **Patterns:** Hunters, Bowies, tacticals, fighters; some miniatures. **Technical:** Grinds D2, 440C and other Damascus. **Prices:** \$75 to \$200; some up to \$500. **Remarks:** First knife sold in 1998. Likes to use height quality stabilized wood. **Mark:** JMK.

KING JR., HARVEY G,
32170 Hwy K4, Alta Vista, KS 66834, Phone: 785-499-5207, Web: www.harveykingknives.com
Specialties: Traditional working and using knives of his design and to customer specs. **Patterns:** Hunters, Bowies and fillet knives. **Technical:** Grinds O1, A2 and D2. Prefers natural handle materials; offers leatherwork. **Prices:** Start at \$100. **Remarks:** Part-time maker; first knife sold in 1988. **Mark:** Name, city, state, and serial number.

KINKER, MIKE,
8755 E County Rd 50 N, Greensburg, IN 47240, Phone: 812-663-5277, Fax: 812-662-8131, mokinker@hsonline.net
Specialties: Working/using knives, straight knives. Starting to make folders. Your design. **Patterns:** Boots, daggers, hunters, skinners, hatchets. **Technical:** Grind 440C and ATS-34, others if required. Damascus, dovetail bolsters, jeweled blade. **Prices:** \$125 to 375; some to \$1000. **Remarks:** Part-time maker; first knife sold in 1991. Doing business as Kinker Knives. **Mark:** Kinker and Kinker plus year.

KINNIKIN, TODD,
EUREKA FORGE, 7 Capper Dr., Pacific, MO 63069-3603, Phone: 314-938-6248
Specialties: Mosaic Damascus. **Patterns:** Hunters, fighters, folders and automatics. **Technical:** Forges own mosaic Damascus with tool steel Damascus edge. Prefers natural, fossil and artifact handle materials. **Prices:** \$1200 to \$2400. **Remarks:** Full-time maker; first knife sold in 1994. **Mark:** Initials connected.

KIOUS, JOE,
1015 Ridge Pointe Rd, Kerrville, TX 78028, Phone: 830-367-2277, kious@hctc.net
Specialties: Investment-quality interframe and bolstered folders. Patterns: Folder specialist, all types. Technical: Both stainless and non-stainless Damascus. Also uses CPM 154CM, M4, and CPM D2. Prices: $1300 to $5000; some to $10,000. Remarks: Full-time maker; first knife sold in 1969. Mark: Last name, city and state or last name only.

KIRK, RAY,
PO Box 1445, Tahlequah, OK 74465, Phone: 918-456-1519, ray@rakerknives.com; Web: www.rakerknives.com
Specialties: Folders, skinners fighters, and Bowies. Patterns: Neck knives and small hunters and skinners. Technical: Forges all knives from 52100 and own Damascus. Prices: $65 to $3000. Remarks: Started forging in 1989; makes own Damascus. Does custom steel rolling. Has some 52100 and Damascus in custom flat bar 52100 for sale Mark: Stamped "Raker" on blade.

KITSMILLER, JERRY,
67277 Las Vegas Dr, Montrose, CO 81401, Phone: 970-249-4290
Specialties: Working straight knives in standard patterns. Patterns: Hunters, boots. Technical: Grinds ATS-34 and 440C only. Prices: $75 to $200; some to $300. Remarks: Spare-time maker; first knife sold in 1984. Mark: JandS Knives.

KLAASEE, TINUS,
PO Box 10221, George 6530, SOUTH AFRICA
Specialties: Hunters, skinners and utility knives. Patterns: Uses own designs and client specs. Technical: N690 stainless steel 440C Damascus. Prices: $700 and up. Remarks: Use only indigenous materials. Hardwood, horns and ivory. Makes his own sheaths and boxes. Mark: Initials and sur name over warthog.

KNAPP, MARK,
Mark Knapp Custom Knives, 1971 Fox Ave, Fairbanks, AK 99701, Phone: 907-452-7477, info@markknappcustomknives.com; Web: www.markknappcustomknives.com
Specialties: Mosaic handles of exotic natural materials from Alaska and around the world. Folders, fixed blades, full and hidden tangs. Patterns: Folders, hunters, skinners, and camp knives. Technical: Forges own Damascus, uses both forging and stock removal with ATS-34, 154CM, stainless Damascus, carbon steel and carbon Damascus. Prices: $800-$3000. Remarks: Full time maker, sold first knife in 2000. Mark: Mark Knapp Custom Knives Fairbanks, AK.

KNAPTON, CHRIS C.,
76 Summerland Dr., Henderson, Auckland, New Zealand, Phone: 098-353-598, knappo@xtra.co.nz
Specialties: Working and fancy straight knives of his own design. Patterns: Utility, hunters, skinners, Persian, Japanese style, all full tang. Technical: Predominate knife steel 12C27, also in use CPM154. High class natural and synthetic handle materials used. All blades made via the stock removal method and flat ground. Prices: $180 - $450; some higher. Remarks: Part-time maker. Mark: Stylized letter K and country name.

KNICKMEYER, HANK,
6300 Crosscreek, Cedar Hill, MO 63016, Phone: 636-285-3210
Specialties: Complex mosaic Damascus constructions. Patterns: Fixed blades, swords, folders and automatics. Technical: Mosaic Damascus with all tool steel Damascus edges. Prices: $500 to $2000; some $3000 and higher. Remarks: Part-time maker; first knife sold in 1989. Doing business as Dutch Creek Forge and Foundry. Mark: Initials connected.

KNICKMEYER, KURT,
6344 Crosscreek, Cedar Hill, MO 63016, Phone: 314-274-0481

KNIGHT, JASON,
110 Paradise Pond Ln, Harleyville, SC 29448, Phone: 843-452-1163, jasonknightknives.com
Specialties: Bowies. Patterns: Bowies and anything from history or his own design. Technical: 1084, 5160, O1, 52102, Damascus/forged blades. Prices: $200 and up. Remarks: Bladesmith. Mark: KNIGHT.

KNIPSCHIELD, TERRY,
808 12th Ave NE, Rochester, MN 55906, Phone: 507-288-7829, terry@knipknives.com; Web: www.knipknives.com
Specialties: Folders and fixed blades and leather working knives. Patterns: Variations of traditional patterns and his own new designs. Technical: Stock removal. Grinds CPM-154CM, ATS-34, stainless Damascus, 01. Prices: $60 to $1200 and higher for upscale folders. Mark: Etchd logo on blade, KNIP with shield image.

KNIPSTEIN, R C (JOE),
731 N Fielder, Arlington, TX 76012, Phone: 817-265-0573;817-265-2021, Fax: 817-265-3410
Specialties: Traditional pattern folders along with custom designs. Patterns: Hunters, Bowies, folders, fighters, utility knives. Technical: Grinds 440C, D2, 154CM and ATS-34. Natural handle materials and full tangs are standard. Prices: Start at $300. Remarks: Part-time maker; first knife sold in 1989. Mark: Last name.

KNOTT, STEVE,
KNOTT KNIVES, 203 Wild Rose, Guyton, GA 31312, Phone: 912-772-7655
Technical: Uses ATS-34/440C and some commercial Damascus, single and double grinds with mirror or satin finishes. Patters: Hunters, boot knives, Bowies, and tantos, slip joint and lock-back folders. Uses a wide variety of handle materials to include ironwood, coca-bola and colored stabilized wood, also horn, bone and ivory upon customer request. Remarks: First knife sold in 1991. Part-time maker.

KNOWLES, SHAWN,
750 Townsbury Rd, Great Meadows, NJ 07838, Phone: 973-670-3307, skcustomknives@gmail.com Web: shawnknowlescustomknives.com

KNUTH, JOSEPH E,
3307 Lookout Dr, Rockford, Il 61109, Phone: 815 874-9597
Specialties: High-art working straight knives of his design or to customer specs. Patterns: Daggers, fighters and swords. Technical: Grinds 440C, ATS-34 and D2. Prices: $150 to $1500; some to $15,000. Remarks: Full-time maker; first knife sold in 1989. Mark: Initials on bolster face.

KOHLS, JERRY,
N4725 Oak Rd, Princeton, WI 54968, Phone: 920-295-3648
Specialties: Working knives and period pieces. Patterns: Hunters-boots and Bowies, your designs or his. Technical: Grinds, ATS-34 440c 154CM and 1095 and commercial Damascus. Remarks: Part-time maker. Mark: Last name.

KOJETIN, W,
20 Bapaume Rd Delville, Germiston 1401, SOUTH AFRICA, Phone: 27118733305/mobile 27836256208
Specialties: High-art and working straight knives of all designs. Patterns: Daggers, hunters and his own Man hunter Bowie. Technical: Grinds D2 and ATS-34; forges and grinds 440B/C. Offers "wrap-around" pava and abalone handles, scrolled wood or ivory, stacked filework and setting of faceted semi-precious stones. Prices: $185 to $600; some to $11,000. Remarks: Spare-time maker; first knife sold in 1962. Mark: Billy K.

KOLITZ, ROBERT,
W9342 Canary Rd, Beaver Dam, WI 53916, Phone: 920-887-1287
Specialties: Working straight knives to customer specs. Patterns: Bowies, hunters, bird and trout knives, boots. Technical: Grinds O1, 440C; commercial Damascus. Prices: $50 to $100; some to $500. Remarks: Spare-time maker; first knife sold in 1979. Mark: Last initial.

KOMMER, RUSS,
4609 35th Ave N, Fargo, ND 58102, Phone: 701-281-1826, russkommer@yahoo.com Web: www.russkommerknives.com
Specialties: Working straight knives with the outdoorsman in mind. Patterns: Hunters, semi-skinners, fighters, folders and utility knives, art knives. Technical: Hollow-grinds ATS-34, 440C and 440V. Prices: $125 to $850; some to $3000. Remarks: Full-time maker; first knife sold in 1995. Mark: Bear paw—full name, city and state or full name and state.

KOPP, TODD M,
PO Box 3474, Apache Jct., AZ 85217, Phone: 480-983-6143, tmkopp@msn.com
Specialties: Classic and traditional straight knives. Fluted handled daggers. Patterns: Bowies, boots, daggers, fighters, hunters, swords and folders. Technical: Grinds 5160, 440C, ATS-34. All Damascus steels, or customers choice. Some engraving and filework. Prices: $200 to $1200; some to $4000. Remarks: Part-time maker; first knife sold in 1989. Mark: Last name in Old English, some others name, city and state.

KOSTER, STEVEN C,
16261 Gentry Ln, Huntington Beach, CA 92647, Phone: 714-840-8621, Fax: Cell: 714-907-7250, kosterknives@verizon.net Web: www.kosterhandforgedknives.com
Specialties: Walking sticks, hand axes, tomahawks. Technical: Use 5160, 52100, 1084, 1095 steels. Prices: $200 to $1000. Remarks: Wood and leather sheaths with silver furniture. ABS Journeyman 2003. California knifemakers member. Mark: Koster squeezed between lines.

KOVACIK, ROBERT,
Erenburgova 23, 98401 Lucenec, SLOVAKIA, Phone: 00421474332566 Mobil:00421470907644800, Fax: 00421470907644800, kovacikart@gmail.com Web: www.robertkovacik.com
Specialties: Engraved hunting knives, guns engraved; Knifemakers. Technical: Fixed blades, folder knives, miniatures. Prices: $350 to $20,000 U.S. Mark: R.

KOVAR, EUGENE,
2626 W 98th St., Evergreen Park, IL 60642, Phone: 708-636-3724/708-790-4115, baldemaster333@aol.com
Specialties: One-of-a-kind miniature knives only. Patterns: Fancy to fantasy miniature knives; knife pendants and tie tacks. Technical: Files and grinds nails, nickel-silver and sterling silver. Prices: $5 to $35; some to $100. Mark: GK.

KOYAMA, CAPTAIN BUNSHICHI,
3-23 Shirako-cho, Nakamura-ku, Nagoya City 453-0817, JAPAN, Phone: 052-461-7070, Fax: 052-461-7070
Specialties: Innovative folding knife. Patterns: General purpose one hand. Technical: Grinds ATS-34 and Damascus. Prices: $400 to $900; some to $1500. Remarks: Part-time maker; first knife sold in 1994. Mark: Captain B. Koyama and the shoulder straps of CAPTAIN.

KRAFT, STEVE,
408 NE 11th St, Abilene, KS 67410, Phone: 785-263-1411
Specialties: Folders, lockbacks, scale release auto, push button auto. **Patterns:** Hunters, boot knives and fighters. **Technical:** Grinds ATS-34, Damascus; uses titanium, pearl, ivory etc. **Prices:** $500 to $2500. **Remarks:** Part-time maker; first knife sold in 1984. **Mark:** Kraft.

KRAPP, DENNY,
1826 Windsor Oak Dr, Apopka, FL 32703, Phone: 407-880-7115
Specialties: Fantasy and working straight knives of his design. **Patterns:** Hunters, fighters and utility/camp knives. **Technical:** Grinds ATS-34 and 440C. **Prices:** $85 to $300; some to $800. **Remarks:** Spare-time maker; first knife sold in 1988. **Mark:** Last name.

KRAUSE, ROY W,
22412 Corteville, St. Clair Shores, MI 48081, Phone: 810-296-3995, Fax: 810-296-2663
Specialties: Military and law enforcement/Japanese-style knives and swords. **Patterns:** Combat and back-up, Bowies, fighters, boot knives, daggers, tantos, wakazashis and katanas. **Technical:** Grinds ATS-34, A2, D2, 1045, O1 and commercial Damascus; differentially hardened Japanese-style blades. **Prices:** Moderate to upscale. **Remarks:** Full-time maker. **Mark:** Last name on traditional knives; initials in Japanese characters on Japanese-style knives.

KREGER, THOMAS,
1996 Dry Branch Rd., Lugoff, SC 29078, Phone: 803-438-4221, tdkreger@bellsouth.net
Specialties: South Carolina/George Herron style working/using knives. Customer designs considered. **Patterns:** Hunters, skinners, fillet, liner lock folders, kitchen, and camp knives. **Technical:** Hollow and flat grinds of ATS-34, CPM154CM, and 5160. **Prices:** $100 and up. **Remarks:** Full-time maker. President of the South Carolina Association of Knifemakers 2002-06. **Mark:** TDKreger.

KREH, LEFTY,
210 Wichersham Way, "Cockeysville", MD 21030

KREIBICH, DONALD L.,
1638 Commonwealth Circle, Reno, NV 89503, Phone: 775-746-0533, dmkreno@sbcglobal.net
Specialties: Working straight knives in standard patterns. **Patterns:** Bowies, boots and daggers; camp and fishing knives. **Technical:** Grinds 440C, 154CM and ATS-34; likes integrals. **Prices:** $100 to $200; some to $500. **Remarks:** Part-time maker; first knife sold in 1980. **Mark:** First and middle initials, last name.

KRESSLER, D F,
Mittelweg 31 i, D-28832 Achim, GERMANY, Phone: 49-4202765742, Fax: 49-042 02/7657 41, info@kresslerknives.com; Web: www.kresslerknives.com
Specialties: High-tech integral and interframe knives. **Patterns:** Hunters, fighters, daggers. **Technical:** Grinds new state-of-the-art steels; prefers natural handle materials. **Prices:** Upscale. **Mark:** Name in logo.

KRETSINGER JR., PHILIP W,
17536 Bakersville Rd, Boonsboro, MD 21713, Phone: 301-432-6771
Specialties: Fancy and traditional period pieces. **Patterns:** Hunters, Bowies, camp knives, daggers, carvers, fighters. **Technical:** Forges W2, 5160 and his own Damascus. **Prices:** Start at $200. **Remarks:** Full-time knifemaker. **Mark:** Name.

KUBASEK, JOHN A,
74 Northhampton St, Easthampton, MA 01027, Phone: 413-527-7917, jaknife01@verizon.net
Specialties: Left- and right-handed LinerLock® folders of his design or to customer specs. Also new knives made with Ripcord patent. **Patterns:** Fighters, tantos, drop points, survival knives, neck knives and belt buckle knives. **Technical:** Grinds 154CM, S30 and Damascus. **Prices:** $395 to $1500. **Remarks:** Part-time maker; first knife sold in 1985. **Mark:** Name and address etched.

KUKULKA, WOLFGANG,
Golf Tower 2, Apt. 107, Greens, PO BOX 126229, Dubai, United Arab Emirates, Phone: 00971-50-2201047, wolfgang.kukulka@hotmail.com
Specialties: Fully handmade from various steels: Damascus Steel, Japanese Steel, 1.2842, 1.2379, K110, K360, M390 microclean **Patterns:** Handles made from stabilized wood, different hard woods, horn and various materials **Technical:** Hardness of blades: 58-67 HRC.

L

LADD, JIM S,
1120 Helen, Deer Park, TX 77536, Phone: 713-479-7286
Specialties: Working knives and period pieces. **Patterns:** Hunters, boots and Bowies plus other straight knives. **Technical:** Grinds D2, 440C and 154CM. **Prices:** $125 to $225; some to $550. **Remarks:** Part-time maker; first knife sold in 1965. Doing business as The Tinker. **Mark:** First and middle initials, last name.

LADD, JIMMIE LEE,
1120 Helen, Deer Park, TX 77536, Phone: 713-479-7186
Specialties: Working knives. **Patterns:** Hunters, skinners and utility knives. **Technical:** Grinds 440C and D2. **Prices:** $75 to $225. **Remarks:** First knife sold in 1979. **Mark:** First and middle initials, last name.

LAINSON, TONY,
114 Park Ave, Council Bluffs, IA 51503, Phone: 712-322-5222
Specialties: Working straight knives, liner locking knives. **Technical:** Grinds 154CM, ATS-34, 440C buys Damascus. Handle materials include Micarta, carbon fiber G-10 ivory pearl and bone. **Prices:** $95 to $600. **Remarks:** Part-time maker; first knife sold in 1987. **Mark:** Name and state.

LAIRSON SR., JERRY,
H C 68 Box 970, Ringold, OK 74754, Phone: 580-876-3426, bladesmt@brightok.net; Web: www.lairson-custom-knives.net
Specialties: Damascus collector grade knives & high performance field grade hunters & cutting competition knives. **Patterns:** Damascus, random, raindrop, ladder, twist and others. **Technical:** All knives hammer forged. Mar Tempering **Prices:** Field grade knives $300. Collector grade $400 & up. **Mark:** Lairson. **Remarks:** Makes any style knife but prefer fighters and hunters. ABS Mastersmith, AKA member, KGA member. Cutting competition competitor.

LAKE, RON,
3360 Bendix Ave, Eugene, OR 97401, Phone: 541-484-2683
Specialties: High-tech working knives; inventor of the modern interframe folder. **Patterns:** Hunters, boots, etc.; locking folders. **Technical:** Grinds 154CM and ATS-34. Patented interframe with special lock release tab. **Prices:** $2200 to $3000; some higher. **Remarks:** Full-time maker; first knife sold in 1966. **Mark:** Last name.

LALA, PAULO RICARDO P AND LALA, ROBERTO P.,
R Daniel Martins 636, Centro, Presidente Prudente, SP-19031-260, BRAZIL, Phone: 0182-210125, Web: http://www.orbita.starmedia/~korth
Specialties: Straight knives and folders of all designs to customer specs. **Patterns:** Bowies, daggers fighters, hunters and utility knives. **Technical:** Grinds and forges D6, 440C, high-carbon steels and Damascus. **Prices:** $60 to $400; some higher. **Remarks:** Full-time makers; first knife sold in 1991. All stainless steel blades are ultra sub-zero quenched. **Mark:** Sword carved on top of anvil under KORTH.

LAMB, CURTIS J,
3336 Louisiana Ter, Ottawa, KS 66067-8996, Phone: 785-242-6657

LAMBERT, JARRELL D,
2321 FM 2982, Granado, TX 77962, Phone: 512-771-3744
Specialties: Traditional working and using straight knives of his design and to customer specs. **Patterns:** Bowies, hunters, tantos and utility/camp knives. **Technical:** Grinds ATS-34; forges W2 and his own Damascus. Makes own sheaths. **Prices:** $80 to $600; some to $1000. **Remarks:** Part-time maker; first knife sold in 1982. **Mark:** Etched first and middle initials, last name; or stamped last name.

LAMBERT, KIRBY,
536 College Ave, Regina Saskatchewan S4N X3, CANADA, kirby@lambertknives.com; Web: www.lambertknives.com
Specialties: Tactical/utility folders. Tactical/utility Japanese style fixed blades. **Prices:** $200 to $1500 U.S. **Remarks:** Full-time maker since 2002. **Mark:** Black widow spider and last name Lambert.

LAMEY, ROBERT M,
15800 Lamey Dr, Biloxi, MS 39532, Phone: 228-396-9066, Fax: 228-396-9022, rmlamey@ametro.net; Web: www.lameyknives.com
Specialties: Bowies, fighters, hard use knives. **Patterns:** Bowies, fighters, hunters and camp knives. **Technical:** Forged and stock removal. **Prices:** $125 to $350. **Remarks:** Lifetime reconditioning; will build to customer designs, specializing in hard use, affordable knives. **Mark:** LAMEY.

LAMPSON, FRANK G,
3215 Saddle Bag Circle, Rimrock, AZ 86335, Phone: 928-567-7395, fglampson@yahoo.com
Specialties: Working folders; one-of-a-kinds. **Patterns:** Folders, hunters, utility knives, fillet knives and Bowies. **Technical:** Grinds ATS-34, 440C and 154CM. **Prices:** $100 to $750; some to $3500. **Remarks:** Full-time maker; first knife sold in 1971. **Mark:** Name in fish logo.

LANCASTER, C G,
No 2 Schoonwinkel St, Parys, Free State, SOUTH AFRICA, Phone: 0568112090
Specialties: High-tech working and using knives of his design and to customer specs. **Patterns:** Hunters, locking folders and utility/camp knives. **Technical:** Grinds Sandvik 12C27, 440C and D2. Offers anodized titanium bolsters. **Prices:** $450 to $750; some to $1500. **Remarks:** Part-time maker; first knife sold in 1990. **Mark:** Etched logo.

LANCE, BILL,
PO Box 4427, Eagle River, AK 99577, Phone: 907-694-1487
Specialties: Ooloos and working straight knives; limited issue sets. **Patterns:** Several ulu patterns, drop-point skinners. **Technical:** Uses ATS-34, Vascomax 350; ivory, horn and high-class wood handles. **Prices:** $85 to $300; art sets to $3000. **Remarks:** First knife sold in 1981. **Mark:** Last name over a lance.

LANDERS, JOHN,
758 Welcome Rd, Newnan, GA 30263, Phone: 404-253-5719
Specialties: High-art working straight knives and folders of his design. **Patterns:** Hunters, fighters and slip-joint folders. **Technical:** Grinds 440C, ATS-34, 154CM and commercial Damascus. **Prices:** $85 to $250; some to $500. **Remarks:** Part-time maker; first knife sold in 1989. **Mark:** Last name.

LANER, DEAN,
1480 Fourth St, Susanville, CA 96130, Phone: 530-310-1917, laner54knives@yahoo.com
Specialties: Fancy working fixed blades, of his design, will do custom orders. **Patterns:** Hunters, fighters, combat, fishing, Bowies, utility, and kitchen knives. **Technical:** Grinds 154CM, ATS-34, D2, buys Damascus. Does mostly hollow grinding, some flat grinds. Uses Micarta, mastodon ivory, hippo ivory, exotic woods. Loves doing spacer work on stick tang knives. A leather or kydes sheath comes with every knife. Life-time warrantee and free sharpening also. **Remarks:** Part-time maker, first knife sold in 1993. **Prices:** $150 to $1000. **Mark:** LANER CUSTOM KNIVES over D next to a tree.

LANG, DAVID,
6153 Cumulus Circle, Kearns, UT 84118, Phone: 801-809-1241, dknifeguy@msn.com
Specialties: Hunters, Fighters, Push Daggers, Upscale Art Knives, Folders. **Technical:** Flat grind, hollow grind, hand carving, casting. **Remarks:** Will work from my designs or to your specifications. I have been making knives 10 years and have gleaned help from Jerry Johnson, Steven Rapp, Earl Black, Steven Johnson, and many others. **Prices:** $225 - $3000. **Mark:** Dland over UTAH.

LANGLEY, GENE H,
1022 N. Price Rd, Florence, SC 29506, Phone: 843-669-3150
Specialties: Working knives in standard patterns. **Patterns:** Hunters, boots, fighters, locking folders and slip-joints. **Technical:** Grinds 440C, 154CM and ATS-34. **Prices:** $125 to $450; some to $1000. **Remarks:** Part-time maker; first knife sold in 1979. **Mark:** Name.

LANGLEY, MICK,
1015 Centre Crescent, Qualicum Beach, B.C., CANADA V9K 2G6, Phone: 250-752-4261
Specialties: Period pieces and working knives. **Patterns:** Bowies, push daggers, fighters, boots. Some folding lockers. **Technical:** Forges 5160, 1084, W2 and his own Damascus. **Prices:** $250 to $2500; some to $4500. **Remarks:** Full-time maker, first knife sold in 1977. **Mark:** Langley with M.S. (for ABS Master Smith)

LANKTON, SCOTT,
8065 Jackson Rd. R-11, Ann Arbor, MI 48103, Phone: 313-426-3735
Specialties: Pattern welded swords, krisses and Viking period pieces. **Patterns:** One-of-a-kind. **Technical:** Forges W2, L6 nickel and other steels. **Prices:** $600 to $12,000. **Remarks:** Part-time bladesmith, full-time smith; first knife sold in 1976. **Mark:** Last name logo.

LAOISLAV, SANTA-LASKY,
Hrochot 264, 976 37 Hrochot, Okres Banska Bystrica, Slovensko (Slovakia), Phone: +421-905-544-280, santa.ladislav@pobox.sk; Web: www.lasky.sk
Specialties: Damascus hunters, daggers and swords. **Patterns:** Carious Damascus patterns. **Prices:** $300 to $6000 U.S. **Mark:** L or Lasky.

LAPEN, CHARLES,
Box 529, W. Brookfield, MA 01585
Specialties: Chef's knives for the culinary artist. **Patterns:** Camp knives, Japanese-style swords and wood working tools, hunters. **Technical:** Forges 1075, car spring and his own Damascus. Favors narrow and Japanese tangs. **Prices:** $200 to $400; some to $2000. **Remarks:** Part-time maker; first knife sold in 1972. **Mark:** Last name.

LAPLANTE, BRETT,
4545 CR412, McKinney, TX 75071, Phone: 972-838-9191, blap007@aol.com
Specialties: Working straight knives and folders to customer specs. **Patterns:** Survival knives, Bowies, skinners, hunters. **Technical:** Grinds D2 and 440C. Heat-treats. **Prices:** $200 to $800. **Remarks:** Part-time maker; first knife sold in 1987. **Mark:** Last name in Canadian maple leaf logo.

LARAMIE, MARK,
301 McCain St., Raeford, NC 28376, Phone: 978-502-2726, mark@malknives.com; Web: www.malknives.com
Specialties: Traditional fancy & art knives. **Patterns:** Slips, back-lock L/L, automatics, single and multi blades. **Technical:** Free hand ground blades of D2, 440, and Damascus. **Mark:** M.A.L. Knives w/fish logo.

LARGIN, KEN,
KELGIN KNIVES, 104 Knife Works Ln, Sevierville, TN 37876, Phone: 765-969-5012, kelginfinecutlery@hotmail.com; Web: wwwkelgin.com
Specialties: Retired from general knife making. Only take limited orders in meteorite Damascus or solid meteorite blades. **Patterns:** Any. **Technical:** Stock removal or forged. **Prices:** $500 & up. **Remarks:** Runs the Kelgin Knife Makers Co-op at Smoky Mtn. Knife Works. **Mark:** K.C. Largin (Kelgin mark retired in 2004).

LARK, DAVID,
6641 Schneider Rd., Kingsley, MI 49649, Phone: 231-342-1076, dblark58@yahoo.com
Specialties: Traditional straight knives, art knives, folders. **Patterns:** All types. **Technical:** Grinds all types of knife making steel and makes damascus. **Prices:** $600 and up. **Remarks:** Full-time maker, custom riflemaker, and engraver. **Mark:** Lark in script and DBL on engraving.

LARSON, RICHARD,
549 E Hawkeye Ave, Turlock, CA 95380, Phone: 209-668-1615, lebatardknives@aol.com
Specialties: Sound working knives, lightweight folders, practical tactical knives. **Patterns:** Hunters, trout and bird knives, fish fillet knives, Bowies, tactical sheath knives, one- and two-blade folders. **Technical:** Grinds ATS-34, A2, D2, CPM 3V and commercial. Damascus; forges and grinds 52100, O1 and 1095. Machines folder frames from aircraft aluminum. **Prices:** $40 to $650. **Remarks:** Full-time maker. First knife made in 1974. Offers knife repair, restoration and sharpening. All knives are serial numbered and registered in the name of original purchaser. **Mark:** Stamped last name or etched logo of last name, city, and state.

LARY, ED,
951 Rangeline Rd, Mosinee, WI 54455, laryblades@hotmail.com
Specialties: Upscale hunters and art knives with display presentations. **Patterns:** Hunters, period pieces. **Technical:** Grinds all steels, heat treats, fancy file work and engraving. **Prices:** Upscale. **Remarks:** Full-time maker since 1974. **Mark:** Hand engraved "Ed Lary" in script.

LAURENT, KERMIT,
1812 Acadia Dr, LaPlace, LA 70068, Phone: 504-652-5629
Specialties: Traditional and working straight knives and folders of his design. **Patterns:** Bowies, hunters, utilities and folders. **Technical:** Forges own Damascus, plus uses most tool steels and stainless. Specializes in altering cable patterns. Uses stabilized handle materials, especially select exotic woods. **Prices:** $100 to $2500; some to $50,000. **Remarks:** Full-time maker; first knife sold in 1982. Doing business as Kermit's Knife Works. Favorite material is meteorite Damascus. **Mark:** First name.

LAWRENCE, ALTON,
201 W Stillwell, De Queen, AR 71832, Phone: 870-642-7643, Fax: 870-642-4023, uncle21@riversidemachine.net; Web: riversidemachine.net
Specialties: Classic straight knives and folders to customer specs. **Patterns:** Bowies, hunters, folders and utility/camp knives. **Technical:** Forges 5160, 1095, 1084, Damascus and railroad spikes. **Prices:** Start at $100. **Remarks:** Part-time maker; first knife sold in 1988. **Mark:** Last name inside fish symbol.

LAY, L J,
602 Mimosa Dr, Burkburnett, TX 76354, Phone: 940-569-1329
Specialties: Working straight knives in standard patterns; some period pieces. **Patterns:** Drop-point hunters, Bowies and fighters. **Technical:** Grinds ATS-34 to mirror finish; likes Micarta handles. **Prices:** Moderate. **Remarks:** Full-time maker; first knife sold in 1985. **Mark:** Name or name with ram head and city or stamp L J Lay.

LAY, R J (BOB),
Box 1225, Logan Lake, B.C., CANADA V0K 1W0, Phone: 250-523-9923, Fax: SAME, rjlay@telus.net
Specialties: Traditional-styled, fancy straight knifes of his design. Specializing in hunters. **Patterns:** Bowies, fighters and hunters. **Technical:** Grinds 440C, ATS-34, S30V, CPM-154CM. Uses exotic handle and spacer material. File cut, prefers narrow tang. Sheaths available. **Price:** $200 to $500, some to $5000. **Remarks:** Full-time maker, first knife sold in 1976. Doing business as Lay's Custom Knives. **Mark:** Signature acid etched.

LEACH, MIKE J,
5377 W Grand Blanc Rd., Swartz Creek, MI 48473, Phone: 810-655-4850
Specialties: Fancy working knives. **Patterns:** Hunters, fighters, Bowies and heavy-duty knives; slip-joint folders and integral straight patterns. **Technical:** Grinds D2, 440C and 154CM; buys Damascus. **Prices:** Start at $300. **Remarks:** Full-time maker; first knife sold in 1952. **Mark:** First initial, last name.

LEAVITT JR., EARL F,
Pleasant Cove Rd Box 306, E. Boothbay, ME 04544, Phone: 207-633-3210
Specialties: 1500-1870 working straight knives and fighters; pole arms. **Patterns:** Historically significant knives, classic/modern custom designs. **Technical:** Flat grinds O1, heat-treats. Filework available. **Prices:** $90 to $350; some to $1000. **Remarks:** Full-time maker; first knife sold in 1981. Doing business as Old Colony Manufactory. **Mark:** Initials in oval.

LEBATARD, PAUL M,
14700 Old River Rd, Vancleave, MS 39565, Phone: 228-826-4137, Fax: Cell phone: 228-238-7461, lebatardknives@aol.com
Specialties: Sound working hunting and fillet knives, folding knives, practical tactical knives. **Patterns:** Hunters, trout and bird knives, fish fillet knives, kitchen knives, Bowies, tactical sheath knives, one- and two-blade folders. **Technical:** Grinds ATS-34, D-2, CPM 3-V, CPM-154CM, and commercial Damascus; forges and grinds 1095, 01, and 52100. **Prices:** $75 to $650; some to $1200. **Remarks:** Full-time maker, first knife made in 1974. Charter member Gulf Coast Custom Knifemakers; Voting member Knifemaker's Guild. **Mark:** Stamped last name, or etched logo of last name, city, and state. **Other:** All knives are serial numbered and registered in the name of the original purchaser.

LEBER, HEINZ,
Box 446, Hudson's Hope, B.C., CANADA V0C 1V0, Phone: 250-783-5304
Specialties: Working straight knives of his design. **Patterns:** 20 models, from capers to Bowies. **Technical:** Hollow-grinds D2 and M2 steel; mirror-finishes and full tang only. Likes moose, elk, stone sheep for handles. **Prices:** $175 to $1000. **Remarks:** Full-time maker; first knife sold in 1975. **Mark:** Initials connected.

LECK, DAL,
Box 1054, Hayden, CO 81639, Phone: 970-276-3663
Specialties: Classic, traditional and working knives of his design and in standard patterns; period pieces. **Patterns:** Boots, daggers, fighters, hunters and push daggers. **Technical:** Forges O1 and 5160; makes his own Damascus. **Prices:** $175 to $700; some to $1500. **Remarks:** Part-time maker; first knife sold in 1990. Doing business as The Moonlight Smithy. **Mark:** Stamped: hammer and anvil with initials.

LEE, RANDY,
PO Box 1873, St. Johns, AZ 85936, Phone: 928-337-2594, Fax: 928-337-5002, randyleeknives@yahoo.com; Web.www.randyleeknives.com
Specialties: Traditional working and using straight knives of his design. **Patterns:** Bowies, fighters, hunters, daggers. **Technical:** Grinds ATS-34, 440C Damascus, and 154CPM. Offers sheaths. **Prices:** $325 to $2500. **Remarks:** Part-time maker; first knife sold in 1979. **Mark:** Full name, city, state.

LELAND, STEVE,
2300 Sir Francis Drake Blvd, Fairfax, CA 94930-1118, Phone: 415-457-0318, Fax: 415-457-0995, Web: www.stephenleland@comcast.net
Specialties: Traditional and working straight knives and folders of his design. **Patterns:** Hunters, fighters, Bowies, chefs. **Technical:** Grinds O1, ATS-34 and 440C. Does own heat treat. Makes nickel silver sheaths. **Prices:** $150 to $750; some to $1500. **Remarks:** Part-time maker; first knife sold in 1987. Doing business as Leland Handmade Knives. **Mark:** Last name.

LEMCKE, JIM L,
10649 Haddington Ste 180, Houston, TX 77043, Phone: 888-461-8632, Fax: 713-461-8221, jimll@hal-pc.org; Web: www.texasknife.com
Specialties: Large supply of custom ground and factory finished blades; knife kits; leather sheaths; in-house heat treating and cryogenic tempering; exotic handle material (wood, ivory, oosik, horn, stabilized woods); machines and supplies for knifemaking; polishing and finishing supplies; heat treat ovens; etching equipment; bar, sheet and rod material (brass, stainless steel, nickel silver); titanium sheet material. Catalog. $4.

LENNON, DALE,
459 County Rd 1554, Alba, TX 75410, Phone: 903-765-2392, devildaddy1@netzero.net
Specialties: Working / using knives. **Patterns:** Hunters, fighters and Bowies. **Technical:** Grinds high carbon steels, ATS-34, forges some. **Prices:** Starts at $120. **Remarks:** Part-time maker, first knife sold in 2000. **Mark:** Last name.

LEONARD, RANDY JOE,
188 Newton Rd, Sarepta, LA 71071, Phone: 318-994-2712

LEONE, NICK,
361 County Road 944, Pontoon Beach, IL 62040, Phone: 618-792-0734, nickleone@sbcglobal.net
Specialties: 18th century period straight knives. **Patterns:** Fighters, daggers, bowies. Besides period pieces makes modern designs. **Technical:** Forges 5160, W2, O1, 1098, 52100 and his own Damascus. **Prices:** $100 to $1000; some to $3500. **Remarks:** Full-time maker; first knife sold in 1987. Doing business as Anvil Head Forge. **Mark:** AHF, Leone, NL

LERCH, MATTHEW,
N88 W23462 North Lisbon Rd, Sussex, WI 53089, Phone: 262-246-6362, Web: www.lerchcustomknives.com
Specialties: Folders and folders with special mechanisms. **Patterns:** Interframe and integral folders; lock backs, assisted openers, side locks, button locks and liner locks. **Technical:** Grinds ATS-34, 1095, 440 and Damascus. Offers filework and embellished bolsters. **Prices:** $900 and up. **Remarks:** Part-time maker; first knife sold in 1995. **Mark:** Last name.

LEU, POHAN,
PO BOX 15423, Rio Rancho, NM 87174, Phone: 949-300-6412, pohanleu@hotmail.com Web: www.leucustom.com
Specialties: Japanese influenced fixed blades made to your cutom specifications. Knives and swords. A2 tool steel, Stock Removal. **Prices:** $180 and up. **Remarks:** Full-time; first knife sold in 2003. **Mark:** LEU or PL.

LEVENGOOD, BILL,
15011 Otto Rd, Tampa, FL 33624, Phone: 813-961-5688, bill.levengood@verison.net; Web: www.levengoodknives.com
Specialties: Working straight knives and folders. **Patterns:** Hunters, Bowies, folders and collector pieces. **Technical:** Grinds ATS-34, S-30V, CPM-154 and Damascus. **Prices:** $175 to $1500. **Remarks:** Full time maker; first knife sold in 1983. **Mark:** Last name, city, state.

LEVIN, JACK,
7216 Bay Pkwy, Brooklyn, NY 11204, Phone: 718-232-8574, levinknives@ymail.com
Specialties: Folders with mechanisms.

LEVINE, BOB,
101 Westwood Dr, Tullahoma, TN 37388, Phone: 931-454-9943, levineknives@msn.com
Specialties: Working left- and right-handed LinerLock® folders. **Patterns:** Hunters and folders. **Technical:** Grinds ATS-34, 440C, D2, O1 and some Damascus; hollow and some flat grinds. Uses fossil ivory, Micarta and exotic woods. Provides custom leather sheath with each fixed knife. **Prices:** Starting at $275. **Remarks:** Full-time maker; first knife sold in 1984. Voting member Knifemakers Guild, German Messermaker Guild. **Mark:** Name and logo.

LEWIS, BILL,
PO Box 63, Riverside, IA 52327, Phone: 319-629-5574, wildbill37@geticonnect.com
Specialties: Folders of all kinds including those made from one-piece of white tail antler with or without the crown. **Patterns:** Hunters, folding hunters, fillet, Bowies, push daggers, etc. **Prices:** $20 to $200. **Remarks:** Full-time maker; first knife sold in 1978. **Mark:** W.E.L.

LEWIS, MIKE,
21 Pleasant Hill Dr, DeBary, FL 32713, Phone: 386-753-0936, dragonsteel@prodigy.net
Specialties: Traditional straight knives. **Patterns:** Swords and daggers. **Technical:** Grinds 440C, ATS-34 and 5160. Frequently uses cast bronze and cast nickel guards and pommels. **Prices:** $100 to $750. **Remarks:** Part-time maker; first knife sold in 1988. **Mark:** Dragon Steel and serial number.

LEWIS, TOM R,
1613 Standpipe Rd, Carlsbad, NM 88220, Phone: 575-885-3616, lewisknives@carlsbadnm.com; Web: www.cavemen.net/lewisknives/
Specialties: Traditional working straight knives. **Patterns:** Outdoor knives, hunting knives and Bowies. **Technical:** Grinds ATS-34 forges 5168 and O1. Makes wire, pattern welded and chainsaw Damascus. **Prices:** $140 to $1500. **Remarks:** Part-time maker; first knife sold in 1980. Doing business as TR Lewis Handmade Knives. **Mark:** Lewis family crest.

LICATA, STEVEN,
LICATA CUSTOM KNIVES, 146 Wilson St. 1st Floor, Boonton, NJ 07005, Phone: 973-588-4909, kniveslicata@aol.com; Web: www.licataknives.com
Specialties: Fantasy swords and knives. One-of-a-kind sculptures in steel. **Prices:** $200 to $25,000.

LIEBENBERG, ANDRE,
8 Hilma Rd, Bordeauxrandburg 2196, SOUTH AFRICA, Phone: 011-787-2303
Specialties: High-art straight knives. **Patterns:** Daggers, fighters and swords. **Technical:** Grinds 440C and 12C27. **Prices:** $250 to $500; some $4000 and higher. Giraffe bone handles with semi-precious stones. **Remarks:** Spare-time maker; first knife sold in 1990. **Mark:** Initials.

LIEGEY, KENNETH R,
288 Carney Dr, Millwood, WV 25262, Phone: 304-273-9545
Specialties: Traditional working/using straight knives of his design and to customer specs. **Patterns:** Hunters, utility/camp knives, miniatures. **Technical:** Grinds 440C. **Prices:** $75 to $150; some to $300. **Remarks:** Spare-time maker; first knife sold in 1977. **Mark:** First and middle initials, last name.

LIGHTFOOT, GREG,
RR #2, Kitscoty, AB, CANADA T0B 2P0, Phone: 780-846-2812; 780-800-1061, Pitbull@lightfootknives.com; Web: www.lightfootknives.com
Specialties: Stainless steel and Damascus. **Patterns:** Boots, fighters and locking folders. **Technical:** Grinds BG-42, 440C, D2, CPM steels, Stellite 6K. Offers engraving. **Prices:** $500 to $2000. **Remarks:** Full-time maker; first knife sold in 1988. Doing business as Lightfoot Knives. **Mark:** Shark with Lightfoot Knives below.

LIKARICH, STEVE,
PO Box 961, Colfax, CA 95713, Phone: 530-346-8480
Specialties: Fancy working knives; art knives of his design. **Patterns:** Hunters, fighters and art knives of his design. **Technical:** Grinds ATS-34, 154CM and 440C; likes high polishes and filework. **Prices:** $200 to $2000; some higher. **Remarks:** Full-time maker; first knife sold in 1987. **Mark:** Name.

LIN, MARCUS,
4616 Rollando Cr., Rolling Hills Estates, CA 90274, Phone: 808-636-0977, marcuslin7@gmail.com; Web: www.linknives.com
Specialties: Working and collector knives. **Patterns:** Hard use folding knives. Camp, hunting, utility knives, daggers, tantos, bowies and integrals. **Technical:** Stock removal. Stonewashed, beadblasted, handrubbed or mirror polished finishes available. Working with A2, D2, M2, ATS-34, CPM alloys and Damasteel. **Prices:** $125 - $1500. **Remarks:** Part-time maker since 2004. Mentored by: R.W. Loveless and Jim Merritt. **Mark:** LIN CALIFORNIA with Chinese characters on left side for "Forest."

LINKLATER, STEVE,
8 Cossar Dr, Aurora, Ont., CANADA L4G 3N8, Phone: 905-727-8929, knifman@sympatico.ca
Specialties: Traditional working/using straight knives and folders of his design. **Patterns:** Fighters, hunters and locking folders. **Technical:** Grinds ATS-34, 440V and D2. **Prices:** $125 to $350; some to $600. **Remarks:** Part-time maker; first knife sold in 1987. Doing business as Links Knives. **Mark:** LINKS.

LISCH, DAVID K,
9239 8th Ave. SW, Seattle, WA 98106, Phone: 206-919-5431, Web: www.davidlisch.com
Specialties: One-of-a-kind collectibles, straight knives of own design and to customer specs. **Patterns:** Hunters, skinners, Bowies, and fighters. **Technical:** Forges all his own Damascus under 360-pound air hammer. Forges and chisels wrought iron, pure iron, and bronze butt caps. **Prices:** Starting at $350. **Remarks:** Full-time blacksmith, part-time bladesmith. **Mark:** D. Lisch J.S.

LISTER JR., WELDON E,
9140 Sailfish Dr, Boerne, TX 78006, Phone: 210-981-2210
Specialties: One-of-a-kind fancy and embellished folders. **Patterns:** Locking and slip-joint folders. **Technical:** Commercial Damascus and O1. All knives embellished. Engraves, inlays, carves and scrimshaws. **Prices:** Upscale. **Remarks:** Spare-time maker; first knife sold in 1991. **Mark:** Last name.

LITTLE, GARY M,
HC84 Box 10301, PO Box 156, Broadbent, OR 97414, Phone: 503-572-2656
Specialties: Fancy working knives. **Patterns:** Hunters, tantos, Bowies, axes and buckskinners; locking folders and interframes. **Technical:** Forges and grinds O1, L6, 1095; makes his own Damascus; bronze fittings. **Prices:** $85 to $300; some to $2500. **Remarks:** Full-time maker; first knife sold in 1979. Doing business as Conklin Meadows Forge. **Mark:** Name, city and state.

LITTLE, LARRY,
1A Cranberry Ln, Spencer, MA 01562, Phone: 508-885-2301, littcran@aol.com
Specialties: Working straight knives of his design or to customer specs. Likes Scagel-style. **Patterns:** Hunters, fighters, Bowies, folders. **Technical:** Grinds and forges L6, O1, 5160, 1095, 1080. Prefers natural handle material especially antler. Uses nickel silver. Makes own heavy duty leather sheath. **Prices:** Start at $125. **Remarks:** Part-time maker. First knife sold in 1985. Offers knife repairs. **Mark:** Little on one side, LL brand on the other.

LIVELY, TIM AND MARIAN,
PO Box 1172, Marble Falls, TX 78654, Web: www.livelyknives.com
Specialties: Multi-cultural primitive knives of their design on speculation. **Patterns:** Old world designs. **Technical:** Hand forges using ancient techniques without electricity; hammer finish. **Prices:** High. **Remarks:** Retired 2009. Offers knifemaking DVD online. **Mark:** Last name.

LIVESAY, NEWT,
3306 S. Dogwood St, Siloam Springs, AR 72761, Phone: 479-549-3356, Fax: 479-549-3357, newt@newtlivesay.com; Web:www.newtlivesay.com
Specialties: Combat utility knives, hunting knives, titanium knives, swords, axes, KYDWX sheaths for knives and pistols, custom orders.

LIVINGSTON, ROBERT C,
PO Box 6, Murphy, NC 28906, Phone: 704-837-4155
Specialties: Art letter openers to working straight knives. **Patterns:** Minis to machetes. **Technical:** Forges and grinds most steels. **Prices:** Start at $20. **Remarks:** Full-time maker; first knife sold in 1988. Doing business as Mystik Knifeworks. **Mark:** MYSTIK.

LOCKETT, STERLING,
527 E Amherst Dr, Burbank, CA 91504, Phone: 818-846-5799
Specialties: Working straight knives and folders to customer specs. **Patterns:** Hunters and fighters. **Technical:** Grinds. **Prices:** Moderate. **Remarks:** Spare-time maker. **Mark:** Name, city with hearts.

LOERCHNER, WOLFGANG,
WOLFE FINE KNIVES, PO Box 255, Bayfield, Ont., CANADA N0M 1G0, Phone: 519-565-2196
Specialties: Traditional straight knives, mostly ornate. **Patterns:** Small swords, daggers and stilettos; locking folders and miniatures. **Technical:** Grinds D2, 440C and 154CM; all knives hand-filed and flat-ground. **Prices:** Vary. **Remarks:** Part-time maker; first knife sold in 1983. Doing business as Wolfe Fine Knives. **Mark:** WOLFE.

LONEWOLF, J AGUIRRE,
481 Hwy 105, Demorest, GA 30535, Phone: 706-754-4660, Fax: 706-754-8470, lonewolfandsons@windstream.net, Web: www.knivesbylonewolf.com www.scrimshawbywei.com
Specialties: High-art working and using straight knives of his design. **Patterns:** Bowies, hunters, utility/camp knives and fine steel blades. **Technical:** Forges Damascus and high-carbon steel. Most knives have hand-carved moose antler handles. **Prices:** $55 to $500; some to $2000. **Remarks:** Full-time maker; first knife sold in 1980. Doing business as Lonewolf and Sons LLC. **Mark:** Stamp.

LONG, GLENN A,
10090 SW 186th Ave, Dunnellon, FL 34432, Phone: 352-489-4272, galong99@att.net
Specialties: Classic working and using straight knives of his design and to customer specs. **Patterns:** Hunters, Bowies, utility. **Technical:** Grinds 440C D2 and 440V. **Prices:** $85 to $300; some to $800. **Remarks:** Part time maker; first knife sold in 1990. **Mark:** Last name inside diamond.

LONGWORTH, DAVE,
PO Box 222, Neville, OH 45156, Phone: 513-876-2372
Specialties: High-tech working knives. **Patterns:** Locking folders, hunters, fighters and elaborate daggers. **Technical:** Grinds O1, ATS-34, 440C; buys Damascus. **Prices:** $125 to $600; some higher. **Remarks:** Part-time maker; first knife sold in 1980. **Mark:** Last name.

LOOS, HENRY C,
210 Ingraham, New Hyde Park, NY 11040, Phone: 516-354-1943, hcloos@optonline.net
Specialties: Miniature fancy knives and period pieces of his design. **Patterns:** Bowies, daggers and swords. **Technical:** Grinds O1 and 440C. Uses sterling, 18K, rubies and emeralds. All knives come with handmade hardwood cases. **Prices:** $90 to $195; some to $250. **Remarks:** Spare-time maker; first knife sold in 1990. **Mark:** Script last initial.

LORO, GENE,
2457 State Route 93 NE, Crooksville, OH 43731, Phone: 740-982-4521, Fax: 740-982-1249, geney@aol.com
Specialties: Hand forged knives. **Patterns:** Damascus, Random, Ladder, Twist, etc. **Technical:** ABS Journeyman Smith. **Prices:** $200 and up. **Remarks:** Loro and hand forged by Gene Loro. **Mark:** Loro. Retired engineer.

LOTT, SHERRY,
1100 Legion Park Rd, Greensburg, KY 42743, Phone: 270-932-2212, info@greenriverleather.com
Specialties: One-of-a-kind, usually carved handles. **Patterns:** Art. **Technical:** Carbon steel, stock removal. **Prices:** Moderate. **Mark:** Sherry Lott. **Remarks:** First knife sold in 1994.

LOVE, ED,
19443 Mill Oak, San Antonio, TX 78258, Phone: 210-497-1021, Fax: 210-497-1021, annaedlove@sbcglobal.net
Specialties: Hunting, working knives and some art pieces. **Technical:** Grinds ATS-34, and 440C. **Prices:** $150 and up. **Remarks:** Part-time maker. First knife sold in 1980. **Mark:** Name in a weeping heart.

LOVESTRAND, SCHUYLER,
1136 19th St SW, Vero Beach, FL 32962, Phone: 772-778-0282, Fax: 772-466-1126, lovestranded@aol.com
Specialties: Fancy working straight knives of his design and to customer specs; unusual fossil ivories. **Patterns:** Hunters, fighters, Bowies and fishing knives. **Technical:** Grinds stainless steel. **Prices:** $450 and up. **Remarks:** Part-time maker; first knife sold in 1982. **Mark:** Name in logo.

LOVETT, MICHAEL,
PO Box 121, Mound, TX 76558, Phone: 254-865-9956, michaellovett@embarqmail.com
Specialties: The Loveless Connection Knives as per R.W. Loveless-Jim Merritt. **Patterns:** All Loveless Patterns and Original Lovett Patterns. **Technical:** Complicated double grinds and premium fit and finish. **Prices:** $1000 and up. **Remarks:** High degree of fit and finish - Authorized collection by R. W. Loveless **Mark:** Loveless Authorized football or double nude.

LOZIER, DON,
5394 SE 168th Ave, Ocklawaha, FL 32179, Phone: 352-625-3576
Specialties: Fancy and working straight knives of his design and in standard patterns. **Patterns:** Daggers, fighters, boot knives, and hunters. **Technical:** Grinds ATS-34, 440C and Damascus. Most pieces are highly embellished by notable artisans. Taking limited number of orders per annum. **Prices:** Start at $250; most are $1250 to $3000; some to $12,000. **Remarks:** Full-time maker. **Mark:** Name.

LUCHAK, BOB,
15705 Woodforest Blvd, Channelview, TX 77530, Phone: 281-452-1779
Specialties: Presentation knives; start of The Survivor series. **Patterns:** Skinners, Bowies, camp axes, steak knife sets and fillet knives. **Technical:** Grinds 440C. Offers electronic etching; filework. **Prices:** $50 to $1500. **Remarks:** Full-time maker; first knife sold in 1983. Doing business as Teddybear Knives. **Mark:** Full name, city and state with Teddybear logo.

LUCHINI, BOB,
1220 Dana Ave, Palo Alto, CA 94301, Phone: 650-321-8095, rwluchin@bechtel.com

LUCIE, JAMES R,
4191 E. Fruitport Rd., Fruitport, MI 49415, Phone: 231-865-6390, scagel@netonecom.net
Specialties: Hand-forges William Scagel-style knives. **Patterns:** Authentic scagel-style knives and miniatures. **Technical:** Forges 5160, 52100 and 1084 and forges his own pattern welded Damascus steel. **Prices:** Start at $750. **Remarks:** Full-time maker; first knife sold in 1975. Believes in sole authorship of his work. ABS Journeyman Smith. **Mark:** Scagel Kris with maker's name and address.

LUCKETT, BILL,
108 Amantes Ln, Weatherford, TX 76088, Phone: 817-594-9288, bill_luckett@hotmail.com Web: www.billluckettcustomknives.com
Specialties: Uniquely patterned robust straight knives. **Patterns:** Fighters, Bowies, hunters. **Technical:** 154CM stainless. **Prices:** $550 to $1500. **Remarks:** Part-time maker; first knife sold in 1975. Knifemakers Guild Member. **Mark:** Last name over Bowie logo.

LUDWIG, RICHARD O,
57-63 65 St, Maspeth, NY 11378, Phone: 718-497-5969
Specialties: Traditional working/using knives. **Patterns:** Boots, hunters and utility/camp knives folders. **Technical:** Grinds 440C, ATS-34 and BG42. File work on guards and handles; silver spacers. Offers scrimshaw. **Prices:** $325 to $400; some to $2000. **Remarks:** Full-time maker. **Mark:** Stamped first initial, last name, state.

LUI, RONALD M,
4042 Harding Ave, Honolulu, HI 96816, Phone: 808-734-7746
Specialties: Working straight knives and folders in standard patterns. **Patterns:** Hunters, boots and liner locks. **Technical:** Grinds 440C and ATS-34. **Prices:** $100 to $700. **Remarks:** Spare-time maker; first knife sold in 1988. **Mark:** Initials connected.

LUMAN, JAMES R,
Clear Creek Trail, Anaconda, MT 59711, Phone: 406-560-1461
Specialties: San Mai and composite end patterns. **Patterns:** Pool and eye Spirograph southwest composite patterns. **Technical:** All patterns with blued steel; all made by him. **Prices:** $200 to $800. **Mark:** Stock blade removal. Pattern welded steel. Bottom ricasso JRL.

LUNDSTROM, JAN-AKE,
Mastmostigen 8, 66010 Dals-Langed, SWEDEN, Phone: 0531-40270
Specialties: Viking swords, axes and knives in cooperation with handle makers. **Patterns:** All traditional-styles, especially swords and inlaid blades. **Technical:** Forges his own Damascus and laminated steel. **Prices:** $200 to $1000. **Remarks:** Full-time maker; first knife sold in 1985; collaborates with museums. **Mark:** Runic.

LUNDSTROM, TORBJORN (TOBBE),
Norrskenet 4, 83013 ARE, Sweden, 9lundstrm@telia.com Web: http://tobbeiare.se/site/

Specialties: Hunters and collectible knives. **Patterns:** Nordic-style hunters and art knives with unique materials such as mammoth and fossil walrus ivory. **Technical:** Uses forged blades by other makers, particularly Mattias Styrefors who mostly uses 15N20 and 20C steels and is a mosaic blacksmith. **Remarks:** First knife made in 1986.

LUNN, GAIL,
434 CR 1422, Mountain Home, AR 72653, Phone: 870-424-2662, gail@lunnknives.com; Web: www.lunnknives.com

Specialties: Fancy folders and double action autos, some straight blades. **Patterns:** One-of-a-kind, all types. **Technical:** Stock removal, hand made. **Prices:** $300 and up. **Remarks:** Fancy file work, exotic materials, inlays, stone etc. **Mark:** Name in script.

LUNN, LARRY A,
434 CR 1422, Mountain Home, AR 72653, Phone: 870-424-2662, larry@lunnknives.com; Web: www.lunnknives.com

Specialties: Fancy folders and double action autos; some straight blades. **Patterns:** All types; his own designs. **Technical:** Stock removal; commercial Damascus. **Prices:** $125 and up. **Remarks:** File work inlays and exotic materials. **Mark:** Name in script.

LUPOLE, JAMIE G,
KUMA KNIVES, 285 Main St., Kirkwood, NY 13795, Phone: 607-775-9368, jlupole@stny.rr.com

Specialties: Working and collector grade fixed blades, ethnic-styled blades. **Patterns:** Fighters, Bowies, tacticals, hunters, camp, utility, personal carry knives, some swords. **Technical:** Forges and grinds 10XX series and other high-carbon steels, grinds ATS-34 and 440C, will use just about every handle material available. **Prices:** $80 to $500 and up. **Remarks:** Part-time maker since 1999. **Marks:** "KUMA" hot stamped, name, city and state-etched, or "Daiguma saku" in kanji.

LUTZ, GREG,
127 Crescent Rd, Greenwood, SC 29646, Phone: 864-229-7340

Specialties: Working and using knives and period pieces of his design and to customer specs. **Patterns:** Fighters, hunters and swords. **Technical:** Forges 1095 and O1; grinds ATS-34. Differentially heat-treats forged blades; uses cryogenic treatment on ATS-34. **Prices:** $50 to $350; some to $1200. **Remarks:** Part-time maker; first knife sold in 1986. Doing business as Scorpion Forge. **Mark:** First initial, last name.

LYLE III, ERNEST L,
LYLE KNIVES, PO Box 1755, Chiefland, FL 32644, Phone: 352-490-6693, ernestlyle@msn.com

Specialties: Fancy period pieces; one-of-a-kind and limited editions. **Patterns:** Arabian/Persian influenced fighters, military knives, Bowies and Roman short swords; several styles of hunters. **Technical:** Grinds 440C, D2 and 154 CM. Engraves. **Prices:** $200 - $7500. **Remarks:** Full-time maker; first knife sold in 1972. **Mark:** Lyle Knives over Chiefland, Fla.

LYNCH, TAD,
140 Timberline Dr., Beebe, AR 72012, Phone: 501-626-1647, lynchknives@yahoo.com Web: lynchknives.com

Specialties: Forged fixed blades. **Patterns:** Bowies, choppers, fighters, hunters. **Technical:** Hand-forged W-2, 1084, 1095 clay quenched 52100, 5160. **Prices:** Starting at $250. **Remarks:** Part-time maker, also offers custom leather work via wife Amy Lynch. **Mark:** T.D. Lynch over anvil.

LYNN, ARTHUR,
29 Camino San Cristobal, Galisteo, NM 87540, Phone: 505-466-3541, lynnknives@aol.com

Specialties: Handforged Damascus knives. **Patterns:** Folders, hunters, Bowies, fighters, kitchen. **Technical:** Forges own Damascus. **Prices:** Moderate.

LYTTLE, BRIAN,
Box 5697, High River, AB, CANADA T1V 1M7, Phone: 403-558-3638, brian@lyttleknives.com; Web: www.lyttleknives.com

Specialties: Fancy working straight knives and folders; art knives. **Patterns:** Bowies, daggers, dirks, sgian dubhs, folders, dress knives, tantos, short swords. **Technical:** Forges Damascus steel; engraving; scrimshaw; heat-treating; classes. **Prices:** $450 to $15,000. **Remarks:** Full-time maker; first knife sold in 1983. **Mark:** Last name, country.

M

MACDONALD, DAVID,
2824 Hwy 47, Los Lunas, NM 87031, Phone: 505-866-5866

MACDONALD, JOHN,
9 David Dr, Raymond, NH 03077, Phone: 603-895-0918

Specialties: Working/using straight knives of his design and to customer specs. **Patterns:** Japanese cutlery, Bowies, hunters and working knives. **Technical:** Grinds O1, L6 and ATS-34. Swords have matching handles and scabbards with Japanese flair. **Prices:** $70 to $250; some to $500. **Remarks:** Part-time maker; first knife sold in 1988. Custom knife cases made from pine and exotic hardwoods for table display or wall hanging. Doing business as Mac the Knife. **Mark:** Initials.

MACKIE, JOHN,
13653 Lanning, Whittier, CA 90605, Phone: 562-945-6104

Specialties: Forged. **Patterns:** Bowie and camp knives. **Technical:** Attended ABS Bladesmith School. **Prices:** $75 to $500. **Mark:** JSM in a triangle.

MACKRILL, STEPHEN,
PO Box 1580, Pinegowrie, JHB 2123, SOUTH AFRICA, Phone: 27-11-474-7139, Fax: 27-11-474-7139, info@mackrill.co.za; Web: www.mackrill.net

Specialties: Art fancy, historical, collectors and corporate gifts cutlery. **Patterns:** Fighters, hunters, camp, custom lock back and LinerLock® folders. **Technical:** N690, 12C27, ATS-34, silver and gold inlay on handles; wooden and silver sheaths. **Prices:** $330 and upwards. **Remarks:** First knife sold in 1978. **Mark:** Mackrill fish with country of origin.

MADRULLI, MME JOELLE,
Residence Ste Catherine B1, Salon De Provence, FRANCE 13330

MAE, TAKAO,
1-119 1-4 Uenohigashi, Toyonaka, Osaka, JAPAN 560-0013, Phone: 81-6-6852-2758, Fax: 81-6-6481-1649, takamae@nifty.com

Remarks: Distinction stylish in art-forged blades, with lacquered ergonomic handles.

MAESTRI, PETER A,
S11251 Fairview Rd, Spring Green, WI 53588, Phone: 608-546-4481

Specialties: Working straight knives in standard patterns. **Patterns:** Camp and fishing knives, utility green-river-styled. **Technical:** Grinds 440C, 154CM and 440A. **Prices:** $15 to $45; some to $150. **Remarks:** Full-time maker; first knife sold in 1981. Provides professional cutler service to professional cutters. **Mark:** CARISOLO, MAESTRI BROS., or signature.

MAGEE, JIM,
741 S. Ohio St., Salina, KS 67401, Phone: 785-820-6928, jimmagee@cox.net

Specialties: Working and fancy folding knives. **Patterns:** Liner locking folders, favorite is his Persian. **Technical:** Grinds ATS-34, Devin Thomas & Eggerling Damascus, titanium. Liners Prefer mother-of-pearl handles. **Prices:** Start at $225 to $1200. **Remarks:** Part-time maker, first knife sold in 2001. Purveyor since 1982. Past president of the Professional Knifemakers Association **Mark:** Last name.

MAGRUDER, JASON,
, Talent, OR, Phone: 719-210-1579, belstain@hotmail.com; jason@magruderknives.com; web: MagruderKnives.com

Specialties: Unique and innovative designs combining the latest modern materials with traditional hand craftsmanship. **Patterns:** Fancy neck knives. Tactical gents folders. Working straight knives. **Technical:** Flats grinds CPM3v, CPM154, ATS34, 1080, and his own forged damascus. Hand carves carbon fiber, titanium, wood, ivory, and pearl handles. Filework and carving on blades. **Prices:** $150 and up. **Remarks:** Part-time maker; first knife sold in 2000. **Mark:** Last name.

MAHOMEDY, A R,
PO Box 76280, Marble Ray KZN, 4035, SOUTH AFRICA, Phone: +27 31 577 1451, arm-koknives@mweb.co.za; Web: www.arm-koknives.co.za

Specialties: Daggers and elegant folders of own design finished with finest exotic materials currently available. **Technical:** Via stock removal, grinds Damasteel, Damascus and the famous hardenable stainless steels. **Prices:** U.S. $650 and up. **Remarks:** Part-time maker. First knife sold in 1995. Voting member knifemakers guild of SA, FEGA member starting out Engraving. **Mark:** Initials A R M crowned with a "Minaret."

MAHOMEDY, HUMAYD A.R.,
PO BOX 76280, Marble Ray 4035, KZN, South Africa, Phone: +27 31 577 1451, arm-koknives@mweb.co.za

Specialties: Tactical folding and fixed blade knives. **Patterns:** Fighters, utilities, tacticals, folders and fixed blades, daggers, modern interpretation of Bowies. **Technical:** Stock-removal knives of Bohler N690, Bohler K110, Bohler K460, Sandvik 12C27, Sandvik RWL 34. Handle materials used are G10, Micarta, Cape Buffalo horn, Water Buffalo horn, Kudu horn, Gemsbok horn, Giraffe bone, Elephant ivory, Mammoth ivory, Arizona desert ironwood, stabilised and dyed burls. **Prices:** $250 - $1000. **Remarks:** First knife sold in 2002. Full-time knifemaker since 2002. First person of color making knives full-time in South Africa. Doing business as HARM EDGED TOOLS. **Mark:** HARM and arrow over EDGED TOOLS.

MAIENKNECHT, STANLEY,
38648 S R 800, Sardis, OH 43946

MAINES, JAY,
SUNRISE RIVER CUSTOM KNIVES, 5584 266th St., Wyoming, MN 55092, Phone: 651-462-5301, jaymaines@fronternet.net; Web: http://www.sunrisecustomknives.com

Specialties: Heavy duty working, classic and traditional fixed blades. Some high-tech and fancy embellished knives available. **Patterns:** Hunters, skinners, fillet, bowies tantos, boot daggers etc. etc. **Technical:** Hollow ground, stock removal blades of 440C, ATS-34 and CPM S-90V. Prefers natural handle materials, exotic hard woods, and stag, rams and buffalo horns. Offers dovetailed bolsters in brass, stainless steel and nickel silver. Custom sheaths from matching wood or hand-stitched from heavy duty water buffalo hide. **Prices:** Moderate to up-scale. **Remarks:** Part-time maker; first knife sold in 1992. Doing business as Sunrise River Custom Knives. Offers fixed blade knives repair and handle conversions. **Mark:** Full name under a Rising Sun logo.

MAISEY, ALAN,
PO Box 197, Vincentia 2540, NSW, AUSTRALIA, Phone: 2-4443 7829, tosanaji@excite.com

Specialties: Daggers, especially krisses; period pieces. Technical: Offers knives and finished blades in Damascus and nickel Damascus. Prices: $75 to $2000; some higher. Remarks: Part-time maker; provides complete restoration service for krisses. Trained by a Japanese Kris smith. Mark: None, triangle in a box, or three peaks.

MAKOTO, KUNITOMO,
3-3-18 Imazu-cho, Fukuyama-city, Hiroshima, JAPAN, Phone: 084-933-5874, kunitomo@po.iijnet.or.jp

MALABY, RAYMOND J,
835 Calhoun Ave, Juneau, AK 99801, Phone: 907-586-6981, Fax: 907-523-8031, malaby@gci.net

Specialties: Straight working knives. Patterns: Hunters, skiners, Bowies, and camp knives. Technical: Hand forged 1084, 5160, O1 and grinds ATS-34 stainless. Prices: $195 to $400. Remarks: First knife sold in 1994. Mark: First initial, last name, city, and state.

MALLETT, J.P.,
3952 San Felipe Rd., Santa Fe, NM 87507, Phone: 505-577-3355

Specialties: Deep hollow grinds with nice lines and file worked spines. Patterns: Makes own damascus. Raindrop, ladder, random, etc. Technical: Has been a grinder for many years. Prices: $100 - $2000. Remarks: Teaching bladesmithing classes beginning January, 2012. Mark: Mallett. Older models stamped M only.

MALLOY, JOE,
1039 Schwabe St, Freeland, PA 18224, Phone: 570-436-6416, jdmalloy@msn.com

Specialties: Working straight knives and lock back folders—plain and fancy—of his design. Patterns: Hunters, utility, Bowie, survival knives, folders. Technical: Grinds ATS-34, 440C, D2 and A2 and Damascus. Makes own leather and kydex sheaths. Prices: $100 to $1800. Remarks: Part-time maker; first knife sold in 1982. Mark: First and middle initials, last name, city and state.

MANARO, SAL,
10 Peri Ave., Holbrook, NY 11741, Phone: 631-737-1180, maker@manaroknives.com

Specialties: Tactical folders, bolstered titanium LinerLocks, handmade folders, and fixed blades with hand-checkered components. Technical: Compound grinds, hidden fasteners and welded components, with blade steels including CPM-154, damascus, Stellite, D2, S30V and O-1 by the stock-removal method of blade making. Prices: $500 and up. Remarks: Part-time maker, made first knife in 2001. Mark: Last name with arrowhead underline.

MANDT, JOE,
3735 Overlook Dr. NE, St. Petersburg, FL 33703, Phone: 813-244-3816, jmforge@mac.com

Specialties: Forged Bowies, camp knives, hunters, skinners, fighters, boot knives, military style field knives. Technical: Forges plain carbon steel and high carbon tool steels, including W2, 1084, 5160, O1, 9260, 15N20, cable Damascus, pattern welded Damascus, flat and convex grinds. Prefers natural handle materials, hand-rubbed finishes, and stainless low carbon steel, Damascus and wright iron fittings. Does own heat treat. Prices: $150 to $750. Remarks: Part-time maker, first knife sold in 206. Mark: "MANDT".

MANEKER, KENNETH,
RR 2, Galiano Island, B.C., CANADA V0N 1P0, Phone: 604-539-2084

Specialties: Working straight knives; period pieces. Patterns: Camp knives and hunters; French chef knives. Technical: Grinds 440C, 154CM and Vascowear. Prices: $50 to $200; some to $300. Remarks: Part-time maker; first knife sold in 1981. Doing business as Water Mountain Knives. Mark: Japanese Kanji of initials, plus glyph.

MANKEL, KENNETH,
7836 Cannonsburg Rd, PO Box 35, Cannonsburg, MI 49317, Phone: 616-874-6955, Fax: 616-8744-4053

MANLEY, DAVID W,
3270 Six Mile Hwy, Central, SC 29630, Phone: 864-654-1125, dmanleyknives@wmconnect.com

Specialties: Working straight knives of his design or to custom specs. Patterns: Hunters, boot and fighters. Technical: Grinds 440C and ATS-34. Prices: $60 to $250. Remarks: Part-time maker; first knife sold in 1994. Mark: First initial, last name, year and serial number.

MANN, MICHAEL L,
IDAHO KNIFE WORKS, PO Box 144, Spirit Lake, ID 83869, Phone: 509 994-9394, Web: www.idahoknifeworks.com

Specialties: Good working blades-historical reproduction, modern or custom design. Patterns: Cowboy Bowies, Mountain Man period blades, old-style folders, designer and maker of "The Cliff Knife", hunter knives, hand ax and fish fillet. Technical: High-carbon steel blades-hand forged 5160. Stock removed 15N20 steel. Also Damascus. Prices: $130 to $670+. Remarks: Made first knife in 1965. Full-time making knives as Idaho Knife Works since 1986. Functional as well as collectible. Each knife truly unique! Mark: Four mountain peaks are his initials MM.

MANN, TIM,
BLADEWORKS, PO Box 1196, Honokaa, HI 96727, Phone: 808-775-0949, Fax: 808-775-0949, birdman@shaka.com

Specialties: Hand-forged knives and swords. Patterns: Bowies, tantos, pesh kabz, daggers. Technical: Use 5160, 1050, 1075, 1095 and ATS-34 steels, cable Damascus. Prices: $200 to $800. Remarks: Just learning to forge Damascus. Mark: None yet.

MARAGNI, DAN,
RD 1 Box 106, Georgetown, NY 13072, Phone: 315-662-7490

Specialties: Heavy-duty working knives, some investor class. Patterns: Hunters, fighters and camp knives, some Scottish types. Technical: Forges W2 and his own Damascus; toughness and edge-holding a high priority. Prices: $125 to $500; some to $1000. Remarks: Full-time maker; first knife sold in 1975. Mark: Celtic initials in circle.

MARCHAND, RICK,
Wildertools, 681 Middleton Lane, Wheatley, Ontario N0P 2P0, Phone: 519-825-9726, rickmarchand@wildertools.com

Specialties: Specializing in multicultural, period stylized blades and accoutrements. Technical: Hand forged from 1070/84 and 5160 steel. Prices: $175 - $900. Remarks: 3 years full-time maker. ABS Apprentice Smith. Mark: Tang stamp: "MARCHAND" along with two Japanese-style characters resembling "W" and "M.".

MARINGER, TOM,
2692 Powell St., Springdale, AR 72764, maringer@arkansas.net; Web: shirepost.com/cutlery.

Specialties: Working straight and curved blades with stainless steel furniture and wire-wrapped handles. Patterns: Subhilts, daggers, boots, swords. Technical: Grinds D-2, A-2, ATS-34. May be safely disassembled by the owner via pommel screw or pegged construction. Prices: $2000 to $3000, some to $20,000. Remarks: Former full-time maker, now part-time. First knife sold in 1975. Mark: Full name, year, and serial number etched on tang under handle.

MARKLEY, KEN,
7651 Cabin Creek Lane, Sparta, IL 62286, Phone: 618-443-5284

Specialties: Traditional working and using knives of his design and to customer specs. Patterns: Fighters, hunters and utility/camp knives. Technical: Forges 5160, 1095 and L6; makes his own Damascus; does file work. Prices: $150 to $800; some to $2000. Remarks: Part-time maker; first knife sold in 1991. Doing business as Cabin Creek Forge. Mark: Last name, JS.

MARLOWE, CHARLES,
10822 Poppleton Ave, Omaha, NE 68144, Phone: 402-933-5065, cmarlowe1@cox.net; Web: www.marloweknives.com

Specialties: Folding knives and balisong. Patterns: Tactical pattern folders. Technical: Grind ATS-34, S30V, CPM154, 154CM, Damasteel, others on request. Forges/grinds 1095 on occasion. Prices: Start at $450. Remarks: First knife sold in 1993. Full-time since 1999. Mark: Turtle logo with Marlowe above, year below.

MARLOWE, DONALD,
2554 Oakland Rd, Dover, PA 17315, Phone: 717-764-6055

Specialties: Working straight knives in standard patterns. Patterns: Bowies, fighters, boots and utility knives. Technical: Grinds D2 and 440C. Integral design hunter models. Prices: $130 to $850. Remarks: Spare-time maker; first knife sold in 1977. Mark: Last name.

MARSH, JEREMY,
6169 3 Mile NE, Ada, MI 49301, Phone: 616-889-1945, steelbean@hotmail.com; Web: www.marshcustomknives.com

Specialties: Locking liner folders, dressed-up gents knives, tactical knives, and dress tacticals. Technical: CPM S30V stainless and Damascus blade steels using the stock-removal method of bladesmithing. Prices: $450 to $1500. Remarks: Self-taught, part-time knifemaker; first knife sold in 2004. Mark: Maker's last name and large, stylized M.

MARSHALL, STEPHEN R,
975 Harkreader Rd, Mt. Juliet, TN 37122

MARTIN, BRUCE E,
Rt. 6, Box 164-B, Prescott, AR 71857, Phone: 501-887-2023

Specialties: Fancy working straight knives of his design. Patterns: Bowies, camp knives, skinners and fighters. Technical: Forges 5160, 1095 and his own Damascus. Uses natural handle materials; filework available. Prices: $75 to $350; some to $500. Remarks: Full-time maker; first knife sold in 1979. Mark: Name in arch.

MARTIN, GENE,
PO Box 396, Williams, OR 97544, Phone: 541-846-6755, bladesmith@customknife.com

Specialties: Straight knives and folders. Patterns: Fighters, hunters, skinners, boot knives, spring back and lock back folders. Technical: Grinds ATS-34, 440C, Damascus and 154CM. Forges; makes own Damascus; scrimshaws. Prices: $150 to $2500. Remarks: Full-time maker; first knife sold in 1993. Doing business as Provision Forge. Mark: Name and/or crossed staff and sword.

MARTIN, HAL W,
781 Hwy 95, Morrilton, AR 72110, Phone: 501-354-1682, hal.martin@sbcglobal.net

Specialties: Hunters, Bowies and fighters. Prices: $250 and up. Mark: MARTIN.

MARTIN, HERB,
2500 Starwood Dr, Richmond, VA 23229, Phone: 804-747-1675, hamjlm@hotmail.com
Specialties: Working straight knives. Patterns: Skinners, hunters and utility. Technical: Hollow grinds ATS-34, and Micarta handles. Prices: $85 to $125. Remarks: Part-time Maker. First knife sold in 2001. Mark: HA MARTIN.

MARTIN, MICHAEL W,
Box 572, Jefferson St, Beckville, TX 75631, Phone: 903-678-2161
Specialties: Classic working/using straight knives of his design and in standard patterns. Patterns: Hunters. Technical: Grinds ATS-34, 440C, O1 and A2. Bead blasted, Parkerized, high polish and satin finishes. Sheaths are handmade. Also hand forges cable Damascus. Prices: $185 to $280 some higher. Remarks: Part-time maker; first knife sold in 1995. Doing business as Michael W. Martin Knives. Mark: Name and city, state in arch.

MARTIN, PETER,
28220 N. Lake Dr, Waterford, WI 53185, Phone: 262-706-3076, Web: www.petermartinknives.com
Specialties: Fancy, fantasy and working straight knives and folders of his design and in standard patterns. Patterns: Bowies, fighters, hunters, locking folders and liner locks. Technical: Forges own Mosaic Damascus, powdered steel and his own Damascus. Prefers natural handle material; offers file work and carved handles. Prices: Moderate. Remarks: Full-time maker; first knife sold in 1988. Doing business as Martin Custom Products. Mark: Martin Knives.

MARTIN, RANDALL J,
51 Bramblewood St, Bridgewater, MA 02324, Phone: 508-279-0682
Specialties: High tech folding and fixed blade tactical knives employing the latest blade steels and exotic materials. Employs a unique combination of 3d-CNC machining and hand work on both blades and handles. All knives are designed for hard use. Clean, radical grinds and ergonomic handles are hallmarks of RJ's work, as is his reputation for producing "Scary Sharp" knives. Technical: Grinds CPM30V, CPM 3V, CPM154CM, A2 and stainless Damascus. Other CPM alloys used on request. Performs all heat treating and cryogenic processing in-house. Remarks: Full-time maker since 2001 and materials engineer. Former helicopter designer. First knife sold in 1976.

MARTIN, TONY,
PO Box 10, Arcadia, MO 63621, Phone: 573-546-2254, arcadian@charter.net; Web: www.arcadianforge.com
Specialties: Specializes in historical designs, esp. puukko, skean dhu. Remarks: Premium quality blades, exotic wood handles, unmatched fit and finish. Mark: AF.

MARTIN, WALTER E,
570 Cedar Flat Rd, Williams, OR 97544, Phone: 541-846-6755

MARTIN, JOHN ALEXANDER,
821 N Grand Ave, Okmulgee, OK 74447, Phone: 918-758-1099, jam@jamblades.com; Web: www.jamblades.com
Specialties: Inlaid and engraved handles. Patterns: Bowies, fighters, hunters and traditional patterns. Swords, fixed blade knives, folders and axes. Technical: Forges 5160, 1084, 10XX, O1, L6 and his own Damascus. Prices: Start at $300. Remarks: Part-time maker. Mark: Two initials with last name and MS or 5 pointed star.

MARZITELLI, PETER,
19929 35A Ave, Langley, B.C., CANADA V3A 2R1, Phone: 604-532-8899, marzitelli@shaw.ca
Specialties: Specializes in unique functional knife shapes and designs using natural and synthetic handle materials. Patterns: Mostly folders, some daggers and art knives. Technical: Grinds ATS-34, S/S Damascus and others. Prices: $220 to $1000 (average $375). Remarks: Full-time maker; first knife sold in 1984. Mark: Stylized logo reads "Marz."

MASON, BILL,
1114 St Louis #33, Excelsior Springs, MO 64024, Phone: 816-637-7335
Specialties: Combat knives; some folders. Patterns: Fighters to match knife types in book *Cold Steel*. Technical: Grinds O1, 440C and ATS-34. Prices: $115 to $250; some to $350. Remarks: Spare-time maker; first knife sold in 1979. Mark: Initials connected.

MASSEY, AL,
Box 14 Site 15 RR#2, Mount Uniacke, Nova Scotia, CANADA B0N 1Z0, Phone: 902-866-4754, armjan@eastlink.ca
Specialties: Working knives and period pieces. Patterns: Swords and daggers of Celtic to medieval design, Bowies. Technical: Forges 5160, 1084 and 1095. Makes own Damascus. Prices: $200 to $500, damascus $300-$1000. Remarks: Part-time maker, first blade sold in 1988. Mark: Initials and JS on Ricasso.

MASSEY, ROGER,
4928 Union Rd, Texarkana, AR 71854, Phone: 870-779-1018
Specialties: Traditional and working straight knives and folders of his design and to customer specs. Patterns: Bowies, hunters, daggers and utility knives. Technical: Forges 1084 and 52100, makes his own Damascus. Offers filework and silver wire inlay in handles. Prices: $200 to $1500; some to $2500. Remarks: Part-time maker; first knife sold in 1991. Mark: Last name, M.S.

MASSEY, RON,
61638 El Reposo St., Joshua Tree, CA 92252, Phone: 760-366-9239 after 5 p.m., Fax: 763-366-4620
Specialties: Classic, traditional, fancy/embellished, high art, period pieces, working/using knives, straight knives, folders, and automatics. Your design, customer specs, about 175 standard patterns. Patterns: Automatics, hunters and fighters. All folders are side-locking folders. Unless requested as lock books slip joint he specializes or custom designs. Technical: ATS-34, 440C, D-2 upon request. Engraving, filework, scrimshaw, most of the exotic handle materials. All aspects are performed by him: inlay work in pearls or stone, handmade Pem' work. Prices: $110 to $2500; some to $6000. Remarks: Part-time maker; first knife sold in 1976.

MATA, LEONARD,
3583 Arruza St, San Diego, CA 92154, Phone: 619-690-6935

MATHEWS, CHARLIE AND HARRY,
TWIN BLADES, 121 Mt Pisgah Church Rd., Statesboro, GA 30458, Phone: 912-865-9098, twinblades@bulloch.net; Web: www.twinxblades.com
Specialties: Working straight knives, carved stag handles. Patterns: Hunters, fighters, Bowies and period pieces. Technical: Grinds D2, CPMS30V, CPM3V, ATS-34 and commercial Damascus; handmade sheaths some with exotic leather, file work. Forges 1095, 1084, and 5160. Prices: Starting at $125. Remarks: Twin brothers making knives full-time under the label of Twin Blades. Charter members Georgia Custom Knifemakers Guild. Members of The Knifemakers Guild. Mark: Twin Blades over crossed knives, reverse side steel type.

MATSUNO, KANSEI,
109-8 Uenomachi Nishikaiden, Gifu-City 501-1168, JAPAN, Phone: 81 58 234 8643

MATSUOKA, SCOT,
94-415 Ukalialii Place, Mililani, HI 96789, Phone: 808-625-6658, Fax: 808-625-6658, scottym@hawaii.rr.com; Web: www.matsuokaknives.com
Specialties: Folders, fixed blades with custom hand-stitched sheaths. Patterns: Gentleman's knives, hunters, tactical folders. Technical: CPM 154CM, 440C, 154, BG42, bolsters, file work, and engraving. Prices: Starting price $350. Remarks: Part-time maker, first knife sold in 2002. Mark: Logo, name and state.

MATSUSAKI, TAKESHI,
MATSUSAKI KNIVES, 151 Ono-Cho Sasebo-shi, Nagasaki, JAPAN, Phone: 0956-47-2938, Fax: 0956-47-2938
Specialties: Working and collector grade front look and slip joint. Patterns: Sheffierd type folders. Technical: Grinds ATS-34 k-120. Price: $250 to $1000, some to $8000. Remarks: Part-time maker, first knife sold in 1990. Mark: Name and initials.

MAXEN, MICK,
2 Huggins Welham Green, "Hatfield, Herts", UNITED KINGDOM AL97LR, Phone: 01707 261213, mmaxen@aol.com
Specialties: Damascus and Mosaic. Patterns: Medieval-style daggers and Bowies. Technical: Forges CS75 and 15N20 / nickel Damascus. Mark: Last name with axe above.

MAXFIELD, LYNN,
382 Colonial Ave, Layton, UT 84041, Phone: 801-544-4176, maxfieldknives@q.com
Specialties: Sporting knives, some fancy. Patterns: Hunters, fishing, fillet, special purpose: some locking folders. Technical: Grinds 440-C, 154-CM, CPM154, D2, CPM S30V, and Damascus. Prices: $125 to $400; some to $900. Remarks: Part-time maker; first knife sold in 1979. Mark: Name, city and state.

MAXWELL, DON,
1484 Celeste Ave, Clovis, CA 93611, Phone: 559-299-2197, maxwellknives@aol.com; Web: maxwellknives.com
Specialties: Fancy folding knives and fixed blades of his design. Patterns: Hunters, fighters, utility/camp knives, LinerLock® folders, flippers and fantasy knives. Technical: Grinds 440C, ATS-34, D2, CPM 154, and commercial Damascus. Prices: $250 to $1000; some to $2500. Remarks: Full-time maker; first knife sold in 1987. Mark: Last name only or Maxwell MAX-TAC.

MAY, CHARLES,
10024 McDonald Rd., Aberdeen, MS 39730, Phone: 662-369-0404, charlesmayknives@yahoo.com; Web: charlesmayknives.blademakers.com
Specialties: Fixed-blade sheath knives. Patterns: Hunters and fillet knives. Technical: Scandinavian-ground D2 and S30V blades, black micarta and wood handles, nickel steel pins with maker's own pocket carry or belt-loop pouches. Prices: $215 to $495. Mark: "Charles May Knives" and a knife in a circle.

MAYNARD, LARRY JOE,
PO Box 493, Crab Orchard, WV 25827
Specialties: Fancy and fantasy straight knives. Patterns: Big knives; a Bowie with a full false edge; fighting knives. Technical: Grinds standard steels. Prices: $350 to $500; some to $1000. Remarks: Full-time maker; first knife sold in 1986. Mark: Middle and last initials.

MAYNARD, WILLIAM N.,
2677 John Smith Rd, Fayetteville, NC 28306, Phone: 910-425-1615
Specialties: Traditional and working straight knives of all designs. **Patterns:** Combat, Bowies, fighters, hunters and utility knives. **Technical:** Grinds 440C, ATS-34 and commercial Damascus. Offers fancy filework; handmade sheaths. **Prices:** $100 to $300; some to $750. **Remarks:** Full-time maker; first knife sold in 1988. **Mark:** Last name.

MAYO JR., HOMER,
18036 Three Rivers Rd., Biloxi, MS 39532, Phone: 228-326-8298
Specialties: Traditional working straight knives, folders and tactical. **Patterns:** Hunters, fighters, tactical, bird, Bowies, fish fillet knives and lightweight folders. **Technical:** Grinds 440C, ATS-34, D-2, Damascus, forges and grinds 52100 and custom makes sheaths. **Prices:** $100 to $1000. **Remarks:** Part-time maker **Mark:** All knives are serial number and registered in the name of the original purchaser, stamped last name or etched.

MAYO JR., TOM,
67 412 Alahaka St, Waialua, HI 96791, Phone: 808-637-6560, mayot001@hawaii.rr.com; Web: www.mayoknives.com
Specialties: Framelocks/tactical knives. **Patterns:** Combat knives, hunters, Bowies and folders. **Technical:** Titanium/stellite/S30V. **Prices:** $500 to $1000. **Remarks:** Full-time maker; first knife sold in 1982. **Mark:** Volcano logo with name and state.

MAYVILLE, OSCAR L,
2130 E. County Rd 910S, Marengo, IN 47140, Phone: 812-338-4159
Specialties: Working straight knives; period pieces. **Patterns:** Kitchen cutlery, Bowies, camp knives and hunters. **Technical:** Grinds A2, O1 and 440C. **Prices:** $50 to $350; some to $500. **Remarks:** Full-time maker; first knife sold in 1984. **Mark:** Initials over knife logo.

MCABEE, WILLIAM,
27275 Norton Grade, Colfax, CA 95713, Phone: 530-389-8163
Specialties: Working/using knives. **Patterns:** Fighters, Bowies, Hunters. **Technical:** Grinds ATS-34. **Prices:** $75 to $200; some to $350. **Remarks:** Part-time maker; first knife sold in 1990. **Mark:** Stylized WM stamped.

MCCALLEN JR., HOWARD H,
110 Anchor Dr, So Seaside Park, NJ 08752

MCCARLEY, JOHN,
4165 Harney Rd, Taneytown, MD 21787
Specialties: Working straight knives; period pieces. **Patterns:** Hunters, Bowies, camp knives, miniatures, throwing knives. **Technical:** Forges W2, O1 and his own Damascus. **Prices:** $150 to $300; some to $1000. **Remarks:** Part-time maker; first knife sold in 1977. **Mark:** Initials in script.

MCCARTY, HARRY,
1479 Indian Ridge Rd, Blaine, TN 37709
Specialties: Period pieces. **Patterns:** Trade knives, Bowies, 18th and 19th century folders and hunting swords. **Technical:** Forges and grinds high-carbon steel. **Prices:** $75 to $1300. **Remarks:** Full-time maker; first knife sold in 1977. Doing business as Indian Ridge Forge. **Mark:** Stylized initials inside a shamrock.

MCCLURE, JERRY,
3052 Isim Rd, Norman, OK 73026, Phone: 405-321-3614, jerry@jmcclureknives.net; Web: www.jmcclureknives.net
Specialties: Gentleman's folder, linerlock with my jeweled pivot system of eight rubies, forged one-of-a-kind Damascus Bowies, and a line of hunting/camp knives. **Patterns:** Folders, Bowie, and hunting/camp **Technical** Forges own Damascus, also uses Damasteel and does own heat treating. **Prices** $500 to $3,000 and up **Remarks** Full-time maker, made first knife in 1965. **Mark** J.MCCLURE

MCCLURE, MICHAEL,
803 17th Ave, Menlo Park, CA 94025, Phone: 650-323-2596, mikesknives@att.net
Specialties: Working/using straight knives of his design and to customer specs. **Patterns:** Bowies, hunters, skinners, utility/camp, tantos, fillets and boot knives. **Technical:** Forges high-carbon and Damascus; also grinds stainless, all grades. **Prices:** Start at $200. **Remarks:** Part-time maker; first knife sold in 1991. ABS Journeyman Smith. **Mark:** Mike McClure.

MCCONNELL JR., LOYD A,
309 County Road 144-B, Marble Falls, TX 78654, Phone: 830-798-8087, ccknives@ccknives.com; Web: www.ccknives.com
Specialties: Working straight knives and folders, some fancy. **Patterns:** Hunters, boots, Bowies, locking folders and slip-joints. **Technical:** Grinds CPM Steels, ATS-34 and BG-42 and commercial Damascus. **Prices:** $450 to $10,000. **Remarks:** Full-time maker; first knife sold in 1975. Doing business as Cactus Custom Knives. Markets product knives under name: Lone Star Knives. **Mark:** Name, city and state in cactus logo.

MCCORNOCK, CRAIG,
MCC MTN OUTFITTERS, 4775 Rt. 212/PO 162, Willow, NY 12495, Phone: 845-679-9758, Mccmtn@aol.com; Web: www.mccmtn.com
Specialties: Carry, utility, hunters, defense type knives and functional swords. **Patterns:** Drop points, hawkbills, tantos, wakizashis, katanas **Technical:** Stock removal, forged and Damascus, (yes, he still flints knap). **Prices:** $200 to $2000. **Mark:** McM.

MCCOUN, MARK,
14212 Pine Dr, DeWitt, VA 23840, Phone: 804-469-7631, mccounandsons@live.com
Specialties: Working/using straight knives of his design and in standard patterns; custom miniatures. **Patterns:** Locking liners, integrals. **Technical:** Grinds Damascus, ATS-34 and 440C. **Prices:** $150 to $500. **Remarks:** Part-time maker; first knife sold in 1989. **Mark:** Name, city and state.

MCCRACKIN, KEVIN,
3720 Hess Rd, House Spings, MO 63051, Phone: 636-677-6066

MCCRACKIN AND SON, V J,
3720 Hess Rd, House Springs, MO 63051, Phone: 636-677-6066
Specialties: Working straight knives in standard patterns. **Patterns:** Hunters, Bowies and camp knives. **Technical:** Forges L6, 5160, his own Damascus, cable Damascus. **Prices:** $125 to $700; some to $1500. **Remarks:** Part-time maker; first knife sold in 1983. Son Kevin helps make the knives. **Mark:** Last name, M.S.

MCCULLOUGH, JERRY,
274 West Pettibone Rd, Georgiana, AL 36033, Phone: 334-382-7644, ke4er@alaweb.com
Specialties: Standard patterns or custom designs. **Technical:** Forge and grind scrap-tool and Damascus steels. Use natural handle materials and turquoise trim on some. Filework on others. **Prices:** $65 to $250 and up. **Remarks:** Part-time maker. **Mark:** Initials (JM) combined.

MCDONALD, RICH,
4590 Kirk Rd, Columbiana, OH 44408, Phone: 330-482-0007, Fax: 330-482-0007
Specialties: Traditional working/using and art knives of his design. **Patterns:** Bowies, hunters, folders, primitives and tomahawks. **Technical:** Forges 5160, 1084, 1095, 52100 and his own Damascus. Fancy filework. **Prices:** $200 to $1500. **Remarks:** Full-time maker; first knife sold in 1994. **Mark:** First and last initials connected.

MCDONALD, ROBERT J,
14730 61 Court N, Loxahatchee, FL 33470, Phone: 561-790-1470
Specialties: Traditional working straight knives to customer specs. **Patterns:** Fighters, swords and folders. **Technical:** Grinds 440C, ATS-34 and forges own Damascus. **Prices:** $150 to $1000. **Remarks:** Part-time maker; first knife sold in 1988. **Mark:** Electro-etched name.

MCDONALD, ROBIN J,
7300 Tolleson Ave NW, Albuquerque, NM 87114-3546
Specialties: Working knives of maker's design. **Patterns:** Bowies, hunters, camp knives and fighters. **Technical:** Forges primarily 5160. **Prices:** $100 to $500. **Remarks:** Part-time maker; first knife sold in 1999. **Mark:** Initials RJM.

MCDONALD, W J "JERRY",
7173 Wickshire Cove E, Germantown, TN 38138, Phone: 901-756-9924, wjmcdonaldknives@email.msn.com; Web: www.mcdonaldknives.com
Specialties: Classic and working/using straight knives of his design and in standard patterns. **Patterns:** Bowies, hunters kitchen and traditional spring back pocket knives. **Technical:** Grinds ATS-34, 154CM, D2, 440V, BG42 and 440C. **Prices:** $125 to $1000. **Remarks:** Full-time maker; first knife sold in 1989. **Mark:** First and middle initials, last name, maker, city and state. Some of his knives are stamped McDonald in script.

MCFALL, KEN,
PO Box 458, Lakeside, AZ 85929, Phone: 928-537-2026, Fax: 928-537-8066, knives@citlink.net
Specialties: Fancy working straight knives and some folders. **Patterns:** Daggers, boots, tantos, Bowies; some miniatures. **Technical:** Grinds D2, ATS-34 and 440C. Forges his own Damascus. **Prices:** $200 to $1200. **Remarks:** Part-time maker; first knife sold in 1984. **Mark:** Name, city and state.

MCFARLIN, ERIC E,
PO Box 2188, Kodiak, AK 99615, Phone: 907-486-4799
Specialties: Working knives of his design. **Patterns:** Bowies, skinners, camp knives and hunters. **Technical:** Flat and convex grinds 440C, A2 and AEB-L. **Prices:** Start at $200. **Remarks:** Part-time maker; first knife sold in 1989. **Mark:** Name and city in rectangular logo.

MCFARLIN, J W,
3331 Pocohantas Dr, Lake Havasu City, AZ 86404, Phone: 928-453-7612, Fax: 928-453-7612, aztheedge@NPGcable.com
Technical: Flat grinds, D2, ATS-34, 440C, Thomas and Peterson Damascus. **Remarks:** From working knives to investment. Customer designs always welcome. 100 percent handmade. Made first knife in 1972. **Prices:** $150 to $3000. **Mark:** Hand written in the blade.

MCGILL, JOHN,
PO Box 302, Blairsville, GA 30512, Phone: 404-745-4686
Specialties: Working knives. **Patterns:** Traditional patterns; camp knives. **Technical:** Forges L6 and 9260; makes Damascus. **Prices:** $50 to $250; some to $500. **Remarks:** Full-time maker; first knife sold in 1982. **Mark:** XYLO.

MCGOWAN, FRANK E,
12629 Howard Lodge Dr, Summer address, Sykesville, MD 21784, Phone: 410-489-4323, fmcgowan11@verizon.net
Specialties: Fancy working knives and folders to customer specs. **Patterns:** Survivor knives, fighters, fishing knives, folders and hunters. **Technical:** Grinds and forges O1, 440C, 5160, ATS-34, 52100, or customer choice. **Prices:** $100 to $1000; some more. **Remarks:** Full-time maker; first knife sold in 1986. **Mark:** Last name.

MCGOWAN, FRANK E,
2023 Robin Ct, Winter address, Sebring, FL 33870, Phone: 443-745-2611, fmcgowan11@verizon.net
Specialties: Fancy working knives and folders to customer specs. **Patterns:** Survivor knives, fighters, fishing knives, folders and hunters. **Technical:** Grinds and forges O1, 440C, 5160, ATS-34, 52100 or customer choice. **Prices:** $100 to $1000, some more. **Remarks:** Full-time maker. First knife sold in 1986. **Mark:** Last name.

MCGRATH, PATRICK T,
8343 Kenyon Ave, Westchester, CA 90045, Phone: 310-338-8764, hidinginLA@excite.com

MCGRODER, PATRICK J,
5725 Chapin Rd, Madison, OH 44057, Phone: 216-298-3405, Fax: 216-298-3405
Specialties: Traditional working/using knives of his design. **Patterns:** Bowies, hunters and utility/camp knives **Technical:** Grinds ATS-34, D2 and customer requests. Does reverse etching; heat-treats; prefers natural handle materials; custom made sheath with each knife. **Prices:** $125 to $250. **Remarks:** Part-time maker. **Mark:** First and middle initials, last name, maker, city and state.

MCGUANE IV, THOMAS F,
410 South 3rd Ave, Bozeman, MT 59715, Phone: 406-586-0248, Web: http://www.thomasmcguane.com
Specialties: Multi metal inlaid knives of handmade steel. **Patterns:** Lock back and LinerLock® folders, fancy straight knives. **Technical:** 1084/1SN20 Damascus and Mosaic steel by maker. **Prices:** $1000 and up. **Mark:** Surname or name and city, state.

MCHENRY, WILLIAM JAMES,
Box 67, Wyoming, RI 02898, Phone: 401-539-8353
Specialties: Fancy high-tech folders of his design. **Patterns:** Locking folders with various mechanisms. **Technical:** One-of-a-kind only, no duplicates. Inventor of the Axis Lock. Most pieces disassemble and feature top-shelf materials including gold, silver and gems. **Prices:** Upscale. **Remarks:** Full-time maker; first knife sold in 1988. Former goldsmith. **Mark:** Last name or first and last initials.

MCINTYRE, SHAWN,
71 Leura Grove, Hawthorn East Victoria, AUSTRALIA 3123, Phone: 61 3 9813 2049/Cell 61 417 041 062, macpower@netspace.net.au; Web: www.mcintyreknives.com
Specialties: Damascus & CS fixed blades and art knives. **Patterns:** Bowies, hunters, fighters, kukris, integrals. **Technical:** Forges, makes own Damascus including pattern weld, mosaic, and composite multi-bars form O1 & 15N20 Also uses 1084, W2, and 52100. **Prices:** $275 to $2000. **Remarks:** Full-time maker since 1999. **Mark:** Mcintyre in script.

MCKEE, NEIL,
674 Porter Hill Rd., Stevensville, MT 59870, Phone: 406-777-3507, mckeenh@peoplepc.com
Specialties: Early American. **Patterns:** Nessmuk, DeWeese, French folders, art pieces. **Technical:** Engraver. **Prices:** $150 to $1000. **Mark:** Oval with initials.

MCKENZIE, DAVID BRIAN,
2311 B Ida Rd, Campbell River B, CANADA V9W-4V7

MCKIERNAN, STAN,
11751 300th St, Lamoni, IA 50140, Phone: 641-784-6873/641-781-0368, slmck@hotmailc.com
Specialties: Self-sheathed knives and miniatures. **Patterns:** Daggers, ethnic designs and individual styles. **Technical:** Grinds Damascus and 440C. **Prices:** $200 to $500, some to $1500. **Mark:** "River's Bend" inside two concentric circles.

MCLENDON, HUBERT W,
125 Thomas Rd, Waco, GA 30182, Phone: 770-574-9796
Specialties: Using knives; his design or customer's. **Patterns:** Bowies and hunters. **Technical:** Hand ground or forged ATS-34, 440C and D2. **Prices:** $100 to $300. **Remarks:** First knife sold in 1978. **Mark:** McLendon or Mc.

MCLUIN, TOM,
36 Fourth St, Dracut, MA 01826, Phone: 978-957-4899, tmcluin@comcast.net; Web: www.mcluinknives.com
Specialties: Working straight knives and folders of his design. **Patterns:** Boots, hunters and folders. **Technical:** Grinds ATS-34, 440C, O1 and Damascus; makes his own mokume. **Prices:** $100 to $400; some to $700. **Remarks:** Part-time maker; first knife sold in 1991. **Mark:** Last name.

MCLURKIN, ANDREW,
2112 Windy Woods Dr, Raleigh, NC 27607, Phone: 919-834-4693, mclurkincustomknives.com
Specialties: Collector grade folders, working folders, fixed blades, and miniatures. Knives made to order and to his design. **Patterns:** Locking liner and lock back folders, hunter, working and tactical designs. **Technical:** Using patterned Damascus, Mosaic Damascus, ATS-34, BG-42, and CPM steels. Prefers natural handle materials such as pearl, ancient ivory and stabilized wood. Also using synthetic materials such as carbon fiber, titanium, and G10. **Prices:** $250 and up. **Mark:** Last name. Mark is often on inside of folders.

MCNABB, TOMMY,
CAROLINA CUSTOM KNIVES, PO Box 327, Bethania, NC 27010, Phone: 336-924-6053, Fax: 336-924-4854, tommy@tmcnabb.com; Web: carolinaknives.com
Specialties: Classic and working knives of his own design or to customer's specs. **Patterns:** Traditional bowies. Tomahawks, hunters and customer designs. **Technical:** Forges his own Damascus steel, hand forges or grinds ATS-34 and other hi-tech steels. Prefers mirror finish or satin finish on working knives. Uses exotic or natural handle material and stabilized woods. **Price:** $300-$3500. **Remarks:** Full time maker. Made first knife in 1982. **Mark"**"Carolina Custom Knives" on stock removal blades "T. McNabb" on custom orders and Damascus knives.

MCRAE, J MICHAEL,
6100 Lake Rd, Mint Hill, NC 28227, Phone: 704-545-2929, scotia@carolina.rr.com; Web: www.scotiametalwork.com
Specialties: Scottish dirks, sgian dubhs, broadswords. **Patterns:** Traditional blade styles with traditional and slightly non-traditional handle treatments. **Technical:** Forges 5160 and his own Damascus. Prefers stag and exotic hardwoods for handles, many intricately carved. **Prices:** Starting at $125, some to $3500. **Remarks:** Journeyman Smith in ABS, member of North Carolina Custom Knifemakers Guild and ABANA. Full-time maker, first knife sold in 1982. Doing business as Scotia Metalwork. **Mark:** Last name underlined with a claymore.

MEERDINK, KURT,
248 Yulan Barryville Rd., Barryville, NY 12719-5305, Phone: 845-557-0783
Specialties: Working straight knives. **Patterns:** Hunters, tactical and neck knives. **Technical:** Grinds ATS-34, 440C, D2, Damascus. **Prices:** $95 to $1100. **Remarks:** Full-time maker, first knife sold in 1994. **Mark:** Meerdink Maker, Rio NY.

MEERS, ANDREW,
2012 S. Illinois Ave., Carbondale, IL 62901, namsuechool@gmail.com
Specialties: Pattern welded blades, in the New England style. **Patterns:** Can do open or closed welding and fancies middle eastern style blades. **Technical:** 1095, 1084, 15n20, 5160, w1, w2 steels **Remarks:** Part-time maker attending graduate school at SIUC; looking to become full-time in the future as well as earn ABS Journeyman status. **Mark:** Korean character for south.

MEIER, DARYL,
75 Forge Rd, Carbondale, IL 62901, Phone: 618-549-3234, Web: www.meiersteel.com
Specialties: One-of-a-kind knives and swords. **Patterns:** Collaborates on blades. **Technical:** Forges his own Damascus, W1 and A203E, 440C, 431, nickel 200 and clad steel. **Prices:** $250 to $450; some to $6000. **Remarks:** Full-time smith and researcher since 1974; first knife sold in 1974. **Mark:** Name or circle/arrow symbol or SHAWNEE.

MELIN, GORDON C,
14207 Coolbank Dr, La Mirada, CA 90638, Phone: 562-946-5753

MELLARD, J R,
17006 Highland Canyon Dr., Houston, TX 77095, Phone: 281-550-9464

MELOY, SEAN,
7148 Rosemary Lane, Lemon Grove, CA 91945-2105, Phone: 619-465-7173
Specialties: Traditional working straight knives of his design. **Patterns:** Bowies, fighters and utility/camp knives. **Technical:** Grinds 440C, ATS-34 and D2. **Prices:** $125 to $300. **Remarks:** Part-time maker; first knife sold in 1985. **Mark:** Broz Knives.

MENEFEE, RICKY BOB,
2440 County Road 1322, Blawchard, OK 73010, rmenefee@pldi.net
Specialties: Working straight knives and pocket knives. **Patterns:** Hunters, fighters, minis & Bowies. **Technical:** Grinds ATS-34, 440C, D2, BG42 and S30V. **Price:** $130 to $1000. **Remarks:** Part-time maker, first knife sold in 2001. Member of KGA of Oklahoma, also Knifemakers Guild. **Mark:** Menefee made or Menefee stamped in blade.

MENSCH, LARRY C,
Larry's Knife Shop, 578 Madison Ave, Milton, PA 17847, Phone: 570-742-9554
Specialties: Custom orders. **Patterns:** Bowies, daggers, hunters, tantos, short swords and miniatures. **Technical:** Grinds ATS-34, stainless steel Damascus; blade grinds hollow, flat and slack. Filework: bending guards and fluting handles with finger grooves. Offers engraving and scrimshaw. **Prices:** $200 and up. **Remarks:** Full-time maker; first knife sold in 1993. Doing business as Larry's Knife Shop. **Mark:** Connected capital "L" and small "m" in script.

MERCER, MIKE,
149 N. Waynesville Rd, Lebanon, OH 45036, Phone: 513-932-2837, mmercer08445@roadrunner.com
Specialties: Miniatures and autos. **Patterns:** All folder patterns. **Technical:** Diamonds and gold, one-of-a-kind, Damascus, O1, stainless steel blades. **Prices:** $500 to $5000. **Remarks:** Carved wax - lost wax casting. **Mark:** Stamp - Mercer.

MERCHANT, TED,
7 Old Garrett Ct, White Hall, MD 21161, Phone: 410-343-0380
Specialties: Traditional and classic working knives. **Patterns:** Bowies, hunters, camp knives, fighters, daggers and skinners. **Technical:** Forges W2 and 5160; makes own Damascus. Makes handles with wood, stag, horn, silver and gem stone inlay; fancy filework. **Prices:** $125 to $600; some to $1500. **Remarks:** Full-time maker; first knife sold in 1985. **Mark:** Last name.

MERZ III, ROBERT L,
1447 Winding Canyon, Katy, TX 77493, Phone: 281-391-2897, bobmerz@consolidated.net; Web: www.merzknives.com
Specialties: Folders. Prices: $350 to $1,400. Remarks: Full time maker; first knife sold in 1974. Mark: MERZ.

MESHEJIAN, MARDI,
5 Bisbee Court 109 PMB 230, Santa Fe, NM 87508, Phone: 505-310-7441, toothandnail13@yahoo.com
Specialties: One-of-a-kind fantasy and high art straight knives & folders. Patterns: Swords, daggers, folders and other weapons. Technical: Forged steel Damascus and titanium Damascus. Prices: $300 to $5000 some to $7000. Mark: Stamped stylized "M."

MESSER, DAVID T,
134 S Torrence St, Dayton, OH 45403-2044, Phone: 513-228-6561
Specialties: Fantasy period pieces, straight and folding, of his design. Patterns: Bowies, daggers and swords. Technical: Grinds 440C, O1, 06 and commercial Damascus. Likes fancy guards and exotic handle materials. Prices: $100 to $225; some to $375. Remarks: Spare-time maker; first knife sold in 1991. Mark: Name stamp.

METHENY, H A "WHITEY",
7750 Waterford Dr, Spotsylvania, VA 22551, Phone: 540842-1440, Fax: 540-582-3095, hametheny@aol.com; Web: www.methenyknives.com
Specialties: Working and using straight knives of his design and to customer specs. Patterns: Hunters and kitchen knives. Technical: Grinds 440C and ATS-34. Offers filework; tooled custom sheaths. Prices: $350 to $450. Remarks: Spare-time maker; first knife sold in 1990. Mark: Initials/full name football logo.

METSALA, ANTHONY,
30557 103rd St. NW, Princeton, MN 55371, Phone: 763-389-2628, acmetsala@izoom.net; Web: www.metsalacustomknives.com
Specialties: Sole authorship one-off mosaic Damascus liner locking folders, sales of makers finished one-off mosaic Damascus blades. Patterns: Except for a couple EDC folding knives, maker does not use patterns. Technical: Forges own mosaic Damascus carbon blade and bolster material. All stainless steel blades are heat treated by Paul Bos. Prices: $250 to $1500. Remarks: Full-time knifemaker and Damascus steel maker, first knife sold in 2005. Mark: A.C. Metsala or Metsala.

METZ, GREG T,
c/o Yellow Pine Bar HC 83, BOX 8080, Cascade, ID 83611, Phone: 208-382-4336, metzenterprise@yahoo.com
Specialties: Hunting and utility knives. Prices: $350 and up. Remarks: Natural handle materials; hand forged blades; 1084 and 1095. Mark: METZ (last name).

MEYER, CHRISTOPHER J,
737 Shenipsit Lake Rd, Tolland, CT 06084, Phone: 860-875-1826, shenipsitforge.cjm@gmail.com
Specialties: Hand forged tool steels. Patterns: Bowies, fighters, hunters, and camp knives. Technical: Forges O1, 1084, W2, Grinds ATS-34, O1, D2, CPM154CM. Remarks: Spare-time maker, sold first knife in 2003. Mark: Name or "Shenipsit forge, Meyer".

MICHINAKA, TOSHIAKI,
I-679 Koyamacho-nishi Tottori-shi, Tottori 680-0947, JAPAN, Phone: 0857-28-5911
Specialties: Art miniature knives. Patterns: Bowies, hunters, fishing, camp knives & miniatures. Technical: Grinds ATS-34 and 440C. Prices: $300 to $900 some higher. Remarks: Part-time maker. First knife sold in 1982. Mark: First initial, last name.

MICHO, KANDA,
7-32-5 Shinzutsumi-cho, Shinnanyo-city, Yamaguchi, JAPAN, Phone: 0834-62-1910

MICKLEY, TRACY,
42112 Kerns Dr, North Mankato, MN 56003, Phone: 507-947-3760, tracy@mickleyknives.com; Web: www.mickleyknives.com
Specialties: Working and collectable straight knives using mammoth ivory or burl woods, LinerLock® folders. Patterns: Custom and classic hunters, utility, fighters and Bowies. Technical: Grinding 154-CM, BG-42 forging O1 and 52100. Prices: Starting at $325 Remarks: Part-time since 1999. Mark: Last name.

MIKOLAJCZYK, GLEN,
4650 W. 7 Mile Rd., Caledonia, WI 53108, Phone: 414-791-0424, Fax: 262-835-9697, glenmikol@aol.com Web: www.customtomahawk.com
Specialties: Pipe hawks, fancy folders, bowies, long blades, hunting knives, all of his own design. Technical: Sole-author, forges own Damascus and powdered steel. Works with ivory, bone, tortoise, horn and antlers, tiger maple, pearl for handle materials. Designs and does intricate file work and custom sheaths. Enjoys exotic handle materials. Prices: Moderate. Remarks: Founded Weg Von Wennig Forge in 2003, first knife sold in 2004. Also, designs and builds mini-forges. Will build upon request. International sales accepted. Mark: Tomahawk and name.

MILES JR., C R "IRON DOCTOR",
1541 Porter Crossroad, Lugoff, SC 29078, Phone: 803-438-5816
Specialties: Traditional working straight knives of his design or made to custom specs. Patterns: Hunters, fighters, utility camp knives and hatches. Technical: Grinds O1, D2, ATS-34, 440C, 1095, and 154 CPM. Forges 18th century style cutlery of high carbon steels. Also forges and grinds old files and farrier's rasps to make knives. Custom leather sheaths. Prices: $100 and up. Remarks: Part-time maker, first knife sold 1997. Member of South Carolina Association of Knifemakers since 1997. Mark: Iron doctor plus name and serial number.

MILITANO, TOM,
CUSTOM KNIVES, 77 Jason Rd., Jacksonville, AL 36265-6655, Phone: 256-435-7132, jeffkin57@aol.com
Specialties: Fixed blade, one-of-a-kind knives. Patterns: Bowies, fighters, hunters and tactical knives. Technical: Grinds 440C, CPM 154CM, A2, and Damascus. Hollow grinds, flat grinds, and decorative filework. Prices: $150 plus. Remarks: Part-time maker. Sold first knives in the mid to late 1980s. Memberships: Founding member of New England Custom Knife Association. Mark: Name engraved in ricasso area - type of steel on reverse side.

MILLARD, FRED G,
27627 Kopezyk Ln, Richland Center, WI 53581, Phone: 608-647-5376
Specialties: Working/using straight knives of his design or to customer specs. Patterns: Bowies, hunters, utility/camp knives, kitchen/steak knives. Technical: Grinds ATS-34, O1, D2 and 440C. Makes sheaths. Prices: $110 to $300. Remarks: Full-time maker; first knife sold in 1993. Doing business as Millard Knives. Mark: Mallard duck in flight with serial number.

MILLER, BOB,
7659 Fine Oaks Pl, Oakville, MO 63129, Phone: 314-846-8934
Specialties: Mosaic Damascus; collector using straight knives and folders. Patterns: Hunters, Bowies, utility/camp knives, daggers. Technical: Forges own Damascus, mosaic-Damascus and 52100. Prices: $125 to $500. Remarks: Part-time maker; first knife sold in 1983. Mark: First and middle initials and last name, or initials.

MILLER, DON,
21049 Uncompahgre Rd., Montrose, CO 81403, Phone: 800-318-8127, www.masterdonknives.com

MILLER, HANFORD J,
Box 97, Cowdrey, CO 80434, Phone: 970-723-4708
Specialties: Working knives in Moran styles, Bowie, period pieces, Cinquedea. Patterns: Daggers, Bowies, working knives. Technical: All work forged: W2, 1095, 5160 and Damascus. ABS methods; offers fine silver repousse, scabboard mountings and wire inlay, oak presentation cases. Prices: $400 to $1000; some to $3000 and up. Remarks: Full-time maker; first knife sold in 1968. Mark: Initials or name within Bowie logo.

MILLER, JAMES P,
9024 Goeller Rd, RR 2, Box 28, Fairbank, IA 50629, Phone: 319-635-2294, Web: www.damascusknives.biz
Specialties: All tool steel Damascus; working knives and period pieces. Patterns: Hunters, Bowies, camp knives and daggers. Technical: Forges and grinds 1095, 52100, 440C and his own Damascus. Prices: $175 to $500; some to $1500. Remarks: Full-time maker; first knife sold in 1970. Mark: First and middle initials, last name with knife logo.

MILLER, M A,
11625 Community Center Dr, Unit #1531, Northglenn, CO 80233, Phone: 303-280-3816
Specialties: Using knives for hunting. 3-1/2"-4" Loveless drop-point. Made to customer specs. Patterns: Skinners and camp knives. Technical: Grinds 440C, D2, O1 and ATS-34 Damascus miniatures. Prices: $225 to $350; miniatures $75 to $150. Remarks: Part-time maker; first knife sold in 1988. Mark: Last name stamped in block letters or first and middle initials, last name, maker, city and state with triangles on either side etched.

MILLER, MICHAEL,
3030 E Calle Cedral, Kingman, AZ 86401, Phone: 928-757-1359, mike@mmilleroriginals.com
Specialties: Hunters, Bowies, and skinners with exotic burl wood, stag, ivory and gemstone handles. Patterns: High carbon steel knives. Technical: High carbon and nickel alloy Damascus and high carbon and meteorite Damascus. Also mosaic Damascus. Prices: $235 to $4500. Remarks: Full-time maker since 2002, first knife sold 2000; doing business as M Miller Originals. Mark: First initial and last name with 'handmade' underneath.

MILLER, MICHAEL E,
910146 S. 3500 Rd., Chandler, OK 74834, Phone: 918-377-2411, mimiller1@brightok.net
Specialties: Traditional working/using knives of his design. Patterns: Bowies, hunters and kitchen knives. Technical: Grinds ATS-34, CPM 440V; forges Damascus and cable Damascus and 52100. Prefers scrimshaw, fancy pins, basket weave and embellished sheaths. Prices: $80 to $300; some to $500. Remarks: Part-time maker; first knife sold in 1984. Doing business as Miller Custom Knives. Member of KGA of Oklahoma and Salt Fork Blacksmith Association. Mark: First and middle initials, last name, maker.

MILLER, NATE,
Sportsman's Edge, 1075 Old Steese Hwy N, Fairbanks, AK 99712, Phone: 907-479-4774, sportsmansedge@gci.net Web: www.alaskasportsmansedge.com
Specialties: Fixed blade knives for hunting, fishing, kitchen and collector pieces. Patterns: Hunters, skinners, utility, tactical, fishing, camp knives-your pattern or mine. Technical: Stock removal maker, ATS-34, 154CM,

440C, D2, 1095, other steels on request. Handle material includes micarta, horn, antler, fossilized ivory and bone, wide selection of woods. **Prices:** $225-$800. **Remarks:** Full time maker since 2002. **Mark:** Nate Miller, Fairbanks, AK.

MILLER, R D,
10526 Estate Lane, Dallas, TX 75238, Phone: 214-348-3496
Specialties: One-of-a-kind collector-grade knives. **Patterns:** Boots, hunters, Bowies, camp and utility knives, fishing and bird knives, miniatures. **Technical:** Grinds a variety of steels to include O1, D2, 440C, 154CM and 1095. **Prices:** $65 to $300; some to $900. **Remarks:** Full-time maker; first knife sold in 1984. **Mark:** R.D. Custom Knives with date or bow and arrow logo.

MILLER, RICK,
516 Kanaul Rd, Rockwood, PA 15557, Phone: 814-926-2059
Specialties: Working/using straight knives of his design and in standard patterns. **Patterns:** Bowies, daggers, hunters and friction folders. **Technical:** Grinds L6. Forges 5160, L6 and Damascus. Patterns for Damascus are random, twist, rose or ladder. **Prices:** $75 to $250; some to $400. **Remarks:** Part-time maker; first knife sold in 1982. **Mark:** Script stamp "R.D.M."

MILLER, RON,
NORTH POLE KNIVES, PO BOX 55301, NORTH POLE, AK 99705, Phone: 907-488-5902, JTMRON@NESCAPE.NET
Specialties: Custom handmade hunting knives built for the extreme conditions of Alaska. Custom fillet blades, tactical fighting knives, custom kitchen knives. Handles are made from mammoth ivory, musk ox, fossilized walrus tusk. Hunters have micarta handles. **Patterns:** Hunters, skinners, fillets, fighters. **Technical:** Stock removal for D2, ATS-34, 109HR, 154CM, and Damascus. **Prices:** $180 and up. **Remarks:** Makes custom sheaths for the above knives. **Mark:** Ron Miller, circle with North Pole Knives with bowie style blade through circle.

MILLER, RONALD T,
12922 127th Ave N, Largo, FL 34644, Phone: 813-595-0378 (after 5 p.m.)
Specialties: Working straight knives in standard patterns. **Patterns:** Combat knives, camp knives, kitchen cutlery, fillet knives, locking folders and butterflies. **Technical:** Grinds D2, 440C and ATS-34; offers brass inlays and scrimshaw. **Prices:** $45 to $325; some to $750. **Remarks:** Part-time maker; first knife sold in 1984. **Mark:** Name, city and state in palm tree logo.

MILLER, SKIP,
13773 Borglum Rd., Keystone, SD 57751, Phone: 605-255-5778, svmlr@mt-rushmore.net
Remarks: Has been making knives since 1994.

MILLER, STEVE,
1376 Pine St., Clearwater, FL 33756, Phone: 727-461-4180, millknives@aol.com
Patterns: Bowies, hunters, skinners, folders. **Technical:** 440-C, ATS-34, Sandvic Stainless, CPM-S30-V, Damascus. Exotic hardwoods, bone, horn, antler, ivory, synthetics. All leather work and sheaths made by me and hand-stitched. **Remarks:** Have been making custom knives for sale since 1990. Part-time maker, hope to go full time in about five and a half years (after retirement from full-time job). **Mark:** Last name inside a pentagram.

MILLER, TERRY,
P.O. Box 262, Healy, AK 99743, Phone: 907-683-1239, terry@denalidomehome.com
Specialties: Alaskan ulas with wood or horn. **Remarks:** New to knifemaking (4 years).

MILLS, LOUIS G,
9450 Waters Rd, Ann Arbor, MI 48103, Phone: 734-668-1839
Specialties: High-art Japanese-style period pieces. **Patterns:** Traditional tantos, daggers and swords. **Technical:** Makes steel from iron; makes his own Damascus by traditional Japanese techniques. **Prices:** $900 to $2000; some to $8000. **Remarks:** Spare-time maker. **Mark:** Yasutomo in Japanese Kanji.

MILLS, MICHAEL,
151 Blackwell Rd, Colonial Beach, VA 22443-5054, Phone: 804-224-0265
Specialties: Working knives, hunters, skinners, utility and Bowies. **Technical:** Forge 5160 differential heat-treats. **Prices:** $300 and up. **Remarks:** Part-time maker, ABS Journeyman. **Mark:** Last name in script.

MINCHEW, RYAN,
2510 Mary Ellen, Pampa, TX 79065, Phone: 806-669-8568, ryan@minchewknives.com Web: www.minchewknives.com
Specialties: Hunters and folders. **Patterns:** Standard hunter, bird, and trout. **Prices:** $150 to $500. **Mark:** Minchew.

MINK, DAN,
PO Box 861, 196 Sage Circle, Crystal Beach, FL 34681, Phone: 727-786-5408, blademkr@gmail.com
Specialties: Traditional and working knives of his design. **Patterns:** Bowies, fighters, folders and hunters. **Technical:** Grinds ATS-34, 440C and D2. Blades and tanges embellished with fancy filework. Uses natural and rare handle materials. **Prices:** $125 to $450. **Remarks:** Part-time maker; first knife sold in 1985. **Mark:** Name and star encircled by custom made, city, state.

MINNICK, JIM,
144 North 7th St, Middletown, IN 47356, Phone: 765-354-4108

Specialties: Lever-lock folding art knives, liner-locks. **Patterns:** Stilettos, Persian and one-of-a-kind folders. **Technical:** Grinds and carves Damascus, stainless, and high-carbon. **Prices:** $950 to $7000. **Remarks:** Part-time maker; first knife sold in 1976. Husband and wife team. **Mark:** Minnick and JMJ.

MIRABILE, DAVID,
1715 Glacier Ave, Juneau, AK 99801, Phone: 907-463-3404
Specialties: Elegant edged weapons. **Patterns:** Fighters, Bowies, claws, tklinget daggers, executive desk knives. **Technical:** Forged high-carbon steels, his own Damascus; uses ancient walrus ivory and prehistoric bone extensively, very rarely uses wood. **Prices:** $350 to $7000. **Remarks:** Full-time maker. Knives sold through art gallery in Juneau, AK. **Mark:** Last name etched or engraved.

MIRABILE, DAVID,
PO BOX 20417, Juneau, AK 99802, Phone: 907-321-1103, dmirabile02@gmail.com
Specialties: Elegant edged weapons and hard use Alaskan knives. **Patterns:** Fighters, personal carry knives, special studies of the Tlinget dagger. **Technical:** Uses W-2, 1080, 15n20, 1095, 5160, and his own Damascus, and stainless/high carbon San Mai.

MITCHELL, JAMES A,
PO Box 4646, Columbus, GA 31904, Phone: 404-322-8582
Specialties: Fancy working knives. **Patterns:** Hunters, fighters, Bowies and locking folders. **Technical:** Grinds D2, 440C and commercial Damascus. **Prices:** $100 to $400; some to $900. **Remarks:** Part-time maker; first knife sold in 1976. Sells knives in sets. **Mark:** Signature and city.

MITCHELL, MAX DEAN AND BEN,
3803 VFW Rd, Leesville, LA 71440, Phone: 318-239-6416
Specialties: Hatchet and knife sets with folder and belt and holster all match. **Patterns:** Hunters, 200 L6 steel. **Technical:** L6 steel; soft back, hand edge. **Prices:** $300 to $500. **Remarks:** Part-time makers; first knife sold in 1965. Custom orders only; no stock. **Mark:** First names.

MITCHELL, WM DEAN,
PO Box 2, Warren, TX 77664, Phone: 409-547-2213
Specialties: Functional and collectable cutlery. Patterns:Personal and collector's designs. Technical:Forges own Damascus and carbon steels. Prices: Determined by the buyer. Remarks:Gentleman knifemaker. ABS Master Smith 1994.Mark: Full name with anvil and MS or WDM and MS.

MITSUYUKI, ROSS,
PO Box 29577, Honolulu, HI 96820, Phone: 808-671-3335, Fax: 808-671-3335, rossman@hawaiiantel.net; Web:www.picturetrail.com/homepage/mrbing
Specialties: Working straight knives and folders/engraving titanium & 416 S.S. **Patterns:** Hunting, fighters, utility knives and boot knives. **Technical:** 440C, BG42, ATS-34, S30V, CPM154, and Damascus. **Prices:** $100 and up. **Remarks:** Spare-time maker, first knife sold in 1998. **Mark:** (Honu) Hawaiian sea turtle.

MIVILLE-DESCHENES, ALAIN,
1952 Charles A Parent, Quebec, CANADA G2B 4B2, Phone: 418-845-0950, Fax: 418-845-0950, amd@miville-deschenes.com; Web: www.miville-deschenes.com
Specialties: Working knives of his design or to customer specs and art knives. **Patterns:** Bowies, skinner, hunter, utility, camp knives, fighters, art knives. **Technical:** Grinds ATS-34, CPMS30V, 0-1, D2, and sometime forge carbon steel. **Prices:** $250 to $700; some higher. **Remarks:** Part-time maker; first knife sold in 2001. **Mark:** Logo (small hand) and initials (AMD).

MOEN, JERRY,
4444 Spring Valley Rd, Dallas, TX 75244, Phone: 972-839-1609, jmoen@moencustomknives.com Web: moencustomknives.com
Specialties: Hunting, pocket knives, fighters tactical, and exotic.

MOJZIS, JULIUS,
B S Timravy 6, 98511 Halic, SLOVAKIA, mojzisj@stoneline.sk; Web: www.juliusmojzis.com
Specialties: Art Knives. **Prices:** USD 2000. **Mark:** MOJZIS.

MONCUS, MICHAEL STEVEN,
1803 US 19 N, Smithville, GA 31787, Phone: 912-846-2408

MONTANO, GUS A,
11217 Westonhill Dr, San Diego, CA 92126-1447, Phone: 619-273-5357
Specialties: Traditional working/using straight knives of his design. **Patterns:** Boots, Bowies and fighters. **Technical:** Grinds 1095 and 5160; grinds and forges cable. Double or triple hardened and triple drawn; hand-rubbed finish. Prefers natural handle materials. **Prices:** $200 to $400; some to $600. **Remarks:** Spare-time maker; first knife sold in 1997. **Mark:** First initial and last name.

MONTEIRO, VICTOR,
31 Rue D'Opprebais, 1360 Maleves Ste Marie, BELGIUM, Phone: 010 88 0441, victor.monteiro@skynet.be
Specialties: Working and fancy straight knives, folders and integrals of his design. **Patterns:** Fighters, hunters and kitchen knives. **Technical:** Grinds ATS-34, 440C, D2, Damasteel and other commercial Damascus, embellishment, filework and domed pins. **Prices:** $300 to $1000, some higher. **Remarks:** Part-time maker; first knife sold in 1989. **Mark:** Logo with initials connected.

MONTELL, TY,
PO BOX 1312, Thatcher, AZ 85559, Phone: 928-792-4509, Fax: Cell: 575-313-4373, montellfamily@aol.com

Specialties: Automatics, slip-joint folders, hunting and miniatures. **Technical:** Stock removal. Steel of choice is CPM-154, Devin Thomas Damascus. **Prices:** $250 and up. **Remarks:** First knife made in 1980. **Mark:** Tang stamp - Montell.

MONTJOY, CLAUDE,
706 Indian Creek Rd, Clinton, SC 29325, Phone: 864-697-6160

Specialties: Folders, slip joint, lock, lock liner and interframe. **Patterns:** Hunters, boots, fighters, some art knives and folders. **Technical:** Grinds ATS-34 and Damascus. Offers inlaid handle scales. **Prices:** $100 to $500. **Remarks:** Full-time maker; first knife sold in 1982. Custom orders, no catalog. **Mark:** Montjoy.

MOONEY, MIKE,
19432 E Cloud Rd, Queen Creek, AZ 85142, Phone: 480-987-3576, mike@moonblades.com; Web: www.moonblades.com

Specialties: Hand-crafted high-performing straight knives of his or customer's design. **Patterns:** Bowies, fighters, hunting, camp and kitchen users or collectible. **Technical:** Flat-grind, hand-rubbed finish, S30V, CMP-154, Damascus, any steel. **Prices:** $300 to $3000. **Remarks:** Doing business as moonblades.com. Commissions are welcome. **Mark:** M. Mooney followed by crescent moon.

MOONEY, MIKE,
19432 E Cloud Rd, Queen Creek, AZ

Specialties: Ono 16". **Patterns:** Mas. **Technical:** Foix. **Prices:** St00. **Remarks:** F0. **Mark:** "Daath.

MOORE, JAMES B,
1707 N Gillis, Ft. Stockton, TX 79735, Phone: 915-336-2113

Specialties: Classic working straight knives and folders of his design. **Patterns:** Hunters, Bowies, daggers, fighters, boots, utility/camp knives, locking folders and slip-joint folders. **Technical:** Grinds 440C, ATS-34, D2, L6, CPM and commercial Damascus. **Prices:** $85 to $700; exceptional knives to $1500. **Remarks:** Full-time maker; first knife sold in 1972. **Mark:** Name, city and state.

MOORE, JON P,
304 South N Rd, Aurora, NE 68818, Phone: 402-849-2616, Web: www.sharpdecisionknives.com

Specialties: Working and fancy straight knives using antler, exotic bone, wood and Micarta. Will use customers antlers on request. **Patterns:** Hunters, skinners, camp Bowies. **Technical:** Hand forged high carbon steel. Makes his own Damascus. **Remarks:** Part-time maker, sold first knife in 2003, member of ABS - apprentice. Does on location knife forging demonstrations. **Mark:** Signature.

MOORE, MARVE,
HC 89 Box 393, Willow, AK 99688, Phone: 907-232-0478, marvemoore@aol.com

Specialties: Fixed blades forged and stock removal. **Patterns:** Hunter, skinners, fighter, short swords. **Technical:** 100 percent of his work is done by hand. **Prices:** $100 to $500. **Remarks:** Also makes his own sheaths. **Mark:** -MM-.

MOORE, MICHAEL ROBERT,
70 Beauliew St, Lowell, MA 01850, Phone: 978-479-0589, Fax: 978-441-1819

MOORE, TED,
340 E Willow St, Elizabethtown, PA 17022, Phone: 717-367-3939, tedmoore@supernet.com; Web: www.tedmooreknives.com

Specialties: Damascus folders, cigar cutters. **Patterns:** Locking folders and slip joint. **Technical:** Grinds Damascus, high-carbon and stainless; also ATS-34 and D2. **Prices:** $250 to $1500. **Remarks:** Part-time maker; first knife sold 1993. Knife and gun leather also. **Mark:** Moore U.S.A.

MORETT, DONALD,
116 Woodcrest Dr, Lancaster, PA 17602-1300, Phone: 717-746-4888

MORGAN, JEFF,
9200 Arnaz Way, Santee, CA 92071, Phone: 619-448-8430

Specialties: Early American style knives. **Patterns:** Hunters, bowies, etc. **Technical:** Carbon steel and carbon steel damascus. **Prices:** $60 to $400

MORGAN, TOM,
14689 Ellett Rd, Beloit, OH 44609, Phone: 330-537-2023

Specialties: Working straight knives and period pieces. **Patterns:** Hunters, boots and presentation tomahawks. **Technical:** Grinds O1, 440C and 154CM. **Prices:** Knives, $65 to $200; tomahawks, $100 to $325. **Remarks:** Full-time maker; first knife sold in 1977. **Mark:** Last name and type of steel used.

MORRIS, C H,
1590 Old Salem Rd, Frisco City, AL 36445, Phone: 334-575-7425

Specialties: LinerLock® folders. **Patterns:** Interframe liner locks. **Technical:** Grinds 440C and ATS-34. **Prices:** Start at $350. **Remarks:** Full-time maker; first knife sold in 1973. Doing business as Custom Knives. **Mark:** First and middle initials, last name.

MORRIS, DARRELL PRICE,
92 Union, St. Plymouth, Devon, ENGLAND PL1 3EZ, Phone: 0752 223546

Specialties: Traditional Japanese knives, Bowies and high-art knives. **Technical:** Nickel Damascus and mokume. **Prices:** $1000 to $4000. **Remarks:** Part-time maker; first knife sold in 1990. **Mark:** Initials and Japanese name—Kuni Shigae.

MORRIS, ERIC,
306 Ewart Ave, Beckley, WV 25801, Phone: 304-255-3951

MORRIS, MICHAEL S.,
609 S. Main St., Yale, MI 48097, Phone: 810-887-7817, mykulmorris@yahoo.com

Specialties: Hunting and Tactical fixed blade knives of his design made from files. **Technical:** All knives hollow ground on 12" wheel. Hand stitches his own sheaths also. **Prices:** From $60 to $350 with most in the $90 to $125 range. **Remarks:** Machinist since 1980, made his first knife in 1984, sold his first knife in 2004. Now full-time maker. **Mark:** Last name with date of manufacture.

MOSES, STEVEN,
1610 W Hemlock Way, Santa Ana, CA 92704

MOSIER, DAVID,
1725 Millburn Ave., Independence, MO 64056, Phone: 816-796-3479, dmknives@aol.com Web: www.dmknives.com

Specialties: Tactical folders and fixed blades. **Patterns:** Fighters and concealment blades. **Technical:** Uses S35VN, CPM 154, S30V, 154CM, ATS-34, 440C, A2, D2, Stainless damascus, and Damasteel. Fixed blades come with Kydex sheaths made by maker. **Prices:** $150 to $1000. **Remarks:** Full-time maker, business name is DM Knives. **Mark:** David Mosier Knives encircling sun.

MOSIER, JOSHUA J,
SPRING CREEK KNIFE WORKS, PO Box 476/608 7th St, Deshler, NE 68340, Phone: 402-365-4386, joshm@sl-kw.com; Web:www.sc-kw.com

Specialties: Working straight and folding knives of his designs with customer specs. **Patterns:** Hunter/utility LinerLock® folders. **Technical:** Forges random pattern Damascus, 01, and 5160. **Prices:** $85 and up. **Remarks:** Part-time maker, sold first knife in 1986. **Mark:** SCKW.

MOULTON, DUSTY,
135 Hillview Lane, Loudon, TN 37774, Phone: 865-408-9779, Web: www.moultonknives.com

Specialties: Fancy and working straight knives. **Patterns:** Hunters, fighters, fantasy and miniatures. **Technical:** Grinds ATS-34 and Damascus. **Prices:** $300 to $2000. **Remarks:** Full-time maker; first knife sold in 1991. Now doing engraving on own knives as well as other makers. **Mark:** Last name.

MOYER, RUSS,
1266 RD 425 So, Havre, MT 59501, Phone: 406-395-4423

Specialties: Working knives to customer specs. **Patterns:** Hunters, Bowies and survival knives. **Technical:** Forges W2 & 5160. **Prices:** $150 to $350. **Remarks:** Part-time maker; first knife sold in 1976. **Mark:** Initials in logo.

MULKEY, GARY,
533 Breckenridge Rd, Branson, MO 65616, Phone: 417-335-0123, gary@mulkeyknives.com; Web: www.mulkeyknives.com

Specialties: Sole authorship Damascus and carbon steel. **Patterns:** Fixed blades (hunters, bowies, and fighters). **Technical:** Prefers 1095 or D2 with Damascus, filework, inlets or clay coated blades available on order. **Prices:** $250 and up. **Remarks:** Full-time maker since 1997. **Mark:** MUL above skeleton key.

MULLER, JODY,
3359 S. 225th Rd., Goodson, MO 65663, Phone: 417-852-4306/417-752-3260, mullerforge2@hotmail.com; Web: www.mullerforge.com

Specialties: Hand engraving, carving and inlays, fancy folders and oriental styles. **Patterns:** One-of-a-kind fixed blades and folders in all styles. **Technical:** Forges own Damascus and high carbon steel. **Prices:** $300 and up. **Remarks:** Full-time Journeyman Smith, knifemaker, does hand engraving, carving and inlay. All work done by maker. **Mark:** Muller J.S.

MUNJAS, BOB,
600 Beebe Rd., Waterford, OH 45786, Phone: 740-336-5538, Web: hairofthebear.com

Specialties: Damascus and carbon steel sheath knives. **Patterns:** Hunters and neck knives. **Technical:** My own Damascus, 5160, 1095, 1984, L6, and W2. Forge and stock removal. Does own heat treating and makes own sheaths. **Prices:** $100 to $500. **Remarks:** Part-time maker. **Mark:** Moon Munjas.

MURSKI, RAY,
12129 Captiva Ct, Reston, VA 22091-1204, Phone: 703-264-1102, rmurski@gmail.com

Specialties: Fancy working/using folders of his design. **Patterns:** Hunters, slip-joint folders and utility/camp knives. **Technical:** Grinds CPM-3V **Prices:** $125 to $500. **Remarks:** Spare-time maker; first knife sold in 1996. **Mark:** Engraved name with serial number under name.

MUTZ, JEFF,
8210 Rancheria Dr. Unit 7, Rancho Cucamonga, CA 91730, Phone: 909-931-9829, jmutzknives@hotmail.com; Web: www.jmutzknives.com

Specialties: Traditional working/using fixed blade and slip-jointed knives of own design and customer specs. **Patterns:** Hunters, skinners, and folders. **Technical:** Grinds 440C. Offers scrimshaw. **Prices:** $145 to $500. **Remarks:** Full-time maker, first knife sold in 1998. **Mark:** First initial, last name over "maker."

MYERS, PAUL,
644 Maurice St, Wood River, IL 62095, Phone: 618-258-1707

Specialties: Fancy working straight knives and folders. **Patterns:** Full range

of folders, straight hunters and Bowies; tie tacks; knife and fork sets. **Technical:** Grinds D2, 440C, ATS-34 and 154CM. **Prices:** $100 to $350; some to $3000. **Remarks:** Full-time maker; first knife sold in 1974. **Mark:** Initials with setting sun on front; name and number on back.

MYERS, STEVE,
903 Hickory Rd., Virginia, IL 62691-8716, Phone: 217-452-3157, Web: www.myersknives.net
    Specialties: Working straight knives and integrals. **Patterns:** Camp knives, hunters, skinners, Bowies, and boot knives. **Technical:** Forges own Damascus and high carbon steels. **Prices:** $250 to $1,000. **Remarks:** Full-time maker, first knife sold in 1985. **Mark:** Last name in logo.

N

NATEN, GREG,
1804 Shamrock Way, Bakersfield, CA 93304-3921
    Specialties: Fancy and working/using folders of his design. **Patterns:** Fighters, hunters and locking folders. **Technical:** Grinds 440C, ATS-34 and CPM440V. Heat-treats; prefers desert ironwood, stag and mother-of-pearl. Designs and sews leather sheaths for straight knives. **Prices:** $175 to $600; some to $950. **Remarks:** Spare-time maker; first knife sold in 1992. **Mark:** Last name above battle-ax, handmade.

NAUDE, LOUIS,
3 Flamingo, Protea Heights, Cape Town, Western Cape 7560, South Africa, Phone: +27-0-21-981-0079, info@louisnaude.co.za Web: www.louisnaude.co.za

NEALY, BUD,
RR1, Box 1439, Stroudsburg, PA 18360, Phone: 570-402-1018, Fax: 570-402-1018, bnealy@ptd.net; Web: www.budnealyknifemaker.com
    Specialties: Original design concealment knives with designer multi-concealment sheath system. **Patterns:** Folders (in addition to others). **Technical:** Grinds CPM 154, S30V & Damascus. **Prices:** $200 to $2500. **Remarks:** Full-time maker; first knife sold in 1980. **Mark:** Name, city, state or signature.

NEASE, WILLIAM,
2336 Front Rd., LaSalle, Ontario Canada N9J 2C4, wnease@hotmail.com Web: www.unsubtleblades.com
    Specialties: Hatchets, choppers, and Japanese-influenced designs. **Technical:** Stock removal. Works A-2, D-2, S-7, O-1, powder stainless alloys, composite laminate blades with steel edges. **Prices:** $125 to $2200. **Remarks:** Part-time maker since 1994. **Mark:** Initials W.M.N. engraved in cursive on exposed tangs or on the spine of blades.

NEDVED, DAN,
206 Park Dr, Kalispell, MT 59901, bushido2222@yahoo.com
    Specialties: Slip joint folders, liner locks, straight knives. **Patterns** Mostly traditional or modern blend with traditional lines. **Technical:** Grinds ATS-34, 440C, 1095 and uses other makers Damascus. **Prices:** $95 and up. Mostly in the $150 to $200 range. **Remarks:** Part-time maker, averages 2 a month. **Mark:** Dan Nedved or Nedved with serial # on opposite side.

NEELY, GREG,
5419 Pine St, Bellaire, TX 77401, Phone: 713-991-2677, gtneely64@comcast.net
    Specialties: Traditional patterns and his own patterns for work and/or collecting. **Patterns:** Hunters, Bowies and utility/camp knives. **Technical:** Forges own Damascus, 1084, 1044, 5160 and some tool steels. Differentially tempers. **Prices:** $225 to $5000. **Remarks:** Part-time maker; first knife sold in 1987. **Mark:** Last name or interlocked initials, MS.

NEILSON, J,
291 Scouten Rd., Wyalusing, PA 18853, Phone: 570-746-4944, mountainhollow@epix.net; Web: www.mountainhollow.net
    Specialties: Working and collectable fixed blade knives. **Patterns:** Hunter/fighters, Bowies, neck knives and daggers. **Technical:** 1084, 1095, 5160, W-2, 52100, maker's own Damascus. **Prices:** $175 to $2500. **Remarks:** ABS Master Smith, full-time maker, first knife sold in 2000, doing business as Neilson's Mountain Hollow. Each knife comes with a sheath. **Mark:** J. Neilson MS.

NELSON, KEN,
PO BOX 272, Pittsville, WI 54466, Phone: 715-323-0538 or 715-884-6448, ken@ironwolfonline.com Web: www.ironwolfonline.com
    Specialties: Working straight knives, period pieces. **Patterns:** Utility, hunters, dirks, daggers, throwers, hawks, axes, swords, pole arms and blade blanks as well. **Technical:** Forges 5160, 52100, W2, 10xx, L6, carbon steels and own Damascus. Does his own heat treating. **Prices:** $50 to $350, some to $3000. **Remarks:** Part-time maker. First knife sold in 1995. Doing business as Iron Wolf Forge. **Mark:** Stylized wolf paw print.

NELSON, TOM,
PO Box 2298, Wilropark 1731, Gauteng, SOUTH AFRICA, Phone: 27 11 7663991, Fax: 27 11 7687161, tom.nelson@telkomsa.net
    Specialties: Own Damascus (Hosaic etc.) **Patterns:** One-of-a-kind art knives, swords and axes. **Prices:** $500 to $1000.

NETO JR., NELSON AND DE CARVALHO, HENRIQUE M.,
R. Joao Margarido No 20-V, Guerra, Braganca Paulista, SP-12900-000, BRAZIL, Phone: 011-7843-6889 or, 011-7843-6889
    Specialties: Straight knives and folders. **Patterns:** Bowies, katanas, jambyias and others. **Technical:** Forges high-carbon steels. **Prices:** $70 to $3000.

Remarks: Full-time makers; first knife sold in 1990. **Mark:** HandN.

NEUHAEUSLER, ERWIN,
Heiligenangerstrasse 15, 86179 Augsburg, GERMANY, Phone: 0821/81 49 97, ERWIN@AUASBURGKNIVES.DE
    Specialties: Using straight knives of his design. **Patterns:** Hunters, boots, Bowies and folders. **Technical:** Grinds ATS-34, RWL-34 and Damascus. **Prices:** $200 to $750. **Remarks:** Spare-time maker; first knife sold in 1991. **Mark:** Etched logo, last name and city.

NEVLING, MARK,
BURR OAK KNIVES, PO Box 9, Hume, IL 61932, Phone: 217-887-2522, burroakknives@aol.com; Web: www.burroakknives.com
    Specialties: Straight knives and folders of his own design. **Patterns:** Hunters, fighters, Bowies, folders, and small executive knives. **Technical:** Convex grinds, Forges, uses only high-carbon and Damascus. **Prices:** $200 to $2000. **Remarks:** Full-time maker, first knife sold 1988. Apprentice Damascus smith to George Werth.

NEWBERRY, ALLEN,
PO BOX 301, Lowell, AR 72745, Phone: 479-530-6439, newberry@newberryknives.com Web: www.newberryknives.com
    Specialties: Fixed blade knives both forged and stock removal. **Patterns:** Traditional patterns as well as newer designs inspired by historical and international blades. **Technical:** Uses 1095, W2, 5160, 154-CM, other steels by request. **Prices:** $150 to $450+. **Remarks:** Many of the knives feature hamons. **Mark:** Newberry with a capital N for forged pieces and newberry with a lower case n for stock removal pieces.

NEWCOMB, CORBIN,
628 Woodland Ave, Moberly, MO 65270, Phone: 660-263-4639
    Specialties: Working straight knives and folders; period pieces. **Patterns:** Hunters, axes, Bowies, folders, buckskinned blades and boots. **Technical:** Hollow-grinds D2, 440C and 154CM; prefers natural handle materials. Makes own Damascus; offers cable Damascus. **Prices:** $100 to $500. **Remarks:** Full-time maker; first knife sold in 1982. Doing business as Corbin Knives. **Mark:** First name and serial number.

NEWHALL, TOM,
3602 E 42nd Stravenue, Tucson, AZ 85713, Phone: 520-721-0562, gggaz@aol.com

NEWTON, LARRY,
1758 Pronghorn Ct, Jacksonville, FL 32225, Phone: 904-221-2340, CNewton1234@aol.com
    Specialties: Traditional and slender high-grade gentlemen's automatic folders, locking liner type tactical, and working straight knives. **Patterns:** Front release locking folders, interframes, hunters, and skinners. **Technical:** Grinds Damascus, ATS-34, 440C and D2. **Prices:** Folders start at $350, straights start at $150. **Remarks:** Retired teacher. Full-time maker. First knife sold in 1989. Won Best Folder for 2008 - Blade Magazine. **Mark:** Last name.

NEWTON, RON,
223 Ridge Ln, London, AR 72847, Phone: 479-293-3001, rnewton@cei.net Web: ronnewtonknives.com
    Specialties: All types of folders and fixed blades. Blackpowder gun knife combos. **Patterns:** Traditional slip joint, multi-blade patterns, antique bowie repros. **Technical:** Forges traditional and mosaid damascus. Performs engraving and gold inlay. **Prices:** $500 and up. **Remarks:** Creates hidden mechanisms in assisted opening folders. **Mark:** NEWTON M.S. in a western invitation font."

NICHOLS, CHAD,
1125 Cr 185, Blue Springs, MS 38828, Phone: 662-538-5966, chadn28@hotmail.com Web: chadnicholsdamascus.com
    Specialties: Gents folders and everyday tactical/utility style knives and fixed hunters. **Technical:** Makes own stainless damascus, mosaic damascus, and high carbon damascus. **Prices:** $450 - $1000. **Mark:** Name and Blue Springs.

NICHOLSON, R. KENT,
PO Box 204, Phoenix, MD 21131, Phone: 410-323-6925
    Specialties: Large using knives. **Patterns:** Bowies and camp knives in the Moran-style. **Technical:** Forges W2, 9260, 5160; makes Damascus. **Prices:** $150 to $995. **Remarks:** Part-time maker; first knife sold in 1984. **Mark:** Name.

NIELSON, JEFF V,
1060 S Jones Rd, Monroe, UT 84754, Phone: 435-527-4242, jvn1u205@hotmail.com
    Specialties: Classic knives of his design and to customer specs. **Patterns:** Fighters, hunters; miniatures. **Technical:** Grinds 440C stainless and Damascus. **Prices:** $100 to $1200. **Remarks:** Part-time maker; first knife sold in 1991. **Mark:** Name, location.

NIEMUTH, TROY,
3143 North Ave, Sheboygan, WI 53083, Phone: 414-452-2927
    Specialties: Period pieces and working/using straight knives of his design and to customer specs. **Patterns:** Hunters and utility/camp knives. **Technical:** Grinds 440C, 1095 and A2. **Prices:** $85 to $350; some to $500. **Remarks:** Full-time maker; first knife sold in 1995. **Mark:** Etched last name.

NILSSON, JONNY WALKER,
Tingsstigen 11, SE-933 33 Arvidsjaur, SWEDEN, Phone: (46) 960-13048, 0960.1304@telia.com; Web: www.jwnknives.com
Specialties: High-end collectible Nordic hunters, engraved reindeer antler. World class freehand engravings. Matching engraved sheaths in leather, bone and Arctic wood with inlays. Combines traditional techniques and design with his own innovations. Master Bladesmith who specializes in forging mosaic Damascus. Sells unique mosaic Damascus bar stock to folder makers. **Patterns:** Own designs and traditional Sami designs. **Technical:** Mosaic Damascus of UHB 20 C 15N20 with pure nickel, hardness HRC 58-60. **Prices:** $1500 to $6000. **Remarks:** Full-time maker since 1988. Nordic Champion (5 countries) numerous times, 50 first prizes in Scandinavian shows. Yearly award in his name in Nordic Championship. Knives inspired by 10,000 year old indigenous Sami culture. **Mark:** JN on sheath, handle, custom wood box. JWN on blade.

NIRO, FRANK,
2469 Waverly Dr., Blind Bay, B.C. Canada V0E1H1, Phone: 250-675-4234, niro@telus.net
Specialties: Liner locking folding knives in his designs in what might be called standard patterns. **Technical:** Enjoys grinding mosaic Damascus with pure nickel of the make up for blades that are often double ground; as well as meteorite for bolsters which are then etched and heat colored. Uses 416 stainless for spacers with inlays of natural materials, gem stones with also file work. Liners are made from titanium are most often fully file worked and anodized. Only uses natural materials particularly mammoth ivory for scales. **Prices:** $500 to $1500 **Remarks:** Full time maker. Has been selling knives for over thirty years. **Mark:** Last name on the inside of the spacer.

NISHIUCHI, MELVIN S,
6121 Forest Park Dr, Las Vegas, NV 89156, Phone: 702-501-3724, msnknives@yahoo.com
Specialties: Collectable quality using/working knives. **Patterns:** Locking liner folders, fighters, hunters and fancy personal knives. **Technical:** Grinds ATS-34 and Devin Thomas Damascus; prefers semi-precious stone and exotic natural handle materials. **Prices:** $375 to $2000. **Remarks:** Part-time maker; first knife sold in 1985. **Mark:** Circle with a line above it.

NOLEN, STEVE,
105 Flowingwells Rd, Pottsboro, TX 75076, Phone: 903-786-2454, blademaster@nolenknives.com; Web: www.nolenknives.com
Specialties: Working knives; display pieces. **Patterns:** Wide variety of straight knives, butterflies and buckles. **Technical:** Grind D2, 440C and 154CM. Offer filework; make exotic handles. **Prices:** $150 to $800; some higher. **Remarks:** Full-time maker; Steve is third generation maker. **Mark:** NK in oval logo.

NORDELL, INGEMAR,
Skarpå 2103, 82041 Färila, SWEDEN, Phone: 0651-23347
Specialties: Classic working and using straight knives. **Patterns:** Hunters, Bowies and fighters. **Technical:** Forges and grinds ATS-34, D2 and Sandvik. **Prices:** $120 to $1500. **Remarks:** Part-time maker; first knife sold in 1985. **Mark:** Initials or name.

NOREN, DOUGLAS E,
14676 Boom Rd, Springlake, MI 49456, Phone: 616-842-4247, gnoren@icsdata.com
Specialties: Hand forged blades, custom built and made to order. Hand file work, carving and casting. Stag and stacked handles. Replicas of Scagel and Joseph Rogers. Hand tooled custom made sheaths. **Technical:** Master smith, 5160, 52100 and 1084 steel. **Prices:** Start at $250. **Remarks:** Sole authorship, works in all mediums, ABS Mastersmith, all knives come with a custom hand-tooled sheath. Also makes anvils. Enjoys the challenge and meeting people.

NORFLEET, ROSS W,
4110 N Courthouse Rd, Providence Forge, VA 23140-3420, Phone: 804-966-2596, rossknife@aol.com
Specialties: Classic, traditional and working/using knives of his design or in standard patterns. **Patterns:** Hunters and folders. **Technical:** Hollow-grinds 440C and ATS-34. **Prices:** $150 to $550. **Remarks:** Part-time maker; first knife sold in 1992. **Mark:** Last name.

NORTON, DON,
95 N Wilkison Ave, Port Townsend, WA 98368-2534, Phone: 306-385-1978
Specialties: Fancy and plain straight knives. **Patterns:** Hunters, small Bowies, tantos and boot knives, fillets. **Technical:** Prefers 440C, Micarta, exotic woods and other natural handle materials. Hollow-grinds all knives except fillet knives. **Prices:** $185 to $2800; average is $200. **Remarks:** Full-time maker; first knife sold in 1980. **Mark:** Full name, Hsi Shuai, city, state.

NOWLAND, RICK,
3677 E Bonnie Rd, Waltonville, IL 62894, Phone: 618-279-3170, ricknowland@frontiernet.net
Specialties: Slip joint folders in traditional patterns. **Patterns:** Trapper, whittler, sowbelly, toothpick and copperhead. **Technical:** Uses ATS-34, bolsters and liners have integral construction. **Prices:** $225 to $1000. **Remarks:** Part-time maker. **Mark:** Last name.

NUNN, GREGORY,
HC64 Box 2107, Castle Valley, UT 84532, Phone: 435-259-8607
Specialties: High-art working and using knives of his design; new edition knife with handle made from anatomized dinosaur bone, first ever made. **Patterns:** Flaked stone knives. **Technical:** Uses gem-quality agates, jaspers and obsidians for blades. **Prices:** $250 to $2300. **Remarks:** Full-time maker; first knife sold in 1989. **Mark:** Name, knife and edition numbers, year made.

O

OATES, LEE,
PO BOX 1391, La Porte, TX 77572, Phone: 281-471-6060, bearoates@att.net Web: www.bearclawknives.com
Specialties: Friction folders, period correct replicas, traditional, working and primitive knives of my design or to customer specs. **Patterns:** Bowies, teflon-coated fighters, daggers, hunters, fillet and kitchen cutlery. **Technical:** Heat treating services for other makers. Forges carbon, 440C, D2, and makes own Damascus, stock removal on SS and kitchen cutlery, Teflon coatings available on custom hunters/fighters, makes own sheaths. **Prices:** $150 to $2500. **Remarks:** Full-time maker and heat treater since 1996. First knife sold in 1988. **Mark:** Harmony (yin/yang) symbol with two bear tracks inside all forged blades; etched "Commanche Cutlery" on SS kitchen cutlery.

O'BRIEN, MIKE J.,
3807 War Bow, San Antonio, TX 78238, Phone: 210-256-0673, obrien8700@att.net
Specialties: Quality straight knives of his design. **Patterns:** Mostly daggers (safe queens), some hunters. **Technical:** Grinds 440c, ATS-34, and CPM-154. Emphasis on clean workmanship and solid design. Likes hand-rubbed blades and fittings, exotic woods. **Prices:** $300 to $700 and up. **Remarks:** Part-time maker, made first knife in 1988. **Mark:** O'BRIEN in semi-circle.

OCHS, CHARLES F,
124 Emerald Lane, Largo, FL 33771, Phone: 727-536-3827, Fax: 727-536-3827, chuckandbelle@juno.com
Specialties: Working knives; period pieces. **Patterns:** Hunters, fighters, Bowies, buck skinners and folders. **Technical:** Forges 52100, 5160 and his own Damascus. **Prices:** $150 to $1800; some to $2500. **Remarks:** Full-time maker; first knife sold in 1978. **Mark:** OX Forge.

OCHS, ERIC,
PO BOX 1311, Sherwood, OR 97140, Phone: 503-925-9790, eric@ochs.com Web: www.ochssherworx.com
Specialties: Hunting and tactical knives including choppers and folding knives. **Patterns:** Primarily full-tang knives, tapered tangs available wth handrub, satin or stonewash finishes and synthetic, wood or bone handles. **Technical:** CPM S30V, CPM S35VN, CPM3V, CPM 154CM and Elmax as well as Damasteel and Chad Nichols Damascus. **Prices:** $100 - $950. **Remarks:** Currently part-time maker; made first knife in 2008 and started selling knives in mid-2009. **Mark:** The words "Ochs Sherworx" separated by an eight point compass insignia.

O'DELL, CLYDE,
176 Ouachita 404, Camden, AR 71701, Phone: 870-574-2754, abcodell@arkansas.net
Specialties: Working knives. **Patterns:** Hunters, camp knives, Bowies, daggers, tomahawks. **Technical:** Forges 5160 and 1084. **Prices:** Starting at $125. **Remarks:** Spare-time maker. **Mark:** Last name.

ODGEN, RANDY W,
10822 Sage Orchard, Houston, TX 77089, Phone: 713-481-3601

ODOM JR., VICTOR L.,
PO Box 572, North, SC 29112, Phone: 803-247-2749, cell 803-608-0829, vlodom3@tds.net Web: www.knifemakercentral.com
Specialties: Forged knives and tomahawks; stock removal knives. **Patterns:** Hunters, Bowies, George Herron patterns, and folders. **Technical:** Use 1095, 5160, 52100 high carbon and alloy steels, ATS-34, and 154 CM. **Prices:** Straight knives $60 and up. Folders $250 and up. **Remarks:** Student of Mr. George Henron. SCAK.ORG. Secretary of the Couth Carolina Association of Knifemakers. **Mark:** Steel stamp "ODOM" and etched "Odom Forge North, SC" plus a serial number.

OGDEN, BILL,
OGDEN KNIVES, PO Box 52, Avis
AVIS, PA 17721, Phone: 570-974-9114
Specialties: One-of-a-kind, liner-lock folders, hunters, skinners, minis. **Technical:** Grinds ATS-34, 440-C, D2, 52100, Damascus, natural and unnatural handle materials, hand-stitched custom sheaths. **Prices:** $50 and up. **Remarks:** Part-time maker since 1992. **Marks:** Last name or "OK" stamp (Ogden Knives).

OGLETREE JR., BEN R,
2815 Israel Rd, Livingston, TX 77351, Phone: 409-327-8315
Specialties: Working/using straight knives of his design. **Patterns:** Hunters, kitchen and utility/camp knives. **Technical:** Grinds ATS-34, W1 and 1075; heat-treats. **Prices:** $200 to $400. **Remarks:** Part-time maker; first knife sold in 1955. **Mark:** Last name, city and state in oval with a tree on either side.

O'HARE, SEAN,
1831 Rte. 776, Grand Manan, NB, CANADA E5G 2H9, Phone: 506-662-8524, sean@ohareknives.com; Web: www.ohareknives.com
Specialties: Fixed blade hunters and folders. **Patterns:** Small to large hunters and daily carry folders. **Technical:** Stock removal, flat ground. **Prices:** $220 USD to $800 USD. **Remarks:** Strives to balance aesthetics, functionality and durability. **Mark:** 1st line - "OHARE KNIVES", 2nd line - "CANADA."

OLIVE, MICHAEL E,
6388 Angora Mt Rd, Leslie, AR 72645, Phone: 870-363-4668
Specialties: Fixed blades. **Patterns:** Bowies, camp knives, fighters and hunters. **Technical:** Forged blades of 1084, W2, 5160, Damascus of 1084, and1572. **Prices:** $250 and up. **Remarks:** Received J.S. stamp in 2005. **Mark:** Olive.

OLIVER, TODD D,
894 Beaver Hollow, Spencer, IN 47460, Phone: 812-829-1762
Specialties: Damascus hunters and daggers. High-carbon as well. **Patterns:** Ladder, twist random. **Technical:** Sole author of all his blades. **Prices:** $350 and up. **Remarks:** Learned bladesmithing from Jim Batson at the ABS school and Damascus from Billy Merritt in Indiana. **Mark:** T.D. Oliver Spencer IN. Two crossed swords and a battle ax.

OLSON, DARROLD E,
PO Box 1539, Springfield, OR 97477, Phone: 541-285-1412
Specialties: Straight knives and folders of his design and to customer specs. **Patterns:** Hunters, liner locks and slip joints. **Technical:** Grinds ATS-34, 154CM and 440C. Uses anodized titanium; sheaths wet-molded. **Prices:** $125 to $550 and up. **Remarks:** Part-time maker; first knife sold in 1989. **Mark:** Name, type of steel and year.

OLSON, JOE,
210 W. Simson Ave, Geyser, MT 59447, Phone: 406-735-4404, joekeri@3rivers.net Web: www.olsonhandmade.com
Specialties: Theme based art knives specializing in mosaic Damascus autos, folders, and straight knives, all sole authorship. **Patterns:** Mas. **Technical:** Foix. **Prices:** $300 to $5000 with most in the $3500 range. **Remarks:** Full-time maker for 15 years. **Mark:** Folders marked OLSON relief carved into back bar. Carbon steel straight knives stamped OLSON, forged hunters also stamped JS on reverse side.

OLSON, ROD,
Box 5973, High River, AB, CANADA T1V 1P6, Phone: 403-652-2744, Fax: 403-646-5838
Specialties: Lockback folders with gold toothpicks. **Patterns:** Locking folders. **Technical:** Grinds ATS-34 blades and spring, filework-14kt bolsters and liners. **Prices:** Mid range. **Remarks:** Part-time maker; first knife sold in 1979. **Mark:** Last name on blade.

OLSZEWSKI, STEPHEN,
1820 Harkney Hill Rd, Coventry, RI 02816, Phone: 401-397-4774, blade5377@yahoo.com; Web: www.olszewskiknives.com
Specialties: Lock back, liner locks, automatics (art knives). **Patterns:** One-of-a-kind art knives specializing in figurals. **Technical:** Damascus steel, titanium file worked liners, fossil ivory and pearl. Double actions. **Prices:** $400 to $20,000. **Remarks:** Will custom build to your specifications. Quality work with guarantee. **Mark:** SCO inside fish symbol. Also "Olszewski."

O'MACHEARLEY, MICHAEL,
129 Lawnview Dr., Wilmington, OH 45177, Phone: 937-728-2818, omachearleycustomknives@yahoo.com
Specialties: Forged and Stock removal; hunters, skinners, bowies, plain to fancy. **Technical:** ATS-34 and 5160, forges own Damascus. **Prices:** $180-$1000 and up. **Remarks:** Full-time maker, first knife made in 1999. **Mark:** Last name and shamrock.

O'MALLEY, DANIEL,
4338 Evanston Ave N, Seattle, WA 98103, Phone: 206-527-0315
Specialties: Custom chef's knives. **Remarks:** Making knives since 1997.

ONION, KENNETH J,
47-501 Hui Kelu St, Kaneohe, HI 96744, Phone: 808-239-1300, shopjunky@aol.com; Web: www.kenonionknives.com
Specialties: Folders featuring speed safe as well as other invention gadgets. **Patterns:** Hybrid, art, fighter, utility. **Technical:** S30V, CPM 154V, Cowry Y, SQ-2 and Damascus. **Prices:** $500 to $20,000. **Remarks:** Full-time maker; designer and inventor. First knife sold in 1991. **Mark:** Name and state.

ORFORD, BEN,
Nethergreen Farm, Ridgeway Cross, Malvern, Worcestershire, England WR13 5JS, Phone: 44 01886 880410, web: www.benorford.com
Specialties: Working knives for woodcraft and the outdoorsman, made to his own designs. **Patterns:** Mostly flat Scandinavian grinds, full and partial tang. Also makes specialist woodcraft tools and hook knives. Custom leather sheaths by Lois, his wife. **Technical:** Grinds and forges 01, EN9, EN43, EN45 plus recycled steels. Heat treats. **Prices:** $25 - $650. **Remarks:** Full-time maker; first knife made in 1997. **Mark:** Celtic knot with name underneath.

ORTEGA, BEN M,
165 Dug Rd, Wyoming, PA 18644, Phone: 717-696-3234

ORTON, RICH,
739 W. Palm Dr., Covina, CA 91722, Phone: 626-332-3441, rorton2@ca.rr.com
Specialties: Straight knives only. **Patterns:** Fighters, hunters, skinners. **Technical:** Grinds ATS-34. Heat treats by Paul Bos. **Prices:** $100 to $1000. **Remarks:** Full-time maker; first knife sold in 1992. Doing business as Orton Knife Works. **Mark:** Last name, city state (maker)

OSBORNE, DONALD H,
5840 N McCall, Clovis, CA 93611, Phone: 559-299-9483, Fax: 559-298-1751, oforge@sbcglobal.net
Specialties: Traditional working using straight knives and folder of his design. **Patterns:** Working straight knives, Bowies, hunters, camp knives and folders. **Technical:** Forges carbon steels and makes Damascus. Grinds ATS-34, 154CM, and 440C. **Prices:** $150 and up. **Remarks:** Part-time maker. **Mark:** Last name logo and J.S.

OSBORNE, WARREN,
#2-412 Alysa Ln, Waxahachie, TX 75167, Phone: 972-935-0899, Fax: 972-937-9004, ossie6@mac.com Web: www.osborneknives.com
Specialties: Investment grade collectible, interframes, one-of-a-kinds; unique locking mechanisms and cutting competition knives. **Patterns:** Folders; bolstered and interframes; conventional lockers, front lockers and back lockers; some slip-joints; some high-art pieces. **Technical:** Grinds CPM M4, BG42, CPM S30V, Damascus - some forged and stock removed cutting competition knives. **Prices:** $1200 to $3500; some to $5000. Interframes $1250 to $3000. **Remarks:** Full-time maker; first knife sold in 1980. **Mark:** Last name in boomerang logo.

OTT, FRED,
1257 Rancho Durango Rd, Durango, CO 81303, Phone: 970-375-9669, fredsknives@durango.net
Patterns: Bowies, hunters tantos and daggers. **Technical:** Forges 1086M, W2 and Damascus. **Prices:** $250 to $1000. **Remarks:** Full-time maker. **Mark:** Last name.

OTT, TED,
154 Elgin Woods Ln., Elgin, TX 78621, Phone: 512-413-2243, tedottknives@aol.com
Specialties: Fixed blades, chef knives, butcher knives, bowies, fillet and hunting knives. **Technical:** Use mainly CPM powder steel, also ATS-34 and D-2. B**Prices:** $250 - $1000, depending on embellishments, including scrimshaw and engraving. **Remarks:** Part-time maker; sold first knife in 1993. Won Blade Show world championship in 2010, along with the Bladesports championship. **Mark:** Ott Knives Elgin Texas.

OUYE, KEITH,
PO Box 25307, Honolulu, HI 96825, Phone: 808-395-7000, keithouyeknives@yahoo.com; Web: www.keithouyeknives.com
Specialties: Folders with 1/8 blades and titanium handles. **Patterns:** Tactical design with liner lock and flipper. **Technical:** Blades are stainless steel ATS 34, CPM154 and S30V. Titanium liners (.071) and scales 3/16 pivots and stop pin, titanium pocket clip. Heat treat by Paul Bos. **Prices:** $450-$600 with engraved knives starting at $995 and up. **Remarks:** Engraving done by C.J. Cai (www.caiengraving.com) and Bruce Shaw Retired, so basically a full time knifemaker. Sold first fixed blade in 2004 and first folder in 2005. **Mark:** Ouye/Hawaii with steel type on back side **Other:** Selected by Blade Magazine (March 2006 issue) as one of five makers to watch in 2006.

OVEREYNDER, T R,
1800 S. Davis Dr, Arlington, TX 76013, Phone: 817-277-4812, Fax: 817-277-4812, trovereynderknives@sbcglobal.net; Web: www.overeynderknives.com
Specialties: Highly finished collector-grade knives. Multi-blades. **Patterns:** Fighters, Bowies, daggers, locking folders, 70 percent collector-grade multi blade slip joints, 25 percent interframe, 5 percent fixed blade **Technical:** Grinds CPM-D2, BG-42, S60V, S30V, CPM154, CPM M4, RWL-34 vendor supplied Damascus. Has been making titanium-frame folders since 1977. **Prices:** $750 to $2000, some to $7000. **Remarks:** Full-time maker; first knife sold in 1977. Doing business as TRO Knives. **Mark:** T.R. OVEREYNDER KNIVES, city and state.

OWENS, DONALD,
2274 Lucille Ln, Melbourne, FL 32935, Phone: 321-254-9765

OWENS, JOHN,
14500 CR 270, Nathrop, CO 81236, Phone: 719-395-0870
Specialties: Hunters. **Prices:** $200 to $375 some to $650. **Remarks:** Spare-time maker. **Mark:** Last name.

OWNBY, JOHN C,
708 Morningside Tr., Murphy, TX 75094-4365, Phone: 972-442-7352, john@johnownby.com; Web: www.johnownby.com
Specialties: Hunters, utility/camp knives. **Patterns:** Hunters, locking folders and utility/camp knives. **Technical:** 440C, D2 and ATS-34. All blades are flat ground. Prefers natural materials for handles—exotic woods, horn and antler. **Prices:** $150 to $350; some to $500. **Remarks:** Part-time maker; first knife sold in 1993. Doing business as John C. Ownby Handmade Knives. **Mark:** Name, city, state.

OYSTER, LOWELL R,
543 Grant Rd, Corinth, ME 04427, Phone: 207-884-8663
Specialties: Traditional and original designed multi-blade slip-joint folders. **Patterns:** Hunters, minis, camp and fishing knives. **Technical:** Grinds O1; heat-treats. **Prices:** $55 to $450; some to $750. **Remarks:** Full-time maker; first knife sold in 1981. **Mark:** A scallop shell.

P

PACKARD, BOB,
PO Box 311, Elverta, CA 95626, Phone: 916-991-5218
Specialties: Traditional working/using straight knives of his design and to customer specs. **Patterns:** Hunters, fishing knives, utility/camp knives. **Technical:** Grinds ATS-34, 440C; Forges 52100, 5168 and cable Damascus. **Prices:** $75 to $225. **Mark:** Engraved name and year.

PADILLA—PATRICK

PADILLA, GARY,
PO Box 5706, Bellingham, WA 98227, Phone: 360-756-7573, gkpadilla@yahoo.com
Specialties: Unique knives of all designs and uses. **Patterns:** Hunters, kitchen knives, utility/camp knives and obsidian ceremonial knives. **Technical:** Grinds 440C, ATS-34, O1 and Damascus. **Prices:** Generally $100 to $200. **Remarks:** Part-time maker; first knife sold in 1977. **Mark:** Stylized name.

PAGE, LARRY,
1200 Mackey Scott Rd, Aiken, SC 29801-7620, Phone: 803-648-0001
Specialties: Working knives of his design. **Patterns:** Hunters, boots and fighters. **Technical:** Grinds ATS-34. **Prices:** Start at $85. **Remarks:** Part-time maker; first knife sold in 1983. **Mark:** Name, city and state in oval.

PAGE, REGINALD,
6587 Groveland Hill Rd, Groveland, NY 14462, Phone: 716-243-1643
Specialties: High-art straight knives and one-of-a-kind folders of his design. **Patterns:** Hunters, locking folders and slip-joint folders. **Technical:** Forges O1, 5160 and his own Damascus. Prefers natural handle materials but will work with Micarta. **Remarks:** Spare-time maker; first knife sold in 1985. **Mark:** First initial, last name.

PAINTER, TONY,
87 Fireweed Dr, Whitehorse Yukon, CANADA Y1A 5T8, Phone: 867-633-3323, jimmies@klondiker.com; Web: www.tonypainterdesigns.com
Specialties: One-of-a-kind using knives, some fancy, fixed and folders. **Patterns:** No fixed patterns. **Technical:** Grinds ATS-34, D2, O1, S30V, Damascus satin finish. Prefers to use exotic woods and other natural materials. Micarta and G10 on working knives. **Prices:** Starting at $200. **Remarks:** Full-time knifemaker and carver. First knife sold in 1996. **Mark:** Two stamps used: initials TP in a circle and painter.

PALM, RIK,
10901 Scripps Ranch Blvd, San Diego, CA 92131, Phone: 858-530-0407, rikpalm@knifesmith.com; Web: www.knifesmith.com
Specialties: Sole authorship of one-of-a-kind unique art pieces, working/using knives and sheaths. **Patterns:** Carved nature themed knives, camp, hunters, friction folders, tomahawks, and small special pocket knives. **Technical:** Makes own Damascus, forges 5160H, 1084, 1095, W2, O1. Does his own heat treating including clay hardening. **Prices:** $80 and up. **Remarks:** American Bladesmith Society Journeyman Smith. First blade sold in 2000. **Mark:** Stamped, hand signed, etched last name signature.

PALMER, TAYLOR,
TAYLOR-MADE SCENIC KNIVES INC., Box 97, Blanding, UT 84511, Phone: 435-678-2523, taylormadewoodeu@citlink.net
Specialties: Bronze carvings inside of blade area. **Prices:** $250 and up. **Mark:** Taylor Palmer Utah.

PANAK, PAUL S,
6103 Leon Rd., Andover, OH 44003, Phone: 330-442-2724, burn@burnknives.com; Web: www.burnknives.com
Specialties: Italian-styled knives. DA OTF's, Italian style stilettos. **Patterns:** Vintage-styled Italians, fighting folders and high art gothic-styles all with various mechanisms. **Technical:** Grinds ATS-34, 154 CM, 440C and Damascus. **Prices:** $800 to $3000. **Remarks:** Full-time maker, first knife sold in 1998. **Mark:** "Burn."

PANCHENKO, SERGE,
5927 El Sol Way, Citrus Heights, CA 95621, Phone: 916-588-8821, serge@sergeknives.com Web: www.sergeknives.com
Specialties: Unique art knives using natural materials, copper and carbon steel for a rustic look. **Patterns:** Art knives, hunting and outdoor knives, Japanese style knives and tactical. **Technical:** Forges and grinds carbon steels. **Prices:** $100 - $600. **Remarks:** Part-time maker, first knife sold in 2008. **Mark:** SERGE

PARDUE, JOE,
PO Box 693, Spurger, TX 77660, Phone: 409-429-7074, Fax: 409-429-5657

PARDUE, MELVIN M,
4461 Jerkins Rd., Repton, AL 36475, Phone: 251-248-2686, mpardue@frontiernet.net; Web: www.pardueknives.com
Specialties: Folders, collectable, combat, utility and tactical. **Patterns:** Lockback, liner lock, push button; all blade and handle patterns. **Technical:** Grinds 154CM, 440C, 12C27. Forges mokume and Damascus. Uses titanium. **Prices:** $400 to $1600. **Remarks:** Full-time maker, Guild member, ABS member, AFC member. First knife made in 1957; first knife sold professionally in 1974. **Mark:** Mel Pardue.

PARKER, CLIFF,
6350 Tulip Dr, Zephyrhills, FL 33544, Phone: 813-973-1682, cooldamascus@aol.com Web: cliffparkerknives.com
Specialties: Damascus gent knives. **Patterns:** Locking liners, some straight knives. **Technical:** Mostly use 1095, 1084, 15N20, 203E and powdered steel. **Prices:** $700 to $2100. **Remarks:** Making own Damascus and specializing in mosaics; first knife sold in 1996. Full-time beginning in 2000. **Mark:** CP.

PARKER, J E,
11 Domenica Cir, Clarion, PA 16214, Phone: 814-226-4837, jimparkerknives@hotmail.com Web:www.jimparkerknives.com
Specialties: Fancy/embellished, traditional and working straight knives of his design and to customer specs. Engraving and scrimshaw by the best in the business. **Patterns:** Bowies, hunters and LinerLock® folders. **Technical:**

Grinds 440C, 440V, ATS-34 and nickel Damascus. Prefers mastodon, oosik, amber and malachite handle material. **Prices:** $75 to $5200. **Remarks:** Full-time maker; first knife sold in 1991. Doing business as Custom Knife. **Mark:** J E Parker and Clarion PA stamped or etched in blade.

PARKER, ROBERT NELSON,
1527 E Fourth St, Royal Oak, MI 48067, Phone: 248-545-8211, rnparkerknives@wowway.com; Web: classicknifedesign@wowway.com
Specialties: Traditional working and using straight knives of his design. **Patterns:** Chutes, subhilts, hunters, and fighters. **Technical:** Grinds ATS-34; GB-42, S-30V, BG-42, ATS, 34-D-Z, no forging, hollow and flat grinds, full and hidden tangs. Hand-stitched leather sheaths. **Prices:** $400 to $1400; some to $2000. **Remarks:** Full-time maker; first knife sold in 1986. I do forge sometimes. **Mark:** Full name.

PARKS, BLANE C,
15908 Crest Dr, Woodbridge, VA 22191, Phone: 703-221-4680
Specialties: Knives of his design. **Patterns:** Boots, Bowies, daggers, fighters, hunters, kitchen knives, locking and slip-joint folders, utility/camp knives, letter openers and friction folders. **Technical:** Grinds ATS-34, 440C, D2 and other carbon steels. Offers filework, silver wire inlay and wooden sheaths. **Prices:** Start at $250 to $650; some to $1000. **Remarks:** Part-time maker; first knife sold in 1993. Doing business as B.C. Parks Knives. **Mark:** First and middle initials, last name.

PARKS, JOHN,
3539 Galilee Church Rd, Jefferson, GA 30549, Phone: 706-367-4916
Specialties: Traditional working and using straight knives of his design. **Patterns:** Hunters, integral bolsters, and personal knives. **Technical:** Forges 1095 and 5168. **Prices:** $275 to $600; some to $800. **Remarks:** Part-time maker; first knife sold in 1989. **Mark:** Initials.

PARLER, THOMAS O,
11 Franklin St, Charleston, SC 29401, Phone: 803-723-9433

PARRISH, ROBERT,
271 Allman Hill Rd, Weaverville, NC 28787, Phone: 828-645-2864
Specialties: Heavy-duty working knives of his design or to customer specs. **Patterns:** Survival and duty knives; hunters and fighters. **Technical:** Grinds 440C, D2, O1 and commercial Damascus. **Prices:** $200 to $300; some to $6000. **Remarks:** Part-time maker; first knife sold in 1970. **Mark:** Initials connected, sometimes with city and state.

PARRISH III, GORDON A,
940 Lakloey Dr, North Pole, AK 99705, Phone: 907-488-0357, ga-parrish@gci.net
Specialties: Classic and high-art straight knives of his design and to customer specs; working and using knives. **Patterns:** Bowies and hunters. **Technical:** Grinds tool steel and ATS-34. Uses mostly Alaskan handle materials. **Prices:** Starting at $225. **Remarks:** Spare-time maker; first knife sold in 1980. **Mark:** Last name, FBKS. ALASKA

PARSONS, LARRY,
1038 W Kyle Way, Mustang, OK 73064, Phone: 405-376-9408, Fax: 405-376-9408, l.j.parsons@sbcglobal.net
Specialties: Variety of sheaths from plain leather, geometric stamped, also inlays of various types. **Prices:** Starting at $35 and up

PARSONS, MICHAEL R,
MCKEE KNIVES, 7042 McFarland Rd., Indianapolis, IN 46227, Phone: 317-784-7943, parsons-michael@att.net
Specialties: Hand-forged fixed-blade and folding knives, all fancy but all are useable knives. **Patterns:** Engraves, carves, wire inlay, and leather work. All knives one-of-a-kind. **Technical:** Blades forged from files, all work hand done. Doing business as McKee Knives. **Prices:** $350 to $2000. **Mark:** McKee.

PARSONS, PETE,
5905 High Country Dr., Helena, MT 59602, Phone: 406-202-0181, Parsons14@MT.net; Web: www.ParsonsMontanaKnives.com
Specialties: Forged utility blades in straight steel or Damascus (will grind stainless on customer request). Folding knives of my own design. **Patterns:** Hunters, fighters, Bowies, hikers, camp knives, everyday carry folders, tactical folders, gentleman's folders. Some customer designed pieces. **Technical:** Forges carbon steel, grinds carbon steel and some stainless. Forges own Damascus. **Mark:** Left side of blade PARSONS stamp or Parsons Helena, MT etch.

PARTRIDGE, JERRY D.,
P.O. Box 977, DeFuniak Springs, FL 32435, Phone: 850-520-4873, jerry@partridgeknives.com; Web: www.partridgeknives.com
Specialties: Fancy and working straight knives and straight razors of his designs. **Patterns:** Hunters, skinners, fighters, chef's knives, straight razors, neck knives, and miniatures. **Technical:** Grinds 440C, ATS-34, carbon Damascus, and stainless Damascus. **Prices:** $250 and up, depending on materials used. **Remarks:** Part-time maker, first knife sold in 2007. **Mark:** Partridge Knives logo on the blade; Partridge or Partridge Knives engraved in script.

PASSMORE, JIMMY D,
316 SE Elm, Hoxie, AR 72433, Phone: 870-886-1922

PATRICK, BOB,
12642 24A Ave, S. Surrey, B.C., CANADA V4A 8H9, Phone: 604-538-6214, Fax: 604-888-2683, bob@knivesonnet.com; Web: www.knivesonnet.com

Specialties: Maker's designs only, No orders. **Patterns:** Bowies, hunters, daggers, throwing knives. **Technical:** D2, 5160, Damascus. **Prices:** Good value. **Remarks:** Full-time maker; first knife sold in 1987. Doing business as Crescent Knife Works. **Mark:** Logo with name and province or Crescent Knife Works.

PATRICK, CHUCK,
4650 Pine Log Rd., Brasstown, NC 28902, Phone: 828-837-7627, chuckandpeggypatrick@gmail.com Web: www.chuckandpeggypatrick.com
Specialties: Period pieces. **Patterns:** Hunters, daggers, tomahawks, pre-Civil War folders. **Technical:** Forges hardware, his own cable and Damascus, available in fancy pattern and mosaic. **Prices:** $150 to $1000; some higher. **Remarks:** Full-time maker. **Mark:** Hand-engraved name or flying owl.

PATRICK, PEGGY,
4650 Pine Log Rd., Brasstown, NC 28902, Phone: 828-837-7627, chuckandpeggypatrick@gmail.com Web: www.chuckandpeggypatrick.com
Specialties: Authentic period and Indian sheaths, braintan, rawhide, beads and quill work. **Technical:** Does own braintan, rawhide; uses only natural dyes for quills, old color beads.

PATRICK, WILLARD C,
PO Box 5716, Helena, MT 59604, Phone: 406-458-6552, Fax: 406-458-7068, wkamar2@onewest.net
Specialties: Working straight knives and one-of-a-kind art knives of his design or to customer specs. **Patterns:** Hunters, Bowies, fish, patch and kitchen knives. **Technical:** Grinds ATS-34, 1095, O1, A2 and Damascus. **Prices:** $100 to $2000. **Remarks:** Full-time maker; first knife sold in 1989. Doing business as Wil-A-Mar Cutlery. **Mark:** Shield with last name and a dagger.

PATTAY, RUDY,
8739 N. Zurich Way, Citrus Springs, FL 34434, Phone: 516-318-4538, dolphin51@att.net; Web: www.pattayknives.com
Specialties: Fancy and working straight knives of his design. **Patterns:** Bowies, hunters, utility/camp knives, drop point, skinners. **Technical:** Hollow-grinds ATS-34, 440C, O1. Offers commercial Damascus, stainless steel soldered guards; fabricates guard and butt cap on lathe and milling machine. Heat-treats. Prefers synthetic handle materials. Offers hand-sewn sheaths. **Prices:** $100 to $350; some to $500. **Remarks:** Full-time maker; first knife sold in 1990. **Mark:** First initial, last name in sorcerer logo.

PATTERSON, PAT,
Box 246, Barksdale, TX 78828, Phone: 830-234-3586, pat@pattersonknives.com
Specialties: Traditional fixed blades and LinerLock folders. **Patterns:** Hunters and folders. **Technical:** Grinds 440C, ATS-34, D2, O1 and Damascus. **Prices:** $250 to $1000. **Remarks:** Full-time maker. First knife sold in 1991. **Mark:** Name and city.

PATTON, DICK AND ROB,
6803 View Ln, Nampa, ID 83687, Phone: 208-468-4123, grpatton@pattonknives.com; Web: www.pattonknives.com
Specialties: Custom Damascus, hand forged, fighting knives, Bowie and tactical. **Patterns:** Mini Bowie, Merlin Fighter, Mandrita Fighting Bowie. **Prices:** $100 to $2000.

PATTON, PHILLIP,
PO BOX 113, Yoder, IN 46798, phillip@pattonblades.com Web: www.pattonblades.com
Specialties: Tactical fixed blades, including fighting, camp, and general utility blades. Also makes Bowies and daggers. Known for leaf and recurve blade shapes. **Technical:** Forges carbon, stainless, and high alloy tool steels. Makes own damascus using 1084/15n20 or O1/L6. Makes own carbon/stainless laminated blades. For handle materials, prefers high end woods and sythetics. Uses 416 ss and bronze for fittings. **Prices:** $175 - $1000 for knives; $750 and up for swords. **Remarks:** Full-time maker since 2005. Two-year backlog. ABS member. **Mark:** "Phillip Patton" with Phillip above Patton.

PAULO, FERNANDES R,
Raposo Tavares No 213, Lencois Paulista, 18680, Sao Paulo, BRAZIL, Phone: 014-263-4281
Specialties: An apprentice of Jose Alberto Paschoarelli, his designs are heavily based on the later designs. **Technical:** Grinds tool steels and stainless steels. Part-time knifemaker. **Prices:** Start from $100. **Mark:** P.R.F.

PAWLOWSKI, JOHN R,
111 Herman Melville Ave, Newport News, VA 23606, Phone: 757-870-4284, Fax: 757-223-5935, www.virginiacustomcutlery.com
Specialties: Traditional working and using straight knives and folders. **Patterns:** Hunters, Bowies, fighters and camp knives. **Technical:** Stock removal, grinds 440C, ATS-34, 154CM and buys Damascus. **Prices:** $150 to $500; some higher. **Remarks:** Part-time maker, first knife sold in 1983, Knifemaker Guild Member. **Mark:** Name with attacking eagle.

PEAGLER, RUSS,
PO Box 1314, Moncks Corner, SC 29461, Phone: 803-761-1008
Specialties: Traditional working straight knives of his design and to customer specs. **Patterns:** Hunters, fighters, boots. **Technical:** Hollow-grinds 440C, ATS-34 and O1; uses Damascus steel. Prefers bone handles. **Prices:** $85 to $300; some to $500. **Remarks:** Spare-time maker; first knife sold in 1983. **Mark:** Initials.

PEASE, W D,
657 Cassidy Pike, Ewing, KY 41039, Phone: 606-845-0387, Web: www.wdpeaseknives.com
Specialties: Display-quality working folders. **Patterns:** Fighters, tantos and boots; locking folders and interframes. **Technical:** Grinds ATS-34 and commercial Damascus; has own side-release lock system. **Prices:** $500 to $1000; some to $3000. **Remarks:** Full-time maker; first knife sold in 1970. **Mark:** First and middle initials, last name and state. W. D. Pease Kentucky.

PEELE, BRYAN,
219 Ferry St, PO Box 1363, Thompson Falls, MT 59873, Phone: 406-827-4633, banana_peele@yahoo.com
Specialties: Fancy working and using knives of his design. **Patterns:** Hunters, Bowies and fighters. **Technical:** Grinds 440C, ATS-34, D2, O1 and commercial Damascus. **Prices:** $110 to $300; some to $900. **Remarks:** Part-time maker; first knife sold in 1985. **Mark:** The Elk Rack, full name, city, state.

PELLEGRIN, MIKE,
MP3 Knives, 107 White St., Troy, IL 62294-1126, Phone: 618-667-6777, Web: MP3knives.com
Specialties: Lockback folders with stone inlays, and one-of-a-kind art knives with stainless steel or damascus handles. **Technical:** Stock-removal method of blade making using 440C, Damasteel or high-carbon damascus blades. **Prices:** $800 and up. **Remarks:** Making knives since 2000. **Mark:** MP (combined) 3.

PENDLETON, LLOYD,
24581 Shake Ridge Rd, Volcano, CA 95689, Phone: 209-296-3353, Fax: 209-296-3353
Specialties: Contemporary working knives in standard patterns. **Patterns:** Hunters, fighters and boots. **Technical:** Grinds and ATS-34; mirror finishes. **Prices:** $400 to $900 **Remarks:** Full-time maker; first knife sold in 1973. **Mark:** First initial, last name logo, city and state.

PENDRAY, ALFRED H,
13950 NE 20th St, Williston, FL 32696, Phone: 352-528-6124
Specialties: Working straight knives and folders; period pieces. **Patterns:** Fighters and hunters, axes, camp knives and tomahawks. **Technical:** Forges Wootz steel; makes his own Damascus; makes traditional knives from old files and rasps. **Prices:** $125 to $1000; some to $3500. **Remarks:** Part-time maker; first knife sold in 1954. **Mark:** Last initial in horseshoe logo.

PENFOLD, MICK,
PENFOLD KNIVES, 5 Highview Close, Tremar, Cornwall PL14 5SJ, ENGLAND/UK, Phone: 01579-345783, Fax: 01579-345783, mickpenfold@btinternet.com; Web: www.penfoldknives.com
Specialties: Hunters, fighters, Bowies. **Technical:** Grinds 440C, ATS-34, Damasteel, and Damascus. **Prices:** $200 to $1800. **Remarks:** Part-time maker. First knives sold in 1999. **Mark:** Last name.

PENNINGTON, C A,
163 Kainga Rd, Kainga Christchurch 8009, NEW ZEALAND, Phone: 03-3237292, capennington@xtra.co.nz
Specialties: Classic working and collectors knives. Folders a specialty. **Patterns:** Classical styling for hunters and collectors. **Technical:** Forges his own all tool steel Damascus. Grinds D2 when requested. **Prices:** $240 to $2000. **Remarks:** Full-time maker; first knife sold in 1988. Color brochure $3. **Mark:** Name, country.

PEPIOT, STEPHAN,
73 Cornwall Blvd, Winnipeg, Man., CANADA R3J-1E9, Phone: 204-888-1499
Specialties: Working straight knives in standard patterns. **Patterns:** Hunters and camp knives. **Technical:** Grinds 440C and industrial hack-saw blades. **Prices:** $75 to $125. **Remarks:** Spare-time maker; first knife sold in 1982. Not currently taking orders. **Mark:** PEP.

PERRY, CHRIS,
1654 W. Birch, Fresno, CA 93711, Phone: 559-246-7446, chris.perry4@comcast.net
Specialties: Traditional working/using straight knives of his design. **Patterns:** Boots, hunters and utility/camp knives. **Technical:** Grinds ATS-34, Damascus, 416ss fittings, silver and gold fittings, hand-rubbed finishes. **Prices:** Starting at $250. **Remarks:** Part-time maker, first knife sold in 1995. **Mark:** Name above city and state.

PERRY, JIM,
Hope Star PO Box 648, Hope, AR 71801, jenn@comfabinc.com

PERRY, JOHN,
9 South Harrell Rd, Mayflower, AR 72106, Phone: 501-470-3043, jpknives@cyberback.com
Specialties: Investment grade and working folders; Antique Bowies and slip joints. **Patterns:** Front and rear lock folders, liner locks, hunters and Bowies. **Technical:** Grinds CPM440V, D2 and making own Damascus. Offers filework. **Prices:** $375 to $1200; some to $3500. **Remarks:** Part-time maker; first knife sold in 1991. Doing business as Perry Custom Knives. **Mark:** Initials or last name in high relief set in a diamond shape.

PERRY, JOHNNY,
PO Box 35, Inman, SC 29349, Phone: 864-431-6390, perr3838@bellsouth.net
Mark: High Ridge Forge.

PERSSON, CONNY,
PL 588, 820 50 Loos, SWEDEN, Phone: +46 657 10305, Fax: +46 657 413 435, connyknives@swipnet.se; Web: www.connyknives.com
Specialties: Mosaic Damascus. **Patterns:** Mosaic Damascus. **Technical:** Straight knives and folders. **Prices:** $1000 and up. **Mark:** C. Persson.

PETEAN, FRANCISCO AND MAURICIO,
R. Dr. Carlos de Carvalho Rosa 52, Centro, Birigui, SP-16200-000, BRAZIL, Phone: 0186-424786
Specialties: Classic knives to customer specs. **Patterns:** Bowies, boots, fighters, hunters and utility knives. **Technical:** Grinds D6, 440C and high-carbon steels. Prefers natural handle material. **Prices:** $70 to $500. **Remarks:** Full-time maker; first knife sold in 1985. **Mark:** Last name, hand made.

PETERSEN, DAN L,
10610 SW 81st, Auburn, KS 66402, Phone: 785-256-2640, dan@petersenknives.com; Web: www.petersenknives.com
Specialties: Period pieces and forged integral hilts on hunters and fighters. **Patterns:** Texas-style Bowies, boots and hunters in high-carbon and Damascus steel. **Technical:** Precision heat treatments. Bainite blades with mantensite cores. **Prices:** $400 to $5000. **Remarks:** First knife sold in 1978. ABS Master Smith. **Mark:** Stylized initials.

PETERSON, CHRIS,
Box 143, 2175 W Rockyford, Salina, UT 84654, Phone: 435-529-7194
Specialties: Working straight knives of his design. **Patterns:** Large fighters, boots, hunters and some display pieces. **Technical:** Forges O1 and meteor. Makes and sells his own Damascus. Engraves, scrimshaws and inlays. **Prices:** $150 to $600; some to $1500. **Remarks:** Full-time maker; first knife sold in 1986. **Mark:** A drop in a circle with a line through it.

PETERSON, ELDON G,
368 Antelope Trl, Whitefish, MT 59937, Phone: 406-862-2204, draino@digisys.net; Web: http://www.kmg.org/egpeterson
Specialties: Fancy and working folders, any size. **Patterns:** Lockback interframes, integral bolster folders, liner locks, and two-blades. **Technical:** Grinds 440C and ATS-34. Offers gold inlay work, gem stone inlays and engraving. **Prices:** $285 to $5000. **Remarks:** Full-time maker; first knife sold in 1974. **Mark:** Name, city and state.

PETERSON, LLOYD (PETE) C,
64 Halbrook Rd, Clinton, AR 72031, Phone: 501-893-0000, wmblade@cyberback.com
Specialties: Miniatures and mosaic folders. **Prices:** $250 and up. **Remarks:** Lead time is 6-8 months. **Mark:** Pete.

PFANENSTIEL, DAN,
1824 Lafayette Ave, Modesto, CA 95355, Phone: 209-575-5937, dpfan@sbcglobal.net
Specialties: Japanese tanto, swords. One-of-a-kind knives. **Technical:** Forges simple carbon steels, some Damascus. **Prices:** $200 to $1000. **Mark:** Circle with wave inside.

PHILIPPE, D A,
PO Box 306, Cornish, NH 03746, Phone: 603-543-0662
Specialties: Traditional working straight knives. **Patterns:** Hunters, trout and bird, camp knives etc. **Technical:** Grinds ATS-34, 440C, A-2, Damascus, flat and hollow ground. Exotic woods and antler handles. Brass, nickel silver and stainless components. **Prices:** $125 to $800. **Remarks:** Full-time maker, first knife sold in 1984. **Mark:** First initial, last name.

PHILLIPS, ALISTAIR,
Amaroo, ACT, 2914, AUSTRALIA, alistair.phillips@knives.mutantdiscovery.com; Web: http://knives.mutantdiscovery.com
Specialties: Slipjoint folders, forged or stock removal fixed blades. **Patterns:** Single blade slipjoints, smaller neck knives, and hunters. **Technical:** Flat grnds O1, ATS-34, and forged 1055. **Prices:** $80 to $400. **Remarks:** Part-time maker, first knife made in 2005 **Mark:** Stamped signature.

PHILLIPS, DENNIS,
16411 West Bennet Rd, Independence, LA 70443, Phone: 985-878-8275
Specialties: Specializes in fixed blade military combat tacticals.

PHILLIPS, DONAVON,
905 Line Prairie Rd., Morton, MS 39117, Phone: 662-907-0322, bigdknives@gmail.com
Specialties: Flat ground, tapered tang working/using knives. **Patterns:** Hunters, Capers, Fillet, EDC, Field/Camp/Survival, Competition Cutters. Will work with customers on custom designs or changes to own designs. **Technical:** Stock removal maker using CPM-M4, CPM-154, and other air-hardening steels. Will use 5160 or 52100 on larger knives. G-10 or rubber standard, will use natural material if requested including armadillo. Kydex sheath is standard, outsourced leather available.†Heat treat is done by maker. **Prices:** $100 - $1000 **Remarks:** Part-time/hobbyist maker. First knife made in 2004; first sold 2007. **Mark:** Mark is etched, first and last name forming apex of triangle, city and state at the base, D in center.

PHILLIPS, RANDY,
759 E. Francis St, Ontario, CA 91761, Phone: 909-923-4381
Specialties: Hunters, collector-grade liner locks and high-art daggers. **Technical:** Grinds D2, 440C and 154CM; embellishes. **Prices:** Start at $200. **Remarks:** Part-time maker; first knife sold in 1981. Not currently taking orders. **Mark:** Name, city and state in eagle head.

PHILLIPS, SCOTT C,
671 California Rd, Gouverneur, NY 13642, Phone: 315-287-1280, Web: www.mangusknives.com
Specialties: Sheaths in leather. Fixed blade hunters, boot knives, Bowies, buck skinners (hand forged and stock removal). **Technical:** 440C, 5160, 1095 and 52100. **Prices:** Start at $125. **Remarks:** Part-time maker; first knife sold in 1993. **Mark:** Before "2000" as above after S Mangus.

PICKENS, SELBERT,
2295 Roxalana Rd, Dunbar, WV 25064, Phone: 304-744-4048
Specialties: Using knives. **Patterns:** Standard sporting knives. **Technical:** Stainless steels; stock removal method. **Prices:** Moderate. **Remarks:** Part-time maker. **Mark:** Name.

PICKETT, TERRELL,
66 Pickett Ln, Lumberton, MS 39455, Phone: 601-794-6125, pickettfence66@bellsouth.net
Specialties: Fix blades, camp knives, Bowies, hunters, & skinners. Forge and stock removal and some firework. **Technical:** 5160, 1095, 52100, 440C and ATS-34. **Prices:** Range from $150 to $550. **Mark:** Logo on stock removal T.W. Pickett and on forged knives Terrell Pickett's Forge.

PIENAAR, CONRAD,
19A Milner Rd, Bloemfontein 9300, SOUTH AFRICA, Phone: 027 514364180, Fax: 027 514364180
Specialties: Fancy working and using straight knives and folders of his design, to customer specs and in standard patterns. **Patterns:** Hunters, locking folders, cleavers, kitchen and utility/camp knives. **Technical:** Grinds 12C27, D2 and ATS-34. Uses some Damascus. Embellishments; scrimshaws; inlays gold. Knives come with wooden box and custom-made leather sheath. **Prices:** $300 to $1000. **Remarks:** Part-time maker; first knife sold in 1981. Doing business as C.P. Knifemaker. Makes slip joint folders and liner locking folders. **Mark:** Initials and serial number.

PIERCE, HAROLD L,
106 Lyndon Lane, Louisville, KY 40222, Phone: 502-429-5136
Specialties: Working straight knives, some fancy. **Patterns:** Big fighters and Bowies. **Technical:** Grinds D2, 440C, 154CM; likes sub-hilts. **Prices:** $150 to $450; some to $1200. **Remarks:** Full-time maker; first knife sold in 1982. **Mark:** Last name with knife through the last initial.

PIERCE, RANDALL,
903 Wyndam, Arlington, TX 76017, Phone: 817-468-0138

PIERGALLINI, DANIEL E,
4011 N. Forbes Rd, Plant City, FL 33565, Phone: 813-754-3908, Fax: 813-754-3908, coolnifedad@wildblue.net
Specialties: Traditional and fancy straight knives and folders of his design or to customer's specs. **Patterns:** Hunters, fighters, skinners, working and camp knives. **Technical:** Grinds 440C, O1, D2, ATS-34, some Damascus; forges his own mokume. Uses natural handle material. **Prices:** $450 to $800; some to $1800. **Remarks:** Part-time maker; sold first knife in 1994. **Mark:** Last name, city, state or last name in script.

PIESNER, DEAN,
1786 Sawmill Rd, Conestogo, Ont., CANADA N0B 1N0, Phone: 519-664-3648, dean47@rogers.com
Specialties: Classic and period pieces of his design and to customer specs. **Patterns:** Bowies, skinners, fighters and swords. **Technical:** Forges 5160, 52100, steel Damascus and nickel-steel Damascus. Makes own mokume gane with copper, brass and nickel silver. Silver wire inlays in wood. **Prices:** Start at $150. **Remarks:** Full-time maker; first knife sold in 1990. **Mark:** First initial, last name, JS.

PITMAN, DAVID,
PO Drawer 2566, Williston, ND 58802, Phone: 701-572-3325

PITT, DAVID F,
6812 Digger Pine Ln, Anderson, CA 96007, Phone: 530-357-2393, handcannons@tds.net Web: bearpawcustoms@tds.net
Specialties: Fixed blade, hunters and hatchets. Flat ground mirror finish. **Patterns:** Hatchets with gut hook, small gut hooks, guards, bolsters or guard less. **Technical:** Grinds A2, 440C, 154CM, ATS-34, D2. **Prices:** $100 to $900. **Remarks:** All work done in-house including heat treat. Guild member since 1982. **Mark:** Bear paw with David F. Pitt Maker.

PLUNKETT, RICHARD,
29 Kirk Rd, West Cornwall, CT 06796, Phone: 860-672-3419; Toll free: 888-KNIVES-8
Specialties: Traditional, fancy folders and straight knives of his design. **Patterns:** Slip-joint folders and small straight knives. **Technical:** Grinds O1 and stainless steel. Offers many different file patterns. **Prices:** $150 to $450. **Remarks:** Full-time maker; first knife sold in 1994. **Mark:** Signature and date under handle scales.

POLK, CLIFTON,
4625 Webber Creek Rd, Van Buren, AR 72956, Phone: 479-474-3828, cliffpolkknives1@aol.com; Web: www.polkknives.com
Specialties: Fancy working folders. **Patterns:** One blades spring backs in five sizes, LinerLock®, automatics, double blades spring back folder with standard drop & clip blade or bird knife with drop and vent hook or cowboy's knives with drop and hoof pick and straight knives. **Technical:** Uses D2 &

ATS-34. Makes all own Damascus using 1084, 1095, O1, 15N20, 5160. Using all kinds of exotic woods. Stag, pearls, ivory, mastodon ivory and other bone and horns. **Prices:** $200 to $3000. **Remarks:** Retired fire fighter, made knives since 1974. **Mark:** Polk.

POLK, RUSTY,
5900 Wildwood Dr, Van Buren, AR 72956, Phone: 870-688-3009, polkknives@yahoo.com; Web: www.facebook.com/polkknives
Specialties: Skinners, hunters, Bowies, fighters and forging working knives fancy Damascus, daggers, boot knives, survival knives, and folders. **Patterns:** Drop point, and forge to shape. **Technical:** ATS-34, 440C, Damascus, D2, 51/60, 1084, 15N20, does all his forging. **Prices:** $200 to $2000. **Mark:** R. Polk

POLLOCK, WALLACE J,
PO BOX 449, Reserve, NM 87830, Phone: 575-654-4039, wally@pollocknives.com Web: www.pollocknives.com
Specialties: Using knives, skinner, hunter, fighting, camp knives. **Patterns:** Use his own patterns or yours. Traditional hunters, daggers, fighters, camp knives. **Technical:** Grinds ATS-34, D-2, BG-42, makes own Damascus, D-2, 0-1, ATS-34, prefer D-2, handles exotic wood, horn, bone, ivory. **Remarks:** Full-time maker, sold first knife 1973. **Prices:** $250 to $2500. **Mark:** Last name, maker, city/state.

POLZIEN, DON,
1912 Inler Suite-L, Lubbock, TX 79407, Phone: 806-791-0766, blindinglightknives.net
Specialties: Traditional Japanese-style blades; restores antique Japanese swords, scabbards and fittings. **Patterns:** Hunters, fighters, one-of-a-kind art knives. **Technical:** 1045-1050 carbon steels, 440C, D2, ATS-34, standard and cable Damascus. **Prices:** $150 to $2500. **Remarks:** Full-time maker. First knife sold in 1990. **Mark:** Oriental characters inside square border.

PONZIO, DOUG,
10219 W State Rd 81, Beloit, WI 53511, Phone: 608-313-3223, prfgdoug@hughes.net; Web: www.ponziodamascus.com
Specialties: Mosaic Damascus, stainless Damascus. **Mark:** P.F.

POOLE, MARVIN O,
PO Box 552, Commerce, GA 30529, Phone: 803-225-5970
Specialties: Traditional working/using straight knives and folders of his design and in standard patterns. **Patterns:** Bowies, fighters, locking folders, bird and trout knives. **Technical:** Grinds 440C, D2, ATS-34. **Prices:** $50 to $150; some to $750. **Remarks:** Part-time maker; first knife sold in 1980. **Mark:** First initial, last name, year, serial number.

POSNER, BARRY E,
12501 Chandler Blvd Suite 104, N. Hollywood, CA 91607, Phone: 818-752-8005, Fax: 818-752-8006
Specialties: Working/using straight knives. **Patterns:** Hunters, kitchen and utility/camp knives. **Technical:** Grinds ATS-34; forges 1095 and nickel. **Prices:** $95 to $400. **Remarks:** Part-time maker; first knife sold in 1987. Doing business as Posner Knives. Supplier of finished mosaic handle pin stock. **Mark:** First and middle initials, last name.

POTIER, TIMOTHY F,
PO Box 711, Oberlin, LA 70655, Phone: 337-639-2229, tpotier@hotmail.com
Specialties: Classic working and using straight knives to customer specs; some collectible. **Patterns:** Hunters, Bowies, utility/camp knives and belt axes. **Technical:** Forges carbon steel and his own Damascus; offers filework. **Prices:** $300 to $1800; some to $4000. **Remarks:** Part-time maker; first knife sold in 1981. **Mark:** Last name, MS.

POTTER, BILLY,
6323 Hyland Dr., Dublin, OH 43017, Phone: 614-589-8324, potterknives@yahoo.com; Web: www.potterknives.com
Specialties: Working straight knives; his design or to customers patterns. **Patterns:** Bowie, fighters, utilities, skinners, hunters, folding lock blade, miniatures and tomahawks. **Technical:** Grinds and forges, carbon steel, L6, 0-1, 1095, 5160, 1084 and 52000. Grinds 440C stainless. Forges own Damascus. Handles: prefers exotic hardwood, curly and birdseye maples. Bone, ivory, antler, pearl and horn. Some scrimshaw. **Prices:** Start at $100 up to $800. **Remarks:** Part-time maker; first knife sold 1996. **Mark:** First and last name (maker).

POWELL, JAMES,
2500 North Robinson Rd, Texarkana, TX 75501

POWELL, ROBERT CLARK,
PO Box 321, 93 Gose Rd., Smarr, GA 31086, Phone: 478-994-5418
Specialties: Composite bar Damascus blades. **Patterns:** Art knives, hunters, combat, tomahawks. **Patterns:** Hand forges all blades. **Prices:** $300 and up. **Remarks:** ABS Journeyman Smith. **Mark:** Powell.

POWERS, WALTER R.,
PO BOX 82, Lolita, TX 77971, Phone: 361-874-4230, carlyn@laward.net Web: waltscustomknives.bladermakers.com
Specialties: Skinners and hunters. Technical: Uses mainly CPMD2 and CPM154, but will occasionally use 3V. Stock removal. **Prices:** $140 - $200. **Remarks:** Part-time maker; first knife made in 2002. **Mark:** Tang mark is W.

PRATER, MIKE,
PRATER AND COMPANY, 81 Sanford Ln., Flintstone, GA 30725, cmprater@aol.com; Web: www.casecustomknives.com
Specialties: Customizing factory knives. **Patterns:** Buck knives, case knives, hen and rooster knives. **Technical:** Manufacture of mica pearl. **Prices:** Varied. **Remarks:** First knife sold in 1980. **Mark:** Mica pearl.

PRESSBURGER, RAMON,
59 Driftway Rd, Howell, NJ 07731, Phone: 732-363-0816
Specialties: BG-42. Only knifemaker in U.S.A. that has complete line of affordable hunting knives made from BG-42. **Patterns:** All types hunting styles. **Technical:** Uses all steels; main steels are D-2 and BG-42. **Prices:** $75 to $500. **Remarks:** Full-time maker; has been making hunting knives for 30 years. Makes knives to your patterning. **Mark:** NA.

PRICE, TIMMY,
PO Box 906, Blairsville, GA 30514, Phone: 706-745-5111

PRIDGEN JR., LARRY,
PO BOX 707, Fitzgerald, GA 31750, Phone: 229-591-0013, pridgencustomknives@gmail.com Web: www.pridgencustomknives.com
Specialties: Bowie and Liner Lock Folders. **Patterns:** Bowie, fighter, skinner, trout, liner lock, and custom orders. **Technical:** I do stock removal and use carbon and stainless Damascus and stainless steel. **Prices:** $250 and up. **Remarks:** Each knife comes with a hand-crafted custom sheath and life-time guarantee. **Mark:** Distinctive logo that looks like a brand with LP and a circle around it.

PRIMOS, TERRY,
932 Francis Dr, Shreveport, LA 71118, Phone: 318-686-6625, tprimos@sport.rr.com or terry@primosknives.com; Web: www.primosknives.com
Specialties: Traditional forged straight knives. **Patterns:** Hunters, Bowies, camp knives, and fighters. **Technical:** Forges primarily 1084 and 5160; also forges Damascus. **Prices:** $250 to $600. **Remarks:** Full-time maker; first knife sold in 1993. **Mark:** Last name.

PRINSLOO, THEUNS,
PO Box 2263, Bethlehem, 9700, SOUTH AFRICA, Phone: 27824663885, theunmesa@telkomsa.net; Web: www.theunsprinsloo.com
Specialties: Fancy folders. **Technical:** Own Damascus and mokume. **Prices:** $450 to $1500.

PRITCHARD, RON,
613 Crawford Ave, Dixon, IL 61021, Phone: 815-284-6005
Specialties: Plain and fancy working knives. **Patterns:** Variety of straight knives, locking folders, interframes and miniatures. **Technical:** Grinds 440C, 154CM and commercial Damascus. **Prices:** $100 to $200; some to $1500. **Remarks:** Part-time maker; first knife sold in 1979. **Mark:** Name and city.

PROVENZANO, JOSEPH D,
39043 Dutch Lane, Ponchatoula, LA 70454, Phone: 225-615-4846
Specialties: Working straight knives and folders in standard patterns. **Patterns:** Hunters, Bowies, folders, camp and fishing knives. **Technical:** Grinds ATS-34, 440C, 154CM, CPM 4400V, CPM420V and Damascus. Hollow-grinds hunters. **Prices:** $110 to $300; some to $1000. **Remarks:** Part-time maker; first knife sold in 1980. **Mark:** Joe-Pro.

PRUYN, PETER,
Brothersville Custom Knives, 1328 NW "B" St., Grants Pass, OR 97526, Phone: 631-793-9052, Fax: 541-479-1889, brothersvilleknife@gmail.com Web: brothersvilleknife.com
Specialties: Fixed blade hunters and working knives. **Technical:** Damascus, hi-carbon and stainless steels. **Prices:** $150 - $350. **Remarks:** Part-time maker, first knife sold in 2009. **Mark:** Anvil with "Brothersville" crested above.

PRYOR, STEPHEN L,
HC Rt 1, Box 1445, Boss, MO 65440, Phone: 573-626-4838, Fax: same, Knives4U3@juno.com; Web: www.stevescutler.com
Specialties: Working and fancy straight knives, some to customer specs. **Patterns:** Bowies, hunting/fishing, utility/camp, fantasy/art. **Technical:** Grinds 440C, ATS-34, 1085, some Damascus, and does filework. Stag and exotic hardwood handles. **Prices:** $250 and up. **Remarks:** Full-time maker; first knife sold in 1991. **Mark:** Stylized first initial and last name over city and state.

PUGH, JIM,
PO Box 711, Azle, TX 76020, Phone: 817-444-2679, Fax: 817-444-5455
Specialties: Fancy/embellished limited editions by request. **Patterns:** 5- to 7-inch Bowies, wildlife art pieces, hunters, daggers and fighters; some commemoratives. **Technical:** Multi color transplanting in solid 18K gold, fine gems; grinds 440C and ATS-34. Offers engraving, fancy file etching and leather sheaths for wildlife art pieces. Ivory and coco bolo handle material on limited editions. Designs animal head butt caps and paws or bear claw guards; sterling silver heads and guards. **Prices:** $60,000 to $80,000 each in the Big Five 2000 edition. **Remarks:** Full-time maker; first knife sold in 1970. **Mark:** Pugh (Old English).

PULIS, VLADIMIR,
CSA 230-95, SL Republic, 96701 Kremnica, SLOVAKIA, Phone: 00421 903 340076, vpulis@host.sk; Web: www.vpulis.host.sk
Specialties: Fancy and high-art straight knives of his design. **Patterns:** Daggers and hunters. **Technical:** Forges Damascus steel. All work done by hand. **Prices:** $250 to $3000; some to $10,000. **Remarks:** Full-time maker; first knife sold in 1990. **Mark:** Initials in sixtagon.

PULLIAM, MORRIS C,
560 Jeptha Knob Rd, Shelbyville, KY 40065, Phone: 502-633-2261, mcpulliam@fastballinternet.com
Specialties: Working knives. **Patterns:** Hunters and tomahawks. **Technical:** Forges L6, W2, 1095, Damascus and bar 320 layer Damascus. **Prices:** $165 to $1200. **Remarks:** Full-time maker; first knife sold in 1974. Makes knives for Native American festivals. Doing business as Knob Hill Forge. Member of Piqua Sept Shawnee of Ohio. Indian name Cherokee name Chewla (Fox). As a member of a state tribe, is an American Indian artist and craftsman by federal law. **Mark:** Small and large - Pulliam.

PURSLEY, AARON,
8885 Coal Mine Rd, Big Sandy, MT 59520, Phone: 406-378-3200
Specialties: Fancy working knives. **Patterns:** Locking folders, straight hunters and daggers, personal wedding knives and letter openers. **Technical:** Grinds O1 and 440C; engraves. **Prices:** $900 to $2500. **Remarks:** Full-time maker; first knife sold in 1975. **Mark:** Initials connected with year.

PURVIS, BOB AND ELLEN,
2416 N Loretta Dr, Tucson, AZ 85716, Phone: 520-795-8290, repknives2@cox.net
Specialties: Hunter, skinners, Bowies, using knives, gentlemen folders and collectible knives. **Technical:** Grinds ATS-34, 440C, Damascus, Dama steel, heat-treats and cryogenically quenches. We do gold-plating, salt bluing, scrimshawing, filework and fashion handmade leather sheaths. Materials used for handles include exotic woods, mammoth ivory, mother-of-pearl, G-10 and Micarta. **Prices:** $165 to $800. **Remarks:** Knifemaker since retirement in 1984. Selling them since 1993. **Mark:** Script or print R.E. Purvis ~ Tucson, AZ or last name only.

PUTNAM, DONALD S,
590 Wolcott Hill Rd, Wethersfield, CT 06109, Phone: 860-563-9718, Fax: 860-563-9718, dpknives@cox.net
Specialties: Working knives for the hunter and fisherman. **Patterns:** His design or to customer specs. **Technical:** Uses stock removal method, O1, W2, D2, ATS-34, 154CM, 440C and CPM REX 20; stainless steel Damascus on request. **Prices:** $250 and up. **Remarks:** Full-time maker; first knife sold in 1985. **Mark:** Last name with a knife outline.

Q

QUAKENBUSH, THOMAS C,
2426 Butler Rd, Ft Wayne, IN 46808, Phone: 219-483-0749

QUARTON, BARR,
PO Box 4335, McCall, ID 83638, Phone: 208-634-3641
Specialties: Plain and fancy working knives; period pieces. **Patterns:** Hunters, tantos and swords. **Technical:** Forges and grinds 154CM, ATS-34 and his own Damascus. **Prices:** $180 to $450; some to $4500. **Remarks:** Part-time maker; first knife sold in 1978. Doing business as Barr Custom Knives. **Mark:** First name with bear logo.

QUATTLEBAUM, CRAIG,
5065 Bennetts Pasture Rd., Suffolk, VA 23435-1443, Phone: 757-686-4635, mustang376@gci.net
Specialties: Traditional straight knives and one-of-a-kind knives of his design; period pieces. **Patterns:** Bowies and fighters. **Technical:** Forges 5168, 1095 and own Damascus. **Prices:** $300 to $2000. **Remarks:** Part-time maker; first knife sold in 1988. **Mark:** Stylized initials.

QUESENBERRY, MIKE,
110 Evergreen Cricle, Blairsden, CA 96103, Phone: 775-233-1527, quesenberry@psln.com; Web: www.quesenberryknives.com
Specialties: Hunters, daggers, Bowies, and integrals. **Technical:** Forges 52100, 1095, 1084, 5160. Makes own Damascus. Will use stainless on customer requests. Does own heat-treating and own leather work. **Prices:** Starting at $300. **Remarks:** Parttime maker. ABS member since 2006. Journeyman Bladesmith **Mark:** Last name.

R

RABUCK, JASON,
W3080 Hay Lake Road, Springbrook, WI 54875, Phone: 715-766-8220, sales@rabuckhandmadeknives.com; web: www.rabuckhandmadeknives.com
Patterns: Hunters, skinners, camp knives, fighters, survival/tactical, neck knives, kitchen knives. Include whitetail antler, maple, walnut, as well as stabilized woods and micarta. **Technical:** Flat grinds 1095, 5160, and 0-1 carbon steels. Blades are finished with a hand-rubbed satin blade finish. Hand stitched leather sheaths specifically fit to each knife. Boot clips, swivel sheaths, and leg ties include some of the available sheath options. **Prices:** $140 - $560. **Remarks:** Also knife restoration (handle replacement, etc.) Custom and replacement sheath work available for any knife. **Mark:** "RABUCK" over a horseshoe

RACHLIN, LESLIE S,
1200 W Church St, Elmira, NY 14905, Phone: 607-733-6889, lrachlin@stry.rr.com
Specialties: Classic and working/using straight knives and folders of his design. **Patterns:** Hunters and utility/camp knives. **Technical:** Grinds 440C. **Prices:** $50 to $700. **Remarks:** Spare-time maker; first knife sold in 1989. Doing business as Tinkermade Knives. **Mark:** LSR

RADER, MICHAEL,
P.O. Box 393, Wilkeson, WA 98396, Phone: 253-255-7064, michael@raderblade.com; Web: www.raderblade.com
Specialties: Swords, kitchen knives, integrals. **Patterns:** Non traditional designs. Inspired by various cultures. **Technical:** Damascus is made with 1084 and 15N-20, forged blades in 52100. **Prices:** $350 - $5,000 **Remarks:** ABS Journeyman Smith **Mark:** "Rader" on one side, "J.S." on other

RADOS, JERRY F,
134 Willie Nell Rd., Columbia, KY 42728, Phone: 606-303-3334, jerry@radosknives.com Web: www.radosknives.com
Specialties: Deluxe period pieces. **Patterns:** Hunters, fighters, locking folders, daggers and camp knives. **Technical:** Forges and grinds his own Damascus which he sells commercially; makes pattern-welded Turkish Damascus. **Prices:** Start at $900. **Remarks:** Full-time maker; first knife sold in 1981. **Mark:** Last name.

RAFN, DAN C.,
Smedebakken 24, 8370 Hadsten, Denmark, contact@dcrknives.com Web: www.dcrknives.com
Specialties: One of a kind collector art knives of own design. **Patterns:** Mostly fantasy style fighters and daggers. But also swords, hunters, and folders. **Technical:** Grinds RWL-34, sleipner steel, damasteel, and hand forges Damascus. **Prices:** Start at $500. **Remarks:** Part-time maker since 2003. **Mark:** Rafn. or DCR. or logo.

RAGSDALE, JAMES D,
160 Clear Creek Valley, Ellijay, GA 30536, Phone: 706-636-3180, jimmarrags@etcmail.com
Specialties: Fancy and embellished working knives of his design or to customer specs. **Patterns:** Hunters, folders and fighters. **Technical:** Grinds 440C, ATS-34 and A2. Uses some Damascus **Prices:** $150 and up. **Remarks:** Full-time maker; first knife sold in 1984. **Mark:** Fish symbol with name above, town below.

RAINVILLE, RICHARD,
126 Cockle Hill Rd, Salem, CT 06420, Phone: 860-859-2776, w1jo@snet.net
Specialties: Traditional working straight knives. **Patterns:** Outdoor knives, including fishing knives. **Technical:** L6, 400C, ATS-34. **Prices:** $100 to $800. **Remarks:** Full-time maker; first knife sold in 1982. **Mark:** Name, city, state in oval logo.

RALEY, R. WAYNE,
825 Poplar Acres Rd, Collierville, TN 38017, Phone: 901-853-2026

RALPH, DARREL,
BRIAR KNIVES, 4185 S St Rt 605, Galena, OH 43021, Phone: 740-965-9970, dr@darrelralph.com; Web: www.darrelralph.com
Specialties: Fancy, high-art, high-tech, collectible straight knives and folders of his design and to customer specs; unique mechanisms, some disassemble. **Patterns:** Daggers, fighters and swords. **Technical:** Forges his own Damascus, nickel and high-carbon. Uses mokume and Damascus; mosaics and special patterns. Engraves and heat-treats. Prefers pearl, ivory and abalone handle material; uses stones and jewels. **Prices:** $250 to six figures. **Remarks:** Full-time maker; first knife sold in 1987. Doing business as Briar Knives. **Mark:** DDR.

RAMONDETTI, SERGIO,
VIA MARCONI N 24, 12013 CHIUSA DI PESIO (CN), ITALY, Phone: 0171 734490, Fax: 0171 734490, info@ramon-knives.com Web: www.ramon-knives.com
Specialties: Folders and straight knives of his design. **Patterns:** Utility, hunters and skinners. **Technical:** Grinds RWL-34 and Damascus. **Prices:** $500 to $2000. **Remarks:** Part-time maker; first knife sold in 1999. **Mark:** Logo (S.Ramon) with last name.

RAMSEY, RICHARD A,
8525 Trout Farm Rd, Neosho, MO 64850, Phone: 417-451-1493, rams@direcway.com; Web: www.ramseyknives.com
Specialties: Drop point hunters. **Patterns:** Various Damascus. **Prices:** $125 to $1500. **Mark:** RR double R also last name-RAMSEY.

RANDALL, PATRICK,
160 Mesa Ave., Newbury Park, CA 91320, Phone: 805-754-8093, pat@patrickknives.com; Web: www.patrickknives.com
Specialties: EDC slipjoint folders, drop point hunters, and dive knives of own design. **Technical:** Materials are mostly O1, A2, and ATS-34. Wood, stag, jigged bone, and micarta handles. **Prices:** $125 to $225. **Remarks:** Part-time maker, 4 years of experience, makes about 50 knives per year.

RANDALL JR., JAMES W,
11606 Keith Hall Rd, Keithville, LA 71047, Phone: 318-925-6480, Fax: 318-925-1709, jw@jwrandall.com; Web: www.jwrandall.com
Specialties: Collectible and functional knives. **Patterns:** Bowies, hunters, daggers, swords, folders and combat knives. **Technical:** Forges 5160, 1084, O1 and his Damascus. **Prices:** $400 to $8000. **Remarks:** Part-time. First knife sold in 1998. **Mark:** JW Randall, MS.

RANDALL MADE KNIVES,
4857 South Orange Blossom Trail, Orlando, FL 32839, Phone: 407-855-8075, Fax: 407-855-9054, Web: http://www.randallknives.com
Specialties: Working straight knives. **Patterns:** Hunters, fighters and Bowies. **Technical:** Forges and grinds O1 and 440B. **Prices:** $170 to $550; some to $450. **Remarks:** Full-time maker; first knife sold in 1937. **Mark:** Randall made, city and state in scimitar logo.

RANDOW, RALPH,
4214 Blalock Rd, Pineville, LA 71360, Phone: 318-640-3369

RANKL, CHRISTIAN,
Possenhofenerstr 33, 81476 Munchen, GERMANY, Phone: 0049 01 71 3 66 26 79, Fax: 0049 8975967265, christian@crankl.de.
Specialties: Tail-lock knives. **Patterns:** Fighters, hunters and locking folders. **Technical:** Grinds ATS-34, D2, CPM1440V, RWL 34 also stainless Damascus. **Prices:** $450 to $950; some to $2000. **Remarks:** Full-time maker; first knife sold in 1989. **Mark:** Electrochemical etching on blade.

RAPP, STEVEN J,
8033 US Hwy 25-70, Marshall, NC 28753, Phone: 828-649-1092
Specialties: Gold quartz; mosaic handles. **Patterns:** Daggers, Bowies, fighters and San Francisco knives. **Technical:** Hollow- and flat-grinds 440C and Damascus. **Prices:** Start at $500. **Remarks:** Full-time maker; first knife sold in 1981. **Mark:** Name and state.

RAPPAZZO, RICHARD,
142 Dunsbach Ferry Rd, Cohoes, NY 12047, Phone: 518-783-6843
Specialties: Damascus locking folders and straight knives. **Patterns:** Folders, dirks, fighters and tantos in original and traditional designs. **Technical:** Hand-forges all blades; specializes in Damascus; uses only natural handle materials. **Prices:** $400 to $1500. **Remarks:** Part-time maker; first knife sold in 1985. **Mark:** Name, date, serial number.

RARDON, A D,
1589 SE Price Dr, Polo, MO 64671, Phone: 660-354-2330
Specialties: Folders, miniatures. **Patterns:** Hunters, buck skinners, Bowies, miniatures and daggers. **Technical:** Grinds O1, D2, 440C and ATS-34. **Prices:** $150 to $2000; some higher. **Remarks:** Full-time maker; first knife sold in 1954. **Mark:** Fox logo.

RARDON, ARCHIE F,
1589 SE Price Dr, Polo, MO 64671, Phone: 660-354-2330
Specialties: Working knives. **Patterns:** Hunters, Bowies and miniatures. **Technical:** Grinds O1, D2, 440C, ATS-34, cable and Damascus. **Prices:** $50 to $500. **Remarks:** Part-time maker. **Mark:** Boar hog.

RAY, ALAN W,
1287 FM 1280 E, Lovelady, TX 75851, awray@rayzblades.com; Web: www.rayzblades.com
Specialties: Working straight knives of his design. **Patterns:** Hunters. **Technical:** Forges 01, L6 and 5160 for straight knives. **Prices:** $200 to $1000. **Remarks:** Full-time maker; first knife sold in 1979. **Mark:** Stylized initials.

REBELLO, INDIAN GEORGE,
358 Elm St, New Bedford, MA 02740-3837, Phone: 508-951-2719, indgeo@juno.com; Web: www.indiangeorgesknives.com
Specialties: One-of-a-kind fighters and Bowies. **Patterns:** To customer's specs, hunters and utilities. **Technical:** Forges his own Damascus, 5160, 52100, 1084, 1095, cable and O1. Grinds S30V, ATS-34, 154CM, 440C, D2 and A2. **Prices:** Starting at $250. **Remarks:** Full-time maker, first knife sold in 1991. Doing business as Indian George's Knives. Founding father and President of the Southern New England Knife-Makers Guild. Member of the N.C.C.A. and A.B.S. **Mark:** Indian George's Knives.

RED, VERNON,
2020 Benton Cove, Conway, AR 72034, Phone: 501-450-7284, knivesvr@conwaycorp.net
Specialties: Custom design straight knives or folders of own design or customer's. **Patterns:** Hunters, fighters, Bowies, folders. **Technical:** Hollow grind, flat grind, stock removal and forged blades. Uses 440C, D-2, ATS-34, 1084, 1095, and Damascus. **Prices:** $150 and up. **Remarks:** Made first knife in 1982, first folder in 1992. Member of (AKA) Arkansas Knives Association. Doing business as Custom Made Knives by Vernon Red. **Mark:** Last name.

REDD, BILL,
2647 West 133rd Circle, Broomfield, Colorado 80020, Phone: 303-469-9803, knifeinfo@reddknives.com; Web: www.reddknives.com

REDDIEX, BILL,
27 Galway Ave, Palmerston North, NEW ZEALAND, Phone: 06-357-0383, Fax: 06-358-2910
Specialties: Collector-grade working straight knives. **Patterns:** Traditional-style Bowies and drop-point hunters. **Technical:** Grinds 440C, D2 and O1; offers variety of grinds and finishes. **Prices:** $130 to $750. **Remarks:** Full-time maker; first knife sold in 1980. **Mark:** Last name around kiwi bird logo.

REED, DAVE,
Box 132, Brimfield, MA 01010, Phone: 413-245-3661
Specialties: Traditional styles. Makes knives from chains, rasps, gears, etc. **Patterns:** Bush swords, hunters, working minis, camp and utility knives. **Technical:** Forges 1075 and his own Damascus. **Prices:** Start at $50. **Remarks:** Part-time maker; first knife sold in 1970. **Mark:** Initials.

REED, JOHN M,
3937 Sunset Cove Dr., Port Orange, FL 32129, Phone: 386-310-4569
Specialties: Hunter, utility, some survival knives. **Patterns:** Trailing Point, and drop point sheath knives. **Technical:** ATS-34, Rockwell 60 exotic wood or natural material handles. **Prices:** $135 to $450. Depending on handle material. **Remarks:** Likes the stock removal method. "Old Fashioned trainling point blades." Handmade and sewn leather sheaths. **Mark:** "Reed" acid etched on left side of blade.

REEVE, CHRIS,
2949 Victory View Way, Boise, ID 83709-2946, Phone: 208-375-0367, Fax: 208-375-0368, crkinfo@chrisreeve.com; Web: www.chrisreeve.com
Specialties: Originator and designer of the One Piece range of fixed blade utility knives and of the Sebenza Integral Lock folding knives made by Chris Reeve Knives. Currently makes only one or two pieces per year himself. **Patterns:** Art folders and fixed blades; one-of-a-kind. **Technical:** Grinds specialty stainless steels, Damascus and other materials to his own design. **Prices:** $1000 and upwards. **Remarks:** Full-time in knife business; first knife sold in 1982. **Mark:** Signature and date.

REEVES, J.R.,
5181 South State Line, Texarkana, Arkansas 71854, Phone: 870-773-5777, jos123@netscape.com
Specialties: Working straight knives of my design or customer design if a good flow. **Patterns:** Hunters, fighters, bowies, camp, bird, and trout knives. **Technical:** Forges and grinds 5160, 1084, 15n20, L6, 52100 and some damascus. Also some stock removal 440C, 01, D2, and 154 CM steels. I offer flat or hollow grinds. Natural handle material to include Sambar stag, desert Ironwood, sheep horn, other stabilized exotic woods and ivory. Custom filework offered. **Prices:** $200 - $1500. **Remarks:** Full-time maker, first knife sold in 1985. **Mark:** JR Reeves.

REGGIO JR., SIDNEY J,
PO Box 851, Sun, LA 70463, Phone: 504-886-5886
Specialties: Miniature classic and fancy straight knives of his design or in standard patterns. **Patterns:** Fighters, hunters and utility/camp knives. **Technical:** Grinds 440C, ATS-34 and commercial Damascus. Engraves; scrimshaws; offers filework. Hollow grinds most blades. Prefers natural handle material. Offers handmade sheaths. **Prices:** $85 to $250; some to $500. **Remarks:** Part-time maker; first knife sold in 1988. Doing business as Sterling Workshop. **Mark:** Initials.

REID, JIM,
6425 Cranbrook St. NE, Albuquerque, NM 87111, jhrabq7@msn.com
Specialties: Fixed-blade knives.

RENNER, TERRY,
707 13th Ave. Cir. W, Palmetto, FL 34221, Phone: 941-729-3226, Fax: 941-723-3230, terrylmusic@gmail.com Web: www.trblades.com
Specialties: Ono 16". **Patterns:** Mas. **Technical:** Foix. **Prices:** St00. **Remarks:** F0. **Mark:** "Daath.

REPKE, MIKE,
4191 N. Euclid Ave., Bay City, MI 48706, Phone: 517-684-3111
Specialties: Traditional working and using straight knives of his design or to customer specs; classic knives; display knives. **Patterns:** Hunters, Bowies, skinners, fighters boots, axes and swords. **Technical:** Grind 440C. Offer variety of handle materials. **Prices:** $99 to $1500. **Remarks:** Full-time makers. Doing business as Black Forest Blades. **Mark:** Knife logo.

REVERDY, NICOLE AND PIERRE,
5 Rue De L'egalite', 26100 Romans, FRANCE, Phone: 334 75 05 10 15, Web: http://www.reverdy.com
Specialties: Art knives; legend pieces. Pierre and Nicole, his wife, are creating knives of art with combination of enamel on pure silver (Nicole) and poetic Damascus (Pierre) such as the "La dague a la licorne." **Patterns:** Daggers, folding knives Damascus and enamel, Bowies, hunters and other large patterns. **Technical:** Forges his Damascus and "poetic Damascus"; where animals such as unicorns, stags, dragons or star crystals appear, works with his own EDM machine to create any kind of pattern inside the steel with his own touch. **Prices:** $2000 and up. **Remarks:** Full-time maker since 1989; first knife sold in 1986. Nicole (wife) collaborates with enamels. **Mark:** Reverdy.

REVISHVILI, ZAZA,
2102 Linden Ave, Madison, WI 53704, Phone: 608-243-7927
Specialties: Fancy/embellished and high-art straight knives and folders of his design. **Patterns:** Daggers, swords and locking folders. **Technical:** Uses Damascus; silver filigree, silver inlay in wood; enameling. **Prices:** $1000 to $9000; some to $15,000. **Remarks:** Full-time maker; first knife sold in 1987. **Mark:** Initials, city.

REXFORD, TODD,
518 Park Dr., Woodland Park, CO 80863, Phone: 719-650-6799, todd@rexfordknives.com; Web: www.rexfordknives.com
Specialties: Dress tactical and tactical folders and fixed blades. **Technical:** I work in stainless steels, stainless damascus, titanium, Stellite and other high performance alloys. All machining and part engineering is done in house.

REXROAT, KIRK,
527 Sweetwater Circle Box 224, Wright, WY 82732, Phone: 307-464-0166, rexknives@vcn.com; Web: www.rexroatknives.com
Specialties: Using and collectible straight knives and folders of his design or to customer specs. **Patterns:** Bowies, hunters, folders. **Technical:** Forges Damascus patterns, mosaic and 52100. **Prices:** $400 and up. **Remarks:** Part-time maker, Master Smith in the ABS; first knife sold in 1984. Doing business as Rexroat Knives. **Mark:** Last name.

REYNOLDS, DAVE,
Rt 2 Box 36, Harrisville, WV 26362, Phone: 304-643-2889, wvreynolds@zoomintevnet.net
Specialties: Working straight knives of his design. **Patterns:** Bowies, kitchen and utility knives. **Technical:** Grinds and forges L6, 1095 and 440C. Heat-treats. **Prices:** $50 to $85; some to $175. **Remarks:** Full-time maker; first knife sold in 1980. Doing business as Terra-Gladius Knives. **Mark:** Mark on special orders only; serial number on all knives.

REYNOLDS, JOHN C,
#2 Andover HC77, Gillette, WY 82716, Phone: 307-682-6076
Specialties: Working knives, some fancy. **Patterns:** Hunters, Bowies, tomahawks and buck skinners; some folders. **Technical:** Grinds D2, ATS-34, 440C and forges own Damascus and knives. Scrimshaws. **Prices:** $200 to $3000. **Remarks:** Spare-time maker; first knife sold in 1969. **Mark:** On ground blades JC Reynolds Gillette, WY, on forged blades, initials make the mark-JCR.

RHEA, LIN,
413 Grant 291020, Prattsville, AR 72129, Phone: 870-699-5095, lwrhea2@windstream.net; Web: www.rheaknives.com
Specialties: Traditional and early American styled Bowies in high carbon steel or Damascus. **Patterns:** Bowies, hunters and fighters. **Technical:** Filework wire inlay. Sole authorship of construction, Damascus and embellishment. **Prices:** $280 to $1500. **Remarks:** Serious part-time maker and rated as a Master Smith in the ABS.

RHO, NESTOR LORENZO,
Primera Junta 589, (6000) Junin, Buenos Aires, ARGENTINA, Phone: (02362) 15670686
Specialties: Classic and fancy straight knives of his design. **Patterns:** Bowies, fighters and hunters. **Technical:** Grinds 420C, 440C, 1084, 51-60, 52100, L6, and W1. Offers semi-precious stones on handles, acid etching on blades and blade engraving. **Prices:** $90 to $500, some to $1500. **Remarks:** Full-time maker; first knife sold in 1975. **Mark:** Name.

RIBONI, CLAUDIO,
Via L Da Vinci, Truccazzano (MI), ITALY, Phone: 02 95309010, Web: www.riboni-knives.com

RICARDO ROMANO, BERNARDES,
Ruai Coronel Rennò 1261, Itajuba MG, BRAZIL 37500, Phone: 0055-2135-622-5896
Specialties: Hunters, fighters, Bowies. **Technical:** Grinds blades of stainless and tools steels. **Patterns:** Hunters. **Prices:** $100 to $700. **Mark:** Romano.

RICHARD, RAYMOND,
31047 SE Jackson Rd., Gresham, OR 97080, Phone: 503-663-1219, rayskee13@hotmail.com; Web: www.hawknknives.com
Specialties: Hand-forged knives, tomahawks, axes, and spearheads, all one-of-a-kind. **Prices:** $200 and up, some to $3000. **Remarks:** Full-time maker since 1994. **Mark:** Name on spine of blades.

RICHARDS, CHUCK,
7243 Maple Tree Lane SE, Salem, OR 97317, Phone: 503-569-5549, chuck@woodforge.com; Web: www.woodchuckforge.com
Specialties: Fixed blade Damascus. One-of-a-kind. **Patterns:** Hunters, fighters. **Prices:** $200 to $1200. **Remarks:** Likes to work with customers on a truly custom knife. **Mark:** A C Richards or ACR.

RICHARDS, RALPH (BUD),
6413 Beech St, Bauxite, AR 72012, Phone: 501-602-5367, DoubleR042@aol.com; Web: SwampPoodleCreations.com
Specialties: Forges 55160, 1084, and 15N20 for Damascus. S30V, 440C, and others. Wood, mammoth, giraffe and mother of pearl handles.

RICHARDSON JR., PERCY,
1117 Kettler St., Navasota, TX 77868, Phone: 936-288-1690, Web: www.richardsonknives@yahoo.com
Specialties: Working straight knives and folders. **Patterns:** Hunters, skinners, bowies, fighters and folders. **Technical:** Grinds 154CM, ATS-34, and D2. **Prices:** $175 - $750 some bowies to $1200. **Remarks:** Part time maker, first knife sold in 1990. Doing business as Richardsons Handmade Knives. **Mark:** Texas star with last name across it.

RICHERSON, RON,
P.O. Box 51, Greenburg, KY 42743, Phone: 270-405-0491, Fax: 270-299-2471, rricherson@windstream.net
Specialties: Collectible and functional fixed blades, locking liners, and autos of his design. **Technical:** Grinds ATS-34, S30V, S60V, CPM-154, D2, 440, high carbon steel, and his and others' Damascus. Prefers natural materials for handles and does both stock removal and forged work, some with embellishments. **Prices:** $160 to $850, some higher. **Remarks:** Full-time maker. Probationary member Knifemakers' Guild and apprentice member American Bladesmith Society. Made first knife in September 2006, sold first knife in

December 2006. **Mark:** Name in oval with city and state. Also name in center of oval Green River Custom Knives.

RICKE, DAVE,
1209 Adams St, West Bend, WI 53090, Phone: 262-334-5739, R.L5710@sbcglobal.net
Specialties: Working knives; period pieces. **Patterns:** Hunters, boots, Bowies; locking folders and slip joints. **Technical:** Grinds ATS-34, A2, 440C and 154CM. **Prices:** $145 and up. **Remarks:** Full-time maker; first knife sold in 1976. Knifemakers Guild voting member. **Mark:** Last name.

RICKS, KURT J.,
Darkhammer Forge, 29 N. Center, Trenton, UT 84338, Phone: 435-563-3471, kopsh@hotmail.com; http://darkhammerworks.tripod.com
Specialties: Fixed blade working knives of all designs and to customer specs. **Patterns:** Fighters, daggers, hunters, swords, axes, and spears. **Technical:** Uses a coal fired forge. Forges high carbon, tool and spring steels. Does own heat treat on forge. Prefers natural handle materials. Leather sheaths available. **Prices:** Start at $50 plus shipping. **Remarks:** A knife should be functional first and pretty second. Part-time maker; first knife sold in 1994. **Mark:** Initials.

RIDER, DAVID M,
PO Box 5946, Eugene, OR 97405-0911, Phone: 541-343-8747

RIDLEY, ROB,
Box 564, Cremona, AB CANADA T0M 0R0, Phone: 403-637-0047, rob@rangeroriginal.com; www.rangeroriginal.com
Specialties: The knives I make are mainly fixed blades, though I'm exploring the complex world of folders. **Technical:** I favour high-end stainless alloys and exotic handle materials because a knife should provide both cutting ability and bragging rights. **Remarks:** I made my first knife in 1998 and still use that blade today. I've gone from full time, to part time, to hobby maker, but I still treasure time in the shop or spent with other enthusiasts.

RIEPE, RICHARD A,
17604 E 296 St, Harrisonville, MO 64701

RIETVELD, BERTIE,
PO Box 53, Magaliesburg 1791, SOUTH AFRICA, Phone: 2783 232 8766, bertie@rietveldknives.com; Web: www.rietveldknives.com
Specialties: Art daggers, Bolster lock folders, Persian designs, embraces elegant designs. **Patterns:** Mostly one-of-a-kind. **Technical:** Sole authorship, work only in own Damascus, gold inlay, blued stainless fittings. **Prices:** $500 - $8,000 **Remarks:** First knife made in 1979. Annual shows attended: ECCKS, Blade Show, Milan Show, South African Guild Show. **Marks:** Logo is elephant in half circle with name, enclosed in Stanhope lens.

RIGNEY JR., WILLIE,
191 Colson Dr, Bronston, KY 42518, Phone: 606-679-4227
Specialties: High-tech period pieces and fancy working knives. **Patterns:** Fighters, boots, daggers and push knives. **Technical:** Grinds 440C and 154CM; buys Damascus. Most knives are embellished. **Prices:** $150 to $1500; some to $10,000. **Remarks:** Full-time maker; first knife sold in 1978. **Mark:** First initial, last name.

RINKES, SIEGFRIED,
Am Sportpl 2, D 91459, Markterlbach, GERMANY

RIZZI, RUSSELL J,
37 March Rd, Ashfield, MA 01330, Phone: 413-625-2842
Specialties: Fancy working and using straight knives and folders of his design or to customer specs. **Patterns:** Hunters, locking folders and fighters. **Technical:** Grinds 440C, D2 and commercial Damascus. **Prices:** $150 to $750; some to $2500. **Remarks:** Part-time maker; first knife sold in 1990. **Mark:** Last name, Ashfield, MA.

ROBBINS, BILL,
192 S. Fairview St, Globe, AZ 85501, Phone: 928-402-0052, billrknifemaker@aol.com
Specialties: Plain and fancy working straight knives. Makes to his designs and most anything you can draw. **Patterns:** Hunting knives, utility knives, and Bowies. **Technical:** Grinds ATS-34, 440C, tool steel, high carbon, buys Damascus. **Prices:** $70 to $450. **Remarks:** Part-time maker, first knife sold in 2001. **Mark:** Last name or desert scene with name.

ROBBINS, HOWARD P,
1310 E. 310th Rd., Flemington, MO 65650, Phone: 417-282-5055, ARobb1407@aol.com
Specialties: High-tech working knives with clean designs, some fancy. **Patterns:** Folders, hunters and camp knives. **Technical:** Grinds 440C. Heat-treats; likes mirror finishes. Offers leatherwork. **Prices:** $100 to $500; some to $1000. **Remarks:** Full-time maker; first knife sold in 1982. **Mark:** Name, city and state.

ROBERTS, CHUCK,
PO Box 7174, Golden, CO 80403, Phone: 303-642-2388, chuck@crobertsart.com; Web: www.crobertsart.com
Specialties: Price daggers, large Bowies, hand-rubbed satin finish. **Patterns:** Bowies and California knives. **Technical:** Grinds 440C, 5160 and ATS-34. Handles made of stag, ivory or mother-of-pearl. **Prices:** $1250. **Remarks:** Full-time maker. Company name is C. Roberts - Art that emulates the past. **Mark:** Last initial or last name.

ROBERTS, GEORGE A,
PO Box 31228, 211 Main St., Whitehorse, YT, CANADA Y1A 5P7, Phone: 867-667-7099, Fax: 867-667-7099, Web: www.yuk-biz.com/bandit blades
Specialties: Mastadon ivory, fossil walrus ivory handled knives, scrimshawed or carved. **Patterns:** Side lockers, fancy bird and trout knives, hunters, fillet blades. **Technical:** Grinds stainless Damascus, all surgical steels. **Prices:** Up to $3500 U.S. **Remarks:** Full-time maker; first knives sold in 1986. Doing business as Bandit Blades. Most recent works have gold nuggets in fossilized Mastodon ivory. Something new using mosaic pins in mokume bolster and in mosaic Damascus, it creates a new look. **Mark:** Bandit Yukon with pick and shovel crossed.

ROBERTS, JACK,
10811 Sagebluff Dr, Houston, TX 77089, Phone: 281-481-1784, jroberts59@houston.rr.com
Specialties: Hunting knives and folders, offers scrimshaw by wife Barbara. **Patterns:** Drop point hunters and LinerLock® folders. **Technical:** Grinds 440-C, offers file work, texturing, natural handle materials and Micarta. **Prices:** $200 to $800 some higher. **Remarks:** Part-time maker, sold first knife in 1965. **Mark:** Name, city, state.

ROBERTS, MICHAEL,
601 Oakwood Dr, Clinton, MS 39056, Phone: 601-540-6222, Fax: 601-213-4891
Specialties: Working and using knives in standard patterns and to customer specs. **Patterns:** Hunters, Bowies, tomahawks and fighters. **Technical:** Forges 5160, O1, 1095 and his own Damascus. Uses only natural handle materials. **Prices:** $145 to $500; some to $1100. **Remarks:** Part-time maker; first knife sold in 1988. **Mark:** Last name or first and last name in Celtic script.

ROBERTS, T. C. (TERRY),
1795 Berry Lane, Fayetteville, AR 72701, Phone: 479-442-4493, carolcroberts@cox.net
Specialties: Working straight knives and folders of the maker's original design. **Patterns:** Bowies, daggers, fighters, locking folders and push buttons as well as gentleman's automatics. **Technical:** Grinds all types of carbon and stainless steels and commercially available Damascus. Works in stone and casts in bronze and silver. Some inlays and engraving. **Prices:** $250 - $2500. **Remarks:** Full-time maker; sold first knife in 1983. **Mark:** Stamp is oval with initials inside.

ROBERTSON, LEO D,
3728 Pleasant Lake Dr, Indianapolis, IN 46227, Phone: 317-882-9899, ldr52@juno.com
Specialties: Hunting and folders. **Patterns:** Hunting, fillet, Bowie, utility, folders and tantos. **Technical:** Uses ATS-34, 154CM, 440C, 1095, D2 and Damascus steels. **Prices:** Fixed knives $75 to $350, folders $350 to $600. **Remarks:** Handles made with stag, wildwoods, laminates, mother-of-pearl. Made first knife in 1990. Member of American Bladesmith Society. **Mark:** Logo with full name in oval around logo.

ROBINSON, CALVIN,
5501 Twin Creek Circle, Pace, FL 32571, Phone: 850 572 1504, calvinshandmadeknives@yahoo.com
Specialties: Working knives of my own design. **Patterns:** Hunters, fishing, folding and kitchen and purse knives. **Technical:** Now using 13-C-26 stainless. **Prices:** $215.00 to $600.00. **Remarks:** Full-time maker. Probationary member of the Knifemaker's Guild. **Mark:** Calvin Robinson Pace, Florida.

ROBINSON, CHARLES (DICKIE),
PO Box 221, Vega, TX 79092, Phone: 806-676-6428, dickie@amaonline.com; Web: www.robinsonknives.com
Specialties: Classic and working/using knives. Does his own engraving. **Patterns:** Bowies, daggers, fighters, hunters and camp knives. **Technical:** Forges O1, 5160, 52100 and his own Damascus. **Prices:** $350 to $850; some to $5000. **Remarks:** Part-time maker; first knife sold in 1988. Doing business as Robinson Knives. ABS Master Smith. **Mark:** Robinson MS.

ROBINSON, CHUCK,
SEA ROBIN FORGE, 1423 Third Ave., Picayune, MS 39466, Phone: 601-798-0060, robi5515@bellsouth.net
Specialties: Deluxe period pieces and working / using knives of his design and to customer specs. **Patterns:** Bowies, fighters, hunters, utility knives and original designs. **Technical:** Forges own Damascus, 52100, O1, L6 and 1070 thru 1095. **Prices:** Start at $225. **Remarks:** First knife 1958. **Mark:** Fish logo, anchor and initials C.R.

ROBINSON III, REX R,
10531 Poe St, Leesburg, FL 34788, Phone: 352-787-4587
Specialties: One-of-a-kind high-art automatics of his design. **Patterns:** Automatics, liner locks and lock back folders. **Technical:** Uses tool steel and stainless Damascus and mokume; flat grinds. Hand carves folders. **Prices:** $1800 to $7500. **Remarks:** First knife sold in 1988. **Mark:** First name inside oval.

ROCHFORD, MICHAEL R,
PO Box 577, Dresser, WI 54009, Phone: 715-755-3520, mrrochford@centurytel.net
Specialties: Working straight knives and folders. Classic Bowies and Moran traditional. **Patterns:** Bowies, fighters, hunters: slip-joint, locking and liner locking folders. **Technical:** Grinds ATS-34, 440C, 154CM and D-2; forges W2, 5160, and his own Damascus. Offers metal and metal and leather sheaths.

Filework and wire inlay. **Prices:** $150 to $1000; some to $2000. **Remarks:** Part-time maker; first knife sold in 1984. **Mark:** Name.

RODEBAUGH, JAMES L,
4875 County Rd, Carpenter, WY 82054

RODEWALD, GARY,
447 Grouse Ct, Hamilton, MT 59840, Phone: 406-363-2192
Specialties: Bowies of his design as inspired from historical pieces. **Patterns:** Hunters, Bowies and camp/combat. Forges 5160 1084 and his own Damascus of 1084, 15N20, field grade hunters AT-34-440C, 440V, and BG42. **Prices:** $200 to $1500. **Remarks:** Sole author on knives, sheaths done by saddle maker. **Mark:** Rodewald.

RODKEY, DAN,
18336 Ozark Dr, Hudson, FL 34667, Phone: 727-863-8264
Specialties: Traditional straight knives of his design and in standard patterns. **Patterns:** Boots, fighters and hunters. **Technical:** Grinds 440C, D2 and ATS-34. **Prices:** Start at $200. **Remarks:** Full-time maker; first knife sold in 1985. Doing business as Rodkey Knives. **Mark:** Etched logo on blade.

ROE JR., FRED D,
4005 Granada Dr, Huntsville, AL 35802, Phone: 205-881-6847
Specialties: Highly finished working knives of his design; period pieces. **Patterns:** Hunters, fighters and survival knives; locking folders; specialty designs like diver's knives. **Technical:** Grinds 154CM, ATS-34 and Damascus. Field-tests all blades. **Prices:** $125 to $250; some to $2000. **Remarks:** Part-time maker; first knife sold in 1980. **Mark:** Last name.

ROEDER, DAVID,
812 W. 45 Pl., Kennewick, WA 99337, d.roeder1980@yahoo.com
Specialties: Fixed blade field and exposition grade knives. **Patterns:** Favorite styles are Bowie and hunter. **Technical:** Forges primarily 5160 and 52100. Makes own Damascus. **Prices:** Start at $150. **Remarks:** Made first knife in September, 1996. **Mark:** Maker's mark is a D and R with the R resting at a 45-degree angle to the lower right of the D.

ROGERS, RAY,
PO Box 126, Wauconda, WA 98859, Phone: 509-486-8069, knives @rayrogers. com; Web: www.rayrogers.com
Specialties: LinerLock® folders. Asian and European professional chef's knives. **Patterns:** Rayzor folders, chef's knives and cleavers of his own and traditional designs, drop point hunters and fillet knives. **Technical:** Stock removal S30V, 440, 1095, O1 Damascus and other steels. Does all own heat treating, clay tempering, some forging G-10, Micarta, carbon fiber on folders, stabilized burl woods on fixed blades. **Prices:** $200 to $450. **Remarks:** Knives are made one-at-a-time to the customer's order. Happy to consider customizing knife designs to suit your preferences and sometimes create entirely new knives when necessary. As a full-time knifemaker is willing to spend as much time as it takes (usually through email) discussing the options and refining details of a knife's design to insure that you get the knife you really want.

ROGERS, RICHARD,
PO Box 769, Magdalena, NM 87825, Phone: 575-838-7237, r.s.rogers@hotmail.com
Specialties: Sheffield-style folders and multi-blade folders. **Patterns:** Folders: various traditional patterns. One-of-a-kind fixed blades: Bowies, daggers, hunters, utility knives. **Technical:** Mainly uses ATS-34 and prefer natural handle materials. **Prices:** $400 and up. **Mark:** Last name.

ROGHMANS, MARK,
607 Virginia Ave, LaGrange, GA 30240, Phone: 706-885-1273
Specialties: Classic and traditional knives of his design. **Patterns:** Bowies, daggers and fighters. **Technical:** Grinds ATS-34, D2 and 440C. **Prices:** $250 to $500. **Remarks:** Part-time maker; first knife sold in 1984. Doing business as LaGrange Knife. **Mark:** Last name and/or LaGrange Knife.

ROHN, FRED,
7675 W Happy Hill Rd, Coeur d'Alene, ID 83814, Phone: 208-667-0774
Specialties: Hunters, boot knives, custom patterns. **Patterns:** Drop points, double edge, etc. **Technical:** Grinds 440 or 154CM. **Prices:** $85 and up. **Remarks:** Part-time maker. **Mark:** Logo on blade; serial numbered.

ROLLERT, STEVE,
PO Box 65, Keensburg, CO 80643-0065, Phone: 303-732-4858, steve@doveknives.com; Web: www.doveknives.com
Specialties: Highly finished working knives. **Patterns:** Variety of straight knives; locking folders and slip-joints. **Technical:** Forges and grinds W2, 1095, ATS-34 and his pattern-welded, cable Damascus and nickel Damascus. **Prices:** $300 to $1000; some to $3000. **Remarks:** Full-time maker; first knife sold in 1980. Doing business as Dove Knives. **Mark:** Last name in script.

ROMEIS, GORDON,
1521 Coconut Dr., Fort Myers, FL 33901, Phone: 239-940-5060, gordonromeis@gmail.com Web: Romeisknives.com
Specialties: Smaller using knives. **Patterns:** I have a number of standard designs that include both full tapered tangs and narrow tang knives. Custom designs are welcome. Many different types. No folders. **Technical:** Standard steel is 440C. Also uses Alabama Damascus steel. **Prices:** Start at $165. **Remarks:** I am a part-time maker however I do try to keep waiting times to a minimum. **Mark:** Either my name, city, and state or simply ROMEIS depending on the knife.

RONZIO, N. JACK,
PO Box 248, Fruita, CO 81521, Phone: 970-858-0921

ROOT, GARY,
644 East 14th St, Erie, PA 16503, Phone: 814-459-0196
Specialties: Damascus Bowies with hand carved eagles, hawks and snakes for handles. Few folders made. **Patterns:** Daggers, fighters, hunter/field knives. **Technical:** Using handforged Damascus from Ray Bybar Jr (M.S.) and Robert Eggerling. Grinds D2, 440C, 1095 and 5160. Some 5160 is hand forged **Prices:** $80 to $300 some to $1000. **Remarks:** Full time maker, first knife sold in 1976. **Mark:** Name over Erie, PA.

ROSE, BOB,
PO BOX 126, Wagontown, PA 19376, Phone: 610-273-1151, medit8@meditationsociety.com Web: www.bobroseknives.com
Patterns: Bowies, fighters, drop point hunters, daggers, bird and trout, camp, and other fixed blade styles. **Technical:** Mostly using 1095 and damascus steel, desert ironwood and other top-of-the-line exotic woods as well as mammoth tooth. **Prices:** $49 - $300. **Remarks:** Been making and selling knives since 2004.

ROSE, DEREK W,
14 Willow Wood Rd, Gallipolis, OH 45631, Phone: 740-446-4627

ROSE II, DOUN T,
Ltc US Special Operations Command (ret), 1795/96 W Sharon Rd SW, Fife Lake, MI 49633, Phone: 231-645-1369, www.epicureanclassic.com www.rosecutlery.com
Specialties: Straight working, collector and presentation knives to a high level of fit and finish. Design in collaboration with customer. **Patterns:** Field knives, Scagel, Bowies, period pieces, axes and tomahawks, fishing and hunting spears. Fine cutlery under "Epicurean Classic" name. **Technical:** Forged and billet ground, high carbon and stainless steel appropriate to end use. Sourced from: Crucible, Frye, Admiral and Starret. Some period pieces from recovered stock. Makes own damascus and mokume gane. **Remarks:** Full-time maker, ABS since 2000, William Scagel Memorial Scholarship 2002, Bill Moran School of Blade Smithing 2003, Apprentice under Master Blacksmith Dan Nickels at Black Rock Forge current. **Mark:** Last name ROSE in block letters with five petal "wild rose" in place of O. Doing business as Rose Cutlery.

ROSENBAUGH, RON,
2806 Stonegate Dr, Crystal Lake, IL 60012, Phone: 815-477-0027, ron@rosenbaughknives.com; Web: www.rosenbaughknives.com
Specialties: Fancy and plain working knives using own designs, collaborations, and traditional patterns. **Patterns:** Bird, trout, boots, hunters, fighters, some Bowies. **Technical:** Grinds high alloy stainless, tool steels, and Damascus; forges 1084, 5160, 52100, carbon and spring steels. **Prices:** $150 to $1000. **Remarks:** Part-time maker, first knife sold in 1004. **Mark:** Last name, logo, city.

ROSENFELD, BOB,
955 Freeman Johnson Rd, Hoschton, GA 30548, Phone: 770-867-2647, www.1bladesmith@msn.com
Specialties: Fancy and embellished working/using straight knives of his design and in standard patterns. **Patterns:** Daggers, hunters and utility/camp knives. **Technical:** Forges 52100, A203E, 1095 and L6 Damascus. Offers engraving. **Prices:** $125 to $650; some to $1000. **Remarks:** Full-time maker; first knife sold in 1984. Also makes folders; ABS Journeyman. **Mark:** Last name or full name, Knifemaker.

ROSS, D L,
27 Kinsman St, Dunedin, NEW ZEALAND, Phone: 64 3 464 0239, Fax: 64 3 464 0239
Specialties: Working straight knives of his design. **Patterns:** Hunters, various others. **Technical:** Grinds 440C. **Prices:** $100 to $450; some to $700 NZ (not U.S. $). **Remarks:** Part-time maker; first knife sold in 1988. **Mark:** Dave Ross, Maker, city and country.

ROSS, STEPHEN,
534 Remington Dr, Evanston, WY 82930, Phone: 307-789-7104
Specialties: One-of-a-kind collector-grade classic and contemporary straight knives and folders of his design and to customer specs; some fantasy pieces. **Patterns:** Combat and survival knives, hunters, boots and folders. **Technical:** Grinds stainless and tool steels. Engraves, scrimshaws. Makes leather sheaths. **Prices:** $160 to $3000. **Remarks:** Part-time-time maker; first knife sold in 1971. **Mark:** Last name in modified Roman; sometimes in script.

ROSS, TIM,
3239 Oliver Rd, Thunder Bay, Ont., CANADA P7G 1S9, Phone: 807-935-2667, Fax: 807-935-3179
Specialties: Fixed blades, natural handle material. **Patterns:** Hunting, fishing, Bowies, fighters. **Technical:** 440C, D2, 52100, Cable, 5160, 1084, 66, W2. **Prices:** $150 to $750 some higher. **Remarks:** Forges and stock removal. **Mark:** Ross Custom Knives.

ROSSDEUTSCHER, ROBERT N,
133 S Vail Ave, Arlington Heights, IL 60005, Phone: 847-577-0404, Web: www.rnrknives.com
Specialties: Frontier-style and historically inspired knives. **Patterns:** Trade knives, Bowies, camp knives and hunting knives, tomahawks and lances. **Technical:** Most knives are hand forged, a few are stock removal. **Prices:** $135 to $1500. **Remarks:** Journeyman Smith of the American Bladesmith Society. **Mark:** Back-to-back "R's", one upside down and backwards, one right side

up and forward in an oval. Sometimes with name, town and state; depending on knife style.

ROTELLA, RICHARD A,
643 75th St, Niagara Falls, NY 14304
Specialties: Working knives of his design. **Patterns:** Various fishing, hunting and utility knives; folders. **Technical:** Grinds ATS-34. Prefers hand-rubbed finishes. **Prices:** $65 to $450; some to $900. **Remarks:** Spare-time maker; first knife sold in 1977. Not taking orders at this time; only sells locally. **Mark:** Name and city in stylized waterfall logo.

ROULIN, CHARLES,
113 B Rt. de Soral, 1233 Geneva, SWITZERLAND, Phone: 022-757-4479, Fax: 079-218-9754, charles.roulin@bluewin.ch; Web: www.coutelier-roulin.com
Specialties: Fancy high-art straight knives and folders of his design. **Patterns:** Bowies, locking folders, slip-joint folders and miniatures. **Technical:** Grinds 440C, ATS-34 and D2. Engraves; carves nature scenes and detailed animals in steel, ivory, on handles and blades. **Prices:** $500 to $3000; some to Euro: 14,600. **Remarks:** Full-time maker; first knife sold in 1988. **Mark:** Symbol of fish with name or name engraved.

ROWE, FRED,
BETHEL RIDGE FORGE, 3199 Roberts Rd, Amesville, OH 45711, Phone: 866-325-2164, fred.rowe@bethelridgeforge.com; Web: www.bethelridgeforge.com
Specialties: Damascus and carbon steel sheath knives. **Patterns:** Bowies, hunters, fillet small kokris. **Technical:** His own Damascus, 52100, O1, L6, 1095 carbon steels, mosaics. **Prices:** $200 to $2000. **Remarks:** All blades are clay hardened. **Mark:** Bethel Ridge Forge.

ROYER, KYLE,
1962 State Route W, Mountain View, MO 65548, Phone: 417-934-6394, Fax: 417-247-5572, royerknifeworks@live.com Web: www.royerknifeworks.com
Specialties: I currently specialize in fixed blades. **Technical:** I forge many different patterns of damascus using mostly 1080 and 15n20. **Remarks:** I am a full-time maker and nineteen years old (12-05-90). I received my ABS Journeyman Smith Stamp at the 2009 Blade Show in Atlanta.

ROZAS, CLARK D,
1436 W "G" St, Wilmington, CA 90744, Phone: 310-518-0488
Specialties: Hand forged blades. **Patterns:** Pig stickers, toad stabbers, whackers, choppers. **Technical:** Damascus, 52100, 1095, 1084, 5160. **Prices:** $200 to $600. **Remarks:** A.B.S. member; part-time maker since 1995. **Mark:** Name over dagger.

RUA, GARY,
396 Snell Street, Fall River, MA 02721, Phone: 508-677-2664
Specialties: Working straight knives of his design. 1800 to 1900 century standard patterns. **Patterns:** Bowies, hunters, fighters, and patch knives. **Technical:** Forges and grinds. Damascus, 5160, 1095, old files. Uses only natural handle material. **Prices:** $350 - $2000. **Remarks:** Part-time maker. (Harvest Moon Forge) **Mark:** Last name.

RUANA KNIFE WORKS,
Box 520, Bonner, MT 59823, Phone: 406-258-5368, Fax: 406-258-2895, info@ruanaknives.com; Web: www.ruanaknives.com
Specialties: Working knives and period pieces. **Patterns:** Variety of straight knives. **Technical:** Forges 5160 chrome alloy for Bowies and 1095. **Prices:** $200 and up. **Remarks:** Full-time maker; first knife sold in 1938. Brand new non catalog knives available on ebay under seller name ruanaknives. For free catalog email regular mailing address to info@ruanaknives.com **Mark:** Name.

RUCKER, THOMAS,
194 Woodhaven Ct., Nacogdoches, TX 75965, Phone: 832-216-8122, admin@knivesbythomas.com Web: www.knivesbythomas.com
Specialties: Personal design and custom design. Hunting, tactical, folding knives, and cutlery. **Technical:** Design and grind ATS34, D2, O1, Damascus, and VG10. **Prices:** $150 - $5,000. **Remarks:** Full-time maker and custom scrimshaw and engraving done by wife, Debi Rucker. First knife done in 1969; first design sold in 1975 **Mark:** Etched logo and signature.

RUPERT, BOB,
301 Harshaville Rd, Clinton, PA 15026, Phone: 724-573-4569, rbrupert@aol.com
Specialties: Wrought period pieces with natural elements. **Patterns:** Elegant straight blades, friction folders. **Technical:** Forges colonial 7; 1095; 5160; diffuse mokume-gane and Damascus. **Prices:** $150 to $1500; some higher. **Remarks:** Part-time maker; first knife sold in 1980. Evening hours studio since 1980. Likes simplicity that disassembles. **Mark:** R etched in Old English.

RUPLE, WILLIAM H,
201 Brian Dr., Pleasanton, TX 78064, Phone: 830-569-0007, bknives@devtex.net
Specialties: Multi-blade folders, slip joints, some lock backs. **Patterns:** Like to reproduce old patterns. Offers filework and engraving. **Technical:** Grinds CPM-154 and other carbon and stainless steel and commercial Damascus. **Prices:** $950 to $2500. **Remarks:** Full-time maker; first knife sold in 1988. **Mark:** Ruple.

RUSS, RON,
5351 NE 160th Ave, Williston, FL 32696, Phone: 352-528-2603, RussRs@aol.com
Specialties: Damascus and mokume. **Patterns:** Ladder, rain drop and butterfly. **Technical:** Most knives, including Damascus, are forged from 52100-E. **Prices:** $65 to $2500. **Mark:** Russ.

RUSSELL, MICK,
4 Rossini Rd, Pari Park, Port Elizabeth 6070, SOUTH AFRICA
Specialties: Art knives. **Patterns:** Working and collectible bird, trout and hunting knives, defense knives and folders. **Technical:** Grinds D2, 440C, ATS-34 and Damascus. Offers mirror or satin finishes. **Prices:** Start at $100. **Remarks:** Full-time maker; first knife sold in 1986. **Mark:** Stylized rhino incorporating initials.

RUSSELL, TOM,
6500 New Liberty Rd, Jacksonville, AL 36265, Phone: 205-492-7866
Specialties: Straight working knives of his design or to customer specs. **Patterns:** Hunters, folders, fighters, skinners, Bowies and utility knives. **Technical:** Grinds D2, 440C and ATS-34; offers filework. **Prices:** $75 to $225. **Remarks:** Part-time maker; first knife sold in 1987. Full-time tool and die maker. **Mark:** Last name with tulip stamp.

RUTH, MICHAEL G,
3101 New Boston Rd, Texarkana, TX 75501, Phone: 903-832-7166/cell:903-277-3663, Fax: 903-832-4710, mike@ruthknives.com; Web: www.ruthknives.com
Specialties: Hunters, bowies & fighters. Damascus & carbon steel. **Prices:** $375 & up. **Mark:** Last name.

RUTH, JR., Michael,
5716 Wilshire, Texarkana, TX 75503, Phone: 903-293-2663, michael@ruthknives.com
Specialties: Custom hand-forged blades, utilizing high carbon and Damascus steels. **Patterns:** Bowies, hunters and fighters ranging from field to presentation-grade pieces. **Technical:** Steels include 5160, 1084, 15n20, W-2, 1095, and O-1. Handle materials include a variety of premium hardwoods, stag, oosik, assorted ivories and micarta. **Prices:** Start at $375. **Mark:** 8-pointed star with capital "R" in center.

RYBAR JR., RAYMOND B,
2328 South Sunset Dr., Came Verde, AZ 86322, Phone: 928-567-6372, ray@rybarknives.com; Web: www.rybarknives.com
Specialties: Straight knives or folders with customers name, logo, etc. in mosaic pattern. **Patterns:** Common patterns plus mosaics of all types. **Technical:** Forges own Damascus. Primary forging of self smelted steel - smelting classes. **Prices:** $200 to $1200; Bible blades to $10,000. **Remarks:** Master Smith (A.B.S.) Primary focus toward Biblically themed blades **Mark:** Rybar or stone church forge or Rev. 1:3 or R.B.R. between diamonds.

RYBERG, GOTE,
Faltgatan 2, S-562 00 Norrahammar, SWEDEN, Phone: 4636-61678

RYDBOM, JEFF,
PO Box 548, Annandale, MN 55302, Phone: 320-274-9639, jry1890@hotmail.com
Specialties: Ring knives. **Patterns:** Hunters, fighters, Bowie and camp knives. **Technical:** Straight grinds O1, A2, 1566 and 5150 steels. **Prices:** $150 to $1000. **Remarks:** No pinning of guards or pommels. All silver brazed. **Mark:** Capital "C" with J R inside.

RYUICHI, KUKI,
504-7 Tokorozawa-Shinmachi, Tokorozawa-city, Saitama, JAPAN, Phone: 042-943-3451

RZEWNICKI, GERALD,
8833 S Massbach Rd, Elizabeth, IL 61028-9714, Phone: 815-598-3239

S

SAINDON, R BILL,
233 Rand Pond Rd, Goshen, NH 03752, Phone: 603-863-1874, dayskiev71@aol.com
Specialties: Collector-quality folders of his design or to customer specs. **Patterns:** Latch release, LinerLock® and lockback folders. **Technical:** Offers limited amount of own Damascus; also uses Damas makers steel. Prefers natural handle material, gold and gems. **Prices:** $500 to $4000. **Remarks:** Full-time maker; first knife sold in 1981. Doing business as Daynia Forge. **Mark:** Sun logo or engraved surname.

SAKAKIBARA, MASAKI,
20-8 Sakuragaoka, 2-Chome Setagaya-ku, Tokyo 156-0054, JAPAN, Phone: 81-3-3420-0375

SAKMAR, MIKE,
903 S. Latson Rd. #257, Howell, MI 48843, Phone: 517-546-6388, Fax: 517-546-6399, sakmarent@yahoo.com; Web: www.sakmarenterprises.com
Specialties: Mokume in various patterns and alloy combinations. **Patterns:** Bowies, fighters, hunters and integrals. **Technical:** Grinds ATS-34, Damascus and high-carbon tool steels. Uses mostly natural handle materials—elephant ivory, walrus ivory, stag, wildwood, oosic, etc. Makes mokume for resale. **Prices:** $250 to $2500; some to $4000. **Remarks:** Part-time maker; first knife sold in 1990. Supplier of mokume. **Mark:** Last name.

SALLEY, JOHN D,
3965 Frederick-Ginghamsburg Rd., Tipp City, OH 45371, Phone: 937-698-4588, Fax: 937-698-4131
Specialties: Fancy working knives and art pieces. **Patterns:** Hunters, fighters, daggers and some swords. **Technical:** Grinds ATS-34, 12C27 and W2; buys Damascus. **Prices:** $85 to $1000; some to $6000. **Remarks:** Part-time maker; first knife sold in 1979. **Mark:** First initial, last name.

SAMPSON, LYNN,
381 Deakins Rd, Jonesborough, TN 37659, Phone: 423-348-8373

Specialties: Highly finished working knives, mostly folders. **Patterns:** Locking folders, slip-joints, interframes and two-blades. **Technical:** Grinds D2, 440C and ATS-34; offers extensive filework. **Prices:** Start at $300. **Remarks:** Full-time maker; first knife sold in 1982. **Mark:** Name and city in logo.

SANDBERG, RONALD B,
24784 Shadowwood Ln, Brownstown, MI 48134-9560, Phone: 734-671-6866, msc2009@comcast.net
Specialties: Good looking and functional hunting knives, filework, mixing of handle materials. **Patterns:** Hunters, skinners and Bowies. **Prices:** $120 and up. **Remarks:** Full lifetime workmanship guarantee. **Mark:** R.B. SANDBERG

SANDERS, BILL,
335 Bauer Ave, PO Box 957, Mancos, CO 81328, Phone: 970-533-7223, Fax: 970-533-7390, billsand@frontier.net; Web: www.billsandershandmadeknives.com
Specialties: Survival knives, working straight knives, some fancy and some fantasy, of his design. **Patterns:** Hunters, boots, utility knives, using belt knives. **Technical:** Grinds 440C, ATS-34 and commercial Damascus. Provides wide variety of handle materials. **Prices:** $170 to $800. **Remarks:** Full-time maker. Formerly of Timberline Knives. **Mark:** Name, city and state.

SANDERS, MICHAEL M,
PO Box 1106, Ponchatoula, LA 70454, Phone: 225-294-3601, sanders@bellsouth.net
Specialties: Working straight knives and folders, some deluxe. **Patterns:** Hunters, fighters, Bowies, daggers, large folders and deluxe Damascus miniatures. **Technical:** Grinds O1, D2, 440C, ATS-34 and Damascus. **Prices:** $75 to $650; some higher. **Remarks:** Full-time maker; first knife sold in 1967. **Mark:** Name and state.

SANDOW, BRENT EDWARD,
50 O'Halloran Road, Howick, Manukau 2014, Auckland, New Zealand, Phone: 64 9 537 4166, Fax: 64 9 533 6655, knifebug@vodafone.co.nz
Specialties: Tactical fixed blades, hunting, camp, Bowie. **Technical:** All blades made by stock removal method. **Prices:** From US $200 upward.

SANDOW, NORMAN E,
63 B Moore St, Howick, Auckland, NEW ZEALAND, Phone: 095328912, sanknife@xtra.co.nz
Specialties: Quality LinerLock® folders. Working and fancy straight knives. Some one-of-a-kind. Embellishments available. **Patterns:** Most patterns, hunters, boot, bird and trout, etc., and to customer's specs. **Technical:** Predominate knife steel ATS-34. Also in use 12C27, D2 and Damascus. High class handle material used on both folders and straight knives. All blades made via the stock removal method. **Prices:** $350 to $2500. **Remarks:** Full-time maker. **Mark:** Norman E Sandow in semi-circular design.

SANDS, SCOTT,
2 Lindis Ln, New Brighton, Christchurch 9, NEW ZEALAND
Specialties: Classic working and fantasy swords. **Patterns:** Fantasy, medieval, celtic, viking, katana, some daggers. **Technical:** Forges own Damascus; 1080 and L6; 5160 and L6; O1 and L6. All hand-polished, does own heat-treating, forges non-Damascus on request. **Prices:** $1500 to $15,000+. **Remarks:** Full-time maker; first blade sold in 1996. **Mark:** Stylized Moon.

SANFORD, DICK,
9 Satsop Court, Montesano, WA 98563, Phone: 360-249-5776, richardsanfo364@centurytel.net
Remarks: Ten years experience hand forging knives

SANTIAGO, ABUD,
Av Gaona 3676 PB A, Buenos Aires 1416, ARGENTINA, Phone: 5411 4612 8396, info@phi-sabud.com; Web: www.phi-sabud.com/blades.html

SANTINI, TOM,
25158 Rose St., Chesterfield, MI 48051, Phone: 586-598-9471, tomsantiniknives@hotmail.com; Web: www.tomsantiniknives.com
Specialties: working/using straight knives, tactical, and some slipjoints **Technical:** Grinds ATS-34, S-90-V, D2, and damascus. I handstitch my leather sheaths. **Prices:** $150 - $500. **Remarks:** Full-time maker, first knife sold in 2004. **Mark:** Full name.

SARGANIS, PAUL,
2215 Upper Applegate Rd, Jacksonville, OR 97530, Phone: 541-899-2831, paulsarganis@hotmail.com; Web: www.sarganis.50megs.com
Specialties: Hunters, folders, Bowies. **Technical:** Forges 5160, 1084. Grinds ATS-34 and 440C. **Prices:** $120 to $500. **Remarks:** Spare-time maker, first knife sold in 1987. **Mark:** Last name.

SASS, GARY N,
2048 Buckeye Dr, Sharpsville, PA 16150, Phone: 724-866-6165, gnsass@yahoo.com
Specialties: Working straight knives of his design or to customer specifications. **Patterns:** Hunters, fighters, utility knives, push daggers. **Technical:** Grinds 440C, ATS-34 and Damascus. Uses exotic wood, buffalo horn, warthog tusk and semi-precious stones. **Prices:** $50 to $250, some higher. **Remarks:** Part-time maker. First knife sold in 2003. **Mark:** Initials G.S. formed into a diamond shape or last name.

SAVIANO, JAMES,
124 Wallis St., Douglas, MA 01516, Phone: 508-476-7644, jimsaviano@gmail.com
Specialties: Straight knives. **Patterns:** Hunters, bowies, fighters, daggers, short swords. **Technical:** Hand-forged high-carbon and my own damascus steel. **Prices:** Starting at $300. **Remarks:** ABS mastersmith, maker since 2000, sole authorship. **Mark:** Last name or stylized JPS initials.

SAWBY, SCOTT,
480 Snowberry Ln, Sandpoint, ID 83864, Phone: 208-263-4171, scotmar@dishmail.net; Web: www.sawbycustomknives.com
 Specialties: Folders, working and fancy. **Patterns:** Locking folders, patent locking systems and interframes. **Technical:** Grinds D2, 440C, CPM154, ATS-34, S30V, and Damascus. **Prices:** $700 to $3000. **Remarks:** Full-time maker; first knife sold in 1974. Engraving by wife Marian. **Mark:** Last name, city and state.

SCARROW, WIL,
c/o LandW Mail Service, PO Box 1036, Gold Hill, OR 97525, Phone: 541-855-1236, willsknife@earthlink.net
 Specialties: Carving knives, also working straight knives in standard patterns or to customer specs. **Patterns:** Carving, fishing, hunting, skinning, utility, swords and Bowies. **Technical:** Forges and grinds: A2, L6, W1, D2, 5160, 1095, 440C, AEB-L, ATS-34 and others on request. Offers some filework. **Prices:** $105 to $850; some higher. Prices include sheath (carver's $40 and up). **Remarks:** Spare-time maker; first knife sold in 1983. Two to eight month construction time on custom orders. Doing business as Scarrow's Custom Stuff and Gold Hill Knife works (in Oregon). Carving knives available at Raven Dog Enterprises. Contact at Ravedog@aol.com. **Mark:** SC with arrow and year made.

SCHALLER, ANTHONY BRETT,
5609 Flint Ct. NW, Albuquerque, NM 87120, Phone: 505-899-0155, brett@schallerknives.com; Web: www.schallerknives.com
 Specialties: Straight knives and locking-liner folders of his design and in standard patterns. **Patterns:** Boots, fighters, utility knives and folders. **Technical:** Grinds CPM154, S30V, and stainless Damascus. Offers filework, hand-rubbed finishes and full and narrow tangs. Prefers exotic woods or Micarta for handle materials, G-10 and carbon fiber to handle materials. **Prices:** $100 to $350; some to $500. **Remarks:** Part-time maker; first knife sold in 1990. **Mark:** A.B. Schaller - Albuquerque NM - handmade.

SCHEID, MAGGIE,
124 Van Stallen St, Rochester, NY 14621-3557
 Specialties: Simple working straight knives. **Patterns:** Kitchen and utility knives; some miniatures. **Technical:** Forges 5160 high-carbon steel. **Prices:** $100 to $200. **Remarks:** Part-time maker; first knife sold in 1986. **Mark:** Full name.

SCHEMPP, ED,
PO Box 1181, Ephrata, WA 98823, Phone: 509-754-2963, Fax: 509-754-3212
 Specialties: Mosaic Damascus and unique folder designs. **Patterns:** Primarily folders. **Technical:** Grinds CPM440V; forges many patterns of mosaic using powdered steel. **Prices:** $100 to $400; some to $2000. **Remarks:** Part-time maker; first knife sold in 1991. Doing business as Ed Schempp Knives. **Mark:** Ed Schempp Knives over five heads of wheat, city and state.

SCHEMPP, MARTIN,
PO Box 1181, 5430 Baird Springs Rd NW, Ephrata, WA 98823, Phone: 509-754-2963, Fax: 509-754-3212
 Specialties: Fantasy and traditional straight knives of his design, to customer specs and in standard patterns; Paleolithic-styles. **Patterns:** Fighters and Paleolithic designs. **Technical:** Uses opal, Mexican rainbow and obsidian. Offers scrimshaw. **Prices:** $15 to $100; some to $250. **Remarks:** Spare-time maker; first knife sold in 1995. **Mark:** Initials and date.

SCHEPERS, GEORGE B,
PO Box 395, Shelton, NE 68876-0395
 Specialties: Fancy period pieces of his design. **Patterns:** Bowies, swords, tomahawks; locking folders and miniatures. **Technical:** Grinds W1, W2 and his own Damascus; etches. **Prices:** $125 to $600; some higher. **Remarks:** Full-time maker; first knife sold in 1981. **Mark:** Schep.

SCHEURER, ALFREDO E FAES,
Av Rincon de los Arcos 104, Col Bosque Res del Sur, C.P. 16010, MEXICO, Phone: 5676 47 63
 Specialties: Fancy and fantasy knives of his design. **Patterns:** Daggers. **Technical:** Grinds stainless steel; casts and grinds silver. Sets stones in silver. **Prices:** $2000 to $3000. **Remarks:** Spare-time maker; first knife sold in 1989. **Mark:** Symbol.

SCHIPPNICK, JIM,
PO Box 326, Sanborn, NY 14132, Phone: 716-731-3715, ragnar@ragweedforge.com; Web: www.ragweedforge.com
 Specialties: Nordic, early American, rustic. **Mark:** Runic R. **Remarks:** Also imports Nordic knives from Norway, Sweden and Finland.

SCHLUETER, DAVID,
2136 Cedar Gate Rd., Madison Heights, VA 24572, Phone: 434-384-8642, drschlueter@hotmail.com
 Specialties: Japanese-style swords. **Patterns:** Larger blades. O-tanto to Tachi, with focus on less common shapes. **Technical:** Forges and grinds carbon steels, heat-treats and polishes own blades, makes all fittings, does own mounting and finishing. **Prices:** Start at $3000. **Remarks:** Sells fully mounted pieces only, doing business as Odd Frog Forge. **Mark:** Full name and date.

SCHMITZ, RAYMOND E,
PO Box 1787, Valley Center, CA 92082, Phone: 760-749-4318

SCHNEIDER, CRAIG M,
5380 N Amity Rd, Claremont, IL 62421, Phone: 217-377-5715, raephtownslam@att.blackberry.net
 Specialties: Straight knives of his own design. **Patterns:** Bowies, hunters,

tactical, bird & trout. **Technical:** Forged high-carbon steel and Damascus. Flat grind and differential heat treatment use a wide selection of handle, guard and bolster material, also offers leather sheaths. **Prices:** $150 to $3000. **Remarks:** Part-time maker; first knife sold in 1985. **Mark:** Stylized initials.

SCHNEIDER, HERMAN,
14084 Apple Valley Rd, Apple Valley, CA 92307, Phone: 760-946-9096
 Specialties: Presentation pieces, Fighters, Hunters. **Prices:** Starting at $900. **Mark:** H.J. Schneider-Maker or maker's last name.

SCHNEIDER, KARL A,
209 N. Brownleaf Rd, Newark, DE 19713, Phone: 302-737-0277, dmatj@msn.com
 Specialties: Traditional working and using straight knives of his design. **Patterns:** Hunters, kitchen and fillet knives. **Technical:** Grinds ATS-34, CM154, 52100, AUS8 - AUS6. Shapes handles to fit hands; uses Micarta, Pakkawood and exotic woods. Makes hand-stitched leather cases. **Prices:** $100 to $300. **Remarks:** Part-time maker; first knife sold in 1974. **Mark:** Name, address; also name in shape of fish.

SCHOEMAN, CORRIE,
Box 28596, Danhof 9310, SOUTH AFRICA, Phone: 027 51 4363528 Cell: 027 82-3750789, corries@intekom.co.za
 Specialties: High-tech folders of his design or to customer's specs. **Patterns:** Linerlock folders and automatics. **Technical:** ATS-34, Damascus or stainless Damascus with titanium frames; prefers exotic materials for handles. **Prices:** $650 to $2000. **Remarks:** Full-time maker; first knife sold in 1984. All folders come with filed liners and back and jeweled inserts. **Mark:** Logo in knife shape engraved on inside of back bar.

SCHOENFELD, MATTHEW A,
RR #1, Galiano Island, B.C., CANADA V0N 1P0, Phone: 250-539-2806
 Specialties: Working knives of his design. **Patterns:** Kitchen cutlery, camp knives, hunters. **Technical:** Grinds 440C. **Prices:** $85 to $500. **Remarks:** Part-time maker; first knife sold in 1978. **Mark:** Signature, Galiano Is. B.C., and date.

SCHOENINGH, MIKE,
49850 Miller Rd, North Powder, OR 97867, Phone: 541-856-3239

SCHOLL, TIM,
1389 Langdon Rd, Angier, NC 27501, Phone: 910-897-2051, tscholl@charter.net
 Specialties: Fancy and working/using straight knives and folders of his design and to customer specs. **Patterns:** Bowies, hunters, tomahawks, daggers & fantasy knives. **Technical:** Forges high carbon and tool steel makes Damascus, grinds ATS-34 and D2 on request. **Prices:** $150 to $6000. **Remarks:** Part-time maker; first knife sold in 1990. Doing business as Tim Scholl Custom Knives. **Mark:** S pierced by arrow.

SCHRADER, ROBERT,
55532 Gross De, Bend, OR 97707, Phone: 541-598-7301
 Specialties: Hunting, utility, Bowie. **Patterns:** Fixed blade. **Prices:** $150 to $600.

SCHRAP, ROBERT G,
CUSTOM LEATHER KNIFE SHEATH CO., 7024 W Wells St, Wauwatosa, WI 53213-3717, Phone: 414-771-6472, Fax: 414-479-9765, knifesheaths@aol.com; Web: www.customsheaths.com
 Specialties: Leatherwork. **Prices:** $35 to $100. **Mark:** Schrap in oval.

SCHROEN, KARL,
4042 Bones Rd, Sebastopol, CA 95472, Phone: 707-823-4057, Fax: 707-823-2914, Web: http://users.ap.net/~schroen
 Specialties: Using knives made to fit. **Patterns:** Sgian dubhs, carving sets, wood-carving knives, fishing knives, kitchen knives and new cleaver design. **Technical:** Forges A2, ATS-34, D2 and L6 cruwear S30V S90V. **Prices:** $150 to $6000. **Remarks:** Full-time maker; first knife sold in 1968. Author of *The Hand Forged Knife*. **Mark:** Last name.

SCHUCHMANN, RICK,
3975 Hamblen Dr, Cincinnati, OH 45255, Phone: 513-553-4316
 Specialties: Replicas of antique and out-of-production Scagels and Randalls, primarily miniatures. **Patterns:** All sheath knives, mostly miniatures, hunting and fighting knives, some daggers and hatchets. **Technical:** Stock removal, 440C and O1 steel. Most knives are flat ground, some convex. **Prices:** $175 to $600 and custom to $4000. **Remarks:** Part-time maker, sold first knife in 1997. Knives on display in the Randall Museum. Sheaths are made exclusively at Sullivan's Holster Shop, Tampa, FL **Mark:** SCAR.

SCHWARZER, LORA SUE,
119 Shoreside Trail, Crescent City, FL 32112, Phone: 386-698-2840, steveschwarzer@GBSO.net
 Specialties: Scagel style knives. **Patterns:** Hunters and miniatures **Technical:** Forges 1084 and Damascus. **Prices:** Start at $400. **Remarks:** Part-time maker; first knife sold in 1997. Journeyman Bladesmith, American Bladesmith Society. Now working with Steve Schwarzer on some projects. **Mark:** Full name - JS on reverse side.

SCHWARZER, STEPHEN,
119 Shoreside Trail, Crescent City, FL 32112, Phone: 386-698-2840, Fax: 386-698-2840, steveschwarzer@gbso.net; Web: www.steveschwarzer.com
 Specialties: Mosaic Damascus and picture mosaic in folding knives. All Japanese blades are finished working with Wally Hostetter considered the top Japanese lacquer specialist in the U.S.A. Also produces a line of carbon steel skinning knives at $300. **Patterns:** Folders, axes and buckskinner knives.

Technical: Specializes in picture mosaic Damascus and powder metal mosaic work. Sole authorship; all work including carving done in-house. Most knives have file work and carving. Hand carved steel and precious metal guards. **Prices:** $1500 to $5000, some higher; carbon steel and primitive knives much less. **Remarks:** Full-time maker; first knife sold in 1976, considered by many to be one of the top mosaic Damascus specialists in the world. Mosaic Master level work. I am now working with Lora Schwarzer on some projects. **Mark:** Schwarzer + anvil.

SCIMIO, BILL,
4554 Creek Side Ln., Spruce Creek, PA 16683, Phone: 814-632-3751, sprucecreekforge@gmail.com Web: www.sprucecreekforge.com
Specialties: Hand-forged primitive-style knives with curly maple, antler, bone and osage handles.

SCORDIA, PAOLO,
Via Terralba 143, 00050 Torrimpietra, Roma, ITALY, Phone: 06-61697231, pands@mail.nexus.it; Web: www.scordia-knives.com
Specialties: Working and fantasy knives of his own design. **Patterns:** Any pattern. **Technical:** Forges own Damascus, welds own mokume and grinds ATS-34, etc. use hardwoods and Micarta for handles, brass and nickel-silver for fittings. Makes sheaths. **Prices:** $100 to $1000. **Remarks:** Part-time maker; first knife sold in 1988. **Mark:** Initials with sun and moon logo.

SCOTT, AL,
2245 Harper Valley Rd, Harper, TX 78631, Phone: 830-928-1742, deadlybeauty@ctesc.net
Specialties: High-art straight knives of his design. **Patterns:** Daggers, swords, early European, Middle East and Japanese knives. **Technical:** Uses ATS-34, 440C and Damascus. Hand engraves; does file work; cuts filigree in the blade; offers ivory carving and precious metal inlay. **Remarks:** Full-time maker; first knife sold in 1994. Doing business as Al Scott Maker of Fine Blade Art. **Mark:** Name engraved in Old English, sometime inlaid in 24K gold.

SCROGGS, JAMES A,
108 Murray Hill Dr, Warrensburg, MO 64093, Phone: 660-747-2568, jscroggsknives@embarqmail.com
Specialties: Straight knives, prefers light weight. **Patterns:** Hunters, hideouts, and fighters. **Technical:** Grinds O1 plus experiments in steels. Uses high and low temperature of salt pots for heat treat. Prefers handles of walnut in English, bastonge, American black. Also uses myrtle, maple, Osage orange. **Prices:** $200 to $1000. **Remarks:** 1st knife sold in 1985. Part-time maker, no orders taken. **Mark:** SCROGGS in block or script.

SCULLEY, PETER E,
340 Sunset Dr, Rising Fawn, GA 30738, Phone: 706-398-0169

SEARS, MICK,
4473 Ernest Scott Rd., Kershaw, SC 29067, Phone: 803-475-4937
Specialties: Scots and confederate reproductions; Bowies and fighters. **Patterns:** Bowies, fighters. **Technical:** Grinds 440C and 1095. **Prices:** $50 to $150; some to $300. **Remarks:** Full-time maker; first knife sold in 1975. Doing business as Mick's Custom Knives. **Mark:** First name.

SEIB, STEVE,
7914 Old State Road, Evansville, IN 47710, Phone: 812-867-2231, sseib@insightbb.com
Specialties: Working straight knives. **Pattern:** Skinners, hunters, bowies and camp knives. **Technical:** Forges high-carbon and makes own damascus. **Remarks:** Part-time maker. ABS member. **Mark:** Last name.

SELF, ERNIE,
950 O'Neill Ranch Rd, Dripping Springs, TX 78620-9760, Phone: 512-940-7134, ernieself@hillcountrytx.net
Specialties: Traditional and working straight knives and folders of his design and in standard patterns. **Patterns:** Hunters, locking folders and slip-joints. **Technical:** Grinds 440C, D2, 440V, ATS-34 and Damascus. Offers fancy filework. **Prices:** $250 to $1000; some to $2500. **Remarks:** Full-time maker; first knife sold in 1982. Also customizes Buck 110's and 112's folding hunters. **Mark:** In oval shape - Ernie Self Maker Dripping Springs TX.

SELLEVOLD, HARALD,
S Kleivesmau:2, PO Box 4134, N5835 Bergen, NORWAY, Phone: 47 55-310682, haraldsellevold@c2i.net; Web:knivmakeren.com
Specialties: Norwegian-styles; collaborates with other Norse craftsmen. **Patterns:** Distinctive ferrules and other mild modifications of traditional patterns; Bowies and friction folders. **Technical:** Buys Damascus blades; blacksmiths his own blades. Semi-gemstones used in handles; gemstone inlay. **Prices:** $350 to $2000. **Remarks:** Full-time maker; first knife sold in 1980. **Mark:** Name and country in logo.

SELZAM, FRANK,
Martin Reinhard Str 23 97631, Bad Koenigshofen, GERMANY, Phone: 09761-5980, frankselzam.de
Specialties: Hunters, working knives to customers specs, hand tooled and stitched leather sheaths large stock of wood and German stag horn. **Patterns:** Mostly own design. **Technical:** Forged blades, own Damascus, also stock removal stainless. **Prices:** $250 to $1500. **Remark:** First knife sold in 1978. **Mark:** Last name stamped.

SENTZ, MARK C,
4084 Baptist Rd, Taneytown, MD 21787, Phone: 410-756-2018
Specialties: Fancy straight working knives of his design. **Patterns:** Hunters, fighters, folders and utility/camp knives. **Technical:** Forges 1085, 1095, 5160,

5155 and his Damascus. Most knives come with wood-lined leather sheath or wooden presentation sheath. **Prices:** Start at $275. **Remarks:** Full-time maker; first knife sold in 1989. Doing business as M. Charles Sentz Gunsmithing, Inc. **Mark:** Last name.

SERAFEN, STEVEN E,
24 Genesee St, New Berlin, NY 13411, Phone: 607-847-6903
Specialties: Traditional working/using straight knives of his design and to customer specs. **Patterns:** Bowies, fighters, hunters. **Technical:** Grinds ATS-34, 440C, high-carbon steel. **Prices:** $175 to $600; some to $1200. **Remarks:** Part-time maker; first knife sold in 1990. **Mark:** First and middle initial, last name in script.

SERVEN, JIM,
PO Box 1, Fostoria, MI 48435, Phone: 517-795-2255
Specialties: Highly finished unique folders. **Patterns:** Fancy working folders, axes, miniatures and razors; some straight knives. **Technical:** Grinds 440C; forges his own Damascus. **Prices:** $150 to $800; some to $1500. **Remarks:** Full-time maker; first knife sold in 1971. **Mark:** Name in map logo.

SEVEY CUSTOM KNIFE,
94595 Chandler Rd, Gold Beach, OR 97444, Phone: 541-247-2649, sevey@charter.net; Web: www.seveyknives.com
Specialties: Fixed blade hunters. **Patterns:** Drop point, trailing paint, clip paint, full tang, hidden tang. **Technical:** D-2, and ATS-34 blades, stock removal. Heat treatment by Paul Bos. **Prices:** $225 and up depending on overall length and grip material. **Mark:** Sevey Custom Knife.

SFREDDO, RODRIGO MENEZES,
Rua 15 De Setembro 66, Centro Nova Petropolis RS, cep g5 150-000, BRAZIL 95150-000, Phone: 011-55-54-303-303-90, www.brazilianbladesmiths.com.br; www.sbccutelaria.org.br
Specialties: Integrals, Bowies, hunters, dirks & swords. **Patterns:** Forges his own Damascus and 52100 steel. **Technical:** Specialized in integral knives and Damascus. **Prices:** From $350 and up. Most around $750 to $1000. **Remarks:** Considered by many to be the Brazil's best bladesmith. ABS SBC Member. **Mark:** S. Sfreddo on the left side of the blade.

SHADLEY, EUGENE W,
26315 Norway Dr, Bovey, MN 55709, Phone: 218-245-1639, Fax: call first, bses@uslink.net
Specialties: Gold frames are available on some models. **Patterns:** Whittlers, stockman, sowbelly, congress, trapper, etc. **Technical:** Grinds ATS-34, 416 frames. **Prices:** Starts at $600. **Remarks:** Full-time maker; first knife sold in 1985. Doing business as Shadley Knives. **Mark:** Last name.

SHADMOT, BOAZ,
MOSHAV PARAN D N, Arava, ISRAEL 86835, srb@arava.co.il

SHARRIGAN, MUDD,
111 Bradford Rd, Wiscasset, ME 04578-4457, Phone: 207-882-9820, Fax: 207-882-9835
Specialties: Custom designs; repair straight knives, custom leather sheaths. **Patterns:** Daggers, fighters, hunters, crooked knives and seamen working knives; traditional Scandinavian-styles. **Technical:** Forges 1095, 5160, and W2. **Prices:** $50 to $325; some to $1200. **Remarks:** Full-time maker; first knife sold in 1982. **Mark:** Swallow tail carving. Mudd engraved.

SHAVER II, JAMES R,
1529 Spider Ridge Rd, Parkersburg, WV 26104, Phone: 304-422-2692, admin@spiderridgeforge.com Web:www.spiderridgeforge.net
Specialties: Hunting and working straight knives in carbon and Damascus steel. **Patterns:** Bowies and daggers in Damascus and carbon steels. **Technical:** Forges 5160 carbon and Damascus in 01 pure nickel 1018. **Prices:** $85 to $125; some to $750. Some to $1000 **Remarks:** Part-time maker; sold first knife in 1998. Believes in sole authorship. **Mark:** Last name.

SHEEHY, THOMAS J,
4131 NE 24th Ave, Portland, OR 97211-6411, Phone: 503-493-2843
Specialties: Hunting knives and ulus. **Patterns:** Own or customer designs. **Technical:** 1095/O1 and ATS-34 steel. **Prices:** $35 to $200. **Remarks:** Do own heat treating; forged or ground blades. **Mark:** Name.

SHEETS, STEVEN WILLIAM,
6 Stonehouse Rd, Mendham, NJ 07945, Phone: 201-543-5882

SHIFFER, STEVE,
PO Box 582, Leakesville, MS 39451, Phone: 601-394-4425, aiifish2@yahoo.com; Web: wwwchoctawplantationforge.com
Specialties: Bowies, fighters, hard use knives. **Patterns:** Fighters, hunters, combat/utility knives. Walker pattern LinerLock® folders. Allen pattern scale and bolster release autos. **Technical:** Most work forged, stainless stock removal. Makes own Damascus. O1 and 5160 most used also 1084, 440c, 154cm, s30v. **Prices:** $125 to $1000. **Remarks:** First knife sold in 2000, all heat treatment done by maker. Doing business as Choctaw Plantation Forge. **Mark:** Hot mark sunrise over creek.

SHINOSKY, ANDY,
3117 Meanderwood Dr, Canfield, OH 44406, Phone: 330-702-0299, andrew@shinosky.com; Web: www.shinosky.com
Specialties: Collectable folders and interframes. **Patterns:** Drop point, spear point, trailing point, daggers. **Technical:** Grinds ATS-34 and Damascus. Prefers natural handle materials. Most knives are engraved by Andy himself. **Prices:** Start at $800. **Remarks:** Part-time maker/engraver. First knife sold in 1992. **Mark:** Name.

SHIPLEY—SLOBODIAN

SHIPLEY, STEVEN A,
800 Campbell Rd Ste 137, Richardson, TX 75081, Phone: 972-644-7981, Fax: 972-644-7985, steve@shipleysphotography
Specialties: Hunters, skinners and traditional straight knives. **Technical:** Hand grinds ATS-34, 440C and Damascus steels. Each knife is custom sheathed by his son, Dan. **Prices:** $175 to $2000. **Remarks:** Part-time maker; like smooth lines and unusual handle materials. **Mark:** S A Shipley.

SHOEMAKER, CARROLL,
380 Yellowtown Rd, Northup, OH 45658, Phone: 740-446-6695
Specialties: Working/using straight knives of his design. **Patterns:** Hunters, utility/camp and early American backwoodsmen knives. **Technical:** Grinds ATS-34; forges old files, O1 and 1095. Uses some Damascus; offers scrimshaw and engraving. **Prices:** $100 to $175; some to $350. **Remarks:** Spare-time maker; first knife sold in 1977. **Mark:** Name and city or connected initials.

SHOEMAKER, SCOTT,
316 S Main St, Miamisburg, OH 45342, Phone: 513-859-1935
Specialties: Twisted, wire-wrapped handles on swords, fighters and fantasy blades; new line of seven models with quick-draw, multi-carry Kydex sheaths. **Patterns:** Bowies, boots and one-of-a-kinds in his design or to customer specs. **Technical:** Grinds A6 and ATS-34; buys Damascus. Hand satin finish is standard. **Prices:** $100 to $1500; swords to $8000. **Remarks:** Part-time maker; first knife sold in 1984. **Mark:** Angel wings with last initial, or last name.

SHOGER, MARK O,
14780 SW Osprey Dr Suite 345, Beaverton, OR 97007, Phone: 503-579-2495, mosdds@msn.com
Specialties: Working and using straight knives and folders of his design; fancy and embellished knives. **Patterns:** Hunters, Bowies, daggers and folders. **Technical:** Forges O1, W2, 1084, 5160, 52100 and 1084/15n20 pattern weld. **Remarks:** Spare-time maker. **Mark:** Last name or stamped last initial over anvil.

SHULL, JAMES,
5146 N US 231 W, Rensselaer, IN 47978, Phone: 219-866-0436, nbjs@netnitco.net Web: www.shullhandforgedknives.com
Specialties: Working knives of hunting, fillet, Bowie patterns. **Technical:** Forges or uses 1095, 5160, 52100 & O1. **Prices:** $100 to $300. **Remarks:** DBA Shull Handforged Knives. **Mark:** Last name in arc.

SIBERT, SHANE,
PO BOX 241, Gladstone, OR 97027, Phone: 503-650-2082, shane.sibert@comcast.net Web: www.sibertknives.com
Specialties: Innovative light weight hiking and backpacking knives for outdoorsman and adventurers, progressive fixed blade combat and fighting knives. One-of-a-kind knives of various configurations. Titanium frame lock folders. **Patterns:** Modern configurations of utility/camp knives, bowies, modified spear points, daggers, tantos, recurves, clip points and spine serrations. **Technical:** Stock removal. Specializes in CPM S30V, CPM S35VN, CPM D2, CPM 3V, stainless Damascus. Micarta, G-10, stabilized wood and titanium. **Prices:** $200 - $1000, some pieces $1500 and up. **Remarks:** Full-time maker, first knife sold in 1994. **Mark:** Stamped "SIBERT" and occasionally uses electro-etch with oval around last name.

SIBRIAN, AARON,
4308 Dean Dr, Ventura, CA 93003, Phone: 805-642-6950
Specialties: Tough working knives of his design and in standard patterns. **Patterns:** Makes a "Viper utility"—a kukri derivative and a variety of straight using knives. **Technical:** Grinds 440C and ATS-34. Offers traditional Japanese blades; soft backs, hard edges, temper lines. **Prices:** $60 to $100; some to $250. **Remarks:** Spare-time maker; first knife sold in 1989. **Mark:** Initials in diagonal line.

SIMMONS, H R,
1100 Bay City Rd, Aurora, NC 27806, Phone: 252-322-5969
Specialties: Working/using straight knives of his design. **Patterns:** Fighters, hunters and utility/camp knives. **Technical:** Forges and grinds Damascus and L6; grinds ATS-34. **Prices:** $150 to $250; some to $400. **Remarks:** Part-time maker; first knife sold in 1987. Doing business as HRS Custom Knives, Royal Forge and Trading Company. **Mark:** Initials.

SIMONELLA, GIANLUIGI,
Via Battiferri 33, 33085 Maniago, ITALY, Phone: 01139-427-730350
Specialties: Traditional and classic folding and working/using knives of his design and to customer specs. **Patterns:** Bowies, fighters, hunters, utility/camp knives. **Technical:** Forges ATS-34, D2, 440C. **Prices:** $250 to $400; some to $1000. **Remarks:** Full-time maker; first knife sold in 1988. **Mark:** Wilson.

SIMS, BOB,
PO Box 772, Meridian, TX 76665, Phone: 254-435-6240
Specialties: Traditional working straight knives and folders in standard patterns. **Patterns:** Locking folders, slip-joint folders and hunters. **Technical:** Grinds D2, ATS-34 and O1. Offers filework on some knives. **Prices:** $150 to $275; some to $600. **Remarks:** Full-time maker; first knife sold in 1975. **Mark:** The division sign.

SINCLAIR, J E,
520 Francis Rd, Pittsburgh, PA 15239, Phone: 412-793-5778
Specialties: Fancy hunters and fighters, liner locking folders. **Patterns:**

Fighters, hunters and folders. **Technical:** Flat-grinds and hollow grind, prefers hand rubbed satin finish. Uses natural handle materials. **Prices:** $185 to $800. **Remarks:** Part-time maker; first knife sold in 1995. **Mark:** First and middle initials, last name and maker.

SINYARD, CLESTON S,
27522 Burkhardt Dr, Elberta, AL 36530, Phone: 334-987-1361, nimoforge1@gulftel.com; Web: www.knifemakersguild
Specialties: Working straight knives and folders of his design. **Patterns:** Hunters, buckskinners, Bowies, daggers, fighters and all-Damascus folders. **Technical:** Makes Damascus from 440C, stainless steel, D2 and regular high-carbon steel; forges "forefinger pad" into hunters and skinners. **Prices:** In Damascus $450 to $1500; some $2500. **Remarks:** Full-time maker; first knife sold in 1980. Doing business as Nimo Forge. **Mark:** Last name, U.S.A. in anvil.

SISKA, JIM,
48 South Maple St, Westfield, MA 01085, Phone: 413-642-3059, siskaknives@comcast.net
Specialties: Traditional working straight knives, no folders. **Patterns:** Hunters, fighters, Bowies and one-of-a-kinds; folders. **Technical:** Grinds D2, A2, 54CM and ATS-34; buys Damascus. Likes exotic woods. **Prices:** $300 and up. **Remarks:** Part-time. **Mark:** Siska in Old English.

SJOSTRAND, KEVIN,
1541 S Cain St, Visalia, CA 93292, Phone: 559-625-5254
Specialties: Traditional and working/using straight knives and folders of his design or to customer specs. **Patterns:** Fixed blade hunters, Bowies, utility/camp knives. **Technical:** Grinds ATS-34, 440C and 1095. Prefers high polished blades and full tang. Natural and stabilized hardwoods, Micarta and stag handle material. **Prices:** $150 to $400. **Remarks:** Part-time maker; first knife sold in 1992. Doing business as Black Oak Blades. **Mark:** SJOSTRAND

SKIFF, STEVEN,
SKIFF MADE BLADES, PO Box 537, Broadalbin, NY 12025, Phone: 518-883-4875, skiffmadeblades@hotmail.com; Web: www.skiffmadeblades.com
Specialties: Custom using/collector grade straight blades and LinerLock® folders of maker's design or customer specifications. **Patterns:** Hunters, utility/camp knives, tactical/fancy art folders. **Prices:** Straight blades $225 and up. Folders $450 and up. **Technical:** Stock removal hollow ground ATS-34, 154 CM, S30V, and tool steel. Damascus-Devon Thomas, Robert Eggerling, Mike Norris and Delbert Ealy. Nickel silver and stainless in-house heat treating. Handle materials: man made and natural woods (stablilized). Horn shells sheaths for straight blades, sews own leather and uses sheaths by "Tree-Stump Leather." **Remarks:** First knife sold 1997. Started making folders in 2000. **Mark:** SKIFF on blade of straight blades and in inside of backspacer on folders.

SKOW, H.A. "TEX",
TEX KNIVES, 3534 Gravel Springs Rd, Senatobia, MS 38668, Phone: 662-301-1568, texknives@bellsouth.net; Web: www.texknives.com
Specialties: One-of-a-kind daggers, Bowies, boot knives and hunters. **Patterns:** Different Damascus patterns (by Bob Eggerling). **Technical:** 440C, 58, 60 Rockwell hardness. Engraving by Joe Mason. **Prices:** Negotiable. **Mark:** TEX.

SLEE, FRED,
9 John St, Morganville, NJ 07751, Phone: 732-591-9047
Specialties: Working straight knives, some fancy, to customer specs. **Patterns:** Hunters, fighters, fancy daggers and folders. **Technical:** Grinds D2, 440C and ATS-34. **Prices:** $285 to $1100. **Remarks:** Part-time maker; first knife sold in 1980. **Mark:** Letter "S" in Old English.

SLOAN, DAVID,
PO BOX 83, Diller, NE 68342, Phone: 402-793-5755, sigp22045@hotmail.com
Specialties: Hunters, choppers and fighters. **Technical:** Forged blades of W2, 1084 and Damascus. **Prices:** Start at $225. **Remarks:** Part-time maker, made first knife in 2002, received JS stamp 2010. **Mark:** Sloan JS.

SLOAN, SHANE,
4226 FM 61, Newcastle, TX 76372, Phone: 940-846-3290
Specialties: Collector-grade straight knives and folders. **Patterns:** Uses stainless Damascus, ATS-34 and 12C27. Bowies, lockers, slip-joints, fancy folders, fighters and period pieces. **Technical:** Grinds D2 and ATS-34. Uses hand-rubbed satin finish. Prefers rare natural handle materials. **Prices:** $250 to $6500. **Remarks:** Full-time maker; first knife sold in 1985. **Mark:** Name and city.

SLOBODIAN, SCOTT,
PO Box 1498, San Andreas, CA 95249, Phone: 209-286-1980, Fax: 209-286-1982, info@slobodianswords.com; Web: www.slobodianswords.com
Specialties: Japanese-style knives and swords, period pieces, fantasy pieces and miniatures. **Patterns:** Small kweikens, tantos, wakazashis, katanas, traditional samurai swords. **Technical:** Flat-grinds 1050, commercial Damascus. **Prices:** Prices start at $1500. **Remarks:** Full-time maker; first knife sold in 1987. **Mark:** Blade signed in Japanese characters and various scripts.

SMALE, CHARLES J,
509 Grove Ave, Waukegan, IL 60085, Phone: 847-244-8013

SMALL, ED,
Rt 1 Box 178-A, Keyser, WV 26726, Phone: 304-298-4254
Specialties: Working knives of his design; period pieces. **Patterns:** Hunters, daggers, buckskinners and camp knives; likes one-of-a-kinds. **Technical:** Forges and grinds W2, L6 and his own Damascus. **Prices:** $150 to $1500. **Remarks:** Full-time maker; first knife sold in 1978. Doing business as Iron Mountain Forge Works. **Mark:** Script initials connected.

SMART, STEVE,
907 Park Row Cir, McKinney, TX 75070-3847, Phone: 214-837-4216, Fax: 214-837-4111
Specialties: Working/using straight knives and folders of his design, to customer specs and in standard patterns. **Patterns:** Bowies, hunters, kitchen knives, locking folders, utility/camp, fishing and bird knives. **Technical:** Grinds ATS-34, D2, 440C and O1. Prefers mirror polish or satin finish; hollow-grinds all blades. All knives come with sheath. Offers some filework. **Prices:** $95 to $225; some to $500. **Remarks:** Spare-time maker; first knife sold in 1983. **Mark:** Name, Custom, city and state in oval.

SMIT, GLENN,
627 Cindy Ct, Aberdeen, MD 21001, Phone: 410-272-2959, wolfsknives@comcast.net
Specialties: Working and using straight and folding knives of his design or to customer specs. Customizes and repairs all types of cutlery. Exclusive maker of Dave Murphy Style knives. **Patterns:** Hunters, Bowies, daggers, fighters, utility/camp, folders, kitchen knives and miniatures, Murphy combat, C.H.A.I.K., Little 88 and Tiny 90-styles. **Technical:** Grinds 440C, ATS-34, O1, A2 also grinds 6AL4V titanium allox for blades. Reforges commercial Damascus and makes own Damascus, cast aluminum handles. **Prices:** Miniatures start at $30; full-size knives start at $50. **Remarks:** Spare-time maker; first knife sold in 1986. Doing business as Wolf's Knives. **Mark:** G.P. SMIT, with year on reverse side, Wolf's Knives-Murphy's way with date.

SMITH, J D,
69 Highland, Roxbury, MA 02119, Phone: 617-989-0723, jdsmith02119@yahoo.com
Specialties: Fighters, Bowies, Persian, locking folders and swords. **Patterns:** Bowies, fighters and locking folders. **Technical:** Forges and grinds D2, his Damascus, O1, 52100 etc. and wootz-pattern hammer steel. **Prices:** $500 to $2000; some to $5000. **Remarks:** Full-time maker; first knife sold in 1987. Doing business as Hammersmith. **Mark:** Last initial alone or in cartouche.

SMITH, J.B.,
21 Copeland Rd., Perkinston, MS 39573, Phone: 228-380-1851
Specialties: Traditional working knives for the hunter and fisherman. **Patterns:** Hunters, Bowies, and fishing knives; copies of 1800 period knives. **Technical:** Grinds ATS-34, 440C. **Prices:** $100 to $800. **Remarks:** Full-time maker, first knife sold in 1972. **Mark:** J.B. Smith MAKER PERKINSTON, MS.

SMITH, JERRY,
JW Smith & Sons Custom Knives, 204 Avenue E, Moody, TX 76557, Phone: 254-493-6295, jerry@jwsmithandsons.com Web: www.jwsmithandsons.com
Specialties: Fixed blade and folding knives. **Technical:** Steels used D2, A2, O1, 154 CM, 154 CPM. Stock removal, heat treat in house, all leather work in house. **Prices:** $240. **Remarks:** Full-time knifemaker. First knife made in 2004. Slogan: "Cut Like You Mean It"

SMITH, JOHN M,
3450 E Beguelin Rd, Centralia, IL 62801, Phone: 618-249-6444, jknife@frontiernet.net
Specialties: Folders. **Patterns:** Folders. **Prices:** $250 to $2500. **Remarks:** First knife sold in 1980. Not taking orders at this time on fixed blade knives. Part-time maker. **Mark:** Etched signature or logo.

SMITH, JOHN W,
1322 Cow Branch Rd, West Liberty, KY 41472, Phone: 606-743-3599, jwsknive@mrtc.com; Web: www.jwsmithknives.com
Specialties: Fancy and working locking folders of his design or to customer specs. **Patterns:** Interframes, traditional and daggers. **Technical:** Grinds 530V and his own Damascus. Offers gold inlay, engraving with gold inlay, hand-fitted mosaic pearl inlay and filework. Prefers hand-rubbed finish. Pearl and ivory available. **Prices:** Utility pieces $375 to $650. Art knives $1200 to $10,000. **Remarks:** Full-time maker. **Mark:** Initials engraved inside diamond.

SMITH, JOSH,
Box 753, Frenchtown, MT 59834, Phone: 406-626-5775, joshsmithknives@gmail.com; Web: www.joshsmithknives.com
Specialties: Mosaic, Damascus, LinerLock folders, automatics, Bowies, fighters, etc. **Patterns:** All kinds. **Technical:** Advanced Mosaic and Damascus. **Prices:** $450 and up. **Remarks:** A.B.S. Master Smith. **Mark:** Josh Smith with last two digits of the current year.

SMITH, LACY,
PO BOX 188, Jacksonville, AL 36265, Phone: 256-310-4619, sales@smith-knives.com

SMITH, LENARD C,
PO Box D68, Valley Cottage, NY 10989, Phone: 914-268-7359

SMITH, MICHAEL J,
1418 Saddle Gold Ct, Brandon, FL 33511, Phone: 813-431-3790, smithknife@hotmail.com; Web: www.smithknife.com
Specialties: Fancy high art folders of his design. **Patterns:** Locking locks and automatics. **Technical:** Uses ATS-34, non-stainless and stainless Damascus; hand carves folders, prefers ivory and pearl. Hand-rubbed satin finish. Liners are 6AL4V titanium. **Prices:** $500 to $3000. **Remarks:** Full-time maker; first knife sold in 1989. **Mark:** Name, city, state.

SMITH, NEWMAN L,
865 Glades Rd Shop #3, Gatlinburg, TN 37738, Phone: 423-436-3322, thesmithshop@aol.com; Web: www.thesmithsshop.com
Specialties: Collector-grade and working knives. **Patterns:** Hunters, slip-joint and lock-back folders, some miniatures. **Technical:** Grinds O1 and ATS-34; makes fancy sheaths. **Prices:** $165 to $750; some to $1000. **Remarks:** Full-time maker; first knife sold in 1984. Partners part-time to handle Damascus blades by Jeff Hurst; marks these with SH connected. **Mark:** First and middle initials, last name.

SMITH, RALPH L,
525 Groce Meadow Rd, Taylors, SC 29687, Phone: 864-444-0819, ralph_smith1@charter.net; Web: www.smithhandcraftedknives.com
Specialties: Working knives: straight and folding knives. Hunters, skinners, fighters, bird, boot, Bowie and kitchen knives. **Technical:** Concave Grind D2, ATS 34, 440C, steel hand finish or polished. **Prices:** $125 to $350 for standard models. **Remarks:** First knife sold in 1976. KMG member since 1981. SCAK founding member and past president. **Mark:** SMITH handcrafted knives in SC state outline.

SMITH, RAYMOND L,
217 Red Chalk Rd, Erin, NY 14838, Phone: 607-795-5257, Bladesmith@wildblue.net; Web: www.theanvilsedge.com
Specialties: Working/using straight knives and folders to customer specs and in standard patterns; period pieces. **Patterns:** Bowies, hunters, skip-joints. **Technical:** Forges 5160, 52100, 1018, 15N20, 1084, ATS 34. Damascus and wire cable Damascus. Filework. **Prices:** $125 to $1500; estimates for custom orders. **Remarks:** Full-time maker; first knife sold in 1991. ABS Master Smith. Doing business as The Anvils Edge. **Mark:** Ellipse with RL Smith, Erin NY MS in center.

SMITH, RICHARD J,
PO BOX 116, Milford, PA 18337, Phone: 908-627-5934, rs@smithknives.com Web: www.smithknives.com
Specialties: Straight working and collector knives with a high level of fit and finish in traditional and collector knives with a high level of fit and finish in traditional and own designs. **Technical:** Grinds CPM 154 CM, ATS-34, 154CM, O1 tool steel and others. **Prices:** $180 to $600. **Remarks:** Part-time maker, first knife sold in 2005. **Mark:** RJ Smith with U.S.A. beneath name.

SMITH, RICK,
BEAR BONE KNIVES, 1843 W Evans Creek Rd., Rogue River, OR 97537, Phone: 541-582-4144, BearBoneSmith@msn.com; Web: www.bearbone.com
Specialties: Classic, historical style Bowie knives, hunting knives and various contemporary knife styles. **Technical:** Blades are either forged or made by stock removal method depending on steel used. Also forge weld wire Damascus. Does own heat treating and tempering using digital oven heat kiln. Stainless blades are sent out for cryogenic "freeze treat." Preferred steels are O1, tool, 5160, 1095, 1084, ATS-34, 154CM, 440C and various high carbon Damascus. **Prices:** $350 to $1500. Custom leather sheaths available for knives. **Remarks:** Full-time maker since 1997. Serial numbers no longer put on knives. Official business name is "Bear Bone Knives." **Mark:** Early maker's mark was "Bear Bone" over capital letters "RS" with downward arrow between letters and "Hand Made" underneath letters. Mark on small knives is 3/8 circle containing "RS" with downward arrow between letters. Current mark since 2003 is "R Bear Bone Smith" arching over image of coffin Bowie knife with two shooting stars and "Rogue River, Oregon" underneath.

SMITH, SHAWN,
2644 Gibson Ave, Clouis, CA 93611, Phone: 559-323-6234, kslc@sbcglobal.net
Specialties: Working and fancy straight knives. **Patterns:** Hunting, trout, fighters, skinners. **Technical:** Hollow grinds ATS-34, 154CM, A-2. **Prices:** $150.00 and up. **Remarks:** Part time maker. **Mark:** Shawn Smith handmade.

SMITH JR., JAMES B "RED",
Rt 2 Box 1525, Morven, GA 31638, Phone: 912-775-2844
Specialties: Folders. **Patterns:** Rotating rear-lock folders. **Technical:** Grinds ATS-34, D2 and Vascomax 350. **Prices:** Start at $350. **Remarks:** Full-time maker; first knife sold in 1985. **Mark:** GA RED in cowboy hat.

SMOCK, TIMOTHY E,
1105 N Sherwood Dr, Marion, IN 46952, Phone: 765-664-0123

SNODY, MIKE,
135 Triple Creek Rd, Fredericksburg, TX 78624, Phone: 361-443-0161, info@snodyknives.com; Web: www.snodyknives.com
Specialties: High performance straight knives in traditional and Japanese-styles. **Patterns:** Skinners, hunters, tactical, Kwaiken and tantos. **Technical:** Grinds BG42, ATS-34, 440C and A2. Offers full or tapered tangs, upgraded handle materials such as fossil ivory, coral and exotic woods. Traditional diamond wrap over stingray on Japanese-style knives. Sheaths available in leather or Kydex. **Prices:** $100 to $1000. **Remarks:** Part-time maker; first knife sold in 1999. **Mark:** Name over knife maker.

custom knifemakers

SNOW, BILL,
4824 18th Ave, Columbus, GA 31904, Phone: 706-576-4390, tipikw@knology.net
Specialties: Traditional working/using straight knives and folders of his design and to customer specs. Offers engraving and scrimshaw. **Patterns:** Bowies, fighters, hunters and folders. **Technical:** Grinds ATS-34, 440V, 440C, 420V, CPM350, BG42, A2, D2, 5160, 52100 and O1; forges if needed. Cryogenically quenches all steels; inlaid handles; some integrals; leather or Kydex sheaths. **Prices:** $125 to $700; some to $3500. **Remarks:** Now also have 530V, 10V and 3V steels in use. Full-time maker; first knife sold in 1958. Doing business as Tipi Knife works. **Mark:** Old English scroll "S" inside a tipi.

SNYDER, MICHAEL TOM,
PO Box 522, Zionsville, IN 46077-0522, Phone: 317-873-6807, wildcatcreek@indy.pr.com

SOAPER, MAX H.,
2375 Zion Rd, Henderson, KY 42420, Phone: 270-827-8143
Specialties: Primitive Longhunter knives, scalpers, camp knives, cowboy Bowies, neck knives, working knives, period pieces from the 18th century. **Technical:** Forges 5160, 1084, 1095; all blades differentially heat treated. **Prices:** $80 to $800. **Remarks:** Part-time maker since 1989. **Mark:** Initials in script.

SOLOMON, MARVIN,
23750 Cold Springs Rd, Paron, AR 72122, Phone: 501-821-3170, Fax: 501-821-6541, mardot@swbell.net; Web: www.coldspringsforge.com
Specialties: Traditional working and using straight knives of his design and to customer specs, also lock back 7 LinerLock® folders. **Patterns:** Single blade folders. **Technical:** Forges 5160, 1095, O1 and random Damascus. **Prices:** $125 to $1000. **Remarks:** Part-time maker; first knife sold in 1990. Doing business as Cold Springs Forge. **Mark:** Last name.

SONNTAG, DOUGLAS W,
902 N 39th St, Nixa, MO 65714, Phone: 417-693-1640, Fax: 417-582-1392, dougsonntag@gmail.com
Specialties: Working knives; art knives. **Patterns:** Hunters, boots, straight working knives; Bowies, some folders, camp/axe sets. **Technical:** Grinds D2, ATS-34, forges own Damascus; does own heat treating. **Prices:** $225 and up. **Remarks:** Full-time maker; first knife sold in 1986. **Mark:** Etched name in arch.

SONTHEIMER, G DOUGLAS,
12604 Bridgeton Dr, Potomac, MD 20854, Phone: 301-948-5227
Specialties: Fixed blade knives. **Patterns:** Whitetail deer, backpackers, camp, claws, fillet, fighters. **Technical:** Hollow Grinds. **Price:** $500 and up. **Remarks:** Spare-time maker; first knife sold in 1976. **Mark:** LORD.

SOPPERA, ARTHUR,
"Pilatusblick", Oberer Schmidberg, CH-9631 Ulisbach, SWITZERLAND, Phone: 71-988 23 27, Fax: 71-988 47 57, doublelock@hotmail.com; Web: www.sopperaknifeart.ch
Specialties: High-art, high-tech knives of his design. **Patterns:** Locking folders, and fixed blade knives. **Technical:** Grinds ATS-34 and commercial Damascus. Folders have button lock of his own design; some are fancy folders in jeweler's fashion. Also makes jewelry with integrated small knives. **Prices:** $300 to $1500, some $2500 and higher. **Remarks:** Full-time maker; first knife sold in 1986. **Mark:** Stylized initials, name, country.

SORNBERGER, JIM,
25126 Overland Dr, Volcano, CA 95689, Phone: 209-295-7819
Specialties: Classic San Francisco-style knives. Collectible straight knives. **Patterns:** Forges 1095-1084/15W2. Makes own Damascus and powder metal. Fighters, daggers, Bowies; miniatures; hunters, custom canes, liner locks folders. **Technical:** Grinds 440C, 154CM and ATS-34; engraves, carves and embellishes. **Prices:** $500 to $20,000 in gold with gold quartz inlays. **Remarks:** Full-time maker; first knife sold in 1970. **Mark:** First Initial, last name, city and state.

SOWELL, BILL,
100 Loraine Forest Ct, Macon, GA 31210, Phone: 478- 994-9863, billsowell@reynoldscable.net
Specialties: Antique reproduction Bowies, forging Bowies, hunters, fighters, and most others. Also folders. **Technical:** Makes own Damascus, using 1084/15N20, also making own designs in powder metals, forges 5160-1095-1084, and other carbon steels, grinds ATS-34. **Prices:** Starting at $150 and up. **Remarks:** Part-time maker. Sold first knife in 1998. Does own leather work. ABS Master Smith. **Mark:** Iron Horse Forge - Sowell - MS.

SPARKS, BERNARD,
PO Box 73, Dingle, ID 83233, Phone: 208-847-1883, dogknifeii@juno.com; Web: www.sparksknives.com
Specialties: Maker engraved, working and art knives. Straight knives and folders of his own design. **Patterns:** Locking inner-frame folders, hunters, fighters, one-of-a-kind art knives. **Technical:** Grinds 530V steel, 440-C, 154CM, ATS-34, D-2 and forges by special order; triple temper, cryogenic soak. Mirror or hand finish. New Liquid metal steel. **Prices:** $300 to $2000. **Remarks:** Full-time maker, first knife sold in 1967. **Mark:** Last name over state with a knife logo on each end of name. Prior 1980, stamp of last name.

SPENCER, KEITH,
PO Box 149, Chidlow Western Australia, AUSTRALIA 6556, Phone: 61 8 95727255, Fax: 61 8 95727266, spencer@knivesaustralia.com.au Web: www.knivesaustralia.com.au
Specialties: Survival & bushcraft bladeware. **Patterns:** Kakadu bushcraft knife, Leilira mini survival knife, Mekong belt knife. **Technical:** D2, RWL-34, Damasteel, Bladesteels H/T 58RC. **Prices:** $150 to $500 AV. **Mark:** Spencer Australia.

SPICKLER, GREGORY NOBLE,
5614 Mose Cir, Sharpsburg, MD 21782, Phone: 301-432-2746

SPINALE, RICHARD,
4021 Canterbury Ct, Lorain, OH 44053, Phone: 440-282-1565
Specialties: High-art working knives of his design. **Patterns:** Hunters, fighters, daggers and locking folders. **Technical:** Grinds 440C and 07; engraves. Offers gold bolsters and other deluxe treatments. **Prices:** $300 to $1000; some to $3000. **Remarks:** Spare-time maker; first knife sold in 1976. **Mark:** Name, address, year and model number.

SPIVEY, JEFFERSON,
9244 W Wilshire, Yukon, OK 73099, Phone: 405-721-4442
Specialties: The Saber tooth: a combination hatchet, saw and knife. **Patterns:** Built for the wilderness, all are one-of-a-kind. **Technical:** Grinds chromemoly steel. The saw tooth spine curves with a double row of biangular teeth. **Prices:** Start at $275. **Remarks:** First knife sold in 1977. As of September 2006 Spivey knives has resumed production of the sabertooth knife. **Mark:** Name and serial number.

SPRAGG, WAYNE E,
252 Oregon Ave, Lovell, WY 82431, Phone: 307-548-7212
Specialties: Working straight knives, some fancy. **Patterns:** Folders. **Technical:** Forges carbon steel and makes Damascus. **Prices:** $200 and up. **Remarks:** All stainless heat-treated by Paul Bos. Carbon steel in shop heat treat. **Mark:** Last name front side w/s initials on reverse side.

SPROKHOLT, ROB,
GATHERWOOD, Burgerweg 5, Netherlands, Netherlands 1754 KB Burgerbrug, Phone: 0031 6 51230225, Fax: 0031 84 2238446, info@gatherwood.nl; Webwww.gatherwood.nl
Specialties: One-of-a-kind knives. Top materials collector grade, made to use. **Patterns:** Outdoor knives (hunting, sailing, hiking), Bowies, man's surviving companions MSC, big tantos, folding knives. **Technical:** Handles mostly stabilized or oiled wood, ivory, Micarta, carbon fibre, g10. Stiff knives are full tang. Characteristic one row of massive silver pins or tubes. Folding knives have a LinerLock® with titanium or Damascus powdersteel liner thumb can have any stone you like. Stock removal grinder: flat or convex. Steel 440-C, RWL-34, ATS-34, PM damascener steel. **Prices:** Start at 320 euro. **Remarks:** Writer of the first Dutch knifemaking book, supply shop for knife enthusiastic. First knife sold in 2000. **Mark:** Gatherwood in an eclipse etched blade or stamped in an intarsia of silver in the spine.

ST. AMOUR, MURRAY,
RR 3, 222 Dicks Rd, Pembroke ON, CANADA K8A 6W4, Phone: 613-735-1061, knives@webhart.net; Web: www.stamourknives.com
Specialties: Working fixed blades. **Patterns:** Hunters, fish, fighters, Bowies and utility knives. **Technical:** Grinds ATS-34, 154CM, CPM-S-30-Y-60-Y-904 and Damascus. **Prices:** $75 and up. **Remarks:** Full-time maker; sold first knife in 1992. **Mark:** Last name over Canada.

ST. CLAIR, THOMAS K,
12608 Fingerboard Rd, Monrovia, MD 21770, Phone: 301-482-0264

ST. CYR, H RED,
1218 N Cary Ave, Wilmington, CA 90744, Phone: 310-518-9525

STAFFORD, RICHARD,
104 Marcia Ct, Warner Robins, GA 31088, Phone: 912-923-6372, Fax: Cell: 478-508-5821, rnrstafford@cox.net
Specialties: High-tech straight knives and some folders. **Patterns:** Hunters in several patterns, fighters, boots, camp knives, combat knives and period pieces. **Technical:** Grinds ATS-34 and 440C. Machine satin finish offered. **Prices:** Starting at $150. **Remarks:** Part-time maker; first knife sold in 1983. **Mark:** R. W. STAFFORD GEORGIA.

STAINTHORP, GUY,
59 Chillington Way, Norton Heights, Stoke-on-Trent ST6 8GJ, guystainthorp@hotmail.com Web: www.stainthorpknives.com
Specialties: Tactical and outdoors knives to his own design. **Patterns:** Hunting, survival and occasionally folding knives. **Technical:** Grinds RWL-34, O1, S30V, Damasteel. Micarta, G10 and stabilised wood/bone for handles. **Prices:** $200 - $1000. **Remarks:** Full-time knifemaker. **Mark:** Squared stylised GS over "Stainthorp".

STALCUP, EDDIE,
PO Box 2200, Gallup, NM 87305, Phone: 505-863-3107, sharon.stalcup@gmail.com
Specialties: Working and fancy hunters, bird and trout. Special custom orders. **Patterns:** Drop point hunters, locking liner and multi blade folders. **Technical:** ATS-34, 154 CM, 440C, CPM 154 and S30V. **Prices:** $150 to $1500. **Remarks:** Scrimshaw, exotic handle material, wet formed sheaths. Membership Arizona Knife Collectors Association. Southern California blades collectors & professional knife makers assoc. **Mark:** E.F. Stalcup, Gallup, NM.

STANCER, CHUCK,
62 Hidden Ranch Rd NW, Calgary, AB, CANADA T3A 5S5, Phone: 403-295-7370, stancerc@telusplanet.net
Specialties: Traditional and working straight knives. **Patterns:** Bowies, hunters and utility knives. **Technical:** Forges and grinds most steels. **Prices:** $175 and up. **Remarks:** Part-time maker. **Mark:** Last name.

STANFORD, PERRY,
405N Walnut #9, Broken Arrow, OK 74012, Phone: 918-251-7983 or 866-305-5690, stanfordoutdoors@valornet; Web: www.stanfordoutdoors.homestead.com
Specialties: Drop point, hunting and skinning knives, handmade sheaths. **Patterns:** Stright, hunting, and skinners. **Technical:** Grinds 440C, ATS-34 and Damascus. **Prices:** $65 to $275. **Remarks:** Part-time maker, first knife sold in 2007. Knifemaker supplier, manufacturer of paper sharpening systems. Doing business as Stanford Outdoors. **Mark:** Company name and nickname.

STANLEY, JOHN,
604 Elm St, Crossett, AR 71635, Phone: 970-304-3005
Specialties: Hand forged fixed blades with engraving and carving. **Patterns:** Scottish dirks, skeans and fantasy blades. **Technical:** Forge high-carbon steel, own Damascus. Prices $70 to $500. **Remarks:** All work is sole authorship. Offers engraving and carving services on other knives and handles. **Mark:** Varies.

STAPEL, CHUCK,
Box 1617, Glendale, CA 91209, Phone: 213-66-KNIFE, Fax: 213-669-1577, www.stapelknives.com
Specialties: Working knives of his design. **Patterns:** Variety of straight knives, tantos, hunters, folders and utility knives. **Technical:** Grinds D2, 440C and AEB-L. **Prices:** $185 to $12,000. **Remarks:** Full-time maker; first knife sold in 1974. **Mark:** Last name or last name, U.S.A.

STAPLETON, WILLIAM E,
BUFFALO 'B' FORGE, 5425 Country Ln, Merritt Island, FL 32953
Specialties: Classic and traditional knives of his design and customer spec. **Patterns:** Hunters and using knives. **Technical:** Forges, O1 and L6 Damascus, cable Damascus and 5160; stock removal on request. **Prices:** $150 to $1000. **Remarks:** Part-time maker, first knife sold 1990. Doing business as Buffalo "B" Forge. **Mark:** Anvil with S initial in center of anvil.

STECK, VAN R,
260 W Dogwood Ave, Orange City, FL 32763, Phone: 407-416-1723, van@thudknives.com
Specialties: Specializing in double-edged grinds. Free-hand grinds: folders, spears, bowies, swords and miniatures. **Patterns:** Tomahawks with a crane for the spike, tactical merged with nature. **Technical:** Hamon lines, folder lock of own design, the arm-lock! **Prices:** $50 - $1500. **Remarks:** Builds knives designed by Laci Szabo or builds to customer design. Studied with Reese Weiland on folders and automatics. **Mark:** GEISHA holding a sword with initials and THUD KNIVES in a circle.

STEFFEN, CHUCK,
504 Dogwood Ave NW, St. Michael, MN, Phone: 763-497-3615
Specialties: Custom hunting knives, fixed blades folders. Specializing in exotic materials. Damascus excellent fit form and finishes.

STEGALL, KEITH,
701 Outlet View Dr, Wasilla, AK 99654, Phone: 907-376-0703, kas5200@yahoo.com
Specialties: Traditional working straight knives. **Patterns:** Most patterns. **Technical:** Grinds 440C and 154CM. **Prices:** $100 to $300. **Remarks:** Spare-time maker; first knife sold in 1987. **Mark:** Name and state with anchor.

STEGNER, WILBUR G,
9242 173rd Ave SW, Rochester, WA 98579, Phone: 360-273-0937, wilbur@wgsk.net; Web: www.wgsk.net
Specialties: Working/using straight knives and folders of his design. **Patterns:** Hunters and locking folders. **Technical:** Makes his own Damascus steel. **Prices:** $100 to $1000; some to $5000. **Remarks:** Full-time maker; first knife sold in 1979. Google search key words-"STEGNER KNIVES." Best folder awards NWKC 2009 and 2010. **Mark:** First and middle initials, last name in bar over shield logo.

STEIER, DAVID,
7722 Zenith Way, Louisville, KY 40219, Web: www.steierknives.com
Specialties: Folding LinerLocks, Bowies, slip joints, lockbacks, and straight hunters. **Technical:** Stock removal blades of 440C, ATS-34, and Damascus from outside sources like Robert Eggerling and Mike Norris. **Prices:** $150 for straight hunters to $1400 for fully decked-out folders. **Remarks:** First knife sold in 1979. **Mark:** Last name STEIER.

STEIGER, MONTE L,
Box 186, Genesee, ID 83832, Phone: 208-285-1769, montesharon@genesee-id.com
Specialties: Traditional working/using straight knives of all designs. **Patterns:** Hunters, utility/camp knives, fillet and chefs. Carving sets and steak knives. **Technical:** Grinds 1095, O1, 440C, ATS-34. Handles of stacked leather, natural wood, Micarta or pakkawood. Each knife comes with right- or left-handed sheath. **Prices:** $110 to $600. **Remarks:** Spare-time maker; first knife sold in 1988. Retired librarian **Mark:** First initial, last name, city and state.

STEIGERWALT, KEN,
507 Savagehill Rd, Orangeville, PA 17859, Phone: 570-683-5156, Web: www.steigerwaltknives.com
Specialties: Carving on bolsters and handle material. **Patterns:** Folders, button locks and rear locks. **Technical:** Grinds ATS-34, 440C and commercial Damascus. Experiments with unique filework. **Prices:** $500 to $5000. **Remarks:** Full-time maker; first knife sold in 1981. **Mark:** Kasteigerwalt

STEINAU, JURGEN,
Julius-Hart Strasse 44, Berlin 0-1162, GERMANY, Phone: 372-6452512, Fax: 372-645-2512
Specialties: Fantasy and high-art straight knives of his design. **Patterns:** Boots, daggers and switch-blade folders. **Technical:** Grinds 440B, 2379 and X90 Cr.Mo.V. 78. **Prices:** $1500 to $2500; some to $3500. **Remarks:** Full-time maker; first knife sold in 1984. **Mark:** Symbol, plus year, month day and serial number.

STEINBERG, AL,
5244 Duenas, Laguna Woods, CA 92653, Phone: 949-951-2889, lagknife@fea.net
Specialties: Fancy working straight knives to customer specs. **Patterns:** Hunters, Bowies, fishing, camp knives, push knives and high end kitchen knives. **Technical:** Grinds O1, 440C and 154CM. **Prices:** $60 to $2500. **Remarks:** Full-time maker; first knife sold in 1972. **Mark:** Signature, city and state.

STEINBRECHER, MARK W,
1122 92nd Place, Pleasant Prairie, WI 53158-4939
Specialties: Working and fancy folders. **Patterns:** Daggers, pocket knives, fighters and gents of his own design or to customer specs. **Technical:** Hollow grinds ATS-34, O1 other makers Damascus. Uses natural handle materials: stag, ivories, mother-of-pearl. File work and some inlays. **Prices:** $500 to $1200, some to $2500. **Remarks:** Part-time maker, first folder sold in 1989. **Mark:** Name etched or handwritten on ATS-34; stamped on Damascus.

STEKETEE, CRAIG A,
871 NE US Hwy 60, Billings, MO 65610, Phone: 417-744-2770, stekknives04@yahoo.com
Specialties: Classic and working straight knives and swords of his design. **Patterns:** Bowies, hunters, and Japanese-style swords. **Technical:** Forges his own Damascus; bronze, silver and Damascus fittings, offers filework. Prefers exotic and natural handle materials. **Prices:** $200 to $4000. **Remarks:** Full-time maker. **Mark:** STEK.

STEPHAN, DANIEL,
2201 S Miller Rd, Valrico, FL 33594, Phone: 727-580-8617, knifemaker@verizon.net
Specialties: Art knives, one-of-a-kind.

STERLING, MURRAY,
693 Round Peak Church Rd, Mount Airy, NC 27030, Phone: 336-352-5110, Fax: Fax: 336-352-5105, sterck@surry.net; Web: www.sterlingcustomknives.com
Specialties: Single and dual blade folders. Interframes and integral dovetail frames. **Technical:** Grinds ATS-34 or Damascus by Mike Norris and/or Devin Thomas. **Prices:** $300 and up. **Remarks:** Full-time maker; first knife sold in 1991. **Mark:** Last name stamped.

STERLING, THOMAS J,
ART KNIVES BY, 120 N Pheasant Run, Coupeville, WA 98239, Phone: 360-678-9269, Fax: 360-678-9269, netsuke@comcast.net; Web: www.bladegallery.com Or www.sterlingsculptures.com
Specialties: Since 2003 Tom Sterling and Dr. J.P. Higgins have created a unique collaboration of one-of-a-kind, ultra-quality art knives with percussion or pressured flaked stone blades and creatively sculpted handles. Their knives are often highly influenced by the traditions of Japanese netsuke and unique fusions of cultures, reflecting stylistically integrated choices of exotic hardwoods, fossil ivories and semi-precious materials, contrasting inlays and polychromed and pyrographed details. **Prices:** $300 to $900. **Remarks:** Limited output ensures highest quality artwork and exceptional levels of craftsmanship. **Mark:** Signatures Sterling and Higgins.

STETTER, J. C.,
115 E College Blvd PMB 180, Roswell, NM 88201, Phone: 505-627-0978
Specialties: Fixed and folding. **Patterns:** Traditional and yours. **Technical:** Forged and ground of varied materials including his own pattern welded steel. **Prices:** Start at $250. **Remarks:** Full-time maker, first knife sold 1989. **Mark:** Currently "J.C. Stetter."

STEWART, EDWARD L,
4297 Audrain Rd 335, Mexico, MO 65265, Phone: 573-581-3883
Specialties: Fixed blades, working knives some art. **Patterns:** Hunters, Bowies, utility/camp knives. **Technical:** Forging 1095-W-2-I-6-52100 makes own Damascus. **Prices:** $85 to $500. **Remarks:** Part-time maker first knife sold in 1993. **Mark:** First and last initials-last name.

STEYN—STYREFORS

STEYN, PETER,
PO Box 76, Welkom 9460, Freestate, SOUTH AFRICA, Phone: 27573522015, Fax: 27573523566, Web: www.petersteynknives.com email: info@petersteynknives.com
Specialties: Fixed blade working knives of own design, tendency toward tactical creative & artistic styles all with hand stitched leather sheaths. **Patterns:** Hunters, skinners, fighters & wedge ground daggers. **Technical:** Grinds 12C27, D2, N690. Blades are bead-blasted in plain or camo patterns & own exclusive crator finish. Prefers synthetic handle materials also uses cocobolo & ironwood. **Prices:** $200-$600. **Remarks:** Full time maker, first knife sold 2005, member of South African Guild. **Mark:** Letter 'S' in shape of pyramid with full name above & 'Handcrafted' below.

STIDHAM, DANIEL,
3106 Mill Cr. Rd., Gallipolis, Ohio 45631, Phone: 740-446-1673, danstidham@yahoo.com
Specialties: Fixed blades, folders, Bowies and hunters. **Technical:** 440C, Alabama Damascus, 1095 with filework. **Prices:** Start at $150. **Remarks:** Has made fixed blades since 1961, folders since 1986. Also sells various knife brands. **Mark:** Stidham Knives Gallipolis, Ohio 45631.

STIMPS, JASON M,
374 S Shaffer St, Orange, CA 92866, Phone: 714-744-5866

STIPES, DWIGHT,
2651 SW Buena Vista Dr, Palm City, FL 34990, Phone: 772-597-0550, dwightstipes@adelphia.net
Specialties: Traditional and working straight knives in standard patterns. **Patterns:** Boots, Bowies, daggers, hunters and fighters. **Technical:** Grinds 440C, D2 and D3 tool steel. Handles of natural materials, animal, bone or horn. **Prices:** $75 to $150. **Remarks:** Full-time maker; first knife sold in 1972. **Mark:** Stipes.

STOCKWELL, WALTER,
368 San Carlos Ave, Redwood City, CA 94061, Phone: 650-363-6069, walter@stockwellknives.com; Web: www.stockwellknives.com
Specialties: Scottish dirks, sgian dubhs. **Patterns:** All knives one-of-a-kind. **Technical:** Grinds ATS-34, forges 5160, 52100, L6. **Prices:** $125 to $500. **Remarks:** Part-time maker since 1992; graduate of ABS bladesmithing school. **Mark:** Shooting star over "STOCKWELL." Pre-2000, "WKS."

STODDART, W B BILL,
2357 Mack Rd #105, Fairfield, OH 45014, Phone: 513-851-1543
Specialties: Sportsmen's working knives and multi-blade folders. **Patterns:** Hunters, camp and fish knives; multi-blade reproductions of old standards. **Technical:** Grinds A2, 440C and ATS-34; makes sheaths to match handle materials. **Prices:** $80 to $300; some to $850. **Remarks:** Part-time maker; first knife sold in 1976. **Mark:** Name, Cincinnati, state.

STOKES, ED,
22614 Cardinal Dr, Hockley, TX 77447, Phone: 713-351-1319
Specialties: Working straight knives and folders of all designs. **Patterns:** Boots, Bowies, daggers, fighters, hunters and miniatures. **Technical:** Grinds ATS-34, 440C and D2. Offers decorative butt caps, tapered spacers on handles and finger grooves, nickel-silver inlays, handmade sheaths. **Prices:** $185 to $290; some to $350. **Remarks:** Full-time maker; first knife sold in 1973. **Mark:** First and last name, Custom Knives with Apache logo.

STONE, JERRY,
PO Box 1027, Lytle, TX 78052, Phone: 830-709-3042
Specialties: Traditional working and using folders of his design and to customer specs; fancy knives. **Patterns:** Fighters, hunters, locking folders and slip joints. Also make automatics. **Technical:** Grinds 440C and ATS-34. Offers filework. **Prices:** $175 to $1000. **Remarks:** Full-time maker; first knife sold in 1973. **Mark:** Name over Texas star/town and state underneath.

STORCH, ED,
RR 4 Mannville, Alberta T0B 2W0, CANADA, Phone: 780-763-2214, storchkn@agt.net; Web: www.storchknives.com
Specialties: Working knives, fancy fighting knives, kitchen cutlery and art knives. Knifemaking classes. **Patterns:** Working patterns, Bowies and folders. **Technical:** Forges his own Damascus. Grinds ATS-34. Builds friction folders. Salt heat treating. **Prices:** $45 to $750 (U.S.). **Remarks:** Part-time maker; first knife sold in 1984. Hosts annual Northwest Canadian Knifemakers Symposium; 60 to 80 knifemakers and families. **Mark:** Last name.

STORMER, BOB,
34354 Hwy E, Dixon, MO 65459, Phone: 636-734-2693, bs34354@gmail.com
Specialties: Straight knives, using collector grade. **Patterns:** Bowies, skinners, hunters, camp knives. **Technical:** Forges 5160, 1095. **Prices:** $200 to $500. **Remarks:** Part-time maker, ABS Journeyman Smith 2001. **Mark:** Setting sun/fall trees/initials.

STOUT, CHARLES,
RT3 178 Stout Rd, Gillham, AR 71841, Phone: 870-386-5521

STOUT, JOHNNY,
1205 Forest Trail, New Braunfels, TX 78132, Phone: 830-606-4067, johnny@stoutknives.com; Web: www.stoutknives.com
Specialties: Folders, some fixed blades. Working knives, some fancy. **Patterns:** Hunters, tactical, Bowies, automatics, liner locks and slip-joints. **Technical:** Grinds stainless and carbon steels; forges own Damascus. **Prices:** $450 to $895; some to $3500. **Remarks:** Full-time maker; first knife

sold in 1983. Hosts semi-annual Guadalupe Forge Hammer-in and Knifemakers Rendezvous. **Mark:** Name and city in logo with serial number.

STOVER, HOWARD,
100 Palmetto Dr Apt 7, Pasadena, CA 91105, Phone: 765-452-3928

STRAIGHT, KENNETH J,
11311 103 Lane N, Largo, FL 33773, Phone: 813-397-9817

STRANDE, POUL,
Soster Svenstrup Byvej 16, Dastrup 4130 Viby Sj., DENMARK, Phone: 46 19 43 05, Fax: 46 19 53 19, Web: www.poulstrande.com
Specialties: Classic fantasy working knives; Damasceret blade, Nikkel Damasceret blade, Lamineret: Lamineret blade with Nikkel. **Patterns:** Bowies, daggers, fighters, hunters and swords. **Technical:** Uses carbon steel and 15C20 steel. **Prices:** NA. **Remarks:** Full-time maker; first knife sold in 1985. **Mark:** First and last initials.

STRAUB, SALEM F.,
324 Cobey Creek Rd., Tonasket, WA 98855, Phone: 509-486-2627, vorpalforge@hotmail.com Web: www.prometheanknives.com
Specialties: Elegant working knives, fixed blade hunters, utility, skinning knives; liner locks. Makes own horsehide sheaths. **Patterns:** A wide range of syles, everything from the gentleman's pocket to the working kitchen, integrals, Bowies, folders, check out my website to see some of my work for ideas. **Technical:** Forges several carbon steels, 52100, W1, etc. Grinds stainless and makes/uses own damascus, cable, san mai, stadard patterns. Likes clay quenching, hamons, hand rubbed finishes. Flat, hollow, or convex grinds. Prefers synthetic handle materials. Hidden and full tapered tangs. **Prices:** $150 - $600, some higher. **Remarks:** Full-time maker. Doing what it takes to make your knife ordering and buying experience positive and enjoyable; striving to exceed expectations. All knives backed by lifetime guarantee. **Mark:** "Straub" stamp or "Promethean Knives" etched. Some older pieces stamped "Vorpal" though no longer using this mark. **Other:** Feel free to call or e-mail anytime. I love to talk knives.

STRICKLAND, DALE,
1440 E Thompson View, Monroe, UT 84754, Phone: 435-896-8362
Specialties: Traditional and working straight knives and folders of his design and to customer specs. **Patterns:** Hunters, folders, miniatures and utility knives. **Technical:** Grinds Damascus and 440C. **Prices:** $120 to $350; some to $500. **Remarks:** Part-time maker; first knife sold in 1991. **Mark:** Oval stamp of name, Maker.

STRIDER, MICK,
STRIDER KNIVES, 120 N Pacific Unit L-7, San Marcos, CA 92069, Phone: 760-471-8275, Fax: 503-218-7069, striderguys@striderknives.com; Web: www.striderknives.com

STRONG, SCOTT,
1599 Beaver Valley Rd, Beavercreek, OH 45434, Phone: 937-426-9290
Specialties: Working knives, some deluxe. **Patterns:** Hunters, fighters, survival and military-style knives, art knives. **Technical:** Forges and grinds O1, A2, D2, 440C and ATS-34. Uses no solder; most knives disassemble. **Prices:** $75 to $450; some to $1500. **Remarks:** Spare-time maker; first knife sold in 1983. **Mark:** Strong Knives.

STROYAN, ERIC,
Box 218, Dalton, PA 18414, Phone: 717-563-2603
Specialties: Classic and working/using straight knives and folders of his design. **Patterns:** Hunters, locking folders, slip-joints. **Technical:** Forges Damascus; grinds ATS-34, D2. **Prices:** $200 to $600; some to $2000. **Remarks:** Part-time maker; first knife sold in 1968. **Mark:** Signature or initials stamp.

STUART, MASON,
24 Beech Street, Mansfield, MA 02048, Phone: 508-339-8236, smasonknives@verizon.net Web: smasonknives.com
Specialties: Straight knives of his design, standard patterns. **Patterns:** Bowies, hunters, fighters and neck knives. **Technical:** Forges and grinds. Damascus, 5160, 1095, 1084, old files. Uses only natural handle material. **Prices:** $350 - 2,000. **Remarks:** Part-time maker. **Mark:** First initial and last name.

STUART, STEVE,
Box 168, Gores Landing, Ont., CANADA K0K 2E0, Phone: 905-440-6910, stevestuart@xplornet.com
Specialties: Straight knives. **Patterns:** Tantos, fighters, skinners, file and rasp knives. **Technical:** Uses 440C, CPM154, CPMS30V, Micarta and natural handle materials. **Prices:** $60 to $400. **Remarks:** Part-time maker. **Mark:** SS.

STYREFORS, MATTIAS,
Unbyn 23, SE-96193 Boden, SWEDEN, infor@styrefors.com
Specialties: Damascus and mosaic Damascus. Fixed blade Nordic hunters, folders and swords. **Technical:** Forges, shapes and grinds Damascus and mosaic Damascus from mostly UHB 15N20 and 20C with contrasts in nickel and 15N20. Hardness HR 58. **Prices:** $800 to $3000. **Remarks:** Full-time maker since 1999. International reputation for high end Damascus blades. Uses stabilized Arctic birch and willow burl, horn, fossils, exotic materials, and scrimshaw by Viveca Sahlin for knife handles. Hand tools and hand stitches leather sheaths in cow raw hide. Works in well equipped former military forgery in northern Sweden. **Mark:** MS.

SUEDMEIER, HARLAN,
762 N 60th Rd, Nebraska City, NE 68410, Phone: 402-873-4372
Patterns: Straight knives. **Technical:** Forging hi carbon Damascus. **Prices:** Starting at $175. **Mark:** First initials & last name.

SUGIHARA, KEIDOH,
4-16-1 Kamori-Cho, Kishiwada City, Osaka, F596-0042, JAPAN, Fax: 0724-44-2677
Specialties: High-tech working straight knives and folders of his design. **Patterns:** Bowies, hunters, fighters, fishing, boots, some pocket knives and liner-lock folders. **Technical:** Grinds ATS-34, COS-25, buys Damascus and high-carbon steels. Prices $60 to $4000. **Remarks:** Full-time maker, first knife sold in 1980. **Mark:** Initial logo with fish design.

SUGIYAMA, EDDY K,
2361 Nagayu, Naoirimachi Naoirigun, Ohita, JAPAN, Phone: 0974-75-2050
Specialties: One-of-a-kind, exotic-style knives. **Patterns:** Working, utility and miniatures. **Technical:** CT rind, ATS-34 and D2. **Prices:** $400 to $1200. **Remarks:** Full-time maker. **Mark:** Name or cedar mark.

SUMMERS, ARTHUR L,
1310 Hess Rd, Concord, NC 28025, Phone: 704-787-9275 Cell: 704-305-0735, arthursummers88@hotmail.com
Specialties: Drop points, clip points, straight blades. **Patterns:** Hunters, Bowies and personal knives. **Technical:** Grinds 440C, ATS-34, D2 and Damascus. **Prices:** $250 to $1000. **Remarks:** Full-time maker; first knife sold in 1988. **Mark:** Serial number is the date.

SUMMERS, DAN,
2675 NY Rt. 11, Whitney Pt., NY 13862, Phone: 607-692-2391, dansumm11@msn.com
Specialties: Period knives and tomahawks. **Technical:** All hand forging. **Prices:** Most $100 to $400.

SUMMERS, DENNIS K,
827 E. Cecil St, Springfield, OH 45503, Phone: 513-324-0624
Specialties: Working/using knives. **Patterns:** Fighters and personal knives. **Technical:** Grinds 440C, A2 and D2. Makes drop and clip point. **Prices:** $75 to $200. **Remarks:** Part-time maker; first knife sold in 1995. **Mark:** First and middle initials, last name, serial number.

SUNDERLAND, RICHARD,
Av Infraganti 23, Col Lazaro Cardenas, Puerto Escondido Oaxaca, MEXICO 71980, Phone: 011 52 94 582 1451, sunamerica@prodigy.net.mx7
Specialties: Personal and hunting knives with carved handles in oosic and ivory. **Patterns:** Hunters, Bowies, daggers, camp and personal knives. **Technical:** Grinds 440C, ATS-34 and O1. Handle materials of rosewoods, fossil mammoth ivory and oosic. **Prices:** $150 to $1000. **Remarks:** Part-time maker; first knife sold in 1983. Doing business as Sun Knife Co. **Mark:** SUN.

SUTTON, S RUSSELL,
4900 Cypress Shores Dr, New Bern, NC 28562, Phone: 252-637-3963, srsutton@suddenlink.net; Web: www.suttoncustomknives.com
Specialties: Straight knives and folders to customer specs and in standard patterns. **Patterns:** Boots, hunters, interframes, slip joints and locking liners. **Technical:** Grinds ATS-34, 440C and stainless Damascus. **Prices:** $220 to $2000. **Remarks:** Full-time maker; first knife sold in 1992. Provides relief engraving on bolsters and guards. **Mark:** Etched last name.

SWEAZA, DENNIS,
4052 Hwy 321 E, Austin, AR 72007, Phone: 501-941-1886, knives4den@aol.com

SWEENEY, COLTIN D,
1216 S 3 St W, Missoula, MT 59801, Phone: 406-721-6782

SWYHART, ART,
509 Main St, PO Box 267, Klickitat, WA 98628, Phone: 509-369-3451, swyhart@gorge.net; Web: www.knifeoutlet.com/swyhart.htm
Specialties: Traditional working and using knives of his design. **Patterns:** Bowies, hunters and utility/camp knives. **Technical:** Forges 52100, 5160 and Damascus 1084 mixed with either 15N20 or O186. Blades differentially heat-treated with visible temper line. **Prices:** $75 to $250; some to $350. **Remarks:** Part-time maker; first knife sold in 1983. **Mark:** First name, last initial in script.

SYLVESTER, DAVID,
465 Sweede Rd., Compton, Quebec CANADA, Phone: 819-837-0304, david@swedevilleforge.com Web: swedevilleforge.com
Patterns: I hand forge all my knives and I like to make hunters and integrals and some Bowies and fighters. I work with W2, 1084, 1095, and my damascus. **Prices:** $200 - $1500. **Remarks:** Part-time maker. ABS Journeyman Smith. **Mark:** D.Sylvester

SYMONDS, ALBERTO E,
Rambla M Gandhi 485, Apt 901, Montevideo 11300, URUGUAY, Phone: 011 598 27103201, Fax: 011 598 2 7103201, albertosymonds@hotmail.com
Specialties: All kinds including puukos, nice sheaths, leather and wood. **Prices:** $300 to $2200. **Mark:** AESH and current year.

SYSLO, CHUCK,
3418 South 116 Ave, Omaha, NE 68144, Phone: 402-333-0647, ciscoknives@cox.net
Specialties: Hunters, working knives, daggers & misc. **Patterns:** Hunters, daggers and survival knives; locking folders. **Technical:** Flat-grinds D2, 440C and 154CM; hand polishes only. **Prices:** $250 to $1000; some to $3000. **Remarks:** Part-time maker; first knife sold in 1978. Uses many natural materials. **Mark:** CISCO in logo.

SZILASKI, JOSEPH,
52 Woods Dr, Pine Plains, NY 12567, Phone: 518-398-0309, Web: www.szilaski.com
Specialties: Straight knives, folders and tomahawks of his design, to customer specs and in standard patterns. Many pieces are one-of-a-kind. **Patterns:** Bowies, daggers, fighters, hunters, art knives and early American-styles. **Technical:** Forges A2, D2, O1 and Damascus. **Prices:** $450 to $4000; some to $10,000. **Remarks:** Full-time maker; first knife sold in 1990. ABS Master Smith and voting member KMG. **Mark:** Snake logo.

T

TABOR, TIM,
18925 Crooked Lane, Lutz, FL 33548, Phone: 813-948-6141, taborknives.com
Specialties: Fancy folders, Damascus Bowies and hunters. **Patterns:** My own design folders & customer requests. **Technical:** ATS-34, hand forged Damascus, 1084, 15N20 mosaic Damascus, 1095, 5160 high carbon blades, flat grind, file work & jewel embellishments. **Prices:** $175 to $1500. **Remarks:** Part-time maker, sold first knife in 2003. **Mark:** Last name

TAKACH, ANDREW,
1390 Fallen Timber Rd., Elizabeth, PA 15037, Phone: 724-691-2271, a-takach@takachforge.com; Web: www.takachforge.com
Specialties: One-of-a-kind fixed blade working knives (own design or customer's). Mostly all fileworked. **Patterns:** Hunters, skinners, caping, fighters, and designs of own style. **Technical:** Forges mostly 5160, 1090, 01, in down pattern welded Damascus, nickle Damascus, and cable and various chain Damascus. Also do some San Mai. **Prices:** $100 to $350, some over $550. **Remarks:** Doing business as Takach Forge. First knife sold in 2004. **Mark:** Takach (stamped).

TAKAHASHI, MASAO,
39-3 Sekine-machi, Maebashi-shi, Gunma 371 0047, JAPAN, Phone: 81 27 234 2223, Fax: 81 27 234 2223
Specialties: Working straight knives. **Patterns:** Daggers, fighters, hunters, fishing knives, boots. **Technical:** Grinds ATS-34 and Damascus. **Prices:** $350 to $1000 and up. **Remarks:** Full-time maker; first knife sold in 1982. **Mark:** M. Takahashi.

TALLY, GRANT,
26961 James Ave, Flat Rock, MI 48134, Phone: 734-789-8961
Specialties: Straight knives and folders of his design. **Patterns:** Bowies, daggers, fighters. **Technical:** Grinds ATS-34, 440C and D2. Offers filework. **Prices:** $250 to $1000. **Remarks:** Part-time maker; first knife sold in 1985. Doing business as Tally Knives. **Mark:** Tally (last name).

TAMBOLI, MICHAEL,
12447 N 49 Ave, Glendale, AZ 85304, Phone: 602-978-4308, mnbtamboli@gmail.com
Specialties: Miniatures, some full size. **Patterns:** Miniature hunting knives to fantasy art knives. **Technical:** Grinds ATS-34 & Damascus. **Prices:** $75 to $500; some to $2000. **Remarks:** Full time maker; first knife sold in 1978. **Mark:** Initials, last name, last name city and state, MT Custom Knives or Mike Tamboli in Japanese script.

TASMAN, KERLEY,
9 Avignon Retreat, Pt Kennedy 6172, Western Australia, AUSTRALIA, Phone: 61 8 9593 0554, Fax: 61 8 9593 0554, taskerley@optusnet.com.au
Specialties: Knife/harness/sheath systems for elite military personnel and body guards. **Patterns:** Utility/tactical knives, hunters small game and presentation grade knives. **Technical:** ATS-34 and 440C, Damascus, flat and hollow grids. **Prices:** $200 to $1800 U.S. **Remarks:** Will take presentation grade commissions. Multi award winning maker and custom jeweler. **Mark:** Maker's initials.

TAYLOR, BILLY,
10 Temple Rd, Petal, MS 39465, Phone: 601-544-0041
Specialties: Straight knives of his design. **Patterns:** Bowies, skinners, hunters and utility knives. **Technical:** Flat-grinds 440C, ATS-34 and 154CM. **Prices:** $60 to $300. **Remarks:** Part-time maker; first knife sold in 1991. **Mark:** Full name, city and state.

TAYLOR, C GRAY,
560 Poteat Ln, Fall Branch, TN 37656, Phone: 423-348-8304, graysknives@aol.com or graysknives@hotmail.com; Web: www.cgraytaylor.com
Specialties: Traditonal multi-blade lobster folders, also art display Bowies and daggers. **Patterns:** Orange Blossom, sleeveboard and gunstocks. **Technical:** Grinds. **Prices:** Upscale. **Remarks:** Full-time maker; first knife sold in 1975. **Mark:** Name, city and state.

TAYLOR, DAVID,
113 Stewart Hill Dr, Rogersville, TN 37857, Phone: 423-921-0733, dtaylor0730@charter.net; Web: www.dtguitars.com
Patterns: Multi-blade folders, traditional patterns. **Technical:** Grinds ATS-34. **Prices:** $400 and up. **Remarks:** First sold knife in 1981 at age 14. Became a member of Knifemakers Guild at age 14. Made first folder in 1983. Full-time pastor of Baptist Church and part-time knifemaker.

TAYLOR, SHANE,
42 Broken Bow Ln, Miles City, MT 59301, Phone: 406-234-7175, shane@taylorknives.com; Web: www.taylorknives.com
Specialties: One-of-a-kind fancy Damascus straight knives and folders. **Patterns:** Bowies, folders and fighters. **Technical:** Forges own mosaic and pattern welded Damascus. **Prices:** $450 and up. **Remarks:** ABS Master Smith, full-time maker; first knife sold in 1982. **Mark:** First name.

TEDFORD, STEVEN,
7486 Bamsey Rd., RR #2, Bewdley, Ontario, Canada K0L 1E0, Phone: 905-342-3696, www.facebook.com
Specialties: Functional outdoorsman knives such as hunters, skinners, Bowies and fillets. One of a kind custom knives and collector's knives.**Technical:** Combination forging and stock removal. Full-tang ATS-34 stainless blades.

TERAUCHI, TOSHIYUKI,
7649-13 219-11 Yoshida, Fujita-Cho Gobo-Shi, JAPAN

TERRILL, STEPHEN,
16357 Goat Ranch Rd, Springville, CA 93265, Phone: 559-539-3116, slterrill@yahoo.com
Specialties: Deluxe working straight knives and folders. **Patterns:** Fighters, tantos, boots, locking folders and axes; traditional oriental patterns. **Technical:** Forges 1095, 5160, Damascus, stock removal ATS-34. **Prices:** $300+.
Remarks: Full-time maker; first knife sold in 1972. **Mark:** Name, city, state in logo.

TERZUOLA, ROBERT,
10121 Eagle Rock NE, Albuquerque, NM 87122, Phone: 505-856-7077, terzuola@earthlink.net
Specialties: Working folders of his design; period pieces. **Patterns:** High-tech utility, defense and gentleman's folders. **Technical:** Grinds CPM154, Damascus, and CPM S30V. Offers titanium, carbon fiber and G10 composite for side-lock folders and tactical folders. **Prices:** $550 to $2000. **Remarks:** Full-time maker; first knife sold in 1980. **Mark:** Mayan dragon head, name.

THAYER, DANNY O,
8908S 100W, Romney, IN 47981, Phone: 765-538-3105, dot61h@juno.com
Specialties: Hunters, fighters, Bowies. **Prices:** $250 and up.

THEIS, TERRY,
21452 FM 2093, Harper, TX 78631, Phone: 830-864-4438
Specialties: All European and American engraving styles. **Prices:** $200 to $2000. **Remarks:** Engraver only.

THEVENOT, JEAN-PAUL,
16 Rue De La Prefecture, Dijon, FRANCE 21000
Specialties: Traditional European knives and daggers. **Patterns:** Hunters, utility-camp knives, daggers, historical or modern style. **Technical:** Forges own Damascus, 5160, 1084. **Remarks:** Part-time maker. ABS Master Smith. **Mark:** Interlocked initials in square.

THIE, BRIAN,
13250 150th St, Burlington, IA 52601, Phone: 319-985-2276, thieknives@gmail.com; Web: www.mepotelco.net/web/tknives
Specialties: Working using knives from basic to fancy. **Patterns:** Hunters, fighters, camp and folders. **Technical:** Forges blades and own Damascus. **Prices:** $250 and up. **Remarks:** ABS Journeyman Smith, part-time maker. Sole author of blades including forging, heat treat, engraving and sheath making. **Mark:** Last name hand engraved into the blade, JS stamped into blade.

THILL, JIM,
10242 Bear Run, Missoula, MT 59803, Phone: 406-251-5475
Specialties: Traditional and working/using knives of his design. **Patterns:** Fighters, hunters and utility/camp knives. **Technical:** Grinds D2 and ATS-34; forges 10-95-85, 52100, 5160, 10 series, reg. Damascus-mosaic. Offers hand cut sheaths with rawhide lace. **Prices:** $145 to $350; some to $1250. **Remarks:** Full time maker; first knife sold in 1962. **Mark:** Running bear in triangle.

THOMAS, DAVID E,
8502 Hwy 91, Lillian, AL 36549, Phone: 251-961-7574, redbluff@gulftel.com
Specialties: Bowies and hunters. **Technical:** Hand forged blades in 5160, 1095 and own Damascus. **Prices:** $400 and up. **Mark:** Stylized DT, maker's last name, serial number.

THOMAS, DEVIN,
PO Box 568, Panaca, NV 89042, Phone: 775-728-4363, hoss@devinthomas.com; Web: www.devinthomas.com
Specialties: Traditional straight knives and folders in standard patterns. **Patterns:** Bowies, fighters, hunters. **Technical:** Forges stainless Damascus, nickel and 1095. Uses, makes and sells mokume with brass, copper and nickel-silver. **Prices:** $300 to $1200. **Remarks:** Full-time maker; first knife sold in 1979. **Mark:** First and last name, city and state with anvil, or first name only.

THOMAS, KIM,
PO Box 531, Seville, OH 44273, Phone: 330-769-9906
Specialties: Fancy and traditional straight knives of his design and to customer specs; period pieces. **Patterns:** Boots, daggers, fighters, swords. **Technical:** Forges own Damascus from 5160, 1010 and nickel. **Prices:** $135 to $1500; some to $3000. **Remarks:** Part-time maker; first knife sold in 1986. Doing business as Thomas Iron Works. **Mark:** KT.

THOMAS, ROCKY,
1716 Waterside Blvd, Moncks Corner, SC 29461, Phone: 843-761-7761
Specialties: Traditional working knives in standard patterns. **Patterns:** Hunters and utility/camp knives. **Technical:** ATS-34 and commercial Damascus. **Prices:** $130 to $350. **Remarks:** Spare-time maker; first knife sold in 1986. **Mark:** First name in script and/or block.

THOMPSON, KENNETH,
4887 Glenwhite Dr, Duluth, GA 30136, Phone: 770-446-6730
Specialties: Traditional working and using knives of his design. **Patterns:** Hunters, Bowies and utility/camp knives. **Technical:** Forges 5168, O1, 1095 and 52100. **Prices:** $75 to $1500; some to $2500. **Remarks:** Part-time maker; first knife sold in 1990. **Mark:** P/W; or name, P/W, city and state.

THOMPSON, LEON,
45723 SW Saddleback Dr, Gaston, OR 97119, Phone: 503-357-2573
Specialties: Working knives. **Patterns:** Locking folders, slip-joints and liner locks. **Technical:** Grinds ATS-34, D2 and 440C. **Prices:** $200 to $600. **Remarks:** Full-time maker; first knife sold in 1976. **Mark:** First and middle initials, last name, city and state.

THOMPSON, LLOYD,
PO Box 1664, Pagosa Springs, CO 81147, Phone: 970-264-5837
Specialties: Working and collectible straight knives and folders of his design. **Patterns:** Straight blades, lock back folders and slip joint folders. **Technical:** Hollow-grinds ATS-34, D2 and O1. Uses sambar stag and exotic woods. **Prices:** $150 to upscale. **Remarks:** Full-time maker; first knife sold in 1985. Doing business as Trapper Creek Knife Co. **Remarks:** Offers three-day knife-making classes. **Mark:** Name.

THOMPSON, TOMMY,
4015 NE Hassalo, Portland, OR 97232-2607, Phone: 503-235-5762
Specialties: Fancy and working knives; mostly liner-lock folders. **Patterns:** Fighters, hunters and liner locks. **Technical:** Grinds D2, ATS-34, CPM440V and T15. Handles are either hardwood inlaid with wood banding and stone or shell, or made of agate, jasper, petrified woods, etc. **Prices:** $75 to $500; some to $1000. **Remarks:** Part-time maker; first knife sold in 1987. Doing business as Stone Birds. Knife making temporarily stopped due to family obligations. **Mark:** First and last name, city and state.

THOMSEN, LOYD W,
30173 Black Banks Rd, Oelrichs, SD 57763, Phone: 605-535-6162, loydt@yahoo.com; Web: horseheadcreekknives.com
Specialties: High-art and traditional working/using straight knives and presentation pieces of his design and to customer specs; period pieces. Hand carved animals in crown of stag on handles and carved display stands. **Patterns:** Bowies, hunters, daggers and utility/camp knives. **Technical:** Forges and grinds 1095HC, 1084, L6, 15N20, 440C stainless steel, nickel 200; special restoration process on period pieces. Makes sheaths. Uses natural materials for handles. **Prices:** $350 to $1000. **Remarks:** Full-time maker; first knife sold in 1995. Doing business as Horsehead Creek Knives. **Mark:** Initials and last name over a horse's head.

THORBURN, ANDRE E.,
P.O. Box 1748, Bela Bela, Warmbaths 0480, SOUTH AFRICA, Phone: 27-82-650-1441, andrethorburn@gmail.com; Web: www.thorburnknives.com
Specialties: Working and fancy folders of own design to customer specs. **Technical:** Uses RWL34, 12C27, 19C27, D2, Danzer36, CPM steels and Carbon and stainless Damascus. **Prices:** Starting at $350. **Remarks:** Full-time maker since 1996, first knife sold in 1990. Member of American Knifemakers Guild and South African, Italian, and German guilds; chairman of Knifemakers Guild of South Africa. **Mark:** Initials and name in a double circle.

THOUROT, MICHAEL W,
T-814 Co Rd 11, Napoleon, OH 43545, Phone: 419-533-6832, Fax: 419-533-3516, mike2row@henry-net.com; Web: wwwsafariknives.com
Specialties: Working straight knives to customer specs. Designed two-handled skinning ax and limited edition engraved knife and art print set. **Patterns:** Fishing and fillet knives, Bowies, tantos and hunters. **Technical:** Grinds O1, D2, 440C and Damascus. **Prices:** $200 to $5000. **Remarks:** Part-time maker; first knife sold in 1968. **Mark:** Initials.

THUESEN, ED,
21211 Knolle Rd, Damon, TX 77430, Phone: 979-553-1211, Fax: 979-553-1211
Specialties: Working straight knives. **Patterns:** Hunters, fighters and survival knives. **Technical:** Grinds D2, 440C, ATS-34 and Vascowear. **Prices:** $150 to $275; some to $600. **Remarks:** Part-time maker; first knife sold in 1979. Runs knifemaker supply business. **Mark:** Last name in script.

TIENSVOLD, ALAN L,
PO Box 355, Rushville, NE 69360, Phone: 308-327-2046
Specialties: Working knives, tomahawks and period pieces, high end Damascus knives. **Patterns:** Random, ladder, twist and many more. **Technical:** Hand forged blades, forges own Damascus. **Prices:** Working knives start at $300. **Remarks:** Received Journeyman rating with the ABS in 2002. Does own engraving and fine work. **Mark:** Tiensvold hand made U.S.A. on left side, JS on right.

TIENSVOLD, JASON,
PO Box 795, Rushville, NE 69360, Phone: 308-327-2046, ironprik@gpcom.net
Specialties: Working and using straight knives of his design; period pieces. Gentlemen folders, art folders. Single action automatics. **Patterns:** Hunters, skinners, Bowies, fighters, daggers, liner locks. **Technical:** Forges own Damascus using 15N20 and 1084, 1095, nickel, custom file work. **Prices:** $200 to $4000. **Remarks:** Full-time maker, first knife sold in 1994; doing business under Tiensvold Custom Knives. **Mark:** J. Tiensvold.

TIGHE, BRIAN,
12-111 Fourth Ave, Suite 376 Ridley Square, St. Catharines, Ont., CANADA L0S 1M0, Phone: 905-892-2734, Web: www.tigheknives.com
Specialties: Folding knives, bearing pivots. High tech tactical folders. **Pat-

terns: Boots, daggers and locking. **Technical:** BG-42, RWL-34, Damasteel, 154CM, S30V, CPM 440V and CPM 420V. Prefers natural handle material inlay; hand finishes. **Prices:** $450 to $4000. **Remarks:** Full-time maker; first knife sold in 1989. **Mark:** Etched signature.

TILL, CALVIN E AND RUTH,
211 Chaping, Chadron, NE 69337
Specialties: Straight knives, hunters, Bowies; no folders **Patterns:** Training point, drop point hunters, Bowies. **Technical:** ATS-34 sub zero quench RC59, 61. **Prices:** $700 to $1200. **Remarks:** Sells only the absolute best knives they can make. Manufactures every part in their knives. **Mark:** RC Till. The R is for Ruth.

TILTON, JOHN,
24041 Hwy 383, Iowa, LA 70647, Phone: 337-582-6785, john@jetknives.com
Specialties: Bowies, camp knives, skinners and folders. **Technical:** All forged blades. Makes own Damascus. **Prices:** $150 and up. **Remarks:** ABS Journeyman Smith. **Mark:** Initials J.E.T.

TINDERA, GEORGE,
BURNING RIVER FORGE, 751 Hadcock Rd, Brunswick, OH 44212-2648, Phone: 330-220-6212
Specialties: Straight knives; his designs. **Patterns:** Personal knives; classic Bowies and fighters. **Technical:** Hand-forged high-carbon; his own cable and pattern welded Damascus. **Prices:** $125 to $600. **Remarks:** Spare-time maker; sold first knife in 1995. Natural handle materials.

TINGLE, DENNIS P,
19390 E Clinton Rd, Jackson, CA 95642, Phone: 209-223-4586, dtknives@earthlink.net
Specialties: Swords, fixed blades: small to medium, tomahawks. **Technical:** All blades forged. **Remarks:** ABS, JS. **Mark:** D. Tingle over JS.

TIPPETTS, COLTEN,
4068 W Miners Farm Dr, Hidden Springs, ID 83714, Phone: 208-229-7772, coltentippetts@gmail.com
Specialties: Fancy and working straight knives and fancy locking folders of his own design or to customer specifications. **Patterns:** Hunters and skinners, fighters and utility. **Technical:** Grinds BG-42, high-carbon 1095 and Damascus. **Prices:** $200 to $1000. **Remarks:** Part-time maker; first knife sold in 1996. **Mark:** Fused initials.

TODD, RICHARD C,
375th LN 46001, Chambersburg, IL 62323, Phone: 217-327-4380, ktodd45@yahoo.com
Specialties: Multi blade folders and silver sheaths. **Patterns:** Jewel setting and hand engraving. **Mark:** RT with letter R crossing the T or R Todd.

TOICH, NEVIO,
Via Pisacane 9, Rettorgole di Caldogna, Vincenza, ITALY 36030, Phone: 0444-985065, Fax: 0444-301254
Specialties: Working/using straight knives of his design or to customer specs. **Patterns:** Bowies, hunters, skinners and utility/camp knives. **Technical:** Grinds 440C, D2 and ATS-34. Hollow-grinds all blades and uses mirror polish. Offers hand-sewn sheaths. Uses wood and horn. **Prices:** $120 to $300; some to $450. **Remarks:** Spare-time maker; first knife sold in 1989. Doing business as Custom Toich. **Mark:** Initials and model number punched.

TOKAR, DANIEL,
Box 1776, Shepherdstown, WV 25443
Specialties: Working knives; period pieces. **Patterns:** Hunters, camp knives, buckskinners, axes, swords and battle gear. **Technical:** Forges L6, 1095 and his Damascus; makes mokume, Japanese alloys and bronze daggers; restores old edged weapons. **Prices:** $25 to $800; some to $3000. **Remarks:** Part-time maker; first knife sold in 1979. Doing business as The Willow Forge. **Mark:** Arrow over rune and date.

TOLLEFSON, BARRY A,
104 Sutter Pl, PO Box 4198, Tubac, AZ 85646, Phone: 520-398-9327
Specialties: Working straight knives, some fancy. **Patterns:** Hunters, skinners, fighters and camp knives. **Technical:** Grinds 440C, ATS-34 and D2. Likes mirror-finishes; offers some fancy filework. Handles made from elk, deer and exotic hardwoods. **Prices:** $75 to $300; some higher. **Remarks:** Part-time maker; first knife sold in 1990. **Mark:** Stylized initials.

TOMBERLIN, BRION R,
ANVIL TOP CUSTOM KNIVES, 825 W Timberdell, Norman, OK 73072, Phone: 405-202-6832, anviltopp@aol.com
Specialties: Hand forged blades, working pieces, standard classic patterns, some swords, and customer designs. **Patterns:** Bowies, hunters, fighters, Persian and eastern-styles. Likes Japanese blades. **Technical:** Forge 1050, 1075, 1084, 1095, 5160, some forged stainless, also do some stock removal in stainless. Also makes own damascus. **Prices:** Start at $275 up to $2000 or higher for swords and custom pieces. **Remarks:** Part-time maker, Mastersmith America Bladesmith Society. Prefers natural handle materials, hand rubbed finishes. Likes temperlines. **Mark:** BRION with MS.

TOMES, P J,
594 High Peak Ln, Shipman, VA 22971, Phone: 434-263-8662, tomgsknives@juno.com; Web: www.tomesknives.com
Specialties: Scagel reproductions. **Patterns:** Front-lock folders. **Technical:** Forges 52100. **Prices:** $150 to $750. **Mark:** Last name, USA, MS, stamped in forged blades.

TOMEY, KATHLEEN,
146 Buford Pl, Macon, GA 31204, Phone: 478-746-8454, ktomey@tomeycustomknives.com; Web: www.tomeycustomknives.com
Specialties: Working hunters, skinners, daily users in fixed blades, plain and embellished. Tactical neck and belt carry. Japanese influenced. Bowies. **Technical:** Grinds O1, ATS-34, flat or hollow grind, filework, satin and mirror polish finishes. High quality leather sheaths with tooling. Kydex with tactical. **Prices:** $150 to $500. **Remarks:** Almost full-time maker. **Mark:** Last name in diamond.

TOMPKINS, DAN,
PO Box 398, Peotone, IL 60468, Phone: 708-258-3620
Specialties: Working knives, some deluxe, some folders. **Patterns:** Hunters, boots, daggers and push knives. **Technical:** Grinds D2, 440C, ATS-34 and 154CM. **Prices:** $85 to $150; some to $400. **Remarks:** Part-time maker; first knife sold in 1975. **Mark:** Last name, city, state.

TONER, ROGER,
531 Lightfoot Pl, Pickering, Ont., CANADA L1V 5Z8, Phone: 905-420-5555
Specialties: Exotic sword canes. **Patterns:** Bowies, daggers and fighters. **Technical:** Grinds 440C, D2 and Damascus. Scrimshaws and engraves. Silver cast pommels and guards in animal shapes; twisted silver wire inlays. Uses semi-precious stones. **Prices:** $200 to $2000; some to $3000. **Remarks:** Part-time maker; first knife sold in 1982. **Mark:** Last name.

TORRES, HENRY,
2329 Moody Ave., Clovis, CA 93619, Phone: 559-297-9154, Web: www.htknives.com
Specialties: Forged high-performance hunters and working knives, Bowies, and fighters. **Technical:** 52100 and 5160 and makes own Damascus. **Prices:** $350 to $3000. **Remarks:** Started forging in 2004. Has mastersmith with American Bladesmith Association.

TOSHIFUMI, KURAMOTO,
3435 Higashioda, Asakura-gun, Fukuoka, JAPAN, Phone: 0946-42-4470

TOWELL, DWIGHT L,
2375 Towell Rd, Midvale, ID 83645, Phone: 208-355-2419
Specialties: Solid, elegant working knives; art knives, high quality hand engraving and gold inlay. **Patterns:** Hunters, Bowies, daggers and folders. **Technical:** Grinds 154CM, ATS-34, 440C and other maker's Damascus. **Prices:** Upscale. **Remarks:** Full-time maker. First knife sold in 1970. Member of AKI. **Mark:** Towell, sometimes hand engraved.

TOWNSEND, ALLEN MARK,
6 Pine Trail, Texarkana, AR 71854, Phone: 870-772-8945

TOWNSLEY, RUSSELL,
PO BOX 185, Concord, AR 72523, Phone: 870-307-8069, circleTRMtownsley@yahoo.com
Specialties: Using knives of his own design. **Patterns:** Hunters, skinners, folders. **Technical:** Hollow grinds D2 and O1. Handle material - antler, tusk, bone, exotic woods. **Prices:** Prices start at $125. **Remarks:** Arkansas knifemakers association. Sold first knife in 2009. Doing business as Circle-T knives. **Mark:** Encircled T.

TRACE RINALDI CUSTOM BLADES,
28305 California Ave, Hemet, CA 92545, Phone: 951-926-5422, Trace@thrblades.com; Web: www.thrblades.com
Technical: Grinds S30V, 3V, A2 and talonite fixed blades. **Prices:** $300-$1000. **Remarks:** Tactical and utility for the most part. **Mark:** Diamond with THR inside.

TRACY, BUD,
495 Flanders Rd, Reno, NV 8951-4784

TREML, GLENN,
RR #14 Site 12-10, Thunder Bay, Ont., CANADA P7B 5E5, Phone: 807-767-1977
Specialties: Working straight knives of his design and to customer specs. **Patterns:** Hunters, kitchen knives and double-edged survival knives. **Technical:** Grinds 440C, ATS-34 and O1; stock removal method. Uses various woods and Micarta for handle material. **Prices:** $150 and up. **Mark:** Stamped last name.

TRINDLE, BARRY,
1660 Ironwood Trail, Earlham, IA 50072-8611, Phone: 515-462-1237
Specialties: Engraved folders. **Patterns:** Mostly small folders, classical-styles and pocket knives. **Technical:** 440 only. Engraves. Handles of wood or mineral material. **Prices:** Start at $1000. **Mark:** Name on tang.

TRISLER, KENNETH W,
6256 Federal 80, Rayville, LA 71269, Phone: 318-728-5541

TRITZ, JEAN JOSE,
Schopstrasse 23, 20255 Hamburg, GERMANY, Phone: 040-49 78 21
Specialties: Scandinavian knives, Japanese kitchen knives, friction folders, swords. **Patterns:** Puukkos, Tollekniven, Hocho, friction folders, swords. **Technical:** Forges tool steels, carbon steels, 52100 Damascus, mokume, San Maj. **Prices:** $200 to $2000; some higher. **Remarks:** Full-time maker; first knife sold in 1989. Does own leatherwork, prefers natural materials. Sole authorship. Speaks French, German, English, Norwegian. **Mark:** Initials in monogram.

TROUT, GEORGE H.,
PO BOX 13, Cuba, OH 45114, Phone: 937-382-2331, gandjtrout@msn.com
Specialties: Working knives, some fancy. **Patterns:** Hunters, drop points, Bowies and fighters. **Technical:** Stock removal: ATS-34, 440C Forged: 5160, W2, 1095, O1 Full integrals: 440C, A2, O1. **Prices:** $150 and up. **Remarks:** Makes own sheaths and mosaic pins. Fileworks most knives. First knife 1985. **Mark:** Etched name and state on stock removal. Forged: stamped name and forged.

TRUJILLO, ALBERT M B,
2035 Wasmer Cir, Bosque Farms, NM 87068, Phone: 505-869-0428, trujilloscutups@comcast.net
Specialties: Working/using straight knives of his design or to customer specs. **Patterns:** Hunters, skinners, fighters, working/using knives. File work offered. **Technical:** Grinds ATS-34, D2, 440C, S30V. Tapers tangs, all blades cryogenically treated. **Prices:** $75 to $500. **Remarks:** Part-time maker; first knife sold in 1997. **Mark:** First and last name under logo.

TRUJILLO, MIRANDA,
6366 Commerce Blvd, Rohnert Park, CA 94928
Specialties: Working/using straight knives of her design. **Patterns:** Hunters and utility/camp knives. **Technical:** Grinds ATS-34 and 440C. Sheaths are water resistant. **Prices:** $145 - $400; some to $600. **Remarks:** Spare-time maker; first knife sold in 1989. Doing business as Alaska Knife and Service Co. **Mark:** NA.

TRUNCALI, PETE,
2914 Anatole Court, Garland, TX 75043, Phone: 214-763-7127, truncaliknives@yahoo.com Web:www.truncaliknives.com
Specialties: Lockback folders, locking liner folders, automatics and fixed blades. Does business as Truncali Custom Knives.

TSCHAGER, REINHARD,
Piazza Parrocchia 7, I-39100 Bolzano, ITALY, Phone: 0471-970642, Fax: 0471-970642, reinhardtschager@virgilio.it
Specialties: Classic, high-art, collector-grade straight knives of his design. **Patterns:** Jewel knife, daggers, and hunters. **Technical:** Grinds ATS-34, D2 and Damascus. Oval pins. Gold inlay. Offers engraving. **Prices:** $900 to $2000; some to $3000. **Remarks:** Spare-time maker; first knife sold in 1979. **Mark:** Gold inlay stamped with initials.

TUOMINEN, PEKKA,
Pohjois-Keiteleentie 20, 72930 Tossavanlahti, FINLAND, Phone: 358405167853, puukkopekka@luukku.com; Web: www.puukkopekka.com
Specialties: Puukko knives. **Patterns:** Puukkos, hunters, leukus, and folders. **Technical:** Forges silversteel, 1085, 52100, and makes own Damascus 15N20 and 1095. Grinds RWL-34 and ATS-34. **Prices:** Starting at $170. **Remarks:** Part-time maker. **Mark:** Name.

TURCOTTE, LARRY,
1707 Evergreen, Pampa, TX 79065, Phone: 806-665-9369, 806-669-0435
Specialties: Fancy and working/using knives of his design and to customer specs. **Patterns:** Hunters, kitchen knives, utility/camp knives. **Technical:** Grinds 440C, D2, ATS-34. Engraves, scrimshaws, silver inlays. **Prices:** $150 to $350; some to $1000. **Remarks:** Part-time maker; first knife sold in 1977. Doing business as Knives by Turcotte. **Mark:** Last name.

TURECEK, JIM,
12 Elliott Rd, Ansonia, CT 06401, Phone: 203-734-8406
Specialties: Exotic folders, art knives and some miniatures. **Patterns:** Trout and bird knives with split bamboo handles and one-of-a-kind folders. **Technical:** Grinds and forges stainless and carbon Damascus. **Prices:** $750 to $1500; some to $3000. **Remarks:** Full-time maker; first knife sold in 1983. **Mark:** Last initial in script, or last name.

TURNBULL, RALPH A,
14464 Linden Dr, Spring Hill, FL 34609, Phone: 352-688-7089, tbull2000@bellsouth.net; Web: www.turnbullknives.com
Specialties: Fancy folders. **Patterns:** Primarily gents pocket knives. **Technical:** Wire EDM work on bolsters. **Prices:** $300 and up. **Remarks:** Full-time maker; first knife sold in 1973. **Mark:** Signature or initials.

TURNER, KEVIN,
17 Hunt Ave, Montrose, NY 10548, Phone: 914-739-0535
Specialties: Working straight knives of his design and to customer specs; period pieces. **Patterns:** Daggers, fighters and utility knives. **Technical:** Forges 5160 and 52100. **Prices:** $90 to $500. **Remarks:** Part-time maker; first knife sold in 1991. **Mark:** Acid-etched signed last name and year.

TURNER, MIKE,
PO BOX 194, Williams, OR 97544, Phone: 541-846-0204, mike@turnerknives.com Web: www.turnerknives.com
Specialties: Forged and stock removed full tang, hidden and thru tang knives. **Patterns:** Hunters, fighters, Bowies, boot knives, skinners and kitchen knives. **Technical:** I make my own Damascus. **Prices:** $200 - $1,000. **Remarks:** Part-time maker, sold my first knife in 2008, doing business as Mike Turner Custom Knives. **Mark:** Name, City, & State.

TYCER, ART,
117 Callaway Ln., Meridianville, AL 35759-1503, Phone: 256-829-1442
Specialties: Fancy working/using straight knives of his design, to customer specs and standard patterns. **Patterns:** Boots, Bowies, daggers, fighters, hunters, kitchen and utility knives. **Technical:** Grinds ATS-34, 440C and a variety of carbon steels. Uses exotic woods with spacer material, stag and

water buffalo. Offers filework. **Prices:** $175 and up depending on size and embellishments or Damascus. **Remarks:** Now making folders (liner locks). Making and using his own Damascus and other Damascus also. Full-time maker. **Mark:** Flying "T" over first initial inside an oval.

TYRE, MICHAEL A,
1219 Easy St, Wickenburg, AZ 85390, Phone: 928-684-9601/602-377-8432, michaeltyre@msn.com
Specialties: Quality folding knives upscale gents folders one-of-a-kind collectable models. **Patterns:** Working fixed blades for hunting, kitchen and fancy Bowies. **Technical:** Grinds prefer hand rubbed satin finishes and use natural handle materials. **Prices:** $250 to $1300.

TYSER, ROSS,
1015 Hardee Court, Spartanburg, SC 29303, Phone: 864-585-7616
Specialties: Traditional working and using straight knives and folders of his design and in standard patterns. **Patterns:** Bowies, hunters and slip-joint folders. **Technical:** Grinds 440C and commercial Damascus. Mosaic pins; stone inlay. Does filework and scrimshaw. Offers engraving and cut-work and some inlay on sheaths. **Prices:** $45 to $125; some to $400. **Remarks:** Part-time maker; first knife sold in 1995. Doing business as RT Custom Knives. **Mark:** Stylized initials.

U

UCHIDA, CHIMATA,
977-2 Oaza Naga Shisui Ki, Kumamoto, JAPAN 861-1204

V

VAGNINO, MICHAEL,
PO Box 67, Visalia, CA 93279, Phone: 559-636-0501, mvknives@lightspeed.net; Web: www.mvknives.com
Specialties: Folders and straight knives, working and fancy. **Patterns:** Folders--locking liners, slip joints, lock backs, double and single action autos. Straight knives--hunters, Bowies, camp and kitchen. **Technical:** Forges 52100, W2, 15N20 and 1084. Grinds stainless. Makes own damascus and does engraving. **Prices:** $275 to $4000 and above. **Remarks:** Full-time maker, ABS Mastersmith. **Mark:** Logo, last name.

VAIL, DAVE,
554 Sloop Point Rd, Hampstead, NC 28443, Phone: 910-270-4456
Specialties: Working/using straight knives of his own design or to the customer's specs. **Patterns:** Hunters/skinners, camp/utility, fillet, Bowies. **Technical:** Grinds ATS-34, 440c, 154 CM and 1095 carbon steel. **Prices:** $90 to $450. **Remarks:** Part-time maker. Member of NC Custom Knifemakers Guild. **Mark:** Etched oval with "Dave Vail Hampstead NC" inside.

VALLOTTON, BUTCH AND AREY,
621 Fawn Ridge Dr, Oakland, OR 97462, Phone: 541-459-2216, Fax: 541-459-7473
Specialties: Quick opening knives w/complicated mechanisms. **Patterns:** Tactical, fancy, working, and some art knives. **Technical:** Grinds all steels, uses others' Damascus. Uses Spectrum Metal. **Prices:** From $350 to $4500. **Remarks:** Full-time maker since 1984; first knife sold in 1981. Co/designer, Applegate Fairbarn folding w/Bill Harsey. **Mark:** Name w/viper head in the "V."

VALLOTTON, RAINY D,
1295 Wolf Valley Dr, Umpqua, OR 97486, Phone: 541-459-0465
Specialties: Folders, one-handed openers and art pieces. **Patterns:** All patterns. **Technical:** Stock removal all steels; uses titanium liners and bolsters; uses all finishes. **Prices:** $350 to $3500. **Remarks:** Full-time maker. **Mark:** Name.

VALLOTTON, SHAWN,
621 Fawn Ridge Dr, Oakland, OR 97462, Phone: 503-459-2216
Specialties: Left-hand knives. **Patterns:** All styles. **Technical:** Grinds 440C, ATS-34 and Damascus. Uses titanium. Prefers bead-blasted or anodized finishes. **Prices:** $250 to $1400. **Remarks:** Full-time maker. **Mark:** Name and specialty.

VALLOTTON, THOMAS,
621 Fawn Ridge Dr, Oakland, OR 97462, Phone: 541-459-2216
Specialties: Custom autos. **Patterns:** Tactical, fancy. **Technical:** File work, uses Damascus, uses Spectrum Metal. **Prices:** From $350 to $700. **Remarks:** Full-time maker. Maker of Protégé 3 canoe. **Mark:** T and a V mingled.

VALOIS, A. DANIEL,
3552 W Lizard Ck Rd, Lehighton, PA 18235, Phone: 717-386-3636
Specialties: Big working knives; various sized lock-back folders with new safety releases. **Patterns:** Fighters in survival packs, sturdy working knives, belt buckle knives, military-style knives, swords. **Technical:** Forges and grinds A2, O1 and 440C; likes full tangs. **Prices:** $65 to $240; some to $600. **Remarks:** Full-time maker; first knife sold in 1969. **Mark:** Anvil logo with last name inside.

VAN CLEVE, STEVE,
Box 372, Sutton, AK 99674, Phone: 907-745-3038

VAN DE MANAKKER, THIJS,
Koolweg 34, 5759 px Helenaveen, HOLLAND, Phone: 0493539369, www.ehijsvandemanakker.com
Specialties: Classic high-art knives. **Patterns:** Swords, utility/camp knives and period pieces. **Technical:** Forges soft iron, carbon steel and Bloom-

ery Iron. Makes own Damascus, Bloomery Iron and patterns. **Prices:** $20 to $2000; some higher. **Remarks:** Full-time maker; first knife sold in 1969. **Mark:** Stylized "V."

VAN DEN ELSEN, GERT,
Purcelldreef 83, 5012 AJ Tilburg, NETHERLANDS, Phone: 013-4563200, gvdelsen@home.nl
Specialties: Fancy, working/using, miniatures and integral straight knives of the maker's design or to customer specs. **Patterns:** Bowies, fighters, hunters and Japanese-style blades. **Technical:** Grinds ATS-34 and 440C; forges Damascus. Offers filework, differentially tempered blades and some mokume-gane fittings. **Prices:** $350 to $1000; some to $4000. **Remarks:** Part-time maker; first knife sold in 1982. Doing business as G-E Knives. **Mark:** Initials GE in lozenge shape.

VAN DER WESTHUIZEN, PETER,
PO Box 1698, Mossel Bay 6500, SOUTH AFRICA, Phone: 27 446952388, pietvdw@telkomsa.net
Specialties: Working knives, folders, daggers and art knives. **Patterns:** Hunters, skinners, bird, trout and sidelock folders. **Technical:** Sandvik, 12627. Damascus indigenous wood and ivory. **Prices:** From $450 to $5500. **Remarks:** First knife sold in 1987. Full-time since 1996. **Mark:** Initial & surname. Handmade RSA.

VAN DIJK, RICHARD,
76 Stepney Ave Rd 2, Harwood Dunedin, NEW ZEALAND, Phone: 0064-3-4780401, Web: www.hoihoknives.com
Specialties: Damascus, Fantasy knives, sgiandubhs, dirks, swords, and hunting knives. **Patterns:** Mostly one-offs, anything from bird and trout to swords, no folders. **Technical:** Forges mainly own Damascus, some 5160, O1, 1095, L6. Prefers natural handle materials, over 35 years experience as goldsmith, handle fittings are often made from sterling silver and sometimes gold, manufactured to cap the handle, use gemstones if required. Makes own sheaths. **Prices:** $300 and up. **Remarks:** Full-time maker, first knife sold in 1980. Doing business as HOIHO KNIVES. **Mark:** Stylized initials RvD in triangle.

VAN EIZENGA, JERRY W,
14281 Cleveland, Nunica, MI 49448, Phone: 616-638-2275
Specialties: Hand forged blades, Scagel patterns and other styles. **Patterns:** Camp, hunting, bird, trout, folders, axes, miniatures. **Technical:** 5160, 52100, 1084. **Prices:** Start at $250. **Remarks:** Part-time maker, sole author of knife and sheath. First knife made 1970s. ABS member who believes in the beauty of simplicity. **Mark:** J.S. stamp.

VAN ELDIK, FRANS,
Ho Flaan 3, 3632BT Loenen, NETHERLANDS, Phone: 0031 294 233 095, Fax: 0031 294 233 095
Specialties: Fancy collector-grade straight knives and folders of his design. **Patterns:** Hunters, fighters, boots and folders. **Technical:** Forges and grinds D2, 154CM, ATS-34 and stainless Damascus. **Prices:** Start at $450. **Remarks:** Spare-time maker; first knife sold in 1979. Knifemaker 30 years, 25 year member of Knifemakers Guild. **Mark:** Lion with name and Amsterdam.

VAN HEERDEN, ANDRE,
P.O. Box 905-417, Garsfontein, Pretoria, SOUTH AFRICA 0042, Phone: 27 82 566 6030, andrevh@iafrica.com; Web: www.andrevanheerden.com
Specialties: Fancy and working folders of his design to customer specs. **Technical:** Grinds RWL34, 19C27, D2, carbon and stainless Damascus. **Prices:** Starting at $350. **Remarks:** Part-time maker; first knife sold in 2003. **Mark:** Initials and name in a double circle.

VAN REENEN, IAN,
6003 Harvard St, Amarillo, TX 79109, Phone: 806-236-8333, ianvanreenen@suddenlink.net Web: www.ianvanreenenknives.com
Specialties: Slipjoints, single and double blades. **Patterns:** Trappers, peanuts, saddle horn trappers. **Technical:** ATS-34 and CPM 154. **Prices:** $400 to $700. **Remarks:** Specializing in slipjoints. **Mark:** VAN REENEN

VAN RIJSWIJK, AAD,
AVR KNIVES, Werf Van Pronk 8, 3134 HE Vlaardingen, NETHERLANDS, Phone: +31 10 4742952, Fax: +31 10 2343648, info@avrknives.com; Web: www.avrknives.com
Specialties: High-art interframe folders of his design. **Patterns:** Hunters and locking folders. **Technical:** Uses semi-precious stones, mammoth ivory, iron wood, etc. **Prices:** $550 to $3800. **Remarks:** Full-time maker; first knife sold in 1993.

VANDERFORD, CARL G,
2290 Knob Creek Rd, Columbia, TN 38401, Phone: 931-381-1488
Specialties: Traditional working straight knives and folders of his design. **Patterns:** Hunters, Bowies and locking folders. **Technical:** Forges and grinds 440C, O1 and wire Damascus. **Prices:** $60 to $125. **Remarks:** Part-time maker; first knife sold in 1987. **Mark:** Last name.

VANDERKOLFF, STEPHEN,
5 Jonathan Crescent, Mildmay Ontario, CANADA N0g 2JO, Phone: 519-367-3401, steve@vanderkolffknives.com; Web: www.vanderkolffknives.com
Specialties: Fixed blades from gent's pocketknives and drop hunters to full sized Bowies and art knives. **Technical:** Primary blade steel 440C, Damasteel or custom made Damascus. All heat treat done by maker and all blades hardness tested. Handle material: stag, stabilized woods or MOP. **Prices:** $150 to $1200. **Remarks:** Started making knives in 1998 and sold first knife in 2000. Winner of the best of show art knife 2005 Wolverine Knife Show.

VANDEVENTER, TERRY L,
3274 Davis Rd, Terry, MS 39170-8719, Phone: 601-371-7414, tvandeventer@comcast.net
Specialties: Bowies, hunters, camp knives, friction folders. **Technical:** 1084, 1095, 15N20 and L6 steels. Damascus and mokume. Natural handle materials. **Prices:** $600 to $3000. **Remarks:** Sole author; makes everything here. First ABS MS from the state of Mississippi. **Mark:** T.L. Vandeventer (silhouette of snake underneath). MS on ricasso.

VANHOY, ED AND TANYA,
24255 N Fork River Rd, Abingdon, VA 24210, Phone: 276-944-4885, vanhoyknives@centurylink.net
Specialties: Traditional and working/using straight knives and folders and innovative locking mechanisms. **Patterns:** Fighters, straight knives, folders, hunters, art knives and Bowies. **Technical:** Grinds ATS-34 and carbon/stainless steel Damascus; forges carbon and stainless Damascus. Offers filework and engraving with hammer and chisel. **Prices:** $250 to $3000. **Remarks:** Full-time maker; first knife sold in 1977. Wife also engraves. Doing business as Van Hoy Custom Knives. **Mark:** Acid etched last name.

VARDAMAN, ROBERT,
2406 Mimosa Lane, Hattiesburg, MS 39402, Phone: 601-268-3889, rv7x@comcast.net
Specialties: Working straight knives of his design or to customer specs. **Patterns:** Bowies, hunters, skinners, utility and camp knives. **Technical:** Forges 52100, 5160, 1084 and 1095. Filework. **Prices:** $100 to $500. **Remarks:** Part-time maker. First knife sold in 2004. **Mark:** Last name, last name with Mississippi state logo.

VASQUEZ, JOHNNY DAVID,
1552 7th St, Wyandotte, MI 48192, Phone: 734-281-2455

VAUGHAN, IAN,
351 Doe Run Rd, Manheim, PA 17545-9368, Phone: 717-665-6949

VEIT, MICHAEL,
3289 E Fifth Rd, LaSalle, IL 61301, Phone: 815-223-3538, whitebear@starband.net
Specialties: Damascus folders. **Technical:** Engraver, sole author. **Prices:** $2500 to $6500. **Remarks:** Part-time maker; first knife sold in 1985. **Mark:** Name in script.

VELARDE, RICARDO,
7240 N Greenfield Dr, Park City, UT 84098, Phone: 435-901-1773, velardeknives@mac.com Web: www.velardeknives.com
Specialties: Investment grade integrals and interframs. **Patterns:** Boots, fighters and hunters; hollow grind. **Technical:** BG on Integrals. **Prices:** $1450 to $5200. **Remarks:** First knife sold in 1992. **Mark:** First initial and last name.

VELICK, SAMMY,
3457 Maplewood Ave, Los Angeles, CA 90066, Phone: 310-663-6170, metaltamer@gmail.com
Specialties: Working knives and art pieces. **Patterns:** Hunter, utility and fantasy. **Technical:** Stock removal and forges. **Prices:** $100 and up. **Mark:** Last name.

VENSILD, HENRIK,
Gl Estrup, Randersvei 4, DK-8963 Auning, DENMARK, Phone: +45 86 48 44 48
Specialties: Classic and traditional working and using knives of his design; Scandinavian influence. **Patterns:** Hunters and using knives. **Technical:** Forges Damascus. Hand makes handles, sheaths and blades. **Prices:** $350 to $1000. **Remarks:** Part-time maker; first knife sold in 1967. **Mark:** Initials.

VESTAL, CHARLES,
26662 Shortsville Rd., Abingdon, VA 24210, Phone: 276-492-3262, charles@vestalknives.com; Web: www.vestalknives.com
Specialties: Hunters and double ground fighters in traditional designs and own designs. **Technical:** Grinds CPM-154, ATS-134, 154-CM and other steels. **Prices:** $300 to $1000, some higher. **Remarks:** First knife sold in 1995.

VIALLON, HENRI,
Les Belins, 63300 Thiers, FRANCE, Phone: 04-73-80-24-03, Fax: 04 73-51-02-02
Specialties: Folders and complex Damascus **Patterns:** His draws. **Technical:** Forge. **Prices:** $1000 to $5000. **Mark:** H. Viallon.

VICKERS, DAVID,
11620 Kingford Dr., Montgomery, TX 77316, Phone: 936-537-4900, jdvickers@gmail.com
Specialties: Working/using blade knives especially for hunters. His design or to customer specs. **Patterns:** Hunters, skinners, camp/utility. **Technical:** Grinds ATS-34, 440C, and D-2. Uses stag, various woods, and micarta for handle material. Hand-stitched sheaths. **Remark:** Full-time maker. **Prices:** $125 - $350. **Mark:** VICKERS

VIELE, H J,
88 Lexington Ave, Westwood, NJ 07675, Phone: 201-666-2906, h.viele@verizon.net
Specialties: Folding knives of distinctive shapes. **Patterns:** High-tech folders and one-of-a-kind. **Technical:** Grinds ATS-34 and S30V. **Prices:** Start at $575. **Remarks:** Full-time maker; first knife sold in 1973. **Mark:** Japanese design for the god of war.

VIKING—WARD

VIKING KNIVES (SEE JAMES THORLIEF ERIKSEN),

VILAR, RICARDO AUGUSTO FERREIRA,
Rua Alemada Dos Jasmins NO 243, Parque Petropolis, Mairipora Sao Paulo, BRAZIL 07600-000, Phone: 011-55-11-44-85-43-46, ricardovilar@ig.com.br.
Specialties: Traditional Brazilian-style working knives of the Sao Paulo state. **Patterns:** Fighters, hunters, utility, and camp knives, welcome customer design. Specialize in the "true" Brazilian camp knife "Soracabana." **Technical:** Forges only with sledge hammer to 100 percent shape in 5160 and 52100 and his own Damascus steels. Makes own sheaths in the "true" traditional "Paulista"-style of the state of Sao Paulo. **Remark:** Full-time maker. **Prices:** $250 to $600. Uses only natural handle materials. **Mark:** Special designed signature styled name R. Vilar.

VILLA, LUIZ,
R. Com. Miguel Calfat, 398 Itaim Bibi, Sao Paulo, SP-04537-081, BRAZIL, Phone: 011-8290649
Specialties: One-of-a-kind straight knives and jewel knives of all designs. **Patterns:** Bowies, hunters, utility/camp knives and jewel knives. **Technical:** Grinds D6, Damascus and 440C; forges 5160. Prefers natural handle material. **Prices:** $70 to $200. **Remarks:** Part-time maker; first knife sold in 1990. **Mark:** Last name and serial number.

VILLAR, RICARDO,
Al. dos Jasmins 243 Mairipora, S.P. 07600-000, BRAZIL, Phone: 011-4851649
Specialties: Straight working knives to customer specs. **Patterns:** Bowies, fighters and utility/camp knives. **Technical:** Grinds D6, ATS-34 and 440C stainless. **Prices:** $80 to $200. **Remarks:** Part-time maker; first knife sold in 1993. **Mark:** Percor over sword and circle.

VILPPOLA, MARKKU,
Arkeologinen Kokeiluverstas, Kuralan Kylamaki, Jaanintie 45, 20540 Turku Finland, Phone: +358 (0)50 566 1563, markku@mvforge.fi Web: www.mvforge.fi
Specialties: All kinds of swords and knives. **Technical:** Forges silver steel, CO, 8%, nickel, 1095, A203E, etc. Mokume (sterling silver/brass/copper). Bronze casting (sand casting, lost-wax casting). **Prices:** Starting at $200.

VINING, BILL,
9 Penny Lane, Methuen, MA 01844, Phone: 978-688-4729, billv@medawebs.com; Web: www.medawebs.com/knives
Specialties: Liner locking folders. Slip joints & lockbacks. **Patterns:** Likes to make patterns of his own design. **Technical:** S30V, 440C, ATS-34. Damascus from various makers. **Prices:** $450 and up. **Remarks:** Part-time maker. **Mark:** VINING or B. Vining.

VISTE, JAMES,
EDGE WISE FORGE, 13401 Mt Elliot, Detroit, MI 48212, Phone: 313-664-7455, grumblejunky@hotmail.com
Mark: EWF touch mark.

VISTNES, TOR,
N-6930 Svelgen, NORWAY, Phone: 047-57795572
Specialties: Traditional and working knives of his design. **Patterns:** Hunters and utility knives. **Technical:** Grinds Uddeholm Elmax. Handles made of rear burls of different Nordic situated woods. **Prices:** $300 to $1100. **Remarks:** Part-time maker; first knife sold in 1988. **Mark:** Etched name and deer head.

VITALE, MACE,
925 Rt 80, Guilford, CT 06437, Phone: 203-457-5591, Web: www.laurelrockforge.com
Specialties: Hand forged blades. **Patterns:** Hunters, utility, chef, Bowies and fighters. **Technical:** W2, 1095, 1084, L6. Hand forged and finished. **Prices:** $100 to $1000. **Remarks:** American Bladesmith Society, Journeyman Smith. Full-time maker; first knife sold 2001. **Mark:** MACE.

VOGT, DONALD J,
9007 Hogans Bend, Tampa, FL 33647, Phone: 813-973-3245, vogtknives@verizon.net
Specialties: Art knives, folders, automatics. **Technical:** Uses Damascus steels for blade and bolsters, filework, hand carving on blade bolsters and handles. Other materials used: jewels, gold, mother-of-pearl, gold-lip pearl, black-lip pearl, ivory. **Prices:** $4,000 to $10,000. **Remarks:** Part-time maker; first knife sold in 1997. **Mark:** Last name.

VOGT, PATRIK,
Kungsvagen 83, S-30270 Halmstad, SWEDEN, Phone: 46-35-30977
Specialties: Working straight knives. **Patterns:** Bowies, hunters and fighters. **Technical:** Forges carbon steel and own Damascus. **Prices:** From $100. **Remarks:** Not currently making knives. **Mark:** Initials or last name.

VOORHIES, LES,
14511 Lk Mazaska Tr, Faribault, MN 55021, Phone: 507-332-0736, lesvor@msn.com; Web: www.lesvoorhiesknives.com
Specialties: Steels. **Patterns:** Liner locks & autos. **Technical:** ATS-34 Damascus. **Prices:** $250 to $1200. **Mark:** L. Voorhies.

VOSS, BEN,
2212 Knox Rd. 1600 Rd. E, Victoria, IL 61485-9644, Phone: 309-879-2940
Specialties: Fancy working knives of his design. **Patterns:** Bowies, fighters, hunters, boots and folders. **Technical:** Grinds 440C, ATS-34 and D2. **Prices:** $35 to $1200. **Remarks:** Part-time maker; first knife sold in 1986. **Mark:** Name, city and state.

VOTAW, DAVID P,
305 S State St, Pioneer, OH 43554, Phone: 419-737-2774
Specialties: Working knives; period pieces. **Patterns:** Hunters, Bowies, camp knives, buckskinners and tomahawks. **Technical:** Grinds O1 and D2. **Prices:** $100 to $200; some to $500. **Remarks:** Part-time maker; took over for the late W.K. Kneubuhler. Doing business as W-K Knives. **Mark:** WK with V inside anvil.

W

WADA, YASUTAKA,
2-6-22 Fujinokidai, Nara City, Nara prefect 631-0044, JAPAN, Phone: 0742 46-0689
Specialties: Fancy and embellished one-of-a-kind straight knives of his design. **Patterns:** Bowies, daggers and hunters. **Technical:** Grinds ATS-34. All knives hand-filed and flat grinds. **Prices:** $400 to $2500; some higher. **Remarks:** Part-time maker; first knife sold in 1990. **Mark:** Owl eyes with initial and last name underneath or last name.

WAGAMAN, JOHN K,
107 E Railroad St, Selma, NC 27576, Phone: 919-965-9659, Fax: 919-965-9901
Specialties: Fancy working knives. **Patterns:** Bowies, miniatures, hunters, fighters and boots. **Technical:** Grinds D2, 440C, 154CM and commercial Damascus; inlays mother-of-pearl. **Prices:** $110 to $2000. **Remarks:** Part-time maker; first knife sold in 1975. **Mark:** Last name.

WAITES, RICHARD L,
PO Box 188, Broomfield, CO 80038, Phone: 303-465-9970, Fax: 303-465-9971, dickknives@aol.com
Specialties: Working fixed blade knives of all kinds including "paddle blade" skinners. Hand crafted sheaths, some upscale and unusual. **Technical:** Grinds 440C, ATS 34, D2. **Prices:** $100 to $500. **Remarks:** Part-time maker. First knife sold in 1998. Doing business as R.L. Waites Knives. **Mark:** Oval etch with first and middle initial and last name on top and city and state on bottom. Memberships; Professional Knifemakers Association and Rocky Mountain Blade Collectors Club.

WALKER, BILL,
431 Walker Rd, Stevensville, MD 21666, Phone: 410-643-5041

WALKER, DON,
2850 Halls Chapel Rd, Burnsville, NC 28714, Phone: 828-675-9716, dlwalkernc@aol.com

WALKER, JIM,
22 Walker Ln, Morrilton, AR 72110, Phone: 501-354-3175, jwalker46@att.net
Specialties: Period pieces and working/using knives of his design and to customer specs. **Patterns:** Bowies, fighters, hunters, camp knives. **Technical:** Forges 5160, O1, L6, 52100, 1084, 1095. **Prices:** Start at $450. **Remarks:** Full-time maker; first knife sold in 1993. **Mark:** Three arrows with last name/MS.

WALKER, MICHAEL L,
925-A Paseo del, Pueblo Sur Taos, NM 87571, Phone: 505-751-3409, Fax: 505-751-3417, metalwerkr@msn.com
Specialties: Innovative knife designs and locking systems; titanium and SS furniture and art. **Patterns:** Folders from utility grade to museum quality art; others upon request. **Technical:** State-of-the-art materials: titanium, stainless Damascus, gold, etc. **Prices:** $3500 and above. **Remarks:** Designer/MetalCrafts; full-time professional knifemaker since 1980; four U.S. patents; invented LinerLock® and was awarded registered U.S. trademark no. 1,585,333. **Mark:** Early mark MW, Walker's Lockers by M.L. Walker; current M.L. Walker or Michael Walker.

WALLINGFORD JR., CHARLES W,
9024 Old Union Rd, Union, KY 41091, Phone: 859-384-4141, Web: www.cwknives.com
Specialties: 18th and 19th century styles, patch knives, rifleman knives. **Technical:** 1084 and 5160 forged blades. **Prices:** $125 to $300. **Mark:** CW.

WALTERS, A F,
PO Box 523, 275 Crawley Rd., TyTy, GA 31795, Phone: 229-528-6207
Specialties: Working knives, some to customer specs. **Patterns:** Locking folders, straight hunters, fishing and survival knives. **Technical:** Grinds D2, 154CM and 13C26. **Prices:** Start at $200. **Remarks:** Part-time maker. Label: "The jewel knife." **Mark:** "J" in diamond and knife logo.

WARD, CHUCK,
PO Box 2272, 1010 E North St, Benton, AR 72018-2272, Phone: 501-778-4329, chuckbop@aol.com
Specialties: Traditional working and using straight knives and folders of his design. **Technical:** Grinds 440C, D2, A2, ATS-34 and O1; uses natural and composite handle materials. **Prices:** $90 to $400, some higher. **Remarks:** Part-time maker; first knife sold in 1990. **Mark:** First initial, last name.

WARD, J J,
7501 S R 220, Waverly, OH 45690, Phone: 614-947-5328
Specialties: Traditional and working/using straight knives and folders of his design. **Patterns:** Hunters and locking folders. **Technical:** Grinds ATS-34, 440C and Damascus. Offers handmade sheaths. **Prices:** $125 to $250; some to $500. **Remarks:** Spare-time maker; first knife sold in 1980. **Mark:** Etched name.

WARD, KEN,
1125 Lee Roze Ln, Grants Pass, OR 97527, Phone: 541-956-8864
Specialties: Working knives, some to customer specs. **Patterns:** Straight, axes, Bowies, buckskinners and miniatures. **Technical:** Grinds ATS-34, Damascus. **Prices:** $100 to $700. **Remarks:** Part-time maker; first knife sold in 1977. **Mark:** Name.

WARD, RON,
PO BOX 21, Rose Hill, VA 24281, Phone: 276-445-4757
Specialties: Classic working and using straight knives, fantasy knives. **Patterns:** Bowies, hunter, fighters, and utility/camp knives. **Technical:** Grinds 440C, 154CM, ATS-34, uses composite and natural handle materials. **Prices:** $50 to $750. **Remarks:** Part-time maker, first knife sold in 1992. Doing business as Ron Ward Blades. **Mark:** Ron Ward Blades, Loveland OH.

WARD, W C,
817 Glenn St, Clinton, TN 37716, Phone: 615-457-3568
Specialties: Working straight knives; period pieces. **Patterns:** Hunters, Bowies, swords and kitchen cutlery. **Technical:** Grinds O1. **Prices:** $85 to $150; some to $500. **Remarks:** Part-time maker; first knife sold in 1969. He styled the Tennessee Knife Maker. **Mark:** TKM.

WARDELL, MICK,
20 Clovelly Rd, Bideford, N Devon EX39 3BU, ENGLAND, Phone: 01237 475312, wardellknives@hotmail.co.uk Web: www.wardellscustomknives.com
Specialties: Folders of his design. **Patterns:** Locking and slip-joint folders, Bowies. **Technical:** Grinds stainless Damascus, S30V and RWL34. Heat-treats. **Prices:** $300 to $2500. **Remarks:** Full-time maker; first knife sold in 1986. **Mark:** M. Wardell - England.

WARDEN, ROY A,
275 Tanglewood Rd, Union, MO 63084, Phone: 314-583-8813, rwarden@yhti.net
Specialties: Complex mosaic designs of "EDM wired figures" and "stack up" patterns and "lazer cut" and "torch cut" and "sawed" patterns combined. **Patterns:** Mostly "all mosaic" folders, automatics, fixed blades. **Technical:** Mosaic Damascus with all tool steel edges. **Prices:** $100 to $1000. **Remarks:** Part-time maker; first knife sold in 1987. **Mark:** WARDEN stamped or initials connected.

WARE, TOMMY,
158 Idlewilde, Onalaska, TX 77360, Phone: 936-646-4649
Specialties: Traditional working and using straight knives, folders and automatics of his design and to customer specs. **Patterns:** Hunters, automatics and locking folders. **Technical:** Grinds ATS-34, 440C and D2. Offers engraving and scrimshaw. **Prices:** $425 to $650; some to $1500. **Remarks:** Full-time maker; first knife sold in 1990. Doing business as Wano Knives. **Mark:** Last name inside oval, business name above, city and state below, year on side.

WARREN, AL,
1423 Sante Fe Circle, Roseville, CA 95678, Phone: 916-784-3217/Cell phone 916-257-5904, Fax: 215-318-2945, al@warrenknives.com; Web: www.warrenknives.com
Specialties: Working straight knives and folders, some fancy. **Patterns:** Hunters, Bowies, fillets, lockback, folders & multi blade. **Technical:** Grinds ATS-34 and S30V.440V. **Prices:** $135 to $3200.**Remarks:** Part-time maker; first knife sold in 1978. **Mark:** First and middle initials, last name.

WARREN, DANIEL,
571 Lovejoy Rd, Canton, NC 28716, Phone: 828-648-7351
Specialties: Using knives. **Patterns:** Drop point hunters. **Prices:** $200 to $500. **Mark:** Warren-Bethel NC.

WARREN (SEE DELLANA), DELLANA,

WASHBURN, ARTHUR D,
ADW CUSTOM KNIVES, 211 Hinman St/PO Box 625, Pioche, NV 89043, Phone: 775-962-5463, knifeman@lcturbonet.com; Web: www.adwcustomknives.com
Specialties: Locking liner folders. **Patterns:** Slip joint folders (single and multiplied), lock-back folders, some fixed blades. Do own heat-treating; Rockwell test each blade. **Technical:** Carbon and stainless Damascus, some 1084, 1095, AEBL, 12C27, S30V. **Prices:** $200 to $1000 and up. **Remarks:** Sold first knife in 1997. Part-time maker. **Mark:** ADW enclosed in an oval or ADW.

WASHBURN JR., ROBERT LEE,
1162 West Diamond Valley Drive, St George, UT 847700, Phone: 435-619-4432, Fax: 435-574-8554, rlwashburn@excite.com; Web:www.washburnknives.com
Specialties: Hand-forged period, Bowies, tactical, boot and hunters. **Patterns:** Bowies, tantos, loot hunters, tactical and folders. **Prices:** $100 to $2500. **Remarks:** All hand forged. 52100 being his favorite steel. **Mark:** Washburn Knives W.

WATANABE, MELVIN,
1297 Kika St., Kailua, HI 96734, Phone: 808-261-2842, meltod808@yahoo.com
Specialties: Fancy folding knives. Some hunters. **Patterns:** Liner-locks and hunters. **Technical:** Grinds ATS-34, stainless Damascus. **Prices:** $350 and up. **Remarks:** Part-time maker, first knife sold in 1985. **Mark:** Name and state.

WATANABE, WAYNE,
PO Box 3563, Montebello, CA 90640, wwknives@gmail.com; Web: www.geocities.com/ww-knives
Specialties: Straight knives in Japanese-styles. One-of-a-kind designs; welcomes customer designs. **Patterns:** Tantos to katanas, Bowies. **Technical:** Flat grinds A2, O1 and ATS-34. Offers hand-rubbed finishes and wrapped handles. **Prices:** Start at $200. **Remarks:** Part-time maker. **Mark:** Name in characters with flower.

WATERS, GLENN,
11 Shinakawa Machi, Hirosaki City 036-8183, JAPAN, Phone: 172-33-8881, gwaters@luck.ocn.ne.jp; Web: www.glennwaters.com
Specialties: One-of-a-kind collector-grade highly embellished art knives. Folders, fixed blades, and automatics. **Patterns:** Locking liner folders, automatics and fixed art knives. **Technical:** Grinds blades from Damasteel, and selected Damascus makers, mostly stainless. Does own engraving, gold inlaying and stone setting, filework, and carving. Gold and Japanese precious metal fabrication. Prefers exotic material, high karat gold, silver, Shyaku Dou, Shibu Ichi Gin, precious gemstones. **Prices:** Upscale. **Remarks:** Designs and makes some-of-a-kind highly embellished art knives often with fully engraved handles and blades. A jeweler by trade for 20 years before starting to make knives. Full-time since 1999, first knife sold in 1994. **Mark:** Glenn Waters maker Japan, G. Waters or Glen in Japanese writing.

WATSON, BERT,
PO Box 26, Westminster, CO 80036-0026, Phone: 303-587-3064, watsonbd21960@q.com
Specialties: Working/using straight knives of his design and to customer specs. **Patterns:** Hunters, utility/camp knives. **Technical:** Grinds O1, ATS-34, 440C, D2, A2 and others. **Prices:** $150 to $800. **Remarks:** Full-time maker. **Mark:** GTK and/or Bert.

WATSON, BILLY,
440 Forge Rd, Deatsville, AL 36022, Phone: 334-365-1482, billy@watsonknives.com; Web: www.watsonknives.com
Specialties: Working and using straight knives and folders of his design; period pieces. **Patterns:** Hunters, Bowies and utility/camp knives. **Technical:** Forges and grinds his own Damascus, 1095, 5160 and 52100. **Prices:** $40 to $1500. **Remarks:** Full-time maker; first knife sold in 1970. Doing business as Billy's Blacksmith Shop. **Mark:** Last name.

WATSON, DANIEL,
350 Jennifer Ln, Driftwood, TX 78619, Phone: 512-847-9679, info@angelsword.com; Web: http://www.angelsword.com
Specialties: One-of-a-kind knives and swords. **Patterns:** Hunters, daggers, swords. **Technical:** Hand-purify and carbonize his own high-carbon steel, pattern-welded Damascus, cable and carbon-induced crystalline Damascus. Teehno-Wootz™ Damascus steel, heat treats including cryogenic processing. European and Japanese tempering. **Prices:** $125 to $25,000. **Remarks:** Full-time maker; first knife sold in 1979. **Mark:** "Angel Sword" on forged pieces; "Bright Knight" for stock removal. Avatar on Techno-Wootz™ Damascus. Bumon on traditional Japanese blades.

WATSON, PETER,
66 Kielblock St, La Hoff 2570, SOUTH AFRICA, Phone: 018-84942
Specialties: Traditional working and using straight knives and folders of his design. **Patterns:** Hunters, locking folders and utility/camp knives. **Technical:** Sandvik and 440C. **Prices:** $120 to $250; some to $1500. **Remarks:** Part-time maker; first knife sold in 1989. **Mark:** Buffalo head with name.

WATSON, TOM,
1103 Brenau Terrace, Panama City, FL 32405, Phone: 850-785-9209, tom@tomwatsonknives.com; Web: www.tomwatsonknives.com
Specialties: Utility/tactical linerlocks. **Patterns:** Tactical and utility. **Technical:** Flat grinds satin finished D2 and Damascus. **Prices:** Starting at $375. **Remarks:** Full time maker. In business since 1978. **Mark:** Name and city.

WATTELET, MICHAEL A,
PO Box 649, 125 Front, Minocqua, WI 54548, Phone: 715-356-3069, redtroll@frontier.com
Specialties: Working and using straight knives of his design and to customer specs; fantasy knives. **Patterns:** Daggers, fighters and swords. **Technical:** Grinds 440C and L6; forges and grinds O1. Silversmith. **Prices:** $75 to $1000; some to $5000. **Remarks:** Full-time maker; first knife sold in 1966. Doing business as M and N Arts Ltd. **Mark:** First initial, last name.

WATTS, JOHNATHAN,
9560 S Hwy 36, Gatesville, TX 76528, Phone: 254-487-2866
Specialties: Traditional folders. **Patterns:** One and two blade folders in various blade shapes. **Technical:** Grinds ATS-34 and Damascus on request. **Prices:** $120 to $400. **Remarks:** Part-time maker; first knife sold in 1997. **Mark:** J Watts.

WATTS, WALLY,
9560 S Hwy 36, Gatesville, TX 76528, Phone: 254-223-9669
Specialties: Unique traditional folders of his design. **Patterns:** One- to five-blade folders and single-blade gents in various blade shapes. **Technical:** Grinds ATS-34; Damascus on request. **Prices:** $150 to $400. **Remarks:** Full-time maker; first knife sold in 1986. **Mark:** Last name.

custom knifemakers

WEBSTER, BILL,
58144 West Clear Lake Rd, Three Rivers, MI 49093, Phone: 269-244-2873, wswebster_5@msn.com Web: www.websterknifeworks.com
Specialties: Working and using straight knives, especially for hunters. His patterns are custom designed. **Patterns:** Hunters, skinners, camp knives, Bowies and daggers. **Technical:** Hand-filed blades made of D2 steel only, unless other steel is requested. Preferred handle material is stabilized and exotic wood and stag. Sheaths are made by Green River Leather in Kentucky. Hand-sewn sheaths by Bill Dehn in Three Rivers, MI. **Prices:** $75 to $500. **Remarks:** Part-time maker, first knife sold in 1978. **Mark:** Originally WEB stamped on blade, at present, Webster Knifeworks Three Rivers, MI laser etched on blade.

WEHNER, RUDY,
297 William Warren Rd, Collins, MS 39428, Phone: 601-765-4997
Specialties: Reproduction antique Bowies and contemporary Bowies in full and miniature. **Patterns:** Skinners, camp knives, fighters, axes and Bowies. **Technical:** Grinds 440C, ATS-34, 154CM and Damascus. **Prices:** $100 to $500; some to $850. **Remarks:** Full-time maker; first knife sold in 1975. **Mark:** Last name on Bowies and antiques; full name, city and state on skinners.

WEILAND JR., J REESE,
PO Box 2337, Riverview, FL 33568, Phone: 813-671-0661, RWPHIL413@ earthlink.net; Web: www.rwcustomknive.som
Specialties: Hawk bills; tactical to fancy folders. **Patterns:** Hunters, tantos, Bowies, fantasy knives, spears and some swords. **Technical:** Grinds ATS-34, 154CM, 440C, D2, O1, A2, Damascus. Titanium hardware on locking liners and button locks. **Prices:** $150 to $4000. **Remarks:** Full-time maker, first knife sold in 1978. Knifemakers Guild member since 1988.

WEINAND, GEROME M,
14440 Harpers Bridge Rd, Missoula, MT 59808, Phone: 406-543-0845
Specialties: Working straight knives. **Patterns:** Bowies, fishing and camp knives, large special hunters. **Technical:** Grinds O1, 440C, ATS-34, 1084, L6, also stainless Damascus, Aebl and 304; makes all-tool steel Damascus; Dendritic D2 from powdered steel. Heat-treats. **Prices:** $30 to $100; some to $500. **Remarks:** Full-time maker; first knife sold in 1982. **Mark:** Last name.

WEINSTOCK, ROBERT,
PO Box 170028, San Francisco, CA 94117-0028, Phone: 415-731-5968, robertweinstock@att.net
Specialties: Folders, slip joins, lockbacks, autos. **Patterns:** Daggers, folders. **Technical:** Grinds A2, O1 and 440C. Chased and hand-carved blades and handles. Also using various Damascus steels from other makers. **Prices:** $3000 to 7000. **Remarks:** Full-time maker; first knife sold in 1994. **Mark:** Last name carved in steel.

WEISS, CHARLES L,
PO BOX 1037, Waddell, AZ 85355, Phone: 623-935-0924, weissknife@live.com
Specialties: High-art straight knives and folders; deluxe period pieces. **Patterns:** Daggers, fighters, boots, push knives and miniatures. **Technical:** Grinds 440C, 154CM and ATS-34. **Prices:** $300 to $1200; some to $2000. **Remarks:** Full-time maker; first knife sold in 1975. **Mark:** Name and city.

WELLING, RONALD L,
15446 Lake Ave, Grand Haven, MI 49417, Phone: 616-846-2274
Specialties: Scagel knives of his design or to customer specs. **Patterns:** Hunters, camp knives, miniatures, bird, trout, folders, double edged, hatchets, skinners and some art pieces. **Technical:** Forges Damascus 1084 and 1095. Antler, ivory and horn. **Prices:** $250 to $3000. **Remarks:** Full-time maker. ABS Journeyman maker. **Mark:** First initials and or name and last name. City and state. Various scagel kris (1or 2).

WERTH, GEORGE W,
5223 Woodstock Rd, Poplar Grove, IL 61065, Phone: 815-544-4408
Specialties: Period pieces, some fancy. **Patterns:** Straight fighters, daggers and Bowies. **Technical:** Forges and grinds O1, 1095 and his Damascus, including mosaic patterns. **Prices:** $200 to $650; some higher. **Remarks:** Full-time maker. Doing business as Fox Valley Forge. **Mark:** Name in logo or initials connected.

WESCOTT, CODY,
5330 White Wing Rd, Las Cruces, NM 88012, Phone: 575-382-5008
Specialties: Fancy and presentation grade working knives. **Patterns:** Hunters, locking folders and Bowies. **Technical:** Hollow-grinds D2 and ATS-34; all knives file worked. Offers some engraving. Makes sheaths. **Prices:** $110 to $500; some to $1200. **Remarks:** Full-time maker; first knife sold in 1982. **Mark:** First initial, last name.

WEST, CHARLES A,
1315 S Pine St, Centralia, IL 62801, Phone: 618-532-2777
Specialties: Classic, fancy, high tech, period pieces, traditional and working/using straight knives and folders. **Patterns:** Bowies, fighters and locking folders. **Technical:** Grinds ATS-34, O1 and Damascus. Prefers hot blued finishes. **Prices:** $100 to $1000; some to $2000. **Remarks:** Full-time maker; first knife sold in 1963. Doing business as West Custom Knives. **Mark:** Name or name, city and state.

WESTBERG, LARRY,
305 S Western Hills Dr, Algona, IA 50511, Phone: 515-295-9276
Specialties: Traditional and working straight knives of his design and in standard patterns. **Patterns:** Bowies, hunters, fillets and folders. **Technical:** Grinds 440C, D2 and 1095. Heat-treats. Uses natural handle materials. **Prices:** $85 to $600; some to $1000. **Remarks:** Part-time maker; first knife sold in 1987. **Mark:** Last name-town and state.

WHEELER, GARY,
351 Old Hwy 48, Clarksville, TN 37040, Phone: 931-552-3092, LR22SHTR@ charter.net
Specialties: Working to high end fixed blades. **Patterns:** Bowies, Hunters, combat knives, daggers and a few folders. **Technical:** Forges 5160, 1095, 52100 and his own Damascus. **Prices:** $125 to $2000. **Remarks:** Full-time maker since 2001, first knife sold in 1985 collaborates/works at B&W Blade Works. ABS Journeyman Smith 2008. **Mark:** Stamped last name.

WHEELER, ROBERT,
289 S Jefferson, Bradley, IL 60915, Phone: 815-932-5854, b2btaz@brmemc.net

WHETSELL, ALEX,
1600 Palmetto Tyrone Rd, Sharpsburg, GA 30277, Phone: 770-463-4881
Specialties: Knifekits.com, a source for fold locking liner type and straight knife kits. These kits are industry standard for folding knife kits. **Technical:** Many selections of colored G10 carbon fiber and wood handle material for kits, as well as bulk sizes for the custom knifemaker, heat treated folding knife pivots, screws, bushings, etc.

WHIPPLE, WESLEY A,
1002 Shoshoni St, Thermopolis, WY 82443, Phone: 307-921-2445, wildernessknife@yahoo.com
Specialties: Working straight knives, some fancy. **Patterns:** Hunters, Bowies, camp knives, fighters. **Technical:** Forges high-carbon steels, Damascus, offers relief carving and silver wire inlay checkering. **Prices:** $300 to $1400; some higher. **Remarks:** Full-time maker; first knife sold in 1989. A.K.A. Wilderness Knife and Forge. **Mark:** Last name/JS.

WHITE, BRYCE,
1415 W Col Glenn Rd, Little Rock, AR 72210, Phone: 501-821-2956
Specialties: Hunters, fighters, makes Damascus, file work, handmade only. **Technical:** L6, 1075, 1095, O1 steels used most. **Patterns:** Will do any pattern or use his own. **Prices:** $200 to $300. Sold first knife in 1995. **Mark:** White.

WHITE, DALE,
525 CR 212, Sweetwater, TX 79556, Phone: 325-798-4178, dalew@taylortel.net
Specialties: Working and using knives. **Patterns:** Hunters, skinners, utilities and Bowies. **Technical:** Grinds 440C, offers file work, fancy pins and scrimshaw by Sherry Sellers. **Prices:** From $45 to $300. **Remarks:** Sold first knife in 1975. **Mark:** Full name, city and state.

WHITE, GARRETT,
871 Sarijon Rd, Hartwell, GA 30643, Phone: 706-376-5944
Specialties: Gentlemen folders, fancy straight knives. **Patterns:** Locking liners and hunting fixed blades. **Technical:** Grinds 440C, S30V, and stainless Damascus. **Prices:** $150 to $1000. **Remarks:** Part-time maker. **Mark:** Name.

WHITE, GENE E,
9005 Ewing Dr, Bethesda, MD 20817-3357, Phone: 301-564-3164
Specialties: Small utility/gents knives. **Patterns:** Eight standard hunters; most other patterns on commission basis. Currently no swords, axes and fantasy knives. **Technical:** Stock removal 440C and D2; others on request. Mostly hollow grinds; some flat grinds. Prefers natural handle materials. Makes own sheaths. **Prices:** Start at $85. **Remarks:** Part-time maker; first knife sold in 1971. **Mark:** First and middle initials, last name.

WHITE, JOHN PAUL,
231 S Bayshore, Valparaiso, FL 32580, Phone: 850-729-9174, johnwhiteknives@gmail.com
Specialties: Forged hunters, fighters, traditional Bowies and personal carry knives with handles of natural materials and fittings with detailed file work. **Technical:** Forges carbon steel and own Damascus. **Prices:** $500 to $3500 **Remarks:** Master Smith, American Bladesmith Society. **Mark:** First initial, last name.

WHITE, LOU,
7385 Red Bud Rd NE, Ranger, GA 30734, Phone: 706-334-2273

WHITE, RICHARD T,
359 Carver St, Grosse Pointe Farms, MI 48236, Phone: 313-881-4690

WHITE, ROBERT J,
RR 1 641 Knox Rd 900 N, Gilson, IL 61436, Phone: 309-289-4487
Specialties: Working knives, some deluxe. **Patterns:** Bird and trout knives, hunters, survival knives and locking folders. **Technical:** Grinds A2, D2 and 440C; commercial Damascus. Heat-treats. **Prices:** $125 to $250; some to $600. **Remarks:** Full-time maker; first knife sold in 1976. **Mark:** Last name in script.

WHITE JR., ROBERT J BUTCH,
RR 1, Gilson, IL 61436, Phone: 309-289-4487
Specialties: Folders of all sizes. **Patterns:** Hunters, fighters, boots and folders. **Technical:** Forges Damascus; grinds tool and stainless steel. **Prices:** $500 to $1800. **Remarks:** Spare-time maker; first knife sold in 1980. **Mark:** Last name in block letters.

WHITENECT, JODY,
Elderbank, Halifax County, Nova Scotia, CANADA B0N 1K0, Phone: 902-384-2511
Specialties: Fancy and embellished working/using straight knives of his design and to customer specs. **Patterns:** Bowies, fighters and hunters. **Technical:** Forges 1095 and O1; forges and grinds ATS-34. Various filework on blades and bolsters. **Prices:** $200 to $400; some to $800. **Remarks:** Part-time maker; first knife sold in 1996. **Mark:** Longhorn stamp or engraved.

WHITESELL, J. DALE,
P.O. Box 455, Stover, MO 65078, Phone: 573-372-5182, dwknives@ heroesonline.us Web: whitesell-knives.webs.com

Specialties: Fixed blade working knives, and some collector pieces. **Patterns:** Hunting and skinner knives and camp knives. **Technical:** Blades ground from O1, 1095, and 440C in hollow, flat and saber grinds. Wood, bone, deer antler, and G10 are basic handle materials. **Prices:** $100 to $250. **Remarks:** Part-time maker, first knife sold in 2003. Doing business as Dale's Knives. **Mark:** Whitesell on the left side of the blade.

WHITLEY, L WAYNE,
1675 Carrow Rd, Chocowinity, NC 27817-9495, Phone: 252-946-5648

WHITLEY, WELDON G,
4308 N Robin Ave, Odessa, TX 79764, Phone: 432-530-0448, Fax: 432-530-0048, wgwhitley@juno.com
Specialties: Working knives of his design or to customer specs. **Patterns:** Hunters, folders and various double-edged knives. **Technical:** Grinds 440C, 154CM and ATS-34. **Prices:** $150 to $1250. **Mark:** Name, address, road-runner logo.

WHITMAN, JIM,
21044 Salem St, Chugiak, AK 99567, Phone: 907-688-4575, Fax: 907-688-4278, Web: www.whitmanknives.com
Specialties: Working straight knives and folders; some art pieces. **Patterns:** Hunters, skinners, Bowies, camp knives, working fighters, swords and hatchets. **Technical:** Grinds AEB-L Swedish, 440C, 154CM, ATS-34, and Damascus in full convex. Prefers exotic hardwoods, natural and native handle materials: whale bone, antler, ivory and horn. **Prices:** Start at $150. **Remarks:** Full-time maker; first knife sold in 1983. **Mark:** Name, city, state.

WHITTAKER, ROBERT E,
PO Box 204, Mill Creek, PA 17060
Specialties: Using straight knives. Has a line of knives for buckskinners. **Patterns:** Hunters, skinners and Bowies. **Technical:** Grinds O1, A2 and D2. Offers filework. **Prices:** $35 to $100. **Remarks:** Part-time maker; first knife sold in 1980. **Mark:** Last initial or full initials.

WHITTAKER, WAYNE,
2900 Woodland Ct, Metamore, MI 48455, Phone: 810-797-5315, lindorwayne@yahoo.com
Specialties: Liner locks and autos. **Patterns:** Folders. **Technical:** Damascus, mammoth, ivory, and tooth. **Prices:** $500 to $1500. **Remarks:** Full-time maker. **Mark:** Inside of backbar.

WHITWORTH, KEN J,
41667 Tetley Ave, Sterling Heights, MI 48078, Phone: 313-739-5720
Specialties: Working straight knives and folders. **Patterns:** Locking folders, slip joints and boot knives. **Technical:** Grinds 440C, 154CM and D2. **Prices:** $100 to $225; some to $450. **Remarks:** Part-time maker; first knife sold in 1976. **Mark:** Last name.

WICK, JONATHAN P.,
300 Cole Ave., Bisbee, AZ 85603, Phone: 520-227-5228, vikingwick@aol.com Web: jpwickbladeworks.com
Specialties: Fixed blades, Bowies, hunters, neck knives, copper clad sheaths, collectibles, most handle styles and materials. **Technical:** Forged blades and own Damascus, along with shibuichi, mokume, lost wax casting. **Prices:** $250 - $1800 and up. **Remarks:** Full-time maker, ABS member, sold first knife in 2008. **Mark:** J P Wick, also on small blades a JP over a W.

WICKER, DONNIE R,
2544 E 40th Ct, Panama City, FL 32405, Phone: 904-785-9158
Specialties: Traditional working and using straight knives of his design or to customer specs. **Patterns:** Hunters, fighters and slip-joint folders. **Technical:** Grinds 440C, ATS-34, D2 and 154CM. Heat-treats and does hardness testing. **Prices:** $90 to $200; some to $400. **Remarks:** Part-time maker; first knife sold in 1975. **Mark:** First and middle initials, last name.

WIGGINS, BILL,
105 Kaolin Lane, Canton, NC 28716, Phone: 828-226-2551, wncbill@bellsouth.net Web: www.wigginsknives.com
Specialties: Forged working knives. **Patterns:** Hunters, Bowies, camp knives and utility knives of own design or will work with customer on design. **Technical:** Forges 1084 and 52100 as well as making own Damascus. **Prices:** $250 - $1500. **Remarks:** Part-time maker. First knife sold in 1989. ABS board member. **Mark:** WigginsJoe

WIGGINS, HORACE,
203 Herndon Box 152, Mansfield, LA 71502, Phone: 318-872-4471
Specialties: Fancy working knives. **Patterns:** Straight and folding hunters. **Technical:** Grinds O1, D2 and 440C. **Prices:** $90 to $275. **Remarks:** Part-time maker; first knife sold in 1970. **Mark:** Name, city and state in diamond logo.

WILCHER, WENDELL L,
RR 6 Box 6573, Palestine, TX 75801, Phone: 903-549-2530
Specialties: Fantasy, miniatures and working/using straight knives and folders of his design and to customer specs. **Patterns:** Fighters, hunters, locking folders. **Technical:** Hand works (hand file and hand sand knives), not grind. **Prices:** $75 to $250; some to $600. **Remarks:** Part-time maker; first knife sold in 1987. **Mark:** Initials, year, serial number.

WILKINS, MITCHELL,
15523 Rabon Chapel Rd, Montgomery, TX, 77316, Phone: 936-588-2696, mwilkins@consolidated.net

WILLEY, WG,
14210 Sugar Hill Rd, Greenwood, DE 19950, Phone: 302-349-4070, Web: www.willeyknives.com
Specialties: Fancy working straight knives. **Patterns:** Small game knives, Bowies and throwing knives. **Technical:** Grinds 440C and 154CM. **Prices:** $350 to $600; some to $1500. **Remarks:** Part-time maker; first knife sold in 1975. Owns retail store. **Mark:** Last name inside map logo.

WILLIAMS, JASON L,
PO Box 67, Wyoming, RI 02898, Phone: 401-539-8353, Fax: 401-539-0252
Specialties: Fancy and high tech folders of his design, co-inventor of the Axis Lock. **Patterns:** Fighters, locking folders, automatics and fancy pocket knives. **Technical:** Forges Damascus and other steels by request. Uses exotic handle materials and precious metals. Offers inlaid spines and gemstone thumb knobs. **Prices:** $1000 and up. **Remarks:** Full-time maker; first knife sold in 1989. **Mark:** First and last initials on pivot.

WILLIAMS, MICHAEL,
Rt. 3 Box 276, Broken Bow, OK 74728, Phone: 580-420-3051, hforge@pine-net.com
Specialties: Functional, personalized, edged weaponry. Working and collectible art. **Patterns:** Bowies, hunters, camp knives, daggers, others. **Technical:** Forges high carbon steel and own forged Damascus. **Prices:** $500 - $12000. **Remarks:** Full-time ABS Master Smith. **Mark:** Williams MS.

WILLIAMS JR., RICHARD,
1440 Nancy Circle, Morristown, TN 37814, Phone: 615-581-0059
Specialties: Working and using straight knives of his design or to customer specs. **Patterns:** Hunters, dirks and utility/camp knives. **Technical:** Forges 5160 and uses file steel. Hand-finish is standard; offers filework. **Prices:** $80 to $180; some to $250. **Remarks:** Spare-time maker; first knife sold in 1985. **Mark:** Last initial or full initials.

WILLIAMSON, TONY,
Rt 3 Box 503, Siler City, NC 27344, Phone: 919-663-3551
Specialties: Flint knapping: knives made of obsidian flakes and flint with wood, antler or bone for handles. **Patterns:** Skinners, daggers and flake knives. **Technical:** Blades have width/thickness ratio of at least 4 to 1. Hafts with methods available to prehistoric man. **Prices:** $58 to $160. **Remarks:** Student of Errett Callahan. **Mark:** Initials and number code to identify year and number of knives made.

WILLIS, BILL,
RT 7 Box 7549, Ava, MO 65608, Phone: 417-683-4326
Specialties: Forged blades, Damascus and carbon steel. **Patterns:** Cable, random or ladder lamented. **Technical:** Professionally heat treated blades. **Prices:** $75 to $600. **Remarks:** Lifetime guarantee on all blades against breakage. All work done by maker; including leather work. **Mark:** WF.

WILLUMSEN, MIKKEL,
Nyrnberggade 23, 2300 Copenhagen S, Denmark, Phone: 4531176333, mw@willumsen-cph.com Web: www.wix.com/willumsen/urbantactical
Specialties: Folding knives, fixed blades, and balisongs. Also kitchen knives. **Patterns:** Primarily influenced by design that is function and quality based. Tactical style knives inspired by classical designs mixed with modern tactics. **Technical:** Uses CPM 154, RW 134, S30V, and carbon fiber titanium G10 for handles. **Prices:** Starting at $600.

WILSON, CURTIS M,
PO Box 383, Burleson, TX 76097, Phone: 817-295-3732, cwknifeman2026@att.net; Web: www.cwilsonknives.com
Specialties: Traditional working/using knives, fixed blade, folders, slip joint, LinerLock® and lock back knives. Art knives, presentation grade Bowies, folder repair, heat treating services. Sub-zero quench. **Patterns:** Hunters, camp knives, military combat, single and multi-blade folders. Dr's knives large or small or custom design knives. **Technical:** Grinds ATS-34, 440C 52100, D2, S30V, CPM 154, mokume gane, engraves, scrimshaw, sheaths leather of kykex heat treating and file work. **Prices:** $150-750. **Remarks:** Part-time maker since 1984. Sold first knife in 1993. **Mark:** Curtis Wilson in ribbon or Curtis Wilson with hand made in a half moon.

WILSON, JAMES G,
PO Box 4024, Estes Park, CO 80517, Phone: 303-586-3944
Specialties: Bronze Age knives; Medieval and Scottish-styles; tomahawks. **Patterns:** Bronze knives, daggers, swords, spears and battle axes; 12-inch steel Misericorde daggers, sgian dubhs, "his and her" skinners, bird and fish knives, capers, boots and daggers. **Technical:** Casts bronze; grinds D2, 440C and ATS-34. **Prices:** $49 to $400; some to $1300. **Remarks:** Part-time maker; first knife sold in 1975. **Mark:** WilsonHawk.

WILSON, JON J,
1826 Ruby St, Johnstown, PA 15902, Phone: 814-266-6410
Specialties: Miniatures and full size. **Patterns:** Bowies, daggers and hunters. **Technical:** Grinds Damascus, 440C and O1. Scrimshaws and carves. **Prices:** $75 to $500; some higher. **Remarks:** Full-time maker; first knife sold in 1988. **Mark:** First and middle initials, last name.

WILSON, MIKE,
1416 McDonald Rd, Hayesville, NC 28904, Phone: 828-389-8145
Specialties: Fancy working and using straight knives of his design or to customer specs, folders. **Patterns:** Hunters, Bowies, utility knives, gut hooks, skinners, fighters and miniatures. **Technical:** Hollow grinds 440C, L6, O1 and D2. Mirror finishes are standard. Offers filework. **Prices:** $50 to $600. **Remarks:** Full-time maker; first knife sold in 1985. **Mark:** Last name.

WILSON, PHILIP C,
SEAMOUNT KNIFEWORKS, PO Box 846, Mountain Ranch, CA 95246, Phone: 209-754-1990, seamount@bigplanet.com; Web: www.seamountknifeworks.com
Specialties: Working knives; emphasis on salt water fillet knives and utility hunters of his design. **Patterns:** Fishing knives, hunters, utility knives. **Technical:** Grinds CPM S-30V, CPM10V, S-90V, CPMS110V, CPM154, CPM M4, M-390, ELMAX. Heat-treats and Rockwell tests all blades. **Prices:** Start at $400. **Remarks:** First knife sold in 1985. Doing business as Sea-Mount Knife Works. **Mark:** Signature.

WILSON, RON,
2639 Greenwood Ave, Morro Bay, CA 93442, Phone: 805-772-3381
Specialties: Classic and fantasy straight knives of his design. **Patterns:** Daggers, fighters, swords and axes, mostly all miniatures. **Technical:** Forges and grinds Damascus and various tool steels; grinds meteorite. Uses gold, precious stones and exotic wood. **Prices:** Vary. **Remarks:** Part-time maker; first knives sold in 1995. **Mark:** Stamped first and last initials.

WILSON, RW,
PO Box 2012, Weirton, WV 26062, Phone: 304-723-2771, rwknives@comcast.net
Specialties: Working straight knives; period pieces. **Patterns:** Bowies, tomahawks and patch knives. **Technical:** Grinds 440C; scrimshaws. **Prices:** $85 to $175; some to $1000. **Remarks:** Part-time maker; first knife sold in 1966. Knifemaker supplier. Offers free knife-making lessons. **Mark:** Name in tomahawk.

WILSON, STAN,
8931 Pritcher Rd, Lithia, FL 33547, Phone: 727-461-1992, swilson@stanwilsonknives.com; Web: www.stanwilsonknives.com
Specialties: Fancy folders and automatics of his own design. **Patterns:** Locking liner folders, single and dual action autos, daggers. **Technical:** Stock removal, uses Damascus, stainless and high carbon steels, prefers ivory and pearl, Damascus with blued finishes and filework. **Prices:** $400 and up. **Remarks:** Member of Knifemakers Guild and Florida Knifemakers Association. Full-time maker will do custom orders. **Mark:** Name in script.

WILSON (SEE SIMONELLA, GIANLUIGI),

WINGO, GARY,
240 Ogeechee, Ramona, OK 74061, Phone: 918-536-1067, wingg_2000@yahoo.com; Web: www.geocities.com/wingg_2000/gary.html
Specialties: Folder specialist. Steel 440C, D2, others on request. Handle bone-stag, others on request. **Patterns:** Trapper three-blade stockman, four-blade congress, single- and two-blade barlows. **Prices:** 150 to $400. **Mark:** First knife sold 1994. Steer head with Wingo Knives or Straight line Wingo Knives.

WINGO, PERRY,
22 55th St, Gulfport, MS 39507, Phone: 228-863-3193
Specialties: Traditional working straight knives. **Patterns:** Hunters, skinners, Bowies and fishing knives. **Technical:** Grinds 440C. **Prices:** $75 to $1000. **Remarks:** Full-time maker; first knife sold in 1988. **Mark:** Last name.

WINKLER, DANIEL,
PO Box 2166, Blowing Rock, NC 28605, Phone: 828-295-9156, danielwinkler@bellsouth.net; Web: www.winklerknives.com
Specialties: Forged cutlery styled in the tradition of an era past as well as producing a custom-made stock removal line. **Patterns:** Fixed blades, friction folders, lock back folders, and axes/tomahawks. **Technical:** Forges, grinds, and heat treats carbon steels, specialty steels, and his own Damascus steel. **Prices:** $350 to $4000+. **Remarks:** Full-time maker since 1988. Exclusively offers leatherwork by Karen Shook. ABS Master Smith; Knifemakers Guild voting member. **Mark:** Hand forged: Dwinkler; Stock removal: Winkler Knives

WINN, MARVIN,
Maxcutter Custom Knives, 8711 Oakwood Ln., Frisco, TX 75035, Phone: 214-471-7012, maxcutter03@yahoo.com Web: www.maxcutterknives.com
Patterns: Hunting knives, some tactical and some miniatures. **Technical:** 1095, 5160, 154 CM, 12C27, CPMS30V and CPM154CM, Damascus or customer specs. Stock removal. **Prices:** $75 - $850. **Remarks:** Part-time maker. First knife made in 2002. **Mark:** Name, city, state.

WINN, TRAVIS A.,
558 E 3065 S, Salt Lake City, UT 84106, Phone: 801-467-5957
Specialties: Fancy working knives and knives to customer specs. **Patterns:** Hunters, fighters, boots, Bowies and fancy daggers, some miniatures, tantos and fantasy knives. **Technical:** Grinds D2 and 440C. Embellishes. **Prices:** $125 to $500; some higher. **Remarks:** Part-time maker; first knife sold in 1976. **Mark:** TRAV stylized.

WINSTON, DAVID,
1671 Red Holly St, Starkville, MS 39759, Phone: 601-323-1028
Specialties: Fancy and traditional knives of his design and to customer specs. **Patterns:** Bowies, daggers, hunters, boot knives and folders. **Technical:** Grinds 440C, ATS-34 and D2. Offers filework; heat-treats. **Prices:** $40 to $750; some higher. **Remarks:** Part-time maker; first knife sold in 1984. Offers lifetime sharpening for original owner. **Mark:** Last name.

WIRTZ, ACHIM,
Mittelstrasse 58, Wuerselen, D-52146, GERMANY, Phone: 0049-2405-462-486, wootz@web.de
Specialties: Medieval, Scandinavian and Middle East-style knives. **Technical:** Forged blades only, Damascus steel, Wootz, Mokume. **Prices:** Start at $200. **Remarks:** Part-time maker. First knife sold in 1997. **Mark:** Stylized initials.

WISE, DONALD,
304 Bexhill Rd, St Leonardo-On-Sea, East Sussex, TN3 8AL, ENGLAND
Specialties: Fancy and embellished working straight knives to customer specs. **Patterns:** Hunters, Bowies and daggers. **Technical:** Grinds Sandvik 12C27, D2 D3 and O1. Scrimshaws. **Prices:** $110 to $300; some to $500. **Remarks:** Full-time maker; first knife sold in 1983. **Mark:** KNIFECRAFT.

WOLF, BILL,
4618 N 79th Ave, Phoenix, AZ 85033, Phone: 623-910-3147, Fax: 623-846-3585, bwcustomknives143@gmail.com Web: billwolfcustomknives.com
Specialties: Investment grade knives. **Patterns:** Own designs or customer's. **Technical:** Grinds stainless and all steels. **Prices:** $400 to ? **Remarks:** First

knife made in 1988. **Mark:** WOLF

WOLF JR., WILLIAM LYNN,
4006 Frank Rd., Lagrange, TX 78945, Phone: 409-247-4626

WOOD, ALAN,
Greenfield Villa, Greenhead, Brampton CA8 7HH, ENGLAND, a.wood@knivesfreeserve.co.uk; Web: www.alanwoodknives.co.uk
Specialties: High-tech working straight knives of his design. **Patterns:** Hunters, utility/camp and bushcraft knives. **Technical:** Grinds 12027, RWL-34, stainless Damascus and O1. Blades are cryogenic treated. **Prices:** $200 to $800; some to $750. **Remarks:** Full-time maker; first knife sold in 1979. Not currently taking orders. **Mark:** Full name with stag tree logo.

WOOD, LARRY B,
PO BOX 222, Jamesville, VA 23398-0222, Phone: 757-442-2660
Specialties: Fancy working knives of his design. **Patterns:** Hunters, buckskinners, Bowies, tomahawks, locking folders and Damascus miniatures. **Technical:** Forges 1095, file steel and his own Damascus. **Prices:** $125 to $500; some to $2000. **Remarks:** Full-time maker; first knife sold in 1974. Doing business as Wood's Metal Studios. **Mark:** Variations of last name, sometimes with blacksmith logo.

WOOD, OWEN DALE,
6492 Garrison St, Arvada, CO 80004-3157, Phone: 303-456-2748, wood.owen@gmail.com; Web: www.owenwoodcustomknives.com
Specialties: Folding knives and daggers. **Patterns:** Own Damascus, specialties in 456 composite blades. **Technical:** Materials: Damascus stainless steel, exotic metals, gold, rare handle materials. **Prices:** $1000 to $9000. **Remarks:** Folding knives in art deco and art noveau themes. Full-time maker from 1981. **Mark:** OWEN WOOD.

WOOD, WEBSTER,
22041 Shelton Trail, Atlanta, MI 49709, Phone: 989-785-2996, mainganikan@src-milp.com
Specialties: Works mainly in stainless; art knives, Bowies, hunters and folders. **Remarks:** Full-time maker; first knife sold in 1980. Retired guild member. All engraving done by maker. **Mark:** Initials inside shield and name.

WORLEY, JOEL A.,
PO BOX 64, Maplewood, OH 45340, Phone: 937-638-9518, j.a.worleyknives@woh.rr.com
Specialties: Bowies, hunters, fighters, utility/camp knives also period style friction folders. **Patterns:** Classic styles, recurves, his design or customer specified. **Technical:** Most knives are fileworked and include a custom made leather sheath. Forges 5160, W2, Cru forge V, files own Damascus of 1080 and 15N20. **Prices:** $250 and up. **Remarks:** Part-time maker. ABS member. First knife sold in 2005. **Mark:** First name, middle initial and last name over a shark incorporating initials.

WRIGHT, KEVIN,
671 Leland Valley Rd W, Quilcene, WA 98376-9517, Phone: 360-765-3589, kevinw@ptpc.com
Specialties: Fancy working or collector knives to customer specs. **Patterns:** Hunters, boots, buckskinners, miniatures. **Technical:** Forges and grinds L6, 1095, 440C and his own Damascus. **Prices:** $75 to $500; some to $2000. **Remarks:** Part-time maker; first knife sold in 1978. **Mark:** Last initial in anvil.

WRIGHT, L T,
1523 Pershing Ave, Steubenville, OH 43952, Phone: 740-282-4947, knifemkr@sbcglobal.net; Web: www.ltwrightknives.com
Specialties: Hunting and tactical knives. **Patterns:** Drop point hunters, bird, trout and tactical. **Technical:** Grinds D2, 440C and O1. **Remarks:** Full-time maker.

WRIGHT, RICHARD S,
PO Box 201, 111 Hilltop Dr, Carolina, RI 02812, Phone: 401-364-3579, rswswitchblades@hotmail.com; Web: www.richardswright.com
Specialties: Bolster release switchblades, tactical automatics. **Patterns:** Folding fighters, gents pocket knives, one-of-a-kind high-grade automatics. **Technical:** Reforges and grinds various makers Damascus. Uses a variety of tool steels. Uses natural handle material such as ivory and pearl, extensive file-work on most knives. **Prices:** $2000 and up. **Remarks:** Full-time knifemaker with background as a gunsmith. Made first folder in 1991. **Mark:** RSW on blade, all folders are serial numbered.

WRIGHT, TIMOTHY,
PO Box 3746, Sedona, AZ 86340, Phone: 928-282-4180
Specialties: High-tech folders and working knives. **Patterns:** Interframe locking folders, non-inlaid folders, straight hunters and kitchen knives. **Technical:** Grinds BG-42, AEB-L, K190 and Cowry X; works with new steels. All folders can disassemble and are furnished with tools. **Prices:** $150 to $1800; some to $3000. **Remarks:** Full-time maker; first knife sold in 1975. **Mark:** Last name and type of steel used.

WUERTZ, TRAVIS,
2487 E Hwy 287, Casa Grande, AZ 85222, Phone: 520-723-4432

WULF, DERRICK,
25 Sleepy Hollow Rd, Essex, VT 05452, Phone: 802-777-8766, dickwulf@yahoo.com Web: www.dicksworkshop.com
Specialties: Makes predominantly forged fixed blade knives using carbon steels and his own Damascus. **Mark:** "WULF".

WYATT, WILLIAM R,
Box 237, Rainelle, WV 25962, Phone: 304-438-5494
Specialties: Classic and working knives of all designs. **Patterns:** Hunters and utility knives. **Technical:** Forges and grinds saw blades, files and rasps. Prefers stag handles. **Prices:** $45 to $95; some to $350. **Remarks:** Part-time maker; first knife sold in 1990. **Mark:** Last name in star with knife logo.

Y

YASHINSKI, JOHN L,
207 N Platt, PO Box 1284, Red Lodge, MT 59068, Phone: 406-446-3916
Specialties: Native American beaded sheaths, painted rawhide sheaths and tack sheaths. **Prices:** Vary.

YEATES, JOE A,
730 Saddlewood Circle, Spring, TX 77381, Phone: 281-367-2765, joeyeates291@cs.com; Web: www.yeatesBowies.com
Specialties: Bowies and period pieces. **Patterns:** Bowies, toothpicks and combat knives. **Technical:** Grinds 440C, D2 and ATS-34. **Prices:** $600 to $2500. **Remarks:** Full-time maker; first knife sold in 1975. **Mark:** Last initial within outline of Texas or last initial.

YESKOO, RICHARD C,
76 Beekman Rd, Summit, NJ 07901

YORK, DAVID C,
PO Box 3166, Chino Valley, AZ 86323, Phone: 928-636-1709, dmatj@msn.com
Specialties: Working straight knives and folders. **Patterns:** Prefers small hunters and skinners; locking folders. **Technical:** Grinds D2. **Prices:** $75 to $300; some to $600. **Remarks:** Part-time maker; first knife sold in 1975. **Mark:** Last name.

YOSHIHARA, YOSHINDO,
8-17-11 Takasago Katsushi, Tokyo, JAPAN

YOSHIKAZU, KAMADA,
540-3 Kaisaki Niuta-cho, Tokushima, JAPAN, Phone: 0886-44-2319

YOSHIO, MAEDA,
3-12-11 Chuo-cho tamashima Kurashiki-city, Okayama, JAPAN, Phone: 086-525-2375

YOUNG, BUD,
Box 336, Port Hardy, BC, CANADA V0N 2P0, Phone: 250-949-6478
Specialties: Fixed blade, working knives, some fancy. **Patterns:** Drop-points to skinners. **Technical:** Hollow or flat grind, 5160, 440C, mostly ATS-34, satin finish. Using supplied damascus at times. **Prices:** $150 to $2000 CDN. **Remarks:** Spare-time maker; making knives since 1962; first knife sold in 1985. Not taking orders at this time, sell as produced. **Mark:** Name.

YOUNG, CLIFF,
Fuente De La Cibeles No 5, Atascadero, San Miguel De Allende, GTO., MEXICO, Phone: 37700, Fax: 011-52-415-2-57-11
Specialties: Working knives. **Patterns:** Hunters, fighters and fishing knives. **Technical:** Grinds all; offers D2, 440C and 154CM. **Prices:** Start at $250. **Remarks:** Part-time maker; first knife sold in 1980. **Mark:** Name.

YOUNG, ERROL,
4826 Storey Land, Alton, IL 62002, Phone: 618-466-4707
Specialties: Traditional working straight knives and folders. **Patterns:** Wide range, including tantos, Bowies, miniatures and multi-blade folders. **Technical:** Grinds D2, 440C and ATS-34. **Prices:** $75 to $650; some to $800. **Remarks:** Part-time maker; first knife sold in 1987. **Mark:** Last name with arrow.

YOUNG, GEORGE,
713 Pinoak Dr, Kokomo, IN 46901, Phone: 765-457-8893
Specialties: Fancy/embellished and traditional straight knives and folders of his design and to customer specs. **Patterns:** Hunters, fillet/camp knives and locking folders. **Technical:** Grinds 440C, CPM440V, and stellite 6K. Fancy ivory, black pearl and stag for handles. Filework: all stellite construction (6K and 25 alloys). Offers engraving. **Prices:** $350 to $750; some $1500 to $3000. **Remarks:** Full-time maker; first knife sold in 1954. Doing business as Young's Knives. **Mark:** Last name integral inside Bowie.

YOUNG, RAYMOND L,
CUTLER/BLADESMITH, 2922 Hwy 188E, Mt. Ida, AR 71957, Phone: 870-867-3947
Specialties: Cutler-Bladesmith, sharpening service. **Patterns:** Hunter, skinners, fighters, no guard, no ricasso, chef tools. **Technical:** Edge tempered 1095, 516C, mosiac handles, water buffalo and exotic woods. **Prices:** $100 and up. **Remarks:** Federal contractor since 1995. Surgical steel sharpening. **Mark:** R.

YURCO, MIKE,
PO Box 712, Canfield, OH 44406, Phone: 330-533-4928, shorinki@aol.com
Specialties: Working straight knives. **Patterns:** Hunters, utility knives, Bowies and fighters, push knives, claws and other hideouts. **Technical:** Grinds 440C, ATS-34 and 154CM; likes mirror and satin finishes. **Prices:** $20 to $500. **Remarks:** Part-time maker; first knife sold in 1983. **Mark:** Name, steel, serial number.

Z

ZACCAGNINO JR., DON,
2256 Bacom Point Rd, Pahokee, FL 33476-2622, Phone: 561-985-0303, zackknife@gmail.com Web: www.zackknives.com
Specialties: Working knives and some period pieces of their designs. **Patterns:** Heavy-duty hunters, axes and Bowies; a line of light-weight hunters, fillets and personal knives. **Technical:** Grinds 440C and 17-4 PH; highly finished in complex handle and blade treatments. **Prices:** $165 to $500; some to $2500. **Remarks:** Part-time maker; first knife sold in 1969 by Don Zaccagnino Sr. **Mark:** ZACK, city and state inside oval.

ZAHM, KURT,
488 Rio Casa, Indialantic, FL 32903, Phone: 407-777-4860
Specialties: Working straight knives of his design or to customer specs. **Patterns:** Daggers, fancy fighters, Bowies, hunters and utility knives. **Technical:** Grinds D2, 440C; likes filework. **Prices:** $75 to $1000. **Remarks:** Part-time maker; first knife sold in 1985. **Mark:** Last name.

ZAKABI, CARL S,
PO Box 893161, Mililani Town, HI 96789-0161, Phone: 808-626-2181
Specialties: User-grade straight knives of his design, cord wrapped and bare steel handles exclusively. **Patterns:** Fighters, hunters and utility/camp knives. **Technical:** Grinds 440C and ATS-34. **Prices:** $90 to $400. **Remarks:** Spare-time maker; first knife sold in 1988. Doing business as Zakabi's Knifeworks LLC. **Mark:** Last name and state inside a Hawaiian sharktooth dagger.

ZAKHAROV, GLADISTON,
Bairro Rio Comprido, Rio Comprido Jacarei, Jacaret SP, BRAZIL 12302-070, Phone: 55 12 3958 4021, Fax: 55 12 3958 4103, arkhip@terra.com.br; Web: www.arkhip.com.br
Specialties: Using straight knives of his design. **Patterns:** Hunters, kitchen, utility/camp and barbecue knives. **Technical:** Grinds his own "secret steel." **Prices:** $30 to $200. **Remarks:** Full-time maker. **Mark:** Arkhip Special Knives.

ZBORIL, TERRY,
5320 CR 130, Caldwell, TX 77836, Phone: 979-535-4157, tzboril@tconline.net
Specialties: ABS Journeyman Smith.

ZEMBKO III, JOHN,
140 Wilks Pond Rd, Berlin, CT 06037, Phone: 860-828-3503, johnzembko@hotmail.com
Specialties: Working knives of his design or to customer specs. **Patterns:** Likes to use stabilized high-figured woods. **Technical:** Grinds ATS-34, A2, D2; forges O1, 1095; grinds Damasteel. **Prices:** $50 to $400; some higher. **Remarks:** First knife sold in 1987. **Mark:** Name.

ZEMITIS, JOE,
14 Currawong Rd, Cardiff Hts, 2285 Newcastle, AUSTRALIA, Phone: 0249549907, jjvzem@bigpond.com
Specialties: Traditional working straight knives. **Patterns:** Hunters, Bowies, tantos, fighters and camp knives. **Technical:** Grinds O1, D2, W2 and 440C; makes his own Damascus. Embellishes; offers engraving. **Prices:** $150 to $3000. **Remarks:** Full-time maker; first knife sold in 1983. **Mark:** First initial, last name and country, or last name.

ZERMENO, WILLIAM D.,
9131 Glenshadow Dr, Houston, TX 77088, Phone: 281-726-2459, will@wdzknives.com Web: www.wdzknives.com
Specialties: Tactical/utility folders and fixed blades. **Patterns:** Frame lock and liner lock folders the majority of which incorporate flippers and utility fixed blades. **Technical:** Grinds CPM 154, S30V, 3V and stainless Damascus. **Prices:** $250 - $600. **Remarks:** Part-time maker; first knife sold in 2008. Doing business as www.wdzknives.com. **Mark:** WDZ over logo.

ZIMA, MICHAEL F,
732 State St, Ft. Morgan, CO 80701, Phone: 970-867-6078, Web: http://www.zimaknives.com
Specialties: Working and collector quality straight knives and folders. **Patterns:** Hunters, lock backs, LinerLock®, slip joint and automatic folders. **Technical:** Grinds Damascus, 440C, ATS-34 and 154CM. **Prices:** $200 and up. **Remarks:** Full-time maker; first knife sold in 1982. **Mark:** Last name.

ZINKER, BRAD,
BZ KNIVES, 1591 NW 17 St, Homestead, FL 33030, Phone: 305-216-0404, bzknives@aol.com
Specialties: Fillets, folders and hunters. **Technical:** Uses ATS-34 and stainless Damascus. **Prices:** $200 to $600. **Remarks:** Voting member of Knifemakers Guild and Florida Knifemakers Association. **Mark:** Offset connected initials BZ.

ZIRBES, RICHARD,
Neustrasse 15, D-54526 Niederkail, GERMANY, Phone: 0049 6575 1371, r.zirbes@freenet.de Web: www.zirbes-knives.com www.zirbes-messer.de
Specialties: Fancy embellished knives with engraving and self-made scrimshaw (scrimshaw made by maker). High-tech working knives and high-tech hunters, boots, fighters and folders. All knives made by hand. **Patterns:** Boots, fighters, folders, hunters. **Technical:** Uses only the best steels for blade material like CPM-T 440V, CPM-T 420V, ATS-34, D2, C440, stainless Damascus or steel according to customer's desire. **Prices:** Working knives and hunters: $200 to $600. Fancy embellished knives with engraving and/or scrimshaw: $800 to $3000. **Remarks:** Part-time maker; first knife sold in 1991. Member of the German Knifemaker Guild. **Mark:** Zirbes or R. Zirbes.

ZOWADA, TIM,
4509 E Bear River Rd, Boyne Falls, MI 49713, Phone: 231-881-5056, tim@tzknives.com Web: www.tzknives.com
Specialties: Working knives and straight razors. **Technical:** Forges O1, L6, his own Damascus and smelted steel "Michi-Gane". **Prices:** $200 to $2500; some to $5000. **Remarks:** Full-time maker; first knife sold in 1980. **Mark:** Gothic, lower case "TZ".

ZSCHERNY, MICHAEL,
1840 Rock Island Dr, Ely, IA 52227, Phone: 319-848-3629, zschernyknives@aol.com
Specialties: Quality folding knives. **Patterns:** Liner-lock and lock-back folders in titanium, working straight knives. **Technical:** Grinds ATS-34 and commercial Damascus, prefers natural materials such as pearls and ivory. **Prices:** Starting at $500. **Remarks:** Full-time maker, first knife sold in 1978. **Mark:** Last name, city and state; folders, last name with stars inside folding knife.

AK

Barlow, Jana Poirier	Anchorage
Brennan, Judson	Delta Junction
Breuer, Lonnie	Wasilla
Broome, Thomas A	Kenai
Cawthorne, Christopher A	Wrangell
Chamberlin, John A	Anchorage
Dempsey, Gordon S	N. Kenai
Desrosiers, Adam	Petersburg
Desrosiers, Haley	Petersburg
Dufour, Arthur J	Anchorage
England, Virgil	Anchorage
Flint, Robert	Anchorage
Gouker, Gary B	Sitka
Grebe, Gordon S	Anchor Point
Harvey, Mel	Nenana
Hibben, Westley G	Anchorage
Hook, Bob	North Pole
Kelsey, Nate	Anchorage
Knapp, Mark	Fairbanks
Lance, Bill	Eagle River
Malaby, Raymond J	Juneau
Mcfarlin, Eric E	Kodiak
Miller, Nate	Fairbanks
Miller, Ron	NORTH POLE
Miller, Terry	Healy
Mirabile, David	Juneau
Mirabile, David	Juneau
Moore, Marve	Willow
Parrish Iii, Gordon A	North Pole
Stegall, Keith	Wasilla
Van Cleve, Steve	Sutton
Whitman, Jim	Chugiak

AL

Batson, James	Madison
Baxter, Dale	Trinity
Bell, Tony	Woodland
Bowles, Chris	Reform
Brothers, Dennis L.	Oneonta
Coffman, Danny	Jacksonville
Conn Jr., C T	Attalla
Daniels, Alex	Town Creek
Dark, Robert	Oxford
Di Marzo, Richard	Birmingham
Durham, Kenneth	Cherokee
Elrod, Roger R	Enterprise
Gilbreath, Randall	Dora
Golden, Randy	Montgomery
Hammond, Jim	Arab
Howard, Durvyn M	Hokes Bluff
Howell, Len	Opelika
Howell, Ted	Wetumpka
Huckabee, Dale	Maylene
Hulsey, Hoyt	Attalla
Mccullough, Jerry	Georgiana
Militano, Tom	Jacksonville
Morris, C H	Frisco City
Pardue, Melvin M	Repton
Roe Jr., Fred D	Huntsville
Russell, Tom	Jacksonville
Sinyard, Cleston S	Elberta
Smith, Lacy	Jacksonville
Thomas, David E	Lillian
Tycer, Art	Meridianville
Watson, Billy	Deatsville

AR

Anders, David	Center Ridge
Ardwin, Corey	North Little Rock
Barnes Jr., Cecil C.	Center Ridge
Brown, Jim	Little Rock
Browning, Steven W	Benton
Bullard, Benoni	Bradford
Bullard, Tom	Flippin
Cabe, Jerry (Buddy)	Hattieville
Cook, James R	Nashville
Copeland, Thom	Nashville
Cox, Larry	Murfreesboro
Crawford, Pat And Wes	West Memphis
Crotts, Dan	Elm Springs
Crowell, James L	Mtn. View
Dozier, Bob	Springdale
Duvall, Fred	Benton
Echols, Roger	Nashville
Edge, Tommy	Cash
Ferguson, Lee	Hindsville
Ferguson, Linda	Hindsville
Fisk, Jerry	Nashville
Fitch, John S	Clinton
Flournoy, Joe	El Dorado
Foster, Ronnie E	Morrilton
Foster, Timothy L	El Dorado
Frizzell, Ted	West Fork
Gadberry, Emmet	Hattieville
Greenaway, Don	Fayetteville
Herring, Morris	Dyer
Hutchinson, Alan	Conway
Lawrence, Alton	De Queen
Livesay, Newt	Siloam Springs
Lunn, Gail	Mountain Home
Lunn, Larry A	Mountain Home
Lynch, Tad	Beebe
Maringer, Tom	Springdale
Martin, Bruce E	Prescott
Martin, Hal W	Morrilton
Massey, Roger	Texarkana
Newberry, Allen	Lowell
Newton, Ron	London
O'Dell, Clyde	Camden
Olive, Michael E	Leslie
Passmore, Jimmy D	Hoxie
Perry, Jim	Hope
Perry, John	Mayflower
Peterson, Lloyd (Pete) C	Clinton
Polk, Clifton	Van Buren
Polk, Rusty	Van Buren
Red, Vernon	Conway
Reeves, J.R.	Texarkana
Rhea, Lin	Prattsville
Richards, Ralph (Bud)	Bauxite
Roberts, T. C. (Terry)	Fayetteville
Solomon, Marvin	Paron
Stanley, John	Crossett
Stout, Charles	Gillham
Sweaza, Dennis	Austin
Townsend, Allen Mark	Texarkana
Townsley, Russell	Concord
Walker, Jim	Morrilton
Ward, Chuck	Benton
White, Bryce	Little Rock
Young, Raymond L	Mt. Ida

AZ

Ammons, David C	Tucson
Bennett, Glen C	Tucson
Birdwell, Ira Lee	Congress
Boye, David	Dolan Springs
Bryan, Tom	Gilbert
Cheatham, Bill	Laveen
Choate, Milton	Somerton
Clark, R W	Surprise
Dawson, Barry	Prescott Valley
Dawson, Lynn	Prescott Valley
Deubel, Chester J.	Tucson
Dodd, Robert F	Camp Verde
Fuegen, Larry	Prescott
Goo, Tai	Tucson
Hancock, Tim	Scottsdale
Hoel, Steve	Pine
Holder, D'Alton	Wickenburg
Hull, Michael J	Cottonwood
Karp, Bob	Phoenix
Kiley, Mike And Jandy	Chino Valley
Kopp, Todd M	Apache Jct.
Lampson, Frank G	Rimrock
Lee, Randy	St. Johns
Mcfall, Ken	Lakeside
Mcfarlin, J W	Lake Havasu City
Miller, Michael	Kingman
Montell, Ty	Thatcher
Mooney, Mike	Queen Creek
Mooney, Mike	Queen Creek
Newhall, Tom	Tucson
Purvis, Bob And Ellen	Tucson
Robbins, Bill	Globe
Rybar Jr., Raymond B	Came Verde
Tamboli, Michael	Glendale
Tollefson, Barry A	Tubac
Tyre, Michael A	Wickenburg
Weiss, Charles L	Waddell
Wick, Jonathan P.	Bisbee
Wolf, Bill	Phoenix
Wright, Timothy	Sedona
Wuertz, Travis	Casa Grande
York, David C	Chino Valley

CA

Abegg, Arnie	Huntington Beach
Abernathy, Paul J	Eureka
Adkins, Richard L	Mission Viejo
Aldrete, Bob	Lomita
Athey, Steve	Riverside
Barnes, Gregory	Altadena
Barron, Brian	San Mateo
Benson, Don	Escalon
Berger, Max A.	Carmichael
Biggers, Gary	Ventura
Bost, Roger E	Palos Verdes
Boyd, Francis	Berkeley
Brack, Douglas D	Ventura
Breshears, Clint	Manhattan Beach
Brooks, Buzz	Los Angles
Brous, Jason	Goleta
Browne, Rick	Upland
Bruce, Richard L.	Yankee Hill
Bruce, Richard L.	Yankee Hill
Butler, Bart	Ramona
Cabrera, Sergio B	Wilmington
Cantrell, Kitty D	Ramona
Caswell, Joe	Newbury
Clinco, Marcus	Venice
Coffey, Bill	Clovis
Cohen, Terry A	Laytonville
Coleman, John A	Citrus Heights
Connolly, James	Oroville
Cucchiara, Matt	Fresno
Davis, Charlie	Santee
De Maria Jr., Angelo	Carmel Valley
Dion, Greg	Oxnard
Dixon Jr., Ira E	Ventura
Dobratz, Eric	Laguna Hills
Doolittle, Mike	Novato
Driscoll, Mark	La Mesa
Dwyer, Duane	San Marcos
Ellis, Dave/Abs Mastersmith	Vista
Ellis, William Dean	Sanger
Emerson, Ernest R	Torrance
English, Jim	Jamul
English, Jim	Jamul
Ernest, Phil (Pj)	Whittier
Essegian, Richard	Fresno
Felix, Alexander	Torrance
Ferguson, Jim	Temecula
Fisher, Theo (Ted)	Montague
Forrest, Brian	Descanso
Fraley, D B	Dixon

Fred, Reed Wyle	Sacramento
Freer, Ralph	Seal Beach
Fulton, Mickey	Willows
Girtner, Joe	Brea
Gofourth, Jim	Santa Paula
Guarnera, Anthony R	Quartzhill
Hall, Jeff	Los Alamitos
Hardy, Scott	Placerville
Harris, Jay	Redwood City
Harris, John	Riverside
Helton, Roy	San Diego
Herndon, Wm R "Bill"	Acton
Hink Iii, Les	Stockton
Hoy, Ken	North Fork
Humenick, Roy	Rescue
Iames, Gary	Tahoe
Jacks, Jim	Covina
Jackson, David	Lemoore
Jensen, John Lewis	Pasadena
Johnson, Randy	Turlock
Kazsuk, David	Perris
Kelly, Dave	Los Angeles
Keyes, Dan	Chino
Kilpatrick, Christian A	Citrus Hieghts
Koster, Steven C	Huntington Beach
Laner, Dean	Susanville
Larson, Richard	Turlock
Leland, Steve	Fairfax
Likarich, Steve	Colfax
Lin, Marcus	Rolling Hills Estates
Lockett, Sterling	Burbank
Luchini, Bob	Palo Alto
Mackie, John	Whittier
Massey, Ron	Joshua Tree
Mata, Leonard	San Diego
Maxwell, Don	Clovis
Mcabee, William	Colfax
Mcclure, Michael	Menlo Park
Mcgrath, Patrick T	Westchester
Melin, Gordon C	La Mirada
Meloy, Sean	Lemon Grove
Montano, Gus A	San Diego
Morgan, Jeff	Santee
Moses, Steven	Santa Ana
Mutz, Jeff	Rancho Cucamonga
Naten, Greg	Bakersfield
Orton, Rich	Covina
Osborne, Donald H	Clovis
Packard, Bob	Elverta
Palm, Rik	San Diego
Panchenko, Serge	Citrus Heights
Pendleton, Lloyd	Volcano
Perry, Chris	Fresno
Pfanenstiel, Dan	Modesto
Phillips, Randy	Ontario
Pitt, David F	Anderson
Posner, Barry E	N. Hollywood
Quesenberry, Mike	Blairsden
Randall, Patrick	Newbury Park
Rozas, Clark D	Wilmington
Schmitz, Raymond E	Valley Center
Schneider, Herman	Apple Valley
Schroen, Karl	Sebastopol
Sibrian, Aaron	Ventura
Sjostrand, Kevin	Visalia
Slobodian, Scott	San Andreas
Smith, Shawn	Clouis
Sornberger, Jim	Volcano
St. Cyr, H Red	Wilmington
Stapel, Chuck	Glendale
Steinberg, Al	Laguna Woods
Stimps, Jason M	Orange
Stockwell, Walter	Redwood City
Stover, Howard	Pasadena
Strider, Mick	San Marcos
Terrill, Stephen	Springville
Tingle, Dennis P	Jackson

Torres, Henry	Clovis
Trace Rinaldi Custom Blades,	Hemet
Trujillo, Miranda	Rohnert Park
Vagnino, Michael	Visalia
Velick, Sammy	Los Angeles
Warren, Al	Roseville
Watanabe, Wayne	Montebello
Weinstock, Robert	San Francisco
Wilson, Philip C	Mountain Ranch
Wilson, Ron	Morro Bay

CO

Anderson, Mark Alan	Denver
Anderson, Mel	Hotchkiss
Booco, Gordon	Hayden
Brock, Kenneth L	Allenspark
Burrows, Chuck	Durango
Dannemann, Randy	Hotchkiss
Davis, Don	Loveland
Dennehy, John D	Loveland
Dill, Robert	Loveland
Fredeen, Graham	Colorado Springs
Fronefield, Daniel	Peyton
Hackney, Dana A.	Monument
High, Tom	Alamosa
Hockensmith, Dan	Carr
Hughes, Ed	Grand Junction
Irie, Michael L	Colorado Springs
Kitsmiller, Jerry	Montrose
Leck, Dal	Hayden
Miller, Don	Montrose
Miller, Hanford J	Cowdrey
Miller, M A	Northglenn
Niro, Frank	Blind Bay
Ott, Fred	Durango
Owens, John	Nathrop
Rexford, Todd	Woodland Park
Roberts, Chuck	Golden
Rollert, Steve	Keenesburg
Ronzio, N. Jack	Fruita
Sanders, Bill	Mancos
Thompson, Lloyd	Pagosa Springs
Waites, Richard L	Broomfield
Watson, Bert	Westminster
Wilson, James G	Estes Park
Wood, Owen Dale	Arvada
Zima, Michael F	Ft. Morgan
Redd, Bill	Broomfield

CT

Buebendorf, Robert E	Monroe
Chapo, William G	Wilton
Cross, Kevin	Higganum
Framski, Walter P	Prospect
Jean, Gerry	Manchester
Meyer, Christopher J	Tolland
Plunkett, Richard	West Cornwall
Putnam, Donald S	Wethersfield
Rainville, Richard	Salem
Turecek, Jim	Ansonia
Vitale, Mace	Guilford
Zembko Iii, John	Berlin

DE

Antonio Jr., William J	Newark
Schneider, Karl A	Newark
Willey, Wg	Greenwood

FL

Adams, Les	Hialeah
Alexander, Oleg, Cossack Blades	
Wellington	
Anders, Jerome	Miramar
Angell, Jon	Hawthorne

Atkinson, Dick	Wausau
Bacon, David R.	Bradenton
Barry Iii, James J.	West Palm Beach
Beers, Ray	Lake Wales
Benjamin Jr., George	Kissimmee
Birnbaum, Edwin	Miami
Blackwood, Neil	Lakeland
Bosworth, Dean	Key Largo
Bradley, John	Pomona Park
Bray Jr., W Lowell	New Port Richey
Brown, Harold E	Arcadia
Burris, Patrick R	Jacksonville
Butler, John	Havana
Chase, Alex	DeLand
Cole, Dave	Satellite Beach
D'Andrea, John	Citrus Springs
Davis Jr., Jim	Zephyrhills
Dietzel, Bill	Middleburg
Doggett, Bob	Brandon
Dotson, Tracy	Baker
Ellerbe, W B	Geneva
Ellis, Willy B	Palm Harbor
Enos Iii, Thomas M	Orlando
Ferrara, Thomas	Naples
Fowler, Charles R	Ft McCoy
Gamble, Roger	Newberry
Gibson Sr., James Hoot	Bunnell
Goers, Bruce	Lakeland
Granger, Paul J	Largo
Greene, Steve	Intercession City
Griffin Jr., Howard A	Davie
Grospitch, Ernie	Orlando
Harris, Ralph Dewey	Brandon
Heaney, John D	Haines City
Heitler, Henry	Tampa
Hodge Iii, John	Palatka
Hostetler, Larry	Fort Pierce
Humphreys, Joel	Lake Placid
Hunter, Richard D	Alachua
Hytovick, Joe "Hy"	Dunnellon
Jernigan, Steve	Milton
Johanning Custom Knives, Tom	Sarasota
Johnson, John R	Plant City
King, Bill	Tampa
Krapp, Denny	Apopka
Levengood, Bill	Tampa
Lewis, Mike	DeBary
Long, Glenn A	Dunnellon
Lovestrand, Schuyler	Vero Beach
Lozier, Don	Ocklawaha
Lyle Iii, Ernest L	Chiefland
Mandt, Joe	St. Petersburg
Mcdonald, Robert J	Loxahatchee
Mcgowan, Frank E	Sebring
Miller, Ronald T	Largo
Miller, Steve	Clearwater
Mink, Dan	Crystal Beach
Newton, Larry	Jacksonville
Ochs, Charles F	Largo
Owens, Donald	Melbourne
Parker, Cliff	Zephyrhills
Partridge, Jerry D.	DeFuniak Springs
Pattay, Rudy	Citrus Springs
Pendray, Alfred H	Williston
Piergallini, Daniel E	Plant City
Randall Made Knives,	Orlando
Reed, John M	Port Orange
Renner, Terry	Palmetto
Robinson, Calvin	Pace
Robinson Iii, Rex R	Leesburg
Rodkey, Dan	Hudson
Romeis, Gordon	Fort Myers
Russ, Ron	Williston
Schwarzer, Lora Sue	Crescent City
Schwarzer, Stephen	Crescent City
Smith, Michael J	Brandon
Stapleton, William E	Merritt Island

Steck, Van R — Orange City
Stephan, Daniel — Valrico
Stipes, Dwight — Palm City
Straight, Kenneth J — Largo
Tabor, Tim — Lutz
Turnbull, Ralph A — Spring Hill
Vogt, Donald J — Tampa
Watson, Tom — Panama City
Weiland Jr., J Reese — Riverview
White, John Paul — Valparaiso
Wicker, Donnie R — Panama City
Wilson, Stan — Lithia
Zaccagnino Jr., Don — Pahokee
Zahm, Kurt — Indialantic
Zinker, Brad — Homestead

GA

Arrowood, Dale — Sharpsburg
Ashworth, Boyd — Powder Springs
Barker, John — Cumming
Barker, Robert G. — Bishop
Bentley, C L — Albany
Bish, Hal — Jonesboro
Bradley, Dennis — Blairsville
Buckner, Jimmie H — Putney
Chamblin, Joel — Concord
Cole, Welborn I — Athens
Crockford, Jack — Chamblee
Daniel, Travis E — Thomaston
Davis, Steve — Powder Springs
Dempsey, David — Macon
Dunn, Charles K — Shiloh
Frost, Dewayne — Barnesville
Gaines, Buddy — Commerce
Glover, Warren D — Cleveland
Greene, David — Covington
Halligan, Ed — Sharpsburg
Hammond, Hank — Leesburg
Hardy, Douglas E — Franklin
Hawkins, Rade — Fayetteville
Hensley, Wayne — Conyers
Hinson And Son, R — Columbus
Hoffman, Kevin L — Savannah
Hossom, Jerry — Duluth
Jones, Franklin (Frank) W — Columbus
Kimsey, Kevin — Cartersville
King, Fred — Cartersville
Knott, Steve — Guyton
Landers, John — Newnan
Lonewolf, J Aguirre — Demorest
Mathews, Charlie And Harry — Statesboro
Mcgill, John — Blairsville
Mclendon, Hubert W — Waco
Mitchell, James A — Columbus
Moncus, Michael Steven — Smithville
Parks, John — Jefferson
Poole, Marvin O — Commerce
Powell, Robert Clark — Smarr
Prater, Mike — Flintstone
Price, Timmy — Blairsville
Pridgen Jr., Larry — Fitzgerald
Ragsdale, James D — Ellijay
Roghmans, Mark — LaGrange
Rosenfeld, Bob — Hoschton
Sculley, Peter E — Rising Fawn
Smith Jr., James B "Red" — Morven
Snow, Bill — Columbus
Sowell, Bill — Macon
Stafford, Richard — Warner Robins
Thompson, Kenneth — Duluth
Tomey, Kathleen — Macon
Walters, A F — TyTy
Whetsell, Alex — Sharpsburg
White, Garrett — Hartwell
White, Lou — Ranger

HI

Evans, Vincent K And Grace — Keaau
Fujisaka, Stanley — Kaneohe
Gibo, George — Hilo
Lui, Ronald M — Honolulu
Mann, Tim — Honokaa
Matsuoka, Scot — Mililani
Mayo Jr., Tom — Waialua
Mitsuyuki, Ross — Honolulu
Onion, Kenneth J — Kaneohe
Ouye, Keith — Honolulu
Watanabe, Melvin — Kailua
Zakabi, Carl S — Mililani Town

IA

Brooker, Dennis — Chariton
Brower, Max — Boone
Clark, Howard F — Runnells
Cockerham, Lloyd — Denham Springs
Helscher, John W — Washington
Lainson, Tony — Council Bluffs
Lewis, Bill — Riverside
Mckiernan, Stan — Lamoni
Miller, James P — Fairbank
Thie, Brian — Burlington
Trindle, Barry — Earlham
Westberg, Larry — Algona
Zscherny, Michael — Ely

ID

Alderman, Robert — Sagle
Alverson, Tim (R.V.) — Moscow
Bloodworth Custom Knives, — Meridian
Burke, Bill — Boise
Eddy, Hugh E — Caldwell
Hawk, Grant And Gavin — Idaho City
Hogan, Thomas R — Boise
Horton, Scot — Buhl
Howe, Tori — Athol
Mann, Michael L — Spirit Lake
Metz, Greg T — Cascade
Patton, Dick And Rob — Nampa
Quarton, Barr — McCall
Reeve, Chris — Boise
Rohn, Fred — Coeur d'Alene
Sawby, Scott — Sandpoint
Sparks, Bernard — Dingle
Steiger, Monte L — Genesee
Tippetts, Colten — Hidden Springs
Towell, Dwight L — Midvale

IL

Andersen, Karl B. — Watseka
Bloomer, Alan T — Maquon
Camerer, Craig — Chesterfield
Cook, Louise — Ozark
Cook, Mike — Ozark
Detmer, Phillip — Breese
Dicristofano, Anthony P — Northlake
Eaker, Allen L — Paris
Fiorini, Bill — Grayville
Hawes, Chuck — Weldon
Heath, William — Bondville
Hill, Rick — Maryville
Knuth, Joseph E — Rockford
Kovar, Eugene — Evergreen Park
Leone, Nick — Pontoon Beach
Markley, Ken — Sparta
Meers, Andrew — Carbondale
Meier, Daryl — Carbondale
Myers, Paul — Wood River
Myers, Steve — Virginia
Nevling, Mark — Hume

Nowland, Rick — Waltonville
Pellegrin, Mike — Troy
Pritchard, Ron — Dixon
Rosenbaugh, Ron — Crystal Lake
Rossdeutscher, Robert N — Arlington Heights
Rzewnicki, Gerald — Elizabeth
Schneider, Craig M — Claremont
Smale, Charles J — Waukegan
Smith, John M — Centralia
Todd, Richard C — Chambersburg
Tompkins, Dan — Peotone
Veit, Michael — LaSalle
Voss, Ben — Victoria
Werth, George W — Poplar Grove
West, Charles A — Centralia
Wheeler, Robert — Bradley
White, Robert J — Gilson
White Jr., Robert J Butch — Gilson
Young, Errol — Alton

IN

Adkins, Larry — Indianapolis
Ball, Ken — Mooresville
Barkes, Terry — Edinburgh
Barrett, Rick L. (Toshi Hisa) — Goshen
Bose, Reese — Shelburn
Bose, Tony — Shelburn
Chaffee, Jeff L — Morris
Claiborne, Jeff — Franklin
Cramer, Brent — Wheatland
Crowl, Peter — Waterloo
Damlovac, Sava — Indianapolis
Darby, Jed — Greensburg
Fitzgerald, Dennis M — Fort Wayne
Fraps, John R — Indianapolis
Good, D.R. — Tipton
Hunt, Maurice — Brownsburg
Imel, Billy Mace — New Castle
Johnson, C E Gene — Chesterton
Kain, Charles — Indianapolis
Keeslar, Steven C — Hamilton
Keeton, William L — Laconia
Kinker, Mike — Greensburg
Mayville, Oscar L — Marengo
Minnick, Jim — Middletown
Oliver, Todd D — Spencer
Parsons, Michael R — Indianapolis
Patton, Phillip — Yoder
Quakenbush, Thomas C — Ft Wayne
Robertson, Leo D — Indianapolis
Seib, Steve — Evansville
Shull, James — Rensselaer
Smock, Timothy E — Marion
Snyder, Michael Tom — Zionsville
Thayer, Danny O — Romney
Young, George — Kokomo

KS

Bradburn, Gary — Wichita
Burrows, Stephen R — Humboldt
Chard, Gordon R — Iola
Courtney, Eldon — Wichita
Craig, Roger L — Topeka
Culver, Steve — Meriden
Darpinian, Dave — Olathe
Davison, Todd A. — Lyons
Dawkins, Dudley L — Topeka
Dick, Dan — Hutchinson
Evans, Phil — Columbus
Hegwald, J L — Humboldt
Herman, Tim — Olathe
Keranen, Paul — Tacumseh
King, Jason M — St. George
King Jr., Harvey G — Alta Vista

Kraft, Steve — Abilene
Lamb, Curtis J — Ottawa
Magee, Jim — Salina
Petersen, Dan L — Auburn

KY

Addison, Kyle A — Hazel
Baskett, Barbara — Eastview
Baskett, Lee Gene — Eastview
Bodner, Gerald "Jerry" — Louisville
Bybee, Barry J — Cadiz
Carson, Harold J "Kit" — Vine Grove
Carter, Mike — Louisville
Coil, Jimmie J — Owensboro
Downing, Larry — Bremen
Dunn, Steve — Smiths Grove
Edwards, Mitch — Glasgow
Finch, Ricky D — West Liberty
Fister, Jim — Simpsonville
France, Dan — Cawood
Frederick, Aaron — West Liberty
Greco, John — Greensburg
Hibben, Daryl — LaGrange
Hibben, Gil — LaGrange
Hibben, Joleen — LaGrange
Hoke, Thomas M — LaGrange
Holbrook, H L — Sandy Hook
Howser, John C — Frankfort
Keeslar, Joseph F — Almo
Lott, Sherry — Greensburg
Pease, W D — Ewing
Pierce, Harold L — Louisville
Pulliam, Morris C — Shelbyville
Rados, Jerry F — Columbia
Richerson, Ron — Greenburg
Rigney Jr., Willie — Bronston
Smith, John W — West Liberty
Soaper, Max H. — Henderson
Steier, David — Louisville
Wallingford Jr., Charles W — Union

LA

Barker, Reggie — Springhill
Blaum, Roy — Covington
Caldwell, Bill — West Monroe
Calvert Jr., Robert W (Bob) — Rayville
Capdepon, Randy — Carencro
Capdepon, Robert — Carencro
Chauvin, John — Scott
Dake, C M — New Orleans
Dake, Mary H — New Orleans
Durio, Fred — Opelousas
Faucheaux, Howard J — Loreauville
Fontenot, Gerald J — Mamou
Gorenflo, James T (Jt) — Baton Rouge
Graves, Dan — Shreveport
Johnson, Gordon A. — Choudrant
Ki, Shiva — Baton Rouge
Laurent, Kermit — LaPlace
Leonard, Randy Joe — Sarepta
Mitchell, Max Dean And Ben — Leesville
Phillips, Dennis — Independence
Potier, Timothy F — Oberlin
Primos, Terry — Shreveport
Provenzano, Joseph D — Ponchatoula
Randall Jr., James W — Keithville
Randow, Ralph — Pineville
Reggio Jr., Sidney J — Sun
Sanders, Michael M — Ponchatoula
Tilton, John — Iowa
Trisler, Kenneth W — Rayville
Wiggins, Horace — Mansfield

MA

Banaitis, Romas — Medway
Cooper, Paul — Woburn
Dailey, G E — Seekonk
Dugdale, Daniel J. — Walpole
Entin, Robert — Boston
Gaudette, Linden L — Wilbraham
Gedraitis, Charles J — Holden
Grossman, Stewart — Clinton
Hinman, Theodore — Greenfield
Jarvis, Paul M — Cambridge
Khalsa, Jot Singh — Millis
Kubasek, John A — Easthampton
Lapen, Charles — W. Brookfield
Little, Larry — Spencer
Martin, Randall J — Bridgewater
Mcluin, Tom — Dracut
Moore, Michael Robert — Lowell
Rebello, Indian George — New Bedford
Reed, Dave — Brimfield
Rizzi, Russell J — Ashfield
Rua, Gary — Fall River
Saviano, James — Douglas
Siska, Jim — Westfield
Smith, J D — Roxbury
Stuart, Mason — Mansfield
Vining, Bill — Methuen

MD

Bagley, R. Keith — White Plains
Barnes, Aubrey G. — Hagerstown
Barnes, Gary L. — New Windsor
Beers, Ray — Monkton
Cohen, N J (Norm) — Baltimore
Dement, Larry — Prince Fredrick
Fuller, Jack A — New Market
Gossman, Scott — Whiteford
Hart, Bill — Pasadena
Hendrickson, E Jay — Frederick
Hendrickson, Shawn — Knoxville
House, Nathan — Lonaconing
Kreh, Lefty — "Cockeysville"
Kretsinger Jr., Philip W — Boonsboro
Mccarley, John — Taneytown
Mcgowan, Frank E — Sykesvile
Merchant, Ted — White Hall
Nicholson, R. Kent — Phoenix
Sentz, Mark C — Taneytown
Smit, Glenn — Aberdeen
Sontheimer, G Douglas — Potomac
Spickler, Gregory Noble — Sharpsburg
St. Clair, Thomas K — Monrovia
Walker, Bill — Stevensville
White, Gene E — Bethesda

ME

Ceprano, Peter J. — Auburn
Coombs Jr., Lamont — Bucksport
Courtois, Bryan — Saco
Fogg, Don — Auburn
Gray, Daniel — Brownville
Hillman, Charles — Friendship
Leavitt Jr., Earl F — E. Boothbay
Oyster, Lowell R — Corinth
Sharrigan, Mudd — Wiscasset

MI

Ackerson, Robin E — Buchanan
Alcorn, Douglas A. — Chesaning
Andrews, Eric — Grand Ledge
Arms, Eric — Tustin
Behnke, William — Kingsley
Booth, Philip W — Ithaca

Buckbee, Donald M — Grayling
Canoy, Andrew B — Hubbard Lake
Carr, Tim — Muskegon
Carroll, Chad — Grant
Casey, Kevin — Hickory Corners
Cashen, Kevin R — Hubbardston
Cook, Mike A — Portland
Cousino, George — Onsted
Cowles, Don — Royal Oak
Dilluvio, Frank J — Prudenville
Ealy, Delbert — Indian River
Erickson, Walter E. — Atlanta
Gordon, Larry B — Farmington Hills
Gottage, Dante — Clinton Twp.
Gottage, Judy — Clinton Twp.
Harm, Paul W — Attica
Harrison, Brian — Cedarville
Hartman, Arlan (Lanny) — Baldwin
Hoffman, Jay — Munising
Hughes, Daryle — Nunica
Krause, Roy W — St. Clair Shores
Lankton, Scott — Ann Arbor
Lark, David — Kingsley
Leach, Mike J — Swartz Creek
Lucie, James R — Fruitport
Mankel, Kenneth — Cannonsburg
Marsh, Jeremy — Ada
Mills, Louis G — Ann Arbor
Morris, Michael S. — Yale
Noren, Douglas E — Springlake
Parker, Robert Nelson — Royal Oak
Repke, Mike — Bay City
Rose Ii, Doun T — Fife Lake
Sakmar, Mike — Howell
Sandberg, Ronald B — Brownstown
Santini, Tom — Chesterfield
Serven, Jim — Fostoria
Tally, Grant — Flat Rock
Van Eizenga, Jerry W — Nunica
Vasquez, Johnny David — Wyandotte
Viste, James — Detroit
Webster, Bill — Three Rivers
Welling, Ronald L — Grand Haven
White, Richard T — Grosse Pointe Farms
Whittaker, Wayne — Metamore
Whitworth, Ken J — Sterling Heights
Wood, Webster — Atlanta
Zowada, Tim — Boyne Falls

MN

Davis, Joel — Albert Lea
Gingrich, Justin — Blue Earth
Hagen, Doc — Pelican Rapids
Hansen, Robert W — Cambridge
Hebeisen, Jeff — Hopkins
Johnson, R B — Clearwater
Knipschield, Terry — Rochester
Maines, Jay — Wyoming
Metsala, Anthony — Princeton
Mickley, Tracy — North Mankato
Rydbom, Jeff — Annandale
Shadley, Eugene W — Bovey
Steffen, Chuck — St. Michael
Voorhies, Les — Faribault

MO

Allred, Elvan — St. Charles
Andrews, Russ — Sugar Creek
Betancourt, Antonio L. — St. Louis
Braschler, Craig W. — Doniphan
Buxton, Bill — Kaiser
Chinnock, Daniel T. — Union
Cover, Raymond A — Festus
Cox, Colin J — Raymore
Davis, W C — El Dorado Springs

Dippold, Al	Perryville
Duncan, Ron	Cairo
Ehrenberger, Daniel Robert	Mexico
Engle, William	Boonville
Hanson Iii, Don L.	Success
Harris, Jeffery A	Chesterfield
Harrison, Jim (Seamus)	St. Louis
Jones, John A	Holden
Kinnikin, Todd	Pacific
Knickmeyer, Hank	Cedar Hill
Knickmeyer, Kurt	Cedar Hill
Martin, Tony	Arcadia
Mason, Bill	Excelsior Springs
Mccrackin, Kevin	House Spings
Mccrackin And Son, V J	House Spings
Miller, Bob	Oakville
Mosier, David	Independence
Mulkey, Gary	Branson
Muller, Jody	Goodson
Newcomb, Corbin	Moberly
Pryor, Stephen L	Boss
Ramsey, Richard A	Neosho
Rardon, A D	Polo
Rardon, Archie F	Polo
Riepe, Richard A	Harrisonville
Robbins, Howard P	Flemington
Royer, Kyle	Mountain View
Scroggs, James A	Warrensburg
Sonntag, Douglas W	Nixa
Steketee, Craig A	Billings
Stewart, Edward L	Mexico
Stormer, Bob	Dixon
Warden, Roy A	Union
Whitesell, J. Dale	Stover
Willis, Bill	Ava

MS

Black, Scott	Picayune
Boleware, David	Carson
Cohea, John M	Nettleton
Davis, Jesse W	Sarah
Evans, Bruce A	Booneville
Flynt, Robert G	Gulfport
Jones, Jack P.	Ripley
Lamey, Robert M	Biloxi
Lebatard, Paul M	Vancleave
May, Charles	Aberdeen
Mayo Jr., Homer	Biloxi
Nichols, Chad	Blue Springs
Phillips, Donavon	Morton
Pickett, Terrell	Lumberton
Roberts, Michael	Clinton
Robinson, Chuck	Picayune
Shiffer, Steve	Leakesville
Skow, H.A. "Tex"	Senatobia
Smith, J.B.	Perkinston
Taylor, Billy	Petal
Vandeventer, Terry L	Terry
Vardaman, Robert	Hattiesburg
Wehner, Rudy	Collins
Wingo, Perry	Gulfport
Winston, David	Starkville

MT

Barnes, Jack	Whitefish
Barnes, Wendell	Clinton
Barth, J.D.	Alberton
Beam, John R.	Kalispell
Beaty, Robert B.	Missoula
Bell, Don	Lincoln
Bizzell, Robert	Butte
Boxer, Bo	Whitefish
Brooks, Steve R	Walkerville
Caffrey, Edward J	Great Falls

Campbell, Doug	McLeod
Carlisle, Jeff	Simms
Christensen, Jon P	Stevensville
Colter, Wade	Colstrip
Conklin, George L	Ft. Benton
Crowder, Robert	Thompson Falls
Curtiss, Steve L	Eureka
Dunkerley, Rick	Lincoln
Eaton, Rick	Broadview
Ellefson, Joel	Manhattan
Fassio, Melvin G	Lolo
Forthofer, Pete	Whitefish
Fritz, Erik L	Forsyth
Gallagher, Barry	Lewistown
Harkins, J A	Conner
Hill, Howard E	Polson
Hintz, Gerald M	Helena
Hulett, Steve	West Yellowstone
Kajin, Al	Forsyth
Kauffman, Dave	Montana City
Kelly, Steven	Bigfork
Luman, James R	Anaconda
Mcguane Iv, Thomas F	Bozeman
Mckee, Neil	Stevensville
Moyer, Russ	Havre
Nedved, Dan	Kalispell
Olson, Joe	Geyser
Parsons, Pete	Helena
Patrick, Willard C	Helena
Peele, Bryan	Thompson Falls
Peterson, Eldon G	Whitefish
Pursley, Aaron	Big Sandy
Rodewald, Gary	Hamilton
Ruana Knife Works,	Bonner
Smith, Josh	Frenchtown
Sweeney, Coltin D	Missoula
Taylor, Shane	Miles City
Thill, Jim	Missoula
Weinand, Gerome M	Missoula
Yashinski, John L	Red Lodge

NC

Baker, Herb	Eden
Barefoot, Joe W.	Wilmington
Best, Ron	Stokes
Bisher, William (Bill)	Denton
Britton, Tim	Bethania
Busfield, John	Roanoke Rapids
Crist, Zoe	Flat Rock
Drew, Gerald	Mill Spring
Edwards, Fain E	Topton
Fox, Paul	Claremont
Gaddy, Gary Lee	Washington
Goode, Brian	Shelby
Greene, Chris	Shelby
Gross, W W	Archdale
Gurganus, Carol	Colerain
Gurganus, Melvin H	Colerain
Guthrie, George B	Bassemer City
Johnson, Tommy	Troy
Laramie, Mark	Raeford
Livingston, Robert C	Murphy
Maynard, William N.	Fayetteville
Mclurkin, Andrew	Raleigh
Mcnabb, Tommy	Bethania
Mcrae, J Michael	Mint Hill
Parrish, Robert	Weaverville
Patrick, Chuck	Brasstown
Patrick, Peggy	Brasstown
Rapp, Steven J	Marshall
Scholl, Tim	Angier
Simmons, H R	Aurora
Sterling, Murray	Mount Airy
Summers, Arthur L	Concord
Sutton, S Russell	New Bern

Vail, Dave	Hampstead
Wagaman, John K	Selma
Walker, Don	Burnsville
Warren, Daniel	Canton
Whitley, L Wayne	Chocowinity
Wiggins, Bill	Canton
Williamson, Tony	Siler City
Wilson, Mike	Hayesville
Winkler, Daniel	Blowing Rock

ND

Kommer, Russ	Fargo
Pitman, David	Williston

NE

Archer, Ray And Terri	Omaha
Hielscher, Guy	Alliance
Jokerst, Charles	Omaha
Marlowe, Charles	Omaha
Moore, Jon P	Aurora
Mosier, Joshua J	Deshler
Schepers, George B	Shelton
Sloan, David	Diller
Suedmeier, Harlan	Nebraska City
Syslo, Chuck	Omaha
Tiensvold, Alan L	Rushville
Tiensvold, Jason	Rushville
Till, Calvin E And Ruth	Chadron

NH

Hill, Steve E	Goshen
Hitchmough, Howard	Peterborough
Hudson, C Robbin	Rummney
Macdonald, John	Raymond
Philippe, D A	Cornish
Saindon, R Bill	Goshen

NJ

Eden, Thomas	Cranbury
Fisher, Lance	Pompton Lakes
Grussenmeyer, Paul G	Cherry Hill
Knowles, Shawn	Great Meadows
Licata, Steven	Boonton
Mcallen Jr., Howard H	So Seaside Park
Polkowski, Al	Chester
Pressburger, Ramon	Howell
Sheets, Steven William	Mendham
Slee, Fred	Morganville
Viele, H J	Westwood
Yeskoo, Richard C	Summit

NM

Black, Tom	Albuquerque
Burnley, Lucas	Albuquerque
Cherry, Frank J	Albuquerque
Cordova, Joseph G	Peralta
Cumming, Bob	Cedar Crest
Digangi, Joseph M	Santa Cruz
Duran, Jerry T	Albuquerque
Dyess, Eddie	Roswell
Fisher, Jay	Clovis
Garner, George	Albuquerque
Goode, Bear	Navajo Dam
Gunter, Brad	Tijeras
Hartman, Tim	Albuquerque
Hethcoat, Don	Clovis
Hume, Don	Albuquerque
Kimberley, Richard L.	Santa Fe
Leu, Pohan	Rio Rancho
Lewis, Tom R	Carlsbad
Lynn, Arthur	Galisteo
Macdonald, David	Los Lunas

Mallett, J.P.	Santa Fe
Mcdonald, Robin J	Albuquerque
Meshejian, Mardi	Santa Fe
Pollock, Wallace J	Reserve
Reid, Jim	Albuquerque
Rogers, Richard	Magdalena
Schaller, Anthony Brett	Albuquerque
Stalcup, Eddie	Gallup
Stetter, J. C.	Roswell
Terzuola, Robert	Albuquerque
Trujillo, Albert M B	Bosque Farms
Walker, Michael L	Pueblo Sur Taos
Wescott, Cody	Las Cruces

NV

Barnett, Van	Reno
Beasley, Geneo	Wadsworth
Bingenheimer, Bruce	Spring Creek
Cameron, Ron G	Logandale
Dellana,	Reno
George, Tom	Henderson
Hrisoulas, Jim	Henderson
Kreibich, Donald L.	Reno
Nishiuchi, Melvin S	Las Vegas
Thomas, Devin	Panaca
Tracy, Bud	Reno
Washburn, Arthur D	Pioche

NY

Baker, Wild Bill	Boiceville
Castellucio, Rich	Amsterdam
Cute, Thomas	Cortland
Davis, Barry L	Castleton
Farr, Dan	Rochester
Faust, Dick	Rochester
Hobart, Gene	Windsor
Johnson, Mike	Orient
Johnston, Dr. Robt	Rochester
Levin, Jack	Brooklyn
Loos, Henry C	New Hyde Park
Ludwig, Richard O	Maspeth
Lupole, Jamie G	Kirkwood
Manaro, Sal	Holbrook
Maragni, Dan	Georgetown
Mccornock, Craig	Willow
Meerdink, Kurt	Barryville
Page, Reginald	Groveland
Phillips, Scott C	Gouverneur
Rachlin, Leslie S	Elmira
Rappazzo, Richard	Cohoes
Rotella, Richard A	Niagara Falls
Scheid, Maggie	Rochester
Schippnick, Jim	Sanborn
Serafen, Steven E	New Berlin
Skiff, Steven	Broadalbin
Smith, Lenard C	Valley Cottage
Smith, Raymond L	Erin
Summers, Dan	Whitney Pt.
Szilaski, Joseph	Pine Plains
Turner, Kevin	Montrose

OH

Bailey, Ryan	Galena
Bendik, John	Olmsted Falls
Busse, Jerry	Wauseon
Collins, Lynn M	Elyria
Coppins, Daniel	Cambridge
Cottrill, James I	Columbus
Downing, Tom	Cuyahoga Falls
Downs, James F	Powell
Etzler, John	Grafton
Foster, R L (Bob)	Mansfield
Francis, John D	Ft. Loramie

Franklin, Mike	Aberdeen
Geisler, Gary R	Clarksville
Gittinger, Raymond	Tiffin
Glover, Ron	Mason
Greiner, Richard	Green Springs
Hinderer, Rick	Shreve
Hudson, Anthony B	Amanda
Humphrey, Lon	Newark
Imboden Ii, Howard L.	Dayton
Johnson, Wm. C. "Bill"	Enon
Jones, Roger Mudbone	Waverly
Kiefer, Tony	Pataskala
Longworth, Dave	Neville
Loro, Gene	Crooksville
Maienknecht, Stanley	Sardis
Mcdonald, Rich	Columbiana
Mcgroder, Patrick J	Madison
Mercer, Mike	Lebanon
Messer, David T	Dayton
Morgan, Tom	Beloit
Munjas, Bob	Waterford
O'Machearley, Michael	Wilmington
Panak, Paul S	Andover
Potter, Billy	Dublin
Ralph, Darrel	Galena
Rose, Derek W	Gallipolis
Rowe, Fred	Amesville
Salley, John D	Tipp City
Schuchmann, Rick	Cincinnati
Shinosky, Andy	Canfield
Shoemaker, Carroll	Northup
Shoemaker, Scott	Miamisburg
Spinale, Richard	Lorain
Stoddart, W B Bill	Fairfield
Strong, Scott	Beavercreek
Summers, Dennis K	Springfield
Thomas, Kim	Seville
Thourot, Michael W	Napoleon
Tindera, George	Brunswick
Trout, George H.	Cuba
Votaw, David P	Pioneer
Ward, J J	Waverly
Worley, Joel A.	Maplewood
Wright, L T	Steubenville
Yurco, Mike	Canfield
Stidham, Daniel	Gallipolis

OK

Baker, Ray	Sapulpa
Burke, Dan	Edmond
Carrillo, Dwaine	Moore
Crenshaw, Al	Eufaula
Damasteel Stainless Damascus,	Norman
Darby, David T	Cookson
Dill, Dave	Bethany
Duff, Bill	Poteau
Gepner, Don	Norman
Giraffebone Inc.,	Norman
Heimdale, J E	Tulsa
Johns, Rob	Enid
Kennedy Jr., Bill	Yukon
Kirk, Ray	Tahlequah
Lairson Sr., Jerry	Ringold
Martin	
Martin, John Alexander	Okmulgee
Mcclure, Jerry	Norman
Menefee, Ricky Bob	Blawchard
Miller, Michael E	Chandler
Parsons, Larry	Mustang
Spivey, Jefferson	Yukon
Stanford, Perry	Broken Arrow
Tomberlin, Brion R	Norman
Williams, Michael	Broken Bow
Wingo, Gary	Ramona

OR

Bell, Michael	Coquille
Bochman, Bruce	Grants Pass
Brandt, Martin W	Springfield
Buchanan, Thad	Prineville
Buchman, Bill	Bend
Buchner, Bill	Idleyld Park
Busch, Steve	Oakland
Carter, Murray M	Hillsboro
Clark, Nate	Yoncalla
Coon, Raymond C	Gresham
Crowner, Jeff	Cottage Grove
Davis, Terry	Sumpter
Dowell, T M	Bend
Eirich, William	Bend
Frank, Heinrich H	Dallas
Gamble, Frank	Salem
Goddard, Wayne	Eugene
Harsey, William H	Creswell
Hilker, Thomas N	Williams
Horn, Jess	Eugene
House, Cameron	Salem
Kelley, Gary	Aloha
Lake, Ron	Eugene
Little, Gary M	Broadbent
Magruder, Jason	Talent
Martin, Gene	Williams
Martin, Walter E	Williams
Ochs, Eric	Sherwood
Olson, Darrold E	Springfield
Pruyn, Peter	Grants Pass
Richard, Raymond	Gresham
Richards, Chuck	Salem
Rider, David M	Eugene
Sarganis, Paul	Jacksonville
Scarrow, Wil	Gold Hill
Schoeningh, Mike	North Powder
Schrader, Robert	Bend
Sevey Custom Knife,	Gold Beach
Sheehy, Thomas J	Portland
Shoger, Mark O	Beaverton
Sibert, Shane	Gladstone
Smith, Rick	Rogue River
Thompson, Leon	Gaston
Thompson, Tommy	Portland
Turner, Mike	Williams
Vallotton, Butch And Arey	Oakland
Vallotton, Rainy D	Umpqua
Vallotton, Shawn	Oakland
Vallotton, Thomas	Oakland
Ward, Ken	Grants Pass

PA

Anderson, Gary D	Spring Grove
Anderson, Tom	Manchester
Appleby, Robert	Shickshinny
Besedick, Frank E	Monongahela
Candrella, Joe	Warminster
Clark, D E (Lucky)	Johnstown
Corkum, Steve	Littlestown
Darby, Rick	Levittown
Derespina, Richard	Willow Grove
Evans, Ronald B	Middleton
Frey Jr., W Frederick	Milton
Godlesky, Bruce F.	Apollo
Goldberg, David	Ft Washington
Gottschalk, Gregory J	Carnegie
Harner, Lloyd R. "Butch"	Hanover
Heinz, John	Upper Black Eddy
Hudson, Rob	Northumberland
Johnson, John R	New Buffalo
Jones, Curtis J	Washington
Malloy, Joe	Freeland
Marlowe, Donald	Dover

Mensch, Larry C — Milton
Miller, Rick — Rockwood
Moore, Ted — Elizabethtown
Morett, Donald — Lancaster
Nealy, Bud — Stroudsburg
Neilson, J — Wyalusing
Ogden, Bill — Avis
Ortega, Ben M — Wyoming
Parker, J E — Clarion
Root, Gary — Erie
Rose, Bob — Wagontown
Rupert, Bob — Clinton
Sass, Gary N — Sharpsville
Scimio, Bill — Spruce Creek
Sinclair, J E — Pittsburgh
Smith, Richard J. — Milford
Steigerwalt, Ken — Orangeville
Stroyan, Eric — Dalton
Takach, Andrew — Elizabeth
Valois, A. Daniel — Lehighton
Vaughan, Ian — Manheim
Whittaker, Robert E — Mill Creek
Wilson, Jon J — Johnstown

RI

Bardsley, Norman P. — Pawtucket
Dickison, Scott S — Portsmouth
Jacques, Alex — Wakefield
Mchenry, William James — Wyoming
Olszewski, Stephen — Coventry
Williams, Jason L — Wyoming
Wright, Richard S — Carolina

SC

Beatty, Gordon H. — Seneca
Branton, Robert — Awendaw
Brend, Walter — Ridge Springs
Cannady, Daniel L — Allendale
Cox, Sam — Gaffney
Denning, Geno — Gaston
Fecas, Stephen J — Anderson
Frazier, Jim — Wagener
Gainey, Hal — Greenwood
George, Harry — Aiken
Gregory, Michael — Belton
Hendrix, Jerry — Clinton
Hendrix, Wayne — Allendale
Hucks, Jerry — Moncks Corner
Kay, J Wallace — Liberty
Knight, Jason — Harleyville
Kreger, Thomas — Lugoff
Langley, Gene H — Florence
Lutz, Greg — Greenwood
Manley, David W — Central
Miles Jr., C R "Iron Doctor" — Lugoff
Montjoy, Claude — Clinton
Odom Jr., Victor L. — North
Page, Larry — Aiken
Parler, Thomas O — Charleston
Peagler, Russ — Moncks Corner
Perry, Johnny — Inman
Sears, Mick — Kershaw
Smith, Ralph L — Taylors
Thomas, Rocky — Moncks Corner
Tyser, Ross — Spartanburg

SD

Boley, Jamie — Parker
Boysen, Raymond A — Rapid Ciy
Ferrier, Gregory K — Rapid City
Miller, Skip — Keystone
Thomsen, Loyd W — Oelrichs

TN

Accawi, Fuad — Clinton
Adams, Jim — Cordova
Bailey, Joseph D. — Nashville
Blanchard, G R (Gary) — Dandridge
Breed, Kim — Clarksville
Byrd, Wesley L — Evensville
Canter, Ronald E — Jackson
Casteel, Dianna — Monteagle
Casteel, Douglas — Monteagle
Claiborne, Ron — Knox
Clay, Wayne — Pelham
Conley, Bob — Jonesboro
Coogan, Robert — Smithville
Corby, Harold — Johnson City
Ewing, John H — Clinton
Harley, Larry W — Bristol
Harley, Richard — Bristol
Heflin, Christopher M — Nashville
Hughes, Dan — Spencer
Hurst, Jeff — Rutledge
Hutcheson, John — Chattanooga
Johnson, David A — Pleasant Shade
Johnson, Ryan M — Signal Mountain
Kemp, Lawrence — Ooltewah
Largin, Ken — Sevierville
Levine, Bob — Tullahoma
Marshall, Stephen R — Mt. Juliet
Mccarty, Harry — Blaine
Mcdonald, W J "Jerry" — Germantown
Moulton, Dusty — Loudon
Raley, R. Wayne — Collierville
Sampson, Lynn — Jonesborough
Smith, Newman L. — Gatlinburg
Taylor, C Gray — Fall Branch
Taylor, David — Rogersville
Vanderford, Carl G — Columbia
Ward, W C — Clinton
Wheeler, Gary — Clarksville
Williams Jr., Richard — Morristown

TX

Adams, William D — Burton
Alexander, Eugene — Ganado
Allen, Mike "Whiskers" — Malakoff
Appleton, Ron — Bluff Dale
Ashby, Douglas — Dallas
Barnes, Jim — Christoval
Barnes, Marlen R. — Atlanta
Barr, Judson C. — Irving
Batts, Keith — Hooks
Blackwell, Zane — Eden
Blum, Kenneth — Brenham
Bratcher, Brett — Plantersville
Broadwell, David — Wichita Falls
Brooks, Michael — Lubbock
Budell, Michael — Brenham
Bullard, Randall — Canyon
Burden, James — Burkburnett
Callahan, F Terry — Boerne
Carey, Peter — Lago Vista
Carpenter, Ronald W — Jasper
Carter, Fred — Wichita Falls
Champion, Robert — Amarillo
Chase, John E — Aledo
Chew, Larry — Granbury
Churchman, T W (Tim) — Bandera
Cole, James M — Bartonville
Connor, John W — Odessa
Connor, Michael — Winters
Costa, Scott — Spicewood
Crain, Jack W — Granbury
Darcey, Chester L — College Station
Davidson, Larry — New Braunfels
Davis, Vernon M — Waco
Dean, Harvey J — Rockdale
Debaud, Jake — Dallas

Delong, Dick — Centerville
Dietz, Howard — New Braunfels
Dominy, Chuck — Colleyville
Dyer, David — Granbury
Eldridge, Allan — Ft. Worth
Elishewitz, Allen — New Braunfels
Epting, Richard — College Station
Eriksen, James Thorlief — Garland
Evans, Carlton — Gainesville
Fant Jr., George — Atlanta
Ferguson, Jim — San Angelo
Fortune Products, Inc., — Marble Falls
Foster, Al — Magnolia
Foster, Norvell C — Marion
Fowler, Jerry — Hutto
Fritz, Jesse — Slaton
Fuller, Bruce A — Baytown
Gann, Tommy — Canton
Garner, Larry W — Tyler
George, Les — Corpus Christi
Graham, Gordon — New Boston
Green, Bill — Sachse
Griffin, Rendon And Mark — Houston
Grimes, Mark — Bedford
Guinn, Terry — Eastland
Halfrich, Jerry — San Marcos
Hamlet Jr., Johnny — Clute
Hand, Bill — Spearman
Hawkins, Buddy — Texarkana
Hayes, Scotty — Tesarkana
Haynes, Jerry — Gunter
Hays, Mark — Austin
Hemperley, Glen — Willis
Hicks, Gary — Tuscola
Horrigan, John — Burnet
Howell, Jason G — Lake Jackson
Hudson, Robert — Humble
Hughes, Lawrence — Plainview
Jackson, Charlton R — San Antonio
Jaksik Jr., Michael — Fredericksburg
Johnson, Gorden W — Houston
Johnson, Ruffin — Houston
Keller, Bill — San Antonio
Kern, R W — San Antonio
Kious, Joe — Kerrville
Knipstein, R C (Joe) — Arlington
Ladd, Jim S — Deer Park
Ladd, Jimmie Lee — Deer Park
Lambert, Jarrell D — Granado
Laplante, Brett — McKinney
Lay, L J — Burkburnett
Lemcke, Jim L — Houston
Lennon, Dale — Alba
Lister Jr., Weldon E — Boerne
Lively, Tim And Marian — Marble Falls
Love, Ed — San Antonio
Lovett, Michael — Mound
Luchak, Bob — Channelview
Luckett, Bill — Weatherford
Martin, Michael W — Beckville
Mcconnell Jr., Loyd A — Marble Falls
Mellard, J R — Houston
Merz Iii, Robert L — Katy
Miller, R D — Dallas
Minchew, Ryan — Pampa
Mitchell, Wm Dean — Warren
Moen, Jerry — Dallas
Moore, James B — Ft. Stockton
Neely, Greg — Bellaire
Nolen, Steve — Pottsboro
Oates, Lee — La Porte
O'Brien, Mike J. — San Antonio
Odgen, Randy W — Houston
Ogletree Jr., Ben R — Livingston
Osborne, Warren — Waxahachie
Ott, Ted — Elgin
Overeynder, T R — Arlington
Ownby, John C — Murphy

Pardue, Joe	Spurger
Patterson, Pat	Barksdale
Pierce, Randall	Arlington
Polzien, Don	Lubbock
Powell, James	Texarkana
Powers, Walter R.	Lolita
Pugh, Jim	Azle
Ray, Alan W	Lovelady
Richardson Jr., Percy	Navasota
Roberts, Jack	Houston
Robinson, Charles (Dickie)	Vega
Rucker, Thomas	Nacogdoches
Ruple, William H	Pleasanton
Ruth, Michael G	Texarkana
Ruth, Jr., Michael	Texarkana
Scott, Al	Harper
Self, Ernie	Dripping Springs
Shipley, Steven A	Richardson
Sims, Bob	Meridian
Sloan, Shane	Newcastle
Smart, Steve	McKinney
Smith, Jerry	Moody
Snody, Mike	Fredericksburg
Stokes, Ed	Hockley
Stone, Jerry	Lytle
Stout, Johnny	New Braunfels
Theis, Terry	Harper
Thuesen, Ed	Damon
Truncali, Pete	Garland
Turcotte, Larry	Pampa
Van Reenen, Ian	Amarillo
Vickers, David	Montgomery
Ware, Tommy	Onalaska
Watson, Daniel	Driftwood
Watts, Johnathan	Gatesville
Watts, Wally	Gatesville
White, Dale	Sweetwater
Whitley, Weldon G	Odessa
Wilcher, Wendell L	Palestine
Wilkins, Mitchell	Montgomery
Wilson, Curtis M	Burleson
Winn, Marvin	Frisco
Wolf Jr., William Lynn	Lagrange
Yeates, Joe A	Spring
Zboril, Terry	Caldwell
Zermeno, William D.	Houston

UT

Allred, Bruce F	Layton
Black, Earl	Salt Lake City
Ence, Jim	Richfield
Ennis, Ray	Ogden
Erickson, L.M.	Ogden
Hunter, Hyrum	Aurora
Johnson, Steven R	Manti
Lang, David	Kearns
Maxfield, Lynn	Layton
Nielson, Jeff V	Monroe
Nunn, Gregory	Castle Valley
Palmer, Taylor	Blanding
Peterson, Chris	Salina
Ricks, Kurt J.	Trenton
Strickland, Dale	Monroe
Velarde, Ricardo	Park City
Washburn Jr., Robert Lee	St George
Winn, Travis A.	Salt Lake City
Jenkins, Mitch	Manti
Johnson, Jerry	Spring City

VA

Apelt, Stacy E	Norfolk
Arbuckle, James M	Yorktown
Ball, Butch	Floyd
Ballew, Dale	Bowling Green
Batley, Mark S.	Wake
Batson, Richard G.	Rixeyville
Beverly Ii, Larry H	Spotsylvania

Catoe, David R	Norfolk
Chamberlain, Charles R	Barren Springs
Davidson, Edmund	Goshen
Douglas, John J	Lynch Station
Eaton, Frank L Jr	Stafford
Foster, Burt	Bristol
Frazier, Ron	Powhatan
Goodpasture, Tom	Ashland
Harris, Cass	Bluemont
Hedrick, Don	Newport News
Hendricks, Samuel J	Maurertown
Herb, Martin	Richmond
Holloway, Paul	Norfolk
Jones, Barry M And Phillip G	Danville
Jones, Enoch	Warrenton
Kearney, Jarod	Swoope
Martin, Herb	Richmond
Mccoun, Mark	DeWitt
Metheny, H A "Whitey"	Spotsylvania
Mills, Michael	Colonial Beach
Murski, Ray	Reston
Norfleet, Ross W	Providence Forge
Parks, Blane C	Woodbridge
Pawlowski, John R	Newport News
Quattlebaum, Craig	Suffolk
Schlueter, David	Madison Heights
Tomes, P J	Shipman
Vanhoy, Ed And Tanya	Abingdon
Vestal, Charles	Abingdon
Ward, Ron	Rose Hill
Wood, Larry B	Jamesville

VT

Bensinger, J. W.	Marshfield
Haggerty, George S	Jacksonville
Kelso, Jim	Worcester
Wulf, Derrick	Essex

WA

Amoureux, A W	Northport
Begg, Todd M.	Spanaway
Ber, Dave	San Juan Island
Berglin, Bruce D	Mount Vernon
Boguszewski, Phil	Lakewood
Bromley, Peter	Spokane
Brothers, Robert L	Colville
Brown, Dennis G	Shoreline
Brunckhorst, Lyle	Bothell
Bump, Bruce D.	Walla Walla
Butler, John R	Shoreline
Campbell, Dick	Colville
Chamberlain, Jon A	E. Wenatchee
Conti, Jeffrey D	Bonney Lake
Conway, John	Kirkland
Crowthers, Mark F	Rolling Bay
D'Angelo, Laurence	Vancouver
Davis, John	Selah
Diaz, Jose	Ellensburg
Diskin, Matt	Freeland
Ferry, Tom	Auburn
Gray, Bob	Spokane
Greenfield, G O	Everett
Hansen, Lonnie	Spanaway
House, Gary	Ephrata
Hurst, Cole	E. Wenatchee
Keyes, Geoff P.	Duvall
Lisch, David K	Seattle
Norton, Don	Port Townsend
O'Malley, Daniel	Seattle
Padilla, Gary	Bellingham
Rader, Michael	Wilkeson
Roeder, David	Kennewick
Rogers, Ray	Wauconda
Sanford, Dick	Montesano
Schempp, Ed	Ephrata

Schempp, Martin	Ephrata
Stegner, Wilbur G	Rochester
Sterling, Thomas J	Coupeville
Straub, Salem F.	Tonasket
Swyhart, Art	Klickitat
Wright, Kevin	Quilcene

WI

Atkins, Jim	Frederic
Boyes, Tom	Addison
Brandsey, Edward P	Janesville
Bruner Jr., Fred Bruner Blades	Fall Creek
Carr, Joseph E.	Menomonee Falls
Coats, Ken	Stevens Point
Delarosa, Jim	Janesville
Haines, Jeff Haines Custom Knives Wauzeka	
Hembrook, Ron	Neosho
Johnson, Richard	Germantown
Kanter, Michael	New Berlin
Kohls, Jerry	Princeton
Kolitz, Robert	Beaver Dam
Lary, Ed	Mosinee
Lerch, Matthew	Sussex
Maestri, Peter A	Spring Green
Martin, Peter	Waterford
Mikolajczyk, Glen	Caledonia
Millard, Fred G	Richland Center
Nelson, Ken	Pittsville
Niemuth, Troy	Sheboygan
Ponzio, Doug	Beloit
Rabuck, Jason	Springbrook
Revishvili, Zaza	Madison
Ricke, Dave	West Bend
Rochford, Michael R	Dresser
Schrap, Robert G	Wauwatosa
Steinbrecher, Mark W	Pleasant Prairie
Wattelet, Michael A	Minocqua

WV

Derr, Herbert	St. Albans
Drost, Jason D	French Creek
Drost, Michael B	French Creek
Elliott, Jerry	Charleston
Jeffries, Robert W	Red House
Liegey, Kenneth R	Millwood
Maynard, Larry Joe	Crab Orchard
Morris, Eric	Beckley
Pickens, Selbert	Dunbar
Reynolds, Dave	Harrisville
Shaver Ii, James R	Parkersburg
Small, Ed	Keyser
Tokar, Daniel	Shepherdstown
Wilson, Rw	Weirton
Wyatt, William R	Rainelle

WY

Alexander, Darrel	Ten Sleep
Ankrom, W.E.	Cody
Banks, David L.	Riverton
Barry, Scott	Laramie
Bartlow, John	Sheridan
Bennett, Brett C	Cheyenne
Draper, Audra	Riverton
Draper, Mike	Riverton
Fowler, Ed A.	Riverton
Friedly, Dennis E	Cody
Kilby, Keith	Cody
Rexroat, Kirk	Wright
Reynolds, John C	Gillette
Rodebaugh, James L	Carpenter
Ross, Stephen	Evanston
Spragg, Wayne E	Lovell
Whipple, Wesley A	Thermopolis

ARGENTINA

Ayarragaray, Cristian L.
(3100) Parana-Entre Rios
Bertolami, Juan Carlos   Neuquen
Gibert, Pedro
Kehiayan, Alfredo
CP B1623GXU Buenos Aires
Rho, Nestor Lorenzo   Buenos Aires
Santiago, Abud   Buenos Aires 1416

AUSTRALIA

Barnett, Bruce   Western Australia
Bennett, Peter   Engadine N.S.W. 2233
Brodziak, David
Albany, Western Australia
Crawley, Bruce R   Croydon 3136 Victoria
Cross, Robert   Tamworth 2340, NSW
Del Raso, Peter
Mt. Waverly, Victoria, 3149
Edmonds, Warrick   Adelaide Hills
Gerner, Thomas   Western Australia
Giljevic, Branko   N.S.W.
Green, William (Bill)   View Bank Vic.
Harvey, Max
Perth 6155, Western Australia
Hedges, Dee   Bedfordale
Husiak, Myron   Victoria
Jones, John   Gympie, Queensland 4570
K B S, Knives   Vic 3450
Maisey, Alan   Vincentia 2540, NSW
Mcintyre, Shawn   Hawthorn East Victoria
Phillips, Alistair   ACT, 2914
Spencer, KeithChidlow Western Australia
Tasman, Kerley   Western Australia
Zemitis, Joe   2285 Newcastle

BELGIUM

Dox, Jan   B 2900 Schoten
Monteiro, Victor 1360 Maleves Ste Marie

BRAZIL

Bodolay, Antal
Belo Horizonte MG-31730-700
Bossaerts, Carl
14051-110, Ribeirao Preto, S.P.
Campos, Ivan   Tatui, SP
Dorneles, Luciano Oliverira
Nova Petropolis, RS
Gaeta, Angelo   SP-17201-310
Gaeta, Roberto   Sao Paulo
Garcia, Mario Eiras
Sao Paulo SP-05516-070
Ikoma, Flavio   Prudonte SP19031-220
Lala, Paulo Ricardo P And
Lala, Roberto P.   SP-19031-260
Neto Jr., Nelson And De Carvalho,
Henrique M.   SP-12900-000
Paulo, Fernandes R   Sao Paulo
Petean, Francisco And Mauricio
SP-16200-000
Ricardo Romano, Bernardes   Itajuba MG
Sfreddo, Rodrigo Menezes
cep g5 150-000
Vilar, Ricardo Augusto Ferreira Mairipora
Sao Paulo
Villa, Luiz   Sao Paulo, SP-04537-081
Villar, Ricardo   S.P. 07600-000
Zakharov, Gladiston   Jacaret SP

CANADA

Arnold, Joe   London, Ont.
Beauchamp, Gaetan   Stoneham, PQ
Beets, Marty   Williams Lake, BC
Bell, Donald   Bedford, Nova Scotia
Berg, Lothar   Kitchener ON
Beshara, Brent (Besh)   NL
Boos, Ralph   Edmonton, Alberta
Bourbeau, Jean Yves Ile Perrot, Quebec
Bradford, Garrick   Kitchener ON
Dallyn, Kelly   Calgary, AB
Debraga, Jose C Trois Rivieres, Quebec
Debraga, Jovan   Quebec
Deringer, Christoph Cookshire, Quebec
Desaulniers, Alain   Cookshire, Quebec
Diotte, Jeff   LaSalle Ontario
Doiron, Donald   Messines, PQ
Doucette, R   Brantford, Ont.
Doussot, Laurent   St. Bruno, Quebec
Downie, James T   Ontario
Frigault, Rick   Niagara Falls, Ont.
Ganshorn, Cal   Regina, Saskatchewan
Garvock, Mark W   Balderson, Ont.
Gilbert, Chantal   Quebec City Quebec
Haslinger, Thomas   Calgary, AB
Hayes, Wally   Essex, Ont.
Hindmarch, Garth   Carlyle SK S0C 0R0
Hofer, Louis   Rose Prairie, B.C.
Jobin, Jacques   Levis Quebec
Kaczor, Tom   Upper London, Ont.
Lambert, Kirby   Regina Saskatchewan
S4N X3
Langley, Mick   Qualicum Beach, B.C.
Lay, R J (Bob)   Logan Lake, B.C.
Leber, Heinz   Hudson's Hope, B.C.
Lightfoot, Greg   Kitscoty, AB
Linklater, Steve   Aurora, Ont.
Loerchner, Wolfgang   Bayfield, Ont.
Lyttle, Brian   High River, AB
Maneker, Kenneth   Galiano Island, B.C.
Marchand, Rick   Wheatley, Ont.
Marzitelli, Peter   Langley, B.C.
Massey, Al   Mount Uniacke, Nova Scotia
Mckenzie, David Brian Campbell River B
Miville-Deschenes, Alain   Quebec
Nease, William   LaSalle, Ont.
O'Hare, Sean   Grand Manan, NB
Olson, Rod   High River, AB
Painter, Tony   Whitehorse Yukon
Patrick, Bob   S. Surrey, B.C.
Pepiot, Stephan   Winnipeg, Man.
Piesner, Dean   Conestogo, Ont.
Ridley, Rob   Cremona
Roberts, George A   Whitehorse, YT
Ross, Tim   Thunder Bay, Ont.
Schoenfeld, Matthew A
Galiano Island, B.C.
St. Amour, Murray   Pembroke ON
Stancer, Chuck   Calgary, AB
Storch, Ed   Alberta T0B 2W0
Stuart, Steve   Gores Landing, Ont.
Sylvester, David   Compton, Quebec
Tedford, Steven   Bewdley, Ontario
Tighe, Brian   St. Catharines, Ont.
Toner, Roger   Pickering, Ont.
Treml, Glenn   Thunder Bay, Ont.
Vanderkolff, Stephen   Mildmay Ontario
Whitenect, Jody   Nova Scotia
Young, Bud   Port Hardy, BC

DENMARK

Andersen, Henrik Lefolii
3480, Fredensborg
Anso, Jens   116, 8472 Sporup
Dyrnoe, Per   DK 3400 Hilleroed
Henriksen, Hans J   DK 3200 Helsinge
Rafn, Dan C.   8370 Hadsten
Strande, Poul   Dastrup 4130 Viby Sj.
Vensild, Henrik   DK-8963 Auning
Willumsen, Mikkel

FINLAND

Tuominen, Pekka   72930 Tossavanlahti
Vilppola, Markku   Jaanintie 45

FRANCE

Bennica, Charles
34190 Moules et Baucels
Chauzy, Alain   21140 Seur-en-Auxios
Chomilier, Alain And Joris
Doursin, Gerard   Pernes les Fontaines
Graveline, Pascal And Isabelle
29350 Moelan-sur-Mer
Headrick, Gary   Juane Les Pins
Madrulli, Mme Joelle Salon De Provence
Reverdy, Nicole And Pierre
Thevenot, Jean-Paul   Dijon
Viallon, Henri

GERMANY

Balbach, Markus   35789
Weilmunster-Laubuseschbach/Ts.
Becker, Franz   84533, Marktl/Inn
Boehlke, Guenter   56412 Grossholbach
Borger, Wolf   76676 Graben-Neudorf
Dell, Wolfgang   D-73277 Owen-Teck
Drumm, Armin   D-89160 Dornstadt
Faust, Joachim   95497 Goldkronach
Fruhmann, Ludwig   84489 Burghausen
Greiss, Jockl   D 77773 Schenkenzell
Hehn, Richard Karl   55444 Dorrebach
Herbst, Peter   91207 Lauf a.d. Pegn.
Joehnk, Bernd   24148 Kiel
Kressler, D F   D-28832 Achim
Neuhaeusler, Erwin   86179 Augsburg
Rankl, Christian   81476 Munchen
Rinkes, Siegfried   Markterlbach
Selzam, Frank   Bad Koenigshofen
Steinau, Jurgen   Berlin 0-1162
Tritz, Jean Jose   20255 Hamburg
Wirtz, Achim   D-52146
Zirbes, Richard   D-54526 Niederkail

GREECE

Filippou, Ioannis-Minas   Athens 17122

HOLLAND

Van De Manakker, Thijs   5759 px
Helenaveen

ISRAEL

Shadmot, Boaz   Arava

ITALY

Albericci, Emilio   24100, Bergamo
Ameri, Mauro   16010 Genova
Ballestra, Santino   18039 Ventimiglia (IM)
Bertuzzi, Ettore 24068 Seriate (Bergamo)
Bonassi, Franco   Pordenone 33170
Fogarizzu, Boiteddu   07016 Pattada
Garau, Marcello   Oristano
Giagu, Salvatore And Deroma Maria
     Rosaria   07016 Pattada (SS)
Ramondetti, Sergio   12013 CHIUSA DI
     PESIO (CN)
Riboni, Claudio   Truccazzano (MI)
Scordia, Paolo   Roma
Simonella, Gianluigi   33085 Maniago
Toich, Nevio   Vincenza
Tschager, Reinhard   I-39100 Bolzano

JAPAN

Aida, Yoshihito
               Itabashi-ku, Tokyo 175-0094
Ebisu, Hidesaku   Hiroshima City
Fujikawa, Shun   Osaka 597 0062
Fukuta, Tak   Seki-City, Gifu-Pref
Hara, Kouji   Gifu-Pref. 501-3922
Hirayama, Harumi
               Saitama Pref. 335-0001
Hiroto, Fujihara   Hiroshima
Isao, Ohbuchi   Fukuoka
Ishihara, Hank   Chiba Pref.
Kagawa, Koichi   Kanagawa
Kanda, Michio   Yamaguchi 7460033
Kanki, Iwao   Hyogo
Kansei, Matsuno   Gitu-city
Kato, Shinichi   Moriyama-ku Nagoya
Katsumaro, Shishido   Hiroshima
Kawasaki, Akihisa   Kobe
Keisuke, Gotoh   Ohita
Koyama, Captain Bunshichi
               Nagoya City 453-0817
Mae, Takao   Toyonaka, Osaka
Makoto, Kunitomo   Hiroshima
Matsuno, Kansei   Gifu-City 501-1168
Matsusaki, Takeshi   Nagasaki
Michinaka, Toshiaki   Tottori 680-0947
Micho, Kanda   Yamaguchi
Ryuichi, Kuki   Saitama
Sakakibara, Masaki   Tokyo 156-0054
Sugihara, Keidoh   Osaka, F596-0042
Sugiyama, Eddy K   Ohita
Takahashi, Masao   Gunma 371 0047
Terauchi, Toshiyuki Fujita-Cho Gobo-Shi
Toshifumi, Kuramoto   Fukuoka
Uchida, Chimata   Kumamoto
Wada, Yasutaka   Nara prefect 631-0044
Waters, Glenn   Hirosaki City 036-8183
Yoshihara, Yoshindo   Tokyo
Yoshikazu, Kamada   Tokushima
Yoshio, Maeda   Okayama

MEXICO

Scheurer, Alfredo E Faes   C.P. 16010
Sunderland, Richard
               Puerto Escondido Oaxaca
Young, Cliff San Miguel De Allende, GTO.

NETHERLANDS

Sprokholt, Rob   Netherlands
Van Den Elsen, Gert   5012 AJ Tilburg
Van Eldik, Frans   3632BT Loenen
Van Rijswijk, Aad   3134 HE Vlaardingen

NEW ZEALAND

Bassett, David J.
               Glendene, Auckland 0645
Gunther, Eddie   2013 Auckland
Knapton, Chris C.   Henderson, Auckland
Pennington, C A
               Kainga Christchurch 8009
Reddiex, Bill   Palmerston North
Ross, D L   Dunedin
Sandow, Brent Edward   Auckland
Sandow, Norman E   Howick, Auckland
Sands, Scott   Christchurch 9
Van Dijk, Richard   Harwood Dunedin

NORWAY

Bache-Wiig, Tom   Eivindvik
Sellevold, Harald   N5835 Bergen
Vistnes, Tor

SPAIN

Cecchini, Gustavo T. Sao Jose Rio Preto

RUSSIA

Kharlamov, Yuri   300007

SLOVAKIA

Albert, Stefan   Filakovo 98604
Bojtos, Arpad   98403 Lucenec
Kovacik, Robert   98401 Lucenec
Laoislav, Santa-Lasky
               Okres Banska Bystrica
Mojzis, Julius
Pulis, Vladimir   96701 Kremnica

SOUTH AFRICA

Arm-Ko Knives,   Marble Ray 4035 KZN
Baartman, George   Limpopo
Bauchop, Robert   Kwazulu-Natal 4278
Beukes, Tinus   Vereeniging 1939
Bezuidenhout, Buzz   Malvern, KZN
Boardman, Guy   New Germany 3619
Brown, Rob E   Port Elizabeth
Burger, Fred   Kwa-Zulu Natal
Burger, Tiaan   Riviera, Pretoria
Dickerson, Gavin   Petit 1512
Fellows, Mike   Mosselbay 6500
Grey, Piet   Naboomspruit 0560
Harvey, Heather   Belfast 1100
Harvey, Kevin   Belfast 1100
Herbst, Gawie   Akasia
Herbst, Thinus   Karenpark 0118, Akasia
Horn, Des
Klaasee, Tinus   George 6530
Kojetin, W   Germiston 1401
Lancaster, C G   Free State
Liebenberg, Andre
               Bordeauxrandburg 2196
Mackrill, Stephen   JHB 2123
Mahomedy, A R   Marble Ray KZN, 4035
Mahomedy, Humayd A.R.   KZN
Naude, Louis   Cape Town
Nelson, Tom   Gauteng
Pienaar, Conrad   Bloemfontein 9300
Prinsloo, Theuns   Bethlehem, 9700
Rietveld, Bertie   Magaliesburg 1791

Russell, Mick   Port Elizabeth 6070
Schoeman, Corrie   Danhof 9310
Steyn, Peter   Freestate
Thorburn, Andre E.   Bela Bela,
     Warmbaths 0480
Van Der Westhuizen, Peter
               Mossel Bay 6500
Van Heerden, Andre Garsfontein, Pretoria
Watson, Peter   La Hoff 2570

SWEDEN

Bergh, Roger   91598 Bygdea
Billgren, Per
Eklund, Maihkel   S-820 41 Farila
Embretsen, Kaj   S-82830 Edsbyn
Hedlund, Anders   Brastad
Hogstrom, Anders T   Johanneshov
Johansson, Anders
               S-772 40 Grangesberg
Lundstrom, Jan-Ake 66010 Dals-Langed
Lundstrom, Torbjorn (Tobbe)
Nilsson, Jonny Walker
               SE-933 33 Arvidsjaur
Nordell, Ingemar   82041 Färila
Persson, Conny   820 50 Loos
Ryberg, Gote   S-562 00 Norrahammar
Styrefors, Mattias
Vogt, Patrik   S-30270 Halmstad

SWITZERLAND

Roulin, Charles   1233 Geneva
Soppera, Arthur   CH-9631 Ulisbach

United Arab Emirates

Kukulka, Wolfgang   Dubai

UNITED KINGDOM

Bailey, I.R.   Colkirk
Barker, Stuart   Oadby, Leicester
Boden, Harry   Derbyshire DE4 2AJ
Farid R, Mehr   Kent
Hague, Geoff   Quarley, SP11 8PX
Harrington, Roger   East Sussex
Heasman, H G   Llandudno, N. Wales
Horne, Grace   Sheffield
Jackson, Jim   High St. Bray
Maxen, Mick   "Hatfield, Herts"
Morris, Darrell Price   Devon
Orford, Ben   Worcestershire
Penfold, Mick Tremar, Cornwall PL14 5SJ
Stainthorp, Guy   Norton Heights
Wardell, Mick   N Devon EX39 3BU
Wise, Donald   East Sussex, TN3 8AL
Wood, Alan   Brampton CA8 7HH

URUGUAY

Gonzalez, Leonardo Williams   CP 20000
Symonds, Alberto E   Montevideo 11300

ZIMBABWE

Burger, Pon   Bulawayo

Not all knifemakers are organization-types, but those listed here are in good standing with these organizations.

the knifemakers' guild

2012 membership

a   Les Adams, Douglas A. Alcorn, Mike "Whiskers" Allen, W. E. Ankrom

b   Robert K. Bagley, Santino e Arlete Ballestra, Norman P. Bardsley, A. T. Barr, James J. Barry, III, John Bartlow, Gene Baskett, Ron Best, Gary Blanchard ,Michael S. Blue, Arpad Bojtos, Philip W. Booth, Tony Bose, Dennis Bradley, Gordon Gayle Bradley, Edward Brandsey, W. Lowell Bray, Jr., George Clint Breshears, Richard E. Browne, Fred Bruner, Jr., John Busfield

c   Harold J. "Kit" Carson, Michael Carter, Chinnock, Howard F. Clark, Wayne Clay, Kenneth R. Coats, Blackie Collins, Bob F. Conley, Gerald Corbit, George Cousino, Colin J. Cox, Pat Crawford

d   Alex K. Daniels, Jack Davenport, Edmund Davidson, John H Davis, William C. Davis, Dan Dennehy, Herbert K. Derr, William J. Dietzel, Frank Dilluvio, Mike Dilluvio, David Dodds, T. M. Dowell, Larry Downing, Tom Downing, James F. Downs, William Duff, Fred Durio

e   Jacob Elenbaas, Jim Elliott, William B. Ellis, James T. Eriksen, Carlton R. Evans

f   Stephen J. Fecas, Lee Ferguson, Linda Ferguson, Michael H. Franklin, John R Fraps, Dennis E. Friedly, Stanley Fujisaka, Bruce A. Fuller, Robert G. Flynt

g   Steve Gatlin, Warren Glover, Stefan Gobec, Richard R. Golden, Gregory J. Gottschalk ,Ernie Grospitch, Kenneth W. Guth

h   Philip (Doc) L. Hagen, Gerald Halfrich, Jim Hammond, Don L Hanson III, Koji Hara, Ralph Dewey Harris, Rade Hawkins, Henry Heitler, Earl Jay Hendrickson, Wayne Hendrix, Wayne G. Hensley, Gil Hibben, R. Hinson, Steven W. Hoel, Kevin Hoffman, Desmond R. Horn, Jerry Hossom, Durvyn Howard, Rob Hudson, Roy Humenick, Joseph Hytovick, Larry Hoststler

i   Billy Mace Imel, Michael Irie

j   James T. Jacks, Brad Johnson, Keith R. Johnson, Ronald B. Johnson, Steven R. Johnson, William "Bill" C. Johnson, Enoch D. Jones, Lonnie L Jones

k   William L. Keeton, Bill Kennedy, Jr., Bill King, Harvey King, J. Kenneth King, Terry Knipschield

l   Kermit Laurent, Paul M LeBetard, Gary E. LeBlanc, Tommy B. Lee, Kevin T. Lesswing, William S. Letcher, William L. Levengood, Yakov Levin, Bob Levine, Steve Linklater, Ken Linton, Wolfgang Loerchner, R. W. Loveless, Schuyler Lovestrand, Don Lozier, Bill Luckett, Gail Lunn, Larry Lunn, Ernest Lyle

m   Stephen Mackrill, Joe Malloy, Tom Maringer, Herbert A. Martin, Charlie B. Mathews, Harry S. Mathews, Jerry McClure, Sandra McClure, Lloyd McConnell, W. J. McDonald, Frank McGowan, Mike Mercer, Ted Merchant, Robert L. Merz, III, Toshiaki Michinaka, James P. Miller, Stephen C. Miller, Dan Mink, Jim Minnick, Jeff Morgan, Riccardo Mainolfi, Jerry Moen

n   Bud Nealy, Corbin Newcomb, Larry Newton, Rick Noland, Ross W Norfleet

o   Clifford W. O'Dell, Charles F. Ochs, III, Ben R. Ogletree, Jr., Warren Osborne, T. R. Overeynder, John E. Owens, Clifford W. O'Dell, Sean O'Hare

p   Larry Page, Cliff Parker, John R. Pawlowski, W. D. Pease, Alfred Pendray, John W. PerMar, Daniel Piergallini, Otakar Pok, Joseph R. Prince, Theunis C. Prinsloo, Jim Pugh, Morris C. Pulliam, Jerry Partridge, Larry Pridgen, Jr.

r   James D. Ragsdale, Steven Rapp, Vernie Reed, John Reynolds, Ron F. Richard, Dave Ricke, Michael Rochford, A. G. Russell, Jason Rabuck

s   Michael A. Sakmar, Hiroyuki Sakurai, Scott W. Sawby, Juergen Schanz, Mike Schirmer, Mark C. Sentz, Yoshinori Seto, Eugene W. Shadley, John I Shore, R. J. Sims, Jim Siska, Steven C. Skiff, Scott Slobodian, Ralph Smith, Marvin Solomon, Arthur Soppera, Jim Sornberger, David Steier, Murray Sterling, Russ Sutton, Charles C. Syslo

t   Robert Terzuola, Leon Thompson, Michael A. Tison, Dan Tompkins, Bobby L. Toole, Reinhard Tschager, Ralph Turnbull

v   Aas van Rijswijk, Donald Vogt

w   George A. Walker, Edward Wallace, Charles B. Ward, Tom Watson, Charles G. Weeber, John S. Weever, Zachary Whitson, Wayne Whittaker, Donnie R. Wicker, RW Wilson, Stan Wilson, Daniel Winkler

y   George L. Young, Mike Yurco

z   Brad Zinker, Michael Zscherny

abs mastersmith listing

a David Anders, Gary D. Anderson, E. R. Russ Andrews II

b Gary Barnes, Aubrey G. Barnes Sr., James L. Batson, Jimmie H. Buckner, Bruce D. Bump, Bill Burke, Bill Buxton

c Ed Caffrey, Murray M. Carter, Kevin R. Cashen, Hsiang Lin (Jimmy) Chin, Jon Christensen, Howard F. Clark, Wade Colter, Michael Connor, James R. Cook, Joseph G. Cordova, Jim Crowell, Steve Culver

d Sava Damlovac, Harvey J. Dean, Christoph Deringer, Bill Dietzel, Audra L. Draper, Rick Dunkerley, Steve Dunn, Kenneth Durham

e Dave Ellis

f Robert Thomas Ferry III, William Fiorini, Jerry Fisk, John S. Fitch, Joe Flournoy, Don Fogg, Burt Foster, Ronnie E. Foster, Ed Fowler, Larry D. Fuegen, Bruce A. Fuller, Jack A. Fuller

g Bert Gaston, Thomas Gerner, Wayne Goddard, Greg Gottschalk

h Tim Hancock, Don .L Hanson III, Heather Harvey, Kevin Harvey, Wally Hayes, E. Jay Hendrickson, Don Hethcoat, John Horrigan, Rob Hudson

j Jim L. Jackson

k Joseph F. Keeslar, Keith Kilby, Ray Kirk, Hank Knickmeyer, Jason Knight, Bob Kramer, Phil Kretsinger

l Jerry Lairson Sr., Mick Langley

m J. Chris Marks, John Alexander Martin, Roger D. Massey, Victor J. McCrackin, Shawn McIntyre, Hanford J. Miller, Wm Dean Mitchell

n Greg Neely, J. Neilson, Ron Newton, Douglas E. Noren

o Charles F. Ochs III

p Alfred Pendray, John L. Perry, Dan Petersen Ph.D., Timothy Potier

r Michael Rader, J. W. Randall, Kirk Rexroat, Linden W. Rhea, Dickie Robinson, James L. Rodebaugh, Raymond B. Rybar Jr.

s James P. Saviano, Stephen C. Schwarzer, Mark C. Sentz, Rodrigo Menezes Sfreddo, Josh Smith, Raymond L. Smith, Bill Sowell, H. Red St. Cyr, Charles Stout,

t Shane Taylor, Jean-paul Thevenot, Jason Tiensvold, Brion Tomberlin, P. J. Tomes, Henry Torres

v Michael V. Vagnino Jr., Terry L. Vandeventer

w James L. Walker, John White, Michael L. Williams, Daniel Winkler

miniature knifemaker's society

Paul Abernathy, Gerald Bodner, Fred Cadwell, Barry Carithers, Kenneth Corey, Don Cowles, David J. Davis, Allen Eldridge, Linda Ferguson, Buddy Gaines, Larry Greenburg, Tom & Gwenn Guinn, Karl Hallberg, Bob Hergert, Laura Holmes, Brian Jacobson, Gary Kelley, R. F. Koebeman, Sterling Kopke, Gary E. Lack, Les Levinson, Henry C. Loos, Howard Maxwell, Mal Mele, Ray Mende, Toshiaki Michinaka, Paul Myer, Noriaki Narushima, Carol A. Olmsted, Allen R. Olsen, Charles Ostendorf, David Perkins, John Rakusan, Mark Rogers, Mary Ann Schultz, Jack Taylor, Valentin V. Timofeyev, Mike Viehman, Michael A. Wattelet, Kenneth P. Whitchard Jr., James D. Whitehead, Steve Williams, Carol A. Winold, Earl and Sue Witsaman, John Yashinski

professional knifemaker's association

Mike Allen, James Agnew, Usef Arie, Ray Archer, Eddie J. Baca, John Bartlow, Donald Bell, Brett C. Bennett, Tom Black, James E. Bliss, Philip Booth, Douglas Brack, Kenneth L. Brock, Ron Burke, Lucas Burnley, Ward Byrd, Craig Camerer, Tim S. Cameron, Ken Cardwell, Rod S. Carter, Del Corsi, Roger L. Craig, Joel Davis, John D. Dennehy, Dan Dennehy, Chester Deubel, Audra L. Draper, Mike J. Draper, Jim English, Ray W. Ennis, James T. Eriksen, Kirby Evers, Lee Ferguson, John Fraps, Scott Gere, Bob Glassman, Sal Glesser, Marge Hartman, Mike Henry, Don Hethcoat, Gary Hicks, Guy E. Hielscher, Alan Hodges, Mike L. Irie, David Johansen, Donald Jones, Jack Jones, Jot Singh Khalsa, Harvey King, Steve Kraft, Jim R. Largent, Ken Linton, Mike A. Lundemann, Jim Magee, Daniel May, Jerry & Sandy McClure, Clayton Miller, Skip Miller, Mark S. Molnar, Tyree L. Montell, Mike Mooney, Gary Moore, Steve Nolen, Rick Nowland, Fred A. Ott, Rob Patton, Dick Patton, James L. Poplin, Bill Redd, Dennis Riley, Terry Roberts, Steve Rollert, Charles R. Sauer, Jerry Schroeder, James Scroggs, Pete Semich, Eddie F. Stalcup, Craig Steketee, J.C. Stetter, Troy Taylor, Robert Terzuola, Roy Thompson, Loyd W. Thomsen, Jim D. Thrash, Ed Thuesen, Dick Waites, Mark Waites, Bill Waldrup, Tommy Ware, David Wattenberg, Hans Weinmueller, Dan Westlind, Harold J. Wheeler, RW Wilson, Denise Wolford, Michael C. Young, Monte Zavatta, Michael F. Zima, Daniel F. Zvonek

state/regional associations

alaska interior knifemakers association
Frank Ownby, Fred DeCicco, Bob Hook, Jenny Day, Kent Setzer, Kevin Busk, Loren Wellnite, Mark Knapp, Matthew Hanson, Mel Harvey, Nate Miller, Richard Kacsur, Ron Miller, Terry Miller, Bob LaFrance, Randy Olsen

alaska knifemakers association
A.W. Amoureux, John Arnold, Bud Aufdermauer, Robert Ball, J.D. Biggs, Lonnie Breuer, Tom Broome, Mark Bucholz, Irvin Campbell, Virgil Campbell, Raymond Cannon, Christopher Cawthorne, John Chamberlin, Bill Chatwood, George Cubic, Bob Cunningham, Gordon S. Dempsey, J.L. Devoll, James Dick, Art Dufour, Alan Eaker, Norm Grant, Gordon Grebe, Dave Highers, Alex Hunt, Dwight Jenkins, Hank Kubaiko, Bill Lance, Bob Levine, Michael Miller, John Palowski, Gordon Parrish, Mark W. Phillips, Frank Pratt, Guy Recknagle, Ron Robertson, Steve Robertson, Red Rowell, Dave Smith, Roger E. Smith, Gary R. Stafford, Keith Stegall, Wilbur Stegner, Norm Story, Robert D. Shaw, Thomas Trujillo, Ulys Whalen, Jim Whitman, Bob Willis

arizona knifemakers association
D. "Butch" Beaver, Bill Cheatham, Dan Dagget, Tom Edwards, Anthony Goddard, Steve Hoel, Ken McFall, Milford Oliver, Jerry Poletis, Merle Poteet, Mike Quinn, Elmer Sams, Jim Sornberger, Glen Stockton, Bruce Thompson, Sandy Tudor, Charles Weiss

arkansas knifemakers association

Mike Allen, David Anders, Robert Ball, Reggie Barker, James Batson, Twin Blades, Craig Braschler, Kim and Gary Breed, Wheeler, Tim Britton, Benoni Bullard, Bill Buxton, J.R. Cook, Gary Crowder, James Crowell, Steve Culver, Jesse Davis, Jim Downie, Bill Duff, Fred Durio, Rodger Echols, Shawn Ellis, Lee Ferguson, Linda Ferguson, Jerry Fisk, Joe Flournoy, Ronnie Foster, James Glisson, Gordon Graham, Bob Ham, Douglas and Gail Hardy, Gary Hicks, Alan Hutchinson, Jack Jones, Lacy Key, Harvey King, Ray Kirk, Bill Kirkes, Jim Krause, Jerry Lairson, Ken Linton, Bill Luckett, Tad Lynch, Jim Magee, Roger Massey, Jerry McClure, Rusty McDonald, W.J. McDonald, Don McIntosh, Tony Metsala, Bill Miller, Skip Miller, Ronnie Mobbs, Sidney Moon, Gary Mulkey, Keith Murr, Steve Myers, Mark Nevling, Allen Newberry, Corbin Newcomb, Ron Newton, Chad Nichols, John Perry, Paul Piccola, Rusty Polk, Bill Post, J.W. Randall, Vernon Red, Lin Rhea, Ralph Richards, Ron Richerson, Bobby Rico, Dennis Riley, T.C. Roberts, Kenny Rowe, Kyle Royer, Mike Ruth, James Scroggs, Richard Self, Tex Skow, Mike Snider, Marvin Snider, Marvin Snider, Marvin Solomon, Craig Steketee, Ed Sticker, Charles Stout, Jeff Stover, Tim Tabor, Brian Thie, Brion Tomberlin, Russell Townsley, Leon Treiber, Pete Truncali, Terry Vandeventer, Charles Vestal, Jim Walker, John White, Mike Williams

australian knifemakers guild inc.

Peter Bald, Col Barn, Bruce Barnett, Denis Barrett, Alistair Bastian, David Brodziak, Stuart Burdett, Jim Deering, Peter Del Raso, Michael Fechner, Keith Fludder, John Foxwell, Thomas Gerner, Branko Giljevic, Stephen Gregory-Jones, Peter Gordon, Barry Gunston, Mal Hannan, Rod Harris, Glenn Henke, Matt James, Peter Kenney, Joe Kiss, Robert Klitscher, Maurie McCarthy, Shawn McIntyre, John McLarty, Ray Mende, Richard Moase, Adam Parker, Jeff Peck, Mike Petersen, Alistair Phillps, Mick Ramage, Wayne Saunders, Murray Shanaughan, Andre Smith, Jim Steele, Rod Stines, Doug Timbs, Stewart Townsend, Hardy Wangermann, Brendan Ware, Ross Yeats

california knifemakers association

Stewart Anderson, Elmer Art, Anton Bosch, Roger Bost, Clint Breshears, Christian Bryant, Mike Butcher, Joe Caswell, Marcus Clinco, Clow Richard, Mike Desensi, Parker Dunbar, Frank Dunkin, Vern Edler III, Stephanie Engnath, Robert Ewing, Chad Fehmie, Alex Felix, Jim Ferguson, Bob Fitlin, Brian Forrest, Dave Gibson, Joe Girtner, Jerry Goettig, Jeanette Gonzales, Russ Green, Tim Harbert, John Harris, Wm. R. 'Bill' Herndon, Neal A. Hodges, Jerid Johnson, Lawrence Johnson, David Kahn, David Kazsuk, Paul Kelso, Steve Koster, Robert Liguori, Harold Locke, R.W. Loveless, Gerald Lundgren, Gordon Melin, Jim Merritt, Russ Moody, Gerald Morgan, Mike Murphy, Tim Musselman, Jeff Mutz, Aram Nigoghossian, Bruce Oakley, Rich Orton, Barry E. Posner, Pat Randall, E. J. Robison, Valente Rosas, Clark Rozas, H. J. Schneider, Red St. Cyr, Chris Stanko, Bill Stroman, Tyrone Swader, Reinhardt Swanson, Tony Swatton, Billy Traylor, Trugrit, Larry White, Stephen A. Williams

canadian knifemakers guild

Joe Arnold, John Benoit, Andre Benoit, Paul Bold, Guillaume Cote, Christoph Deringer, Alain Desaulniers, Sylvain Dion, Jim Downie, Eric Elson, Paul-Aime Fortier, Rick Frigault, Thomas Haslinger, Paul H. Johnston, Kirby Lambert, Greg Lightfoot, Steve Linklater, Wolfgang Loerchner, Brian Lyttle, David MacDonald, Antoine Marcal, James McGowan, Edward McRae, Mike Mossington, William Nease, Simone Raimondi, George Roberts, Paul Savage, Murray St. Amour, Stephen Stuart, David Sylvester, Brian Tighe, Stephen Vanderkolff, Craig Wheatley, Peter Wile, Elizabeth Loerchner, Fred Thynne, Rick Todd

florida knifemaker's association

Dick Atkinson, George Bachley, Mitch Baldwin, James Barry III, Dwayne Batten, Terry Betts, James H. Beusse Jr., Howard Bishop, Dennis Blaine, Dennis Blankenhem, Stephen A. Bloom, Dean Bosworth, John Boyce, W. Lowell Bray, Jr., Patrick R. Burris, Steve Butler, Norman Caesar, Tim Caldwell, Jason Clark, Lowell Cobb, William Cody, David Cole, Steve Corn, Jack Davenport, John Davis, Kenny Davis, Cary Desmon, Tim Caldwell, Jacob Elenbaas, Jim Elliot, William Ellis, Lynn Emrich, Tom Enos, Gary Esker, Frank Fischer, Todd Fischer, Mike Fisher, Travis Fletcher, Roger Gamble, Tony Garcia, James"Hoot" Gibson, Pedro Dick Gonzalez, Paul J. Granger, Ernie Grospitch, David Gruber, Chuck Harnage, Fred Harrington, R. Dewey Harris, Henry Heitler, Kevin Hoffman, Edward O. Holloway, Larry Hostetler, Stewart R. Hudson, Julie Hyman, Joe "Hy" Hytovick, Tom Johanning, Richard Johnson, Roy Kelleher, Paul Kent, Bill King, Bryan Komula, George H. Lambert, William S. Letcher, Bill Levengood, Glenn A. Long, Ernie Lyle, Bob Mancuso, Stephen Mathewson, Michael Matthews, James McNiel, Faustina Mead, Steve Miller, Dan Mink, Martin L. Murphy, Gary Nelson, Larry Newton, J. Cliff Parker, Jerry D. Partridge, John W. PerMar Jr., Larry Patterson, Dan Piergallini, Terry Lee Renner, Calvin J. Robinson, Vince Ruano, Roberto Sanchez, Russell Sauls, Dave Semones, Stuart Shaw, Ann Sheffield, Brad Shepherd, Bill Simons, Jimmie H. Smith, Fred Stern, Kent Swicegood, Timothy Tabor, , Dale Thomas, Wayne Timmerman, Michael Tison, Ralph Turnbull, Louis Vallet, Donald Vogt, Bruce Wassberg, Stan Wilson, Denny Young, Brad Zinker

georgia custom knifemakers' guild

Don R. Adams, Doug Adams, Dennis Bradley, Aaron Brewer, Mike Brown, Robert Busbee, Henry Cambron, Jim Collins, John Costa, Jerry Costin, Scott Davidson, Charles K. Dunn, Will Dutton, Emory Fennell, Stephan Fowler, Dean Gates, Warren Glover, George Hancox, Rade Hawkins, Wayne Hensley, Ronald Hewitt, Kevin Hoffman, Frank Jones, Davin Kates, Dan Masson, Charlie Mathews, Harry Mathews, Leroy Mathews, David McNeal, Dan Mink, James Mitchell, Ralph Mitchell, Sandy Morrisey, Jerry Partridge, Wes Peterson, James Poplin, Joan Poythress, Carey Quinn, Jim Ragsdale, Carl Rechsteiner, David Roberts, Andrew Roy, Joe Sangster, Jamey Saunders, Craig Schneeberger, Randy Scott, Ken Simmons, Nelson Simmons, Jim Small, Bill Snow, Don Tommey, Alex Whetsel, Mike Wilson, Patrick & Hillary Wilson, Robert A. Wright

knife group association of oklahoma

Mike "Whiskers" Allen, Ed Allgood, David Anders, Rocky Anderson, Tony and Ramona Baker, Jerry Barlow, Troy Brown, Dan Burke, Tom Buchanan, F. L. Clowdus Bill Coye, Gary Crowder, Steve Culver, Marc Cullip, David Darby, Voyne Davis, Dan Dick, Dave Dill, Lynn Drury, Bill Duff, Beau Erwin, David Etchieson, Harry Fentress, Lee Ferguson, Linda Ferguson, Daniel Fulk, Gary Gloden, Steve Hansen, Paul Happy, Calvin Harkins, Ron Hebb, Billy Helton, Ed Hites, Tim Johnston, Les Jones, Jim Keen, Bill Kennedy, Stew Killiam, Barbara Kirk, Ray Kirk, Nicholas Knack, Jerry Lairson, Sr., Al Lawrence, Ken Linton, Ron Lucus, Aidan Martin, Barbara Martin, Duncan Martin, John Martin, Jerry McClure, Sandy McClure, Rick Menefee, Ben Midgley, Michael E. Miller, Roy Miller, Ray Milligan, Duane Morganflash, Gary Mulkey, Jerald Nickels, Jerry Parkhurst, Chris Parson, Larry Parsons, Jerry Paul, Larry Paulen, Paul Piccola, Cliff Polk, Roland Quimby, Ron Reeves, Lin Rhea, Mike Ruth, Dan Schneringer, Terry Schreiner, Allen Shafer, Shawn Shropshire, Randell Sinnett, Clifford Smith, Jeremy Steely, Doug Sonntag, Perry Stanford, Mike Stegall, Gary Steinmetz, Mike Stott, Dud Hart Thomas, Brian Tomberlin, Tom Upton, Chuck Ward, Brett Wheat-Simms, Jesse Webb, Rob Weber, Joe Wheeler, Bill Wiggins, Joe Wilkie, Gary Wingo, Daniel Zvonek

knifemakers' guild of southern africa

Jeff Angelo, John Arnold, George Baartman, Francois Basson, Rob Bauchop, George Beechey, Arno Bernard, Buzz Bezuidenhout, Harucus Blomerus, Chris Booysen, Thinus Botha, Ian Bottomley, Peet Bronkhorst, Rob Brown, Fred Burger, Sharon Burger, Trevor Burger, William Burger, Brian Coetzee, Larry Connelly, Andre de Beer, André de Villiers, Melodie de Witt, Gavin Dickerson, Roy Dunseith, Mike Fellows, Leigh Fogarty, Werner Fourie, Andrew Frankland, Brian Geyer, Ettoré Gianferrari, Dale Goldschmidt, Stan Gordon, Nick Grabe, John Grey, Piet Gray, Heather Harvey, Kevin Harvey, Dries Hattingh, Gawie Herbst, Thinus Herbst, Greg Hesslewood, Des Horn, Nkosi Jubane, Billy Kojetin, Mark Kretschmer, Steven Lewis, Garry Lombard, Steve Lombard, Ken Madden, Abdur-Rasheed Mahomedy, Peter Mason, Edward Mitchell, George Muller, Günther Muller, Tom Nelson, Andries Olivier, Jan Olivier, Christo Oosthuizen, Cedric Pannell, Willie Paulsen, Nico Pelzer, Conrad Pienaar, David Pienaar, Jan Potgieter, Lourens Prinsloo, Theuns Prinsloo, Hilton Purvis, Derek Rausch, Chris Reeve, Bertie Rietveld, Melinda Rietveld, Dean Riley, John Robertson, Corrie Schoeman, Eddie Scott, Harvey Silk, Mike Skellern, Toi Skellern, Carel Smith, Ken Smythe, Graham Sparks, Peter Steyn, André Thorburn, Hennie Van Brakel, Fanie Van Der Linde, Johan van der Merwe, Van van der Merwe, Marius Van der Vyver, Louis Van der Walt, Cor Van Ellinckhuijzen, Andre van Heerden, Danie Van Wyk, Ben Venter, Willie Venter, Gert Vermaak, René Vermeulen, Erich Vosloo, Desmond, Waldeck, Albie Wantenaar, Henning Wilkinson, John Wilmot, Wollie Wolfaardt, Owen Wood

midwest knifemakers association

E.R. Andrews III, Frank Berlin, Charles Bolton, Tony Cates, Mike Chesterman, Ron Duncan, Larry Duvall, Bobby Eades, Jackie Emanuel, James Haynes, John Jones, Mickey Koval, Ron Lichlyter, George Martoncik, Gene Millard, William Miller, Corbin Newcomb, Chris Owen, A.D. Rardon, Archie Rardon, Max Smith, Ed Stewart, Charles Syslo, Melvin Williams

montana knifemaker's association

Peter C. Albert, Chet Allinson, Marvin Allinson, Tim & Sharyl Alverson, Bill Amoureux, Jan Anderson, Wendell Barnes, Jim & Kay Barth, Bob & Marian Beaty, Don Bell, Brett Bennett, Robert Bizzell, BladeGallery, Paul Bos, Daryl & Anna May Boyd, Chuck Bragg, Frederick Branch, Peter Bromley, Bruce Brown, Emil Bucharksky, Bruce & Kay Bump, Bill Burke, Alpha Knife Supply Bybee, Ed Caffrey, Jim & Kate Carroll, Murray Carter, Jon & Brenda Christensen, Norm Cotterman, Seith Coughlin, Bob Crowder, Mike Dalimata, John Davis, Maria DesJardins, Rich & Jacque Duxbury, Dan Erickson, Mel & Darlene Fassio, E.V. Ford, Eric Fritz, Dana & Sandy Hackney, Doc & Lil Hagen, Gary & Betsy Hannon, Eli Hansen, J.A. Harkins, Tedd Harris, Sam & Joy Hensen, Loren Higgins, Mickey Hines, Gerald & Pamela Hintz, Gary House, Tori Howe, Kevin Hutchins, Al Inman, Frank & Shelley Jacobs, Karl Jermunson, Keith Johnson, Don Kaschmitter, Steven Kelly, Dan & Penny Kendrick, Monte Koppes, Donald Kreuger, David Lisch, James Luman, Robert Martin, Max McCarter, Neil McKee, Larry McLaughlin, Mac & Nancy McLaughlin, Phillip Moen, Gerald Morgan, Randy Morgan, Dan & Andrea Nedved, Daniel O'Malley, Joe Olson, Collin Paterson, Willard & Mark Patrick, Jeffrey & Tyler Pearson, Brian Pender, James Poling, Chance & Kerri Priest, Richard Prusz, Greg Rabatin, Jim Raymond, Jim Rayner, Darren Reeves, John Reynolds, Ryan Robison, Gary Rodewald, Buster Ross, Ruana Knifeworks, Charles Sauer, Dean Schroeder, Michael Sheperes, Mike Smith, Gordon St. Clair, Terry Steigers, George Stemple, Dan & Judy Stucky, Art & Linda Swyhart, Jim Thill, Cary Thomas, James & Tammy Venne, Bill & Lori Waldrup, Jonathan & Doris Walther, Kenneth Ward, Michael Wattelet, Darlene Weinand, Gerome & Darlene Weinand, Daniel & Donna Westlind, Matt & Michelle Whitmus, Dave Wilkes, Mike & Sean Young

national independent cutlery association

Ron & Patsy Beck, Bob Bennett, Dave Bishop, Steve Corn, Dave Harvey, C.J. McKay, Mike Murray, Gary Parker, Rachel Schindler, Joe Tarbell

new england bladesmiths guild

Phillip Baldwin, Gary Barnes, Paul Champagne, Jimmy Fikes, Don Fogg, Larry Fuegen, Rob Hudson, Midk Langley, Louis Mills, Dan Maragni, Jim Schmidt, Wayne Valachovic and Tim Zowada

north carolina custom knifemakers' guild

Dr. James Batson, Wayne Bernauer, Tom Beverly, William "Bill" Bisher, Jamin Bracket, Mark Cary, Thomas Clegg, Ray Clontz, Travis Daniel, David Driggs, Russell Gardner, Talmage M. Hall, Koji Hara, John Hege, Curtis Iovito, Tommy Johnson, Barry and Phillip Jones, Frank Joyce, Carol Kelly, Tony Kelly, Robert Knight, Leon Lassiter, Gregory Manley, Mathew Manley, Aubrey McDonald, Tommy McNabb, Arthur McNeil, Christopher McNeil, William Morris, Van Royce Morton, Charles Ostendorf, James Poplin, Murphy Ragsdale, Kenneth Steve Randall, Bruce Ryan, Joel Sandifer, Tim Scholl, Andy Sharpe, Gene Smith, Octavio F. Soares, Arthur Summers, Russ Sutton, Bruce Turner.

ohio knifemakers association

Raymond Babcock, Van Barnett, Harold A. Collins, Larry Detty, Tom Downing, Jim Downs, Patty Ferrier, Jeff Flannery, James Fray, Bob Foster, Raymond Guess, Scott Hamrie, Rick Hinderer, Curtis Hurley, Ed Kalfayan, Michael Koval, Judy Koval, Larry Lunn, Stanley Maienknecht, Dave Marlott, Mike Mercer, David Morton, Patrick McGroder, Charles Pratt, Darrel Ralph, Roy Roddy, Carroll Shoemaker, John Smith, Clifton Smith, Art Summers, Jan Summers, Donald Tess, Dale Warther, John Wallingford, Earl Witsaman, Joanne Yurco, Mike Yurco

saskatchewan knifemakers guild

Vern Alton, Al Bakke, Marty Beets, Clarence Broeksma, Irv Brunas, Emil Bucharsky, Jim Clow, Murray Cook, Bob Crowder, Herb Davison, Ray Dilling, Kevin Donald, Brian Drayton, Dallas Dreger, Ray Fehler, Cal Ganshorn, Dale Garling, Wayne Hamilton, Robert Hazell, Bryan Hebb, Garth Hindmarch, John Hopkins, Cliff Kaufmann, Doug Kirkness, Donald Kreuger, Paul Laronge, Pat Macnamara, David McLellan, Ed McRae, Len Meeres, Arnold Miller, Robert Minnes, Ron Nelson, Morris Nesdole, Blaine Parry, Greg Penner, Barry Popick, Jim Quickfall, Ryan Reich, Rob Ridley, Marilyn Ridley, Robert Robson, Carl Sali, Eugene Schreiner, Kim Senft, Don Spasoff, Anthony Wachowicz, Ken Watt, Andy Weeks, Trevor Whitfield, David Wilkes, Merle Williams

south carolina association of knifemakers

Douglas Bailey, Ken Black, Bobby Branton, Richard Bridwell, Gordo Brooks, Dan Cannady, Rodger Cassey, John Conn, Allen Corbet, Bill Dauksch, Geno Denning, Charlie Douan, Gene Ellison, Eddy Elsmore, Robbie Estabrook Jr., Lewis Fowler, Jim Frazier, Tally Grant, Jerry Hendrix, Wayne Hendrix, Johnny Johnson, Lonnie Jones, John Keaton, Jason Knight, Col. Thomas Kreger, Gene Langley, Tommy Lee, David Manley, Bill Massey, C.R. Miles, Gene Miller, Claude Montjoy, Patrick Morgan, Barry Meyers, Paul Nystrom Jr., Lee O'Quinn, Victor Odom Jr., Larry Page, James Rabb, Ricky Rankin, Rick Rockwood, John Sarratt, Gene Scaffe, Mick Sears, Ralph Smith, David Stroud, Rocky Thomas, Allen Timmons, Justin Walker, Mickey Walker, Woody Walker, Syd Willis Jr.

tennessee knifemakers association

John Bartlow, Doug Casteel, Harold Crisp, Larry Harley, John W. Walker, Harold Woodward, Harold Wright

texas knifemakers & collectors association

Doug Arnew, Doug Ashby, Ed Barker, George Blackburn, Zane Blackwell, Garrett Blackwell, David Blair, Gayle Bradley, Craig Brewer, Nathan Burgess, Stanley Buzek, Dennis Clark, Dwain Coats, Emil Colmenares, Stewart Crawford, Chester Darcey, Wesley Davis, Rorick Davis, Brian Davis, Harvey Dean, James Drouillard II, Stan Edge, Carlton Evans, Jesse Everett Jr., Sammy Fischer, Christopher Flo, Norvell Foster, Theodore Friesenhahn, Jason Fry, Les George, Mark Grimes, Don Halter, Johnny Hamlet, Glenn Hemperley, Roy Hinds, Darrel Holmquist, Mark Hornung, Karl Jakubik, Mickey Kaehr, Bill Keller, David Kinn, Greg Ledet, Jim Lemcke, Ken Linton, Michael LoGiudice, Paul Long, Eliot Maldonado, Glenn Marshall, Newton Martin, Riley Martin, Bob Merz, Jerry Moen, Don Morrow, Ted Munson, Clifford O'Dell, Tom Overeynder, John Ownby, Ronnie Packard, Glenn Parks, Pat Patterson, Garrett Patterson, Troy Patterson, Steven Patterson, William Petersen III, Jeff Petzke, Paul Piccola, Bill and Pat Post, Gary Powell, Rusty Preston, Martin Rizo, Thomas Rucker, Bill Ruple, Merle Rush, James Schiller, Dwight Schoneweis, Richard Self, Kirby Simmons, Adam Starr, Linda Stone, Wayne Stone, Johnny Stout, Katie Stout, Luke Swenson, Leon Treiber, Larry Turcotte, Charles Turnage, Jimmy Vasquez, David Vickers, Austin Walter, John Walts, Chuck Ward, Bruce Weber, John Weever, Harold Wheeler, Marvin Winn, John Wootters

photo index

The firms listed here are special in the sense that they make or market special kinds of knives made in facilities they own or control either in the U.S. or overseas. Or they are special because they make knives of unique design or function. The second phone number listed is the fax number.

sporting cutlers

A.G. RUSSELL KNIVES INC
2900 S. 26th St
Rogers, AR 72758-8571
800-255-9034 or 479-631-0130;
fax 479-631-8493
ag@agrussell.com; www.agrussell.com
The oldest knife mail-order company, highest quality. Free catalog available. In these catalogs you will find the newest and the best. If you like knives, this catalog is a must

AL MAR KNIVES
PO Box 2295
Tualatin, OR 97062-2295
503-670-9080; 503-639-4789
www.almarknives.com
Featuring our Ultralight™ series of knives. Sere 2000™ Shrike, Sere™, Operator™, Nomad™ and Ultraligh series™

ANZA KNIVES
C Davis
Dept BL 12 PO Box 710806
Santee, CA 92072-0806
619-561-9445; 619-390-6283
sales@anzaknives.com;
www.anzaknives.com

B&D TRADING CO.
3935 Fair Hill Rd
Fair Oaks, CA 95628

BARTEAUX MACHETES, INC.
1916 SE 50th St
Portland, OR 97215
503-233-5880
barteaux@machete.com; www.machete.com
Manufacture of machetes, saws, garden tools

BEAR & SON CUTLERY
(FORMERLY BEAR MGC CUTLERY)
PO Box 600
5111 Berwyn Rd Suite 110
College Park, MD 20740 USA
800-338-6799; 301-486-0901
www.knifecenter.com
Folding pocket knives, fixed blades, specialty products

BECK'S CUTLERY & SPECIALTIES
McGregor Village Center
107 Edinburgh South Dr
Cary, NC 27511
919-460-0203; 919-460-7772
beckscutlery@mindspring.com;
www.beckscutlery.com

BENCHMADE KNIFE CO. INC.
300 Beavercreek Rd
Oregon City, OR 97045
800-800-7427
info@benchmade.com;
www.benchmade.com
Sports, utility, law enforcement, military, gift and semi custom

BERETTA U.S.A. CORP.
17601 Beretta Dr
Accokeek, MD 20607
800-636-3420 Customer Service
www.berettausa.com
Full range of hunting & specialty knives

BEST KNIVES / GT KNIVES
PO Box 151048
Fort Myers, FL 33914
800-956-5696; fax 941-240-1756
info@bestknives.com;
www.bestknives.com/gtknives.com
Law enforcement & military automatic knives

BLACKJACK KNIVES
PO Box 3
Greenville, WV 24945
304-832-6878; Fax 304-832-6550
knifeware@verizon.net;
www.knifeware.com

BLUE GRASS CUTLERY CORP.
20 E Seventh St PO Box 156
Manchester, OH 45144
937-549-2602; 937-549-2709 or 2603
sales @bluegrasscutlery.com;
www.bluegrasscutlery.com
Manufacturer of Winchester Knives, John Primble Knives and many contract lines

BOB'S TRADING POST
308 N Main St
Hutchinson, KS 67501
620-669-9441
www.gunshopfinder.com
Tad custom knives with Reichert custom sheaths one at a time, one-of-a-kind

BOKER USA INC
1550 Balsam St
Lakewood, CO 80214-5917
303-462-0662; 303-462-0668
sales@bokerusa.com; www.bokerusa.com
Wide range of fixed blade and folding knives for hunting, military, tactical and general use

BROWNING
One Browning Place
Morgan, UT 84050
800-333-3504; Customer Service:
801-876-2711 or 800-333-3288
www.browning.com
Outdoor hunting & shooting products

BUCK KNIVES INC.
660 S Lochsa St
Post Falls, ID 83854-5200
800-326-2825; Fax: 208 262-0555
www.buckknives.com
Sports cutlery

BULLDOG BRAND KNIVES
6715 Heritage Business Ct
Chattanooga, TN 37421
423-894-5102; 423-892-9165
Fixed blade and folding knives for hunting and general use

BUSSE COMBAT KNIFE CO.
11651 Co Rd 12
Wauseon, OH 43567
419-923-6471; 419-923-2337
www.bussecombat.com
Simple & very strong straight knife designs for tactical & expedition use

CAMILLUS CUTLERY CO.
54 W Main St.
Camillus, NY 13031
315-672-8111; 315-672-8832
customerservice@camillusknives.com

CAS IBERIA INC.
650 Industrial Blvd
Sale Creek, TN 37373
423-332-4700
www.cashanwei.com
Extensive variety of fixed-blade and folding knives for hunting, diving, camping, military and general use. Japan ese swords and European knives.

CASE CUTLERY
W R & Sons
PO Box 4000
Owens Way
Bradford, PA 16701
800-523-6350; Fax: 814-368-1736
consumer-relations@wrcase.com
www.wrcase.com
Folding pocket knives

CHICAGO CUTLERY CO.
5500 Pearl St.
Rosemont, IL 60018
847-678-8600
www.chicagocutlery.com
Sport & utility knives.

CHRIS REEVE KNIVES
2949 S. Victory View Way
Boise, ID 83709-2946
208-375-0367; Fax: 208-375-0368
crknifo@chrisreeve.com;
www.chrisreeve.com
Makers of the award winning Yarborough/ Green Beret Knife; the One Piece Range; and the Sebenza and Mnandi folding knives

COAST CUTLERY CO
PO Box 5821
Portland, OR 97288
800-426-5858
www.coastcutlery.com
Variety of fixed-blade and folding knives and multi-tools for hunting, camping and general use

COLD STEEL INC
3036-A Seaborg Ave.
Ventura, CA 93003
800-255-4716 or 805-650-8481
customerservice@coldsteel.com;
www.coldsteel.com
Wide variety of folding lockbacks and fixed-blade hunting, fishing and neck knives, as well as bowies, kukris, tantos, throwing knives, kitchen knives and swords

COLONIAL KNIFE COMPANY
DIVISION OF COLONIAL CUTLERY
INTERNATIONAL
PO Box 960
North Scituate, RI 02857
866-421-6500; Fax: 401-737-0054
colonialcutlery@aol.com;
www.colonialcutlery@aol.com or

www.colonialknifecompany.com
*Collectors edition specialty knives. Special
promotions. Old cutler, barion, trappers,
military knives. Industrial knives-electrician.*

COLUMBIA RIVER KNIFE & TOOL
18348 SW 126th Place
Tualatin, OR 97026
800-891-3100; 503-685-5015
info@crkt.com; www.crkt.com
*Complete line of sport, work and tactical
knives*

CONDOR™ TOOL & KNIFE
Rick Jones, Natl. Sales Manager
6309 Marina Dr
Orlando, FL 32819
407-876-0886
rtj@earthlink.net

CRAWFORD KNIVES, LLC
205 N Center Drive
West Memphis, AR 72301
870-732-2452
www.crawfordknives.com
Folding knives for tactical and general use

CUT CO. CORPORATION
1116 E State St
Olean, NY 14760
716-372-3111; 716-373-6155
www.cutco.com
Household cutlery / sport knives

DAVID BOYE KNIVES
PO Box 1238
Dolan Springs, AZ 86441-1238
800-853-1617 or 928-767-4273
boye@ctaz.com; www.boyeknives.com
Boye Dendritic Cobalt boat knives

DUNN KNIVES
Steve Greene
PO Box 204; 5830 NW Carlson Rd
Rossville KS 66533
800-245-6483
steve.greene@dunnknives.com;
www.dunnknives.com
Custom knives

EMERSON KNIVES, INC.
PO Box 4180
Torrance, CA 90510-4180
310-212-7455; Fax: 310-212-7289
www.emersonknives.com
*Hard use tactical knives; folding & fixed
blades*

EXTREMA RATIO SAS
Mauro Chiostri/Maurizio Castrati
Via Tourcoing 40/p
59100 Prato
ITALY
0039 0574 584639; Fax: 0039 0574 581312
info@extremaratio.com
*Tactical/military knives and sheaths, blades
and sheaths to customers specs*

FALLKNIVEN AB
Havrevägen 10
S-961 42 Boden
SWEDEN
46-921 544 22; Fax: 46-921 544 33
info@fallkniven.se; www.fallkniven.com
High quality stainless knives

FROST CUTLERY CO
PO Box 22636
Chattanooga, Tn 37422
800-251-7768; Fax: 423-894-9576
www.frostcutleryco.com
*Wide range of fixed-blade and folding knives
with a multitude of handle materials*

GATCO SHARPENERS
PO Box 600
Getzville, NY 14068
716-877-2200; Fax: 716-877-2591
gatco@buffnet.net;
www.gatcosharpeners.com
*Precision sharpening systems, diamond
sharpening systems, ceramic sharpening
systems, carbide sharpening systems,
natural Arkansas stones*

GERBER LEGENDARY BLADES
14200 SW 72nd Ave
Portland, OR 97224
503-639-6161; Fax: 503-684-7008
www.gerberblades.com
*Knives, multi-tools, axes, saws, outdoor
products*

GROHMANN KNIVES LTD.
PO Box 40
116 Water St
Pictou, Nova Scotia B0K 1H0
CANADA
888-756-4837; Fax: 902-485-5872
www.grohmannknives.com
*Fixed-blade belt knives for hunting and
fishing, folding pocketknives for hunting and
general use. Household cutlery.*

H&B FORGE CO.
235 Geisinger Rd
Shiloh, OH 44878
419-895-1856
hbforge@direcway.com; www.hbforge.com
*Special order hawks, camp stoves, fireplace
accessories, muzzleloading accroutements*

HISTORIC EDGED WEAPONRY
1021 Saddlebrook Dr
Hendersonville, NC 28739
828-692-0323; 828-692-0600
histwpn@bellsouth.net
*Antique knives from around the world;
importer of puukko and other knives from
Norway, Sweden, Finland and Lapland; also
edged weaponry book "Travels for Daggers"
by Eiler R. Cook*

JOY ENTERPRISES-FURY CUTLERY
Port Commerce Center III
1862 M.L. King Jr. Blvd
Riviera Beach, FL 33404
800-500-3879; Fax: 561-863-3277
mail@joyenterprises.com;
www.joyenterprises.com;
www.furycutlery.com
*Fury™ Mustang™ extensive variety of
fixed-blade and folding knives for hunting,
fishing, diving, camping, military and general
use; novelty key-ring knives. Muela Sporting
Knives. KA-BAR KNIVES INC. Fury Tactical,
Muela of Spain, Mustang Outdoor Adventure*

KA-BAR KNIVES INC
200 Homer St
Olean, NY 14760
800-282-0130; Fax: 716-790-7188
info@ka-bar.com; www.ka-bar.com

KATZ KNIVES, INC.
10924 Mukilteo Speedway #287
Mukilteo, WA 98275
480-786-9334; 480-786-9338
katzkn@aol.com; www.katzknives.com

KELLAM KNIVES CO.
902 S Dixie Hwy
Lantana, FL 33462
800-390-6918; Fax: 561-588-3186
info@kellamknives.com;
www.kellamknives.com
*Largest selection of Finnish knives;
handmade & production*

KERSHAW/KAI CUTLERY CO.
7939 SW Burns Way
Wilsonville, OR 97070

KLOTZLI (MESSER KLOTZLI)
Hohengasse 3 CH 3400
Burgdorf
SWITZERLAND
(34) 422-23 78; Fax: (34) 422-76 93
info@klotzli.com; www.klotzli.com
*High-tech folding knives for tactical and
general use*

KNIFEWARE INC
PO Box 3
Greenville, WV 24945
304-832-6878; Fax: 304-832-6550
knifeware@verizon.net; www.knifeware.com
*Blackjack and Big Country Cross reference
Big Country Knives see Knifeware Inc.*

KNIGHTS EDGE LTD.
5696 N Northwest Highway
Chicago, IL 60646-6136
773-775-3888; Fax: 773-775-3339
sales@knightsedge.com;
www.knightsedge.com
*Medieval weaponry, swords, suits of armor,
katanas, daggers*

KNIVES OF ALASKA, INC.
Charles or Jody Allen
3100 Airport Dr
Denison, TX 75020
800-572-0980; 903-786-7371
info@knivesofalaska.com;
www.knivesofalaska.com
High quality hunting & outdoorsmen's knives

KNIVES OF ALASKA, INC.
Charles or Jody Allen
3100 Airport Dr
Denison, TX 75020
800-572-0980; 903-786-7371
info@knivesofalaska.com;
www.knivesofalaska.com
High quality hunting & outdoorsmen's knives

KNIVES PLUS
2467 40 West
Amarillo, TX 79109
800-687-6202
www.knivesplus.com
*Retail cutlery and cutlery accessories since
1987; free catalog available*

LAKOTA (BRUNTON CO.)
620 E Monroe Ave
Riverton, WY 82501
307-856-6559
AUS 8-A high-carbon stainless steel blades

LEATHERMAN TOOL GROUP, INC.
PO Box 20595
Portland, OR 97294-059 0595 5
800-847-8665; Fax: 503-253-7830
mktg@leatherman.com;
www.leatherman.com
Multi-tools

LONE WOLF KNIVES
Doug Hutchens, Marketing Manager
9373 SW Barber Street, Suite A
Wilsonville, OR 97070
503-431-6777
customerservice@lonewolfknives.com;
www.lonewolfknives.com

LONE STAR WHOLESALE
P.O. Box 587
Amarillo, TX 79105
806-356-9540; Fax 806-359-1603
knivesplus@knivesplus.com
Great prices, dealers only, most major brands

MARBLE'S OUTDOORS
420 Industrial Park
Gladstone, MI 49837
906-428-3710; Fax: 906-428-3711
info@marblescutlery.com;
www.marblesoutdoors.com

MASTER CUTLERY INC
701 Penhorn Ave
Secaucus, NJ 07094
888-271-7229; Fax: 201-271-7666
www.mastercutlery.com
Largest variety in the knife industry

**MASTERS OF DEFENSE KNIFE CO.
(BLACKHAWK PRODUCTS GROUP)**
4850 Brookside Court
Norfolk, VA 23502
800-694-5263; 888-830-2013
cs@blackhawk.com; www.modknives.com
Fixed-blade and folding knives for tactical and general use

MCCANN INDUSTRIES
132 S 162nd PO Box 641
Spanaway, WA 98387
253-537-6919; Fax: 253-537-6993
mccann.machine@worldnet.att.net;
www.mccannindustries.com

MEYERCO MANUFACTURING
4481 Exchange Service Dr
Dallas, TX 75236
214-467-8949; 214-467-9241
www.meyercousa.com
Folding tactical,rescue and speed-assisted pocketknives; fixed-blade hunting and fishing designs; multi-function camping tools and machetes

MICROTECH KNIVES
300 Chestnut Street Ext.
Bradford, PA 16701
814-363-9260; Fax: 814-363-9284
mssweeney@microtechknives.com;
www.microtechknives.com
Manufacturers of the highest quality production knives

MORTY THE KNIFE MAN, INC.
80 Smith St
Farmingdale, NY 11735
631-249-2072
clkiff@mtkm.com;
www.mortytheknifeman.com

MUSEUM REPLICAS LTD.
P.O. Box 840
2147 Gees Mill Rd
Conyers, GA 30012
800-883-8838; Fax: 770-388-0246
www.museumreplicas.com
Historically accurate & battle-ready swords & daggers

MYERCHIN, INC.
14765 Nova Scotia Dr
Fontana, CA 92336
909-463-6741; 909-463-6751
myerchin@myerchin.com;
www.myerchin.com
Rigging/ Police knives

NATIONAL KNIFE DISTRIBUTORS
125 Depot St
Forest City, NC 28043
800-447-4342; 828-245-5121
nkdi@nkdi.com; www.nkdi.com
Benchmark pocketknives from Solingen, Germany

NORMARK CORP.
10395 Yellow Circle Dr
Minnetonka, MN 55343-9101
800-874-4451; 612-933-0046
www.rapala.com
Hunting knives, game shears and skinning ax

ONTARIO KNIFE CO.
PO Box 145
Franklinville, NY 14737
800-222-5233; 800-299-2618
sales@ontarioknife.com;
www.ontarioknife.com
Fixed blades, tactical folders, military & hunting knives, machetes

OUTDOOR EDGE CUTLERY CORP.
4699 Nautilus Ct. S #503
Boulder, CO 80301
800-447-3343; 303-530-7667
info@outdooredge.com;
www.outdooredge.com

PACIFIC SOLUTION MARKETING, INC.
1220 E. Belmont St.
Ontario, CA 91761
Tel: 877-810-4643
Fax: 909-930-5843
sales@pacificsolution.com
www.pacificsolution.com
Wide range of folding pocket knives, hunting knives, tactical knives, novelty knives, medieval armors and weapons as well as hand forged samurai sword and tantos.

PILTDOWN PRODUCTIONS
Errett Callahan
2 Fredonia Ave
Lynchburg, VA 24503
434-528-3444
www.errettcallahan.com

QUEEN CUTLERY COMPANY
PO Box 500
Franklinville, NY 14737
800-222-5233; 800-299-2618
sales@ontarioknife.com;
www.queencutlery.com
Pocket knives, collectibles, Schatt & Morgan, Robeson, club knives

QUIKUT
118 East Douglas Road
Walnut Ridge, AR 72476
800-338-7012; Fax: 870-886-9162
www.quikut.com

RANDALL MADE KNIVES
4857 South Orange Blossom Trail
Orlando, FL 32839
407-855-8075; Fax: 407-855-9054
grandall@randallknives.com;
www.randallknives.com
Handmade fixed-blade knives for hunting, fishing, diving, military and general use

REMINGTON ARMS CO., INC.
PO Box 700
870 Remington Drive
Madison, NC 27025-0700
800-243-9700; Fax: 336-548-7801
www.remington.com

SANTA FE STONEWORKS
3790 Cerrillos Rd.
Santa Fe, NM 87507
800-257-7625; Fax: 505-471-0036
knives@rt66.com;
www.santafestoneworks.com
Gem stone handles

SARCO CUTLERY LLC
449 Lane Dr
Florence AL 35630
256-766-8099
www.sarcoknives.com
Etching and engraving services, club knives, etc. New knives, antique-collectible knives

SOG SPECIALTY KNIVES & TOOLS, INC.
6521 212th St SW
Lynnwood, WA 98036
425-771-6230; Fax: 425-771-7689
info@sogknives.com; www.sogknives.com
SOG assisted technology, Arc-Lock, folding knives, specialized fixed blades, multi-tools

SPYDERCO, INC.
820 Spyderco Way
Golden, CO 80403
800-525-7770; 303-278-2229
sales@spyderco.com;
www.spyderco.com
Knives and sharpeners

SWISS ARMY BRANDS INC.
Service Center
65 Trap Falls Road
Shelton, CT 06484
800-442-2706; Fax: 800-243-4006
www.swissarmy.com
Folding multi-blade designs and multi-tools for hunting, fishing, camping, hiking, golfing and general use. One of the original brands (Victorinox) of Swiss Army Knives

TAYLOR BRANDS LLC
1043 Fordtown Road
Kingsport, TN 37663
800-251-0254; Fax: 423-247-5371
info@taylorbrandsllc.com;
www.taylorbrands.com
Fixed-blade and folding knives for tactical, rescue, hunting and general use. Also provides etching, engraving, scrimshaw services.

TIGERSHARP TECHNOLOGIES
1002 N Central Expwy Suite 499
Richardson TX 75080
888-711-8437; Fax: 972-907-0716
www.tigersharp.com

TIMBERLINE KNIVES
PO Box 600
Getzville, NY 14068-0600
800-548-7427; Fax: 716-877-2591
www.timberlineknives.com
High technology production knives for professionals, sporting, tradesmen & kitchen use

TINIVES
1725 Smith Rd
Fortson, GA 31808
888-537-9991; 706-322-9892
info@tinives.com; www.tinives.com
High-tech folding knives for tactical, law enforcement and general use

TRU-BALANCE KNIFE CO.
6869 Lake Bluff Dr
Comstock Park, MI 49321
(616) 647-1215

TURNER, P.J., KNIFE MFG., INC.
P.O. Box 1549
164 Allred Rd
Afton, WY 83110
307-885-0611
pjtkm@silverstar.com;
www2.silverstar.com/turnermfg

UTICA CUTLERY CO
820 Noyes St
PO Box 10527
Utica, NY 13503-1527

800-879-2526; Fax: 315-733-6602
info@uticacutlery.com; www.uticacutlery.com
Wide range of folding and fixed-blade designs, multi-tools and steak knives

WARNER, KEN
PO Box 3
Greenville, WV 24945
304-832-6878; 304-832-6550
www.knifeware.com

WENGER NORTH AMERICA
15 Corporate Dr
Orangeburg, NY 10962
800-267-3577 or 800-447-7422
www.wengerna.com
One of the official makers of folding multi-blade Swiss Army knives

WILD BOAR BLADES / KOPROMED USA
1701 Broadway PMB 282
Vancouver, WA 98663
360-735-0570; Fax: 360-735-0390
info@wildboarblades.com;
wildboarblades@aol.com;
www.wildboarblade.com
Wild Boar Blades is pleased to carry a full line of Kopromed knives and kitchenware imported from Poland

WORLD CLASS EXHIBITION KNIVES
Cary Desmon
941-504-2279
www.withoutequal.com

Carries an extensive line of Pius Lang knives

WILLIAM HENRY FINE KNIVES
3200 NE Rivergate St
McMinnville, OR 97128
888-563-4500; Fax: 503-434-9704
www.williamhenryknives.com
Semi-custom folding knives for hunting and general use; some limited editions

WUU JAU CO. INC
2600 S Kelly Ave
Edmond, OK 73013
800-722-5760; Fax: 877-256-4337
mail@wuujau.com; www.wuujau.com
Wide variety of imported fixed-blade and folding knives for hunting, fishing, camping, and general use. Wholesale to knife dealers only

WYOMING KNIFE CORP.
101 Commerce Dr
Ft. Collins, CO 80524
970-224-3454; Fax: 970-226-0778
wyoknife@hotmail.com;
www.wyomingknife.com

XIKAR INC
PO Box 025757
Kansas City MO 64102
888-676-7380; 816-474-7555
info@xikar.com; www.xikar.com
Gentlemen's cutlery and accessories

importers

A.G. RUSSELL KNIVES INC
2900 S. 26th St.
Rogers, AR 72758-8571
800-255-9034 or 479-631-0130;
fax 479-631-8493
ag@agrussell.com; www.agrussell.com
The oldest knife mail-order company, highest quality. Free catalog available. In these catalogs you will find the newest and the best. If you like knives, this catalog is a must. Celebrating over 40 years in the industry

ADAMS INTERNATIONAL KNIFEWORKS
8710 Rosewood Hills
Edwardsville, IL 62025
Importers & foreign cutlers

AITOR-BERRIZARGO S.L.
P.I. Eitua PO Box 26
48240 Berriz Vizcaya
SPAIN
946826599; 94602250226
info@aitor.com; www.aitor.com
Sporting knives

ATLANTA CUTLERY CORP.
P.O.Box 839
Conyers, Ga 30012
800-883-0300; Fax: 770-388-0246
custserve@atlantacutlery.com;
www.atlantacutlery.com
Exotic knives from around the world

BAILEY'S
PO Box 550
Laytonville, CA 95454
800-322-4539; 707-984-8115
baileys@baileys-online.com;
www.baileys-online.com

BELTRAME, FRANCESCO
Fratelli Beltrame F&C snc Via dei Fabbri
15/B-33085 MANIAGO (PN)
ITALY
39 0427 701859
www.italianstiletto.com

BOKER USA, INC.
1550 Balsam St
Lakewood, CO 80214-5917
303-462-0662; 303-462-0668
sales@bokerusa.com; www.bokerusa.com
Ceramic blades

CAMPOS, IVAN DE ALMEIDA
R. Stelio M. Loureiro, 205
Centro, Tatui
BRAZIL
00-55-15-33056867
www.ivancampos.com

C.A.S. IBERIA, INC.
650 Industrial Blvd
Sale Creek, TN 37373
423-332-4700; 423-332-7248
info@casiberia.com; www.casiberia.com

CAS/HANWEI, MUELA
Catoctin Cutlery
PO Box 188
Smithsburg, MD 21783

CLASSIC INDUSTRIES
1325 Howard Ave, Suite 408
Burlingame, CA 94010

COAST CUTLERY CO.
8033 NE Holman St.
Portland, OR 97218
800-426-5858
staff@coastcutlery.com;
www.coastcutlery.com

COLUMBIA PRODUCTS CO.
PO Box 1333
Sialkot 51310
PAKISTAN

COLUMBIA PRODUCTS INT'L
PO Box 8243
New York, NY 10116-8243
201-854-3054; Fax: 201-854-7058
nycolumbia@aol.com;
http://www.columbiaproducts.homestead.com/cat.html
Pocket, hunting knives and swords of all kinds

COMPASS INDUSTRIES, INC.
104 E. 25th St
New York, NY 10010
800-221-9904; Fax: 212-353-0826
jeff@compassindustries.com;
www.compassindustries.com
Imported pocket knives

CONAZ COLTELLERIE
Dei F.Lli Consigli-Scarperia
Via G. Giordani, 20
50038 Scarperia (Firenze)
ITALY
36 55 846187; 39 55 846603
conaz@dada.it; www.consigliscarpeia.com
Handicraft workmanship of knives of the ancient Italian tradition. Historical and collection knives

CONSOLIDATED CUTLERY CO., INC.
696 NW Sharpe St
Port St. Lucie, FL 34983
772-878-6139

CRAZY CROW TRADING POST
PO Box 847
Pottsboro, TX 75076
800-786-6210; Fax: 903-786-9059
info@crazycrow.com; www.crazycrow.com
Solingen blades, knife making parts & supplies

DER FLEISSIGEN BEAVER
(The Busy Beaver)
Harvey Silk
PO Box 1166
64343 Griesheim
GERMANY
49 61552231; 49 6155 2433
Der.Biber@t-online.de
Retail custom knives. Knife shows in Germany & UK

EXTREMA RATIO SAS
Mauro Chiostri; Mavrizio Castrati
Via Tourcoing 40/p
59100 Prato (PO)
ITALY
0039 0574 58 4639; 0039 0574 581312
info@extremarazio.com;
www.extremaratio.com
Tactical & military knives manufacturing

FALLKNIVEN AB
Havrevagen 10
S-96142 Boden
SWEDEN
46 92154422; 46 92154433
info@fallkniven.se
www.fallkniven.com
High quality knives

FREDIANI COLTELLI FINLANDESI
Via Lago Maggiore 41
I-21038 Leggiuno
ITALY

GIESSER MESSERFABRIK GMBH, JOHANNES
Raiffeisenstr 15
D-71349 Winnenden
GERMANY
49-7195-1808-29
info@giesser.de; www.giesser.de
Professional butchers and chef's knives

HIMALAYAN IMPORTS
3495 Lakeside Dr
Reno, NV 89509
775-825-2279
unclebill@himalayan-imports.com; www.
himilayan-imports.com

IVAN DE ALMEIDA CAMPOS-KNIFE DEALER
R. Xi De Agosto
107, Centro, Tatui, Sp 18270
BRAZIL
55-15-251-8092; 55-15-251-4896
campos@bitweb.com.br
Custom knives from all Brazilian knifemakers

JOY ENTERPRISES
1862 M.L. King Blvd
Riviera Beach, FL 33404
800-500-3879; 561-863-3277
mail@joyenterprises.com;

www.joyenterprises.com
Fury™, Mustang™, Hawg Knives, Muela

KELLAM KNIVES CO.
902 S Dixie Hwy
Lantana, FL 33462
800-390-6918; 561-588-3186
info@kellamknives.com;
www.kellamknives.com
Knives from Finland; own line of knives

KNIFE IMPORTERS, INC.
11307 Conroy Ln
Manchaca, TX 78652
512-282-6860, Fax: 512-282-7504
Wholesale only

KNIGHTS EDGE
5696 N Northwest Hwy
Chicago, IL 60646
773-775-3888; 773-775-3339
www.knightsedge.com
Exclusive designers of our Rittersteel, Stagesteel and Valiant Arms and knightedge lines of weapon

LEISURE PRODUCTS CORP.
PO Box 1171
Sialkot-51310
PAKISTAN

L. C. RISTINEN
Suomi Shop
17533 Co Hwy 38
Frazee MN 56544
218-538-6633; 218-538-6633
icrist@wcta.net
Scandinavian cutlery custom antique, books and reindeer antler

LINDER, CARL NACHF.
Erholungstr. 10
D-42699 Solingen
GERMANY
212 33 0 856; Fax: 212 33 71 04
info@linder.de; www.linder.de

MARTTIINI KNIVES
PO Box 44 (Marttiinintie 3)
96101 Rovaniemi
FINLAND

MATTHEWS CUTLERY
4401 Sentry Dr, Suite K
Tucker, GA 30084-6561
770-939-6915

MESSER KLÖTZLI
PO Box 104
Hohengasse 3, Ch-3402 Burgdorf
SWITZERLAND
034 422 2378; 034 422 7693
info@klotzli.com; www.klotzli.com

MURAKAMI, ICHIRO
Knife Collectors Assn. Japan
Tokuda Nishi 4 Chome, 76 Banchi, Ginancho
Hashimagun, Gifu
JAPAN
81 58 274 1960; 81 58 273 7369
www.gix.orjp/~n-resin/

MUSEUM REPLICAS LIMITED
2147 Gees Mill Rd
Conyers, GA 30012
800-883-8838
www.museumreplicas.com

NICHOLS CO.
Pomfret Rd
South Pomfret, VT 05067
Import & distribute knives from EKA (Sweden), Helle (Norway), Brusletto (Norway), Roselli (Finland). Also market Zippo products, Snow, Nealley axes and hatchets and snow & Neally axes

NORMARK CORP.
Craig Weber
10395 Yellow Circle Dr
Minnetonka, MN 55343

PRODUCTORS AITOR, S.A.
Izelaieta 17
48260 Ermua
SPAIN
943-170850; 943-170001
info@aitor.com
Sporting knives

PROFESSIONAL CUTLERY SERVICES
9712 Washburn Rd
Downey, CA 90241
562-803-8778; 562-803-4261
Wholesale only. Full service distributor of domestic & imported brand name cutlery. Exclusive U.S. importer for both Marto Swords and Battle Ready Valiant Armory edged weapons

SCANDIA INTERNATIONAL INC.
5475 W Inscription Canyon Dr
Prescott, AZ 86305
928-442-0140; Fax: 928-442-0342
mora@cableone.net; www.frosts-scandia.
com
Frosts knives of Sweden

STAR SALES CO., INC.
1803 N. Central St
Knoxville, TN 37917
800-745-6433; Fax: 865-524-4889
www.starknives.com

SVORD KNIVES
Smith Rd., RD 2
Waiuku, South Auckland
NEW ZEALAND
64 9 2358846; Fax: 64 9 2356483
www.svord.com

SWISS ARMY BRANDS LTD.
The Forschner Group, Inc.
One Research Drive
Shelton, CT 06484
203-929-6391; 203-929-3786
www.swissarmy.com

TAYLOR BRANDS, LLC
1043 Fordtown Road
Kingsport, TN 37663
800-251-0254; Fax: 423-247-5371
info@taylorbrandsllc.com;
www.taylorbrands.com
Fixed-blade and folding knives for tactical, rescue, hunting and general use. Also provides etching, engraving, scrimshaw services.

UNITED CUTLERY CORP.
1425 United Blvd
Sevierville, TN 37876
865-428-2532; 865-428-2267
order@unitedcutlery.com;
www.unitedcutlery.com
Harley-Davidson ® Colt ®, Stanley ®, U21 ®, Rigid Knives ®, Outdoor Life ®, Ford ®, hunting, camping, fishing, collectible & fantasy knives

UNIVERSAL AGENCIES INC
4690 S Old Peachtree Rd, Suite C
Norcross, GA 30071-1517
678-969-9147; Fax: 678-969-9169
info@knifecupplies.com;
www.knifesupplies.com;
www.thunderforged.com; www.uai.org
*Serving the cutlery industry with the finest
selection of India Stag, Buffalo Horn,
Thurnderforged ™ Damascus. Mother of Pearl,
Knife Kits and more*

VALOR CORP.
1001 Sawgrass Corp Pkwy
Sunrise, FL 33323
800-899-8256; Fax: 954-377-4941
www.valorcorp.com
Wide variety of imported & domestic knives

WENGER N. A.
15 Corporate Dr
Orangeburg, NY 10962
800-431-2996
www.wengerna.com
Swiss Army ™ Knives

WILD BOAR BLADES
1701 Broadway, Suite 282
Vancouver, WA 98663
888-476-4400; 360-735-0390
usakopro@aol.com;
www.wildboarblades.com
*Carries a full line of Kopromed knives and
kitchenware imported from Poland*

WORLD CLASS EXHIBITION KNIVES
Cary Desmon
941-504-2279
www.withoutequal.com
Carries an extensive line of Pius Lang knives

ZWILLING J.A. HENCKELS USA
171 Saw Mill River Rd
Hawthorne, NY 10532
800-777-4308; Fax: 914-747-1850
info@jahenckels.com;
www.jahenckels.com
*Kitchen cutlery, scissors, gadgets, flatware and
cookware*

knife making supplies

AFRICAN IMPORT CO.
Alan Zanotti
22 Goodwin Rd
Plymouth, MA 02360
508-746-8552; 508-746-0404
africanimport@aol.com
Ivory

ALABAMA DAMASCUS STEEL
PO Box 54
WELLINGTON, AL 36279
256-892-2950
sales@alabamadamascussteel.com
www.alabamadamascussteel.com
*We are a manufacturer of damascus steel
billets & blades. We also offer knife supplies.
We can custom make any blade design that
the customer wants. We can also make custom
damascus billets per customer specs.*

AMERICAN SIEPMANN CORP.
65 Pixley Industrial Parkway
Rochester, NY 14624
800-724-0919; Fax: 585-247-1883
www.siepmann.com
*CNC blade grinding equipment, grinding
wheels, production blade grinding services.
Sharpening stones and sharpening equipment*

ANKROM EXOTICS
Pat Ankrom
22900 HWY 5
Centerville, IA 52544
641-436-0235
ankromexotics@hotmail.com
www.ankromexotics.com
*Stabilized handle material; Exotic burls
and hardwoods from around the world;
Stabilizing services available*

ATLANTA CUTLERY CORP.
P.O.Box 839
Conyers, Ga 30012
800-883-0300; Fax: 770-388-0246
custserve@atlantacutlery.com;
www.atlantacutlery.com

BATAVIA ENGINEERING
PO Box 53
Magaliesburg, 1791
SOUTH AFRICA
27-14-5771294
bertie@batavia.co.za; www.batavia.co.za
*Contact wheels for belt grinders and surface
grinders; damascus and mokume*

BLADEMAKER, THE
Gary Kelley
17485 SW Phesant Ln
Beaverton, OR 97006
503-649-7867
garykelly@theblademaker.com;
www.theblademaker.com
*Period knife and hawk blades for hobbyists
& re-enactors and in dendritic D2 steel.
"Ferroulithic" steel-stone spear point, blades
and arrowheads*

BOONE TRADING CO., INC.
PO Box 669
562 Coyote Rd
Brinnon, WA 98320
800-423-1945; Fax: 360-796-4511
www.boonetrading.com
Ivory of all types, bone, horns

BORGER, WOLF
Benzstrasse 8
76676 Graben-Neudorf
GERMANY
wolf@messerschmied.de;
www.messerschmied.de

BOYE KNIVES
PO Box 1238
Dolan Springs, AZ 86441-1238
800-853-1617; 928-767-4273
info@boyeknives.com;
www.boyeknives.com
Dendritic steel and Dendritic cobalt

BRONK'S KNIFEWORKS
Lyle Brunckhorst
Country Village
23706 7th Ave SE, Suite B
Bothell, WA 98021
425-402-3484
bronks@bronksknifeworks.com;
www.bronksknifeworks.com
Damascus steel

CRAZY CROW TRADING POST
PO Box 847
Pottsboro, TX 75076
800-786-6210; Fax: 903-786-9059
info@crazycrow.com; www.crazycrow.com
Solingen blades, knife making parts & supplies

CULPEPPER & CO.
Joe Culpepper
P.O. Box 690
8285 Georgia Rd.
Otto, NC 28763
828-524-6842; Fax: 828-369-7809
culpepperandco@verizon.net
www.knifehandles.com http://www.
knifehandles.com
www.stingrayproducts.com <http://www.
stingrayproducts.com>
*Mother of pearl, bone, abalone, stingray, dyed
stag, blacklip, ram's horn, mammoth ivory,
coral, scrimshaw*

CUSTOM FURNACES
PO Box 353
Randvaal, 1873
SOUTH AFRICA
27 16 365-5723; 27 16 365-5738
johnlee@custom.co.za
Furnaces for hardening & tempering of knives

DAMASCUS-USA CHARLTON LTD.
149 Deans Farm Rd
Tyner, NC 27980-9607
252-221-2010
rcharlton@damascususa.com;
www.damascususa.com

DAN'S WHETSTONE CO., INC.
418 Hilltop Rd
Pearcy, AR 71964
501-767-1616; 501-767-9598
questions@danswhetstone.com;
www.danswhetstone.com
Natural abrasive Arkansas stone products

**DIAMOND MACHINING TECHNOLOGY,
INC. DMT**
85 Hayes Memorial Dr
Marlborough, MA 01752
800-666-4DMT
dmtsharp@dmtsharp.com;
www.dmtsharp.com
*Knife and tool sharpeners-diamond, ceramic
and easy edge guided sharpening kits*

DIGEM DIAMOND SUPPLIERS
7303 East Earll Drive
Scottsdale, Arizona 85251
602-620-3999
eglasser@cox.net
*#1 international diamond tool provider. Every
diamond tool you will ever need 1/16th of an
inch to 11'x9'. BURRS, CORE DRILLS, SAW
BLADES, MILLING SHAPES, AND WHEELS*

DIXIE GUN WORKS, INC.
PO Box 130
Union City, TN 38281
800-238-6785; Fax: 731-885-0440
www.dixiegunworks.com
Knife and knifemaking supplies

EZE-LAP DIAMOND PRODUCTS
3572 Arrowhead Dr
Carson City, NV 89706
800-843-4815; Fax: 775-888-9555
sales@eze-lap.com; www.eze-lap.com
Diamond coated sharpening tools

FLITZ INTERNATIONAL, LTD.
821 Mohr Ave
Waterford, WI 53185
800-558-8611; Fax: 262-534-2991
info@flitz.com; www.flitz.com
Metal polish, buffing pads, wax

FORTUNE PRODUCTS, INC.
205 Hickory Creek Rd
Marble Falls, TX 78654-3357
830-693-6111; Fax: 830-693-6394
www.accusharp.com
AccuSharp knife sharpeners

GALLERY HARDWOODS
Larry Davis
Acworth, GA
www.galleryhardwoods.com
Stabilized exotic burls and woods

GILMER WOOD CO.
2211 NW St Helens Rd
Portland, OR 97210
503-274-1271; Fax: 503-274-9839
www.gilmerwood.com

GREEN RIVER LEATHER, INC.
1100 Legion Park Rd.
Greensburg, KY 42743
270-932-2212; Fax: 270-299-2471
sherrylott@alltel.net;
www.greenriverleather.com
Complete line of veg tan and exotic leathers, shethmaking hardware, thread, dyes, finishes, etc.

GRS CORP.
D.J. Glaser
PO Box 1153
Emporia, KS 66801
800-835-3519; Fax: 620-343-9640
glendo@glendo.com; www.glendo.com
Engraving, equipment, tool sharpener, books/ videos

HALPERN TITANIUM INC.
Les and Marianne Halpern
PO Box 214
4 Springfield St
Three Rivers, MA 01080
888-283-8627; Fax: 413-289-2372
info@halperntitanium.com;
www.halperntitanium.com
Titanium, carbon fiber, G-10, fasteners; CNC milling

HAWKINS KNIVE MAKING SUPPLIES
110 Buckeye Rd
Fayetteville, GA 30214
770-964-1177; Fax: 770-306-2877
Sales@hawkinsknifemakingsupplies.com
www.HawkinsKnifeMakingSupllies.com
All styles

HILTARY-USGRC
6060 East Thomas Road
Scottsdale, AZ 85251
Office: 480-945-0700
Fax: 480-945-3333
usgrc@cox.net
Gibeon Meteorite, Recon Gems, Diamond cutting tools, Exotic natural minerals, garaffe bone. Atomic absorbtion/ spectographic analyst, precisious metal

HOUSE OF TOOLS LTD.
#54-5329 72 Ave. S.E.
Calgary, Alberta
CANADA T2C 4X
403-640-4594; Fax: 403-451-7006

INDIAN JEWELERS SUPPLY CO.
Mail Order: 601 E Coal Ave
Gallup, NM 87301-6005
2105 San Mateo Blvd NE
Albuquerque, NM 87110-5148
505-722-4451; 505-265-3701
orders@ijsinc.com; www.ijsinc.com
Handle materials, tools, metals

INTERAMCO INC.
5210 Exchange Dr
Flint, MI 48507
810-732-8181; 810-732-6116
solutions@interamco.com
Knife grinding and polishing

JANTZ SUPPLY / KOVAL KNIVES
PO Box 584
309 West Main
Davis, OK 73030
800-351-8900; 580-369-2316
jantz@brightok.net; www.knifemaking.com
Pre shaped blades, kit knives, complete knifemaking supply line

JOHNSON, R.B.
I.B.S. Int'l. Folder Supplies
Box 11
Clearwater, MN 55320
320-558-6128; 320-558-6128
Threaded pivot pins, screws, taps, etc.

JOHNSON WOOD PRODUCTS
34897 Crystal Rd
Strawberry Point, IA 52076
563-933-6504

K&G FINISHING SUPPLIES
1972 Forest Ave
Lakeside, AZ 85929
800-972-1192; 928-537-8877
csinfo@knifeandgun.com;
www.knifeandgun.com
Full service supplies

KOWAK IVORY
Roland and Kathy Quimby
(April-Sept): PO Box 350
Ester, AK 99725
907-479-9335
(Oct-March)
PO Box 693
Bristow, OK 74010
918-367-2684
sales@kowakivory.com;
www.kowakivory.com
Fossil ivories

LITTLE GIANT POWER HAMMER
Harlan "Sid" Suedmeier
420 4th Corso
Nebraska City, NE 68410
402-873-6603
www.littlegianthammer.com
Rebuilds hammers and supplies parts

LIVESAY, NEWT
3306 S Dogwood St
Siloam Springs, AR 72761
479-549-3356; 479-549-3357
Combat utility knives, titanium knives, sportsmen knives, custom made orders taken on knives and after market Kydex© sheaths for commercial or custom cutlery

LOHMAN CO., FRED
3405 NE Broadway
Portland, OR 97232
503-282-4567; Fax: 503-287-2678
lohman@katana4u.com;
www.japanese-swords.com

M MILLER ORIGINALS
Michael Miller
2960 E Carver Ave
Kingman AZ 86401
928-757-1359
mike@milleroriginals.com;
www.mmilleroriginals.com
Supplies stabilized juniper burl blocks and scales

MARKING METHODS, INC.
Sales
301 S. Raymond Ave
Alhambra, CA 91803-1531
626-282-8823; Fax: 626-576-7564
experts@markingmethods.com;
www.markingmethods.com
Knife etching equipment & service

MASECRAFT SUPPLY CO.
254 Amity St
Meriden, CT 06450
800-682-5489; Fax: 203-238-2373
info@masecraftsupply.com;
www.masecraftsupply.com
Natural & specialty synthetic handle materials & more

MEIER STEEL
Daryl Meier
75 Forge Rd
Carbondale, IL 62903
618-549-3234; Fax: 618-549-6239
www.meiersteel.com

NICO, BERNARD
PO Box 5151
Nelspruit 1200
SOUTH AFRICA
011-2713-7440099; 011-2713-7440099
bernardn@iafrica.com

NORRIS, MIKE
Rt 2 Box 242A
Tollesboro, KY 41189
606-798-1217
Damascus steel

NORTHCOAST KNIVES
17407 Puritas Ave
Cleveland, Ohio 44135
www.NorthCoastKnives.com
Tutorials and step-by-step projects. Entry level knifemaking supplies.

OSO FAMOSO
PO Box 654
Ben Lomond, CA 95005
831-336-2343
oso@osofamoso.com;
www.osofamoso.com
Mammoth ivory bark

OZARK KNIFE & GUN
3165 S Campbell Ave
Springfield, MO 65807
417-886-CUTT; 417-887-2635
danhoneycutt@sbcglobal.net
28 years in the cutlery business, Missouri's oldest cutlery firm

PARAGON INDUSTRIES, INC. L. P.
2011 South Town East Blvd
Mesquite, TX 75149-1122
800-876-4328; Fax: 972-222-0646
info@paragonweb.com;
www.paragonweb.com
Heat treating furnaces for knifemakers

POPLIN, JAMES / POP'S KNIVES & SUPPLIES
103 Oak St
Washington, GA 30673
706-678-5408; Fax: 706-678-5409
www.popsknifesupplies.com

PUGH, JIM
PO Box 711
917 Carpenter
Azle, TX 76020
817-444-2679; Fax: 817-444-5455
Rosewood and ebony Micarta blocks,rivets for Kydex sheaths, 0-80 screws for folders

RADOS, JERRY
7523E 5000 N. Rd
Grant Park, IL 60940
815-405-5061
jerry@radosknives.com;
www.radosknives.com
Damascus steel

REACTIVE METALS STUDIO, INC.
PO Box 890
Clarksdale, AZ 86324
800-876-3434; 928-634-3434; Fax: 928-634-6734
info@reactivemetals.com; www.reactivemetals.com

R. FIELDS ANCIENT IVORY
Donald Fields
790 Tamerlane St
Deltona, FL 32725
386-532-9070
donaldfields@aol.com
Selling ancient ivories; Mammoth, fossil & walrus

RICK FRIGAULT CUSTOM KNIVES
3584 Rapidsview Dr
Niagara Falls, Ontario
CANADA L2G 6C4
905-295-6695
zipcases@zipcases.com;
www.zipcases.com
Selling padded zippered knife pouches with an option to personalize the outside with the marker, purveyor, stores-address, phone number, email web-site or any other information needed. Available in black cordura, mossy oak camo in sizes 4"x2" to 20"x4.5"

RIVERSIDE MACHINE
201 W Stillwell
DeQueen, AR 71832
870-642-7643; Fax: 870-642-4023
uncleal@riversidemachine.net
www.riversidemachine.net

ROCKY MOUNTAIN KNIVES
George L. Conklin
PO Box 902, 615 Franklin
Ft. Benton, MT 59442
406-622-3268; Fax: 406-622-3410
bbgrus@ttc-cmc.net
Working knives

RUMMELL, HANK
10 Paradise Lane
Warwick, NY 10990
845-469-9172
hank@newyorkcustomknives.com;
www.newyorkcustomknives.com

SAKMAR, MIKE
1451 Clovelly Ave
Rochester, MI 48307
248-852-6775; Fax: 248-852-8544
mikesakmar@yahoo.com
Mokume bar stock. Retail & wholesale

SANDPAPER, INC. OF ILLINOIS
P.O. Box 2579
Glen Ellyn, IL 60138
630-629-3320; Fax: 630-629-3324
sandinc@aol.com; www.sandpaperinc.com
Abrasive belts, rolls, sheets & discs

SCHEP'S FORGE
PO Box 395
Shelton, NE 68876-0395

SENTRY SOLUTIONS LTD.
PO Box 214
Wilton, NH 03086
800-546-8049; Fax: 603-654-3003
info@sentrysolutions.com;
www.sentrysolutions.com
Knife care products

SHEFFIELD KNIFEMAKERS SUPPLY, INC.
PO Box 741107
Orange City, FL 32774
386-775-6453
email@sheffieldsupply.com;
www.sheffieldsupply.com

SHINING WAVE METALS
PO Box 563
Snohomish, WA 98291
425-334-5569
info@shiningwave.com;
www.shiningwave.com
A full line of mokume-gane in precious and non-precious metals for knifemakers, jewelers and other artists

SMITH ABRASIVES, INC. / SMITH WHETSTONE, INC.
1700 Sleepy Valley Rd
Hot Springs, AR 71901
www.smithabrasives.com

SMOLEN FORGE, INC.
Nick Smolen
S1735 Vang Rd
Westby, WI 54667
608-634-3569; Fax: 608-634-3869
smoforge@mwt.net;
www.smolenforge.com
Damascus billets & blanks, Mokume gane billets

SOSTER SVENSTRUP BYVEJ 16
Søster Svenstrup Byvej 16
4130 Viby Sjælland
Denmark
45 46 19 43 05; Fax: 45 46 19 53 19
www.poulstrande.com

STAMASCUS KNIFEWORKS INC.
Ed VanHoy
24255 N Fork River Rd
Abingdon, VA 24210
276-944-4885; Fax: 276-944-3187
stamascus@hughes.net;
www.stamascus-knive-works.com
Blade steels

STOVER, JEFF
PO Box 43
Torrance, CA 90507
310-532-2166
edgedealer1@yahoo.com;
www.edgedealer.com
Fine custom knives, top makers

TEXAS KNIFEMAKERS SUPPLY
10649 Haddington Suite 180
Houston TX 77043
713-461-8632; Fax: 713-461-8221
sales@texasknife.com;
www.texasknife.com
Working straight knives. Hunters including upswept skinners and custom walking sticks

TRU-GRIT, INC.
760 E Francis Unit N
Ontario, CA 91761
909-923-4116; Fax: 909-923-9932
www.trugrit.com
The latest in Norton and 3/M ceramic grinding belts. Also Super Flex, Trizact, Norax and Micron belts to 3000 grit. All of the popular belt grinders. Buffers and variable speed motors. ATS-34, 440C, BG-42, CPM S-30V, 416 and Damascus steel

FINE TURNAGE PRODUCTIONS
Charles Turnage
1210 Midnight Drive
San Antonio, TX 78260
210-352-5660
cat41259@aol.com
www.fineturnage.com
Specializing in stabilized mammoth tooth and bone, mammoth ivory, fossil brain coral, meteorite, etc.

UNIVERSAL AGENCIES INC
4690 S Old Peachtree Rd, Suite C
Norcross, GA 30071-1517
678-969-9147; Fax: 678-969-9169
info@knifecupplies.com;
www.knifesupplies.com;
www.thunderforged.com; www.uai.org
Serving the cutlery industry with the finest selection of India Stag, Buffalo Horn, Thurnderforged ™ Damascus. Mother of Pearl, Knife Kits and more

WASHITA MOUNTAIN WHETSTONE CO.
PO Box 20378
Hot Springs, AR 71903-0378
501-525-3914; Fax: 501-525-0816
wmw@hsnp

WEILAND, J. REESE
PO Box 2337
Riverview, FL 33568
813-671-0661; 727-595-0378
rwphil413@earthlink.net
Folders, straight knives, etc.

WILD WOODS
Jim Fray
9608 Monclova Rd
Monclova, OH 43542
419-866-0435

WILSON, R.W.
PO Box 2012
113 Kent Way
Weirton, WV 26062
304-723-2771

WOOD CARVERS SUPPLY, INC.
PO Box 7500-K
Englewood, FL 34223
800-284-6229; 941-460-0123
info@woodcarverssupply.com;
www.woodcarverssupply.com
Over 2,000 unique wood carving tools

WOOD LAB
Michael Balaskovitz
P.O. Box 222
Hudsonville, MI 49426
616-322-5846
michael@woodlab.biz;
www.woodlab.biz
Acrylic stabilizing services and materials

WOOD STABILIZING SPECIALISTS INT'L, LLC
2940 Fayette Ave
Ionia, IA 50645
800-301-9774; 641-435-4746
mike@stabilizedwood.com;
www.stabilizedwood.com
Processor of acrylic impregnated materials

ZOWADA CUSTOM KNIVES
Tim Zowada
4509 E. Bear River Rd
Boyne Falls, MI 49713
231-348-5416
tim@tzknives.com; www.tzknives.com
Damascus, pocket knives, swords, Lower case gothic tz logo

mail order sales

A.G. RUSSELL KNIVES INC
2900 S. 26th St
Rogers, AR 72758-8571
800-255-9034 or 479-631-0130;
fax 479-631-8493
ag@agrussell.com; www.agrussell.com
The oldest knife mail-order company, highest quality. Free catalog available. In these catalogs you will find the newest and the best. If you like knives, this catalog is a must

ARIZONA CUSTOM KNIVES
Julie Hyman
2225 A1A South
Suite B-5
St. Augustine, FL 32080
904-826-4178
sharptalk@arizonacustomknifes.com;
www.arizonacustomknives.com
Color catalog $5 U.S. / $7 Foreign

ARTISAN KNIVES
Ty Young
575 Targhee Twn Rd
Alta, WY 83414
304-353-8111
ty@artisanknives.com;
www.artisanknives.com
Feature master artisan knives and makers in a unique "coffee table book" style format

ATLANTA CUTLERY CORP.
P.O.Box 839
Conyers, Ga 30012
800-883-0300; Fax: 770-388-0246
custserve@atlantacutlery.com;
www.atlantacutlery.com

ATLANTIC BLADESMITHS/PETER STEBBINS
50 Mill Rd
Littleton, MA 01460
978-952-6448
Sell, trade, buy; carefully selected handcrafted, benchmade and factory knives

BALLARD CUTLERY
1495 Brummel Ave.
Elk Grove Village, IL 60007
847-228-0070

BECK'S CUTLERY SPECIALTIES
107 S Edinburgh Dr
Cary, NC 27511
919-460-0203; Fax: 919-460-7772
beckscutlery@mindspring.com;
www.beckscutlery.com
Knives

BLADEGALLERY, INC. / EPICUREAN EDGE, THE
107 Central Way
Kirkland, WA 98033
425-889-5980; Fax: 425-889-5981
info@bladegallery.com;
www.bladegallery.com
Bladegallery.com specializes in hand-made one-of-a-kind knives from around the world. We have an emphasis on forged knives and high-end gentlemen's folders

BLUE RIDGE KNIVES
166 Adwolfe Rd
Marion, VA 24354
276-783-6143; 276-783-9298
onestop@blueridgeknives.com;
www.blueridgeknives.com
Wholesale distributor of knives

BOB NEAL CUSTOM KNIVES
PO Box 20923
Atlanta, GA 30320
770-914-7794
bob@bobnealcustomknives.com;
www.bobnealcustomknives.com
Exclusive limited edition custom knives-sets & single

BOB'S TRADING POST
308 N Main St
Hutchinson, KS 67501
620-669-9441
bobstradingpost@cox.net;
www.gunshopfinder.com
Tad custom knives with reichert custom sheaths one at a time, one of a kind

BOONE TRADING CO., INC.
PO Box 669
562 Coyote Rd
Brinnon, WA 98320
800-423-1945; Fax: 360-796-4511
www.boonetrading.com
Ivory of all types, bone, horns

CARMEL CUTLERY
Dolores & 6th
PO Box 1346
Carmel, CA 93921
831-624-6699; 831-624-6780
ccutlery@ix.netcom.com;
www.carmelcutlery.com
Quality custom and a variety of production pocket knives, swords; kitchen cutlery; personal grooming items

CUSTOM KNIFE CONSIGNMENT
PO Box 20923
Atlanta, GA 30320
770-914-7794; 770-914-7796
bob@customknifeconsignment.com; www.customknifeconsignment.com
We sell your knives

CUTLERY SHOPPE
3956 E Vantage Pointe Ln
Meridian, ID 83642-7268
800-231-1272; Fax: 208-884-4433
order@cutleryshoppe.com;
www.cutleryshoppe.com
Discount pricing on top quality brands

CUTTING EDGE, THE
2900 South 26th St
Rogers, AR 72758-8571
800-255-9034; Fax: 479-631-8493
ce_info@cuttingedge.com;
www.cuttingedge.com
After-market knives since 1968. They offer about 1,000 individual knives for sale each month. Subscription by first class mail, in U.S. $20 per year, Canada or Mexico by air mail, $25 per year. All overseas by air mail, $40 per year. The oldest and the most experienced in the business of buying and selling knives. They buy collections of any size, take knives on consignment. Every month there are 4-8 pages in color featuring the work of top makers

DENTON, JOHN W.
703 Hiawassee Estates
Hiawassee, GA 30546
706-781-8470
jwdenton@windstream.net
Loveless knives

DUNN KNIVES INC.
PO Box 204
5830 NW Carlson Rd
Rossville, KS 66533
800-245-6483
steve.greene@dunnknives.com;
www.dunnknives.com

FAZALARE, ROY
PO Box 7062
Thousand Oaks, CA 91359
805-496-2002 after 7pm
ourfaz@aol.com
Handmade multiblades; older case; Fight'n Rooster; Bulldog brand & Cripple Creek

FROST CUTLERY CO.
PO Box 22636
Chattanooga, TN 37422
800-251-7768; Fax: 423-894-9576
www.frostcutlery.com

GENUINE ISSUE INC.
949 Middle Country Rd
Selden, NY 11784
631-696-3802; 631-696-3803
gicutlery@aol.com
Antique knives, swords

GEORGE TICHBOURNE CUSTOM KNIVES
7035 Maxwell Rd #5
Mississauga, Ontario L5S 1R5
CANADA
905-670-0200
sales@tichbourneknives.com;
www.tichbourneknives.com
Canadian custom knifemaker has full retail knife store

GODWIN, INC. G. GEDNEY
PO Box 100
Valley Forge, PA 19481
610-783-0670; Fax: 610-783-6083
sales@gggodwin.com;
www.gggodwin.com
18th century reproductions

GOLCZEWS KNIVES
Larry Golczewski, dba New Jersey Knifer
30 Quigley Rd.
Hewitt, NJ 07421
973-728-2386
Medium- to high-priced custom and handmade knives, some production if made in USA, Japan, Germany, or Italy. Practical to tactical. Consignments welcome. Also buy, design, and appraise.

GRAZYNA SHAW/QUINTESSENTIAL CUTLERY
715 Bluff St.
Clearwater, MN 55320
201-655-4411; Fax: 320-558-6128; www.quintcut.com
Specializing in investment-grade custom knives and early makers

GUILD KNIVES
Donald Guild
320 Paani Place 1A
Paia, HI 96779
808-877-3109
don@guildknives.com;
www.guildknives.com
Purveyor of custom art knives

HOUSE OF TOOLS LTD.
#136, 8228 Macleod Tr. SE
Calgary, Alberta, Canada
T2H 2B8

JENCO SALES, INC. / KNIFE IMPORTERS, INC. / WHITE LIGHTNING
PO Box 1000
11307 Conroy Ln
Manchaca, TX 78652
303-444-2882
kris@finishlineusa.com
www.whitelightningco.com
Wholesale only

KELLAM KNIVES CO.
902 S Dixie Hwy
Lantana, FL 33462
800-390-6918; 561-588-3186
info@kellamknives.com;
www.kellamknives.com
Largest selection of Finnish knives; own line of folders and fixed blades

KNIFEART.COM
13301 Pompano Dr
Little Rock AR 72211
501-221-1319; Fax: 501-221-2695
www.knifeart.com
Large internet seller of custom knives & upscale production knives

KNIFEPURVEYOR.COM LLC
646-872-0476
mdonato@knifepurveyor.com; www.knifepurveyor.com
Owned and operated by Michael A. Donato (full-time knife purveyor since 2002). We buy, sell, trade, and consign fine custom knives. We also specialize in buying and selling valuable collections of fine custom knives. Our goal is to make every transaction a memorable one.

KNIVES PLUS
2467 I 40 West
Amarillo, TX 79109
800-687-6202
salessupport@knivesplus.com; www.knivesplus.com
Retail cutlery and cutlery accessories since 1987

KRIS CUTLERY
2314 Monte Verde Dr
Pinole, CA 94564
510-758-9912 Fax: 510-223-8968
kriscutlery@aol.com; www.kriscutlery.com
Japanese, medieval, Chinese & Philippine

LONE STAR WHOLESALE
2407 W Interstate 40
Amarillo, TX 79109
806-356-9540
Wholesale only; major brands and accessories

MATTHEWS CUTLERY
4401 Sentry Dr
Tucker, GA 30084-6561
770-939-6915

MOORE CUTLERY
PO Box 633
Lockport, IL 60441
708-301-4201
www.knives.cx
Owned & operated by Gary Moore since 1991 (a full-time dealer). Purveyor of high quality custom & production knives

MORTY THE KNIFE MAN, INC.
4 Manorhaven Blvd
Pt Washington, NY 11050
516-767-2357; 516-767-7058

MUSEUM REPLICAS LIMITED
2147 Gees Mill Rd
Conyers, GA 30012
800-883-8838
www.museumreplicas.com
Historically accurate and battle ready swords & daggers

NORDIC KNIVES
1634-C Copenhagen Drive
Solvang, CA 93463
805-688-3612; Fax: 805-688-1635
info@nordicknives.com;
www.nordicknives.com
Custom and Randall knives

PARKERS' KNIFE COLLECTOR SERVICE
6715 Heritage Business Court
Chattanooga, TN 37422
615-892-0448; Fax: 615-892-9165

PLAZA CUTLERY, INC.
3333 S. Bristol St., Suite 2060
South Coast Plaza
Costa Mesa, CA 92626
866-827-5292; 714-549-3932
dan@plazacutlery.com;
www.plazacutlery.com
Largest selection of knives on the west coast. Custom makers from beginners to the best. All customs, William Henry, Strider, Reeves, Randalls & others available online by phone

RANDALL KNIFE SOCIETY
PO Box 158
Meadows of Dan, VA 24120
276-952-2500
payrks@gate.net;
www.randallknifesociety.com
Randall, Loveless, Scagel, moran, antique pocket knives

ROBERTSON'S CUSTOM CUTLERY
4960 Sussex Dr
Evans, GA 30809
706-650-0252; 706-860-1623
rccedge@csranet.com; www.robertsoncustomcutlery.com
World class custom knives, Vanguard knives-Limited exclusive design

SMOKY MOUNTAIN KNIFE WORKS, INC.
2320 Winfield Dunn Pkwy
PO Box 4430
Sevierville, TN 37864
800-251-9306; 865-453-5871
info@smkw.com; www.eknifeworks.com
The world's largest knife showplace, catalog and website

VOYLES, BRUCE
PO Box 22007
Chattanooga, TN 37422
423-238-6753; Fax: 423-238-3960
bruce@jbrucevoyles.com;
www.jbrucevoyles.com
Knives, knife auctions

knife services

appraisers

Levine, Bernard, P.O. Box 2404, Eugene, OR, 97402, 541-484-0294, brlevine@ix.netcom.com

Russell, A.G., Knives Inc, 2900 S. 26th St., Rogers, AR 72758-8571, phone 800-255-9034 or 479-631-0130, fax 479-631-8493, ag@agrussell.com, www.agrussell.com

Vallini, Massimo, Via G. Bruno 7, 20154 Milano, ITALY, 02-33614751, massimo_vallini@yahoo.it, Knife expert

custom grinders

McGowan Manufacturing Company, 4854 N Shamrock Pl #100, Tucson, AZ, 85705, 800-342-4810, 520-219-0884, info@mcgowanmfg.com, www.mcgowanmfg.com, Knife sharpeners, hunting axes

Peele, Bryan, The Elk Rack, 215 Ferry St. P.O. Box 1363, Thompson Falls, MT, 59873

Schlott, Harald, Zingster Str. 26, 13051 Berlin, GERMANY, 049 030 9293346, harald.schlott@T-online.de, Custom grinder, custom handle artisan, display case/box maker, etcher, scrimshander

Wilson, R.W., P.O. Box 2012, Weirton, WV, 26062

custom handles

Cooper, Jim, 1221 Cook St, Ramona, CA, 92065-3214, 760-789-1097, (760) 788-7992, jamcooper@aol.com

Burrows, Chuck, dba Wild Rose Trading Co, 289 Laposta Canyon Rd, Durango, CO, 81303, 970-259-8396, chuck@wrtcleather.com, www.wrtcleather.com

Fields, Donald, 790 Tamerlane St, Deltona, FL, 32725, 386-532-9070, donaldfields@aol.com, Selling ancient ivories; mammoth & fossil walrus

Grussenmeyer, Paul G., 310 Kresson Rd, Cherry Hill, NJ, 08034, 856-428-1088, 856-428-8997, pgrussentne@comcast.net, www.pgcarvings.com

Holland, Dennis K., 4908-17th Pl., Lubbock, TX, 79416

Imboden II, Howard L., hi II Originals, 620 Deauville Dr., Dayton, OH, 45429

Kelso, Jim, 577 Collar Hill Rd, Worcester, VT, 05682, 802-229-4254, (802) 223-0595

Knack, Gary, 309 Wightman, Ashland, OR, 97520

Marlatt, David, 67622 Oldham Rd., Cambridge, OH, 43725, 740-432-7549

Mead, Dennis, 2250 E. Mercury St., Inverness, FL, 34453-0514

Myers, Ron, 6202 Marglenn Ave., Baltimore, MD, 21206, 410-866-6914

Saggio, Joe, 1450 Broadview Ave. #12, Columbus, OH, 43212, jvsag@webtv.net, www.j.v.saggio@worldnet.att.net, Handle Carver

Schlott, Harald, Zingster Str. 26, 13051 Berlin, GERMANY, 049 030 9293346, harald.schlott@T-online.de, Custom grinder, custom handle artisan, display case/box maker, etcher, scrimshander

Snell, Barry A., 4801 96th St. N., St. Petersburg, FL, 33708-3740

Vallotton, A., 621 Fawn Ridge Dr., Oakland, OR, 97462

Watson, Silvia, 350 Jennifer Lane, Driftwood, TX, 78619

Wilderness Forge, 315 North 100 East, Kanab, UT, 84741, 435-644-3674, bhatting@xpressweb.com

Williams, Gary, (GARBO), PO Box 210, Glendale, KY, 42740-2010

display cases and boxes

Bill's Custom Cases, P O Box 603, Montague, CA, 96064, 530-459-5968, billscustomcases@earthlink.net

Brooker, Dennis, Rt. 1, Box 12A, Derby, IA, 50068

Chas Clements' Custom Leathercraft, Chas, 1741 Dallas St., Aurora, CO, 80010-2018, 303-364-0403, GRYPHONS@HOME.NET, Display case/box maker, Leatherworker, Knife appraiser

Freund, Steve, Tomway LLC, 1646 Tichenor Court, Atlanta, GA, 30338, 770-393-8349, steve@tomway.com, www.tomway.com

Gimbert, Nelson, P.O. Box 787, Clemmons, NC, 27012

McLean, Lawrence, 12344 Meritage Ct, Rancho Cucamonga, CA, 91739, 714-848-5779, lmclean@charter.net

Miller, Michael K., M&M Kustom Krafts, 28510 Santiam Highway, Sweet Home, OR, 97386

Miller, Robert, P.O. Box 2722, Ormond Beach, FL, 32176

Retichek, Joseph L., W9377 Co. TK. D, Beaver Dam, WI, 53916

Robbins, Wayne, 11520 Inverway, Belvidere, IL, 61008

S&D Enterprises, 20 East Seventh St, Manchester, OH, 45144, 937-549-2602, 937-549-2602, sales@s-denterprises.com, www.s-denterprises.com, Display case/ box maker. Manufacturer of aluminum display, chipboard type displays, wood displays. Silk screening or acid etching for logos on product

Schlott, Harald, Zingster Str. 26, 13051 Berlin, GERMANY, 049 030 9293346, harald.schlott@T-online.de, Custom grinder, custom handle artisan, display case/box maker, etcher, scrimshander

engravers

Adlam, Tim, 1705 Witzel Ave., Oshkosh, WI, 54902, 920-235-4589, www.adlamngraving.com

Alfano, Sam, 36180 Henry Gaines Rd., Pearl River, LA, 70452

Allard, Gary, 2395 Battlefield Rd., Fishers Hill, VA, 22626

Alpen, Ralph, 7 Bentley Rd., West Grove, PA, 19390, 610-869-7141

Baron, David, Baron Technology Inc., 62 Spring Hill Rd., Trumbull, CT, 06611, 203-452-0515, bti@baronengraving.com, www.baronengraving.com, Polishing, plating, inlays, artwork

Bates, Billy, 2302 Winthrop Dr. SW, Decatur, AL, 35603, bbrn@aol.com, www.angelfire.com/al/billybates

Bettenhausen, Merle L., 17358 Ottawa, Tinley Park, IL, 60477

Blair, Jim, PO Box 64, 59 Mesa Verde, Glenrock, WY, 82637, 307-436-8115, jblairengrav@msn.com

Bonshire, Benita, 1121 Burlington, Muncie, IN, 47302

Boster, A.D., 3000 Clarks Bridge Rd Lot 42, Gainesville, GA, 30501, 770-532-0958

Brooker, Dennis B., Rt. 1 Box 12A, Derby, IA, 50068

Churchill, Winston G., RFD Box 29B, Proctorsville, VT, 05153

Collins, Michael, Rt. 3075, Batesville Rd., Woodstock, GA, 30188

Cupp, Alana, PO Box 207, Annabella, UT, 84711

Dashwood, Jim, 255 Barkham Rd., Wokingham, Berkshire RG11 4BY, ENGLAND

Dean, Bruce, 13 Tressider Ave., Haberfield, N.S.W. 2045, Sydney, AUSTRALIA, 02 97977608

DeLorge, Ed, 6734 W Main St, Houma, LA, 70360, 504-223-0206

Dickson, John W., PO Box 49914, Sarasota, FL, 34230

Dolbare, Elizabeth, PO Box 502, Dubois, WY, 82513-0502

Downing, Jim, PO Box 4224, Springfield, MO, 65808, 417-865-5953, www.thegunengraver.com, Scrimshander

Duarte, Carlos, 108 Church St., Rossville, CA, 95678

Dubben, Michael, 414 S. Fares Ave., Evansville, IN, 47714

Dubber, Michael W., 8205 Heather Pl, Evansville, IN, 47710-4919

Eklund, Maihkel, Föne 1111, S-82041 Färila, SWEDEN, www.art-knives.com

Eldridge, Allan, 1424 Kansas Lane, Gallatin, TN, 37066

Ellis, Willy B, Willy B's Customs by William B Ellis, 4941 Cardinal Trail, Palm Harbor, FL, 34683, 727-942-6420, www.willyb.com

Engel, Terry (Flowers), PO Box 96, Midland, OR, 97634

Flannery Engraving Co., Jeff, 11034 Riddles Run Rd., Union, KY, 41091, engraving@fuse.net, http://home.fuse.net/ engraving/

Foster, Norvell, Foster Enterprises, PO Box 200343, San Antonio, TX, 78220

Fountain Products, 492 Prospect Ave., West Springfield, MA, 01089

Gipe, Sandi, Rt. 2, Box 1090A, Kendrick, ID, 83537

Glimm, Jerome C., 19 S. Maryland, Conrad, MT, 59425

Gournet, Geoffroy, 820 Paxinosa Ave., Easton, PA, 18042, 610-559-0710, www.geoffroygournet.com

Halloran, Tim 316 Fence line Dr. Blue Grass, IA 52726 563-381-5202

Harrington, Fred A., Winter: 3725 Citrus, Summer: 2107 W Frances Rd Mt Morris MI 48458-8215, St. James City, FL, 33956, Winter: 239-283-0721 Summer: 810-686-3008

Henderson, Fred D., 569 Santa Barbara Dr., Forest Park, GA, 30297, 770-968-4866

Hendricks, Frank, 396 Bluff Trail, Dripping Springs, TX, 78620, 512-858-7828

Holder, Pat, 7148 W. Country Gables Dr., Peoria, AZ, 85381

Ingle, Ralph W., 151 Callan Dr., Rossville, GA, 30741, 706-858-0641, riengraver@aol.com, Photographer

Johns, Bill, 1716 8th St, Cody, WY, 82414, 307-587-5090

Kelly, Lance, 1723 Willow Oak Dr., Edgewater, FL, 32132

Kelso, Jim, 577 Coller Hill Rd, Worcester, VT, 05682

Koevenig, Eugene and Eve, Koevenig's Engraving Service, Rabbit Gulch, Box 55, Hill City, SD, 57745-0055

Kostelnik, Joe and Patty, RD #4, Box 323, Greensburg, PA, 15601

Kudlas, John M., 55280 Silverwolf Dr, Barnes, WI, 54873, 715-795-2031, jkudlas@cheqnet.net, Engraver, scrimshander

Lark, David, 6641 Schneider Rd., Kingsley, MI 49649, Phone: 231-342-1076 dblark58@yahoo.com

Limings Jr., Harry, 959 County Rd. 170, Marengo, OH, 43334-9625

Lindsay, Steve, 3714 West Cedar Hills Drive, Kearney, NE, 68847

Lyttle, Brian, Box 5697, High River AB CANADA, T1V 1M7

Lytton, Simon M., 19 Pinewood Gardens, Hemel Hempstead, Herts. HP1 1TN, ENGLAND

Mason, Joe, 146 Value Rd, Brandon, MS, 39042, 601-824-9867, www.joemasonengraving.com

McCombs, Leo, 1862 White Cemetery Rd., Patriot, OH, 45658

McDonald, Dennis, 8359 Brady St., Peosta, IA, 52068

McKenzie, Lynton, 6940 N Alvernon Way, Tucson, AZ, 85718

McLean, Lawrence, 12344 Meritage Ct, Rancho Cucamonga, CA, 91739, 714-848-5779, lmclean@charter.net

Meyer, Chris, 39 Bergen Ave., Wantage, NJ, 07461, 973-875-6299

Minnick, Joyce, 144 N. 7th St., Middletown, IN, 47356

Morgan, Tandie, P.O. Box 693, 30700 Hwy. 97, Nucla, CO, 81424

Morton, David A., 1110 W. 21st St., Lorain, OH, 44052

Moulton, Dusty, 135 Hillview Ln, Loudon, TN, 37774, 865-408-9779

Muller, Jody & Pat, PO Box 35, Pittsburg, MO, 65724, 417-852-4306/417-752-3260, mullerforge@hotmail.com, www.mullerforge.com

Nelida, Toniutti, via G. Pasconi 29/c, Maniago 33085 (PN), ITALY

Nilsson, Jonny Walker, Tingsstigen 11, SE-933 33 Arvidsjaur, SWEDEN, +(46) 960-13048, 0960.13048@telia.com, www.jwnknives.com

Nott, Ron, Box 281, Summerdale, PA, 17093

Parsons, Michael R., McKee Knives, 7042 McFarland Rd, Indianapolis, IN, 46227, 317-784-7943

Patterson, W.H., P.O. Drawer DK, College Station, TX, 77841

Peri, Valerio, Via Meucci 12, Gardone V.T. 25063, ITALY

Pilkington Jr., Scott, P.O. Box 97, Monteagle, TN, 37356, 931-924-3400, scott@pilkguns.com, www.pilkguns.com

Poag, James, RR1, Box 212A, Grayville, IL, 62844

Potts, Wayne, 1580 Meade St Apt A, Denver, CO, 80204

Rabeno, Martin, Spook Hollow Trading Co, 530 Eagle Pass, Durango, CO, 81301

Raftis, Andrew, 2743 N. Sheffield, Chicago, IL, 60614

Roberts, J.J., 7808 Lake Dr., Manassas, VA, 20111, 703-330-0448, jjrengraver@aol.com, www.angelfire.com/va2/ engraver

Robidoux, Roland J., DMR Fine Engraving, 25 N. Federal Hwy. Studio 5, Dania, FL, 33004

Rosser, Bob, Hand Engraving, 2809 Crescent Ave Ste 20, Homewood, AL, 35209-2526, www.hand-engravers.com

Rudolph, Gil, 20922 Oak Pass Ave, Tehachapi, CA, 93561, 661-822-4949, www.gtraks@csurfers.net

Rundell, Joe, 6198 W. Frances Rd., Clio, MI, 48420

Schickl, L., Ottingweg 497, A-5580 Tamsweg, AUSTRIA, 0043 6474 8583, Scrimshander

Schlott, Harald, Zingster Str. 26, 13051 Berlin, GERMANY, 049 030 9293346, 049 030 9293346, harald.schlott@T-online. de, www.gravur-kunst-atelier.de.vu, Custom grinder, custom handle artisan, display case/box maker, etcher, scrimshander

Schönert, Elke, 18 Lansdowne Pl., Central, Port Elizabeth, SOUTH AFRICA

Shaw, Bruce, P.O. Box 545, Pacific Grove, CA, 93950, 831-646-1937, 831-644-0941

Shostle, Ben, 1121 Burlington, Muncie, IN, 47302

Simmons, Rick W., 3323 Creek Manor Dr., Kingwood, TX, 77339, 504-261-8450, exhibitiongrade@gmail.com www. exhibitionengraver.com

Slobodian, Barbara, 4101 River Ridge Dr., PO Box 1498, San Andreas, CA 95249, 209-286-1980, fax 209-286-1982, barbara@dancethetide.com. Specializes in Japanese-style engraving.

Smith, Ron, 5869 Straley, Ft. Worth, TX, 76114

Smitty's Engraving, 21320 Pioneer Circle, Hurrah, OK, 73045, 405-454-6968, smittys.engraving@prodigy.net, www.smittys-engraving.us

Spode, Peter, Tresaith Newland, Malvern, Worcestershire WR13 5AY, ENGLAND

Swartley, Robert D., 2800 Pine St., Napa, CA, 94558

Takeuchi, Shigetoshi, 21-14-1-Chome kamimuneoka Shiki shi, 353 Saitama, JAPAN

Theis, Terry, 21452 FM 2093, Harper, TX, 78631, 830-864-4438

Valade, Robert B., 931 3rd Ave., Seaside, OR, 97138, 503-738-7672, (503) 738-7672

Waldrop, Mark, 14562 SE 1st Ave. Rd., Summerfield, FL, 34491

Warenski, Julie, 590 East 500 N., Richfield, UT, 84701, 435-896-5319, julie@warenskiknives.com, www.warenskiknives.com

Warren, Kenneth W., P.O. Box 2842, Wenatchee, WA, 98807-2842, 509-663-6123, (509) 663-6123

Whitehead, James 2175 South Willow Ave. Space 22 Fresno, CA 93725 559-412-4374 jdwmks@yahoo.com

Whitmore, Jerry, 1740 Churchill Dr., Oakland, OR, 97462

Winn, Travis A., 558 E. 3065 S., Salt Lake City, UT, 84106

Wood, Mel, P.O. Box 1255, Sierra Vista, AZ, 85636

Zietz, Dennis, 5906 40th Ave., Kenosha, WI, 53144

Zima, Russ, 7291 Ruth Way, Denver, CO, 80221, 303-657-9378, www.rzengraving.com

etchers

Baron Technology Inc., David Baron, 62 Spring Hill Rd., Trumbull, CT, 06611

Fountain Products, 492 Prospect Ave., West Springfield, MA, 01089

Hayes, Dolores, P.O. Box 41405, Los Angeles, CA, 90041

Holland, Dennis, 4908 17th Pl., Lubbock, TX, 79416

Kelso, Jim, 577 Collar Hill Rd, Worcester, VT, 05682

Larstein, Francine, FRANCINE ETCHINGS & ETCHED KNIVES, 368 White Rd, Watsonville, CA, 95076, 800-557-1525/831-426-6046, 831-684-1949, francine@francinetchings.com, www.boyeknivesgallery.com

Lefaucheux, Jean-Victor, Saint-Denis-Le-Ferment, 27140 Gisors, FRANCE

Mead, Faustina L., 2550 E. Mercury St., Inverness, FL, 34453-0514, 352-344-4751, scrimsha@infionline.net, www.scrimshaw-by-faustina.com

Myers, Ron, 6202 Marglenn Ave., Baltimore, MD, 21206, (acid) etcher

Nilsson, Jonny Walker, Tingsstigen 11, SE-933 33 Arvidsjaur, SWEDEN, +(46) 960-13048, 0960.13048@telia.com, www.jwnknives.com

Schlott, Harald, Zingster Str. 26, 13051 Berlin, GERMANY, 049 030 9293346, harald.schlott@T-online.de, Custom grinder, custom handle artisan, display case/box maker, etcher, scrimshander

Vallotton, A., Northwest Knife Supply, 621 Fawn Ridge Dr., Oakland, OR, 97462

Watson, Silvia, 350 Jennifer Lane, Driftwood, TX, 78619

heat treaters

Bay State Metal Treating Co., 6 Jefferson Ave., Woburn, MA, 01801

Bos Heat Treating, Paul, Shop: 1900 Weld Blvd., El Cajon, CA, 92020, 619-562-2370 / 619-445-4740 Home, PaulBos@BuckKnives.com

Holt, B.R., 1238 Birchwood Drive, Sunnyvale, CA, 94089

Kazou, Okaysu, 12-2 1 Chome Higashi, Ueno, Taito-Ku, Tokyo, JAPAN, 81-33834-2323, 81-33831-3012

Metal Treating Bodycote Inc., 710 Burns St., Cincinnati, OH, 45204

O&W Heat Treat Inc., One Bidwell Rd., South Windsor, CT, 06074, 860-528-9239, (860) 291-9939, owht1@aol.com

Progressive Heat Treating Co., 2802 Charles City Rd, Richmond, VA, 23231, 804-545-0010, 804-545-0012

Texas Heat Treating Inc., 303 Texas Ave., Round Rock, TX, 78664

Texas Knifemakers Supply, 10649 Haddington, Suite 180, Houston, TX, 77043

Tinker Shop, The, 1120 Helen, Deer Park, TX, 77536

Valley Metal Treating Inc., 355 S. East End Ave., Pomona, CA, 91766

Wilderness Forge, 315 North 100 East, Kanab, UT, 84741, 435-644-3674, bhatting@xpressweb.com

Wilson, R.W., P.O. Box 2012, Weirton, WV, 26062

leather workers

Abramson, David, 116 Baker Ave, Wharton, NJ, 07885, lifter4him1@aol.com, www.liftersleather.com

Bruner, Rick, 7756 Aster Lane, Jenison, MI, 49428, 616-457-0403

Burrows, Chuck, dba Wild Rose Trading Co, 289 Laposta Canyon Rd, Durango, CO, 81303, 970-259-8396, chuck@wrtcleather.com

Clements' Custom Leathercraft, Chas, 1741 Dallas St., Aurora, CO, 80010-2018

Cole, Dave, 620 Poinsetta Dr., Satellite Beach, FL 32937, 321-773-1687, www.dcknivesandleather.blademakers.com. Custom sheath services.

Cooper, Harold, 136 Winding Way, Frankfort, KY, 40601

Cooper, Jim, 1221 Cook St, Ramona, CA, 92065-3214, 760-789-1097, 760-788-7992, jamcooper@aol.com

Cow Catcher Leatherworks, 3006 Industrial Dr, Raleigh, NC, 27609

Cubic, George, GC Custom Leather Co., 10561 E. Deerfield Pl., Tucson, AZ, 85749, 520-760-0695, gcubic@aol.com

Dawkins, Dudley, 221 N. Broadmoor Ave, Topeka, KS, 66606-1254, 785-235-3871, dawkind@sbcglobal.net, ABS member/knifemaker forges straight knives

Evans, Scott V, Edge Works Mfg, 1171 Halltown Rd, Jacksonville, NC, 28546, 910-455-9834, (910) 346-5660, edgeworks@coastalnet.com, www.tacticalholsters.com

Genske, Jay, 283 Doty St, Fond du Lac, WI, 54935, 920-921-8019/Cell Phone 920-579-0144, jaygenske@hotmail.com, Custom Grinder, Custom Handle Artisan

Green River Leather, 1100 Legion Park Road, PO BOX 190, Greensburg, KY, 42743, Phone: 270-932-2212 fax: 270-299-2471 info@greenriverleather.com

Hawk, Ken, Rt. 1, Box 770, Ceres, VA, 24318-9630

Homyk, David N., 8047 Carriage Ln., Wichita Falls, TX, 76306

John's Custom Leather, John R. Stumpf, 523 S. Liberty St, Blairsville, PA, 15717, 724-459-6802, 724-459-5996

Kelley, Jo Ann, 52 Mourning Dove Dr., Watertown, WI 53094, 920-206-0807, ladybug@ticon.net, www.hembrookcustomknives.com. Custom leather knife sheaths $40 to $100; making sheaths since 2002.

Kravitt, Chris, HC 31 Box 6484, Rt 200, Ellsworth, ME, 04605-9805, 207-584-3000, 207-584-3000, sheathmkr@aol.com, www.treestumpleather.com, Reference: Tree Stump Leather

Larson, Richard, 549 E. Hawkeye, Turlock, CA, 95380

Layton, Jim, 2710 Gilbert Avenue, Portsmouth, OH, 45662

Lee, Randy, P.O. Box 1873, 270 N 9th West, St. Johns, AZ, 85936, 928-337-2594, 928-337-5002, randylee@randyleeknives.com, info@randyleeknives.com, Custom knifemaker; www.randyleeknives.com

Long, Paul, 108 Briarwood Ln W, Kerrville, TX, 78028, 830-367-5536, PFL@cebridge.net

Lott, Sherry, 1100 Legion Park Rd., Greenburg, KY 42743, phone 270-932-2212, fax 270-299-2471, sherrylott@alltel.net

Mason, Arne, 258 Wimer St., Ashland, OR, 97520, 541-482-2260, (541) 482-7785, www.arnemason.com

McGowan, Liz, 12629 Howard Lodge Dr., Winter Add-2023 Robin Ct Sebring FL 33870, Sykesville, MD, 21784, 410-489-4323

Metheny, H.A. "Whitey", 7750 Waterford Dr., Spotsylvania, VA, 22553, 540-582-3228 Cell 540-542-1440, 540-582-3095, nametheny@aol.com, www.methenyknives.com

Miller, Michael K., 28510 Santiam Highway, Sweet Home, OR, 97386

Mobley, Martha, 240 Alapaha River Road, Chula, GA, 31733

Morrissey, Martin, 4578 Stephens Rd., Blairsville, GA, 30512

Niedenthal, John Andre, Beadwork & Buckskin, Studio 3955 NW 103 Dr., Coral Springs, FL, 33065-1551, 954-345-0447, a_niedenthal@hotmail.com

Neilson, Tess, RR2 Box 16, Wyalusing, PA, 18853, 570-746-4944, www.mountainhollow.net, Doing business as Neilson's Mountain Hollow

Parsons, Larry, 1038 W. Kyle, Mustang, OK 73064 405-376-9408 s.m.parsons@sbcglobal.net

Parsons, Michael R., McKee Knives, 7042 McFarland Rd, Indianapolis, IN, 46227, 317-784-7943

Poag, James H., RR #1 Box 212A, Grayville, IL, 62844

Red's Custom Leather, Ed Todd, 9 Woodlawn Rd., Putnam Valley, NY, 10579, 845-528-3783

Rowe, Kenny, 3219 Hwy 29 South, Hope, AR, 71801, 870-777-8216, 870-777-0935, rowesleather@yahoo.com, www.knifeart.com or www.theedgeequipment.com

Schrap, Robert G., 7024 W. Wells St., Wauwatosa, WI, 53213-3717, 414-771-6472, (414) 479-9765, knifesheaths@aol.com, www.customsheaths.com

Strahin, Robert, 401 Center St., Elkins, WV, 26241, *Custom Knife Sheaths

Tierney, Mike, 447 Rivercrest Dr., Woodstock ON CANADA, N4S 5W5

Turner, Kevin, 17 Hunt Ave., Montrose, NY, 10548

Velasquez, Gil, 7120 Madera Dr., Goleta, CA, 93117

Walker, John, 17 Laber Circle, Little Rock, AR, 72210, 501-455-0239, john.walker@afbic.com

Watson, Bill, #1 Presidio, Wimberly, TX, 78676

Whinnery, Walt, 1947 Meadow Creek Dr., Louisville, KY, 40218

Williams, Sherman A., 1709 Wallace St., Simi Valley, CA, 93065

miscellaneous

Hendryx Design, Scott, 5997 Smokey Way, Boise, ID, 83714, 208-377-8044, www.shdsheaths@msn.com

Kydex Sheath Maker

Robertson, Kathy, Impress by Design, PO Box 1367, Evans, GA, 30809-1367, 706-650-0982, (706) 860-1623, impressbydesign@comcast.net, Advertising/graphic designer

Strahin, Robert, 401 Center St., Elkins, WV, 26241, 304-636-0128, rstrahin@copper.net, *Custom Knife Sheaths

photographers

Alfano, Sam, 36180 Henery Gaines Rd., Pearl River, LA, 70452

Allen, John, Studio One, 3823 Pleasant Valley Blvd., Rockford, IL, 61114

Balance Digital, Rob Szajkowski, 261 Riverview Way, Oceanside, CA 92057, 760-815-6131, rob@balancedigital.com, www. balancedigital.com

Bilal, Mustafa, Turk's Head Productions, 908 NW 50th St., Seattle, WA, 98107-3634, 206-782-4164, (206) 783-5677, mustafa@turkshead.com, www.turkshead.com, Graphic design, marketing & advertising

Bogaerts, Jan, Regenweg 14, 5757 Pl., Liessel, HOLLAND

Box Photography, Doug, 1804 W Main St, Brenham, TX, 77833-3420

Brown, Tom, 6048 Grants Ferry Rd., Brandon, MS, 39042-8136

Butman, Steve, P.O. Box 5106, Abilene, TX, 79608

Calidonna, Greg, 205 Helmwood Dr., Elizabethtown, KY, 42701

Campbell, Jim, 7935 Ranch Rd., Port Richey, FL, 34668

Cooper, Jim, Sharpbycoop.com photography, 9 Mathew Court, Norwalk, CT, 06851, jcooper@sharpbycoop.com, www. sharpbycoop.com

Courtice, Bill, P.O. Box 1776, Duarte, CA, 91010-4776

Crosby, Doug, RFD 1, Box 1111, Stockton Springs, ME, 04981

Danko, Michael, 3030 Jane Street, Pittsburgh, PA, 15203

Davis, Marshall B., P.O. Box 3048, Austin, TX, 78764

Earley, Don, 1241 Ft. Bragg Rd., Fayetteville, NC, 28305

Ehrlich, Linn M., 1850 N Clark St #1008, Chicago, IL, 60614, 312-209-2107

Etzler, John, 11200 N. Island Rd., Grafton, OH, 44044

Fahrner, Dave, 1623 Arnold St., Pittsburgh, PA, 15205

Faul, Jan W., 903 Girard St. NE, Rr. Washington, DC, 20017

Fedorak, Allan, 28 W. Nicola St., Amloops BC CANADA, V2C 1J6

Fox, Daniel, Lumina Studios, 6773 Industrial Parkway, Cleveland, OH, 44070, 440-734-2118, (440) 734-3542, lumina@en.com

Freiberg, Charley, PO Box 42, Elkins, NH, 03233, 603-526-2767, charleyfreiberg@tos.net

Gardner, Chuck, 116 Quincy Ave., Oak Ridge, TN, 37830

Gawryla, Don, 1105 Greenlawn Dr., Pittsburgh, PA, 15220

Goffe Photographic Associates, 3108 Monte Vista Blvd., NE, Albuquerque, NM, 87106

Graham, James, 7434 E Northwest Hwy, Dallas, TX, 75231, 214-341-5138, jamie@jamiephoto.com, www.jamiephoto.com, Product photographer

Graley, Gary W., RR2 Box 556, Gillett, PA, 16925

Griggs, Dennis, 118 Pleasant Pt Rd, Topsham, ME, 04086, 207-725-5689

Hanusin, John, Reames-Hanusin Studio, PO Box 931, Northbrook, IL, 60065 0931

Hardy, Scott, 639 Myrtle Ave., Placerville, CA, 95667

Hodge, Tom, 7175 S US Hwy 1 Lot 36, Titusville, FL, 32780-8172, 321-267-7989, egdoht@hotmail.com

Holter, Wayne V., 125 Lakin Ave., Boonsboro, MD, 21713, 301-416-2855, mackwayne@hotmail.com

Hopkins, David W, Hopkins Photography inc, 201 S Jefferson, Iola, KS, 66749, 620-365-7443, nhoppy@netks.net

Kerns, Bob, 18723 Birdseye Dr., Germantown, MD, 20874

LaFleur, Gordon, 111 Hirst, Box 1209, Parksville BC CANADA, V0R 270

Lear, Dale, 6544 Cora Mill Rd, Gallipolis, OH, 45631, 740-245-5482, dalelear@yahoo.com, Ebay Sales

LeBlanc, Paul, No. 3 Meadowbrook Cir., Melissa, TX, 75454

Lester, Dean, 2801 Junipero Ave Suite 212, Long Beach, CA, 90806-2140

Leviton, David A., A Studio on the Move, P.O. Box 2871, Silverdale, WA, 98383, 360-697-3452

Long, Gary W., 3556 Miller's Crossroad Rd., Hillsboro, TN, 37342

Long, Jerry, 402 E. Gladden Dr., Farmington, NM, 87401

Lum, Billy, 16307 Evening Star Ct., Crosby, TX, 77532

McCollum, Tom, P.O. Box 933, Lilburn, GA, 30226

Mitch Lum Website and Photography, 22115 NW Imbrie Dr. #298, Hillsboro, OR 97124, mitch@mitchlum.com, www.mitchlum. com, 206-356-6813

Moake, Jim, 18 Council Ave., Aurora, IL, 60504

Moya Inc., 4212 S. Dixie Hwy., West Palm Beach, FL, 33405

Norman's Studio, 322 S. 2nd St., Vivian, LA, 71082

Owens, William T., Box 99, Williamsburg, WV, 24991

Pachi, Francesco, Loc. Pometta 1, 17046 Sassello (SV) ITALY Tel-fax: 0039 019 720086 www.pachi-photo.com

Palmer Studio, 2008 Airport Blvd., Mobile, AL, 36606

Payne, Robert G., P.O. Box 141471, Austin, TX, 78714

Pigott, John, 9095 Woodprint LN, Mason, OH, 45040

Point Seven, 6450 Weatherfield Ct., Unit 2A, Maumee, OH, 43537, 419-243-8880, 877-787-3836, www.pointsevenstudios. com

Professional Medica Concepts, Patricia Mitchell, P.O. Box 0002, Warren, TX, 77664, 409-547-2213, pm0909@wt.net

Rasmussen, Eric L., 1121 Eliason, Brigham City, UT, 84302

Rhoades, Cynthia J., Box 195, Clearmont, WY, 82835

Rice, Tim, PO Box 663, Whitefish, MT, 59937

Richardson, Kerry, 2520 Mimosa St., Santa Rosa, CA, 95405, 707-575-1875, kerry@sonic.net, www.sonic.net/~kerry

Ross, Bill, 28364 S. Western Ave. Suite 464, Rancho Palos Verdes, CA, 90275

Rubicam, Stephen, 14 Atlantic Ave., Boothbay Harbor, ME, 04538-1202

Rush, John D., 2313 Maysel, Bloomington, IL, 61701

Schreiber, Roger, 429 Boren Ave. N., Seattle, WA, 98109

Semmer, Charles, 7885 Cyd Dr., Denver, CO, 80221

Silver Images Photography, 2412 N Keystone, Flagstaff, AZ, 86004

Slobodian, Scott, 4101 River Ridge Dr., P.O. Box 1498, San Andreas, CA, 95249, 209-286-1980, (209) 286-1982, www. slobodianswords.com

Smith, Earl W., 5121 Southminster Rd., Columbus, OH, 43221

Smith, Randall, 1720 Oneco Ave., Winter Park, FL, 32789

Storm Photo, 334 Wall St., Kingston, NY, 12401

Surles, Mark, P.O. Box 147, Falcon, NC, 28342

Third Eye Photos, 140 E. Sixth Ave., Helena, MT, 59601

Thurber, David, P.O. Box 1006, Visalia, CA, 93279

Tighe, Brian, RR 1, Ridgeville ON CANADA, L0S 1M0, 905-892-2734, www.tigheknives.com

Towell, Steven L., 3720 N.W. 32nd Ave., Camas, WA, 98607, 360-834-9049, sltowell@netscape.com

Valley Photo, 2100 Arizona Ave., Yuma, AZ, 85364

Verno Studio, Jay, 3030 Jane Street, Pittsburgh, PA, 15203

Ward, Chuck, 1010 E North St, PO Box 2272, Benton, AR, 72018, 501-778-4329, chuckbop@aol.com

Weyer International, 6466 Teal Rd., Petersburgh, MI, 49270, 419-534-2020, law-weyerinternational@msn.com, Books

Wise, Harriet, 242 Dill Ave., Frederick, MD, 21701

Worley, Holly, Worley Photography, 6360 W David Dr, Littleton, CO, 80128-5708, 303-257-8091, 720-981-2800, hsworley@aol. com, Products, Digital & Film

scrimshanders

Adlam, Tim, 1705 Witzel Ave., Oshkosh, WI, 54902, 920-235-4589, www.adlamngraving.com

Alpen, Ralph, 7 Bentley Rd., West Grove, PA, 19390, 610-869-7141

Anderson, Terry Jack, 10076 Birnamwoods Way, Riverton, UT, 84065-9073

Bailey, Mary W., 3213 Jonesboro Dr., Nashville, TN, 37214, mbscrim@aol.com, www.members.aol.com/mbscrim/ scrim.html

Baker, Duane, 2145 Alum Creek Dr., Cambridge Park Apt. #10, Columbus, OH, 43207

Barrows, Miles, 524 Parsons Ave., Chillicothe, OH, 45601

Brady, Sandra, P.O. Box 104, Monclova, OH, 43542, 419-866-0435, (419) 867-0656, sandyscrim@hotmail.com, www. knifeshows.com

Beauchamp, Gaetan, 125 de la Riviere, Stoneham, PQ, G0A 4P0, CANADA, 418-848-1914, (418) 848-6859, knives@ gbeauchamp.ca, www.beauchamp.cjb.net

Bellet, Connie, PO Box 151, Palermo, ME, 04354 0151, 207-993-2327, phwhitehawk@gwl.net

Benade, Lynn, 2610 Buckhurst Dr, Beachwood, OH, 44122, 216-464-0777, llbnc17@aol.com

Bonshire, Benita, 1121 Burlington Dr., Muncie, IN, 47302

Boone Trading Co. Inc., P.O. Box 669, Brinnon, WA, 98320, 800-423-1945, ww.boonetrading.com

Bryan, Bob, 1120 Oak Hill Rd., Carthage, MO, 64836

Burger, Sharon, Cluster Box 1625, Forest Hills/KLOOF 3624, KZN, South Africa, cell: +27 83 7891675, tel/fax: +27 31 7621349, scribble@iafrica.com, www.kgsa.co.za/members/sharonburger

Byrne, Mary Gregg, 1018 15th St., Bellingham, WA, 98225-6604

Cable, Jerry, 332 Main St., Mt. Pleasant, PA, 15666

Caudill, Lyle, 7626 Lyons Rd., Georgetown, OH, 45121

Cole, Gary, PO Box 668, Naalehu, HI, 96772, 808-929-9775, 808-929-7371, www.community.webshots.com/album/11836830uqyeejirsz

Collins, Michael, Rt. 3075, Batesville Rd., Woodstock, GA, 30188

Conover, Juanita Rae, P.O. Box 70442, Eugene, OR, 97401, 541-747-1726 or 543-4851, juanitaraeconover@yahoo.com

Courtnage, Elaine, Box 473, Big Sandy, MT, 59520

Cover Jr., Raymond A., Rt. 1, Box 194, Mineral Point, MO, 63660

Cox, J. Andy, 116 Robin Hood Lane, Gaffney, SC, 29340

Dietrich, Roni, Wild Horse Studio, 1257 Cottage Dr, Harrisburg, PA, 17112, 717-469-0587, ronimd@aol

DiMarzo, Richard, 2357 Center Place, Birmingham, AL, 35205

Dolbare, Elizabeth, PO Box 502, Dubois, WY, 82513-0502

Eklund, Maihkel, Föne 1111, S-82041 Färila, SWEDEN, +46 6512 4192, maihkel.eklund@swipnet.se, www.art-knives.com

Eldridge, Allan, 1424 Kansas Lane, Gallatin, TN, 37066

Ellis, Willy b, Willy B's Customs by William B Ellis, 4941 Cardinal Trail, Palm Harbor, FL, 34683, 727-942-6420, www.willyb.com

Fisk, Dale, Box 252, Council, ID, 83612, dafisk@ctcweb.net

Foster Enterprises, Norvell Foster, P.O. Box 200343, San Antonio, TX, 78220

Fountain Products, 492 Prospect Ave., West Springfield, MA, 01089

Gill, Scott, 925 N. Armstrong St., Kokomo, IN, 46901

Halligan, Ed, 14 Meadow Way, Sharpsburg, GA, 30277, ehkiss@bellsouth.net

Hands, Barry Lee, 26192 East Shore Route, Bigfork, MT, 59911

Hargraves Sr., Charles, RR 3 Bancroft, Ontario CANADA, K0L 1C0

Harless, Star, c/o Arrow Forge, P.O. Box 845, Stoneville, NC, 27048-0845

Harrington, Fred A., Summer: 2107 W Frances Rd, Mt Morris MI 48458 8215, Winter: 3725 Citrus, St. James City, FL, 33956, Winter 239-283-0721, Summer 810-686-3008

Hergert, Bob, 12 Geer Circle, Port Orford, OR, 97465, 541-332-3010, hergert@harborside.com, www.scrimshander.com

Hielscher, Vickie, 6550 Otoe Rd, P.O. Box 992, Alliance, NE, 69301, 308-762-4318, g-hielsc@bbcwb.net

High, Tom, 5474 S. 112.8 Rd., Alamosa, CO, 81101, 719-589-2108, scrimshaw@vanion.com, www.rockymountainscrimshaw.com, Wildlife Artist

Himmelheber, David R., 11289 40th St. N., Royal Palm Beach, FL, 33411

Holland, Dennis K., 4908-17th Place, Lubbock, TX, 79416

Hutchings, Rick "Hutch", 3007 Coffe Tree Ct, Crestwood, KY, 40014, 502-241-2871, baron1@bellsouth.net

Imboden II, Howard L., 620 Deauville Dr., Dayton, OH, 45429, 937-439-1536, Guards by the "Last Wax Technic"

Johnson, Corinne, W3565 Lockington, Mindora, WI, 54644

Johnston, Kathy, W. 1134 Providence, Spokane, WA, 99205

Karst Stone, Linda, 903 Tanglewood Ln, Kerrville, TX, 78028-2945, 830-896-4678, 830-257-6117, karstone@ktc.com

Kelso, Jim, 577 Coller Hill Rd, Worcester, VT, 05682

Kirk, Susan B., 1340 Freeland Rd., Merrill, MI, 48637

Koevenig, Eugene and Eve, Koevenig's Engraving Service, Rabbit Gulch, Box 55, Hill City, SD, 57745-0055

Kostelnik, Joe and Patty, RD #4, Box 323, Greensburg, PA, 15601

Lemen, Pam, 3434 N. Iroquois Ave., Tucson, AZ, 85705

Martin, Diane, 28220 N. Lake Dr., Waterford, WI, 53185

McDonald, René Cosimini-, 14730 61 Court N., Loxahatchee, FL, 33470

McFadden, Berni, 2547 E Dalton Ave, Dalton Gardens, ID, 83815-9631

McGowan, Frank, 12629 Howard Lodge Dr., Winter Add-2023 Robin Ct Sebring FL 33870, Sykesville, MD, 21784, 863-385-1296

McGrath, Gayle, PMB 232 15201 N Cleveland Ave, N Ft Myers, FL, 33903

McLaran, Lou, 603 Powers St., Waco, TX, 76705

McWilliams, Carole, P.O. Box 693, Bayfield, CO, 81122

Mead, Faustina L., 2550 E. Mercury St., Inverness, FL, 34453-0514, 352-344-4751, scrimsha@infionline.net, www.scrimshaw-by-faustina.com

Mitchell, James, 1026 7th Ave., Columbus, GA, 31901

Moore, James B., 1707 N. Gillis, Stockton, TX, 79735

Ochonicky, Michelle "Mike", Stone Hollow Studio, 31 High Trail, Eureka, MO; 63025, 636-938-9570, www.bestofmissourihands.com

Ochs, Belle, 124 Emerald Lane, Largo, FL, 33771, 727-530-3826, chuckandbelle@juno.com, www.oxforge.com

Pachi, Mirella, Via Pometta 1, 17046 Sassello (SV), ITALY, 019 720086, WWW.PACHI-KNIVES.COM

Parish, Vaughn, 103 Cross St., Monaca, PA, 15061

Peterson, Lou, 514 S. Jackson St., Gardner, IL, 60424

Pienaar, Conrad, 19A Milner Rd., Bloemfontein 9300, SOUTH AFRICA, Phone: 027 514364180 fax: 027 514364180

Poag, James H., RR #1 Box 212A, Grayville, IL, 62844

Polk, Trena, 4625 Webber Creek Rd., Van Buren, AR, 72956

Purvis, Hilton, P.O. Box 371, Noordhoek, 7979, SOUTH AFRICA, 27 21 789 1114, hiltonp@telkomsa.net, www.kgsa.co.za/member/hiltonpurvis

Ramsey, Richard, 8525 Trout Farm Rd, Neosho, MO, 64850

Ristinen, Lori, 14256 County Hwy 45, Menahga, MN, 56464, 218-538-6608, lori@loriristinen.com, www.loriristinen.com

Roberts, J.J., 7808 Lake Dr., Manassas, VA, 22111, 703-330-0448, jjrengraver@aol.com, www.angelfire.com/va2/ engraver

Rudolph, Gil, 20922 Oak Pass Ave, Tehachapi, CA, 93561, 661-822-4949, www.gtraks@csurfers.net

Rundell, Joe, 6198 W. Frances Rd., Clio, MI, 48420

Saggio, Joe, 1450 Broadview Ave. #12, Columbus, OH, 43212, 614-481-1967, jvsaggio@earthlink.net, www.j.v.saggio@worldnet.att.net

Sahlin, Viveca, Konstvaktarevagem 9, S-772 40 Grangesberg, SWEDEN, 46 240 23204, www.scrimart.use

Satre, Robert, 518 3rd Ave. NW, Weyburn SK CANADA, S4H 1R1

Schlott, Harald, Zingster Str. 26, 13051 Berlin, 929 33 46, GERMANY, 049 030 9293346, 049 030 9293346, harald.schlott@t-online.de, www.gravur-kunst-atelier.de.vu

Schulenburg, E.W., 25 North Hill St., Carrollton, GA, 30117

Schwallie, Patricia, 4614 Old Spartanburg Rd. Apt. 47, Taylors, SC, 29687

Selent, Chuck, P.O. Box 1207, Bonners Ferry, ID, 83805

Semich, Alice, 10037 Roanoke Dr., Murfreesboro, TN, 37129

Shostle, Ben, 1121 Burlington, Muncie, IN, 47302

Smith, Peggy, 676 Glades Rd., #3, Gatlinburg, TN, 37738

Smith, Ron, 5869 Straley, Ft. Worth, TX, 76114

Stahl, John, Images In Ivory, 2049 Windsor Rd., Baldwin, NY, 11510, 516-223-5007, imivory@msn.com, www.imagesinivory.org

Steigerwalt, Jim, RD#3, Sunbury, PA, 17801

Stuart, Stephen, 15815 Acorn Circle, Tavares, FL, 32778, 352-343-8423, (352) 343-8916, inkscratch@aol.com

Talley, Mary Austin, 2499 Countrywood Parkway, Memphis, TN, 38016, matalley@midsouth.rr.com

Thompson, Larry D., 23040 Ave. 197, Strathmore, CA, 93267

Toniutti, Nelida, Via G. Pascoli, 33085 Maniago-PN, ITALY

Trout, Lauria Lovestrand, 1555 Delaney Dr, No. 1723, Talahassee, FL, 32309, 850-893-8836, mayalaurie@aol.com

Tucker, Steve, 3518 W. Linwood, Turlock, CA, 95380

Tyser, Ross, 1015 Hardee Court, Spartanburg, SC, 29303

Velasquez, Gil, Art of Scrimshaw, 7120 Madera Dr., Goleta, CA, 93117

Wilderness Forge, 475 NE Smith Rock Way, Terrebonne, OR, 97760, bhatting@xpressweb.com

Williams, Gary, PO Box 210, Glendale, KY, 42740, 270-369-6752, garywilliam@alltel.net

Winn, Travis A., 558 E. 3065 S., Salt Lake City, UT, 84106

Young, Mary, 4826 Storeyland Dr., Alton, IL, 62002

organizations

AMERICAN BLADESMITH SOCIETY
c/o Office Manager, Cindy Sheely; P. O. Box 160, Grand Rapids, Ohio 45522; cindy@americanbladesmith.com; (419) 832-0400; Web: www.americanbladesmith.com

AMERICAN KNIFE & TOOL INSTITUTE***
David Kowalski, Comm. Coordinator, AKTI; DEPT BL2, PO Box 432, Iola, WI 54945-0432;715-445-3781; Web: communications@akti.org; www. akti.org

AMERICAN KNIFE THROWERS ALLIANCE
c/o Bobby Branton; 4976 Seewee Rd; Awendaw, SC 29429; www.AKTA-USA.com

ARIZONA KNIFE COLLECTOR'S ASSOCIATION
c/o D'Alton Holder, President, 7148 W. Country Gables Dr., Peoria, AZ 85381; Web: www.akca.net

ART KNIFE COLLECTOR'S ASSOCIATION
c/o Mitch Weiss, Pres.; 2211 Lee Road, Suite 104; Winter Park, FL 32789

BAY AREA KNIFE COLLECTOR'S ASSOCIATION
Doug Isaacson, B.A.K.C.A. Membership, 36774 Magnolia, Newark, CA 94560; Web: www.bakca.org

ARKANSAS KNIFEMAKERS ASSOCIATION
David Etchieson, 60 Wendy Cove, Conway, AR 72032; Web: www.arkansasknifemakers.com

AUSTRALASIAN KNIFE COLLECTORS
PO BOX 149 CHIDLOW 6556 WESTERN AUSTRALIA TEL: (08) 9572 7255; FAX: (08) 9572 7266. International Inquiries: TEL: + 61 8 9572 7255; FAX: + 61 8 9572 7266, akc@knivesaustralia.com.au

CALIFORNIA KNIFEMAKERS ASSOCIATION
c/o Clint Breshears, Membership Chairman; 1261 Keats St; Manhattan Beach CA 90266; 310-372-0739; breshears@mindspring.com
Dedicated to teaching and improving knifemaking

CANADIAN KNIFEMAKERS GUILD
c/o Peter Wile; RR # 3; Bridgewater N.S. CANADA B4V 2W2; 902-543-1373; www.ckg.org

CUSTOM KNIFE COLLECTORS ASSOCIATION
c/o Jim Treacy, PO Box 5893, Glen Allen, VA 23058-5893; E-mail: customknifecollectorsassociation@yahoo.com; Web: www.customknifecollectorsassociation.com
The purpose of the CKCA is to recognize and promote the artistic significance of handmade knives, to advnace their collection and conservation, and to support the creative expression of those who make them. Open to collectors, makers purveyors, and other collectors. Has members from eight countries. Produced a calednar which features custom knives either owned or made by CKCA members.

CUTTING EDGE, THE
1920 N 26th St, Lowell, AR 72745; 479-631-0055; 479-636-4618; ce-info@cuttingedge.com
After-market knives since 1968. We offer about 1,000 individual knives each month. The oldest and the most experienced in the business of buying and selling knives. We buy collections of any size, take knives on consignment or we will trade. Web: www.cuttingedge.com

FLORIDA KNIFEMAKERS ASSOCIATION
c/o President, Dan Mink, PO Box 861, Crystal beach, Florida, 34681 (727) 786 5408; Web: www.floridaknifemakers.org

JAPANESE SWORD SOCIETY OF THE U.S.
PO Box 712; Breckenridge, TX 76424

KNIFE COLLECTORS CLUB INC, THE
1920 N 26th St; Lowell AR 72745; 479-631-0130; 479-631-8493; ag@agrussell.com; Web:www.club@k-c-c.com
The oldest and largest association of knife collectors. Issues limited edition knives, both handmade and highest quality production, in very limited numbers. The very earliest was the CM-1, Kentucky Rifle

KNIFE WORLD
PO Box 3395; Knoxville, TN 37927; 800-828-7751; 865-397-1955; 865-397-1969; knifepub@knifeworld.com
Publisher of monthly magazine for knife enthusiasts and world's largest knife/cutlery bookseller. Web: www.knifeworld.com

KNIFEMAKERS GUILD
c/o Beverly Imel, Knifemakers Guild, Box 922, New Castle, IN 47362; (765) 529-1651; Web: www.knifemakersguild.com

KNIFEMAKERS GUILD OF SOUTHERN AFRICA, THE
c/o Carel Smith; PO Box 1744; Delmars 2210; SOUTH AFRICA; carelsmith@therugby.co.za; Web:www.kgsa.co.za

KNIVES ILLUSTRATED
265 S. Anita Dr., Ste. 120; Orange, CA 92868; 714-939-9991; 714-939-9909; knivesillustrated@yahoo.com; Web:www.knivesillustrated.com
All encompassing publication focusing on factory knives, new handmades, shows and industry news, plus knifemaker features, new products, and travel pieces

MONTANA KNIFEMAKERS' ASSOCIATION, THE
14440 Harpers Bridge Rd; Missoula, MT 59808; 406-543-0845
Annual book of custom knife makers' works and directory of knife making supplies; $19.99

NATIONAL KNIFE COLLECTORS ASSOCIATION
PO Box 21070; Chattanooga, TN 37424; 423-892-5007; 423-899-9456; info@nationalknife.org; Web: www.nationalknife.org

NEO-TRIBAL METALSMITHS
PO Box 44095; Tucson, AZ 85773-4095; Web: www.neo-tribalmetalsmiths.com

NEW ENGLAND CUSTOM KNIFE ASSOCIATION
George R. Rebello, President; 686 Main Rd; Brownville, ME 04414; Web: www.knivesby.com/necka.html

NORTH CAROLINA CUSTOM KNIFEMAKERS GUILD
c/o 2112 Windy Woods Drive, Raleigh, NC 27607 (919) 834-4693; Web: www.ncknifeguild.org

NORTH STAR BLADE COLLECTORS
PO Box 20523, Bloomington, MN 55420

OHIO KNIFEMAKERS ASSOCIATION
c/o Jerry Smith, Anvils and Ink Studios, P.O. Box 7887, Columbus, Ohio 43229-7887; Web: www.geocities.com/ohioknives/

OREGON KNIFE COLLECTORS ASSOCIATION

Web: www.oregonknifeclub.org

RANDALL KNIFE SOCIETY

PO Box 158, Meadows of Dan, VA 24120 email: payrks@ gate.net; Web: www.randallknifesociety.com

ROCKY MOUNTAIN BLADE COLLECTORS ASSOCIATION

Mike Moss. Pres., P.O. Box 324, Westminster, CO 80036

RESOURCE GUIDE AND NEWSLETTER / AUTOMATIC KNIVES

2269 Chestnut St., Suite 212; San Francisco, CA 94123; 415-731-0210; Web: www.thenewsletter.com

SOUTH CAROLINA ASSOCIATION OF KNIFEMAKERS

c/o Victor Odom, Jr., Post Office Box 572, North, SC 29112 (803) 247-5614; Web: www.scak.org

SOUTHERN CALIFORNIA BLADES

SC Blades, PO Box 1140, Lomita, CA 90717; Web: www. scblades.com

TEXAS KNIFEMAKERS & COLLECTORS ASSOCIATION

2254 Fritz Allen Street, Fort Worth, Texas 76114; Web: www. tkca.org

TACTICAL KNIVES

Harris Publications; 1115 Broadway; New York, NY 10010; Web: www.tacticalknives.com

TRIBAL NOW!

Neo-Tribal Metalsmiths; PO Box 44095; Tucson, AZ 85733-4095; Web: www.neo-tribalmetalsmiths.com

WEYER INTERNATIONAL BOOK DIVISION

6466 Teal Rd., Petersburgh, MI 49270, 419-534-2020, Web: www.weyerinternational.com

publications

BLADE

700 E. State St., Iola, WI 54990-0001; 715-445-2214; Web: www.blademag.com
The world's No. 1 knife magazine

CUTLERY NEWS JOURNAL (BLOG)

www.cutlerynewsjournal.blog
Covers significant happenings from the world of knife collecting, in addition to editorials, trends, events, auctions, shows, cutlery history, and reviews

KNIFE WORLD

PO Box 3395, Knoxville, TN 37927; www.knifeworld.com

KNIVES ILLUSTRATED

265 S. Anita Dr., Ste. 120, Orange, CA 92868; 714-939-9991; knivesillustrated@yahoo.com; Web: www.knivesillustrated. com
All-encompassing publication focusing on factory knives, new handmades, shows and industry news

RESOURCE GUIDE AND NEWSLETTER / AUTOMATIC KNIVES

2269 Chestnut St., Suite 212, San Francisco, CA 94123; 415-731-0210; Web: www.thenewsletter.com

TACTICAL KNIVES

Harris Publications, 1115 Broadway, New York, NY 10010; Web: www.tacticalknives.com

WEYER INTERNATIONAL BOOK DIVISION

2740 Nebraska Ave., Toledo, OH 43607-3245